Other Souths

Other Souths

Diversity and Difference in the U.S. South,
Reconstruction to Present

EDITED BY PIPPA HOLLOWAY

The University of Georgia Press / *Athens and London*

Credits for previously published works appear on pages
443–444 and constitute an extension of this copyright page.

© 2008 by the University of Georgia Press
Athens, Georgia 30602
All rights reserved
Set in Minion Pro by Newgen-Austin
Printed and bound by Sheridan Books
The paper in this book meets the guidelines for permanence
and durability of the Committee on Production Guidelines
for Book Longevity of the Council on Library Resources.

Printed in the United States of America
12 11 10 09 08   C   5 4 3 2 1
12 11 10 09 08   P   5 4 3 2 1

Library of Congress Cataloging-in-Publication Data

Other Souths : diversity and difference in the U.S. South,
Reconstruction to present / edited by Pippa Holloway.
    p. cm.
Includes bibliographical references and index.
ISBN-13: 978-0-8203-2984-0 (hardcover : alk. paper)
ISBN-10: 0-8203-2984-3 (hardcover : alk. paper)
ISBN-13: 978-0-8203-3052-5 (pbk. : alk. paper)
ISBN-10: 0-8203-3052-3 (pbk. : alk. paper)
1. Pluralism (Social sciences)—Southern States—History.
2. Southern States—Social conditions—1865–1945. 3. Southern
States—Social conditions—1945– 4. Southern States—
History—1865–1951. 5. Southern States—History—1951–
I. Holloway, Pippa.
F220.A1O86 2008
975'.043—dc22   2007038707

British Library Cataloging-in-Publication Data available

CONTENTS

Other Souths

Introduction

Pippa Holloway

In recent years, historical scholarship on the South has come to reflect the true diversity of this region. While for many the word *southerner* may
still conjure up the traditional, white stereotypes—bourbon-sipping gentle-
men, delicate southern belles, and slow-witted rednecks—historians have reminded us that the South is composed of individuals from different races,
backgrounds, sexual orientations, and cultures. New historical scholarship on
the South not only explores the range of life in the South but also reflects it, as
historians have utilized an assortment of approaches to further our understanding of this region. Some of this wide-ranging and provocative scholarship can be found in the pages that follow.

A central goal of this collection is to fit new scholarship on a variety of
southern topics into the chronological and event-driven framework around
which many students and teachers organize their understanding of the past.
The historians represented here engage well-recognized topics in American
history: wars, reform efforts, social movements, and political milestones. Cultural topics are considered as well, including the development of consumer
capitalism, the history of rock and roll, and the history of sport. This focus and
organization underscores the value of southern history to the larger national
narrative. In short, these historians argue, studies of the South tell much about
the American nation.

Although this collection is organized chronologically, the articles here also
demonstrate key themes in recent historical scholarship, particularly the recognition that our understanding of the past is enhanced by studies of gender,
race, ethnicity, class, and sexuality. This scholarship goes well beyond the
"contributory" history that marked some of the first explorations into women's
history, African American history, and the history of the working class. Rather
than inserting select individuals into an already-established historical narrative, much of this work transforms the narrative itself. In particular, scholarship that has used race and gender as categories of analysis has brought new
perspectives to key events in southern history while moving long-overlooked
events into prominence. Accordingly, some of the articles selected here offer
new views on, for example, Reconstruction, the First World War, and the Black
Freedom Movement, while others argue for the significance of topics such as

1

the construction of whiteness and lesbian and gay history to our understanding of the South.

Another result of putting race, class, gender, sexuality, and ethnicity at the center of historical inquiry is scholarship that explores the social construction and social function of these categories. Modern societies have used such social divisions to sort individuals and to create social hierarchies. Studies of the past have asked how the definition of these social categories has changed over time, and they have examined the social and/or political ends served by particular constructions of these social categories.

Indeed, one might imagine a reordering of the essays in this volume into sections on race, class, gender, sexuality, and ethnicity, but for one critical fact. Central to this scholarship is the question of interrelations between these categories. Analyses of gender and race, for instance, can ask how racial differences have been constructed in gendered terms. Considering ethnicity can enhance our understanding of race and class, while studies of class illuminate key issues in the history of gender. An examination of sexuality can bring unique aspects of all these topics into focus. For example, historians of sexuality have argued the fear that sexual behavior might cross or weaken boundaries of race, class, and gender has been a powerful cause of sexual surveillance and discipline.

The title of this book pays homage to Carl Degler's 1974 work *The Other South: Southern Dissenters in the Nineteenth Century*. Degler reminded historians of the diversity of political thought in the South—even within the relatively homogenous class of white southern men—by chronicling the experiences of white southerners who stood outside the mainstream of nineteenth-century politics, particularly on the issue of race. Though Degler was not the first historian to document political diversity among white southerners, his insistence that "the South is not and never has been a monolith" is still a valuable reminder to students of American history.

The political diversity of southerners is illustrated in a variety of ways in the following selections. Two articles demonstrate, in particular, the different political positions held by southern whites. Andrew Doyle considers disputes at Auburn University in the 1920s over the football team. He connects the unpopularity and forced resignation of university president Spright Dowell with Dowell's disdain for college football and his conservative social morality. Dowell found himself out of step with a student body that was challenging strict campus discipline, Prohibition, and rural values while demanding sexual liberalization, democratic campus governance, and the right to have fun. Even issues of academic curriculum came into the debate, as Dowell committed resources to the School of Agriculture (more in step with his rural outlook) at the expense of the school's engineering program, which was considered a training ground for future members of the urban middle class.

Jeanette Keith's work examines conscription in the rural South during the First World War and finds that class shaped both perceptions of the war and how southerners experienced the conflict. Lower-class rural southerners were more likely to oppose the war; they resisted the draft and sometimes even turned to armed resistance. In contrast, upper and middle class whites used a variety of techniques, including control of the local draft boards, to avoid military service.

Just as class affected the view of white southerners toward the First World War, race shaped the impact of military service in the Second World War on southerners, as Jennifer E. Brooks documents in her study of African American and white veterans in Georgia. Her work verifies other scholarship that has argued that African Americans returned from Europe determined to fight racial injustice at home. However, her most significant contribution is her argument that some white veterans came home with new ideas about both race and governance that led them to challenge the existing political order. Veterans of both races brought a new kind of intellectual diversity that changed the political landscape.

One example of how scholarship on gender and race can transform the historical narrative is Leslie Schwalm's article on freedwomen in the South Carolina low country. Schwalm argues that African American women helped define the terms of Reconstruction by insisting on changes in their work environment. Women who worked in the fields and those who worked in plantation residences challenged the conditions of their labor relationships, a struggle that served to set the terms of freedom in the changed political context after the Civil War. Schwalm joins other scholars of African American women in re-shaping our understanding of what politics is, how political change happens, and who political actors are.

Just as Schwalm's work shows that experiences in the daily lives of women made a distinct contribution to defining the terms of the newly won freedom, Lu Ann Jones, too, finds larger lessons in everyday life in the South. Her study of southern itinerant commerce in the first half of the twentieth century inserts the rural South into the history of American consumer culture. Mining a variety of sources, including oral histories, Jones finds that itinerant commerce had tremendous appeal to women and African Americans of both sexes, as these southerners had less access to the commercial world of the town or city. Female consumers in the South—black and white—shaped the nature of commerce and consumer culture.

The significance of one life—that of a Virginia prisoner named John Henry—is explored in Scott Reynolds Nelson's article. Nelson traces the legend of John Henry to a real prisoner who worked building tunnels for the Chesapeake and Ohio Railway. Locating the man behind the myth leads

Nelson to consider the relationship between folklore and history and to investigate diverse approaches to historical sources. He also finds that the phrase *rock and roll* was used to describe the action of drills operated by pairs of workers; their movements were coordinated by rhythmic singing. Finally, this article includes discussions of the convict labor system in the South and the financing of southern penitentiaries, topics relevant as officials debated who would pay for the return and burial of bodies such as that of John Henry.

Nelson's work serves as a reminder of the geographic and economic diversity of the South. It is a region of agricultural flatlands but also mountain ranges, such as the ones where John Henry toiled. The definition of the South itself is also a topic for consideration. Three articles in this collection focus on Florida, a state often excluded from examinations of the South. The work of Scott H. Dewey, Stacy Braukman, and Danielle L. McGuire locate topics in Florida's past that illustrate southern themes and demonstrate how experiences in Florida shed light on the history of the larger region.

The work of both J. Douglas Smith and Sarah Gualtieri ask how southerners wrestled with defining whiteness and blackness in the twentieth century. Their work is part of a larger body of scholarship on the social construction of race that has investigated how social systems create and refine racial classification. Gualtieri begins her study with the case of George Dow, a Syrian immigrant who sought to convince a South Carolina judge that he was white. Under immigration law of the time, whiteness was a requirement for naturalization. Gualtieri underscores the significance of the 1910s and 1920s as an era in which racial categories were in flux, and J. Douglas Smith's study of interracial marriage laws in Virginia leads him to concur that this period was marked by a "mutability of race relations." Smith finds that white activists who embraced the crusade for racial purity persuaded the legislature to redefine whiteness to exclude anyone with any non-white ancestor, even an ancestor many generations earlier. They argued that without state action, interracial sex and marriage would undermine white supremacy, ultimately destroying the white race.

A similar set of questions about the perceived connections between political and social subversion are raised by Stacy Braukman in her article on the fear of lesbian teachers in Florida. Florida's "Johns Commission," originally established to investigate the NAACP and undermine the civil rights struggle, turned its focus in the 1960s to rooting out homosexual teachers in high schools and colleges. Investigators asked startlingly explicit questions of teachers and even some students. Braukman concludes that these interrogations illustrate the postwar "conflations" of male and female homosexuality into a single category of sexually deviant subversives.

Braukman identifies schools as a key location where anxieties about homosexuality, communism, and integration connected. Schools figure into a number of the articles here as sites where social struggles played out. While Doyle focuses his study of football at Auburn University, Alex Macaulay examines the Citadel and the reactions of students at this military school to the Vietnam Antiwar movement. Though the South Carolina campus was initially hostile to the antiwar movement, by the 1970s cadets exhibited diverse opinions on the war. Macaulay attributes this in part to a growing culture of dissent on campus; as students began to question certain aspects of the college administration, they opened up the intellectual space for challenges to the war. But, Macaulay also argues that student dissent tapped into a uniquely southern military tradition that embraced rebellion against authority.

An entirely different kind of academic environment comes under consideration in Susan Cahn's work. This article looks at a 1931 arson trial at Samarcand Manor, a North Carolina girls' reformatory. The trial exposed "sexual delinquency" among the young residents of the reformatory, prompting a state-wide debate over whether delinquent working-class girls were uniquely corrupt ("Fiends Incarnate") or normal girls who misbehaved. Should these girls be offered the privileges and protections accorded other white citizens, or were they racial degenerates that should be incarcerated and sexually sterilized?

The work of Cahn and Braukman are not only linked by their shared focus on educational environments but also by the fact that they demonstrate the importance of historical studies of sexuality. In both contexts, activities perceived as sexually deviant were interpreted as being politically threatening. Private behaviors seemed to have public implications, and those who controlled the state used their power to restrict and punish such sexual transgressions. Particularly notable is the fact that in both cases white female sexual deviance came under public scrutiny. Though such a focus is not unique to the South, in this region white leaders felt that activities that undermined the image of the "Southern Lady" posed a challenge to the racial hierarchy.

The import given white female respectability stands in contrast to the centuries-long failure in the South to recognize sexual assault on African American women. While white women were considered pure and unsexual, African American women were thought to be lascivious and oversexual, indifferent to sexual assault if not actually inviting it. Danielle L. McGuire seeks to identify a shift in this order. Beginning in the 1940s African American communities began to rally behind African American women's resistance to sexual exploitation. The culture of dissemblance that required silence about issues of African American sexuality began to crumble as black men and women rallied against such violence. Florida A&M students, for example, led protests and threatened a boycott demanding the prosecution of white men who assaulted African American students. Resistance to sexual violence represented "battles over manhood and womanhood" that were at the heart of the African American freedom struggle.

While McGuire looks the agents of racial change in the 1950s and 1960s, Kevin M. Kruse considers those who reacted to it in Atlanta, Georgia. When public spaces (such as parks, buses, swimming pools, and golf courses) desegregated, whites who opposed integration pushed for the construction of segregated private alternatives. Kruse argues that this retreat from public institutions laid the groundwork for the "tax revolt"—a movement more often associated with the 1970s and 1980s—as white individuals who refused to use integrated public institutions sought to avoid paying for them. Ignoring these racist roots of tax resistance has allowed its conservative proponents to claim their agenda is "colorblind" and devoid of biases of race or class.

Struggles over the limits of federal authority in the South have often centered on racial issues. Following *Brown v. Board of Education,* for example, some white southerners joined "white citizens' councils" to protect what they saw as a local tradition of segregation against Supreme Court–mandated desegregation. Scott H. Dewey's article suggests we explore the intersection of local and federal power in another context as well: in the area of environmental policy. In the early 1950s Central Florida farmers realized that emissions from the rapidly growing phosphate industry were damaging citrus trees and cattle. Environmental protection was primarily the task of the states in this era, as federal mandates were weak and its authority limited primarily to conducting research. Dewey shows that Florida's state government proved largely ineffective at curbing these damaging emissions, and he concludes that absent federal pressure, states are unreliable sources of environmental protection.

Ronald Reagan famously observed in his 1981 inaugural address that "government is not the solution to our problem; government is the problem." The work of Dewey and Kruse demonstrate how historical scholarship on the South can help us understand the national political climate of the late twentieth and early twenty-first centuries. Kruse shows that Reagan's comments built on an ideological framework already constructed in locations such as Atlanta, and Dewey suggests that recent efforts to shrink the size of the federal government may reverse important progress made on protecting the environment.

Raymond A. Mohl contributes the article of this volume that looks to the future of the South and predicts a "*nuevo* New South." More than a decade of accelerating Hispanic immigration has begun to change the economic, political, and social structure of the region. The long division of the South along the binary of black and white may be disappearing as new migrants enter even the most isolated small towns. Among the many questions these changes mean for the region concerns southern distinctiveness. Will the South meld into the rest of the "Latinized" nation or will these new generations of southerners make their own contribution to the maintenance of a unique regional culture? Such questions will doubtless be the subject of forthcoming scholarship in southern history.

"Sweet Dreams of Freedom"

Freedwomen's Reconstruction of Life and Labor in Lowcountry South Carolina

Leslie Schwalm

In his memoir of Civil War and Reconstruction, rice planter Charles Manigault offered what he regarded as some of the "leading Characteristicks of The NEGRO, and . . . The Times, through which we have recently passed." For Manigault, those characteristics were exemplified by his former slave Peggy, who offered ample evidence of how emancipation and Confederate defeat had turned Manigault's world upside down. Manigault noted that as the war came to a close, former slaves plundered and destroyed planter homes throughout his lowcountry South Carolina neighborhood. Peggy "seized as Her part of the spoils my wife's Large & handsome Mahogany Bedstead & Mattrass & arranged it in her own Negro House on which she slept for some time" and in which Manigault bitterly imagined she enjoyed "her Sweet Dreams of freedom." Peggy also confiscated from the Manigault residence "some Pink Ribands, & tied in a dozens bows the wooly head of her Daughter, to the admiration of the other Negroes." Lastly, Manigault noted Peggy's response when he, joined by his son and a former overseer (and Confederate officer), came onto the farm and "immediately began to pitch the Negro Effects" into two wagons, intending to evict the freedpeople. Only Peggy ("the lady of the Big Mahogany Bed") tried to intervene: "placing her arms akimbo, said 'She would go off to the Provost Marshal in town & stop our unlawful proceedings with their property in their own homes.'"[1]

Peggy's appropriation of her former mistresses' furniture, her use of contraband ribbons to style her daughter's hair, and her public challenge to Manigault's authority all signaled to Manigault that Peggy was pursuing her freedom with a literal vengeance, or what Manigault described as "recklessness and Ingratitude." In the actions of freedwomen like Peggy, and also in the responses that she and freedwomen like her provoked from former owners and from the civilian and military agents of Reconstruction, lies one of the most underexplored dynamics of the South's transition from slavery to freedom and the subject of this essay: the influence of former slave women's defining acts of freedom on the South's transition to a free labor society.

In the last 15 years, historians have produced an impressive body of work reexamining the South's transition from slavery to freedom during and after the Civil War, work that has yielded new information and a richer understanding of the complex process, and implications, of American emancipation.[2] Yet much of this scholarship, despite its emphasis on the multifaceted involvement of former slaves in shaping the South's transition to a free society, has omitted the actions and experiences of half of the four million who passed from slavery to freedom. Too often the transition from slavery to freedom has been investigated and portrayed as though slave women did not share that experience or failed to contribute to the process; enslaved African American women like Peggy, it would seem, had little if any specific or general influence on the shape of the path slaves forged which led from slavery to freedom.[3]

Historians' failure to come to terms with freedwomen's role in the wartime and postbellum South has not been entirely a matter of omission. Despite the dearth of research, many scholars have characterized freedwomen's role in the postbellum conflict as allegedly withdrawing and retreating from the labor force, a conclusion that relies upon the infallibility of contemporary observations by northern and southern whites, and also on census-based estimates of freedwomen's labor-force participation.[4] Even with limited evidence, scholars have freely interpreted freedwomen's motivations and expectations based on their alleged withdrawal from the paid workforce. Some posit that freedwomen gladly yielded to the demands of their husbands that they withdraw from agricultural employment, that they voluntarily collaborated with their husbands' postemancipation claims to the privileges and prerogatives of a patriarchally ordered family and household. Others suggest that freedwomen were imitating white behavior, anxious to claim for themselves the privileges they perceived in elite white women's domesticity—not the least of which was an escape from the physical demands of field work and the demeaning labor of domestic service.[5] The work of Jacqueline Jones and Gerald Jaynes has offered a significant departure from speculation, given their more focused investigations into the actions of freedwomen in the postwar South. Both have turned their attention to freedwomen's creative attempts to choose productive and reproductive labor in their own and their families' best interests. Yet while Jones posits that "Only at home could [freedwomen] exercise considerable control over their own lives and those of their husbands and children and impose a semblance of order on the physical world," Jaynes has persuasively argued that freedwomen's actions must be evaluated in the context of specific postwar agricultural economies, offering an important challenge to the somewhat deterministic assumption that all freedwomen acted alike.[6] The conclusion that freedwomen's refusal to work in the manner demanded or prescribed by southern or northern whites actually culminated in women's wholesale withdrawal from labor markets across the South is premature, and its acceptance as "common knowledge" has deterred closer investigation of freedwomen's influence over and participation in wartime and postbellum conflict.

With the themes of withdrawal and retreat used to characterize women's postbellum experience, freedwomen like Peggy have been easily ignored as actors on the public landscape, the landscape from which historians typically identify the "facts" of Reconstruction. Yet Peggy's actions were both "public" and, as this essay will argue, typical for lowcountry freedwomen. In the actions of freedwomen like Peggy we find clues to some of the many ways in which former slave women distinguished their freedom from their slavery— from the vengeful ransacking of their former owners' homes, to the significance of dress and hair style in claiming and asserting a new personal dignity, to "reckless" confrontations with the plantation whites who had defined the day-to-day nature of exploitation under slavery. Recent research suggests there were also other important arenas in which former slave women tried to give meaning and substance to their freedom. Sharon Holt has revealed how freedwomen's (and men's) efforts to increase their autonomy and their resources were intertwined with their desire to build, staff, and sustain schools, churches, mutual and benevolent societies, and a host of other independent institutions. Elsa Barkley Brown has reminded us that when Radical Reconstruction opened the political arena to freedmen, freedwomen also brought forward their own claims to citizenship, to political meetings and rallies, to voter registration, and to the polls.[8] Work, which had been so central to women's experience of slavery, was also critical to women's definition of freedom. In lowcountry South Carolina, freedwomen escalated the battle to define black freedom when they sought autonomous control over plantation lands, when they negotiated and reconstructed plantation and domestic labor, and when they defended the new autonomy of their families and household economies from exploitation by planters and unwelcome intervention by northern agents of Reconstruction. In seeking control over their field labor on lowcountry rice plantations, women sought to distance themselves from the power and control of former slaveowning whites outside of the rice fields as much as in them.

Determined to pursue freedom on their own terms, freedwomen who sought the means and the opportunity to live and subsist as free from white intervention as possible encountered considerable opposition from several sources. Opposition came from white vigilantes, planters, mistresses, and overseers all anxious for the return of a reliable and subordinate labor force, and from U.S. soldiers and agents of the Freedmen's Bureau who were frustrated by former slaves' unwillingness to embrace the tenets of the free labor society many Northerners envisioned for the postwar South. The letters, reports, complaints, and official responses generated by freedwomen's observers and antagonists offer a rich record of freedwomen's efforts to reconstruct life and labor in lowcountry South Carolina. They also reveal that an important part of the work of defining freedom lies in freedwomen's determined efforts to reveal and disrupt the relations of power and domination that had marked their lives as enslaved laborers in the rice fields and planter residences of low-country plantations.[9] When freedwomen insisted on working "in their own way and at such times as they think fit," they were articulating a politics of Reconstruction in which women's experience of gender, race, and a history of enslavement were inseparable. They made the issue of reconstructing work their own, an integral part of their desire and intent to secure black freedom.

The women who had been held in slavery in mainland lowcountry South Carolina were situated in a region marked by a specific geography, a unique African American culture, and a particular plantation setting organized around a single crop cultivated under a distinctive system of slave labor. African American women enslaved elsewhere in the South were faced with a very different set of circumstances before, during, and after the Civil War. The rice-planting region of lowcountry South Carolina contained some of the South's largest plantations and wealthiest planters, and before the war, some of its largest, most stable, and culturally autonomous slave communities.[10] On the eve of the war, rice agriculture rested squarely on the shoulders of slave women whose lives were spent in the fields and ditches that marked the distinctive lowcountry terrain. As in other advanced plantation regimes, slave women on rice plantations were a significant proportion of "prime" field hands. However, to paraphrase from the introduction to an anthology on slave labor in the Americas, it was the particulars of slaves' labor which "determined, in large measure, the course of their lives."[11] Slave labor in the rice fields was organized under the task system, so that the work of preparing fields, and cultivating and processing the rice crop, was assigned to women by the task—portion of an acre for hoeing, a certain number of linear feet for ditch-digging, a certain number of rice sheaves cut and tied. This distinguished slave women's task labor from women's dawn-to-dusk gang labor in almost every other plantation economy. The pace of task labor was set by slaves, who—with considerable effort—could often complete their tasks by mid-afternoon. For slave women, this translated into more daylight hours for the labor of raising and caring for families and for a variety of activities related to independent production.

Slave women's work in the rice fields and the elaborate residences of rice planters not only shaped their experience of slavery but also influenced their wartime struggle to escape or destroy slavery. The naval blockade of southern ports and the subsequent disruption of trade, the withdrawal of white men from agriculture to military service, and demands by the Confederate military and state authorities for slave labor and slave-produced goods all disrupted the long-established patterns of plantation life and labor in the lowcountry.[12] The forced removal of lowcountry slaves to the state's more protected interior further undermined the traditional cycle of rice agriculture as well as the local ties which for many generations had anchored lowcountry plantation production and slavery. With the occupation of Port Royal by Union forces early in the war, the threat posed by the proximity of the enemy exacerbated the war's domestic interruptions in South Carolina.

For country slave men and women, these wartime conditions translated into incremental disruptions of the traditions, customary rights, social relations, and domestic networks that they had forged over several generations of struggle against slavery. Yet even as wartime shortages forced a deterioration in the standard of living in the slave quarters, slave women accelerated the wartime collapse of slavery by slowing plantation production, resisting the new forms of exploitation introduced during the war, and escaping lowcountry plantations in unprecedented numbers and making their way to the fleet of federal ships blockading the coast. When slave women seized the opportunities presented by the war to further weaken the institution of slavery or to secure their own freedom, it was not only slavery which they hoped to leave behind but also the worsening conditions of life on lowcountry plantations. Long before emancipation became a part of Union policy, slave women were struggling to alter the conditions of life and labor on South Carolina plantations.

It bears stressing that war affected not only the material conditions of lowcountry slave life but also the relationships of power that were integral to slavery. As planters became increasingly unable to purchase or afford the most basic necessities; as they became subject to impressment of their plantation products and slaves; as they, their overseers, and their sons became vulnerable to conscription; and, as increasing numbers of plantation mistresses assumed unprecedented and unanticipated responsibility for plantation operations in light of the absence of husbands and sons, slaves watched the weakening of their masters' ability to dominate. Slave women not only observed, but tested and acted upon, the wartime crisis of plantation mastery. Overseers and planter families alike complained during the war of slave women disrupting the peaceful operation of their plantations, threatening to run away, and slowing the pace of work.[13] One rice plantation mistress complained early in the war of the "license" increasingly taken by slaves; they "all think this a crisis in their lives that must be taken advantage of. . . . [T]imes and slaves, have changed" since secession.[14] The weaknesses in the bedrock of slavery exposed by the war were seized upon and widened by slave women who were determined to make the war's trajectory towards emancipation irreversible.

Thousands of slave women fled lowcountry plantations during the war and made their way to the Union-occupied Sea Islands, beginning their transition from slavery to freedom under the dominion of northern missionaries, civilians, and military authorities. Unlike native Sea Islanders who staked out their own portion of plantation lands and continued to live in their slave quarters, slave women from the mainland rice plantations constituted a refugee population. They found living quarters in refugee camps, abandoned buildings, or temporary barracks, and pieced together a living from the employment they found in the Quartermaster's Department, as regimental laundresses or cooks, from the pay of their enlisted kin or husbands, or by marketing provisions to Union soldiers stationed on the islands. Yet their appreciation for the protection, schooling, and charity offered by northern military and civilian authorities did not slow women's response when the freedom offered under northern tutelage was less than what they expected. Whether this meant shaming the northern missionary women who pointedly ignored the pressing needs of young "unmarried" slave mothers, challenging military authorities who tried to prevent their entry into soldiers' camps to sell provisions or to "see and be seen," or leading groups of women to protest unacceptably low wages, these refugees from mainland slavery were hardly content to await passively the redefinition of black life and labor by others. Before the war had ended, these contraband women were already engaged in the process of defining and defending their freedom.[15]

Women's pursuit of freedom gained momentum and breadth in the immediate aftermath of the war. The final dissolution of lowcountry slavery in early 1865, coinciding with the chaotic closing weeks of war in the wake of Sherman's advance through the state, inspired newly freed slave women to attack former overseers, raid planter residences and storehouses, and confiscate or destroy planter property. From the smallest luxuries to the most expensive furnishings, freedwomen clothed themselves and their children in confiscated and previously forbidden finery "in pride of their freedom." In the aftermath of the war, former slave women's defining acts of freedom were also found in their efforts to reunite their families, separated before or during the war; in the strategies they adopted to endure calamitous material conditions and to evade violent attacks by white reactionaries and northern soldiers; and in the ways they reorganized and reallocated their agricultural, domestic, and household labor.

For most lowcountry freedpeople, women and men, land was critical to the freedom and independence they sought for themselves, their families, and their communities. Lowcountry freedpeople shared a definition of freedom as their right, not simply to survive, but to work and thrive without white intervention on the land they had worked as slaves and where generations of their ancestors had lived, worked, and died.[16] On the Sea Islands and on the mainland, from Georgetown to the Savannah River, freedpeople held public meetings, organized commissions, appointed delegations, and formed paramilitary guards to protest the accelerating process of restoration under the terms of Johnsonian Reconstruction and to prevent returning white landowners from setting foot on the islands and usurping their own claims to the land.[17] As federal Reconstruction policy accelerated the restoration of so-called "abandoned lands" to white planters, freedpeople were forced either to relinquish their claims or defend them. Freedwomen figured in many of the conflicts that flared in defense of those claims. They physically forced planters or overseers off the plantation, threatened violent confrontations with bureau agents and armed guards of U.S. soldiers, and individually refused to cooperate with white landowners.[18]

Women's vigorous resistance to restoration was evident in a violent confrontation that developed on Keithfield plantation. In March 1865, former slaves had driven the white overseer off the plantation, and for the rest of the year a community of about 150 freedpeople lived on and independently worked the plantation, cultivating at least a partial crop of rice.[19] But early in 1866 Keithfield's absentee planter, a widow, asked a neighboring planter to help her retake control of Keithfield. She could not have chosen a figure more hated by local freedpeople, for this neighbor, Francis Parker, Sr., had helped carry out the ritualized public execution of recaptured fugitive slaves during the war. Adding to the potential for conflict, Parker attempted (with the approval of the local bureau agent) to install as overseer Dennis Hazel, a former slave driver.[20]

In March 1866, according to Parker and Hazel's account of the conflict, Parker sent his son and Hazel to deliver work orders to the people at Keithfield, but the men's authority was repudiated by Abram, whom the freedpeople had appointed their foreman. Parker's son threatened to bring Abram before the local provost marshal and "break him" but left the plantation before doing so. Abram called the women and men in from the field. The work gang turned their tools—"Axes hatchets hoes and poles"—into weapons, and attacked Hazel, threatening to kill him. Hazel escaped and that afternoon returned to the plantation with Parker's son and two soldiers. On their appearance, the freedpeople assaulted them with their tools and pelted them with bricks and stones. Sukey and Becky entered the fray armed with heavy clubs. Joined by Jim, they exhorted their fellow laborers to join the fight, "declaring that the time was come and they must yield their lives if necessary—that a life was lost but once, and they must try and kill" the intruders. The crowd was joined by eight or ten "infuriated women," including Charlotte Simons, Susan Lands, Clarrisa Simons, Sallie Mayzck, Quashuba and Magdalen Moultrie, who were armed with heavy clubs and hoes, and backed by four or five men. The women made a point of their particular hatred for the former slave driver Hazel by focusing their attack on him; the soldiers' efforts to defend him from their blows were "entirely ineffectual." Parker pleaded with the women to let up their attack on Hazel, promising to leave and let Freedmen's Bureau authorities settle the matter, but, as he recalled, "the mob was not to be reasoned with." The freedmen encouraged the women; "kill him, now is your time, don't let him get away." Three times, Parker called on the freedmen to "exert themselves," to stop and force back what he described as "the maddened women." The freedmen replied to Parker that he "had no business over there anyhow—that no white man could control them now they were free." Sukey and Becky then shifted their attack from Hazel to Parker. Sukey seized a hickory stick out of Parker's hands and beat him with it over his back; both she and Becky delivered a series of heavy blows to his head. One of the soldiers, "his face covered with blood" and apparently disarmed by the freedpeople, "beseeched his comrade to shoot" at the mob, but Parker insisted no shooting take place, "fearing such a measure might further madden the desperate mob." Parker and Hazel turned to make a hasty retreat, begging the men to keep the women back, but before Parker could escape he was "struck very heavily over [his] right eye with a club in the hands of a woman Becky—the blow bringing blood instantly, and making [him] stagger with blindness[.]" He noted that "vigorous efforts to strike me again were continued by women among whom I recognized Sukey, Becky, Quashuba, Charlotte, Susan." Now fearing for his life, Parker (followed by Hazel) made the only escape he could, by jumping into the river and swimming out to their boat, "under a shower of missiles." Parker and Hazel left the soldiers to make their own escape by foot, bloodied and disarmed by the freedpeople.

Later, an armed guard of U.S. soldiers temporarily settled the incident by arresting several of the ringleaders. Three of the freedmen were charged with inciting the freedwomen to violence; five of the women served sentences in the local jail. Although the Freedmen's Bureau agent called the violence attending Keithfield's restoration "unusual," reports from across the lowcountry noted the vigor of women's participation as freedpeople resisted rice planters who attempted to reclaim their plantations and to reinstate overseers and former slave drivers. The reports confirmed the fears of Freedmen's Bureau agents who knew that freedpeople were cultivating so-called abandoned lands "in anticipation of being left to enjoy the fruits of their labors"; agents anticipated that the return of planters would inevitably lead to "serious difficulties" but seemed surprised at the role played by freedwomen.[21]

Some freedwomen faced more immediate battles when former owners remained on the plantations at the close of the war. Freedwomen's involvement in the conflicts was noted by the overseers, former owners, and white elites who were as outraged at freedwomen's purposeful violation of antebellum rituals of deference and subordination as by the actual content of their demands.

Although conflict and resistance had been part of the fabric of day-to-day life under slavery, by the late summer of 1865, freedwomen were clashing with former slaveowners and other whites in a new, more public, and openly declared arena. Freedwomen like Peggy had added a new public strategy of insubordination and direct confrontation to their antebellum repertoire of evasive tactics and deceptive appearances.[22] They challenged former slaveowners' and overseers' expectations of ritualized, deferential behavior as they set out in clear terms and with definitive action how they believed life and labor should differ in freedom from their experience under slavery.

In the fall and early winter of 1865, lowcountry planters complained with growing frequency that freedpeople left the plantations without permission, refused work orders, and made threats against planters. Planters complained the freedpeople "not only will not work now, but tell you so openly & plainly." [23] They accused former slaves of being saucy, insolent, intractable, disobedient, and dangerous. Even in this general climate of conflict and resistance, men and women of the lowcountry planter class, white overseers, soldiers, and agents of the Freedmen's Bureau all complained pointedly about the insubordinate behavior of former slave women. Freedwoman Jane, who rejected work orders and slapped her white mistress, was denounced by her employers as "an audacious creature." [24] Mary Ann "boldly [and] unblushingly" confronted her former owner in the field, refused his assignment of work unrelated to the present crop, and "frequently contradicted [him] and spoke to [him] as roughly and as defiantly as if [he] had been the meanest old negro in the country." He was as alarmed by Mary Ann's defiant bearing towards him as by her insistence on determining for herself which work she would and would not perform.[25] Another planter characterized freedwomen as idle and insolent vagrants, playing sick and doing no work; the driver's wife thought she was "too fine a lady to think of doing any work," and even Eve, while admittedly "an old woman," he described as "very impertinent." [26] It was the behavior of women like these that prompted the agent on one lowcountry plantation to complain that "[t]he more kindness offered to them the more ingratitude & abuse we receive," an unwitting admission that freedwomen were challenging the facade of reciprocal relations that had masked the abusive and exploitative nature of antebellum paternalism.

Beyond their insistence on bringing radical change to their relationships with lowcountry elites, lowcountry freedwomen's reputation for insubordination was in part a consequence of the specific kinds of demands they made in postwar labor arrangements. Freedpeople needed to innovate new family economies to cope with conditions of starvation and want; they sought a balance between their ties to specific communities and plantation lands and their need for cash, or food and basic goods. After the harvest, freedmen (husbands and fathers) left the plantations in pursuit of day labor, sold firewood or fruit to passing steamers or in nearby towns, or found other temporary avenues into the cash economy. Freedwomen—often wives and mothers—remained on the plantations and assumed a frontline role in ongoing plantation battles over the shape of postemancipation labor while caring for family and tending independent crops.[27] Some families on mainland plantations managed to plant "private crops of their own," and the men were said to "hire out now & then . . . to neighbors" while freedwomen and children remained on the plantation.[28] This strategy not only exacerbated planters' concern about securing essential postharvest labor from freedpeople but also placed freedwomen in direct conflict with planters.

Freedwomen fueled the escalating labor conflict by their refusal to perform postharvest domestic chores for planters. Planters had customarily assigned female slaves a range of postharvest labor that included spinning and weaving, the manufacture of clothing, butchering and preserving meat, and other kinds of domestic production critical to the maintenance and support of plantation operations. That labor had eaten into the hours slavewomen might otherwise have spent with, and working for, their own families. In the fall of 1865, freedwomen who had contracted to work as field hands were no longer willing to perform "double duty" in domestic production for their employers. This included freedwoman Mary Ann, who "shewed the virago from the start"; according to her former owner, "she has refused to rake[,] fence[,] or do any work," leading him to fear that her behavior "will poison all the rest of the people of the place." [29] Freedwomen on one of the Allston plantations brought an end to the extra burden of postharvest wool production, first by killing off the plantation sheep and then eating them. One planter's wife reported that in order to get former slaves to work even half tasks in the field, chores related to domestic production, such as spinning, had to be totally abandoned. Another planter's wife found herself reported to a local bureau agent for trying to compel female field hands to do her spinning and weaving. Even young women like sixteen-year-old Margaret Brown rejected "weaving after night" for her employer, who took her refusal as provocation enough to beat her with his bare hands and with a stick.[30] Freedwomen's contributions to lowcountry labor conflicts did not go unnoticed or unanswered. According to bureau and military records, many freedwomen paid a dear price for the audacity of insisting on their right to define free labor on their own terms. Their experience of violence at the hands of an outraged employer was not unusual. Hagar Barnwell had been ordered by her former owner to go into the kitchen and work, but "she refused . . . as she had contracted to work in the field." When Barnwell vowed she would leave the plantation rather than work in his kitchen, the man threatened her with his pistol, stated he would kill her if not for the need to get his crop in, and then he took her to a shed and tied her up by her thumbs so that her feet barely touched the ground. Barnwell eventually escaped but appealed to three different army officers as well as a local magistrate before she found someone willing to investigate her mistreatment.[31] In another instance, "a Woman named Sarah . . . was tied up by the thumbs" by a planter and two accomplices, as punishment for violating plantation rules; "Sarah was pregnant and . . . she was kept suspended for nearly two hours," reported the agent; "in consequence of this brutality the birth of the child was forced." The infant "was dead when delivered," and Sarah was "not . . . expected to live."[32] Their refusal to withdraw from disputes over the meaning of black freedom meant that freedwomen became targets for physical attack, resulting in a record of brutality that historians of the postbellum South are only beginning to plumb.[33]

Planters and overseers were so intent on regaining control of plantation lands (and bureau and military personnel so determined that this was in the best interests of all lowcountry residents) that many failed to anticipate what freedwomen soon demonstrated: Restoration was only an incremental concession, the beginning of a longer process of negotiation on lowcountry plantations.[34] Between 1865 and 1867, it was not unusual for planters, their land restored, to discover that freedpeople "were not willing to make any contracts, inasmuch as the contract system would tend to bring them into a state of slavery again."[35] Along the Santee River, a region the Georgetown bureau agent described as "in a very unsettled state," planters discovered how quickly freedpeople could render restoration a hollow victory for planters. Many planters simply found that they could not negotiate with freedpeople; "the word of the planters to the freedpeople has no weight." The apparent accidental burning of a Santee River planter residence, following restoration, dissuaded other planters from returning.[36]

The owner of two Waccamaw River plantations returned in early 1866 to discover that nearly sixty women and men, formerly his slaves, had resided on and worked the plantations in his absence, and now, "in a state of utter insubordination, refused to contract, claiming the right to remain on the places." They insisted "they will only work in their own way & at such times as they think fit, without the supervision of an agent or any white man & insist upon renting the lands, they to fix the amount to be paid us according to their notions of justice."[37] Although ultimately forced by the course of Reconstruction politics and their determined northern benefactors to relinquish control over the plantations and instead work for planters under the labor contract system, freedwomen disregarded the terms of the contracts and persisted in laboring on their own terms, while also focusing debate and open conflict on the nature of plantation labor and their new relationships to overseers, former slave drivers, employers, and former owners. The responses of military and civilian agents of Reconstruction to freedwomen's actions similarly underwent a noticeable change. In 1865, observers viewed freedpeople's resistance to restoration and contract labor primarily as a threat to the immediate peace and good order of a region still recovering from war, posing an obstacle to the military's efforts to prevent further starvation and reduce the chaos of the southern countryside. But by 1866, their continued resistance to the restoration of the lowcountry plantation economy was construed by some of the military and civilian agents of Reconstruction as a conscious and ill-informed rejection of the tenets of free labor during the crucial, first full year of freedom.[38]

Although both freedmen and freedwomen insisted on setting the terms of their labor in accordance with their own ideas about what freedom meant, it was freedwomen's refusal to work as they had under slavery that planters and northern agents of Reconstruction commented on most frequently and most bitterly. More than one planter complained to the Freedmen's Bureau that he was "forced to discharge my freedwomen for neglect and refusal to do less than reasonable tasks."[39] Planter E.B. Heyward's complaints in 1867 were typical:

> The women have got rather lazy and try your patience severely. The work progresses very slowly and they seem perfectly indifferent. . . . The women appear most lazy, merely because they are allowed the opportunity. They wish to stay in the house, or in the garden all the time—If you chide them, they say "Eh ch! Massa, aint I mus' mind de fowl, and look a' me young corn aint I mus' watch um." And to do this, the best hand on the place will stay at home all day and every day.

Heyward also noted that the "men are scarcely much better"; men and women both seemed to "feel bound as a slave and work under constraint, are impudent, careless and altogether very provoking." As a consequence, Heyward was cautious in his interactions with former slaves, saying, "If the women get mad . . . they run in their holes like Fiddlers and won't come out. I therefore never quarrel. . . . I avoid all difficulties, and make a kind of retreating fight." The freedwomen working on his cousin's plantation were scarcely much better; they "come out on a kind of frolic and sow and cover his rice doing it of course abominably. All the work is badly done."[40]

John DeForest, a bureau agent in upcountry South Carolina, was among the first to label freedwomen's rejection of a "prime" hand's labor and seeming withdrawal from field labor as the "evil of female loaferism." DeForest—whose memoir is often cited by historians as contemporary evidence of women's universal withdrawal from field labor—noted that "myriads of women who once earned their own living now have aspirations to be like white ladies and, instead of using the hoe, pass the days in dawdling over their trivial housework, or gossiping among their neighbors." DeForest's characterization of women's social and reproductive labor as "trivial" was undoubtedly as firmly rooted in the devaluation of (white) women's unpaid housework in the North as in the judgment he was also making about freedwomen's unpaid labor in and connected to the support of their households. Both issues were important to the way northern and southern whites viewed the decisions freedwomen were making.

What was the extent of women's withdrawal from the lowcountry work force? Even DeForest was careful to add that he "did not mean that all women were thus idle; the larger proportion were still laboring afield, as of old; rigid necessity held them up to it." The withdrawal of some women from the waged workforce, he concluded, was gaining popularity among freedpeople just as it had "among us white men and brethren."[41] Most contemporary observers commenting on freedwomen's seeming withdrawal from field labor failed to qualify its extent, as DeForest had; planters from across the state reported that freedwomen would simply stay in their cabins if starvation did not drive them to work. Freedwomen "generally decline to work altogether and depend on their lords [husbands] for their support," reported one planter in 1866, although another nearby planter relied on a plantation labor force composed of two freedwomen to every freedman.[42]

Freedwomen's efforts to shape their labor on lowcountry rice plantations from within the contract labor system are partially documented in the surviving labor contracts filed by lowcountry planters with the Freedman's Bureau between 1865 and 1868. Although labor contracts offer at best an incomplete record of labor arrangements in the postwar era, they do suggest some important trends in the labor force participation of men and women, trends that appear consistent with the descriptive examples from other sources provided so far.[43]

Freedwomen's enrollment on the labor contracts for Georgetown District (see table 1) suggests that they were continuing to work in the lowcountry rice fields but increasingly rejected full-time field labor. From 1866 to 1868, freedwomen's names were consistently nearly half of those signed to the contracts—which was very close to the proportion of slave women who were working in the rice fields before the war. Nonetheless, their intent to decrease the amount of agricultural labor they performed for planters was demonstrated by contracting not as prime or full hands, but as three-quarter or half hands. In fact, according to their enrollment on the labor contracts, men as well as women insisted on working less than they had as slaves. While a significant proportion of contracting freedwomen continued to work as full hands, many insisted on working less than a full hand would. Drawing on a subset of the labor contracts (those where the workers were indicated as contracting as full or partial hands), we learn that the percentage of freedwomen contracting as full

TABLE 1. Georgetown Labor Contracts, 1866–1868

	1866		1867		1868	
Number of contracts with rating (total number of contracts)	57 (171)		45 (88)		14 (38)	
	Women	Men	Women	Men	Women	Men
Number of rated hands (total rated and unrated)	800 (2088)	749 (2267)	812 (1461)	669 (1409)	191 (586)	161 (601)
Percentage contracting as full hands	68.75	81	54.4	81.3	34	70
Percentage contracting as ¾ hands	11	6	16.2	6.27	31.9	18
Percentage contracting as ½ hands	17.75	7.87	27	9.27	29.3	11
Percentage contracting as ¼ hands	2.5	2.8	1.9	3.1	4.7	—

Source: Georgetown Labor Contracts, 1866–1868.

hands on Georgetown plantations had declined from nearly 69 percent of the women who contracted to work in the fields in 1866, to 34 percent in 1868. During the same years, in this same subset of all contracted hands, the percentage of freedmen contracting as full hands also declined, but at a much lower rate—from 81 percent to 70 percent.[44]

Further evidence that lowcountry freedwomen had not retreated from the battle to transform plantation labor was seen in their refusal to labor under former slave drivers and overseers, and their insistence on selecting their own foremen—regardless of the fact that most of the bureau-approved labor contracts for 1866 and 1867 gave that prerogative to their employers. Planters anticipated former slaves' refusal to work under their former overseers; as one planter warned, "I suppose there is no doubt of the ill will of the slaves to him—and in any case I do not think you could expect to renew your relations there or elsewhere through any overseer formerly employed. . . . The petty despot who came between you & them will never be submitted to."[45] But the refusal of southern whites to admit the specific grounds for freedpeople's hatred of former overseers—overseers' exploitation of the productive and reproductive labor of slaves, their oftentimes sexually-charged domination, coercion, and violence against slave women—was also a denial of the extent to which freedpeople now rejected the relations of domination so critical to their experience of slavery.[46] While southern white men defended the sensitivities of white women to the wartime horrors so recently perpetrated by northern whites (southern white women "would be averse, for the present at least, to intimate social relations with those who have been . . . connected with the suffering which they have endured"), African American women were afforded no such protection.[47] When freedwomen claimed the right to live and work free from their former tormentors, whites responded with derision. Freedwomen on El Dorado plantation secured the right to work under a foreman of their own choosing, but the plantation mistress ridiculed the fact that "the 'foreman' escorts the women with an air of gallantry" to the fields, directing their labor "in the most courteous manner," addressing them as "ladies" even as they wielded their hoes in the field.[48]

In fact, the fight against the reinstatement of antebellum overseers and slave drivers was a struggle in which freedwomen gained particular notoriety. Freedwomen explicitly challenged the power and authority of their former overseers, purposefully and publicly violating the ritualized behavior of subservience, obedience, and submission demanded from them while slaves, at the same time escalating the protracted battle over the terms and conditions of their labor. Some overseers found freedwomen's verbal attacks on their authority so sharp as to threaten "manhood and common sense." Even agents of the Freedmen's Bureau concurred, reporting that while freedmen were "tolerably civil" towards former masters, "the women, especially those advanced in age, are abusive, with remarkable aptitude at 'billingsgate,'" the vituperative verbal weaponry exercised by women in London's famous open-air fish market.[49] Edwin Tilton, 12 years the overseer on Waverly plantation, complained in January 1866 that he was "subject of the most gross abuse" by the freedwomen, formerly slaves on the plantation, who candidly expressed their feelings about his employment on the plantation. On another plantation, freedwomen rebuked the white overseer when he attempted to revoke privileges they had won in slavery, such as the right to the open range of their poultry and farm animals on the plantations; in addition, they had become fierce defenders of their right to perform their labor without his supervision. One freedwoman "has ordered me out of her task, saying if I come in her task again she would put me in the ditch." When the same overseer tried to take a seat in a boat being used to transport seed rice, one of the freedwomen demanded to know, as he reported, "who told me to sit down in the boat." Daunted by freedwomen's determined efforts to undermine his authority on the plantation, this particular overseer appealed for the support of an armed guard from local military authorities.[50]

Freedwomen's repudiation of the legitimacy of overseers' authority may have been prompted by reasons beyond their outrage at their experiences of exploitation; freedwomen may also have been acting strategically on behalf of their communities, aware that sometimes the risks were different for freedmen and freedwomen who challenged whites. One overseer explained that while freedwomen challenged him, "I did not mind it so much, but when the men took to backing up the women by some of the same talk I asserted my rights as an American Citizen under abuse by at once knocking down and trouncing one of the abusers" (the same overseer suggested that the provost marshal would "be surprised" at the "actions and language" of the freedwomen and freedmen). Still, overseers could and did take their revenge with freedwomen who spoke their minds.[51]

Freedwomen's opposition to the reinstatement of former overseers, like their opposition to the return of planters, also indicated their concerns about developments outside the rice fields. The symbolic violation of freedpeople's homes became one avenue by which planters and their agents attempted to circumscribe the consequences of emancipation, avenge freedpeople's depredations on planter residences at the close of the war, and reclaim some of their antebellum power over former slaves—both in and outside the rice fields. Former owners and overseers entered and searched freedpeople's homes ostensibly to reclaim stolen property. Of course, given the enthusiasm with which freedpeople had ransacked the planter residences at the close of the war, it was possible—even probable—that many planters actually were trying to recover stolen property. But no less important than the reclamation of that property was the significance of planters and overseers claiming the right to enter and search freedpeople's homes and even their persons. In the process of these searches, planters and their agents performed a ritualistic return to antebellum relations of power on lowcountry plantations, reclaiming their prerogative to violate, and denying freedpeople's claims to the privilege of an inviolable family sphere. One such search was decried by freedman George Singleton as "not only unlawful and cruel but also indecent." Despite his protests and those of the two midwives attending his wife in childbirth, her bed and her person were searched by three white men, allegedly looking for stolen cotton. In this instance and many others, the search also served as an instrument of terror.[52]

Searches were sometimes accomplished with the assistance of an armed guard from a local military post, provoking the disappointment—and outrage—of lowcountry freedpeople who felt betrayed by soldiers' complicity in what they clearly regarded as an invasion and an undesirable return to the past.[53] When a search of this type occurred on Hagley plantation early in 1866, there was trouble "when the freedpeople resisted the soldiers while the latter were making a search of the former's houses for furniture belonging to the estate. One of the men, Corporal Freck, was severely beaten by them, and later in the darkness of the evening missiles were thrown" at an officer and the planter.[54] On another plantation, a planter and a bureau agent made a search of the freedpeople's homes, removing property that the planter identified as stolen. They ordered the freedpeople to carry the items back to the planter residence, but the people refused, saying that their work was done for the day. According to the bureau agent, the freedpeople were "most unruly and impertinent"; they "acknowledged that they had no right in the furniture but wanted to be obstinate." Having accomplished the search on this plantation, the bureau agent then went to a neighboring plantation and performed the same service there.[55] It was not unusual for the bureau to approve planter and overseers' searches of freedpeople's homes on the pretext of recovering supposedly stolen crops or to approve labor contracts that included clauses permitting planters to freely enter and search the homes of contracting freedpeople.[56]

While field laborers endeavored to derail the patterns of invasion and exploitation that had been so common to antebellum life and threatened their freedom, freedwomen who worked in planter residences developed their own strategies to reshape life and labor. Just before the war, from one-third to one-half of the slave workforce on lowcountry rice plantations consisted of domestic servants, artisans, and other slaves with specialized work assignments; these slaves, involved in plantation operations outside the rice fields or waiting on the families of planters or overseers, had an experience of slavery very different from that of field hands.[57] Without the apparent separation between "master's time" and their own time that the task system permitted, house servants faced a more personal and daily struggle to limit the demands made of them. Female house servants were subject to a forced intimacy with slaveowning families, including a degree of vulnerability to sexual exploitation.

With the arrival of Union troops, former slave women began to abandon the mask of subservience they had been forced to wear as domestic slaves, and, in the immediate aftermath of war, female domestic servants, like field hands, first resorted to a work stoppage. Some servants preferred to leave their former owners and find new employers rather than fight with former owners over what they would and would not continue to do now that they were free. Planters' families frequently complained to each other of having to perform their own domestic labor, "their servants having all left them." Since planters viewed the training of new servants as burdensome, some forcibly prevented their former servants from seeking employment elsewhere. Fifteen-year-old Rebecca Jane Grant knew "we had been done freed," but still her uncle "stole me by night from my Missus," so that she could return to her own family.[58] Other planters asked ex-Confederate guerrillas to track down and punish or return house servants who fled their former owners.[59]

Some freedwomen who tried to exercise their new mobility suffered the painful consequences of a domestic slave's constant proximity to slaveowners. Mistresses who had treated the children of their domestic slaves as pets resisted separation from those children when freedwomen decided it was time to leave. Even worse, the children themselves may have resisted separation, having formed strong attachments to the white women who undoubtedly had more time to spend with them than did their enslaved mothers. Wartime diarist Mary Chesnut recorded the drama of a three-year-old child, "a great pet," who "did not wish to go even with his mother." The child was "torn" from the arms of the mistress by "ruthless Yanks" and turned over to his mother. The mother—whose torment and fury over slavery's interference with her child's loyalties and attachments can only be imagined—was described by the mistress as running away with her child, "whipping this screaming little rebel darky every foot of the way." Like other former slaves who found their freedom so quickly revoked, this mother and her child were soon forcibly returned by rebel pickets. The three-year-old was denied the opportunity to renew his confused attachments; both mother and child were banished from the house by the angry and jealous mistress.[60]

When house servants began to reappear voluntarily at planter residences during the summer and fall of 1865 in search of employment, they tried to implement important changes in their work and in their relations with the white women who now employed, rather than owned, them. Former mistresses complained (mostly to each other) that former slave women studiously transgressed the rituals of subservience; they "just drop down into a chair if they come to talk to you about anything & are as free as possible."[61] In attempting to distinguish their work as wage laborers from their experience of slavery, freedwomen focused many of their efforts on undermining the fundamental demand for the undivided attention and loyalty of domestic servants. Freedwomen challenged this expectation in two fundamental ways: by trying to focus their employment on the tasks to be performed rather than the people to be served; and by explicitly preferring labor arrangements designed to accommodate their own familial interests and responsibilities.

To the consternation of many women of the planter families, freedwomen insisted that domestic service be broken down into specific tasks or skills: washing, cooking, cleaning, and nursing became separate jobs. For example, Hagar, a former slave and house servant, insisted she "was not strong enough" to do the laundry and refused to wash "even a towel fit to look at." She could carry water and clean the rooms, but she would not do the laundry, nor would she turn and beat the mattresses. Months later, her employer still had not found a house servant who would agree to do washing as well as cooking.[62] Freedwomen also began to insist on their right to reject particularly arduous or demeaning labor, prompting complaints by women of one planter family when a domestic servant refused to wash her employer's "necessaries"—her menstrual rags.[63] Freedwomen may have gained considerable satisfaction not only from freeing themselves of what they felt was demeaning labor but also from knowing that former slaveowning women were now forced to perform such labor on their own.

Making their family responsibilities an explicit consideration in their labor arrangements, some freedwomen insisted, for example, on bringing their children along to their employer's house, or limiting the hours or days they worked, as they tried to balance the demands of wage work and child care.[64] Many white women began to view the families of domestic servants as encumbrances and distractions; they tried their best to employ servants without families, a "quality" some prospective employers valued above cleanliness, industry, and even deference.[65] Employers resented the demands of young children on their domestic servants ("her infant monopolizes her attentions," one plantation mistress complained), but welcomed the employment of mothers who were willing to put their older children to work as well.[66]

Freedwomen in domestic service also challenged the very nature of their relationship to planter families, seeking a new level of dignity even as servants. "Have you noticed with the Negroes at home," inquired one planter's wife to another, "that when you call they will never answer, every body [sic] up here finds it the case, they seem to think it is a sign of their freedom, heard one of them say, 'My Miss don't like it because I won't answer, but I ain't got no call to answer now.'" White employers sometimes faced the difficult choice of firing servants or finding a way to put up with the changes freedom was bringing into their households; others began what seemed like an endless search for the perfectly deferential and obedient servant, as promising servants proved themselves too assertive for the job ("she was too impudent for anything"). White women treasured those servants they could hire who still acted "humble & civil." [67]

When freedwomen employed as domestic servants attempted to define their own terms of labor, their efforts were made all the more difficult by the fact that plantation mistresses—no less than planters—were unwilling to concede the end of slavery and their loss of ownership and control over former slaves. When freedwomen struck at the core of the antebellum mythology of domestic servitude—that slave women had no lives, priorities, or identity outside their service to white families—slaveowners-turned-employers planned and schemed to prevent the return of formerly enslaved servants to their family and friends. Freedwomen became the target of considerable hostility and bitter resentment when they chose to abandon their former owners in search of their own families and lives.[68] Setting new boundaries and new terms on their household labor, freedwomen also challenged their employers' presumptions of intimacy and mutual dependency with their former slaves, while at the same time undermining the plantation mistress's veneer of authority in her ability to command and manage a household of servants.[69] Thus, the "servant problem" described by so many elite white South Carolinians in the postbellum period referred not only to the shrinking supply of labor, but also to the assertiveness of freedwomen in shaping the terms and conditions of their employment.

When freedwomen sought control over their paid and unpaid labor, they were driven not only by their determination to shape the meaning of free labor in lowcountry rice fields and planter residences but also by the increased demands on their domestic production in households stripped of the most basic tools and necessities. White observers seemed convinced that it was a desire not to work that motivated freedwomen, rather than an effort to negotiate the terms of their contracted work, or the necessity of devoting more of their time and resources to the direct care and support of their families, households, and independent crops. But when Union troops moved through the lowcountry at the close of the war, they had laid waste to the region's plantation infrastructure. Union soldiers destroyed or stole the household possessions of innumerable lowcountry slaves. Soldiers confiscated what little reserve of food or farm animals and poultry remained; even pots, pans, bedding, and mattresses were stripped from slave quarters. For many freedwomen, the material condition of their households was worse than it had been in slavery, and military and bureau officials had quickly forgotten their own role in making this so. However, the physical devastation of the countryside, the shortage of food and clothing and the most basic necessities, and the poor crops of the 1860s all heavily increased freedwomen's labor in their own homes. With their own survival and that of their families in the balance, laziness or an escape from hard work were luxuries they could not easily afford.

Freedwomen's "sweet Dreams of freedom" may be difficult to recover from the historical record, but their impact on South Carolina's transition to a free labor society cannot be denied. Far from passive or retreating figures withdrawing to the shadows of southern life, freedwomen played a visible and instrumental role in the reconstruction of life and labor in the postbellum South. They fought for greater freedom of movement between their household and family economies and the plantation economy, for greater insularity from the supervision of overseers and other hated figures from their recent past, and for the freedom to make their own decisions about how best to allocate their time and their labor. In nearly every arena of postbellum conflict, freedwomen also struggled to replace the antebellum configuration of plantation power relations with a new autonomy for African American women, one which protected their freedom both in the rice fields and plantation residences and outside them. Freedwomen assumed both the right to define black freedom and the responsibility for defending it, and our histories of slavery, war and Reconstruction have yet to acknowledge their bold lessons about the meaning of freedom in America.

Notes

I would like to thank Elsa Barkley Brown, Daniel Letwin, Steven Hahn, and Tera Hunter for their comments on earlier versions of this research presented at the 1992 North American Labor History Conference and the 1992 meeting of the Southern Historical Association. I would also like to thank Kathleen Brown, Noralee Frankel, Linda Gordon, Leslie Reagan, Susan Smith, and Doris Stormoen for their suggestions and support. This research was funded in part by a grant from the National Endowment for the Humanities.

1. Charles Manigault, "The Close of the War—The Negro, etc.," Manigault Family Papers, Records of Ante-Bellum Southern Plantations, Series (Ser.) J, Pt. 4, Reel (R) 1.

2. See, for example, Ira Berlin, Joseph P. Reidy, and Leslie S. Rowland, eds., *Freedom: A Documentary History of Emancipation, 1861–1867, Ser. II: The Black Military Experience* (Cambridge: Cambridge University Press, 1982); Ira Berlin, Barbara J. Fields, Thavolia Glymph, Joseph P. Reidy, and Leslie S. Rowland, eds., *Freedom: A Documentary History of Emancipation, 1861–1867, Ser. I, vol. 1: The Destruction of Slavery* (Cambridge: Cambridge University Press, 1985); Ira Berlin, Thavolia Glymph, Steven F. Miller, Joseph P. Reidy, Leslie S. Rowland, and Julie Saville, eds., *Freedom: A Documentary History of Emancipation, 1861–1867, Ser. I, vol. 3: The Wartime Genesis of Free Labor: The Lower South* (Cambridge: Cambridge University Press, 1990); Barbara Jeanne Fields, *Slavery and Freedom on the Middle Ground: Maryland during the Nineteenth Century* (New Haven: Yale University Press, 1985); Eric Foner, *Nothing but Freedom: Emancipation and Its Legacy* (Baton Rouge: Louisiana State University Press, 1983) and *Reconstruction: America's Unfinished Revolution, 1863–1877* (New York: Harper and Row, 1988); Thavolia Glymph and John J. Kushma, eds., *Essays on the Postbellum Southern Economy* (College Station: University of Texas Press, 1985).

3. The conflicts and alliances among and between southern and northern participants in Reconstruction also continue to be described as though women were not a part of the social landscape and as though gender was peripheral to the expression of power and domination in American cultures. The important exceptions include Jacqueline Jones, *Labor of Love, Labor of Sorrow: Black Women, Work, and the Family from Slavery to the Present* (New York: Basic Books, 1985); Susan A. Mann, "Slavery, Sharecropping, and Sexual Inequality," *Signs: A Journal of Women in Culture and Society* 14, no. 4 (1989): 774–98; Noralee Frankel, "The Southern Side of 'Glory': Mississippi African-American Women during the Civil War," in *"We Specialize in the Wholly Impossible": A Reader in Black Women's History*, ed. Darlene Clark Hine, Wilma King, and Linda Reed (Brooklyn: Carlson Publishing, 1995), 335–42; Laura F. Edwards, "Sexual Violence, Gender, Reconstruction, and the Extension of Patriarchy in Granville County, North Carolina," *North Carolina Historical Review* LXVIII, no. 3 (1991): 234–60; Catherine Clinton, "Reconstructing Freedwomen," in *Divided Houses: Gender and the Civil War*, ed. Catherine Clinton and Nina Silber (New York: Oxford

University Press, 1992), 306–19; Victoria E. Bynum, *Unruly Women: The Politics of Social and Sexual Control in the Old South, 1840–1865* (Chapel Hill: University of North Carolina Press, 1992), and Elsa Barkley Brown, "Negotiating and Transforming the Public Sphere: African American Political Life in the Transition from Slavery to Freedom," *Public Culture* 7 (1994): 107–46. See also Drew Gilpin Faust, "'Trying to Do a Man's Business': Slavery, Violence, and Gender in the American Civil War," *Gender & History* 4, no. 2 (1992): 197–214.

4. See Roger L. Ransom and Richard Sutch, *One Kind of Freedom: The Economic Consequences of Emancipation* (Cambridge: Cambridge University Press, 1977), 44–47 and 232–36, for their estimate of the rate of freedwomen's retreat from the paid workforce in select districts of the Cotton South. Their study is often used to support assertions about the prevalence of women's withdrawal, despite the implicit and explicit limitations of their estimates. Ransom and Sutch did not address, for example, how variations in family size and household make-up, plantation size, or the process and organization of agricultural production affected the amount of work performed by women in slavery or freedom, nor examine the propagandistic intent of such sources as Freedmen's Bureau estimates of work. Historians have tended to overlook the limitations of Ransom and Sutch's findings. Jacqueline Jones uses *One Kind of Freedom* as the basis for her assertion about the prevalence of withdrawal (in *Labor of Love, Labor of Sorrow*) but also emphasizes that first-hand observations about withdrawal were common (58–63). Both Lawrence Powell (*New Masters: Northern Planters during the Civil War and Reconstruction* [New Haven: Yale University Press, 1980], 108–9) and Jones attempt to contextualize women's withdrawal in terms of the exploitation and oppression they encountered in the postbellum organization of free labor.

5. See, for example, William Cohen, *At Freedom's Edge: Black Mobility and the Southern White Quest for Racial Control, 1861–1875* (Baton Rouge: Louisiana State University Press, 1991), 14; and Herbert G. Gutman, *The Black Family in Slavery and Freedom, 1750–1925* (New York: Pantheon Press, 1976), 167–68. Leon F. Litwack suggests that by insisting on the withdrawal of their wives from the workforce, freedmen attempted to "reinforce their position as the head of the family in accordance with the accepted norms of the dominant society" (Leon F. Litwack, *Been in the Storm So Long: The Aftermath of Slavery* [New York: Knopf, 1979], 245), but in a following paragraph also portrays withdrawal as a strategy by which freedwomen gained control over the allocation and conditions of their paid labor.

6. Jones, *Labor of Love, Labor of Sorrow,* 58; see also Ira Berlin, Steven F. Miller, and Leslie S. Rowland, "Afro-American Families in the Transition from Slavery to Freedom," *Radical History Review* 42 (1988): 89–121. In his work *Branches without Roots: Genesis of the Black Working Class in the American South* (New York: Oxford University Press, 1986), Gerald Jaynes challenges the presumption of universality by historians who have described freedwomen's work choices. He contrasts the rate of women's participation in different plantation systems and finds significantly less participation by women in postbellum sugar, as opposed to cotton, plantation agriculture (228–33). Jaynes also argues that the purchasing power of women's wage work lagged behind the value of women's unpaid social and reproductive labor, making "withdrawal" from the

wage labor force and increased work in independent gardens and cash crops a logical and rational choice.

7. Sharon Ann Holt, "Making Freedom Pay: Freedpeople Working for Themselves, North Carolina, 1865–1900," *The Journal of Southern History* LX, no. 2 (1994): 228–62; and Elsa Barkley Brown, "Negotiating and Transforming the Public Sphere."

8. See Geo. E. Pingree to Maj. Edw. Deane, 31 August 1867, R 35, National Archives Microfilm Publication (M) 869, and "Recent Election in South Carolina: Testimony Taken by the Select Committee on the Recent Election in South Carolina," House Miscellaneous Document No. 31, 44th Congress, 2d Session (Washington, D.C.: Government Printing Office, 1877), 15, 19, 24, 27, 35, 38, 40, 55, 63.

9. See Leslie A. Schwalm, "The Meaning of Freedom: African-American Women and Their Transition from Slavery to Freedom in Lowcountry South Carolina" (Ph.D. diss., University of Wisconsin, 1991).

10. On emancipation and Reconstruction in lowcountry South Carolina, see Willie Lee Rose, *Rehearsal for Reconstruction: The Port Royal Experiment* (Indianapolis: Bobbs-Merrill, 1976); Joel Williamson, *After Slavery: The Negro in South Carolina during Reconstruction, 1861–1877* (Chapel Hill: University of North Carolina Press, 1965); Thomas C. Holt, *Black over White: Negro Political Leadership in South Carolina during Reconstruction* (Urbana: University of Illinois Press, 1977); Charles Joyner, *Down by the Riverside: A South Carolina Slave Community* (Urbana: University of Illinois Press, 1984); John Scott Strickland, "Traditional Culture and Moral Economy: Social and Economic Change in the South Carolina Lowcountry, 1865–1910," in *The Countryside in the Age of Capitalist Transformation,* ed. Steven Hahn and Jonathon Prude (Chapel Hill: University of North Carolina Press, 1985), 141–78 and "'No More Mud Work': The Struggle for the Control of Labor and Production in Low Country South Carolina, 1863–1880," in *The Southern Enigma: Essays on Race, Class, and Folk Culture,* ed. Walter J. Fraser, Jr. and Winfred B. Moore, Jr. (Westport, Conn.: Greenwood Press, 1983), 43–62; Philip Morgan, "Work and Culture: The Task System and the World of Lowcountry Blacks, 1700 to 1880," *William and Mary Quarterly,* 3rd Ser. 39 (1982): 563–99; and Julie Saville, *The Work of Reconstruction: From Slave to Wage Laborer in South Carolina, 1860–1870* (Cambridge: Cambridge University Press, 1994).

11. Ira Berlin and Philip D. Morgan, "Labor and the Shaping of Slave Life in the Americas," in *Cultivation and Culture: Labor and the Shaping of Slave Life in the Americas,* ed. Ira Berlin and Philip D. Morgan (Charlottesville: University Press of Virginia, 1993), 1.

12. See Richard H. Sewell, *A House Divided: Sectionalism and Civil War, 1848–1865* (Baltimore: The Johns Hopkins University Press, 1988), 101–25; Paul W. Gates, *Agriculture and the Civil War* (New York: Alfred A. Knopf, 1965), 3–45; Emory M. Thomas, *The Confederate Nation, 1861–1865* (New York: Harper and Row, 1979), 236–42; and James L. Roardk, *Masters without Slaves: Southern Planters in the Civil War and Reconstruction* (New York: Norton, 1977).

13. J. H. Easterby, ed., *The South Carolina Rice Plantation As Revealed in the Papers of Robert F.W. Allston* (Chicago: University of Chicago Press, 1945), 291–92, 309, 312, 314, 316; Adele Petigru Allston to Charles Allston, 8 July 1863, and Adele Petigru Allston

to Benjamin Allston, 30 June 1864, both in R.F.W. Allston Family Papers, South Caroliniana Library, University of South Carolina (SCL); William Capers to Louis Manigault, 20 August and 24 September 1863, Louis Manigault Papers, Ser. F, Part (Pt.) II, R6, Records of Ante-Bellum Southern Plantations.

14. James M. Clifton, ed., *Life and Labor on Argyle Island: Letters and Documents of a Savannah River Rice Plantation, 1833–1867* (Savannah: The Beehive Press, 1978), 320; C. Vann Woodward, ed., *Mary Chestnut's Civil War* (New Haven: Yale University Press, 1981), 48, 78, 234, 464; Mary Elliott Johnstone to Mamma [Mrs. William Elliott], 1861 or 1862, Elliott and Gonzales Family Papers [Ser. 1.7, Folder 67], Southern Historical Collection, University of North Carolina (SHC).

15. Elizabeth Hyde Botume, First Days amongst the Contrabands (1893; reprint, New York; Arno, 1968), 124–27; Ira Berlin et al., eds., *The Wartime Genesis of Free Labor*, 316–19; Virginia M. Adams, ed., *On the Altar of Freedom: A Black Soldier's Civil War Letters from the Front: Corporal James Henry Gooding* (Amherst: University of Massachusetts Press, 1991), 110–11; Rupert Sargent Holland, ed., *Letters and Diaries of Laura M. Towne* (1912; reprint, New York: Negro Universities Press, 1969), 20–22, 56, 140, 144–45; Elizabeth Ware Pearson, ed., *Letters and Diaries from Port Royal, 1862–1866* (1906; reprint, New York: Arno Press, 1969), 250, 303–4; see also Leslie A. Schwalm, *"A Hard Fight for We": Women's Transition from Slavery to Freedom in South Carolina* (University of Illinois Press, forthcoming), chap. 4.

16. *Charleston Daily Courier,* 31 May 1866.

17. Following Johnson's February 1866 veto of the Freedmen's Bureau Bill, including the bill's 3-year extension on the possessory titles freedpeople held to Sea Island lands, the bureau and the military department in the state yielded to the inevitability of restoration. By March 1866, the possessory titles to Sea Island land held by freedpeople were subject to closer scrutiny, and those who held no title or who had settled on land other than that specified in the title were subject to eviction. See Martin Abbott, *The Freedmen's Bureau in South Carolina, 1865–1872* (Chapel Hill: University of North Carolina Press, 1967), 60–62; Foner, *Reconstruction*, 161–63; and Williamson, *After Slavery*, 84–86.

18. Lt. Col. B. F. Smith to Maj. Genl. Devens, 20 January 1866, Letters Received, Ser. 2392, 4th Subdist., Mil. Dist. of Charleston SC, National Archives Record Group (RG) 393, Pt. II, No. 142; and George C. Fox to Lt. Col. A.J. Willard, 2 November 1865, Registered Letters Received, Ser. 3202, Georgetown SC Subasst. Comr., RG 105.

19. W. C. Munnerlyn to Maj. Genl. Saxton, 29 December 1865, Unregistered Letters Received, R 21, M 869; Geo. C. Fox, Monthly Land Report for the State of South Carolina, 31 October 1865, Misc. Records, Ser. 3212, Georgetown SC Sub-asst. Comr., RG 105.

20. George C. Rogers, Jr., The History of Georgetown County, South Carolina (Columbia: University of South Carolina Press, 1970), 407; testimony of Job Mayzeck, 11 March 1873, and testimony of Dennis Hazel, 12 March 1873, both in claim of Job Mayzeck, Disallowed Claims, RG 233; and testimony of Dennis Hazel, 18 March 1873, claim of Alonzo Jackson, Southern Claims Commission, RG 217.

21. Testimony of Dennis Hazel, 4 April 1866; Statement of Francis S. Parker, Jr., 4 April 1866; Charges and Specifications against Jim, Job, and Stewart, 2 April 1866;

Charges against Sukey, 1 April 1866; Charges against Becky, 1 April 1866; Francis S. Parker, Jr., to Col. Smith, 31 March 1866, and undated, unsigned list of fourteen names, all in Letters Received, Ser. 2392, 4th Subdist., Mil. Dist. of Charleston SC, RG 393, Pt. 2, No. 142 [C1606]. See also Lt. Col. Smith to Capt. M. N. Rice, 7 April 1866, vol. 156 Department of the South (DS), pp. 62–63, Letters Sent, Ser. 2389, 4th Subdist., Mil. Dist. of Charleston SC, RG 393, Pt. 2, No. 142; Capt. B.F. Smith to Major H.W. Smith, 6 April 1866, Reports of Conditions and Operations, Georgetown, R 34, M 869; and Capt. B.F. Smith, "Semi-Monthly Report of Persons Arrested," 15 May 1866, Reports of Arrests of Civilians, Ser. 4161, Department of the Carolinas, RG 393, Pt. I. Lt. Col. A.J. Willard to Capt. Geo. W. Hooker, 20 October 1865, Vol. 156 DS, pp. 8–10, Letters Sent, Ser. 2389, 4th Sub-dist., Mil. Dist. of Charleston SC, RG 393, Pt. II, No. 142 [C-1614]. Bracketed letters and numbers (e.g., [C-1614]) refer to file numbers assigned to documents copied from the national Archives by the editors of the Freedmen and Southern Society Project at the University of Maryland, source of the multi-volume history, *Freedom: A Documentary History of Emancipation, 1861–1867.*

22. James C. Scott (*Domination and the Arts of Resistance: Hidden Transcripts* [New Haven: Yale University Press, 1990]) offers a theory of confrontations between dominant and subordinate groups which is helpful to understanding the changing relations between former slaveowners and former slaves in the postbellum South.

23. Williams Middleton to J. Frances Fisher, 17 November 1865, Middleton Family Papers, South Carolina Historical Society (SCHS).

24. Entry for 24 August 1865, James Chaplin Beecher Memorandum Book, 1865–1866, James Chaplin Beecher Papers, Perkins Library, Duke University (PL).

25. Wm. G. Robert to Captain [Upham], 20 November 1865, Ser. 2384, Letters Received, Subdistrict of Coosawatchie, RG 393, Pt. 2, No. 141 [C-1581].

26. Statement by W.M. Roberston, 15 September 1865, and "List of Negroes with their Characters," undated, both enclosed in Lt. W. Wood to Lt. S. Baker, 16 September 1865, Letters Received, Ser. 2384, Subdistrict of Coosawatchie SC, RG 393, DS, Pt. II, No. 141 [C-1593].

27. One planter complained to military authorities that "All male hands but two have left the place . . . so I have my houses, filled with women and children, 12 (twelve) women who are full hands, but will not work, 6 (six) half hands, 4 (four) old and crippled, 21 (twenty-one) children fit for not work of any kind, 43 (forty-three) in all" (Benj. R. Bostick to Capt. Upham, 17 October 1865, Letters Received, Ser. 2384, Subdistrict of Coosawatchie SC, RG 393, DS, Pt. 2, No. 141 [C-585]).

28. J.S. Bostick to Capt., n.d. [September 1865?], Letters Received, Ser. 2384, Subdistrict of Coosawatchie SC, RG 393, DS, Pt. 2, No. 141 [C-1588].

29. William Robert to Capt. Upham, 13 and 28 September 1865, and to Captain [Upham], 20 November 1865, all in Letters Received, Ser. 2384, Subdistrict of Coosawatchie SC, RG 393, Pt. 2, No. 141 [C-1581].

30. Elizabeth Catherine Porcher to Philip Edward Porcher, 23 March 1865, typed transcript, Folder 19, Palmer Family Papers, SCL; Easterby, ed., *The South Carolina Rice Plantation,* 208; Col. James C. Beecher to Gilbert Pillsbury, 11 August 1865, and G. Pillsbury to Col. James C. Beecher, 16 August 1865, both in R 34, M 869; entry for

10 August 1865, James Chaplin Beecher Memorandum Book, 1865–66, James Chaplin Beecher Papers, PL.

31. G. G. Batchelder to Maj. Genl. R. Saxton, 10 October 1865, R 20, M 869.

32. G. Pillsbury to Maj. H.W. Smith, 30 December 1865, Unregistered Letters Received, R 20, M 869.

33. This issue has been explored by Catherine Clinton, "Reconstructing Freedwomen," in Clinton and Silber, eds., *Divided Houses,* 306–19, and by Laura F. Edwards, "Sexual Violence," 237–60. For an example of violence against lowcountry freedwomen, see Lt. Col. Garrett Nagle, Report of Outrages Committed, 31 July 1866, Colleton District, Ser. 3353, RG 105.

34. Planters' exaggerated hopes for what restoration could accomplish are well documented in Daniel E. Huger Smith, Alice R. Huger Smith, and Arney R. Childs, eds., *Mason Smith Family Letters, 1860–1868* (Columbia: University of South Carolina Press, 1950).

35. Major James P. Roy to Lt. Col. W.L.M. Burger, 9 December 1865 and 1 February 1866, both in Letters Received, Ser. 4109, Dept. of SC, RG 393, Pt. 1.

36. *Charleston Daily Courier,* 24 January 1866; William Bull Pringle to Gen. Sickles, 18 January 1866, RG 98; Bvt. Lt. Col. B.F. Smith to 1st Lt. M.N. Rice, 21 January 1866, Vol. 156 DS, pp. 40–41, Letters Sent, Ser. 2389, 4th Subdist., Military Dist. of Charleston, RG 393, Pt. 2, No. 142 [c-1616]; Bvt. Lt. Col. B.F. Smith to 1st Lt. M.N. Rice, 21 January 1866, Vol. 156, DS, pp. 40–41, Letters Sent, Ser. 2389, 4th Subdistrict, Military Dist. of Charleston, RG 393, Pt. 2, No. 142 [c-1616]; Wm. R. Maxwell to Genl. Sickles and Genl. Bennet, 1 March 1866, Letters Received, Ser. 2392, RG 393, Pt. II, No. 142.

37. W. St. J. Mazyck to Col. Smith, 4 February 1866, Letters Received, Ser. 2392, 4th Subdist., Mil. Dist. of Charleston SC, RG 393, Pt. II, No. 142.

38. Maj. Gen. D.E. Sickles to James L. Orr, 17 December 1865, South Carolina Governors' Papers; Capt. D.T. Corbin to Maj. H.W. Smith, 28 February 1866, Mt. Pleasant, Reports of Conditions and Operations, R 34 M 869; Gen. R.K. Scott, Circular Letter to the Landlords and Laborers of the State of South Carolina, 26 December 1866, *Charleston Daily Courier,* 5 January 1867; Gen. R.K. Scott to Maj. Gen. O.O. Howard, 21 February 1866, reprinted in U.S., Senate, Senate Executive Documents, 39th Congress, 1st Session, No. 27, p. 25.

39. [?] McKim to Capt. F.W. Liedtke, 25 June 1866, and J. Calhoun Cain to Capt. F.W. Liedtke, 11 August 1866, both in Letters Received, Ser. 3277, Moncks Corner SC, Subasst. Comr., RG 105.

40. Barney [Edward Barnwell Heyward] to Tab [Catherine Heyward], 5 May 1867, Heyward Family Papers, SCL.

41. John William DeForest, A Union Officer in the Reconstruction (New Haven: Yale University Press, 1948), 94.

42. *Charleston Daily Courier,* 25 May 1866; Olney Harleston to General R. K. Scott, 21 January 1867, Testimony, Reports, and Other Records Relating to Court Cases and Complaints, Ser. 3284, Moncks Corner SC, Subasst. Comr., RG 105.

43. The labor contracts discussed here are located in Ser. 3210 and 3211, Labor Contracts, Georgetown SC Subasst. Comr., RG 105. Information from additional contracts

which are not themselves extant can be found in the Reports of Contracts Approved in the Subdistricts, Ser. 2930, SC Assist. Commr., RG 105, reproduced in R 42, M 869. The problems associated with this particular kind of evidence include the casual enforcement of contract terms and constant efforts by both employers and employees to overturn the contract terms; whether the contracts were representative of labor arrangements, given the likelihood that many plantations operated without contracts; and difficulties in transcribing the documents, particularly in identifying the assignees by sex.

44. The data represented here are an imperfect and incomplete representation of postbellum labor arrangements. Judging from the total number of contracts which are extant for Georgetown District, there were more plantations operating without labor contracts than operating with. For these and other reasons, the contracts can only be considered a closed universe, rather than representative of all plantation labor in this particular lowcountry district.

45. E. Francis Fischer to Williams Middleton, 10 February 1866, Middleton Family Papers, SCHS.

46. On rape, violence, and women's experience of slavery, see Catherine Clinton, "'Southern Dishonor': Flesh, Blood, Race, and Bondage," in *In Joy and In Sorow: Women, Family, and Marriage in the Victorian South*, ed. Carol Blesser (New York: Oxford University Press, 1991), 52–68.

47. Rev. C. W. Howard, "Conditions and Resources of Georgia," Report of the Commissioner of Agriculture for the Year 1866 (Washington, D.C.: Department of the South, 1867), 567–80.

48. C. P. [illeg.] to Mary Elliott Johnstone, 2 March 1868, Ser. 1.8, Elliott-Gonzales Papers, SHC.

49. Edwin M. Tilton to Col. Smith, 18 January 1866, Vol. 156 DS, Letters Sent, Ser. 2392, Post of Georgetown SC, RG 393, Pt. 2, No. 142; and Gen. James C. Beecher to Lieut. M.N. Rice, 21 January 1866, Letters and Reports Received, Ser. 4112, Department of SC, RG 393, Pt. 1.

50. B. H. Pinners to Col. Smith, 1 May 1866, Letters Received, Ser. 2392, Post of Georgetown SC, RG 393, Pt. II, No. 142.

51. Edwin M. Tilton to Col. Smith, 16 January 1866 and B.H. Pinners to Col. Smith, 1 May 1866, both in Letters Received, Ser. 2392, Post of Georgetown SC, RG 393, Pt. II, No. 142.

52. See George Singleton vs. John Henry Porcher and Samuel Ravenel, Proceedings of Provost Courts, Military Tribunals, and Post Court Martial Cases tried in North and South Carolina, Ser. 4251 A, Judge Advocate, RG 393. For another example of how white men used the pretense of searching freedpeople's homes as a means of terrorizing them, see freedman Austin Elmore's charges against Peter Bird, who entered the Elmore home; beat Austin, his wife, and mother with a pistol and an iron; and smashed earthenware, provisions, and other property in the cabin; see Affidavit by Austin Elmore, 24 December 1866, Misc. Records, Ser. 3353, Summerville SC, Subasst. Comr., RG 105.

53. For an example of the violence which accompanied these searches, see Affidavit of Austin Elmore, 24 September 1866, Colleton Dist., Ser. 3353, RG 105.

54. Lt. Col. B. F. Smith to Lt. M. N. Rice, 20 February 1866, vol. 156 DS, pp. 53–54, Letters Sent, Ser. 2389, 4th Subdist., Mil. Dist. of Charleston, RG 393, Pt. 2, No. 142 [c-1616].

55. C. V. Wilson to Major O'Brien, 18 July 1866, Testimony, Reports, and Other Records Relating to Court Cases and Complaints, Ser. 3284, Moncks Corner SC, Subasst. Comr., RG 105.

56. Entry for 10 October 1866, vol. 239, Register of Complaints, Ser. 3283, Moncks Corner SC, Subasst. Comr., RG 105; Smith et al., eds., *Mason Smith Family Letters*, 264–65; Contract between A.G. Heriot and Freedmen, 1 February 1866, Labor Contracts, Ser. 3211, Georgetown SC, Subassist. Commr., RG 105.

57. Based on slave lists from plantations belonging to Charles Manigault in 1845 (Clifton, ed., *Life and Labor on Argyle Island*, 31–32), and plantations belonging to James R. Sparkman in 1847 and 1858 ("Task Hands 1847 June," 1827–1845, and "Dirleton 1858" and "Task Hands Birdfield January 1 1858," 1857–1859, James Ritchie Sparkman Papers, Ser. A, Pt. II, R6, Records of Ante-Bellum Southern Plantations).

58. George P. Rawick, ed., *The American Slave: A Composite Autobiography* (Westport, Conn.: Greenwood Press, 1972), *South Carolina*, Vol. 2, Pt. 2: 179–80. In Virginia Ingraham Burr, ed., *The Secret Eye: The Journal of Ella Gertrude Clanton Thomas, 1848–1889* (Chapel Hill: University of North Carolina Press, 1990), Thomas describes a very similar postwar scenario where a young girl, a house servant and previously her slave, conspires with her mother—sold away for bad behavior—and "escaped" from the Thomas household, much to Thomas's disappointment (267–68).

59. Susan R. Jervey and Charlotte St. J. Ravenel, *Two Diaries from Middle St. John's, Berkeley, South Carolina, February–May 1865* (Charletson, South Carolina: St. John's Hunting Club, 1921), 42.

60. C. Vann Woodward and Elisabeth Muhlenfeld, eds., *The Private Mary Chesnut: The Unpublished Civil War Diaries* (New York: Oxford University Press, 1984), 246.

61. Elizabeth Catherine Porcher to Hattie, 25 October 1865, Palmer Family Papers, SCL.

62. Alice A. Palmer to Hattie, 20 July and 2 August 1865, Folder 19, Palmer Family Papers, SCL.

63. Alice A. Palmer to Hattie, 17 October 1866, and Elizabeth Catherine Porcher to Hattie, 25 October 1865, both in Palmer Family Papers, SCL. See also Major Jos. Totten to Inspector General, 9 May 1866, T-19 1866, Letters Received, Ser. 15, RG 159 [J-51], for a description of the changes freedwomen made in domestic service.

64. Elizabeth Catherine Porcher to [My Dear Hattie], 5 August [1866], and E. L. Porcher to Hariet [?], [1870], Palmer Family Papers, SCL; Meta M. Grimball to J.B. Grimball, 5 January 1866, John Berkeley Grimball Papers, PL.

65. Hattie [Harriet Rutledge Elliott Gonzales] to Mama [Ann Hutchinson Smith Elliott], Monday 11th [1867–68], Ser. 1.8, Elliott-Gonzales Papers, SHC.

66. Mary Elliott Johnstone to Mrs. William Elliott, 10 January 1866, Ser. 1.7, Elliott-Gonzales Papers, SHC, and E.C.P. to Hattie, [1866] and 24 May 1868, both in Palmer Family Papers, SCL.

67. Alice Palmer to [My Dear Hattie], 19 September 1866, and E.C.P. to Hattie, 25 September [1866], and 28 November 1867, all in Palmer Family Papers, SCL.

68. Mary Elliott Johnstone to Mrs. William Elliott, 10 January 1866, and Mary Elliott Johnstone to Ralph E. Elliott, 9 July 1865, both in Ser. 1.7, Elliot-Gonzales Papers, SHC.

69. Elizabeth Fox-Genovese has explored white women's identities as household mistresses in *Within the Plantation Household: Black and White Women of the Old South* (Chapel Hill: University of North Carolina Press, 1988); see also Emily Elliott to Mary Eliott Johnstone, 21 September 1866, Elliott-Gonzales Papers, SHC.

Who Was John Henry?

Railroad Construction, Southern Folklore, and the Birth of Rock and Roll

Scott Reynolds Nelson

Legend describes John Henry as a powerful black man whose hammer cleared the way for the Chesapeake & Ohio Railroad. Hammer met chisel, million-year-old mountains yielded, and John Henry sang to the rhythm all the while.

> Ain't no hammer
> Ain't no hammer
> In these mountains
> In these mountains
> Rings like mine

But the years following the Civil War witnessed a new sound in the mountains of West Virginia. Engineers experimented with steam-powered rock drills and threatened to replace the hammer man and shaker team immortalized by the John Henry story. In the legend, John Henry challenged one of the new drills to a race and so began the great contest between man and machine. At day's end, the man had drilled fourteen feet and the steam drill had made only nine. Though victorious, an exhausted John Henry collapsed—his head "spinning 'round"—and, with his last words, asked for a cool drink of water. The end had come, and the story tells how his body was taken to the White House and buried in the sand. Not to be forgotten, John Henry's grave beckoned to passing steam engines: "Every locomotive came roarin' by / says yonder lies a steel-drivin' man."

The song "John Henry" and the accompanying legend has resonated with gang laborers and folk singers, labor organizers and fiddle bands, dime novelists and blues musicians. Among these radically dissimilar people, the story of a battle between a powerful black workingman and a newfangled steam drill has been adopted, transformed, and retransmitted. Over four hundred versions of the song exist, dating back to the 1920s. John Henry's race with a steam drill, his victory, and his death immediately afterward have functioned as a legend about the conflict between workers and modern machinery.

38

The story has been variously interpreted as a tale about workers' adversaries: bosses, white men, corporations, and new technology. The folklorist Archie Green has called the ballad of John Henry the prototypical labor song, a nearly universal story of the problems of American workers. Scholars have also noted the tale's coded sexual language—of hammers, drilling, and the love of Polly Ann—that may have made it a universally appealing story for young men. In Philadelphia, men ask one another, "How's your hammer hanging?" Cardiologists have coined the term "John Henry syndrome" to describe black men's propensities for hypertension and heart attack. A line of oversized dress shirts and slacks carries John Henry's name on the pockets. In the schoolrooms of working-class Cleveland and rural West Virginia, teachers describe his exploits to inspire black boys and girls to think about their history. The story has been adapted as a play, a musical, a Disney cartoon, a half-dozen children's books, and a comic book character.[1] The American Folklife Center calls it the most researched American folk song.[2] But who was John Henry?

Between 1927 and 1933, two folklorists and their students sought to answer that question. But despite extensive oral interviews, newspaper advertisements, letters to railroad managers and former workers, neither researcher found proof that John Henry was a real person who beat a steam drill and then died. The Big Bend Tunnel on the C&O railroad had been dug between 1870 and 1873, but there was no conclusive evidence of a steam drill, a steel driller named John Henry, or a contest between them. These two researchers—a sociologist, Guy Johnson, and a professor of literature, Louis Chappell—published their oral interviews and dozens of versions of the song, and moved on.

Historians tend to regard music as background rather than raw material. Appropriated for book titles by countless historians, music itself is seldom seen as a primary source. But if we piece together labor folklore, the manuscript census of population (previously unavailable), Virginia penitentiary records (restricted until recently), Virginia county court records, the engineering records of the C&O railroad (which Johnson and Chappell believed to have been lost), and the lyrics to the song itself, we do find John Henry, a man shipped west to do grading and tunnel work on the C&O. He was not, however, a free black man of massive proportions. He was a man whose death marked a terrible, largely unrecorded tragedy in the mountains between Virginia and West Virginia.

John Henry was a convict laborer leased to the C&O railroad by the Virginia penitentiary. Arrested as a young man in Prince George County, Virginia, in 1866, he was tried in the newly constituted county courts under the notorious "black codes,"[3] for housebreaking and larceny. Sent to the state penitentiary in Richmond for a ten-year term, he served two before being shipped off to work as a gang laborer on the C&O. By 1870, contractors shipped their hired convicts to the Lewis Tunnel, on the border between Virginia and West Virginia, where prisoners really did work alongside steam drills and also died by the hundreds. John Henry disappeared from penitentiary records before his sentence was complete, because, like the many other prisoners marked "transferred," he probably died on the job.

In the song, the tunnel where John Henry died is the Big Bend, but in fact he died working on the Lewis Tunnel, which was dug in the same years. Big Bend Tunnel works better as a lyric, and as many later versions of the song demonstrate, workers turned their own tunnels, or nearby tunnels, into the tunnel that killed John Henry.[4] Thus, while the event occurred in Lewis Tunnel, it was probably first sung at the Big Bend Tunnel nearby. Multiple sources confirm that the Lewis Tunnel was the source of the song. In fact, when Johnson and Chappell were doing their research in the late 1920s, many local informants mentioned the Lewis Tunnel, dug by convicts, as the source of the song; both Johnson and Chappell failed to follow these leads.[5] Some of Chappell's informants from the 1920s recalled that John Henry was a convict, but Chappell dismissed these black informants as unreliable, preferring to trust "white citizens in good standing" only.[6] Chappell, arriving on the railroad line first, ignored and insulted black informants. He followed the lead of whites interested in calling attention to the town of Talcott, West Virginia. Johnson, arriving later, found black informants unwilling to talk about the man or the legend. Both researchers received bowdlerized versions of the tale.

By reexamining the sources and listening to those old informants, and to the song itself, we can discover where the bodies were buried, including John Henry's. This is one of the uglier stories of civil engineering, of a modern corporate railroad system built from the dead. The real story of John Henry is even more disturbing than the tragic ballad itself.

John Henry Appears to Folklorists

The John Henry legend first came to the attention of folklore scholars in 1909, when Louise Rand Bascom, a Wellesley student home for the summer in Highlands, North Carolina, published a couplet of a song that she had heard about. Bascom said she had heard of a fiddle tune and ballad, but had only a phrase of it: "Johnie Henry was a hard-workin' man, / He died with a hammer in his hand."[7] Fiddlers played the songs at yearly conventions in the mountains of southwestern North Carolina, and Bascom had asked a few people about it. A brief examination of Bascom's own life suggests that she may have heard of the fiddle tune from the family's white maid, whose two sons were apparently fiddlers. Bascom quipped then that a song about hard work could not really be native to the hills of North Carolina.[8]

Four years later, in 1913, Eber Carle Perrow, a University of Louisville English professor and lover of folk songs, picked up the trail. He transcribed from memory a brief John Henry song he had heard in east Tennessee in 1905, and a longer version he had acquired in 1912 from someone in Kentucky. "Among the workmen on the railroads in the South," he wrote, "there has been formed a considerable body of verse about John Henry, a famous steel-driving man."[9] After Perrow's discovery, a flood of longer versions came from the Kentucky folklorist Josiah Combs, the University of Texas's John Lomax, Hampton University's Natalie Curtis Burlin, and Duke University's Frank C. Brown.[10]

For a song that had not been copyrighted or apparently widely performed in cities (no sheet music has been discovered before 1922), English professors at colleges throughout the South found that they were only minutes away from workers who could recite the song from memory. From black men in Mississippi, "mountain whites" in Kentucky, black miners in Virginia, and track liners on the C&O railroad came a collection of songs with as many as a dozen verses, most of which had the structure of a ballad.[11] Perrow had been the first to recover a separate group of "hammer songs," two-stanza or three-stanza songs sung to the accompaniment of a sledge hammer, which referred to the death of John Henry from overwork.[12] In 1915 William Aspenwall Bradley, a poet and collector of folk stories, provided the first description of the song's performance. He was in Berea, Kentucky, in front of a city jail, when he first overheard the song:

> There a group of village boys would congregate, pick the banjo, sing, and execute the infinitely varied steps of the "hoe-down," while the other boys behind the bars would look out through the narrow windows and join in all the jokes and laughter. Sometimes the banjo would be on the inside instead of on the outside, and there was one youth, "Bad Bill," a favorite performer, who was certain on such occasions to respond to the clamorous request, "Sang Bill, now *you* sang!" with an exceedingly popular composition entitled "John Henry," or "The Steam Drill."[13]

Folklorists found the song among fiddle players in the mountains of North Carolina, Virginia, West Virginia, and Kentucky as well as among railroad hands as far west as Texas.

The chronology gets messier as the song became more famous, but the earliest recorded versions provide more clues to the possible sites where the legend originated. The jazz and blues legend W. C. Handy copyrighted the first printed score of the folk song in 1922 as "John Henry blues."[14] Handy believed that John Henry worked in West Virginia.[15] In 1924 Atlanta's Fiddlin' John Carson—one of the first "hillbilly" artists on phonograph and radio—recorded a version of the song, as did Gid Tanner and Riley Puckett, who later formed the famous string band "Gid Tanner and His Skillet Lickers." Both Carson and the Skillet Lickers helped establish the sound that would become country music.

In that same year, a black street musician from Cleveland named Sam Jones recorded the earliest solo "blues" songs, including one he called "John Henry." A one-man band, Sam Jones performed on the streets of Cleveland with a kazoo, harmonica, guitar, and a stovepipe that "created a tone somewhere between a wax-papered comb and a sweetly distorted tuba."[16] He recorded under the name of Stovepipe No. 1 at a session in Columbia studios in New York in August, though the song was never cut as a record. Jones became one of the first artists to record what became known as the blues, or country blues. Later in 1924, Ernest Thompson, a blind minstrel from North Carolina, made a recording of the song, though his imprint was not cut as a record either.[17] Though the song spread on radio and phonograph, many local versions of it persisted throughout the United States, mostly in the South and mostly among black workingmen.

John Henry as Ulysses

In 1926, a University of North Carolina sociologist, Guy Benton Johnson, heard construction workers sing work songs he had never heard before as they built buildings on the Chapel Hill campus. Hailing from as far away as Tennessee and Georgia, they had come as day laborers to build the campus in its years of rapid expansion. Johnson, with his mentor Howard Odum, collected many work songs near the building sites and near Odum's house, which stood a few feet from the barracks the college had erected for students to live in. Johnson combined the songs and stories he had collected with a batch of transcriptions Odum had made as early as 1906. The two published a collection of two books of African American work songs, the first published collection of African American labor folklore. In their second book, *Negro Workaday Songs,* published in 1926, Johnson suggested that one of the favorites, John Henry, might serve as the model for a Black Ulysses, the hero that writers in the Harlem Renaissance were searching for.[18] In 1927 Louis Watson Chappell submitted an article to Odum and Johnson suggesting that John Henry was a real person who had lived and died building the Big Bend Tunnel in West Virginia. Chappell had just begun interviewing local people in and around the work site.[19] In the same year, Johnson sent dozens of letters to performers and C&O employees hoping to collect a large batch of John Henry songs. Johnson then took graduate students up to the Big Bend Tunnel to interview the same locals that Chappell had interviewed about the story. At the same time, Johnson sponsored a contest in black newspapers and at black colleges, promising a prize for the most complete version of the John Henry legend. He also promised a prize for the oldest printed version of the ballad.[20]

Chappell used his own connections, largely among whites near Talcott, to gather dozens of stories about John Henry and versions of the ballad.[21] Johnson and Chappell, using slightly different methods but with a common assumption about the song's origin in West Virginia, found many contradictory versions of the story. Both ended their works believing, but unable to prove, that a contest had taken place in the Big Bend Tunnel in Summers County, West Virginia, in 1871 or 1872. The largest problem was the evidence of a contest. No direct evidence suggested that a steam drill was ever used on the Big Bend Tunnel. Contemporary reports suggested that the soil was not particularly hard and that while labor was scarce, delivering a large enough steam engine, along with hoses and drilling equipment, into remote Summers County may have been impractical.[22] An engineer who worked on the site as a water boy declared that there had never been steam drills used there.[23] The resident engineer at the site stated that steam drills had never been tried there.[24]

Chappell's book came out in 1933, published in Germany. While Chappell had more versions of the song, the book itself wandered a great deal, mostly sniping at Johnson and criticizing black informants for being superstitious and inclined to lie. Chappell spoke about the trustworthiness of the white men he interviewed and how white observers' secondhand stories of John Henry were preferable to the uneven and contradictory firsthand stories of black residents of Virginia and West Virginia.[25] Chappell's only extended report from an African American source came from William Lawson of Charleston, West Virginia, a story Chappell was disinclined to believe. Lawson began his story by describing a gunfight between his brother and another steel driver over whose drilling led to the completion of the tunnel. He then described a contest shortly afterward between John Henry and a steam drill.

> When I went there they had a steam drill in the tunnel at the east end. They piped the steam in. They had a little coffee-pot engine on the outside. They didn't use it in the heading, but on the bench and on the sides.
>
> John Henry drove steel with the steam drill one day, and beat it down, but got too hot and died. He fell out right at the mouth of the tunnel. They put a bucket of cold water on him.
>
> His wife come to the tunnel that day, and they said she carried his body away, I don't know. I never saw anybody buried at the tunnel except my brother. They said they shipped some of them away, but I didn't see anybody shipped away. . . .
>
> The time John Henry killed his self was his own fault, 'cause he bet the man with the steam drill he could beat him down. John Henry never let no man beat him down, but the steam drill won't no good nohow.

John Henry was always singing or mumbling something when he was whipping steel. He would sing over and over the same thing sometimes. He'd sing

"My old hammer ringing in the mountains,
Nothing but my hammer falling down."

A colored boy 'round there added on and made up the John Henry song after he got killed, and all the muckers sung it.

C. R. Mason was the boss man at the tunnel. He was a good-hearted old man, but he was a tough man. He'd spit on you all the time he was talking to you. His son was named Clay Mason.

Chappell printed the interview but dismissed it as the least credible. While other sources mentioned C. R. Mason, Chappell reported that the story could not be trusted. After all, Mason had not contracted on the Big Bend Tunnel in West Virginia but on the Lewis Tunnel in Virginia, one mile from the border of West Virginia. Guy Johnson also found a detailed report from an engineer named C. E. Waugh, who had worked as a water boy at the time. Waugh had worked as a contractor on the C&O for more than forty years and declared that during that time Mason had told him many times about John Henry's beating the steam drill and his untimely death.[26]

But Johnson and Chappell focused on places rather than people, and because the Big Bend Tunnel in West Virginia was mentioned in many of the songs, both men interviewed near that site.[27] Many had heard the song there and put together elaborate but contradictory stories about John Henry's life.[28] When Johnson asked officials on the C&O about Mason and the Big Bend Tunnel, he was told that his informants must be mistaken: Mason had never contracted on the Big Bend Tunnel but worked on the Lewis Tunnel.[29] When Johnson asked the C&O officials for engineering records, they replied that none existed. The search for John Henry appeared to be a dead end.[30]

But William Lawson's account has much to recommend it. He used contemporary jargon of tunnel engineers, including the expressions "heading," "bench," "coffeepot engine," "whipping steel," and "muckers." He appeared to understand mining and tunnel construction, and his description of the tunneling method—an outside engine that piped steam in for running the drill—very closely matches the steam drills used on the Lewis Tunnel after 1870. A pipe sent compressed air (not steam) into the tunnel, which then pushed the drills inside.[31]

While many historians and folklorists have discussed the John Henry story since then, the search for the real John Henry seems to have ended there. Johnson and Chappell thought the Big Bend Tunnel was the site of the contest, but the oral testimony was contradictory and inconclusive, and most engineers on the site declared that no contest took place there.

Finding John Henry

In 1998, while writing about hammer songs and the John Henry legend for a talk at the Social Science History Association, I found what appeared to be a strange coincidence. Many of the longer versions of the song referred to "the White House," as in Onah L. Spencer's version, which he heard sung by black "railroad construction employees, teamsters, and laborers from contracting jobs" in Baptist Hill in Cincinnati, Ohio:

> They took John Henry to the White House,
> And buried him in the san'
> And every locomotive come roarin' by,
> Says there lays that steel drivin' man,
> Says there lays that steel drivin' man.

The same reference is in Gid Tanner and Riley Puckett's recorded version:

> Took John Henry to the white house,
> Rolled him in the sand.
> The men from the east and the ladies from the west
> Came to see that good steel-drivin' man.[32]

It also appeared in Leadbelly's version sung in the 1940s:

> Now they taken John Henry to the white house
> And they buried him in the sand
> And every locomotive comes a rollin' by says
> There lies that steel drivin' man, Lord, Lord
> There lies that steel drivin' man (2x).[33]

One more version from Johnson, one from Lomax, and four more in Chappell repeat the passage.[34] Guy Johnson dismissed the mention of the White House as the "wishful grandeur" of its chroniclers.[35] One of Chappell's white informants notes, "The White House is where the President lives. John Henry and the other Negroes there in the tunnel used to sing about it, and about going there too."[36]

I was humming the tune with an old postcard of the Virginia penitentiary six inches from my nose, and it dawned on me that the image featured a white house, a railroad track, and sand running alongside of it. I already knew that the Virginia penitentiary provided nearly all of its convicts to the C&O railroad.

I found the plans to the Virginia penitentiary in a master's thesis and learned that the new workshop was built in 1825 out of stone from the old courthouse. It was plastered with lime, giving the building a bright white appearance—a white house. The penitentiary had stood at the top of one of the seven hills of Richmond and would have been visible from a long distance. Later, in 1877, after complaints by the city council about burials on the premises, the penitentiary established a new burying ground for convicts.[37] Where the old convicts were buried was unrecorded.

From friends and newspaper accounts, I learned that the building had been torn down and sold to the Ethyl Corporation in 1989. Richmond newspapers carried a story that in 1992 construction workers digging a drainage ditch at the Ethyl site had uncovered over a hundred unidentified skeletons. In later discussions with the archaeologist Katherine Beidelman, I learned that four hundred bodies were buried along Byrd Street. Contemporary maps confirmed that the bodies lay near the lines of a downtown connection railroad. They stood next to the old white house, not where the railroad is pictured on the lower left but on the opposite side of the white house. Trains descended from a hill toward the penitentiary, literally "roaring by" the white house on their way into Richmond. Bodies had been laid in boxes with sizes that ranged, Beidelman told me, "from an orange crate to a grand piano." Coffin fragments inside suggested that some were reburied. Boxes were stacked sometimes two deep, with a thin layer of sand between them.[38]

After some perseverance, I found an archivist at the Library of Virginia who would let me examine the penitentiary records. Using a pencil, she helpfully

Figure 1. John Henry *by Frank Long. Courtesy of Warren and Julie Payne, Payne Fine Arts, Louisville, Kentucky.*

Figure 2. The white house at the Virginia Penitentiary.
Courtesy Scott Reynolds Nelson, private collection.

crossed out the line in the finding aid that declared the records sealed.[39] The
records showed an inmate named "John Wm. Henry."

> John William Henry c[olored] (#497)
> When received: 1866 Nov. 16
> Where sentenced: Prince George
> Crime: Housebreak & larceny
> Term: 10 years
> Nativity: US
> State or Province: New Jersey
> County Dist or city: Elizabeth City
> Height: 5 ft 1 ¼
> Age: 19
> Complexion: Black
> Col of Hair: Black
> Col of eyes: Black
> Marks or other peculiar descriptions: a small scar on left arm above elbow.
> A small one on right arm above wrist.
> When Pensioned, discharged, or died: Transferred [in pencil][40]

John Henry was short, and born in New Jersey! The manuscript census for 1870
listed him as John Henry, a resident of the Virginia penitentiary. A close comparison of the census page to the prisoner register shows that the census taker
simply copied the pages from the prison register directly into the census. While
John Henry's name appeared in the Richmond census, the prison register

shows that he was actually contracted out to work on the C&O railroad in 1868, charged to Capt. Goodlow, an employee of C. R. Mason, railroad contractor.[41]

Civil Engineering in the Age of John Henry

Much of the rest of the story of John Henry falls into place when one changes the location of the contest from the Big Bend Tunnel to the nearby Lewis Tunnel. I began to search for sources using the names mentioned in versions of the song and by the black informants whom Chappell had dismissed as unreliable and who had later refused to talk to Johnson. The song mentions Captain Tommy Walters, and contemporaries mentioned C. R. Mason. The company reports of the C&O named H. D. Whitcomb as chief engineer. Contemporary newspaper reports mentioned that the general superintendent of construction was A. H. Perry.[42] Searching for information on these names, I found what Johnson and Chappell had declared to be lost forever: the engineering reports made by construction superintendents to the chief engineer on the C&O. They were in an unlikely place, the Western Reserve Historical Society in Cleveland, Ohio.[43] These records revealed how convicts and steam drills, working side by side, cut through the Lewis Tunnel. The penitentiary records revealed how the men who did the hand labor died in the process.

Tunneling proceeded in three stages: the "attack" with drills and hammers, the blast with nitroglycerin, and the clearing by muckers. The key innovation in tunneling after the 1860s came from the application of nitroglycerin to rock faces, which increased the yield from blasting by a factor of ten.[44] The reduction of time in the first phase—the attack—became the goal of tunnel engineers from Switzerland to California.

In the attack phase, a hammer man swung a sledgehammer at a drill that a "shaker" or "buddy" held in his hands and between his legs. At least three holes—called shot holes—were needed, each three to four feet long, depending on the hardness of the rock. The vertical hole at the center of the rock face went straight in. Upper holes went upward at a forty-five- to sixty-degree angle. Lower holes went downward at a similar angle. Depending on the nature of the rock, holes had to extend between three and a half to four feet into the rock face. In the Big Bend Tunnel these holes were packed with gunpowder, but the hard rock of the Lewis Tunnel required the more expensive and dangerous compounds of dynamite and dualin (nitroglycerin mixed with gunpowder).[45]

As the hammer man swung the hammer, the shaker would occasionally move the drill between blows. He either "rocked" the drill from side to side to clear rubble or "rolled" the drill by twisting it slightly inside the hole. The hammer man sometimes sang to set his pace. Song allowed the shaker to know when he had a moment to move the drill. As the drill penetrated the rock and became dull, the hammer man would replace it with a longer drill. An attack generally required as many as five drills. When three or more shot holes had been sunk to their limit, an explosives crew moved in. While speed was vital for hammer and shaker, explosives crews moved slowly, packing either vials of nitroglycerin or tubes of dualin into the holes. An electrical charge ignited the fuse; staggered fuse sizes made for a series of ordered blasts. The explosives team counted the blasts before reentering the hole made by the blast. Muckers and rail cars then rushed to the face to load rock and sand into baskets and then into the cars.[46]

As blasting became more powerful, that part of the process sped up considerably. The use of railway cars in the mucking process shortened the time after the blasts. Hand drilling the blast holes became the bottleneck in the process. One civil engineer in 1867 called hand drilling "the most difficult portion of the labor and that which consumes the most time."[47] On the major tunnels of the late nineteenth century—the Mount Cenis and the Hoosac—miners would drill for hours at a time, while the blasting crew worked perhaps an hour a day.[48] Speeding up the drilling process became critical.

The solution to the bottleneck seemed to lie in the steam drill. The power of steam engines had been the marvel of the last two centuries, but transferring that power to something other than a wheel had proved impractical. Every bend or fork cost energy, and one could not put a steam engine into the man-sized tunnels that miners and blasters pushed into mountains. In an age before the practical transmission of electricity, engineers and mechanics determined that the best way to transfer steam power over a distance was to transfer the steam itself over a distance. Engineers connected powerful steam engines to long vacuum pipes. As steam rushed through the pipe it pushed a rod forward; when the steam was released a vacuum pulled the rod backward. A number of systems for transferring steam into pipes emerged, but all terminated by delivering a percussive force to a steel chisel, much like the one that miners had been hammering into rock for a dozen centuries.[49]

A competing steam drill, sometimes called a diamond drill, was also in development. A Swiss watchmaker who collected dozens of ugly black diamonds created a device that used their sharp edges. Mounting them around a piston, a drill could spin inside of a small pilot hole, pushing rapidly into the most difficult rock. This rotating motion worked best in softer rock or rock that was crumbly. Modern oil drills still use this basic process. As early as 1868, Huntington's contractors asked both percussive and rotating drill manufacturers to run tests on the tunnels. The contractors planned to blast and drill their way through to the Ohio River.[50]

Both steam drills were what we would today call kluges—fiendishly complex devices designed to solve a basic problem. (The term allegedly derives from an intricate tangle of cams and driveshafts called a "Kluge paper feeder" that fed paper into mechanical printing presses in the 1930s.)[51] In the years that John Henry spent in the penitentiary, both kluges were tried, and neither worked consistently. The steam pipes for the steam drill broke down frequently, and the diamond drill often broke at the sharp end.

Both kinds of drills lacked the flexibility that one found in the skilled two-man hammer teams that had been tunneling through mountains for decades. As the hammer man swung a sledgehammer down onto the chisel, a shaker shifted the drill between blows to improve the drill's bite. The civil engineer and inventor Herman Haupt broke down the three kinds of actions of the shaker, actions that steam drills tried to emulate. The first action, rocking, required the shaker to rock the drill back and forward to clear away bits of broken rock. The second action, rolling, rotated the drill to push it deeper into the hole. The third action, feeding, allowed the drill to penetrate.[52]

Song coordinated the movements. White observers in the 1840s noted the presence of singing deep underground in the Chesterfield mines, though they declared black miners tuneless.[53] The descendants of these singing miners became the skilled men on the C&O tunneling sites, men who either supervised or worked alongside unskilled workers, free and convict.

The phrases of black miners' hammer songs coordinated the complex movements of drilling. Sometimes the hammer man drove the steel with his sledge, telling his partner with his rhythm and lyrics when the next blow would come. Other times a third man would sing for hammer man and shaker. Between blows the shaker would work his magic, either rocking or rolling. Hammer songs, as Archie Green has demonstrated, echoed the work process. Thus many hammer songs describe the rolling that the partner, or "buddy," did with the drill: "Roll on buddy, don't you roll so slow, / Baby, how can I roll when my wheel won't go?"[54]

The story of "rock and roll" is a complicated one, but as many folklorists have demonstrated, black blues performances from the 1910s to the 1940s borrowed phrases from everyday work songs.[55] By the 1950s the style, cadence, and phrases in these black blues performances were, according to Green, "beginning to seep out of black communities to reach mass audiences of white teenagers" through performers like Bill Haley and Elvis Presley. More directly, country artists like the Buckle Busters, the Skillet Lickers, Tennessee Ernie Ford, and Merle Travis appropriated black work songs of mines and railroad camps and turned them into country music.[56] The phrase *rock and roll* was used to describe the actions of a steel driller, but it also became a double entendre, describing sexual penetration. The sexual meaning has come to be regarded as the primary source of the term, and the context of the mines and work camps of Southern railroads has been largely forgotten.

While discussion of the source of the term *rock and roll* must remain conjectural, rocking and rolling were phrases that suggested how skilled hammer teams in 1871 could defeat a steam drill. Initially, convicts like John Henry started as unskilled and extra labor for the C&O, grading track, clearing pits, or working as muckers to clear away broken rock before becoming hammer men. A group of black men with hammers, drills, and song formed a complex machine that the high technology of the 1870s could not match. A contracting engineer might imagine that steam drills could replace the skilled labor of miners, that he could work without their rock and roll. But he was wrong.

Convicts in Tunnel Construction

Sixty-five-year-old Claiborne R. Mason (as the chief contractor for convicts) would work more than one hundred men to death as he supervised the completion of the Lewis Tunnel. Mason was a self-taught railroad contractor who had bossed slaves and free blacks in his mines in Chesterfield County, Virginia. He had also used them to build railroads east of Covington, Virginia, before the war. In seasons when he needed extra labor, he leased free black convicts from the penitentiary. During the war he controlled thousands of drafted slaves, rebuilding bridges for Stonewall Jackson.[57] A reporter described him as "a short, stout, firmly built man, with a head like a Senator's, plain of dress, direct and brief of speech, with that undeniable air of ease that comes to a man who has acquired all he knows from experience."

Indeed, Mason's long experience controlling men and recapturing runaways made him an able if brutal labor boss for the C&O. Many Southerners already hated and feared Mason for what he had done to stop Confederate desertions. In the last two years of the Civil War, General Robert E. Lee had given Mason broad orders to hunt deserters in Albemarle County in western Virginia near Charlottesville. Mason had dutifully captured dozens of soldiers absent without leave, as well as those who had given them aid. He then brought them to the nearest town, posted notice of their execution, and hanged them. In the mountains, bitterness toward Mason lasted for decades. A major stockholder in the C&O, Mason's résumé was not a liability for the railroad.[58]

On December 1, 1868, the presidency of the C&O was handed over to W. C. Wickham, a stand-in for the interests of C. P. Huntington.[59] The Chesapeake & Ohio Railway was incorporated shortly afterward, when Huntington formally took command. On the same day that the state handed over the state-funded sections of the C&O railroad to Wickham, John Henry, along with fifteen other men, was loaded onto the railroad cars at the Richmond penitentiary. Dozens of other convicts were already at work on the line.[60]

A peculiar wrinkle added to the contract that day ensured that John Henry would be forever tied to the city of Richmond. Shortly after the prisoners had started flowing from the penitentiary to the C&O, some escaped from Mason's guards. The state of Virginia, nearly impoverished, had had to pay to recapture them. Thus just before John Henry departed the prison walls, the governor added a new provision to the contract between the state and the railroad. Contractors like Mason would post a bond that guaranteed the safe return of prisoners and pay all the expenses for the state's attempts to recapture them. Governor Wells wrote that contracts have "stipulated damages of one hundred dollars for each *prisoner not returned*" (emphasis in original). This way Mason could not claim that a prisoner had died when he had simply escaped. Mason and his lieutenant agreed, eager to get the men, and signed the contract on the day it was written. They may not have understood then that the contract would require that the corpses of the many prisoners who died in the coming years would have to be returned to Richmond, to avoid the exorbitant fee of one hundred dollars each. (One hundred dollars in 1868 was more than a year's labor by a convict.) This contract was the reason John Henry's body would be shipped back to the white house and buried in the sand. His resting place would be the grounds of the Richmond penitentiary.[61]

Building the C&O, 1871–73

The frenzied construction of the mountain sections of the C&O railroad started in December 1868, after Huntington acquired the company. The chief engineer divided the remaining track-laying into three divisions: Alleghany, Greenbrier, and New River. The company put out yearly contracts, which the division engineers could revise monthly. They inspected the site while the contractors tunneled, bridged, graded, and tracked. The engineers dutifully gathered the gossip that traveled up and down the line. They reported monthly on the contractors who got drunk, those who abandoned their contracts, and those who seemed to be failing—not an uncommon occurrence. As contractors faced problems with supplies or labor, they quickly went bankrupt. In less than a month county sheriffs would arrive to seize contractors' mules, scrapers, and shanties. Every bankruptcy pushed the company further and further toward the use of convict labor.

Thousands of free black men came to work on the line at first, but trouble brewed quickly. Early on in the construction, the assistant engineer issued a circular requiring contractors to pay no more than "one dollar and board per day for ordinary laborers." He also set the hours of labor at "six o'clock AM till sunset allowing one hour for dinner."[62] When workers balked about the pay, Huntington threatened to bring impoverished Irishmen from the slums of

New York. Some Irish workers were in fact brought in to work on the western end of the line, but most men who built the C&O in 1868 were former slaves.[63]

When it came to tunneling, black men with experience in the Chesterfield County mines were especially welcome. Claiborne Mason saw managing these men as his particular skill, for he had bossed slaves, free blacks, and convicts for years as they dug coal out of the pits of the county. These black colliers brought the songs and traditions of almost two hundred years of coal mining from the James River up to the mountains with them.[64] Mason mixed skilled free laborers from the county with unskilled convicts.

Along with their traditions, workers bought their liquor (and had their fights) in the ordinaries and public houses that sprang up in the mountains almost overnight. County sheriffs could hardly keep track of them. For every legitimate and licensed establishment, like Mason's own grog shop at the foot of Lewis Tunnel, there were two or three crossroads shanties run by Irishmen with names like Finn and Fox. Sheriffs hauled them to court for selling ardent spirits without a license.[65] These, too, became places where music was shared between the black colliers of Chesterfield County, the Irish American brick masons from near the Ohio River, and the black carpenters and blacksmiths from plantations downstate. The convicts from Richmond might have been paid extra for skilled work, but because they were not allowed to leave the work site, they could spend it only in Mason's grog shop.[66]

Between 1868 and 1872, the Lewis Tunnel and one other consumed the attention of Chief Engineer Whitcomb and President Huntington. The Lewis Tunnel at the foot of Lewis Mountain promised to pierce the eastern entrance to the Appalachian chain. The entrance would be nearly a mile long when complete. Further west, the Big Bend (or Great Bend) Tunnel would shave miles from the route that the Greenbrier River had etched around the Great Bend mountain. The C&O hoped to pierce the great bend and head straight to the Ohio River. As the division engineer C. A. Sharp put it to Whitcomb, "If you want a monument, let this Big Bend Tunnel serve to carry your name down to posterity."[67] But no one remembers H. D. Whitcomb. The Big Bend Tunnel carried only John Henry's name down to posterity.

While the Big Bend Tunnel was longer, the Lewis Tunnel proved more difficult to build. Huntington had contractors grade and lay track to the major tunnels. Temporary track ran over the mountains while construction was in progress. Concerned about the Lewis Mountain's harder rock, Huntington immediately sought out steam drills. He had Whitcomb contact John Tilsby, an agent for Burleigh rock drills, to get quotes. Tilsby outlined how the drills worked. While hand labor made about fifty feet per month, he bragged that in the Hoosac tunnel in Pennsylvania his drill made "as much as 7 feet per day" and allowed blasts that made tunnels wider and taller than could be made by human hands.[68] By October 1869, Tilsby's associate brought in a man who had superintended "tunnels through the Sierra Nevada on the CPRR."[69] This must have reassured Huntington, since he made his first fortune when the Central Pacific had passed through the Sierra Nevada. Everything seemed to be falling into place.

By March 1870, contracts went out for drilling, and the contractor C. P. Durham received the bid for the Lewis Tunnel. "We expect to use the Burleigh drills," Durham told the chief engineer. His hope was to not drill shafts down from the top of the mountain at all, as hand tunneling usually required. He would drill straight across and "progress with more rapidity than by going down the shafts and doing the work by hand."[70] The Burleigh drills used steam forced through a pipe the size of a drain spout to a chamber with a metal drill inside. A valve action pushed the drill forward into the rock with a percussive force that, it was hoped, would far exceed that of one man with a hammer. Through most of 1870, free workers apparently tunneled, while convicts did support tasks. In March, for example, Mason's convicts dug out pits east of the tunnel. There they mined the rock that would be used for bridges. Convicts also built shanties in nearby Millboro as the steam drill experiment proceeded.[71]

But something was wrong with the percussive drills; they did not work as fast as Whitcomb had hoped, and just a week later he sought out agents for a rotating drill. The Severance & Holt Diamond Drilling Company sent its diamond drills out to the site after a brief demonstration in Richmond. With the same technological exuberance as the Burleigh agent, William Holt gushed about his diamond drills.

> Our firm would make very liberal arrangements with your co. to furnish all the drilling apparatus for the *entire work* and wd. *guarantee* its entire success, enabling yr. contractors to do their work far more *quickly* & *cheaply* than they can possibly do it with any other machine. Our machines are especially adapted to *through cuts* and *tunnels*—boring in the latter 3 to 5 holes simultaneously at steady rate of eight to ten feet *per hour* in *each hole*. The extreme simplicity of our drilling apparatus enables it to be operated by cheap labor, and renders repairing unnecessary.

Durham declared that he would try his best to use these new drills but that he lacked iron to lay track to the tunnel. By the summer of 1870, things had progressed from bad to worse. Water flooded the tunnel's western end, and steam engines were required to pump it out. Moreover, five of Mason's convicts had escaped from nearby Millboro and were at large in the mountains.[72] Finally, neither steam drill was working reliably. By the end of the summer, Huntington determined that Durham and company had not really made a fair test of the drills and that Durham's contract should be terminated.[73]

Labor troubles also proliferated along the line. On the Big Bend Tunnel, the men went on strike in the summer. Drilling in the shafts produced silica that floated in the tunnels long after drilling and blasting. Miners, black and white, declared that the tunnels had "bad air" and marched out, demanding two dollars a day and a resolution of the problem.[74] On the Lewis Tunnel, Durham had proved unable to get enough laborers at the prescribed rate of a dollar a day.[75] Huntington proposed turning over the Lewis Tunnel contract to an old associate, J. J. Gordon, who wanted to "bring Chinese laborers from California immediately." "I would probably consent to pay him a small advance on the rates agreed upon with Durham," Huntington wrote, "in consideration of the good effect it would have upon other labor."[76] While Irish workers on the CPRR had refused to work near nitroglycerin, Chinese workers, who were often bound to contractors by debt and could be threatened with deportation, had submitted to the dangerous blasts. In Huntington's mind, no doubt, Chinese laborers were a small step above slaves.

But by the summer of 1870, Huntington came to understand that "coolie labor" would not do the drilling for him. Chinese workers from California were unavailable, and to get them from China, he would have to contract them almost a year in advance. The Franco-Prussian War in Europe greatly unsettled the bond markets, which meant that he could not gather the funds to import Chinese workers.[77]

Thus Huntington had to find cheap, pliable labor closer to home. Virginia's overloaded penal system supplied the solution. In 1870 alone, over two thousand black men had come to the Virginia penitentiary to serve long sentences for small crimes, so many that the state could not house them. Burnham Wardwell, the humanitarian warden who along with the governor had instituted year-round labor contracts and demanded that workers be returned if injured, had just left office.[78] Wardwell's replacement, George F. Strother, was more pliable. Strother's reports to the governor dwelt on his great ability to cut costs and mentioned nothing about conditions.[79] So Whitcomb met with Claiborne Mason in August 1870, and they decided that J. J. Gordon, experienced with steam drills and coolie laborers, would take over the tunnel. He would try the steam drills again alongside a mix of free workers (who understood drilling) and Mason's convicts, who could neither strike nor demand higher wages, since they received none.

The Contest

The real contest between steam drills and convicts began, then, in August 1870. As Mason finished grading and filling outside the Lewis Tunnel, he brought two hundred convicts directly to the site.[80] Gordon built up a whole town to support his drills. A correspondent described the tunnel and the temporary track that ran over it, adding that Gordon had assembled entire "machine-shops . . . at which a locomotive might be built." To a man who traveled over the tunnel, the activity that transpired beneath him was remarkable:

> 150 feet beneath him are nearly 200 toilers boring through the earth, and showing by patient and persevering labor the triumphs of man over seemingly insurmountable obstacles. Besides the approaches to the tunnel, there are three shafts, measuring in depth 70, 125 and 145 feet respectively. One hundred and twenty men are at work inside constantly, night and day. The difficulty in working Lewis tunnel, as is doubtless known, is the almost unprecedented hardness of the material through which it has been worked. It has the appearance of blue granite, and is so hard that it almost resists the ordinary drill.[81]

Convicts who worked alongside the drill were housed near the tunnel itself and occasionally escaped, as did white convicts in August 1871.[82]

Neither the steam drills nor the convicts worked as planned. Gordon's partner told a correspondent for the *Richmond Dispatch* that he was happy enough with the free black and convict laborers, "despite many drawbacks."[83] One principal drawback was price. Gordon had the contract to drill and was paid by the cubic foot, but Mason and his partner owned the convicts. Gordon probably paid Mason's convicts by the day, but Gordon got paid by the C&O for every foot he drilled.

Though Gordon gave them a fair test, the steam drills failed again and again. He had thought that the Sierra Madres in California were remote and that the rock there was hard, but he had never been to the edge of the Alleghenies. Gordon continually faced engine problems, probably from the dust generated by the drills themselves. He found he could not get replacement boilers. "I am very anxious to get that boiler to run Burleigh Drill in East approach," he wrote Whitcomb in October 1871, "if you have done anything in regards the furnishing it please inform me, if not I will have to double on it with hammers."

The phrase "double on it with hammers" is telling. Gordon was apparently drilling two sets of holes on the rock face of the east approach, one with convicts, one with the Burleigh drill. Before the boiler failed, Gordon would have run a steam drill on one side and a hammer team on the other. Thus in the summer of 1871, before the boiler failed on the east approach, both men and drills worked side by side. The steam drill set on the right hand side,

> John Henry was on the left.
> He said, "I will beat that steam drill down
> Or hammer my fool self to death."

The men that made that steam drill,
Thought it was mighty fine;
John Henry sunk a fourteen-foot hole
And the steam drill only made nine.[84]

By October 1871, Gordon had run out of steam. The western tunneling expert who "thought his drill was mighty fine" was hemorrhaging money by hiring workers from Mason. Gordon asked to be excused from the contract by the middle of the month.[85]

Once Gordon had abandoned his contract, Mason and his partner Gooch did the work entirely with their many convicts. Because Mason and his partner had not bid on the price of drilling, the convict owners and C&O officials haggled over prices. As division engineer Peyton Randolph told the chief engineer in October, "The rock is hard but drills and blasts well and I consider $4 [per foot] an outside price for it. Yesterday Gooch talked about $5 but I laughed at him."[86] Randolph knew that Mason and Gooch got their convicts for twenty-five cents a day and had hundreds of them to spare.

The steam drills left the tunnel by the end of October 1871. The race was over. Nearly two hundred men, mostly convicts, now finished the tunnel for Huntington. Thousands of free laborers graded, laid track, and finished the surfacing of the other tunnels. Men had triumphed over machines, but at a terrible cost. For two years, between the last month of steam drill operation and the completion of the tunnel—between September 1871 and September 1873—close to one hundred convicts died.

John Henry, O, John Henry!
Blood am runnin' red!
Falls right down with his hammah to th' groun',
Says, "I've beat him to th' bottom but I'm dead,—
Lawd,—Lawd,—
I've beat him to th' bottom but I'm dead."

John Henry kissed his hammah;
Kissed it with a groan;
Sighed a sigh and closed his weary eyes,
Now po' Lucy has no man to call huh own,—
Lawd,—Lawd,—
Po' Lucy has no man to call huh own.[87]

As a closed society of prisoners, the Lewis Tunnel probably produced few memorable songs. The nearby Big Bend Tunnel, with free black and white laborers, was likely where the song about this terrible event was first put together. The contractor in charge of the Big Bend was Captain William R. Johnson Jr., who used mostly free workers to build his tunnel. Johnson did take thirty Virginia prisoners from the penitentiary in 1868 and another fourteen in 1869. Johnson, like Mason, had gotten his start bossing slaves in the Confederacy's engineering corps.[88] After the initial drilling at the Lewis Tunnel, some black workers came up to the Big Bend Tunnel after the failed effort with the steam drills in 1871. One man, a roundhouse cook named Cal Evans, traveled from Lewis Tunnel to the Big Bend Tunnel. When Lewis Chappell interviewed him, he said little, though Chappell noted that Evans's storytelling "is a matter of general knowledge in the community."[89] Evans may have been shy if he had heard about one of Chappell's interviews. It ended when Chappell yelled "Another damn lie!" at one of his black informants and sent him away.[90] While Guy Johnson was no racist, Chappell had already been in the area for a year and had made clear to the community whom he trusted and what he thought of black witnesses. Chappell may have driven many black informants away or made them less likely to talk to a white folklorist who came along later.

To the White House

It is difficult to determine exactly how over one hundred of convicts died building the Lewis Tunnel. The surgeon's report for the penitentiary made a careful list of the men who died in prison, but only gave total figures for the men who died on the C&O railroad.

The Virginia penitentiary's board of directors reported that from 1871 to 1873 death rates were increasing rapidly, but that their penitentiary was not to blame. "Less than half of the deaths during the year were caused by disease contracted in the building," the surgeon reported. "All the cases of scurvy we have had in this institution were contracted while the men were at work on the Chesapeake & Ohio railroad. They were returned on account of the disease. Dropsy, appearing in three cases . . . was [actually] the result of scurvy; [and] also several of the cases of consumption." Thus prisoners died of scurvy, a result of malnutrition. Some convicts who appeared in the death tables "died of dis[ease] contracted while at work on rr" or "ret[urne]d from Lewis tunnel in dying condition."[91] So while the deaths could not be laid at the feet of the penitentiary, the bodies could be.

The surgeon's report stated that many of the men who died in his care had been injured on the C&O and returned to the penitentiary to die. Others returned as corpses, or parts of corpses, as blasting accidents and cave-ins surely killed others. But the prison surgeon only saw men who had returned alive to the penitentiary. The single greatest cause of death the prison surgeon saw was "consumption," the nineteenth-century shorthand for death that originated in a wasting away of the lungs. While many cases of consumption can be attributed to the tuberculosis bacterium (discovered in 1882), miners knew that the mines themselves could be dangerous to men's lungs. Agricola, the founder of geology in the 1550s, noted that "there were women in the Carpathian mountains who had married seven husbands, all of whom had died from consumption."[92] This miners' consumption was caused not by bacteria or close confinement but by the silica loosed by blasting rock. The men who went on strike at the Big Bend Tunnel understood that "bad air" put dust in your lungs that could kill you. These miners demanded that tunnels be washed down or ventilated before they entered them. But convicts could not strike. Some escaped, some were killed by guards for what the railroad labeled "mutiny," but the remainder entered tunnels where tiny bits of microscopic rock floated in the air, entered their lungs, and, over a period of six months to three years, strangled them. These prisoners died gasping for air, unable to get oxygen through bronchial tubes that were clogged with microscopic rock.[93] By contract, they had to be returned to the Virginia penitentiary in Richmond, "the white house." If they were not sent back, the C&O faced a one-hundred-dollar fine per man. Nearly one hundred men came back between 1871 and 1873, most of them dead. Dozens more died shortly afterward.

John Henry did not die inside the Virginia prison, because his name is not listed in the surgeon's report. He does, however, disappear from prison records by 1874, with no mention of pardon, parole, or release. His corpse, then, must have been one of the counted but unnamed bodies shipped back to the penitentiary by rail. Other men returned from the Lewis Tunnel to the penitentiary with advanced cases of consumption and died in the hospital ward. John Henry, if he lived past the contest, might have died on the way back to the penitentiary. Otherwise, he would have died in a prison shanty outside the Lewis Tunnel, asking for one last cool drink of water before he died.

> John Henry hammered in the mountains
> Till the hammer caught on fire.
> Very last words I heard him say,
> "Cool drink of water 'fore I die,
> Cool drink of water 'fore I die."[94]

John Wm. Henry, prisoner and railroad man, raced a steam drill at the Lewis Tunnel in the late summer of 1871. He beat the steam drill, but he and more than one hundred other railroad men died doing it. And so the harsh sentences meted out by Virginia's Reconstruction courts became death sentences in the Appalachian Mountains. The biggest problem, as the superintendent saw it, was what to do with the bodies. They were taken to the white house that lay along the track of the Richmond, Fredericksburg & Potomac Railroad and buried in the sand, and no one was the wiser. Only a song, stubbornly sung by railroad men, convicts, and miners, kept the story alive.

Notes

The author would like to thank the following people for reading drafts or providing help with understanding the John Henry material: Bruce Baker, Seth Bruggeman, Ed Cabbell, Robert Cantwell, Jennifer Cutting, Leon Fink, Harold Forsythe, Kelly Gray, Jeff Guy, Cindy Hahamovitch, Joe Hickerson, Rhys Isaac, Nelson Lichtenstein, Jennifer Luff, Charlie McGovern, Kate McPherson, Deirdre Mullane, Gunther Peck, Kimberley Phillips, Nick Salvatore, and James Spady.

1. Trudier Harris, personal conversation with author, May 1985, Chapel Hill, NC; Lisa Lindsay, personal conversation with author, November 21, 1998, Chicago; "The John Henry shirt," John Henry vertical files, American Folklife Center, Library of Congress; Pierre Priest, personal conversation with author, December 13, 2002, Cleveland, OH; Archie Green, *Wobblies, Pile Butts, and Other Heroes: Laborlore Explorations* (Urbana: University of Illinois Press, 1993), 51–54. After the "death" of Superman in 1993, the man of steel was resurrected into four different characters, including a modern-day John Henry. See Louise Simonson, Jon Bogdanove, and Dennis Janke, *Superman: The Man of Steel* 22 (New York: DC Comics, 1993). The most influential analyses of John Henry have been Lawrence Levine, *Black Culture and Black Consciousness* (New York: Oxford University Press, 1977), 422–25; and Leon Litwack, *Trouble in Mind: Black Southerners in the Age of Jim Crow* (New York: Knopf, 1998), 436–44. A good summary of John Henry's fate in literature, poetry, and prose is Brett Williams, *John Henry: A Bio-Bibliography* (Westport, CT: Greenwood, 1983).

2. Joe Hickerson and Jennifer Cutting, personal conversation with author, September 25, 2003, American Folklife Center, Library of Congress.

3. The black codes denied black men and women most of the rights guaranteed in the Bill of Rights, including those against unlawful search and seizure, and the right to testify in court. Anger at the black codes in the South helped usher in the Civil Rights Act and the Fourteenth Amendment. See especially Eric Foner, *Reconstruction: America's Unfinished Revolution, 1863–1877* (New York: Harper & Row, 1988), 198–227.

4. Thus later tunnels in Georgia, Alabama, Missouri, Arkansas, and Colorado all claim John Henry. George Herring, a historian of U.S. foreign policy, found a number of state markers recently (Herring, personal conversation with author, February 29, 2004, Lexington, KY).

5. Guy Benton Johnson, *John Henry: Tracking Down a Negro Legend* (Chapel Hill: University of North Carolina Press, 1929), 31–32; on Mason of Lewis Tunnel, see 48–49, 53. Louis Watson Chappell, *John Henry: A Folk-lore Study* (1933; repr., Port Washington, NY: Kennikat, 1968), 13; on dismissing Cal Evans's account because he came from near Lewis Tunnel, see 37–39, 43–46, 73–74, 86. Chappell ridiculed the testimony of black informants, preferring "the stable citizenry of a conservative community" (49), namely, "white citizens in good standing in their respective communities" (55).

6. Chappell, *John Henry,* 26–27, 30.

7. Archie Green, *Only a Miner: Studies in Recorded Coal-Mining Songs* (Urbana: University of Illinois Press, 1972), 332; Williams, *John Henry,* 47. Louise Bascom was born c. 1885 in Highlands, NC; her first published play was "Masonic Ring, or the Adventures of a College Bride," printed in 1910. She also published stories in *Harper's Monthly Magazine* between 1913 and 1915.

8. Bascom's "informant," a "certain woman" whom she has "known . . . for a dozen years or more," is probably the family's servant listed in the 1900 census, Naomi Wilson, who would have been fifty-five at the time that Bascom's article came out. The informant notes having a number of boys who are fiddle players, and Wilson is listed in that census as having five boys. From Bascom's obituary it is clear that Bascom went to boarding school in Salt Lake City and then Wellesley, probably graduating in 1907, and came home to North Carolina for the summers. Census and obituary come from John M. Stewart, "Research Notes on Louise Rand Bascom" (author's possession). Stewart is a descendant. Bascom was unique among collectors, noting the methods of transmission of songs. Later scholars have noted the problem of how collecting worked: most collectors in the early years were university professors. These collectors "seldom surprised the folksong; he [*sic*] had it recalled for him by self-conscious informants on their best behavior and without their instruments of the devil. He collected not just half the folksong, as often charged, but sometimes only a third of it" (Donald K. Wilgus, *Anglo-American Folksong Scholarship since 1898* [New Brunswick, NJ: Rutgers University Press, 1959], 154).

9. Eber Carle Perrow, "Songs and Rhymes from the South," *Journal of American Folklore* 26, no. 100 (1913): 163; Green, *Only a Miner,* 333; Norm Cohen, *Long Steel Rail: The Railroad in American Folksong,* 2nd ed. (Urbana: University of Illinois Press, 2000), 65. I have found no biography of Perrow. Born in 1880, he was a student of William Ellery Leonard at the University of Wisconsin. He taught at the University of Louisville, but retired around 1919 to live on a farm in Talking Rock, Georgia. See Eber Carle Perrow, "Unto the Hills" (n.p.: privately printed, 1955), pamphlet collection, Duke University Library, Durham, NC.

10. Williams, *John Henry,* 47–48; Green, *Wobblies, Pile Butts, and Other Heroes,* 53. Duke University was called Trinity College when Brown and N. I. White began collecting.

11. Perrow had versions from correspondents in Mississippi and Kentucky; Curtis Burlin had a version from a student who heard the song in the mines of Virginia; Lomax had the songs of C&O track liners. Ballads usually have four stanzas with an *xaxa, xbxb* structure, where *a* rhymes with *a, b* with *b,* and the *x* stanzas do not rhyme. The first and third measures usually have four beats, and the second and fourth have three. Because the ballad has a regular set of strong accents, without syllables, it is easy to fit words into them. Some versions of the John Henry song double the last stanza.

12. Chappell and Green believe these hammer songs to be unrelated to the ballads. Johnson believed that the ballad evolved from work songs. See Green, *Only a Miner,* 337.

13. William Aspenwall Bradley, "Song-Ballets and Devil's Ditties," *Harper's Monthly Magazine,* no. 780 (1915): 901–14.

14. On Handy, see Green, *Wobblies, Pile Butts, and Other Heroes,* 53. Joe Hickerson, a folklorist who had previously run the Archive of Folk Culture at the Library of

Congress, showed me a copyright card for a score with the title "John Henry" that came from Canada that was considerably earlier than 1922, but the score is not at the library.

15. Guy B. Johnson to W. C. Handy, Care A&C Boni, July 25, 1927, Guy Benton Johnson Papers, Southern Historical Collection, University of North Carolina, Chapel Hill (hereafter cited as Johnson papers, SHC-UNC).

16. Liner notes from *Stovepipe No. 1: Complete Recorded Works (1924–1950) & the Jug Washboard Band (1928),* Document Records, 1995.

17. For the timing of the recordings, see Cohen, *Long Steel Rail,* 74. A complete discography of over four hundred different versions of the John Henry ballad is listed in *Long Steel Rail* (77–89). Cohen suggests that Ernest Thompson was black, calling him a "blind North Carolina minstrel," but this may be the blind white performer from North Carolina also named Ernest Thompson. See "Ernest Thompson: Forgotten Pioneer," *Journal of Country Music* 18 (1996): 41–51.

18. Lynn Moss Sanders, *Howard W. Odum's Folklore Odyssey: Transformation to Tolerance through African American Folk Studies* (Athens: University of Georgia Press, 2003), 40–44.

19. Chappell accused Johnson of stealing the idea from him, saying that he had begun studying the legend in September 1925 and that a nineteen-page report of his work written in February 1927 "fell into the hands of Dr. Johnson" (Chappell, *John Henry,* 6–33). From Johnson's papers, including dated letters, it is clear that Johnson had begun the project before Chappell issued his report. See folder 1052, Johnson papers, SHC-UNC. Lynn Sanders interviewed Johnson about these charges in 1986, and while Johnson did read Chappell's paper, he points out that he had begun gathering versions of the song before Chappell got involved. See Sanders, *Howard W. Odum's Folklore Odyssey,* 40–44.

20. "John Henry Prize Contest," folder 1063, Johnson papers, SHC-UNC.

21. Local legend has it that Chappell himself stole many versions from his colleague Patrick Ward Gainer (Avery Gaskin, personal conversation with author, October 20, 2002, John Henry folk festival, Morgantown, West Virginia).

22. "Capt. William J. Brightwell," in *Old and New,* vol. 3 of *The History of West Virginia* (New York: American Historical Society, 1923), 540–41; Henry S. Drinker, *Tunneling, Explosive Compounds, and Rock Drills,* 3rd ed. (New York: John Wiley and Sons, 1893), 964–65.

23. West Virginia field notes, page headed "Mr. Bill Winner," folder 1047, Johnson papers, SHC-UNC.

24. James P. Nelson, Chesapeake & Ohio Railway to G. B. Johnson, January 6, 1928, folder 1056, Johnson papers, SHC-UNC.

25. Chappell, *John Henry,* 13–14, 33–34, 37–39, 49–55, 71–79, 85–86.

26. Johnson, *John Henry,* 31–32. This report is secondhand, from C. E. Waugh, a contractor from Orange, Virginia. Waugh mentions a contest between John Henry and the Irishman Mike Olery (probably O'Leary), and then a contest between Henry and the steam drill shortly afterward. Johnson asked specifically about a contest at the Big Bend Tunnel. Waugh's letter responding to the note does say that the contest took place at the Big Bend Tunnel. Mason, however, was a contractor on the Lewis Tunnel.

27. Both researchers considered claims that the contest took place in Alabama in the 1880s, which also had a few firsthand accounts, but gave up on that site when they could find no evidence of a Cruzee mountain in Alabama. See Johnson, *John Henry*, 19–22; see also John Garst, "Chasing John Henry in Alabama and Mississippi: A Personal Memoir of Work in Progress," *Tributaries: Journal of the Alabama Folklife Association* 5 (2002): 92–129.

28. The best account of the five white informants is Chappell, *John Henry*, 49–56.

29. C. C. Huntley to G. B. Johnson, October 26, 1927, James P. Nelson to G. B. Johnson, January 6, 1928, Johnson papers, Folder 1056, SHC-UNC.

30. Johnson, *John Henry*, 49.

31. Using compressed air generated from a steam engine has little to recommend it. It is much less thermally efficient than using a wheel and leather straps; it is prone to breakdown; and it is difficult to get force that can be turned on and off as the drill is repositioned.

32. Johnson, *John Henry*, 107.

33. Transcribed from *Shout On: Leadbelly Legacy, Vol. 3*, Smithsonian Folkways CD.

34. See Johnson, *John Henry*, 108; and Chappell, *John Henry*, 112, 116, 120, 122; John Lomax, "Some Types of American Folk-Song," *Journal of American Folklore*, no. 107 (1915): 13.

35. Johnson, *John Henry*, 150.

36. Chappell, *John Henry*, 54.

37. The buildings that I saw in the postcard were in different places. In 1878, for example, the workshops had burned in a fire that consumed shops and machinery and were replaced by a new white house. See Mary Agnes Grant, *History of the State Penitentiary of Virginia* (manuscript, College of William and Mary, 1936), 94–101, 146.

38. Katherine Beidelman, phone conversation with author, November 22, 1998. The place of the Richmond penitentiary in this story is not a coincidence. I am indebted to Richard Wilkes of Glen Allen, Virginia, for helping me identify the RF&P's connecting railroad, which ran freight and passenger trains starting in April 1867. He noted to me that given the steep grade of the tracks, trains would have gone roaring by the white house. For convicts who came to Richmond penitentiary after 1878, after the white house was burned down, after the new burying ground was established just outsidethe walls of the penitentiary and along the street, the story of a man's burial would have been different. This may account for a different lyric that appears in only one version of the song. Melvin T. Hairston of Raleigh, West Virginia, gives these stanzas.

They took John Henry from the big white house
And they put him in the tunnel for to drive
With two nine-pound hammers hanging by his side
And the steam drill pointing to the sky, *etc.*
Oh shaker, huh turner, let her go down,
Oh shaker, huh turner, let her go down.
. . .

nd Compiler," *Niles Register* 65

f his interpretation of this line is

nusic is extensive. A useful histo-
onship between folk music, work
f Jon Michael Spenser, *Re-search-
Press, 1996).

he American Civil War (London:
h, January 13, 1885.
ry of the Commonwealth, Execu-
imond; *Richmond Dispatch*, Janu-
luring the War between the States,
m/~jcrosswell/Hist/obranch.html

al Stoneman, commander of Vir-
rs of October and November 1868
) Railroad, folder 1, 1868–1875, Li-
eman's original, confidential letter
:Allister Schofield Papers, Letters
Congress. The letter itself is not in
es the contents. It is in Schofield to
eld Papers, Letters Sent, container
ofield's reassurance to James Lyon
er 20, 1868.
numbered pages in Prisoner Regis-
ns, Library of Virginia.
o His Excellency H. H. Wells, Gov.
the Commonwealth, Executive Pa-

:after cited as HDW), 28 July 1870,

, 2 vols. (Newport News, VA: Mari-
Tunnel, VA, to HDW, July 4, 1870,

sapeake and Ohio Railroad," *Scrib-

ook, vol. 6, 1859–73, Library of Vir-

ebruary 22, 1869, WRHS.
/RHS.

69. Jos. F. Nounnan to HDW, October 16, 1869, WRHS.

70. C. P. Durham to HDW, April 5, 1870, WRHS.

71. [Peyton Randolph] to HDW, April 6, 1870, WRHS.

72. *Staunton Spectator,* June 14, 1870.

73. C. P. Huntington to HDW, June 25, 1870, WRHS.

74. Peyton Randolph to HDW, May 23, 1870, WRHS.

75. C. P. Durham to HDW, July 15, 1870, WRHS.

76. C. P. Huntington to HDW, July 7, 1870, WRHS.

77. C. P. Huntington to HDW, August 10, 1870, WRHS; Lee & Hustons, Thorndike PO, Cabell co, WV, to HDW, August 20, 1870, WRHS.

78. Secretary of the Commonwealth, Executive Journal, 1864–67, Minute Book, February 1870, Library of Virginia, Richmond.

79. "Report of the Board of Directors of the Virginia Penitentiary, w/ accompanying Documents for the Year ending Sept. 30, 1872" (Richmond, VA: RF Walker Superintendent of Public Printing, 1872), 5–6; "Report . . . Year ending Sept. 30, 1873," 3–5.

80. Three hundred eighty prisoners worked on the railroad from September 30, 1871, to September 30, 1872 ("Report . . . Year ending Sept. 30, 1872," 13).

81. *Richmond Dispatch,* October 12, 1871.

82. *Staunton Vindicator,* September 1, 1871.

83. *Richmond Dispatch,* October 12, 1871.

84. Chappell, *John Henry,* 108.

85. Huntington to Whitcomb, August 30, 1871, WRHS.

86. Peyton Randolph to HDW, n.d., in folder 6 with other letters from October 1871, WRHS.

87. Johnson, *John Henry,* 94.

88. *Richmond Dispatch,* April 10, 1872; Francis Earl Lutz, *Chesterfield: An Old Virginia County* (Richmond, VA: W. Byrd Press, 1954), 260; Prisoner Register, Penitentiary Records, Department of Corrections, Library of Virginia, Richmond.

89. Chappell, *John Henry,* 14.

90. This bizarre story is described in Chappell's book. See Chappell, *John Henry,* 84–85.

91. "Report . . . Year ending Sept. 30, 1872," bound in *Annual Reports of Officers, Boards & Institutions of the Cmwlth of Virginia* (Richmond, VA: RF Walker Superintendent of Public Printing, 1872).

92. "The Origins of Rock Drilling," *Digging Deeper: Newsletter of Australian Mining Consultants, Pty. Ltd.* (July 1998): 2–3.

93. This process is described in detail in Martin Cherniack, *The Hawk's Nest Incident: America's Worst Industrial Disaster* (New Haven, CT: Yale University Press, 1986).

94. Johnson, *John Henry,* 118.

ng ground

e street,
" etc.

ong was altered to fit the new circum-
n many particulars how convicts would
t. See Johnson, *John Henry,* 108.
e on December 23, 2003.
, Department of Corrections, Library of

contracts with railroads and canals.

first search. According to the director,
was uncataloged and unavailable to re-
atalog was released. The catalog states that
collection and thus "bring under control
imulated. Until this was done, however, a
nserviceable." Wickham's correspondence
on Palmer, a collector who had previously
el McCormick, personal conversation with
Quotation from Kermit J. Pike, *A Guide to
Reserve Historical Society* (Cleveland, OH:

Rise of the Tunnelling Industry* (New York:

ounds, and Rock Drills,* 278–81.
achinery: Description of Perforators and
ing. Devised by Herman Haupt, Civil Engi-
ean" (Philadelphia: HG Leisenring's Steam
nan Haupt Papers, Yale University; Drinker,
k Drills,* 281–84.
27.

for the Advancement of Science Meeting at
paper, "On the Application of Machinery to
upt, folder 75, Herman Haupt Papers, Yale

September 15, 1869, October 5, 1869; C. P.
iam J. Holt to Whitcomb, April 9, 1870; all in
pondence, 1869–1874, Western Reserve His-
cited as WRHS).
an.net/jargon/terms/k/kluge.html (accessed

Gender, Race, and Itinerant Commerce in the Rural New South

Lu Ann Jones

Few strangers crossed the hardscrabble landscape that Harry Crews evoked in his memoir of childhood in south Georgia during the 1930s and 1940s. Crews remembered that the Jewish peddler, driving a team of mismatched mules, "came into [his] little closed world smelling of strangeness and far places." Bolts of cloth, needles, thimbles, spools of thread, forks, knives, spoons, a grinding stone that "could sharpen anything," staples, nails, mule harnesses, "and a thousand other things" filled the inside of the peddler's wagon. Frying pans, boiling pots, washtubs, and mason fruit jars festooned the outside.[1]

It was Harry's mother, Myrtice Crews, who negotiated for these treasures. The peddler "did business almost exclusively with women," Crews recollected, "and whatever they needed, they could always find in the Jew's wagon. If they didn't have the money to pay for what they needed, he would trade for eggs or chickens or cured meat or canned vegetables and berries." To arrive at a price, the peddler and Crews's mother performed a ritual of bargaining. No matter how much Myrtice Crews protested "I ain't got the money," she often succumbed to the peddler's invitation to feel a bolt of cloth; and, after more haggling, he might offer to take corn and hay to feed his mules in payment for the fabric. Harry's mother signaled the end of the transactions when she "silently took two brown chicken eggs out of her apron and gave them to him" in exchange for peppermint balls. "With the candies melting on our tongues," Crews wrote, "we stood and watched him go, feeling as though we had ourselves just been on a long trip, a trip to the world we knew was out there but had never seen," a trip financed with the products of his mother's labor.[2]

Modest negotiations like those conducted by Myrtice Crews in her backyard occurred routinely during the first half of the twentieth century. Ubiquitous but elusive, transactions with itinerant merchants have been overlooked by scholars who assume that country stores took center stage in the rural New South. Analyzing stories about itinerant commerce rather than treating them as quaint anecdotes enriches the understanding of the New South's consumer economy and broadens the cast of characters who shaped it. Recent studies

demonstrate that southern country stores were economic institutions and social spaces where white men held the upper hand.[3] Oral history interviews,
reminiscences, regional fiction, and trade literature illuminate a universe of
buying and selling where itinerant merchants prevailed, where the farm
household was a place of consumption as well as production, and where male
dominance and white supremacy might be challenged.

A consideration of itinerant commerce joins a lively historical literature that
charts the complex story of how consumer culture spread across the United
States. Once preoccupied with middle-class shoppers in the urban Northeast,
scholars have discovered that the story's subplots vary by region, race, gender,
and class, revolve around the agency of buyers as well as the power of businesses, and unfold at different times in different places. This essay focuses less
on cultural historians' questions about theories of consumerism and the
meanings of goods than on the concerns of social historians—the nature of
buying and selling, the power relationships that defined those transactions,
and the context in which they occurred. It highlights human relationships
rather than anonymous representatives of the market.[4]

Several kinds of mobile merchants operated in the rural South well into the
twentieth century. Some, like the Jewish peddler of Harry Crews's youth, were
independent entrepreneurs who sold from their packs or wagons. Other itinerants operated what were popularly known as "rolling stores," portable exten-
sions of permanent businesses. Still other "traveling men" represented large
manufacturing firms that offered a diverse line of goods and provided elaborate advice on sales techniques. Two firms whose retailers frequented rural
southern homes were the W. T. Rawleigh Company and the J. R. Watkins Medical Company, both headquartered in the upper Midwest but boasting factories and distribution centers all over the United States, with several strategically located to take advantage of southern markets.[5]

Itinerant merchants extended the world of manufactured goods into the
countryside. Although they certainly did business with any willing customer,
they appealed to women and African American buyers who entertained fewer
options as consumers than did white men. Itinerant sellers accommodated the
needs of black and white farm women, whose patronage of town and country
stores was often limited by constraints on their travel and by their discomfort
in commercial places where men gathered to do business and pass the time.
Because traveling merchants took the products of women's labor in trade,
women customers were able to combine domestic production with consumption in a mix that suited their needs and pocketbooks. Contrary to the assumptions of cultural historians that sellers always had the upper hand, these
customers were shrewd buyers rather than easy dupes, and they enjoyed the
challenge of bargaining with traders. Besides the goods that filled a peddler's

pack or a sales agent's sample case, these merchants also arrived with news from beyond the immediate neighborhood, a commodity prized by women who kept close to home. Furthermore, African American men found doing business with mobile merchants attractive because what and where itinerants sold provided alternatives to trading with country storekeepers whose racist assumptions shaped access to credit and goods.

Itinerant merchants in the New South joined a long line of mobile sellers that began with peddlers. American business practice and lore usually associate peddlers with antebellum Yankee entrepreneurs who sold clocks, tinware, patent medicines, cloth, and notions to country people. In the early nineteenth century peddlers served an economic purpose as distributors for small-scale manufacturers and importers. But as historian Jackson Lears has argued, they also were the heralds of a nascent consumer culture and touchstones for the anxiety and ambivalence that the spread of a market economy generated. Here today and gone tomorrow, itinerants crossed the boundaries between local neighborhoods and the cosmopolitan world; they represented the "magic" of the marketplace, with its mixture of danger and allure. Peddlers inspired a rich folklore and humor that mirrored the apprehensions that accompanied the quickened pace of nineteenth-century commerce. In literary representations and the popular imagination, peddlers aroused suspicion as outsiders and shrewd tricksters who supposedly found women, in particular, to be vulnerable to their verbally seductive sales pitches.[6]

As peddlers extended the market's reach into the antebellum South, anxieties about both race and gender aroused suspicions. Newspaper editors and storekeepers accused peddlers of "cheating women and children."[7] At least one husband agreed. In 1826 a Georgia man accused peddlers of convincing his young bride "to buy a considerable quantity of store-goods" without his "knowledge or approbation" and was so incensed that he took out a newspaper advertisement warning vendors away from his house for eighteen months.[8] Peddlers also stirred distrust among slaveholders. Planters feared that itinerants trafficked with slaves who offered pilfered livestock in trade and worried that peddlers were abolitionists in disguise sowing the seeds of rebellion among bondmen. In the wake of insurrection panics, slaveholders cast skeptical eyes on itinerant merchants, who were strangers in their midst. After John Brown's 1859 raid at Harpers Ferry, for example, whites in several Georgia towns questioned and harassed traveling salesmen from the North, who were thought to sympathize with the abolitionist. An idle remark was enough to provoke a committee of white citizens in Columbus, Georgia, to scrutinize the "many persons from the free States now traveling through our neighborhood for the ostensible purpose of selling books, maps, rat traps, etc.," and such harassment inspired the salesmen to catch the next train or steamship home.[9]

What those who study peddlers have ignored—but is implicit in their accounts—is that the harshest critics of itinerants were white men who constructed unsavory images of peddlers and their female and African American clientele in an effort to control access to the marketplace. Centering the analysis of consumption around gender and consumers' perspectives, however, places peddlers in a different light. Perhaps peddlers posed a danger because they took their wares to buyers who were not male heads of households. By extending the market, peddlers and their patrons undercut the domestic authority of men. From the vantage point of women and slaves, peddlers were welcomed visitors. The same was true for their postbellum descendents.[10]

Although the popular literature of the New South perpetuated images of peddlers as duplicitous tricksters, these portrayals camouflage the precarious social conditions of their work. After the Civil War, recent newcomers from Eastern Europe got footholds in business by peddling in the South. With little capital to invest, immigrant peddlers often catered to poor whites and African Americans, economically marginal figures like themselves. Stereotyped as shady dealers, peddlers were in reality vulnerable salesmen who were easy targets of criminals as they traveled alone hauling merchandise and carrying money. Such was the fate of Francis Brice, an Irish peddler who sold his wares in southeastern North Carolina. In 1878 as Brice passed through a remote marsh, two local men shot him, wrenched a pistol from his hand, and clubbed him with his own walking stick. After stealing Brice's money, the robbers left him to die. Similar bad fortune befell Samuel Tucker, a Jewish peddler from Richmond, Virginia, whose route traversed the North Carolina piedmont. During an 1892 selling trip, Tucker sought overnight lodgings in Franklin County and was robbed and murdered where he rested. The culprits tossed his body into a vine-choked ravine, where it went undetected for months.[11] As these cases suggest, representing peddlers as tricksters endowed them with more social power than they actually wielded.

Popular mythology also distorts other characteristics of peddlers' work. Like the itinerant whom Harry Crews remembered, many peddlers became familiar outsiders rather than feared strangers. Though customers surely did not count them as neighbors and frequently associated immigrants with exotic, foreign places, between spring and fall of each year peddlers often traveled predictable circuits that brought them back to the same customers month after month. For example, in the early twentieth century a man known only as "Peddler Black" was a regular visitor in Owen County, Kentucky. Although residents later debated his ethnicity and pondered his "mysterious origins," at least one woman asserted that "he *was not a stranger to us*."[12]

General stores had sprouted at nearly every dusty crossroad by the 1880s and 1890s, but itinerant merchants continued to find a niche in the New South.

Even as railroads connected the region to national markets and the South crawled with drummers who sold wholesale to storekeepers, access to the manufactured goods that expanded briskly after the Civil War varied according to place, race, class, and gender. Members of the new middle class who lived in the South's burgeoning towns and cities could patronize stores and specialty shops that their country cousins could only imagine. Country stores offered lines of merchandise that ranged from patent medicines to plow points, but peddlers and other sales agents brought their wares right to the homes of customers for whom the rural retail outlets were alien places.[13]

General stores, as historian Ted Ownby has noted, "were not settings for racial equality." Nor were they settings for gender equality. Black and white men struck bargains with merchants who provided credit for farm supplies, groceries, and dry goods in exchange for liens on their crops. White men gathered around stoves to play checkers or loafed on porches, passing the time with ribald humor and neighborhood gossip, the conversations sometimes lubricated with whiskey. Although white storekeepers welcomed African American men as customers, they kept a tight fist on credit, monitored their purchases, directed them towards inferior goods, and did little to ease the tensions that black men felt as "conspicuous outsiders." In the era of Jim Crow, the stores became stages where southerners choreographed steps in a new dance of race relations. Sometimes black and white men mixed freely and without conflict, but all too often African Americans suffered verbal epithets or physical jostling that diminished any joy attached to buying.[14]

Bastions of male customs and habits, country stores were not particularly hospitable places for women to shop either. In his classic study of southern country stores, Thomas D. Clark noted that women approached these centers of commerce with reluctance and uneasiness. "They stood near the front door with embarrassed grins on their faces showing clearly mixed feelings of eager curiosity and shocked modesty," Clark wrote. "They were caught in the unhappy situation of not knowing whether to stay until someone came to serve them or to leave the store." In the 1930s and 1940s when photographers from the Farm Security Administration (FSA) traveled the back roads of the South, they found men lounging on store porches and gathered inside; women were hardly to be found. The woman who did venture across a store's threshold might, in William Faulkner's words, have to pass "the squatting men . . . spitting across the heelgnawed porch" and training their "ranked battery of maneyes" on her.[15]

Practical constraints joined ideology to restrict rural women's visits to stores. Preoccupied with childbearing and childrearing much of their adult lives, rural women simply had less chance to get away from home. Basic household maintenance filled their time. When Sara Brooks was growing up in the

Alabama Black Belt during the 1920s, her mother rarely accompanied her father to town on Saturdays. Brooks's mother reserved the day for cleaning the house, sweeping the yard, and cooking Sunday dinner.[16]

Although the products of women's labor often provided the currency for trade, men usually did the shopping. Sara Brooks reported that before her father went to the store, he asked his wife, "'Now what to get?' [and] [s]he would write him a little list and give it to him." In eastern North Carolina, A. C. and Grace Griffin established a similar pattern in the 1930s and maintained it for years. "[W]hen we first got married we didn't have any transportation [the] first five years," Grace Griffin explained. "On Saturday morning [A. C.] and his daddy would go to town in the mule and cart and buy the week's groceries. Then we had a young couple . . . move close to us . . . . He and A. C. would go to town together on Saturday morning a lot of times and each one would carry whatever eggs we had left over from the hens that week and buy the groceries. Well, the pattern was set by the time we got an automobile and I learned how to drive it."[17]

The shopping arrangement that the Griffins worked out also followed from expectations about proper public behavior, which differed for men and women. When women went to town to grocery shop, Grace Griffin had been raised to believe, they should dress up, whereas men were free to wear their work clothes away from home. If A. C. did the shopping, she was spared the trouble of outfitting herself for a "public" appearance.[18]

Itinerant merchants understood these facts of economic and social life and turned farm households into sites of consumption as well as production. In reminiscences of rural life in the early-twentieth-century South, peddlers remained familiar figures. Filtered through the lens of childhood, recollections ascribed magical qualities to peddlers who inspired fascination and fantasy. The peddler's visit to the Wake County farm where Bernice Kelly Harris grew up in the late nineteenth century remained a vivid memory for the North Carolina writer forty years later. When the peddler opened his packs, Harris recalled, "It was Aladdin's lamp, an adventure in wonderland, a glimpse into the goldhaired prince's palace beside the sea. For the rings and things conjured up a way of life that glittered." The peddler, according to Harris, "was not so much a person to the children as a symbol, like Santa Claus."[19] Harris was not alone in her fond memories. Itinerant sellers "who visited the farms of those days and brightened the lives of those who lived there" figured prominently in Caroline S. Coleman's reminiscences about a turn-of-the-century childhood in the South Carolina piedmont. The peddlers who "linked the remote countryside with the marts of trade" in her part of the world were usually Italians, Syrians, or Irishmen. Children playing in the yard often spied the peddlers first and relayed the exciting news to their grandmother. As the peddler unfastened his pack, Coleman remembered, "we watched in wide eyed wonder" as he revealed the "riches of Araby."[20]

For children like Harris and Coleman, peddlers represented miraculous gift-bearers. But for adult women their visits provided opportunities to bargain for household necessities and a few small luxuries and to embroider their roles as good domestic managers. While young Bernice Harris enjoyed the aroma of soaps and admired the ribbons, lace, and brooches that the peddler displayed, her mother calculated which goods she could afford to buy and which trinkets she had to pass up. After engaging in a form of window-shopping in her own home, Bernice appreciated that her mother "had spent her butter and egg money to let us enjoy looking at the wares." When the peddler arrived at the home of Caroline Coleman's grandmother, the older woman invited him to turn her parlor into a show room for the fine shawls, towels, tablecloths, pillowshams, combs, and beads that he pulled from his pack. Word of the peddler's visit traveled the "grapevine telegraph," and soon "every colored woman on the place" came to examine his stock and to join the "fine art" of trading with him. Buying turned into a collective activity, and several women matching bargaining wits with a peddler might have afforded them some advantage. After dickering and buying had ended, Coleman's grandmother offered to board the peddler for the night, her gesture of hospitality repaid with stories "of his home country in the great world beyond our doors" and with a gift such as fine linen towels.[21]

Hassan Mohamed was a Lebanese peddler who gained a foothold in southern commerce. Soon after he landed in New York City in 1911, Mohamed headed to the Mississippi Delta, where friends helped him get a start. A Clarksdale, Mississippi, storekeeper "gave him $27 worth of merchandise in [a] little suitcase," and Mohamed set out on foot to sell. A limited command of English and an unfamiliarity with American currency put Mohamed at the mercy of his customers—a dilemma that turned the image of the crafty peddler on its head. "He said he didn't know the five dollars from the ten [dollar bill] or the one," recalled his widow, Ethel Wright Mohamed. "But he said he felt like any house he stopped, they'd buy whatever they bought out of the suitcase, [and] they would make the change and he felt like everyone was honest. He didn't think anybody beat him out of any money."[22]

Black sharecroppers who worked Delta plantations patronized Mohamed, and he counted one woman in particular as a "special" customer. If she and her family were working in the fields when he arrived, Mohamed napped in the shade until she came to the house. "Then he would go up on the porch," Ethel Wright Mohamed explained, "and she would have some of the neighbors come, and they'd buy everything out of his suitcase right there. And he said she would run her hand up under the rug and get the money she had hid in the house. And he thought that was the most wonderful thing he'd ever seen. And so that was her bank . . . and that was his store." Within three years, Mohamed had earned enough to buy a wagon, allowing him to expand the line of goods he carried and the territory he covered. By 1922 he was able to buy a store in the hamlet of Shaw and to settle permanently.[23]

Trading with peddlers was especially appealing to women. They could weigh their choices in the privacy of their backyards or front porches. They shaped the space where goods were displayed, calibrated the value, and gauged their own capacity to spend. They might even practice their bartering prowess before an appreciative audience of neighbors. On home turf, women incorporated commerce into a domestic economy where they operated from a position of strength and helped define the terms of trade.

The peddlers' lessons were not lost on store owners. Some rural storekeepers realized that they could tap their market's full potential only if they took their merchandise to women's homes. At these "rolling stores"—trucks or wagons fitted out with merchandise—customers could buy according to their financial means or personal whims. Hal Edmonds's grandfather knew that the farmwives and daughters in the North Carolina mountains rarely made trips to the country store or to the Madison County towns of Mars Hill and Marshall. But every week O. S. Edmonds took a scaled-down version of his permanent store to customers, trading merchandise for eggs, chickens, and butter. In the 1940s, Hal worked as a clerk for his grandfather. "Most all that traded in the regular store," Hal Edmonds explained, "they was mostly men. Men would come to the store and stay about all day and their wives, whatever they wanted, they would write it down or tell the men. Women very seldom ever come to the store. Like in the rolling [store] business, it was all different. It was all women."[24]

Because Edmonds kept regular weekly routes, women anticipated his arrival and met him at the end of their lanes, ready to offer baskets of eggs or coops of live chickens in trade. "They'd like to come out right beside the house," Edmonds recalled, "sit down beside the road. See, you started up a little road up one of these hollers, and they could hear you coming. Wasn't no traffic." From the shelves and aisle of the specially rigged truck, Edmonds supplied primarily the same merchandise that stocked the shelves of his "regular store." He also took special orders for bulky items, such as a hundred-pound bag of salt during hog-killing season, or custom goods, such as shoes, which he delivered the following week. The rolling store business continued in Madison County until the 1950s, when better roads and more automobiles eased travel and chain grocery stores were established.[25]

Rolling stores also served rural customers in south Georgia, where Mioma Thompson grew up the daughter of farm wage hands during the 1930s. Her mother patronized stores in the town of Tifton and the rolling stores that stopped at their house. Rolling stores, Thompson remembered, "carried material, flour and sugar, flavoring, or this liniment. A lot of people back then was bad to rub with liniment. Just whatever they could put on that store that would keep, that's what they'd take." By the time the mobile store arrived, "Mama would always save her money and her eggs. Course, we had what we wanted to eat. But about time for [the rolling store] to come, she'd go to saving them eggs up and put her a chicken in the coop, fatten it up. That's the way she got what she needed." Mioma's mother controlled the egg money and used its proceeds to buy staple goods and to indulge a child's sweet tooth when the mobile merchant visited.[26]

Buying at the "rolling store" was both a way to acquire needed goods and a form of entertainment. In East Tennessee until the mid-1940s Della Sarten traded butter and eggs with a man who ran a rolling store "that was just packed full." A man from Sevierville "come along with cloth, had anything like they had in a grocery store," Sarten recalled. "[H]e come around once a week. . . . I had eggs. Sometimes I'd sell two or three hens. Then I'd have a list wrote out, and I'd just call it off, and they'd just hand it out, and on they'd go." To the merchant's dismay, not everyone made their choices as quickly as Sarten did, and he recounted to Sarten his experiences with other customers: "My next door neighbor, she'd climb up in their truck, and she'd look at the cloth and she looked at everything for about an hour. He said one day, 'If everybody was like you, we'd get along.' They'd come back in Sevierville way in the night, you know, people taking so long to trade."[27] In contrast to the pragmatic Sarten, her neighbor turned the storekeeper's visit into a leisure activity. Either way, the seller had to keep the customer happy.

A third kind of itinerant merchant was a common visitor to rural southern homes—agents who represented large manufacturing enterprises and specialized in a line of goods. Salesmen of musical instruments, lightening rods, and patent medicines pervaded the autobiographical novels and folk plays of North Carolinian Bernice Kelly Harris. When a stranger appeared in the fictional community of Beulah Ridge, for example, the women speculated that he must be selling farm periodicals or Canadian lace. Like peddlers, these "traveling men" often doubled as entertainers; their skills as raconteurs and musicians complemented their sales pitches, and customers prized their talents, company, and the news they brought with them as much as the merchandise they sold. In Harris's play *Pair of Quilts,* Sudie Johnson rated the traveling men who boarded in her home. "I thought the 'Native Herb' man was real entertainin' with his fast pieces on the fiddle, and the lightnin' rod agent with han'chief tricks," Sudie said, "but the grapherphone man's got 'em all beat with his funny jokes."[28]

Like the members of her own family, the women of Harris's fiction welcomed sales agents, but her fictional men often tried to ban them or banished them outright. One woman of the neighborhood reported that the squire of Beulah Ridge "stopped agents from comin' on his land, told 'em to stay way from the Ridge just like he owned it all." In Harris's novel *Purslane,* the patriarch John Fuller so despised solicitors that he "had once put up a sign at the road: 'No agents allowed here.' " The warning had backfired, however, attracting rather than deterring curious salesmen. The "Native Herb" man was among those who ignored the posting and annoyed Fuller by interrupting his plowing with his sales pitch. But when the agent "mentioned indigestion," John's wife Dele "entered the conversation," Harris wrote. "The result was she took the agency for the herb pills," which "became a family and neighborhood standby" for all manner of ailments and also turned a profit for Dele. How frequently women sold medicines is uncertain. In *Mothers of the South: Portraiture of the White Tenant Farm Woman,* sociologist Margaret Jarman Hagood described the pitch of a woman selling salves, tooth powders, and a tonic called Vi-Ava.[29]

These fictional sales agents were in some ways prototypes of the men who sold the products of the Rawleigh and Watkins companies. To this day older rural southerners recollect regular visits by "the Rawleigh man" and "the Watkins man." Although they often put these sellers in the same category as peddlers and rolling store merchants, salesmen for Rawleigh and Watkins were, in many respects, a breed apart. When they arrived at farm houses with their sample cases, they were retailers acting on behalf of large companies whose founders had coached them in the latest sales techniques. These itinerant merchants represented the so-called incorporation of America and a new, intensified phase in the creation of a national market for brand-name consumer goods. But gender, race, and local customs shaped the way southerners encountered the market.[30]

Although Rawleigh and Watkins retailers visited the rural South frequently, the parent companies were located in the upper Midwest. Based in northern Illinois, the W. T. Rawleigh Company headquarters was less than two hundred miles from the J. R. Watkins Medical Company hometown of Winona, Minnesota. W. T. Rawleigh began modestly in the late nineteenth century, peddling to farmers the medicines that his first wife—whom he later divorced—manufactured and bottled in their home near Freeport. By the early twentieth century, Rawleigh envisioned the sales potential, and the company began building factories in cities across the United States and Canada. The birth and development of the J. R. Watkins Medical Company followed a similar path, starting with a popular liniment in 1868 and expanding its inventory and sales territory in the early twentieth century.[31]

A dizzying array of products rolled off the Rawleigh and Watkins assembly lines. There were spices and flavorings to season foods; toiletries to soften and perfume the body; salves, liniments, laxatives, and cough syrups to relieve human aches and afflictions; and veterinary dips, disinfectants, and powders to treat the diseases of livestock. In 1921 the Rawleigh Company manufactured 125 different products; during a visit by "the Rawleigh man" customers could buy everything from blood-purifying tonics to vanilla flavoring and lemon extract, cinnamon and nutmeg, White Rose and Anna May Bouquet perfumes, shampoo and face lotion, and a powder to rid chickens of lice.[32]

By 1912 both companies had established factories and branches in Memphis, Tennessee. Rawleigh boasted that its "beautiful and artistic" manufacturing plant there, surrounded by "a spreading lawn," was "the handsomest factory building in the South, being pronounced perfect by the State Factory Inspection." While the Memphis plant positioned the company to tap markets in the mid-South, a Richmond factory put the company within easy reach of retailers and customers in the upper South. Similarly, the Watkins company declared that its Memphis and Baltimore branches had "helped greatly in developing an enormous business in the southern states long before any other concerns operating by the wagon method had even made a start" and had "made the south solid for Watkins." Yet, the company announced, it could still employ hundreds of salesmen because there was "a lot of virgin territory in the South awaiting the coming of 'The Watkins way.'"[33]

Both companies published manuals designed to entice men to join their sales teams and to instruct them in the most effective selling techniques. In 1906 W. T. Rawleigh wrote his first selling guide and another followed in 1921, its 319 pages full of tips guaranteed to increase sales. Rawleigh's suggestions were exhaustive, and he anticipated every contingency. By 1926 the *Rawleigh Methods* guide filled 1,917 pages and in bulk it resembled a thick brick. Meanwhile, Watkins published a similar—albeit slimmer—sales manual entitled *The Open Door to Success* about 1914.[34]

Like manufacturers of their era who "literally celebrated the 'mass' in 'mass production,'" Rawleigh and Watkins impressed employees and customers with the vastness of their companies. The Rawleigh enterprise, for example, began with expeditions to Madagascar, Sumatra, and other foreign lands in search of the most pungent spices, and then the company produced an extensive line of goods in large factories and coordinated complicated distribution systems that ran like well-oiled machines. The process ended when Rawleigh retailers established successful routes that delivered products to customers. Sketches of the Rawleigh and Watkins factories illustrated their publications, visually reinforcing the scale and scope of the operations and encouraging sales agents to consider themselves part of modern American businesses based on mass production and factory-made goods.[35]

Rawleigh and Watkins sought to distance themselves from unflattering images of itinerant merchants by stressing that their agents represented the vanguard of modern marketing methods. "Our men are not mere peddlers," insisted the Watkins company. "They are high class salesmen with a real service to render the public." Rawleigh assured customers that the retailer of his products was "No stranger, or irresponsible, transient agent, or peddler to take your money and be gone," but "a neighbor and a friend. . . . He is not an outsider."[36]

Rawleigh coached his retailers in the principles of so-called scientific salesmanship, encouraging sellers to follow precise rules rather than relying on techniques and patter that they invented themselves. A good agent, according to the 1921 guide, "must be more than a mere order-taker—he must be a *creator and builder* of business, he must be able to influence and persuade others to buy his goods, he must create interest, then desire, and afterwards decision or action." With practice and experience, Rawleigh assured new agents, "you will be able to read character," design an effective presentation, and judge "your chances of making sales . . . almost instantly after you have met your customer."[37]

Rawleigh and Watkins manuals featured the stories of outstanding agents. Not surprisingly, their experiences endorsed company sales recommendations. Both firms encouraged retailers to make as many "Time and Trial" sales as possible. Customers who accepted goods on trial agreed to pay in full on the agent's next visit only if they had used the products and found them satisfactory. Agents shared tips on ways to dissolve customer resistance to buying and to collect money owed for products sold on credit. Indeed, testimonials usually took the form of long dialogues between the agent and his customers that read like scripts for novice sellers to follow. Although agents were encouraged to seek food and lodging with families along their routes, they were discouraged from indulging in evening entertainments; swapping stories or playing music were not part of the "modern" salesman's repertoire. Rather, the agent in these exemplary stories spent his time demonstrating products or preparing customers for sales that he would conclude before his departure in the morning.[38]

The Rawleigh company counted both men and women among its customers, but testimonials by agents suggest that husbands were more skeptical of itinerants than were their wives. Men, according to these accounts, might refuse to buy from peddlers or "wagon men" because they preferred to patronize established storekeepers in their communities or suspected the quality of the products sold by itinerants. On the other hand, the trade literature portrayed women as customers who recognized the superiority of the Rawleigh spices, flavorings, and medicines.[39]

When a "Rawleigh man" or "Watkins man" pulled up to a southern farmhouse, he had a bag of sales tricks at his disposal—if he heeded the voluminous advice offered. The recollections of a Chatham County, North Carolina, woman whose grandparents bought from "the Rawleigh man" during the 1930s and 1940s suggest that agents followed some of the recommendations. Gladys Hackney Thomas recalled that the Rawleigh retailer who called on her family patiently described his products but did not dawdle. "He was always in a hurry," she remembered. "He took time to show his goods," but as soon as purchases were made, "he was on his way." The behavior of this "Rawleigh man" resembles the sales guide's directive to "be active and business-like" when making customer calls. "Do not loaf or loiter around one moment after finishing your business," the guide instructed. "Time is valuable, do not waste yours or compel others to waste theirs, but move on." In addition, the North Carolina agent met the Rawleigh dress code of "neat but not showy," a style with which rural customers would feel comfortable. "He didn't wear overalls like farmers did," Thomas remembered, "but he didn't wear a tie, either." [40]

Oral history accounts suggest that women especially welcomed the visits of Rawleigh and Watkins retailers because they were breaks in household routines and opportunities to make autonomous purchases. Moreover, contrary to stereotype, women appear to have been discriminating customers who judged products and evaluated their efficacy with care. The "Rawleigh man" passed through Gladys Thomas's community about once every three months, and the women "were so thrilled" that they telephoned neighbors as soon as someone spotted him in the vicinity. He often arrived mid-morning, and Thomas's grandmother and aunts would interrupt their cooking to inspect the goods and make their purchases. Rawleigh salves and liniments were treasured items in the family medicine chest, and Thomas's grandmother liked to add Rawleigh cake colorings to batter or frosting, a touch that set her cakes apart from the crowd on Sundays when a church dinner followed preaching. [41]

The Watkins agent who visited the eastern North Carolina home of Edythe Hollowell Jones in the 1920s was sometimes a source of amusement, but his products were highly valued. The family joked that the salesman planned his route in order to arrive at noon. "I've heard my mother say when he was in our neighborhood, she swore he heard our dinner bell ring and made it there in time to eat dinner," recalled Edythe Jones. "Oh, yeah! Mama'd always ask him to come in and have dinner and he'd eat." Irene Barber Hollowell selected "all kinds of spices," trusted Rawleigh salves to relieve congested chests and soothe burns, and "swore by" the veterinary tablets and powders she bought to cure her chickens of parasites. Examining the Rawleigh products brought to her door gave Irene Hollowell "an opportunity to make a few purchasing decisions" otherwise denied her when her husband filled the grocery list. [42]

Rural southerners used consumer goods to their own ends, incorporating purchased medicines into a pharmacopeia that still included homemade remedies. New consumer possibilities did not eclipse older practices. Although Gladys Thomas's grandmother bought Rawleigh tonics and salves, she continued to gather wild mullein leaves and cherry tree bark to be boiled into a syrup for coughs. The fictional Dele Fuller purchased indigestion pills from the "Native Herb" man, but she and her female relatives searched the woods when they needed ingredients for a special salve that relieved aching muscles and joints or a tea that soothed sore throats. Even store-bought medicines were applied in dosages and according to methods that reflected the accumulated wisdom of farm women. Rather than being susceptible to bogus sales pitches, many farm women evaluated the curative powers of commercial remedies and made choices based on time-tested observations and experiences.[43]

Although Rawleigh advised salesmen to accept payment in goods instead of cash only as a last resort, agents nonetheless found themselves bartering with customers for whom eggs, chickens, or smoked meat were the only currency. In south Georgia, Clyde Purvis's mother swapped eggs for Rawleigh products. During the Great Depression, Jessie Gosney's father ran a Rawleigh route near Stuttgart, Arkansas. Using hyperbole to describe the lengths to which her father went to cater to his poor clients, Gosney said that he "would get paid in dogs and cats and strawberries, rotten strawberries. Mother never will forgive him for that." Barter and mass marketing went hand in hand.[44] Photographs suggest the popularity of Watkins products in the South and illustrate how farm families used company advertising as a kind of vernacular household decoration. In 1938 FSA photographer Russell Lee recorded a husband, wife, and six children in "a small, plainly furnished, but comfortable house" near New Iberia, Louisiana. The only adornment on the wall behind them was a Watkins calendar. When FSA photographer Jack Delano captured the image of "Mrs. Fanny Parrot, the wife of an ex-slave" near Siloam, Georgia, in May 1941, the subject posed before a fireplace. Above the mantel hung a Watkins calendar, and suspended below it was a Watkins almanac.[45]

As black southerners entered the market as consumers, albeit on unequal terms with whites, the Rawleigh company took note. During a trip to his Memphis plant in the 1920s, W. T. Rawleigh became convinced that southern African Americans represented a lucrative market for the company's line of goods. When he published the 1926 edition of his sales guide, he entitled a chapter "Southern Collection Methods." Drawn largely from retailer testimonials, the chapter encouraged Rawleigh men to overcome reservations they might have about dealing with black customers and described the best ways to sell to and collect from them.[46]

The advice reflected a contradictory blend of entrepreneurial respect and racist suspicion and coercion typical of white southern country store owners. "[T]reat the negro right," began the circuitous counsel of J. W. McCall of

Tennessee. "Of course keep them in their place. Sell them the Products and let them know you expect their money and treat them as negroes should be treated. Treat them with the same consideration in a business transaction as white people." Although the sales manual cautioned southern Rawleigh retailers "against using old fashioned plantation managers' methods of extending long credits and of allowing Consumers to . . . pay only once a year" after fall harvest, agents who had profited from a large trade with black customers described taking out mortgages and notes as one way to assure reimbursement for products sold on time. On some plantations, Rawleigh men consulted with managers and owners before selling to their tenants and convinced them to agree "that the accounts . . . would be guaranteed by the manager and held out of [the tenant's] crop or wages."[47]

Rawleigh men who shared their methods of collecting payments revealed that they subjected black customers to bullying tactics never imagined for white buyers. A Georgia agent who tried to win the confidence of black clients and to treat them fairly nonetheless resorted to threats of suing "careless" blacks who failed to pay their bills. An Alabama salesman treated his recalcitrant patrons "firmly" and provided an example of a firm collection strategy. "One day," he recalled, "I had to get out of my wagon and whip one fellow to make him see my way, but from then on, I never had any trouble." To encourage retailers to tap the African American market, Rawleigh first contended that many black customers were as trustworthy as whites and then sanctioned legal and physical coercion should there be exceptions to this general principle.[48]

Rawleigh's philosophy toward black customers compounded the disadvantages that African Americans suffered in a marketplace where landlords and merchants commonly practiced deceit and usury. Yet, Rawleigh did provide African Americans buying options that included the range of goods they could purchase and the site of consumption itself. While some retailers sought the consent and cooperation of plantation managers before approaching tenants, others met black buyers in spaces that blacks controlled and that were away from the watchful eyes of whites. S. B. Pearson of Alabama, for example, delivered products to and collected payments from black customers at a local church or schoolhouse.[49]

Regardless of the conditions of trade, African Americans may have welcomed the alternative to general stores that Rawleigh men and other sales agents offered. Merchants who "furnished" credit and supplies to farm families often monitored their purchases in order to limit the amount of debt accumulated through the year. For example, the southern Mississippi storekeeper who "furnished" N. J. Booth in the 1930s and 1940s restricted the purchases that the black farmer and his wife could make, although they owned their own land. The merchant, Booth recalled, refused to sell his wife groceries that "he figured we could do without. . . . [S]he might [make a list that included] something to make a cake or something like that. He took that off. Flour and lard, he would leave that on. But something extra, he always looked at the bill and he took that off." The merchant "had to okay the bill every time my wife or Brother Henry's wife [wanted to buy anything]—and he did the poor white the same way." Wayland Spivey, an African American sharecropper in eastern North Carolina in the 1940s, described a similar experience. The landlord "would give me a purchase order to go to the store and get food, and that was all I could get."[50] Given such restrictions, black farmers might welcome a "Rawleigh man" and a chance to buy flavorings and spices to beat into cake batter.

Not all itinerants undermined racial hierarchies, but peddlers, rolling store owners, and agents of national companies at least provided white women and African Americans with options that were denied to them at country stores. Stores flourished and fostered a new consumer economy and culture in the South's cities and towns; at the same time, an older way of buying and selling persisted and assumed new forms as itinerants "linked the remote countryside with the marts of trade." Too often, historians of commerce in the New South have treated stories about mobile merchants and their customers as picturesque artifacts of an earlier era. But taken seriously, these stories reveal that humble consumers shaped the marketplace and enticed sellers to offer goods on their turf and on their terms. Careful observations of transactions conducted with itinerant merchants add new layers of meaning to the picture of consumerism in the rural South and demonstrate that women and African Americans were agents in the marketplace who stretched its boundaries rather than buckled to its constraints. As Myrtice Crews and her boy Harry knew every time the Jewish peddler drove into their yard, the southern country store was but one constellation in the region's universe of buying and selling.

Notes

1. Harry Crews, *A Childhood: The Biography of a Place* (New York, 1978), 73–74 (first quotation on p. 73; second and third quotations on p. 74). Many colleagues have commented on drafts of this essay. I wish to thank Peter Coclanis, Jacquelyn Dowd Hall, Cliff Kuhn, Susan Levine, Bill Mansfield, Marla Miller, Laura J. Moore, Mary Murphy, Ted Ownby, Joseph T. Rainer, Anastatia Sims, and five anonymous reviewers for the *Journal of Southern History*. Grants from East Carolina University's Department of History, Division of Research and Graduate Studies, and College of Arts and Sciences supported research and writing.

2. Ibid., 74–76 (first quotation on p. 74; second quotation on p. 75; third and fourth quotations on p. 76).

3. The classic study remains Thomas D. Clark, *Pills, Petticoats, and Plows: The Southern Country Store* (Indianapolis and New York, 1944). Recent studies include

Edward L. Ayers, *The Promise of the New South: Life After Reconstruction* (New York and Oxford, 1992), Chap. 4; Grace Elizabeth Hale, *Making Whiteness: The Culture of Segregation in the South, 1890–1940* (New York, 1998), 168–79; and Ted Ownby, *American Dreams in Mississippi: Consumers, Poverty, and Culture, 1830–1998* (Chapel Hill and London, 1999), Chaps. 1–4.

4. Excellent introductions to the literature are Tom Pendergast, "Consuming Questions: Scholarship on Consumerism in America to 1940," *American Studies International*, XXXVI (June 1998), 23–43; and Peter N. Stearns, "Stages of Consumerism: Recent Work on the Issues of Periodization," *Journal of Modern History*, LXIX (March 1997), 102–17. On the cultural history of consumerism see Jackson Lears, *Fables of Abundance: A Cultural History of Advertising in America* (New York, 1994). Studies sensitive to gender, class, region, and race include Susan Porter Benson, "Living on the Margin: Working-Class Marriages and Family Survival Strategies in the United States, 1919–1941," in Victoria de Grazia, with Ellen Furlough, eds., *The Sex of Things: Gender and Consumption in Historical Perspective* (Berkeley, Los Angeles, London, 1996), 212–43; Lizabeth Cohen, "Encountering Mass Culture at the Grassroots: The Experience of Chicago Workers in the 1920s," *American Quarterly*, XLI (March 1989), 6–33; Cohen, "The Class Experience of Mass Consumption: Workers as Consumers in Interwar America," in Richard Wightman Fox and T. J. Jackson Lears, eds., *The Power of Culture: Critical Essays in American History* (Chicago and London, 1993), 135–60; Hal S. Barron, *Mixed Harvest: The Second Great Transformation in the Rural North, 1870–1930* (Chapel Hill and London, 1997), Chaps. 5–6; Thomas J. Schlereth, "Country Stores, County Fairs, and Mail-Order Catalogues: Consumption in Rural America," in Simon J. Bronner, ed., *Consuming Visions: Accumulation and Display of Goods in America, 1880–1920* (New York and London, 1989), 339–75; Susan Atherton Hanson, "Home Sweet Home: Industrialization's Impact on Rural Households, 1865–1925" (Ph.D. diss., University of Maryland, 1986); and Robert E. Weems, Jr., *Desegregating the Dollar: African American Consumerism in the Twentieth Century* (New York and London, 1998).

5. Portions of this article are taken from Chap. 2 of Lu Ann Jones, "Re-visioning the Countryside: Southern Women, Rural Reform, and the Farm Economy in the Twentieth Century" (Ph.D. diss., University of North Carolina at Chapel Hill, 1996). Determining the precise number of itinerant merchants is difficult, and even official numbers must be taken with a grain of salt. According to U.S. censuses, the number of peddlers and hucksters increased in several southern states between 1890 and 1930. For example, in 1890 and 1930 respectively, there were in Alabama, 440 and 813 peddlers and hucksters; in Arkansas, 150 and 258; in Georgia, 689 and 1,114; in Kentucky, 835 and 857; in North Carolina, 287 and 343; and in Tennessee, 773 and 998. For figures see U.S. Department of the Interior, Census Office, *Compendium of the Eleventh Census: 1890. Part III* (Washington, D.C., 1897), 402, 403, 411, 426, and 434; and U. S. Department of Commerce, Bureau of the Census, *Fifteenth Census of the United States: 1930, Population, Volume IV, Occupation by State* (Washington, D.C., 1933), 113, 154, 381, 591, 1204, and 1518. Sales agents are listed separately, although changing census categories make comparisons over time difficult. In 1920, there were in Alabama, 454; Arkansas, 329;

Georgia, 966; Kentucky, 480; North Carolina, 374; South Carolina, 221; and Tennessee, 916. See Department of Commerce, Bureau of the Census, *Fourteenth Census of the United States Taken in the Year 1920, Vol. IV, Population, 1920, Occupations* (Washington, D.C., 1923), 68, 69, 86, 105, and 122. Scholars who have focused on the Northeast have argued that peddlers were obsolete by the latter nineteenth century. See Alfred D. Chandler Jr., *The Visible Hand: The Managerial Revolution in American Business* (Cambridge, Mass., and London, 1977), 217; David Jaffee, "Peddlers of Progress and the Transformation of the Rural North, 1760–1860," *Journal of American History,* LXXVIII (September 1991), 533; and Lears, *Fables of Abundance,* 102. A study that finds itinerants thriving in the mid-nineteenth-century Midwest is Cheryl Lyon-Jenness, "A Telling Tirade: What Was the Controversy Surrounding Nineteenth-Century Midwestern Tree Agents Really All About?" *Agricultural History,* LXXII (Fall 1998), 675–707.

6. Penrose Scull, with Prescott C. Fuller, *From Peddlers to Merchant Princes: A History of Selling in America* (New York and Chicago, 1967), 25–33; Chandler, *Visible Hand,* 56; Richardson Wright, *Hawkers and Walkers in Early America: Strolling Peddlers, Preachers, Lawyers, Doctors, Players, and Others, from the Beginning to the Civil War* (Philadelphia, 1927); Lears, *Fables of Abundance,* 40–101, esp. 63–74; and Jaffee, "Peddlers of Progress and the Transformation of the Rural North," 511–35, esp. 528–31.

7. Lewis E. Atherton, "Itinerant Merchandising in the Ante-bellum South," *Bulletin of the Business Historical Society,* XIX (April 1945), 35–59 (Atherton's words quoted here, from p. 54).

8. Milledgeville *Georgia Journal,* July 11, 1826, p. 4. Thanks to Joseph T. Rainer for providing this reference.

9. Atherton, "Itinerant Merchandising in the Ante-bellum South," 43, 47, and 53–56; on retaliation against itinerants in the wake of John Brown's raid see Clarence L. Mohr, *On the Threshold of Freedom: Masters and Slaves in Civil War Georgia* (Athens and London, 1986), 5; and Columbus (Ga.) *Daily Sun,* December 5, 1859, p. 3.

10. On the importance of viewing consumption from the perspective of buyers see Susan Porter Benson, "Consuming Questions: Thoughts on Gender, Class, and Race in the Social History of Consumption," paper presented at the annual meeting of the American Historical Association, Cincinnati, December 27–30, 1988 (copy in author's possession). For a study of peddlers in the antebellum South that analyzes the power dynamics of gender, race, and consumerism see Joseph T. Rainer, "Yankee Peddlers and Antebellum Southern Consumers in the Arena of Exchange," paper presented at Shopping and Trade in Early America Symposium, George Mason University, Fairfax, Va., March 14, 1997 (copy in author's possession); and Rainer, "The Honorable Fraternity of Moving Merchants: Yankee Peddlers in the Old South, 1800–1860" (Ph.D. diss., College of William and Mary, 1999).

11. For an example of the perpetuation of the trickster image see Bernice Kelly Harris, *Folk Plays of Eastern Carolina,* edited with an introduction by Frederick H. Koch (Chapel Hill, 1940), 200–228. An informal history of and tribute to peddlers in America, which observes that Jewish peddlers served African Americans and poor

whites, is Harry Golden, *Forgotten Pioneer* (Cleveland and New York, 1963), 41. Accounts of these murders are in F. Roy Johnson, *Tales of Country Folks Down Carolina Way* (Murfreesboro, [N.C.], 1978), 48–49; W. F. Shelton, *The Day the Black Rain Fell* (Louisburg, N.C., 1984), 7–12. For other accounts of murdered peddlers see Atherton, "Itinerant Merchandising in the Ante-bellum South," 41–43; Jane Adams, ed., *All Anybody Ever Wanted of Me Was to Work: The Memoirs of Edith Bradley Rendleman* (Carbondale and Edwardsville, Ill., 1996), 49; and Robert Coltman, "A '90s Murder Mystery: 'The Peddler and His Wife'," *Old Time Music*, XXX (Autumn 1978), 13–15.

12. Neil R. Grobman, "Peddler Black of Owen County: 'Not a Stranger to Us'," *Kentucky Folklore Record*, XXIV (January–March, 1978), 2–5 (quotations on p. 4, emphasis in original). On peddlers traveling a circuit see James E. Spears, "Where Have All the Peddlers Gone?" ibid., XXI (July–September 1975), 77–81. For another account of a familiar peddler known as "old George" see Floyd C. Watkins and Charles Hubert Watkins, *Yesterday in the Hills* (Athens, 1973), 157–58.

13. Ayers, *Promise of the New South*, 81–82; Clark, *Pills, Petticoats, and Plows*; and Ownby, *American Dreams in Mississippi*, 82–97. As several historians have noted, the mail-order businesses of Sears, Roebuck and Company and Montgomery Ward & Company brought a world of manufactured goods to the homes of rural southerners. Ordering from a catalog provided women and African Americans some autonomy and anonymity as consumers and allowed them to bypass local stores. Nonetheless, mail-order customers had to pay in cash and could not evaluate the quality of goods until they arrived—two shortcomings that buying from itinerants avoided. On mail-order buying in the South see Ayers, *Promise of the New South*, 87–88; Hale, *Making Whiteness*, 176–78; and Ownby, *American Dreams in Mississippi*, 75–76. That rural southerners often dubbed the mail-order catalogues "wish books" suggests how close and yet how far away the goods they offered might be for people of humble means.

14. Ownby, *American Dreams in Mississippi*, 61–81 (quotations on p. 72); and Hale, *Making Whiteness*, 168–79.

15. Clark, *Pills, Petticoats, and Plows*, 36; and William Faulkner, *Light in August* (New York, 1932), 20 and 23. Pictures of country stores by Farm Security Administration photographers include Dorothea Lange, "A country store located on a dirt road, on Sunday afternoon," LC-USF-34–19911-C, Gordonton, N.C., July 1939; Jack Delano, "The interior of a general store," LC-USF-34–40652-D, Stem, N.C., May 1940; Delano, "The interior of the general store. High school boys on holiday because it is election day," LC-USF-34–40575-D, Stem, N.C., May 1940; Delano, "Mr. Jackson in his general store," LC-USF-34–44483-D, Siloam, Ga., June 1941, Farm Security Administration/ Office of War Information Collection, Division of Prints and Photographs (Library of Congress, Washington, D.C.); hereinafter cited as FSA/OWI with appropriate Library of Congress catalog number. Ted Ownby explores poor and middling rural men as the family shoppers in antebellum general stores and notes that the custom was still intact in the 1930s; see *American Dreams in Mississippi*, 7–32 and 102. To be sure, general stores were not entirely foreign to women, but poster-size advertisements featuring "cheesecake" images may have also added to female patron's discomfort; see Russell Lee, "A Negro woman trading a sack of pecans for groceries in the general store,"

LC-USF-34–31759-D, Jareau, La., October 1938; and Lee, "A sign in a country store," LC-USF-33–11805-M5, Vacherie, La., September 1938, FSA/OSI.

16. Thordis Simonsen, ed., *You May Plow Here: The Narrative of Sara Brooks* (New York and London, 1986), 56–58.

17. Ibid., 57; and transcript of the A. C. and Grace Griffin interviews by author, December 8 and 10, 1986, pp. 108–9, Oral History of Southern Agriculture (Division of the History of Technology, National Museum of American History, Washington, D.C.).

18. Transcript of Griffin interviews, 109.

19. Harris, *Folk Plays of Eastern Carolina*, xvii (quotations); Bernice Kelly Harris, *Southern Savory* (Chapel Hill, 1964), 19–26. For a thoughtful literary biography see Valerie Raleigh Yow, *Bernice Kelly Harris: A Good Life Was Writing* (Baton Rouge, 1999).

20. Caroline S. Coleman, with a foreword by William F. Gaines, *Five Petticoats on Sunday* (Greenville, S.C., 1962), vii, 23, and 24.

21. Harris, *Southern Savory*, 21; and Coleman, *Five Petticoats on Sunday*, 24 (first two quotations) and 25 (third and fourth quotations).

22. Transcript of Ethel Wright Mohamed interview by author, October 23, 1987, pp. 9–10, Oral History of Southern Agriculture.

23. Ibid., 10.

24. Hal Edmonds interview with author, August 4, 1994 (tape recording and typed notes in author's possession). See also James E. Spears, "Rolling Store: A Reminiscence," *Kentucky Folklore Record*, XXIV (January–March 1978), 20–21.

25. Edmonds interview.

26. Transcript of Mioma Thompson interview by author, January 24, 1987, pp. 15–17 (quotations on p. 16), Oral History of Southern Agriculture.

27. Transcript of Della Sarten interview by author, May 1, 1987, pp. 31–32, Oral History of Southern Agriculture.

28. Bernice Kelly Harris, *Sweet Beulah Land* (Garden City, N. J., 1943), 6; Harris, *Folk Plays of Eastern Carolina*, 201 (quotation). See also Harris, *Purslane* (Chapel Hill, 1939), 211–12. In his memoir *Red Hills and Cotton: An Upcountry Memory* (New York, 1942), 115, Ben Robertson recalled that his grandmother patronized sales agents because she wanted "to encourage them to come again, for peddlers brought news, and my grandmother was interested in news of every kind and especially enjoyed gossip."

29. Harris, *Sweet Beulah Land*, 26; Harris, *Purslane*, 211 and 212; and Margaret Jarman Hagood, *Mothers of the South: Portraiture of the White Tenant Farm Woman* (Chapel Hill, 1939; rpt., New York, 1977), 133–36.

30. For mention of Rawleigh and Watkins salesmen see transcript of Thompson interview, 16; transcript of Clyde Purvis interview by author, January 26, 1987, p. 93; and transcript of Jessie and Kenneth Gosney interview by author, October 1, 1987, p. 8, all three in Oral History of Southern Agriculture. On changes in manufacturing and marketing in the late nineteenth century see Alan Trachtenberg, *The Incorporation of America: Culture and Society in the Gilded Age* (New York, 1982); Susan Strasser, *Satisfaction Guaranteed: The Making of the American Mass Market* (New York, 1989); and

Daniel J. Boorstin, *The Americans: The Democratic Experience* (New York, 1973), 89–164. For the importance of taking class, ethnicity, race, and context into account when studying consumerism see Cohen, "Encountering Mass Culture at the Grassroots."

31. *The Rawleigh Industries* (Freeport, Ill., 1932), 8–13; J. R. Watkins Medical Company, *The Open Door to Success* (Winona, Minn., [191?]), 1–20; and *A Merry Christmas and a Happy New Year from the J. R. Watkins Co. and Your Watkins Dealer* ([Winona, Minn.], 1938). On Rawleigh's first wife see Mrs. John W. (Mary X.) Barrett, ed., *The History of Stephenson County, 1970* (Freeport, Ill., 1972), 530–31; and obituary of Mrs. Minnie B. Rawleigh, Freeport *Journal Standard*, November 19, 1947, p. 20. Locating information about these companies has required persistence, serendipity, and friendly assistance. I found Rawleigh and Watkins publications in places as diverse as the Library of Congress and Smithsonian Institution, Washington, D.C.; Baker Library, Harvard University, Cambridge, Mass.; and an antique store in Pittsboro, N.C. Thanks to Dorothy Glastetter, a volunteer at the Freeport, Ill., public library, and to Tena Barratt, reference librarian there, who provided materials on the Rawleigh Company and its founder, and to Marie Dorsch, archivist at the Winona County Historical Society, for supplying copies of vintage and recent publications from the Watkins Company, which still does business as Watkins Products, Inc.

32. [W. T. Rawleigh], *Guide Book to Help Rawleigh Retailers: A Book on Salesmanship* (Freeport, Ill., 1921), 23–26, 284; *Rawleigh's 1927 Good Health Guide, Almanac, Cookbook* (Freeport, Ill., 1927); *Rawleigh's Stock and Poultry Raisers' Guide* (Freeport, Ill., n.d.), copy of stock and poultry raisers' guide in Folder 19, Box 2, Dairy files, Warshaw Collection (Archives Center, National Museum of American History, Washington, D.C.); and Watkins Company, *Open Door to Success*, 46–49.

33. *Rawleigh's Stock and Poultry Raisers' Guide*, 18 and 19; and Watkins Company, *Open Door to Success*, 16, 17, and 28.

34. [Rawleigh], *Guide Book to Help Rawleigh Retailers* (1921); W. T. Rawleigh, *Rawleigh Methods: A Guidebook for Rawleigh Customers* (Freeport, Ill., and other cities, 1926); and Watkins Company, *Open Door to Success*. Rawleigh's first guide is mentioned on page 11 of the 1921 *Guide Book to Help Rawleigh Retailers*.

35. Strasser, *Satisfaction Guaranteed*, 110–13 (quotation on p. 112); *Rawleigh Industries*, 6–13; *Rawleigh's Stock and Poultry Raisers' Guide*, 17–20; and Watkins Company, *Open Door to Success*, 4–30 and 45.

36. Watkins Company, *Open Door to Success*, 19; and *Rawleigh's 1927 Good Health Guide*, 2.

37. [Rawleigh], *Guide Book to Help Rawleigh Retailers*, 42 (first quotation, emphasis in original) and 47 (second and third quotations). On scientific salesmanship see ibid., Chap. 8. On the development of modern selling techniques and advice guides for commercial travelers see Timothy B. Spears, *100 Years on the Road: The Traveling Salesman in American Culture* (New Haven and London, 1995), Chap. 7.

38. For letters written—or purportedly written—by successful retailers see [Rawleigh], *Guide Book to Help Rawleigh Retailers*, 115–214, esp. 129–31, 176, and 195–96; and Watkins Company, *Open Door to Success*, 51–127.

39. [Rawleigh], *Guide Book to Help Rawleigh Retailers*, 119, 137–38, 144, and 199.

40. Gladys Hackney Thomas interview by author, November 17, 1994 (tape recording in author's possession); [Rawleigh], *Guide Book to Help Rawleigh Retailers*, 88, 89, and 253.

41. Tape recording of Thomas interview.

42. Transcript of Edythe Hollowell Jones interview by author, July 1, 1982, p. 8 (in author's possession) (second quotation); and Edythe Hollowell Jones, letter to author, 1988 (in author's possession) (all other quotations).

43. Thomas interview; Harris, *Purslane*, 13, 90–91, and 266; and Jones, letter to author.

44. [Rawleigh], *Guide Book to Help Rawleigh Retailers*, 200; Jones, letter to author; transcript of Purvis interview, 93; and transcript of Gosney interview, 8.

45. Russell Lee, LC-USF-34-31787-D, "The family [caption obscured] and six children. They own 20 acres of ground on which there is a small, plainly furnished, but comfortable house." New Iberia (vicinity), La., October 1938; and Jack Delano, "Mrs. Fanny Parrott, the wife of an ex-slave," LC-USF-34–44162-D, Siloam (vicinity), Ga., May 1941, FSA/OWI.

46. Rawleigh, *Rawleigh Methods*, 1581–1625. The Watkins Company may have also directed particular attention to southern African Americans. Watkins Company, *Open Door to Success*, 39, lists two intriguing sales pamphlets—*Handling the Trade in the South* and *Handling the Watkins Line in Georgia*—but efforts to locate them have been unsuccessful. For an overview of race and consumerism see Weems, *Desegregating the Dollar*.

47. Rawleigh, *Rawleigh Methods*, 1590 (first two quotations), 1583 (third quotation), 1594, 1608, and 1623 (fourth quotation).

48. Ibid., 1603 and 1612.

49. Ibid., 1595 and 1599.

50. Transcript of N. J. and Jarutha Booth interview by author, October 27, 1987, pp. 13–14; and transcript of Wayland Spivey interview by author, December 9, 1986, p. 34, both in Oral History of Southern Agriculture. On the general practice of merchants limiting purchases by tenants see Clark, *Pills, Petticoats, and Plows*, 55–58.

Becoming "White"

Race, Religion, and the Foundations of Syrian/Lebanese Ethnicity in the United States

Sarah Gualtieri

No one was white before he/she came to America. It took generations, and a vast amount of coercion, before this became a white country.
James Baldwin, "On Being White and Other Lies"

On 14 September 1915, George Dow, a Syrian[1] immigrant living in South Carolina, appeared before a circuit court judge and waited to hear the fate of his petition for naturalization. Twice already, it had been denied in a lower court because he was deemed racially ineligible for citizenship. Specifically, Dow had been refused naturalization on the grounds that he did not meet the racial requirement of the United States law, which limited naturalization to "aliens being free white persons, and to aliens of African nativity and to persons of African descent."[2] George Dow could not, therefore, be accepted into the fold of American citizenry. The Syrian community—which by conservative estimates numbered around 150,000 persons nationwide—was outraged by the refusal to naturalize Dow.[3] His was not the first case to ignite a community response, but around it Syrian immigrants mobilized to a degree that was unprecedented. Their efforts would ultimately prove effective, for in this, George Dow's final appeal, the judge ruled that Syrians "were to be classed as white persons," and were eligible for naturalization.[4] Although it was not the last time a Syrian appeared before the courts attempting to litigate his (the cases involved men only) racial status, the Dow case established a weighty legal precedent in favor of Syrian whiteness.

Much of the literature on Syrian and Lebanese immigrants in the United States celebrates the final ruling in George Dow's case. Declaring the Syrians to be "white persons" (at the Court of Appeals level) is interpreted as a righting of a historic wrong inflicted upon a hard-working and highly assimilable community and a victory over discrimination and prejudice.[5] In some instances, the Syrian struggle for recognition as "white persons" is described as an early assertion of ethnic pride.[6] The underlying logic in each of these interpretations, though, is that the Syrians were "in fact" white and simply needed to be recognized as such by the courts. My analysis starts from the opposite premise—that the racial classification of Syrians as "white" was by no means obvious to the applicants for citizenship or to the officials who heard their cases. This essay argues that Syrians, like other immigrant groups, became white only after they had successfully claimed whiteness and when law and custom confirmed it. This did not happen without considerable debate. If, as the literature argues, the ruling in *Dow v. United States* represented a victory for Syrians, it was because it had been preceded by so much uncertainty as to their racial classification. I suggest in the conclusion that, while Syrians had cause to celebrate the legal recognition of their whiteness, there were (and still are) reasons to be profoundly ambivalent about the process by which their claims to whiteness were made.

To begin, this essay focuses on the following question: why did Syrians, and not other immigrant groups appearing in the courts at roughly the same time, emerge on the white side of the "color line"? What scientific, legal, and religious rationales made the Syrian claim of whiteness possible? The first section answers this question through an analysis of the judicial rulings in Syrian naturalization cases heard between 1909 and 1915. Following Ian F. Haney López, the cases will be referred to as "racial prerequisite cases" since they revolved around the question of whether or not the applicant met the racial requirement of the naturalization statute.[8]

Racial classification was not, of course, an affair of the courts only. Legal decisions were influential in producing and disseminating a discourse on race, but they alone cannot fully explain how and why Syrians participated in this discourse and produced knowledge about themselves as racial beings. The second part of this essay, therefore, explores the reaction of Syrians to the naturalization issue, specifically to its racial dimensions. Simply put, Syrians wanted to be recognized as white because it made them eligible for citizenship and the privileges it afforded (such as the right to vote and travel more freely); but being white was not the only way to gain naturalization. It was also possible, since the amendment of the naturalization statute in 1875, to argue for naturalization on the basis of African nativity or descent. Yet, not a single applicant in the racial prerequisite cases, Syrian or otherwise, attempted to make this argument.[9] One could argue that it would have been inherently illogical for Syrians to argue for naturalization on the basis of African nativity or descent since Syria was not in Africa. However, as this essay attempts to show, arguments in favor of Syrian whiteness were rooted more in ideology than logic, for there was nothing more fanciful, ridiculous, and illogical than the idea that whiteness could be linked to a single skull—that of a Georgian woman found in the Caucasus.[10]

The main reason Syrians chose to stake their claim to citizenship on the basis of membership in the "white race" was that there was something compelling, even alluring, about whiteness that went beyond the strategic and the practical. Historian David Roediger, drawing on W. E. B. Du Bois, has called this the "wages of whiteness"—the psychological compensation of being "not black" in a racist, exploitative society.[11] This theory helps explain why working-class immigrants claimed whiteness, but there is also the question of how they did so. As Roediger and Noel Ignatiev's work on the Irish shows, immigrants participated in and transformed institutions and cultural traditions that marked them as "white" and blacks as "others."[12] "To enter the white race," Ignatiev reminds us, "was a strategy to secure an advantage in a competitive society," and whiteness was, ultimately, the "result of choices made."[13] This essay examines a chapter in the history of how Syrians "entered the white race" in America and it is especially concerned with how they participated as actors in this history. For example, Syrians wrote letters, published articles, hired lawyers, formed associations, and raised money all to support the claim of whiteness. Moreover, as will be argued below, they initially made sense of American racial categories by using their own understandings of difference. They did not simply "buy into" American notions of race but tried to incorporate these ideas into preexisting patterns of thinking or interpretive grids.

The Syrian naturalization cases are therefore important for understanding the development of Syrian ethnicity through the use of key institutions like the press, voluntary associations, and religious organizations, but the racialization of Syrians before the law had broader implications. Members of a small immigrant community, Syrians were disproportionately represented (just under one third) in the racial prerequisite cases heard in United States federal courts between 1909 and 1923. More importantly, the first Syrian racial prerequisite case was also the first case in which an applicant for citizenship prevailed by successfully litigating his status as a "white person."[14] It is not an exaggeration, then, to say that the Syrian cases played a significant role in the legal construction of the "white race." The rulings in these cases, which drew on legal precedent, the scientific literature of the day, and the nebulous category of "common knowledge," are relevant not only to the study of Syrians as immigrants and ethnics but to the broader study of the taxonomy of whiteness as a whole.

The Legal Ground of Whiteness: From "Science" to "Common Knowledge"

The question of whether or not Syrians met the racial requirement of the naturalization law did not become a controversial one until the first decade of the twentieth century. Syrians who had applied for citizenship before 1909 had been granted it without much deliberation.[15] The new decade, however, was very different. Anxieties over America's "foreign element" intensified, and nativists sharpened their rhetoric with demands for restriction on immigration and greater surveillance of the foreign born. This reinvigorated nativism produced elaborate theories of the contaminating effect of what was called the "new immigration" from southern and eastern Europe. Members of the northern intelligentsia, for example, churned out literature on Anglo-Saxon "race suicide" and flirted with the proponents of eugenics. Southern whites were, in contrast, principally concerned with cracks in the color line. Particularly threatening to white southerners was the "inbetweenness" of the new immigrants, that is, their status as neither white nor black in the southern racial scheme.[16] The ambiguous racial status of Italians, East European Jews, and Syrians stemmed from the perception that they possessed cultures and habits that were fundamentally at odds with the southern way of life and that they would not abide by the "white man's code."[17] Nativists lashed out at this alleged "immigrant menace" in public denunciations and behind-the-scenes schemes that involved intimidation and violence. North Carolina Senator F. M. Simmons, for example, exclaimed that the new immigrants were "nothing more than the degenerate progeny of the Asiatic hoards [sic], . . . the spawn of the Phoenician curse."[18]

Senator Simmons' use of a biological metaphor "spawn" was telling, and completely in keeping with the most vitriolic nativist language of the day, which linked immigration to contagion and disease. Government health officials helped fuel this prejudice by quarantining entire immigrant neighborhoods, ostensibly to control a disease that they believed was spread by immigrant habits.[19] Chinese and Russian Jews were especially pathologized in this regard, and it was possible that Syrian immigrants could suffer the same fate. Already, Syrians were being refused entry into the United States at an increasing rate as carriers of trachoma, a "loathsome and dangerous contagious disease."[20] The fear of being excluded prompted many Syrians to attempt entering the United States via Mexico.[21] For others, trachoma separated them from members of their family and sent them sailing out of United States ports-of-entry to South America and as far away as Australia.[22] As Alan Krant has argued, the "disease-status" of a particular immigrant group, whether real or imagined, served as a gauge of desirability both into the country and into the polity.

The concern with controlling immigration found institutional support in 1906 with the creation of the Bureau of Immigration and Naturalization in the Department of Commerce and Labor. Chief among the Bureau's responsibilities was the administration of a new naturalization law aimed at curtailing many of the abuses that had plagued the naturalization process in the nineteenth century. The law of 1906 banned, for example, naturalization heatings held within thirty days of a general election in a court's area of jurisdiction. Such a measure would, it was hoped, discourage political bosses from rounding up immigrants and herding them to court to secure their naturalization papers, and thereafter their votes. The naturalization law was to be newly codified and administered by an extensive bureaucracy, which included three hundred naturalization examiners stationed throughout the country.[23] It was in this context of heightened nativism and bureaucratic reform that Syrian racial identity was first challenged in a federal court.

The case of Costa Najour, a Syrian from Mount Lebanon, was heard in Atlanta, Georgia, in December 1909.[24] Najour had been denied naturalization in a lower court on the grounds that he did not meet the requirements of the revised naturalization statute. Najour appealed, and his case went to the Fifth Circuit Court where Judge William T. Newman granted him naturalization on the grounds that Syrians were members of the "white race." The rationale for Judge Newman's holding fell overwhelmingly on the side of what was considered "scientific evidence." He rejected the idea that the statute referred to skin color and was adamant that "fair or dark complexion should not be allowed to control [the decision]."[25] This construction would be used in other rulings and given the rather ponderous wording that race was not to be determined by "ocular inspection alone."

Judge Newman's decision helped alter the discourse on racial classification by distinguishing between skin color and race.[26] It is important to note, however, that he followed his statement on color with this caveat: "providing the person seeking naturalization comes within the classification of the white or Caucasian race."[27] In other words, color did not necessarily matter if it could be determined by some other rationale that the applicant was white and possessed the personal qualifications deemed necessary for naturalization. In cases where personal qualifications were in doubt and the applicant was deemed unworthy of citizenship, color continued to serve as an additional marker of ineligibility. When, for example, Syrian applicant Faras Shahid was denied naturalization in a South Carolina district court in 1913, the judge emphasized that he was "somewhat darker than is the usual mulatto of one-half mixed blood between the white and the negro races."[28] Even Judge Newman, whose ruling in the Najour case seemed to move away from color as the defining marker of race, began his decision with a description of Najour as "not particularly dark." He may have distinguished between skin color and race, but a basic pattern persisted in the racial prerequisite cases: the ascription of darkness increased the chances of ineligibility, while that of lightness decreased them. The lawyer for the government in the Najour case knew as much.

After a four-hour testimony by Costa Najour that seemed only to confirm his eligibility to naturalize, the exasperated lawyer, desperate to prove that Najour was not white, asked him to take off his shirt and show his body to the court. Najour began to comply, but was stopped in the early stages of undress by Judge Newman who wanted no such theatrics in his courtroom.[29]

What was perhaps more important in Judge Newman's ruling—as far as altering the legal discourse on racial classification goes—was his use of the category Caucasian. In deciding whether or not Najour was part of the "white race," Judge Newman, like many other judges across the country, looked to the literature of ethnology. He drew on A. H. Keane's *The World's Peoples* to reach the conclusion that Syrians were "part of the Caucasian or white race."[30] The use of "or" was significant, for it indicated that being Caucasian and being white were held to be one and the same thing. This equation was not new in the world of ethnology, and it had been used in combination with other rationales in previous racial prerequisite cases.[31] What was different in the Najour case was that Judge Newman made it possible to use membership in something called the "Caucasian race" as the sole criterion for judging whether or not someone was white for the purposes of naturalization.

Several judges followed Judge Newman's lead, but an equal number rejected this formulation and dismissed altogether the relevance of "scientific evidence." Judge Henry Smith, for example, ruling in the Shahid case cited above, ridiculed the idea that being Caucasian automatically meant someone was white. The very idea of a Caucasian race was suspect to him, the result, he would later write, "of a strange intellectual hocus pocus."[32] The ultimate test of whiteness, in his view, was one of geography, and the deciding factor was whether or not the applicant was from Europe or a descendant of a European immigrant. There was, therefore, no need to "examine his [the applicant's] complexion with a microscope nor measure his skull or his limbs and features."[33] Since the Syrians were, in his estimation, clearly not European but "Asiatic," they were not entitled to the privileges of citizenship.[34] To arrive at this ruling that whiteness was linked to European descent, Judge Smith relied on two other rationales that would become increasingly popular in the racial prerequisite cases: common knowledge and congressional intent.

The term "congressional intent" referred to the meaning of the Naturalization Act as it was first formulated by Congress in 1790. In Judge Smith's words: "The real question is: What does the statute mean, to whom did the terms 'free white persons' refer in 1790, in the understandings of the makers of the law."[35] He answered the question through an imaginary journey into the mind of a member of Congress at the end of the eighteenth century. Such a man, he argued, would have known nothing of the ethnological or linguistic theories that undergirded modern racial classification. He would, for example, "certainly have repudiated the idea that a black Ceylonese or dark South Persian was in the language of the enthusiastic supporters of the theory that all speakers of Aryan languages are of one race, an "Aryan brother."[36] Judge Smith was so sure of this he claimed it was all something to which "an average citizen" in 1790 could agree. He thus shifted from his original position that what mattered was the intention of the framers of the law to one that emphasized the understanding of the "common man." This was not the first time that common knowledge was tacked on to congressional intent to strengthen a judge's interpretation of the statute. Aware of the ambiguity of his own ruling, Judge Smith concluded with the suggestion that an appeal be taken to the Supreme Court where a settlement to "this most vexed and difficult question could be reached."[37]

The issue was vexed because the naturalization statute could be interpreted in so many different ways. While some judges relied on scientific evidence, others used congressional intent, common knowledge, or some combination of all three to determine the race of an applicant for naturalization. Complicating matters was the category of personal qualifications that, like color, was not supposed to figure prominently in the determination of race but was repeatedly used to assist in the decision. Syrian applicant Tom Ellis's religious, professional and moral profile, for example, clearly influenced the decision on his racial eligibility in an Oregon district court in July 1910. Indeed, so intertwined were the criteria in the judge's ruling that it is difficult to discern where one ends and the other begins.

Ellis, described as "a Turkish subject . . . a Syrian, a native of the province of Palestine, and a Maronite,"[38] had come up against the argument that he was ineligible for citizenship because he was not of European descent. Lawyers for the district attorney made no attempt to argue that Ellis was not "of the white race." In fact, they openly admitted that immigration officers considered Syrians to be white. Their argument was that he was not the right kind of white, that is, he did not descend from white Europeans. The importance of being of European descent was soon made clear in the district attorney's interpretation of the statute. The meaning of the words "free white persons" "comprehended such only of the white races who, from tradition, teaching, and environment, would be predisposed toward our form of government, and thus readily assimilate with the people of the United States."[39] Whereas Judge Smith had couched his preference for European immigrants in the language of congressional intent, lawyers for the government in the Ellis case were much more explicit in their use of race as a marker of a particular cultural and political disposition. In the logic of their argument, whiteness was linked to geography (Europe) which, in their minds, produced moral and intellectual traits essential for participation in the American polity. More to the point, it was assumed that white Europeans were familiar with, and predisposed toward, republican forms of government.

Non-Europeans were, in contrast, deemed to be dubious products of despotic regimes, politically unsophisticated, and likely to taint the cherished pool of American citizenry. The government lawyer's insistence on the connection between whiteness and fitness for self-government was a well-worn strategy. Indeed, it was firmly embedded in the discourse of American citizenship.[40] The district attorney in the Najour case had also used this argument, claiming that Najour, as a subject of the Muslim Ottoman sultan, was incapable of understanding American institutions and government. Despite a ruling in Najour's favor,[41] whiteness as fitness for self-government continued to figure prominently in the legal debates on racial eligibility for citizenship until the 1950s.

Fortunately for Ellis, Judge Wolverton ruled that if Congress had intended the statute to mean Europeans only, it would have specified such. He granted Ellis citizenship, but his ruling reveals how it was possible to reject the specific formulation of the government argument while accepting its underlying assumptions—that "personal qualifications" were an indication of a person's racial eligibility for naturalization. What ultimately tilted the decision in Ellis' favor was Judge Wolverton's conviction that he was "possessed of the highest qualities which go to make an excellent citizen . . . well disposed toward the principles and policies of this government."[42] Having already decided that Ellis was of "Semitic stock, a markedly white type of the race," the judge went on to extol Ellis's personal qualifications, noting that he was a "good and highly respected citizen of the community." Tom Ellis spoke English, was a practicing Christian and of "good morals, sober and industrious." In short, he possessed "all the essential qualifications to entitle him to naturalization." He was, in Judge Wolverton's view, exactly the type of person Congress had intended to become a citizen. Remarkably oblivious to the debates—scientific, judicial, and congressional—that suggested otherwise, Judge Wolverton believed that the words "free white persons" were devoid of ambiguity and were of "plain and simple signification."[43] He did not pause to consider how far the "personal qualifications" of the applicant had influenced the legal construction of his whiteness.

Taken as a whole, the Syrian racial prerequisite cases heard in federal courts between 1909 and 1915 show that buried beneath the reasoned rationales of the legal ruling lay contradictions, ambiguities, and discrepancies. Quite simply, the courts were having difficulty deciding who was a "white person." There was, however, a basic pattern amid the confusion. Judges were turning more and more to the rationales of congressional intent and common knowledge (and away from science) to determine racial eligibility for naturalization. While, for example, ethnology had so neatly assisted Costa Najour in his bid for citizenship, it was completely discarded in *Ex Parte Shahid*. This move away from scientific explanations of race was evident in other cases as well and would culminate in the 1923 United States Supreme Court decision in the case of South Asian applicant Bhagat Singh Thind. Since the Thind case would significantly redefine racial eligibility for citizenship, a brief outline of the case (and its relevance for Syrians) is in order.

Thind was born in India, immigrated to the United States in 1913, and petitioned for naturalization in 1920. He was successful at the district court level, but lawyers for the federal government appealed and the case eventually reached the United States Supreme Court in January 1923 where the decision of the lower court was reversed. The Court claimed that, although science considered Indians to be "Caucasian," Thind was not a "free white person" in the "understanding of the common man."[44] He was therefore ineligible to citizenship. Ironically, only a few months earlier in the Takao Ozawa case, the Supreme Court had affirmed the power of what it called "scientific authorities" when it argued that Japanese persons were not Caucasian (but Mongolian) and therefore not white.[45] In the Ozawa case, "white" and "Caucasian" were synonymous, but in the Thind case clearly they were not. These two Supreme Court rulings suggest that, when science failed to reinforce popular beliefs about racial difference, it was disregarded, but when it confirmed them, it was conveniently embraced. This was not a mere subtlety in an arcane legal tradition but a decision that had real and often disastrous consequences in the lives of immigrants. At least sixty-five Indian immigrants, for example, were stripped of their citizenship between 1923 and 1927, prompting one, Vaisho Das Bagai, to commit suicide.[46]

Mention must also be made of a secondary ruling given in the *United States v. Thind* case. When the Circuit Court of Appeals submitted its certificate to the Supreme Court, it requested instruction on two questions. The first was whether or not a "high-caste Hindu, of full Indian blood" was a white person within the meaning of section 2169, Revised Statutes. The second concerned the applicability of the Act of 1917, which had designated certain geographic areas, the inhabitants of which would be barred from entering the United States as immigrants.[47] Specifically, the lower court wanted to know whether the Act disqualified from naturalization "Hindus" who had entered the country legally, that is, prior to the passage of the said Act. It was, in fact, the Supreme Court's response to the first question that generated the lengthier and weightier response, but the second question was not ignored. In the final paragraph of the ruling, the Court made an explicit connection between eligibility for immigration into the United States and suitability for naturalization. "It is not without significance," Justice Sutherland wrote,

that Congress, by the Act of February 5, 1917 . . . has now excluded from admission into this country all natives of Asia within designated limits of latitude and longitude, including the whole of India. This not only constitutes conclusive evidence of the congressional attitude of opposition to Asiatic immigration generally, but is persuasive of a similar attitude toward Asiatic naturalization as well, since it is not likely that Congress would be willing to accept as citizens class of persons whom it rejects as immigrants.[48]

The inclusion of India in the Asiatic "barred zone" had thus informed Justice Sutherland's thinking on racial eligibility for naturalization. Significantly, Syria had fallen outside the zone, a decision that furnished additional proof for the Syrian claim of whiteness. In 1923, for example, when a poorly informed Judge Smith tried once again to prevent the naturalization of a Syrian applicant, he was confronted with the same argument made by Justice Sutherland only in reverse: Syrians were eligible to immigrate into the United States, so they were therefore eligible to naturalize. The applicant, F. W. Basha, was naturalized and the Syrian eligibility question never again reached the courts.[49]

It is beyond the scope of this essay to trace in detail the racial underpinnings of immigration legislation passed between 1917 and 1924.[50] The examples cited above are among the many that show the intricate connections between immigration and naturalization law and, specifically, their shared racial logic. Both the Act of 1917 and the Supreme Court rulings on eligibility for naturalization deployed a racial construction of Asians that was narrow and rigid, while simultaneously allowing for flexibility in determining the racial status of European immigrant groups. As Mae Ngai argues in her discussion of the 1924 Immigration Act, this led to a reconstruction of racial categories whereby race and nationality were conflated for Asians (and Mexicans), but disaggregated for "white" Europeans.[51] The legal construction of Asians as non-white would continually mark them as "outsiders," thus rendering them targets of discriminatory legislation.[52]

The demise of scientific explanations of race in favor of those rooted in congressional intent and common knowledge did not bode well for South Asian and Japanese immigrants. The same cannot be said for Syrians whose encounter with naturalization law during roughly the same period eventually led to a legal consensus that they were white. It is especially curious that the Syrians did not meet the same fate as the South Asians since, in cases where their whiteness was affirmed (Najour for example), judges had relied overwhelmingly on science to argue that Syrians were Caucasian and therefore white. The logic that was ultimately rejected by the Supreme Court in the Thind case continued to be applied to the Syrians. Parallels between the Syrian and South Asian cases had been apparent not only at the level of legal argumentation. Influential Syrians in New York had actually assisted the naturalization of a South Asian applicant in 1910 in the hope that his case would influence future rulings in Syrian cases.[53] They were right. The case of Bhicaji Franyi Balsara, described as a "Parsee," was cited as a precedent in at least two federal cases affirming the whiteness of Syrians and, hence, their eligibility for naturalization.[54] It was, however, completely overlooked as a legal precedent in the most important case involving a South Asian, that of Bhagat Singh Thind. The twisted labyrinth of legal reasoning on the question of whiteness had led to a position that, were it not for its underlying prejudice, might be dismissed as patently absurd: some South Asians (notably non-Hindus) remained white, and their whiteness (in the form of a legal precedent) could help prove the whiteness of other immigrant groups like the Syrians, but not—as the Thind case clearly demonstrated—the whiteness of fellow South Asians!

What explains this apparent discrepancy? Why did the courts begin to place Syrians in the category of those "commonly understood" to be white and not Indians (labeled, often erroneously, as "high caste Hindus")? An important part of the explanation for this Syrian "victory" lies in the record of their involvement in the racial prerequisite cases. Armed with expert lawyers, *amici curiae*, and a belief in their special status as the mediators of the Christian tradition, Syrians actively participated in arguments for inclusion in the "white race."[55] The following section discusses this participation and, more generally, the ways in which Syrian immigrants positioned themselves within, and made sense of, United States racial categories.

Syrian Understandings of "Whiteness:" Fusing Religious and Racial Difference

The involvement of Syrian community leaders in George Dow's case, which helped settle the question of Syrian whiteness from a legal standpoint, was part of an effort that began earlier under less litigious circumstances. One of the first arguments for inclusion in the "white race" came from a Syrian doctor in Birmingham, Alabama, in 1907. In a carefully worded letter to the editor, in the *Birmingham Age-Herald*, H. A. Elkourie challenged the views of the popular Alabama congressman, John L. Burnett, staunch backer of the proposed literacy test which would restrict entry into the United States to literate persons only. Elkourie argued that the test was an inadequate measure of a person's qualifications and he added in good humor that, "my experience has shown me that scoundrels exist among the educated in greater proportion than amongst the uneducated."[56] The more important issue for the doctor, however, was Congressman Burnett's claim that Syrians (along with Jews, Poles, and Russians) "belonged to a distinct race other than the white race." Elkourie responded by emphasizing Syrian compatibility with "western" civilization and by invoking a religious argument that would become key in Syrian understandings of whiteness.

The first step was to argue that the Syrians were Semites. Then, citing "authorities" from Gibbon to Webster, he placed the Semites within a branch of the "white race." But, Elkourie's argument went beyond the purely ethnological, for at the core of his defense of the Semitic peoples was a description of their contribution to civilization. From the Phoenicians to Jesus Christ, he wrote, the "Semitic was the original civilizer, developer and intermediator of culture and learning."[57] The power of this argument derived not from a claim to any special phenotype but on a reclaiming of a Semitic origin and an emphasis on the Syrian connection to the Holy Land and to Christianity. However, Elkourie's argument was not merely an attempt to emphasize Syrian religious affinity with southern whites: it was an attempt to understand difference—in this case racial difference—the way Syrians had traditionally done so, that is, in religious terms.

Syrian immigrants had come from a society where social classification was rooted in religious, not racial difference. This owed much to the Ottoman millet system, devised in the wake of the Ottoman conquest of Constantinople as a uniquely Muslim form of governance over a vast multiethnic, multireligious empire. Officially, each religious community (millet) was granted autonomy in the regulation of matters pertaining to civil status, such as marriage, divorce, and inheritance. In practice, leaders of the different millets controlled a much broader administrative base, overseeing, for example, education, charity, and even the collection of taxes. Individuals, therefore, owed ultimate allegiance to the millet and not to the Ottoman state per se. While the origins of the term "millet," and even its usefulness in describing an administrative system, have been greatly disputed,[58] the fundamental salience of religion as a marker of identity in the late-Ottoman Arab provinces remains uncontested. There were indeed other ways of marking difference: a certain inflection in the voice could disclose a village of origin, just as a well-maintained fez indicated membership in the growing and self-conscious *efendiyya* (westernized) class; but religion, and more particularly sect, remained the most important tool for drawing boundaries between us and them.

This impulse to identify difference in religious terms was not abandoned when Syrians set foot on American shores but was deployed in new ways. Elkourie's argument for inclusion in the "white race," for example, was made on the basis of membership in the Christian fold. While this argument would not hold up in a court of law as constituting decisive proof of whiteness, it became a pillar of Syrian legal argumentation and community self-construction. The sense of Christian entitlement to share in whiteness was markedly evident in the Dow case, which became a cause célèbre for the Syrian immigrant elite in 1914. Determined to settle the question of eligibility for citizenship once and for all, lawyers for George Dow and the Syrian American Associations (which was backing his case) formulated an elaborate defense of Syrian whiteness. Their argument for why Dow should be included in the term "white persons" had five points, which are worth listing in full,

1) That the term "white persons" in the statute means persons of the "Caucasian race," and persons white in color.

2) That he is a Semite or a member of one of the Semitic nations.

3) That the Semitic nations are all members of the "Caucasian" or white race.

4) That the matter has been settled in their favor as the European Jews have been admitted without question since the passage of the statute and that the Jews are one of the Semitic peoples.

5) That the history and position of the Syrians, their connection through all time with the peoples to whom the Jewish and Christian peoples owe their religion, make it inconceivable that the statute could have intended to exclude them.[59]

This complex argument incorporated nearly all the rationales used in previous attempts to prove Syrian whiteness. There was first the three-part equation that Syrians were Semites, hence Caucasian and therefore white. This had worked in cases where the judge had relied heavily on ethnology, but it was useless in front of judges like Smith who relied on the rationale of congressional intent. The second important component of the Syrian argument was the cultural one, the insistence that their "history and position" made them eligible for the privilege of citizenship. The third part of the argument turned on legal precedent, namely, that European Jews (who were also Semites) had been naturalized and that the same should hold for Syrians. This argument, however, played into the hands of Judge Smith whose definition of white always turned on the question of European descent. In his opinion, a European Jew was first and foremost a European, "racially, physiologically, and psychologically a part of the peoples he lives among."[60] A far more interesting argument would have been that Arabic-speaking Levantine Jews had already been naturalized, but for reasons that are unclear, neither the Syrians nor their lawyers chose this strategy.

Judge Smith denied Dow's petition for naturalization in this rehearing which the Syrian American Associations had so vigorously supported. Smith actually began his ruling with an acknowledgement of the "deep feeling manifested on the part of Syrian immigrants" but went on to argue that they had misinterpreted the decision of the court. The Syrians claimed that they had suffered "humiliation" and "mortification" in the wake of the decision that they did not belong to the "white race." Judge Smith countered that this had not been the wording of the decision, but rather that "a modern Syrian was an

Asiatic, and was thus not included in the term 'white persons' as contained in section 2169 of the U.S. Revised Statutes as amended in 1875."[61] He followed this clarification with a telling interpretation of the Syrian position: "The true ground of this supposed humiliation is that the applicant and his associates conceive the refusal of this privilege to mean that they do not belong to a white race but to a colored and what they consider an inferior race."[62] The judge's musings were not without merit. Syrians did perceive exclusion from naturalization to mean that they were deficient, unwelcome, and uncultured. That is why their early arguments for inclusion in the "white race" revolved around the issue of the contribution of Semitic peoples to the western world, especially western Christendom. The claim that the Syrians interpreted the defeat in the courts to mean that they were "colored" and therefore members of an inferior race was entirely different. This was a construction that was familiar to southern whites, but Syrian immigrants had to learn it. In Elkourie's defense of Syrian whiteness, there was no mention of color, nor did he resort to the strategy of defining whiteness as the absence of blackness. The "others" from which he attempted to distance Syrians were not blacks and Asians but prostitutes and anarchists. As refusals to naturalize Syrians increased, however, the ways in which Syrian whiteness was defined both within the community and without shifted. No longer did Syrians simply claim whiteness by asserting their Christian credentials; they began to do so in terms that explicitly excluded blacks and Asians.

Nowhere was this more evident than in the letter-writing campaign initiated by the Syrian Society for National Defense (SSND) in the wake of George Dow's first defeat. The society was organized in March 1914 in Charleston, South Carolina, to "defend our [Syrian] historic, civil and social rights."[63] The immediate goal of the SSND was to reverse Judge Smith's decision in the Dow case and support an appeal in Washington.[64] SSND secretary, Najib al-Sarghani, kept readers of the popular Arabic-language paper, *al-Hoda,* (The Guidance) up to date on the case and he made repeated appeals for money to support the legal defense. Syrians in the South were especially generous, and their names, along with the size of their contributions, were acknowledged in the pages of the paper.

al-Sarghani's appeals for support were first and foremost appeals to defend the Syrian sense of honor (*al-difa' 'an al-sharaf*). "We have found ourselves at the center of an attack on the Syrian honor," he wrote,[65] and a concerted effort was needed to reverse the shame of the decision excluding Syrians from citizenship. al-Sarghani and other members of the SSND were especially worried about the ramifications of yet another ruling (possibly at the Supreme Court level) that Syrians were nonwhite. In their view, this would affect Syrian commerce, restrict their ability to travel, encourage slander, and bring embarrassment to Syrian children.[66] More worrisome, however, was the possibility that such a ruling would render the Syrian "no better than blacks (*al-zunuj*) and Mongolians (*al-mughuli*). Rather, blacks will have rights that the Syrian does not have."[67]

al-Sarghani's statements reveal the change in Syrian thinking on race, whereby the claim to whiteness was framed explicitly against other racialized groups, namely, blacks and Asians. He argued that there could be no worse dishonor than for blacks to have rights that Syrians did not yet fully possess, an argument that boosted the Syrian claim to citizenship while it simultaneously called into question the appropriateness of black and Asian citizenship. Securing status as "white persons" was no longer just about securing the right to naturalize; it was about distancing Syrians from blacks and Asians in the discourse on race. Hence, the argument in favor of Syrian whiteness in the Arabic-language press became more and more about defending the Syrian's status as "a pure Caucasian," racially distinct from two other groups of people understood (both in the understanding of the common man and according to scientific rationales) to be emphatically "not white."[68]

This shift to a more racial, rather than a purely religious or civilizational, understanding of Syrian whiteness was further evidenced in a book that appeared in the midst of the Dow controversy. Published in both English and Arabic, it aimed to clarify (before Dow's case went to the Circuit Court of Appeals) the racial classification of the Syrians. The book was written by Kahlil A. Bishara at the urging of Naoum Mokarzel, editor and owner of *al-Hoda* and president of the Syrian American Associations. The goal of the book in the English introduction was to "set forth with a fairly high degree of precision, the evidence conducive to the determination of the racial identity of the modern Syria."[69] The Arabic introduction dispensed with the niceties and stated the purpose more forcefully. The book was a "reply to those who have denied that the Syrian emigrant is Caucasian, and have made him out to be of Mongolian origin, whereby they have made him ineligible for American citizenship."[70]

This was not the only place where the English version differed from the Arabic. In an impressive list of figures described as evincing the Semitic "pliability combined with iron fixity of propose," Bishara cited Moses, Elijah, Hannibal, Amos, Paul, Peter, and John. The Arabic version was identical except that it also included the name of the Muslim prophet, Muhammad. The omission was an interesting and strategic move. Having already made gains by promoting the Christian credentials of Syrian immigrants, it is likely that Bishara did not want to jeopardize their standing by aligning them with Muslims, especially not at a time when the Anglo-American judiciary (and the American public's) perception of Islam was steeped in ignorance and superstition.[71] Like others before him, then, Bishara stressed the Syrian connection to the Holy

Land, to Christianity, and to "western" civilization. But the larger argument in his book (especially the Arabic version) evinced a new development in the debate on Syrian racial identity. The early Syrian arguments for inclusion in the white race had emphasized industry, religiosity, and sobriety—qualities that had to do with what their proponents believed was the measure of a group's ability to contribute effectively to the American nation, not of membership in the "white race" as such. Increasingly, though, Syrians saw the denial of their whiteness to mean that they were Asian or black, and not, as Elkourie had seen it, heathens, derelicts, and drunks. Syrians thus generated a different definition of their whiteness; one that hinged on the question of who was "not white." It was this argument that carried the day in George Dow's final appeal in 1915 where it was affirmed, at the federal court level, that he was indeed a "white person."

Conclusions

For most scholars of Syrian and Lebanese immigration to the United States, the "race crisis" was simply an unfortunate chapter in the otherwise successful history of first-wave immigrant assimilation in the United States. "The events of those few critical years," writes Alixa Naff, "constituted an aberration," which "hardly dented the spirit of self-esteem of the Syrians."[72] They had, in other words, surmounted an annoying obstacle in the path of full-fledged integration into the American mainstream.

This essay argues that the racial prerequisite cases were of much wider significance for principally two reasons. First, they helped determine the legal definition of whiteness during a period of heightened nativism, and second, they encouraged Syrians to view themselves as white in relation to other groups. The crisis may have "vanished" (to use Naff's words), but the saliency of race for Syrians did not. In Georgia, for example, they were targets of Ku Klux Klan threats and violence long after George Dow secured his victory in court in 1915.[73] And, in Florida, the lynching of Syrian immigrant, Nola Romey, served as a terrible reminder that the whiteness of Syrians was inconclusive, particularly in a South still steeped in the politics of Jim Crow.[74] Indeed, the seemingly provisional quality of Syrian whiteness, despite *Dow v. United States*, prompted Syrian immigrants (especially the elite among them) to reaffirm their coveted racial status as whites. They did not challenge the premise that whiteness was a legitimate prerequisite for citizenship and the privileges it afforded, only, as Mathew Jacobson has pointedly remarked, "that their rightful share in whiteness was being denied them."[75]

Advancing arguments in favor of Syrian suitability to "share in whiteness" was certainly on Naoum Mokarzel's mind when, in 1920, he wrote a letter to the French Consul in New York City, beseeching his intervention on the part of Syrians in Panama. The Panamanian government had passed a restrictive law on immigration, which barred Syrians and "other Asians" from entering the country. Mokarzel asked for Consul Liébert's intervention: "Will you take charge of the matter yourself and see that the Lebanese and Syrians are treated as they ought to be? They are not only from the white race," he continued, "but from the cream of that race, and I am sending you a book written on the subject."[76] The book was no doubt Kalil Bishara's—the same one Naoum Mokarzel had commissioned to serve as evidence in the United States racial prerequisite cases. By this time, Syrian arguments for inclusion in the "white race" based on their Christian credentials had given way to arguments rooted in the language of racial hierarchies. Moreover, Syrians claimed that they were white, not only to safeguard their right to naturalize as Americans, but because whiteness had become more central to how they thought of themselves as Syrians. It is thus not altogether surprising that in the aftermath of the Romey lynching, the most extensive coverage in the Syrian-American press conveyed not so much outrage at the barbarity of the crime (which had taken the life of Nicholas, as well as his wife), but bewilderment—the sense that he had been the victim of racial misidentification, and that his murderers had not understood that he was really white. In the words of one commentator, writing in the newspaper *ash-Shaab*: "The Syrian is not a negro whom Southerners feel they are justified in lynching when he is suspected of an attack on a white woman. The Syrian is a civilized white man who has excellent traditions and a glorious historical background and should be treated as among the best elements of the American nation."[77]

In sum, the legal decision in *Dow v. United States* corresponded to, and was even made possible by, a decision on the part of individual Syrians to think of themselves as white in the "popular" sense of the term, or—as the legal phrasing of the day put it—"in the understanding of the common man." Ultimately, this demanded that Syrians construct and make sense of their whiteness in relation to others who were non-white, and, as the statement in *ash-Shaab* made clear, whiteness had little meaning unless it stood in opposition to a racialized Other. Perhaps that is why, forty years after he was granted naturalization and deemed to be a "free white person," Costa Najour described the verdict as one that refuted the idea that he was "yellow."[78] For Najour, and many other Syrians, being "white" meant that they inevitably participated in the racialization of those who remained "not white." While this may have helped Syrians assimilate more quickly, it unfortunately helped perpetuate a discourse of exclusion in which other immigrant groups were marked as "others," ineligible for citizenship and full membership in the American nation. Thus, one of the paradoxical, if unintended, consequences of the Syrian struggle for whiteness was that it helped refine the legal arguments that repeatedly called into question the suitability of non-Europeans to "become American." The paradoxes inherent in the Syrian encounter with naturalization law will become more apparent by analyzing one final case; that of Yemeni immigrant, Ahmed Hassan, heard in Detroit, Michigan, in 1942. This case revealed that, close to three decades after Syrian Christians had scored a crucial legal victory in favor of their whiteness, other Arabic-speaking groups, particularly Muslim ones, would not fare so well in the courts or in the understanding of the "common man."

Hassan's physical appearance rendered him at a disadvantage from the start. After noting that the petitioner was "an Arab," Judge Tuttle declared that he was "undisputedly dark brown in color,"[79] confirming, once more, that while skin color was not supposed to determine racial eligibility to naturalize, it figured prominently in cases where petitions for citizenship were denied. In the Hassan case, darkness of skin definitely did matter, so much so that the judge argued that "a strong burden of proof devolves upon him [Hassan] to establish that he is a white person within the meaning of the [Naturalization] act."[80]

There was one important argument that could have helped establish Hassan's eligibility to naturalize, namely, the position of the southwestern part of the Arabian Peninsula outside the Asiatic barred zone. Placement in relation to the barred zone had already been used as a rationale in other racial prerequisite cases, such as the Basha case, which affirmed the eligibility to naturalize of a Syrian immigrant and, more significantly, the Thind case, which deemed Indians ineligible to citizenship because India fell within the zone. In the Hassan case, however, placement outside the zone was declared irrelevant, and the judge resorted to more familiar interpretations of congressional intent and common knowledge. Two factors, in particular, stood out as controlling the decision against Hassan: the fact that he was Muslim and the distance of Yemen from a European border. "Apart from the dark skin of the Arabs," Judge Tuttle opined, "it is well known that they are a part of the Mohammedan world and that a wide gulf separates their culture from that of the predominately Christian peoples of Europe."[81] In addition, and revealing that discussions of race were very often connected to anxieties over sex and marriage, Judge Tuttle argued that (Muslim) Arabs could not be expected to intermarry with "our population and be assimilated into our civilization."[82] It is not clear what evidence, if any, the judge used to make such an assertion. Rates of outmarriage were, in fact, quite high among Muslim Arab immigrants (and even higher among their children) and there was even a perception among Muslim men that they were more likely to marry "American" women because they did not immigrate with their wives, or send for them, as was more often the case with Syrian Christians.[83]

Rather than base his argument in the realities of the Arab immigrant experience, Judge Tuttle preferred to rely on suppositions and the old imperialist conviction that closeness to Europe meant closeness to "civilization" and membership in the "white race." In making this argument, he did of course have the weight of other legal rulings behind him, and he cited the case of an Armenian immigrant, Tatos O. Cartozian, as an important precedent. Heard in an Oregon district court in 1925, *United States v. Cartozian* had affirmed the whiteness of Armenians thanks largely to the testimony of noted Columbia University anthropologist, Franz Boas. Carefully combining ethnological and common knowledge rationales, Boas argued that Armenians were white because of their "European origin" and "Alpine stock." The judge placed great weight on Boas's testimony, as well as on the historic "aloothess" of the Armenians from the Turks, their proximity to Europe, Christian background, and tendency to "intermarry with white people everywhere." [84] It is worth noting that the judge presiding over the Cartozian case was the one who had ruled in favor of Syrian applicant, Tom Ellis. Also cited in *United States v. Cartozian* was the Halladjian case, which had been used to affirm the eligibility of a Syrian petitioner in 1910. [85] While the cases of Armenians and Syrians were frequently used to support each other, they were never mentioned in *In re Ahmad Hassan*, although there were clearly grounds to do so. Why, in this instance, were the Syrian racial prerequisite cases not relevant in the case of a Muslim Arab? The reason appears deceptively simple: in the legal discourse of the 1940s, the term "Arab" did not mean, as it does today in its most general sense, speakers of Arabic, but persons born in the Arabian Peninsula and, increasingly, Arabic-speaking Muslims from Palestine. The different categorization of Muslim and Christian Arabs was also more complicated, as subsequent debates would show. Establishing the whiteness of both groups, at the same time, would require a new argument—a task taken on, not by Arab-American associations, but by the Immigration and Naturalization Service.

Less than one year after Hassan's case was heard in Michigan, the INS published a lengthy statement on the eligibility of Arabs to naturalize. Strikingly at odds with the ruling in *In re Ahmed Hassan,* the article began by stating that the "Immigration and Naturalization Service and the Board of Immigration Appeals take the view that a person of the Arabian race is eligible to naturalization." [86] It then proceeded to link eligibility to the provisions of the Thind case and shift the terms of the debate to ones derived from an emerging discourse of anti-Fascism. With regard to Thind, the INS considered Arabia's exclusion from the barred zone to be "highly significant" and cited Justice Sutherland's now famous opinion that had linked eligibility for immigration into the United States to eligibility to naturalize. But, the INS knew that placement in relation to the zone was not enough and proceeded (ironically much as Judge Tuttle had) to link geography to a particular cultural pedigree which, in its view, boosted the eligibility of certain immigrant groups to citizenship. Not surprisingly, compatibility with European civilization was at the top of the list. Here, the article did cite the Syrians and Armenians as examples of peoples eligible to naturalization "chiefly because of their European contacts" and added that, by the same logic, "the Arabians . . . would seem the most likely candidates" for citizenship.[87]

It is important to stress that the Syrian and Armenian racial prerequisite cases were not directly cited as precedents by the INS, nor were the Syrians viewed as another "Arab" group that had successfully claimed whiteness through the courts and could, therefore, support the claims of Palestinians and Yemenis. Rather, it was, according to the INS, the history of "European contact" that the Syrians, Armenians, and "Arabians" all shared that rendered them white. The INS thus reamed to the argument that whiteness could be measured in cultural terms and used a yardstick divided, metaphorically, in increments of "contribution to western civilization." Since the "Semitic races" were situated at the beginning of this yardstick, that is, in the early history of western civilization (but clearly not in its present), they could be classed as white. Finally, in an appeal to out-dated but still popular theories of ethnology, the INS cited a 1941 decision of the Board of Appeals that had affirmed the admissibility of a certain Majid Ramsay Sharif to the United States, because "Arabians [are] closely related to the Jews . . . whose eligibility to citizenship has never been questioned."[88] All of the components of this INS argument were applied a year later in a Massachusetts court, where the petition for naturalization of another Muslim Arab, Mohamed Mohriez, was granted.[89]

To be sure, the desire to include Muslim Arabs in the category of those eligible to naturalization, so evident in the INS's article and Mohriez case, was also linked to wartime concern over the devastating effects of European racism. The *Monthly Review,* for example, concluded its statement on Arab eligibility with palpable unease with the ruling against Hasan, noting that "it comes at a time when the evil results of race discrimination are disastrously apparent." In a more reflexive vein, Judge Wyzanski, writing in favor of Mohriez, argued that "we as a country have learned that policies of rigid exclusion are not only false to our profession of democratic liberalism but repugnant to our vital interests as a world power."[90] Granting Mohriez' petition for citizenship was a way to "fulfill the promise that we shall treat all men as created equal."[91]

The controversy over the eligibility of Muslim Arabs to naturalize was interesting in the way it both did, and did not, revisit the arguments made in the Syrian racial prerequisite cases. The INS position in favor of Arab whiteness, for example, was remarkably similar to the argument made for Syrians in the Dow case. The main difference was that the INS was willing to incorporate

Muslim Arabs into this definition, provided that they were cast as players in the march of Christian, western civilization. In other words, Muslim Arabs were deemed white when their religious identity was effaced. In this way, they became, to use Joseph Massad's term, "honorary whites," those accepted into the body politic but under suspicion that they did not quite deserve it.[92] Whereas the Christian identity of Syrian applicants in the racial prerequisite cases had been central to their argument for whiteness, and had indeed helped them secure it, Muslim Arabs were at their whitest when stripped of their religious affiliation and rendered part of the western fantasy of an original "Semitic" race.

The new emphasis on "racial equality" (that is equality between those admitted to the "white race") could not change the more provisional status of Muslim Arab whiteness. The "not-quite-white" status of this group would become increasingly apparent in the post-World War Two era, with the rise in discrimination and ethnic stereotyping in the workplace and media. The conflation of Muslim/Arab/Other that lay at the heart of this stereotype was linked to a complex set of factors, including widespread American support of Zionist aspirations, suspicion of pan-Arab ideals, and resentment toward the oil-rich Arab Gulf states. This history of discrimination has been aptly chronicled by other scholars,[93] as has the impressive record of resistance and activism on the part of second-wave immigrants and their children.[94]

Less attention has been paid to the implications of first-wave Arab immigrant racialization as whites in the United States. It seems especially appropriate to do so in the wake of intensive efforts by leading Arab-American organizations to change the classification of Arabs as "Caucasian" on the United States Census to either a separate "Middle Eastern" or "Arab-American" category.[95] This had obvious strategic implications: minority status would render Arabs eligible for federally funded programs and provide greater protection under anti-discrimination laws. Moreover, for many Arab Americans, the desire to disassociate from the category "white" is rooted in a basic disconnect between their own self-perception as a people marked as outsiders and "un-American" and the official racial status accorded them.[96] While the disavowal of whiteness is a provocative and, in many circles, welcome development, it should not be done without serious reflection on the history of how and why Arabs became white in the first place. Arab whiteness is, after all, a legacy of the Syrian encounter with naturalization law, an encounter in which members of an immigrant group strategically chose to pursue the privileges of citizenship by defining themselves as distinct from nonwhites, notably blacks and Asians. There is still much to be learned about how the racialization of Arabs as white (and "not-quite-white") shaped their relationships with other groups in the United States and with each other.

Notes

The author wishes to thank Rashid Khalidi, Kathleen Neils Conzen, Michael Suleiman, Leora Auslander, María Elena Martínez, and two anonymous readers at the *Journal of American Ethnic History* for reading and commenting on this essay. Participants in the American Historical Association's 1998 panel, "Arab *Mahjars*/Diasporas in the Americas" (Jeff Lesser, Theresa Alfaro Velcamp, Gladys Jozami, and Nadim Shehadi) gave good advice in the early stages of this study. Thanks also to the staffs at the National Museum of American History, Archives Center (Washington), and the Center for Migration Studies (Staten Island) for their assistance.

1. "Syrian" refers to persons originating from the late-Ottoman provinces of bilad al-Sham, or geographical Syria. This area included the present states of Syria, Lebanon, Israel/Palestine, and Jordan. While the majority of emigrants from bilad al-Sham to the United States were from what became the Republic of Lebanon, they described themselves as "Syrian" and were referred to as such in the sources used for this essay. Arabic words are transliterated according to the system found in the *International Journal of Middle East Studies,* although, aside from *'ayn* and *hamza,* all diacritical marks have been omitted. Arabic names are transliterated as family members chose to do so.

2. This was section 2169 of the Revised Statutes (1878). The first naturalization law was passed in 1790 and provided that, to be naturalized, an alien must be "a free white person." After the adoption of the fourteenth amendment, the act of 1870 extended naturalization "to aliens of African nativity and to persons of African descent." See Luella Gettys, *The Law of Citizenship in the United States* (Chicago, 1934), p. 70; U.S. House, Citizenship of the United States, Expatriation, and Protection Abroad, 59 Cong. 2 Sess. H. Doc. 326 (Washington, D.C., 1906), pp. 98–99.

3. The question of how many Syrian immigrants entered the United States in the pre-World War One period is answered with widely diverging numbers. The U.S. Immigration Commission claimed that 56,909 Syrians had entered the country between 1899 and 1910, while the Thirteenth Census of 1910, under the category of "foreign stock" of Syrian origin, gave a figure of 46,727. See United States Immigration Commission, 1907–1910, Abstract of Reports, vol. 1 (Washington, D.C., 1911), p. 95; United States Bureau of the Census, Thirteenth Census of the United States, 1910: Population, vol. 1 (Washington, D.C., 1913), p. 963. Syrian community estimates were consistently higher. Rev. Basil Kherbawi, for example, relying on figures from Syrian voluntary associations and churches, estimated the Syrian population in the United States to be 200,000 in 1913. In *Tarikh al-wilayat al-muttahida* [History of the United States], (New York, 1913). Part of the reason for the inaccuracy of U.S. government statistics lies in the fact that Syrians were not distinguished from other Ottoman subjects until 1899.

4. *Dow v. United States,* 226 Fed. 148 (1915).

5. This began with Philip Hitti's classic study *The Syrians in America* (New York, 1924), p. 89; and Joseph Ferris' series entitled "The Syrian Naturalization Question in the United States" published in the journal *The Syrian World* v.2, nos.8 and 9 (1928): 3–11, 18–24. See also Adele Younis' notes in appendix 4 in *The Coming of the*

Arabic-Speaking Peoples to the United States, ed. Philip Kayal (Staten Island, N.Y., 1995), pp. 297–301.

6. Alixa Naff, *Becoming American: The early Arab Immigrant Experience* (Carbondale, Ill., 1985), p. 259.

7. In terms of race, I have been influenced by work that traces ideas about race and practices of racism to the specific cultural and social formation of a given society. See David Theo Goldberg, ed. *Anatomy of Racism* (Minneapolis, 1990); M. Omi and H. Winant, *Racial Formation in the United States: From the 1960s to the 1990s* (New York, 1994); and the critique of the aforementioned in Thomas C. Holt, "Marking: Race, Race-making, and the Writing of History," *"American Historical Review,"* 100, 1 (1995): 1–20.

8. Ian F. Haney López, *White by Law: The Legal Construction of Race* (New York, 1996), 3.

9. Much later, in 1938, a petitioner did attempt to naturalize on the basis of African descent but was refused. The court ruled that persons one-quarter African and three-quarters Native American were not eligible for citizenship on the basis of "African descent." *In re Cruz,* cited in Haney López, *White By Law,* 240, fn. 2.

10. This theory was first advanced by Johann Friedrich Blumenbach, professor of medicine at the University of Gottingen, in the late eighteenth century. Theories that attributed racial difference to variations in the size and shape of human skulls ("craniometry" or "craniology") had an unusually long life in both Europe and the United States. Not until the 1880s was craniometry—as a method of classifying races—seriously challenged by anthropologists. However, this did not mean that attempts to "measure" race were completely abandoned, and craniometry often gave way to the study not of skulls but of brains. See Thomas F. Gosset, *Race: The History of an Idea in America,* new ed. (New York, 1968 [1963]), pp. 69–77.

11. David R. Roediger, *The Wages of Whiteness: Race and the Making of the American Working Class* (London, 1991), p. 13.

12. Both authors emphasize the role of the Catholic church and the Democratic party in helping the Irish learn to value their whiteness. See Roediger, *The Wages of Whiteness,* pp. 140–144. Roediger, in a section indebted to psychoanalytic theory, also argues that the Irish "projected" their desire for a preindustrial past onto blacks—a desire he sees at work in the simultaneous development of popular blackface minstrelsy among the "white" working class and notions of white supremacy. See *The Wages of Whiteness,* chapter 6.

13. Noel Ignatiev, *How the Irish Became White* (New York, 1995), p. 2.

14. Haney Lopez, *White by Law,* p. 68. There were thirteen racial prerequisite cases heard before Najour's. The petitioners were: three Chinese, three Japanese, one Burmese, one Hawaiian, one Mexican, two mixed Native American and white, one mixed Asian and white.

15. The largest concentration of naturalized Syrians was in the North. New York City, for example, had approximately 300 naturalized Syrians by 1901. U.S. House, Industrial Commission on Immigration, Reports, vol. XV. 57 Cong. 1 Sess. Doc. 184 (Washington, D.C., 1901), p. 445.

16. John Higham, *Strangers in the Land: Patterns of American Nativism* (New York, 1993), p. 165.

17. Italians, for example, often worked beside and competed with blacks for jobs. Their commercial dealings with blacks could lead to violent reprisals from whites, as was the case in Tallulah, Louisiana, where five Sicilian storekeepers were lynched. Higham, *Strangers in the Land,* p. 169.

18. Ibid., p. 165.

19. See Alan M. Kraut, *Silent Travelers: Germs, Genes and the "Immigrant Menace"* (New York, 1994), chapter 4.

20. Trachoma (an infectious eye disease) as well as favus, venereal diseases, parasitic infections, and tuberculosis were all considered "Class A" conditions, that is, conditions warranting exclusion, by the United States Public Health Service. See Amy Fairchild, "Science at the Borders: Immigrant Medical Inspection and Defense of the Nation, 1891–1930," (Ph.D. diss., Columbia University, 1997).

21. Interview with Farah S., 1 March 1997, Damascus, Syria; Sarah E. John, "Arabic-Speaking Immigration to El Paso Area, 1900–1935," in *Crossing the Waters,* ed. Eric J. Hooglund (Washington, 1987), pp. 106–107; Alice Abraham. Transcript of interview by Alixa Naff, Los Angeles, CA, 1962, Naff Arab-American Collection, Series 4/C, Archives Center, National Museum of American History, Smithsonian Institution, Washington, D.C.

22. According to records from the Department of Commerce and Labor 4,648 (almost one in ten) Syrians were turned back in the period between 1899 and 1907. Of these, 1,578 persons were debarred on account of trachoma. See Louise Seymour Houghton, "Syrians in the United States," The Survey, v.26, no. 14 (1911), p. 490.

23. Reed Ueda, "Naturalization and Citizenship," in *Harvard Encyclopedia of American Ethnic Groups,* ed. Stephen Thernstrom (Cambridge, Mass., 1980), p. 740.

24. The case of Syrian immigrant George Shishim, a police officer in Venice, California, was heard before Najour's in the Supreme Court of Los Angeles. While the Shishim case is an important one, especially because it generated a good deal of debate in the local press, this essay will focus on cases heard in U.S. district and circuit courts. On the Shishim case see Joseph R. Haiek, *Arab-American Almanac,* 4th ed. (Glendale, Calif., 1992), pp. 21–23.

25. *In re Najour,* 174 Fed. 735 (1909).

26. On this point, see Haney López, *White By Law,* p. 68.

27. *In re Najour,* p. 735.

28. Ex parte Shahid, 205 Fed. 813 (1913).

29. Costa Najour to Adele Younis (in Arabic), January 1961, Syrian-American Archival Collection (SAAC), Gr. II, Series C, folder 203, Center for Migration Studies (CMS), Staten Island, NY.

30. *In re Najour,* p. 735.

31. *In Re Ah Yup,* cited in Haney López, *White By Law,* p. 210.

32. He was quoting from Huxley's *Methods and Results of Ethnology.* See In re Dow, 213 Fed. 358 (1914).

33. Ibid., p. 366.

34. The classification of Syrians as "Asiatic" could be deduced from the 1910 U.S. Census, which considered Syria part of "Turkey in Asia." However, it is clear from the census that for the purpose of population statistics, Syrians were considered white, since immigrants from "Turkey in Asia" were listed in the category "foreign-born white."

35. *In re Dow*, p. 365.

36. Ibid.

37. Ibid., 367.

38. *In re Ellis*, 179 Fed. 1002 (1910).

39. Ibid., p. 1003.

40. Matthew Frye Jacobson, *Whiteness of a Different Color: European Immigrants and the Alchemy of Race* (Cambridge, Mass., 1998), pp. 68–74. See also Souad Joseph's fascinating study of how representations of Arabs as "not quite free" has impeded their integration into the category of American citizen. "Against the Grain of the Nation— The Arab," in *Arabs in America: Building a New Future,* ed. Michael W. Suleiman (Philadelphia, 1999), pp. 257–271.

41. Judge Newman dismissed the argument, claiming that if being a Turkish subject disqualified one from naturalization, "the extension of the Turkish Empire over people unquestionably of the white race would deprive them of the privilege of naturalization." *In re Najour,* p. 736.

42. *In re Ellis*, p. 1004.

43. Ibid.

44. *United States v. Thind*, 261 U.S. 204 (1923).

45. *Takao Ozawa v. United States,* 260 U.S. 178 (1922).

46. Haney López, *White By Law*, p. 91; David R. Roediger, "Whiteness and Ethnicity in the History of 'White Ethnics' in the United States," in *Towards the Abolition of Whiteness: Essays on Race, Politics and Working Class History* (London, 1994), p. 182.

47. See "The Comprehensive Immigration Act of 1917," in *Immigration: Select Documents and Case Records,* ed. Edith Abbott (Chicago, 1924), p. 217.

48. *United States v. Thind*, p. 215.

49. Joseph Ferris, "Syrian Naturalization Question in the United States," The Syrian World 2, no. 9 (1928), p. 22; Helen Hatab Samhan, "Not Quite White: Racial Classification and the Arab-American Experience," in *Arabs in America*, p. 217.

50. For a more detailed discussion of the Thind and Ozawa cases, see Jeff H. Lesser, "Always 'Outsiders': Asians, Naturalization, and the Supreme Court," *Amerasia,* 12, no. 1(1985–86): pp. 83–100.

51. Mae M. Ngai, "The Architecture of Race in American Immigration Law: A Reexamination of the Reed Johnson Act of 1924," *Journal of American History,* 86, no. 1 (1999): 67–92.

52. See Lesser's discussion of the continuities between naturalization and Japanese internment cases in "Always 'Outsiders'," pp. 92–93.

53. *United States v. Balsara*, 180 Fed. 696 (1910).

54. *In re Ellis*, 1003; *Dow v. United States*, p. 148.

55. The vast majority of "first wave," that is, pre–World War II, Syrian immigrants to the United States were Christian of either the Greek Orthodox, Greek Catholic

(*Melkite*) or Maronite denominations. Lucius Miller's comprehensive 1904 study of the Greater New York community found Melkites in the majority, followed by the Maronites, Eastern Orthodox, and a much smaller number of Protestants. Out of a total population of 2,482 persons, there were only seven Muslims and approximately one hundred Syrian Jews. In Worcester, MA, another area of early Syrian settlement, the Orthodox were in the majority. These two examples, however, may not be representative of other communities in the United States, and there is still much work to be done on how the religious composition of the migration changed over time. See Philip M. P. Kayal and Joseph M. Kayal, *The Syrian-Lebanese in America* (Boston, 1975), p. 78; Lucius Hopkins Miller, *A Study of the Syrian Population of Greater New York* (New York, 1904), p. 22; Najib E. Saliba, *Emigration from Syria and the Syrian-Lebanese Community of Worcester, MA* (Ligonier, Pa., 1992), p. 39.

56. "Elkourie Takes Burnett to Task," *Birmingham Age-Herald*, 20 Oct. 1907. This was the second of two letters written by Elkourie. The first appeared under the title "Dr. Elkourie Defends Syrian Immigrants" in the *Birmingham Ledger*, 20 Sept. 1907. According to Nancy Faires Conklin, the two letters were collected in a pamphlet and distributed under the title "In Defense of the Semitic and the Syrian Especially." See Conklin and Faires, "'Colored' and Catholic: The Lebanese in Birmingham, Alabama," in *Crossing the Waters,* ed. Eric J. Hooglund (Washington, D.C., 1987), p. 76.

57. "Elkourie Takes Burnett to Task."

58. Benjamin Braude, for example, argues that there was no unified Ottoman administrative system but rather "a set of arrangements, largely local, with considerable variation over time and place." See his article "Foundation Myths of the Millet System," in *Christians and Jews in the Ottoman Empire* v. 2, ed. Benjamin Braude and Bernard Lewis (New York, 1982), pp. 72–74.

59. *In re Dow*, p. 357.

60. Ibid., p. 363.

61. Ibid., p. 356.

62. Ibid.

63. *Al-Hoda*, 11 March 1914, p. 3.

64. *Al-Hoda*, 4 April 1914, p. 3.

65. *Al-Hoda*, 11 March 1914, p. 3.

66. Ibid.

67. Ibid.

68. See, for example, *al-Hoda*, 17 September 1914, p. 8.

69. Kalil A. Bishara, *The Origin of the Modern Syrian* (New York, 1914), p. 5.

70. Kalil A. Bishara, *Asl al-suriy al-hadith* (New York, 1914), p. 5.

71. Michael Suleiman, "Early Arab-Americans: the Search for Identity," in *Crossing the Waters,* p. 45. The most common perception was that Islam was an impediment to progress and that its adherents were prone to debauchery. These ideas could be found in the accounts of American missionaries as well as in enormously popular literary works like Robert Hitchens' *The Garden of Allah* (1904) and Mark Twain's *The Innocents Abroad*. See Terry Hammons, "'A Wild Ass of a Man': American Images of Arabs to 1948," (Ph.D. diss., University of Oklahoma, 1978).

72. Naff, *Becoming American,* p. 259. Kayal and Kayal devote two paragraphs to the naturalization cases and attribute the debates over Syrian racial identity to "the general anti-immigrant climate prevalent in the country at the time." While noting that "legally and politically the question was important," they minimize the participation of Syrians in the debates and add, rather cryptically, that "socially, the Syrian Christians—often blond and blue-eyed—were not particularly handicapped." See *The Syrian-Lebanese in America,* p. 74. Helen Hatab Samhan, in one of the few studies that problematizes the racial classification of Arabs as "white," oddly concurs with Naff by arguing that "this 'yellow race' crisis, while the most intensely discriminatory experience of the early Arab immigrants, did not have a very penetrating effect on their identity nor on their civic assimilation." See "Not Quite White," p. 217.

73. In 1923, for example, the home of a Syrian family in Marietta, Georgia, was dynamited, allegedly by the KKK. Jusserand to Poincaré, 3 January 1923, Levant 1918–1940, Syrie-Liban (SL), v. 407, Ministére des Affaires Étrangéres (MAE), Paris.

74. Reported in *The Syrian World* 3, no. 12 (June 1929), p. 47.

75. Matthew Frye Jacobson, *Whiteness of a Different Color,* p. 239.

76. Letter from S. Mokarzel to Gaston Liébert, 29 September 1920 (contained in dispatch to the French Consul in Panama), Levant 1918–1940, Syrie-Liban, v.128, MAE, p. 93.

77. Excerpted in *The Syrian World* 3, no. 12 (June 1929), p. 42.

78. Costa Najour to Adele Younis (in Arabic), January 1961, SAAC, Gr. II, Series C, folder 203, CMS, Staten Island.

79. *In re Ahmad Hassan,* 48 F. Supp. 843 (1942).

80. Ibid., p. 845.

81. Ibid.

82. Ibid.

83. Lawrence Oschinsky, "Islam in Chicago" (M.A. Thesis, University of Chicago, 1947), p. 27; Abdo Elkholy, *The Arab Moslems in the United States: Religion and Assimilation* (New Haven, 1966), pp. 29–33.

84. *United States v. Cartozian,* 6 F. 2d. 919 (1925).

85. *In re Halladjian,* 174 Fed. 834 (1909). The case involved four Armenian applicants and was heard in Circuit Court, D. Massachusetts. It was cited in *In re Mudarri* 176 Fed. 465

86. "The Eligibility of Arabs to Naturalization," Department of Justice, Immigration and Naturalization Service, Monthly Review 1, no. 4 (Oct. 1943), p. 12. Italics in original.

87. Ibid.

88. Ibid. Both the INS and the naturalization courts appeared oblivious to the power of institutionalized anti-Semitism to construct Jews as nonwhite. As Karen Brodkin argues, the systematic exclusion of Jews from professional, educational, and social spaces reserved for "authentic" (usually Protestant) whites contributed to their racialization. Not until after the Second World War, with the rise in philo-Semitism and the ascendancy of Jews into the American middle-class, did Jews become, in her estimation, fully "white." See her *How Jews Became White Folks and What that Says About Race in America,* (New Brunswick, N.J., 1998).

89. *Ex parte Mohriez*, 54 F. Supp. 941 (1944).

90. Ibid., p. 943.

91. Ibid.

92. Joseph Massad, "Palestinians and the Limits of a Racialized Discourse," *Social Text*, 34 (1993): 94–114. Massad argues that "honorary white" status was first conferred on European Jews who became objects of Gentile white support and sympathy in the post-holocaust era. It has, in his opinion, only recently been conferred on Palestinians as objects of Israeli human rights violations. I am suggesting that naturalization law defined Muslim Arabs as "honorary whites" much earlier, but that their whiteness was not considered as legitimate as that of the Syrian Christians, who claimed it earlier and more successfully.

93. E.C. Hagopian, "Minority Rights in a Nation-State: The Nixon Administration's Campaign against the Arab-Americans," *Journal of Palestine Studies* 5, nos. 1–2 (1975): 97–114; Jack Shaheen, *The TV Arab* (Bowling Green, Ohio, 1984); Michael W. Suleiman, *The Arabs in the Mind of America* (Brattleboro, Vt., 1988); Nabeel Abraham, "Anti-Arab Racism and Violence in the United States," in *The Development of Arab-American Identity*, ed. Ernest McCarus (Ann Arbor, Mich.,), pp. 155–214.

94. Nabeel Abraham, "Arab-American Marginality: Mythos and Praxis," in *Arab Americans: Continuity and Change*, ed. Baha Abu-Laban and Michael W. Suleiman, AAUG Monograph Series, no. 24 (Belmont, Mass., 1989), pp. 17–43; Janice J. Terry, "Community and Political Activism Among Arab Americans in Detroit," in *Arabs in America*, pp. 241–254.

95. Michael W. Suleiman, "Introduction: The Arab Immigrant Experience," in *Arabs in America*, p.15; Therese Saliba, "Resisting Invisibility," p. 309; and Helen Hatah Samhan, "Not Quite White," pp. 222–23. For an interesting discussion of how the debate on racial classification points to a split within the Arab-American community between those in favor of maintaining formal classification as "whites" and those wishing to ally with people of color, see Lisa Suhair Majaj, "Arab-American Ethnicity: Locations, Coalitions, and Cultural Negotiations," in *Arabs in America*, p. 322.

96. Samhan, "Not Quite White," p. 222. Arab-American feminists, in particular, have embraced the term "people of color" to identify and forge alliances with other minority groups. See, for example, the collection edited by Joanna Kadi, *Food for Our Grandmothers* (Boston, 1994).

The Politics of Southern Draft Resistance, 1917–1918

Class, Race, and Conscription in the Rural South

Jeanette Keith

In the darkness of an early summer morning in 1918, a truck loaded with fifty soldiers lumbered up into the hills north of Atlanta, Georgia, part of a federal-state expedition into rural Cherokee County, a reported center of resistance to the World War I draft. After interrogating suspected deserters' families and intimidating a local antidraft activist, troops and law enforcement agents loaded up again and drove even deeper into the hills, in search of another deserter's home. At this point, what had been a successful raid took an unexpected turn. To reach the next target, the convoy had to pass over a wooden bridge spanning the Etowah River. The heavy truck carrying the soldiers crashed through the bridge and fell into the river below, killing three soldiers and seriously injuring eight. At the scene of the crash, an agent from the Justice Department's Bureau of Investigation noted that farmers seemed to appear from nowhere to rescue the injured men. Suspicious, he investigated the timbers supporting the bridge and found that they had been sawed almost through. When he asked an elderly man at the scene about the bridge's condition, he was told that the timbers had been damaged during the Civil War. The agent discounted this possibility and recorded his suspicion of sabotage.[1]

The agent's report wound up in the files of the Bureau of Investigation, one of scores of reports on draft resistance in the rural South. Those files, combined with information from the records of other agencies involved in World War I mobilization, present a view of the World War I home front that significantly diverges from the accepted narrative of overwhelming support for the policies of Woodrow Wilson's administration. Behind the patriotic pageant staged by war mobilization agencies are transcripts of resistance.[2]

Alone among the combatants in World War I, Americans locate the Great War's significance, not in the trenches of France, but on the home front. Historians studying the modern managerial state find its origins in the Wilson administration's war mobilization measures, while others see in the government's wartime suppression of liberties a foreshadowing of the Cold War and the national security state. Taking one or the other of those aspects of the home front as theme, historians have produced admirable works that nonetheless raise as many questions as they answer. The most significant of them can be simply summarized: To what extent did the American public support Mr. Wilson's war and the mobilization methods used to pursue it?[3]

Consider the standard book on the World War I draft, John Whiteclay Chambers II's *To Raise an Army,* a well-written, thoroughly researched, whiggish policy history. Chambers acknowledges that the draft was unpopular with the American people. He estimates that between 2.4 and 3.6 million men avoided service by refusing to register. Citing statistics compiled by the provost marshal general's (PMG) office, Chambers notes that 337,649 men "deserted," either by failing to show up for induction (considered desertion during World War I) or by running away from training camps. As he notes, about 12 percent of the 2.8 million men drafted thus "deserted." Nonetheless, Chambers considers the conscription policy successful since it allowed the United States to raise an army by 1918. From a political standpoint, however, the very existence of so much draft evasion cannot be dismissed as irrelevant. If most Americans supported the war, as home front historians assume, then why the high rate of draft evasion?[4]

Similar questions arise out of the historiography of wartime civil liberty violations. While historians of American radicalism tend to depict wartime repression as just one more battle in the nation's ongoing suppression of the Left, most historians have evoked "hysteria" to explain why local councils of defense and other agencies of mobilization squelched dissent, leftist or not, with such vigor. "Hysteria" makes sense only if we believe that war mobilization agencies had no reason impelling them (for example) to stir up mobs against those who refused to buy Liberty bonds. As an explanation, it assumes overwhelming public support for the war. Remove that assumption, and the actions of local-level councils of defense in encouraging repression appear to be rational, if brutal and unconstitutional, applications of power in aid of state goals. Keep that assumption, and we still must account for simultaneous outbreaks of hysteria in almost every community in the United States. Either way, hysteria as an explanation is problematic.[5]

Reexamining the American home front requires new questions. How did the politics of the times play into mobilization policy? How did regional cultures affect the operation of rationalized national bureaucracies? Did the very implementation of mobilization policies create dissent, and if so, why?

To aid such a reexamination, I study the implementation of one policy, conscription, in one region, the South, defined here as the states of the old Confederacy. By focusing on the rural South, home to at least three-quarters of the regional population, I hope to provide insight into how a policy designed to shelter industry from the draft affected farmers. In addition, the overwhelming pre-dominance of the native-born among rural southerners mitigates the possibil-ity of divided loyalties as a factor in dissent. Perhaps influenced by the South's reputation as the nation's most militaristic region, historians have tended to discount known incidents of draft resistance in the South as isolated, sporadic, unimportant, and attributable to the ignorance of the populations involved. I will argue the contrary. Opposition to the draft in the South began as a political movement, and it reached such a level that governors of three southern states asked for federal troops to put down armed bands of deserters.[6]

It would be easy to see southern draft resistance as one more chapter in white southerners' long struggle against the central government. The political leaders of the antidraft movement did label conscription an unconstitutional extension of federal power, an argument drawn from the arsenal of states' rights rhetoric. But there is no reason to believe that the South's reluctant con-scripts would have been more willing to go to France had they been mustered by the states, rather than the federal government. I contend that the majority of southern draft resisters opposed conscription, not because the draft was federal, but because it forced them to support a cause they considered irrele-vant at best, dubious at worst. It is a truism that ordinary Americans do not care about foreign policy, but as this essay will illustrate, sometimes they do, as when that policy leads to war. Many ordinary white southerners opposed United States entry into the Great War. They thought that the war was being fought for economic interests not their own, and they struggled against being forced to serve in it. Their counterparts across the color line, black farmers and laborers, agreed with this critique and added to it a disinclination to serve a country that denied them full citizenship.

Ironically, the Wilson administration's attempts to domesticate the draft by running conscription through local draft boards only exacerbated southern rural draft resistance. Draft boards, chosen from small-town elites, operated in ways that seemed highly suspicious to farmers of both races. The adminis-tration of the draft in the South proved riddled with class biases in favor of the region's white middle class. Meanwhile, the racial biases embedded in draft board decisions and in federal policies not only worked to the detriment of black men but also increased the burden of conscription on poor whites. The result was widespread evasion, desertion, and (in places) armed resistance.

In telling this story, I will be moving from the national to the local, from the political to the social, in a narrative that takes us back to the presence of fed-eral agents in the hills of rural Georgia and to the deaths of American soldiers at the Etowah bridge. The decision to conscript an army in 1917 followed upon two years of national debate over the structure of the United States military. "Preparedness" advocates, strongest in the Republican party and in the Northeast, pushed for "universal military training and service" (UMT&S), a policy that would have required all young American men to undergo military training for service in a continental reserve army. Most preparedness advocates cited nationalistic motives for supporting military reform: universal military service would teach young men discipline, Americanize immigrants, and break down class and regional divisions. Factions in the movement, however, supported UMT&S as a step toward conscription. Between 1915 and 1917, preparedness supporters so muddled together the concepts of UMT&S and selective service that in the 1917 congressional debates over the draft, supporters of conscription referred to it as "universal service" when it was just the opposite, a selection of men rather than a levy en masse. By that time conscription supporters had begun to point to the British experience in the Great War to bolster their arguments for selection. As preparedness advocates saw it, the British volunteer system had drawn disproportionately from skilled workers while allowing slackers to opt out. Without a draft, they argued, the United States would replicate the British experience. They implied that the sons of the British American middle class would volunteer while immigrants and unskilled workers stayed home. Thus preparedness supporters included those who wanted to create a rational, efficient army without damaging the nation's industrial base, those who favored universal service to facilitate nation building, and those who thought a draft would more equitably distribute the burden of service across class and ethnic lines.[7]

The antipreparedness cause attracted socialists, feminists, and pacifists, but it derived its political clout from its popularity among southern rural whites. It was their representatives, the agrarian Democrats ensconced in the party leadership in the House and Senate, who blocked most preparedness proposals from 1913 through 1916. Southern Democratic leaders in the House and Senate especially opposed plans that called for the abolition of the National Guard, a force both politically powerful and popular throughout the nation. Southern political leaders found the guard useful for racial reasons: since the guard was under state control, southern governors could ensure that it remained an all-white military force. But the congressmen's constituents had other concerns, as their letters to the man who led congressional opposition to preparedness, House majority leader Claude Kitchin of rural Scotland Neck, North Carolina, indicate.[8]

Rural southerners worried most about the uses to which this new model army might be put. Conceding that in an emergency the nation could call men to the defense of the homeland, they opposed proposals to raise a mass conscript standing army during peacetime as both a violation of American military tradition and a temptation to the power-hungry, who might subvert national policy to their own interests. As Hugh W. White, a member of the

Virginia House of Delegates from rural Rockbridge County, wrote to Kitchin in December 1915, "I believe that a declaration of war by this country is the objective point on the part of the great manufacturing interests of this country with a view to a restoration of a high tariff and a consequent monopoly and profit of millions." As the point man for antipreparedness in Congress, Kitchin received dozens of similar missives from across the South begging him to save the common people from the machinations of the rich. The fact that the boards of preparedness lobbying groups tended to be filled with northeastern industrialists, munitions manufacturers, and investment bankers did nothing to allay suspicion that preparedness was a Wall Street plot.[9]

It is impossible to say how many rural southerners opposed preparedness, but the political impact of southerners' antimilitarism may be gauged by the behavior of their congressmen. In the winter of 1915–1916, Kitchin and other congressional agrarian leaders fought their own popular president over the issue, forcing him to make substantial changes in the preparedness program he brought before Congress. In essence, the congressmen saved the National Guard and scotched Wilson's proposed volunteer continental army. Wilson's secretary of war quit in disgust when the president accepted this compromise.[10]

Nor did antimilitarist sentiment fade away as the Wilson administration moved toward war in the spring of 1917. Kitchin and a handful of rural southerners joined middle western congressmen and senators to vote against Wilson's requested declaration of war. A much larger number of congressmen and senators from agrarian districts in the Middle West and South lined up, regardless of party, against conscription. Chambers suggests that southern congressmen and senators who personally supported the draft found it necessary to oppose conscription publicly for fear of their constituents' wrath. At any rate, the southern agrarian opposition to conscription was so great that the House Military Affairs Committee, dominated by southern Democrats, refused to report Wilson's conscription legislation. Instead, committee chair Hubert S. Dent Jr. of Alabama proposed a compromise measure calling for the use of volunteers to be followed by conscription only if the volunteer system failed. It fell to a Republican member of the committee, Julius Kahn, to introduce Wilson's draft bill in the form of an amendment to Dent's bill. The Senate Military Affairs Committee approved Wilson's bill but with strong opposition from southern and midwestern members, who supported an amendment similar to the Dent plan.[11]

At this point in spring 1917, more intensely regional notes appeared in the debates over war and conscription in Congress and in the letters sent by southerners to their representatives. Among the new themes race played an important, but not overwhelming, role. Some southern congressmen based their opposition to the draft on the fear of black soldiers (a position most vehemently articulated by Sen. James Vardaman of Mississippi), while prodraft southern Democrats turned the argument on its head, insisting that conscription would protect white women by removing black men in the same proportion as whites. But race seems to have been less important than different understandings of history in determining where a person stood on conscription in 1917. While pro-war southerners evoked the spirits of the valiant Civil War dead in speeches and letters supporting the draft, southern antimilitarists drew upon memories of the Civil War to justify their aversion to war and especially to conscription. As an aged Confederate veteran wrote to Kitchin, "I know what it takes to face and charge a line of battle, or retreat, for I was in the Civil War. Entered in 61 came out in 65 a cripple for life. . . . I don't want to see my sons and the sons of our country men to see such slaughter as I and those who fought the late war." Wilson administration supporters cited the Confederate draft to prove that conscription was not unsouthern, while antidraft congressmen used the Confederate draft to show that conscription would not work.[12]

Southerners opposed to conscription also registered their protests in geographically specific and class-conscious terms. Thus a North Carolina tile manufacturer wrote to his congressman that the war had been "gotten up" by New Yorkers so that they could continue their trips abroad. The North, he wrote, wanted "the government to draft the young boys from each state; in other words she wants the South to go over there and fight that she may have her freedom, etc." However, the geography of opposition to conscription was not a simple matter of South versus North. The preparedness campaign had convinced many middle-class town folk of the rationality and social utility of the draft, while others of this group supported conscription out of loyalty to Woodrow Wilson, a highly popular figure among the regional middle class. When preparedness lobbies sent telegrams to business leaders throughout the South urging them to pressure their congressmen to vote for conscription, the result was an outpouring of mail and telegrams the likes of which the Capitol had never seen. As Congressman Jeff McLemore of Texas noted, his prodraft mail came "principally from board[s] of trade and chambers of commerce and other commercial bodies," while letters "from the country have come chiefly from farmers, and were against conscription." Speaking for the North Carolina Farmer's Union, its president, H. Q. Alexander, sent the entire state congressional delegation a letter denouncing conscription: "If this war was to protect the free institutions of America, our homes, women and children, selective conscription might be justified; but in that case there would be no need of conscription."[13]

Understanding that the Selective Draft Act of 1917 had been designed in part to shelter industrial labor, many agrarian House members feared that the army would be filled with conscripted farmers. In the end, the Wilson administration brought rural representatives over by promising that essential farm labor, like industrial labor, would be exempted. Many southern congressmen took that to mean that farmers as a group would not be drafted and so informed their constituents. On the question of drafting blacks, Wilson administration officials told southern leaders what they wanted to hear, ultimately producing a mixed and confusing message: some senators believed that African Americans would not be drafted at all but would be exempted as essential agricultural labor; others received assurances that the ratio of blacks and whites in the South would not be disturbed, which seemed to indicate that blacks and whites would be drafted according to their proportion in the region's population. When the president's plan for selective service finally came to the floor of the House, it passed 313 to 109. Even then, the negative votes came from rural districts in the South and Midwest.[14]

As it became clear that the Selective Draft Act might pass, savvy members of the southern white political elite hurried to place their sons and friends as officers in the National Guard or army. Uncertain as to the mechanism of obtaining commissions, many wrote to their governors, congressmen, and senators. Sen. John Sharp Williams of Mississippi cited this behavior as a reason for voting for conscription, noting sarcastically, "I have had enough applications for commissions to furnish the entire army we are going to raise. Nobody has bothered me about getting in as a private." While some of the powerful just wanted to assure their boys' rank, others expressed their desire to keep their sons safe in class-related terms. As a constituent who asked Gov. Thomas Rye of Tennessee to intervene with the army to place a man in the quartermaster corps stated, "I think one of the great problems of this war, and probably the outstanding problem, is to keep young men who have had special training for the important business enterprises that must be carried on from filling out the ranks of soldiers while the men who have not had any special training for anything stay back to do things for which they are not fitted."[15]

While public patriotism and private string pulling seem to have been common among the southern middle class, few left as clear a record of how the two could be combined, without any overt consciousness of hypocrisy, as did Eugene Cunningham Branson, professor of rural economics and sociology at the University of North Carolina. Branson served on the North Carolina Council of Defense and worked to mobilize public opinion in favor of the war. While publicly calling for patriotism and sacrifice, Branson conspired with his son's employer to place his son in jobs that would be likely to earn the young man an industrial deferment. Branson noted that his son might want to enlist: "This boy is willing enough to give his life to his country, but he'll serve humanity better alive than dead, I think." To explain himself to his son's employer, Branson noted that his wife was frantic with fear for the boy's life.[16]

Mrs. Branson was not the only mother worried about the fate of her son as the nation prepared for war. Rural southern whites' letters to their congressmen after the passage of the Selective Draft Act expressed sorrow, fear, and anger. A North Carolina minister informed North Carolina Rep. Edwin Yates Webb: "I have been in many parts of our State and in South Carolina and Virginia recently and I tell you the people are SAD." The minister continued, "Many mothers are desperate, and the thought of an unjustifiable, useless war to be backed up by CONSCRIPTION of our boys into a fight of which they do not approve, and the expenditure of sums, such as the world has never heard of, for War, of the PEOPLE'S money, has spread like a Pall all over our country." Another of Webb's constituents summed up years of southern rural white resentment, scrawling his protest in pencil on cheap lined paper:

It is inconseivable to think that the people are agoin to fight in foreign contry for and idile or principel that their own government falls far short of given them. . . . The Southern and Western farmer has been drinking the very bittrest dregs of the cup of humiliation for 40 yars but he has never had it put over and rubed in as it has been don now.[17]

The implementation of the draft in the South did nothing to allay antimilitarists' suspicions; instead it provoked resentment, evasion, and, ultimately, violent resistance. The Selective Draft Act of 1917 authorized the conscription of men aged twenty-one to thirty, inclusive, under the supervision of Provost Marshal General Enoch Crowder. After registering at his local voting precinct on June 5, each man received a draft number. The order of induction was determined by a lottery held in Washington. To rule on requests for exemption, Crowder created county-level exemption boards. Decisions made there could be appealed to district boards, which also automatically reviewed all exemptions awarded on the local level. The men who served on county and district boards were officially appointed by the president, but in practice the president chose members from lists supplied by state governors. Since no regulations specified the composition of draft boards, their composition varied from state to state. For example, in Georgia draft boards included a local physician, the county sheriff, and the superior court clerk (who was also registrar of deeds). In Tennessee, boards were composed of doctors, lawyers, and businessmen; in Alabama, of the county sheriff, the county health officer, and the circuit court clerk. In effect exemption board members were political appointees, not precisely the "friends and neighbors" memorialized in World War I propaganda nor "volunteers": when exemption board members tried to quit, Crowder informed them that they should consider themselves conscripted for the duration.[18]

In September 1917 Crowder and his staff developed a four-tiered classification system, based on occupation and familial status, to be used by draft boards in deciding who was eligible for exemption. Under this plan, the most conscriptable men would be placed in class I and the least in class IV. At the end of the war, Crowder announced that only men from class I had been called to service. Therefore, some historians have concluded that in World War I the United States drafted only unmarried men, a statement that appears even in John Keegan's recent military history of the war. That is both inaccurate and illustrative of the difficulties of reading conscription policy from the top down. In fact, many married men entrained for camp in August and September 1917.[19]

Crowder and his staff began with the assumption that men would be exempted, not for *marriage,* but for *dependency.* It was up to local draft boards to decide who fit that category, but Crowder's office insisted that dependency claims should not be awarded lightly. In July 1917 the PMG's office ruled that men whose relatives or in-laws could take care of their wives and children should not be awarded dependency exemptions, nor should men whose wives had land that could be rented to produce income, nor men whose pay as soldiers would supply adequate support for their dependents. Despite President Wilson's public statement of hope that no married men would be drafted, one senator complained to Wilson's private secretary: "The trouble is that the President says one thing and Crowder gives instructions to the local boards that are the opposite. Crowder is naturally trying to get an army, and he is taking advantage of technicalities in order to get it."[20]

In the rural South the most significant of the PMG's rulings was the one disallowing exemptions to married men whose families could be adequately supported by their army pay. In practice, this meant that if a married man earned less than about $30 a month, he could be denied a dependency exemption. Few rural day laborers, sharecroppers, and small farmers made more than $1 a day, as they would have had to do to claim exemption. As a result, as Crowder noted in 1918, "many registrants both white and colored, have been put in Class I on the ground that their allotment and allowances while in the Army would furnish an equivalent support to their dependents." Thus the federal government encouraged draft boards to choose those to be sent into harm's way on the basis of income.[21]

The Wilson administration's assurance that farmers would be exempted also proved false, as Rep. Frank Clark of Florida protested in a letter to President Wilson in September 1917: "the rules and regulations issued by the War Department do not at all comport with the declarations of the proponents of the [conscription] bill." Concerned citizens of Faxon, Tennessee, informed their governor in 1917, "We have been told that such farmers as are in Benton County are not considered [as entitled to agricultural exemptions] by the government." The Selective Service based agricultural exemptions on the farmer's ability to produce for market. Many white southern farmers in hill-country and mountain districts practiced semisubsistence agriculture, concentrating on feeding their families first, and earned cash from nonfarm employment in logging or mining. Tenant farmers of both races neither owned their land nor completely controlled what crops were planted there. Only the wealthiest southern "farmers," such as the planters who still dominated agriculture in the Deep South, could hope to obtain an agricultural exemption under Selective Service regulations requiring that farmers prove that they produced "an appreciable amount of agricultural produce over and above what is necessary for the maintenance of those living on the place." [22]

The federal government's system of allocating draft quotas combined with southern whites' racial prejudices to magnify the impact of conscription upon the region. The federal government set quotas based on a state's population of draft-age men and on the number of volunteers a state had already sent to service. States with many men already in the National Guard and the regular services received low quotas. Southern white men had not rushed to volunteer, and southern black men had not been allowed to: Most southern states had no black National Guard units, and the federal government stopped accepting recruits to the black regiments in the regular army in the spring of 1917. Therefore state draft quotas were higher in proportion to population in the South than in other parts of the nation. [23]

Charged with allocating exemptions under regulations intrinsically prejudicial to the poor, exemption board members quickly discovered that they had taken on a difficult job. Many southern men of both races simply did not want to serve and became "slackers" with full community support. Out of 557 rural county draft board reports, 214, or 40.7 percent, reported that communities encouraged young men to file for exemptions from service. [24]

Throughout the region, draft boards reported that large numbers of men requested exemption from service. The Saluda County, South Carolina, board noted that the "general attitude of this community seems to be to get out of the service if possible, and let the other fellow do the fighting." The Princess Anne County, Virginia, draft board's statement, while lengthier than most, was not unusual in content:

> Claims for exemption nearly unanimous, that the board had a very hard time considering, and did not get much support from the community in general. . . . [T]he people should be made to know and to understand that we are at war with a strong enemy, we need men and it is very tiresome for a local board to have 90 per cent of the drafted men asking for exemption.

From Texas, the Gregg County board wrote, "Everybody that had any shadow of a claim lost no time filing," and the Shelby County board wrote, "In the towns the general attitude of the people was against filing claims. In the rural districts it was largely in favor of filing claims and in a majority of cases neighbors would go to extremes in assisting a registrant in obtaining a discharge." [25]

The capriciousness of local draft boards added to public resentment. Since Provost Marshal General Crowder urged local boards to use their own best judgment in adapting rules to local circumstances, World War I conscription lacked any uniformity; decisions made on who was drafted and who could stay home varied from county to county. In addition, serious complaints about the political motivations of draft boards surfaced in Arkansas, East Tennessee, and Texas. A Justice Department agent reported that the Crittenden County, Arkansas, draft board, which contained members from both of the county's political factions, was corrupt and useless: one member "knows no more about the workings of the Local Exemption Board . . . than a Jack Rabbit," while another, when pressed to process exemptions, would "sober up and in half a day classify men like they were sheep and goats." In East Tennessee, a Republican enclave in a Democratic state, the district board became seriously entangled in partisan politics. The Knoxville city commission requested a federal investigation when the district board, all but one of them Democrats, ruled on over two thousand cases per day. The provost marshal general's office concurred that this was taking efficiency too far and suggested that some cases be reopened. The Milam County, Texas, board summarized the region's experience in its 1917 report: *politics and sympathy is an ever present factor.*" [26]

Accusations of political favoritism shaded into accusations of class bias: those who had political pull also had money. While it is nearly impossible to prove or disprove contentions that draft boards conscripted men based on their politics, federal government regulations mandated class bias by denying married men with low incomes exemptions for dependency. As interpreted by local draft boards, however, federal regulations took a peculiarly southern rural and racial spin.

It was impossible for southern draft boards to exempt all married men, since a majority, 52.5 percent, of southern men of draft age (21–30) were married. As the Walker County, Alabama, draft board informed Crowder, "We recall instances in this county where the man was only 28 years old and was the father of 4 or 5 children in wedlock, and the Lord only knows how many out of it." By contrast, outside the South, 43.84 percent of the registrants were married. (In the highly urbanized states of Massachusetts and New York, 39.91 and 40.99 percent of the registrants, respectively, were married.) As a result, southern draft boards exempted a smaller percentage of married men than did boards elsewhere in the nation. In the South, 86.52 percent of married registrants were exempted; outside the region, 91.15 percent were. Inside the South, the range of exemptions for married registrants ran from Florida's low of 82.32 percent to

North Carolina's high of 90.75 percent. In contrast, South Dakota exempted 94.29 percent of married registrants. Faced with the necessity of taking some married men, draft boards struggled to determine which ones.[27]

Some draft boards made their choices based upon concepts of manhood and of family that strayed far from the Selective Service's simple equation of income (money earned) with support. In James County, Tennessee, the draft board felt that family discipline required a man's touch: "In fact a woman can not control children as a man can and in bringing them up they need a father, no matter whether dependent for support or not." Several draft boards refused to draft married men because their families needed them for protection. Some draft boards based exemption on virility: men who had been married for several years without producing children might as well be sent to the front, since as the Caldwell County, Texas, board said, "what use are they anyway?" Other draft boards, in direct contradiction to Selective Service regulations, thought the sons of the rich should be drafted first. In many cases, boards followed the PMG's suggestion that they consider the capacity of the extended family to support the wives and children of soldiers and expressed frustration that they were unable to call fathers and fathers-in-law before them and question them about their ability and willingness to take care of a soldier's immediate dependents. Other draft boards considered the marriage tie less important than the support sons owed to aged parents.[28]

The Wilkes County, North Carolina, board summarized the feeling of many draft boards throughout the South when it reported, "In general, we believe that policy should be pursued which does less violence, not to individual, but to the community feeling." Thus at least one draft board in Virginia exempted married sharecroppers on the grounds that their wives would have to leave the area and find housing in the city; the board believed that the women, unused to urban life, would have a hard time managing in town even with their husbands' allotments. Of course, this policy also benefited landowners by exempting their tenants from the draft, a policy also documented in the south Georgia plantation belt. "Community feeling" in many cases was shorthand for the interests and needs of local elites. Therefore, draft boards used conscription to rid their communities of the shiftless, immoral, and criminal. As the board in Franklin County, Tennessee, explained, "Where a man was a good citizen and had more than one child we would discharge him. If he was a bad citizen it didn't make any difference how many children he had, we took him." Others used economic criteria, but in a special way—they refused to draft men whose families might become charity cases.[29]

The majority of southern draft boards, however, made their choices based upon the potential conscript's class or, as they put it, "station." Draft boards seemed to define station as a combination of income (as mandated by federal regulations), accustomed standard of consumption, and character: boards considered the conscript's "earning capacity, his standard of life, his willingness to work and the station and condition of those dependent upon him." In addition, station could include residence in town. Farmers charged that boards drafted their sons while exempting store clerks and bank tellers, particularly if they were the sons of prominent local men. In September 1918 "farmers and citizens" from Clay County, Arkansas, sent a petition to the provost marshal general alleging that married men with children had been called to camp "and refused even a few days in which to wind up their crop" while town men without dependents had not been drafted. In Frederick County, Virginia, the local draft board added its weight to citizens' complaints that a local rich man's son had received an agricultural deferment from the district board after he quit his job as a banker and bought a farm from his father for $1. The board stated that the district board "persistently exempted rich men's sons in this county, which has brought about a great deal of criticism in regard to the Draft Law . . . as most of the rich men's sons spend most of their time riding around in Automobiles and amount to very little as an Agricultural Asset."[30]

Southern draft boards' concepts of "station" were of particular salience in their treatment of the region's poorest and least influential men. During World War I African American men were drafted in disproportionate numbers; one-third of black registrants were conscripted, as compared to one-quarter of the whites. Since approximately 80 percent of the nation's African American population lived in the South, historians have attributed the draft's inequities to racism, noting that in five southern states (Florida, Georgia, Louisiana, Mississippi, and South Carolina) more blacks were drafted than whites. However, if draft boards had applied Selective Service regulations fairly, they would still have drafted black men in disproportionate numbers. Given regional wage standards, a totally color-blind draft operating in a totally color-blind state would have taken proportionately more black men than whites in the nation as a whole, since most black men in the nation lived in its poorest region and were the poorest people in that region.[31]

But southern draft boards were not color-blind. Some draft boards openly announced their intention to "take care of the white registrants and send the negros to answer the call," as in Taliaferro County, Georgia, where the first call-up had consisted of sixty-four blacks and four whites. Moreover, boards habitually considered the race of a registrant as being part of his station in life, especially when considering exemptions for dependency. As the Montgomery County, Alabama, board stated: "The majority of registrants within the jurisdiction of this Board are africans and their average wages are around $30 per month. Where a registrant had only a wife, it was considered that the husband in the army could send the wife more than he had heretofore contributed, and further, that negro women are always in demand as cooks. The matter of lone-liness during the absence of the husband was not taken into consideration." In Monroe County, Alabama, the draft board conscripted childless married white men and black men who had only one child: "Not that we intend to dis-criminate between the races, but because it is a matter of common knowledge that it requires more for a white man and his wife to live than it does a negro man and his wife, due to their respective station in life." [32]

Less likely than whites to receive deferments based on dependency, black men were more likely to be exempted from the draft because of the inter-vention of white employers. From Arkansas, a Little Rock attorney wrote to Emmett J. Scott, the provost marshal general's liaison with the black commu-nity, "The injustice is all the more flagrant because if a Negro is a tenant or works for some influential white man, he can 'get by the board' as they put it. The Negro who is somewhat independent, has his own farm or business, is the one who is hard hit." [33]

Federal records bear out these accusations. In Leon County, Texas, the local draft board used conscription to keep black men from leaving jobs on planta-tions belonging to their friends and political cronies. In Houston County, Alabama, the draft board apparently exempted or conscripted black men at the request of prominent whites, as a hotel owner in Dothan, Alabama, testified: "I asked [the board chairman] if he could not let Ulasas finish my crop, as I had no one to attend to it while I was sick. I told him that I had four negroes around the hotel and that he could substitute either one of these for Ulasas. . . . [T]he negro went back to the farm and stayed four or five weeks." [34]

Southern draft boards certainly practiced racial discrimination, but during World War I racism cut in peculiar ways. Many southern draft boards and many southern politicians believed that black men could not be used effectively as combat soldiers and suggested that they be employed as laborers. The Craig-head County, Arkansas, draft board protested against conscripting blacks at all, alleging that "the negro soldier is a danger to any community; the officers seem unable to control them, and their natural brutality asserts itself when in pack and with arms." The board concluded, "They are quite necessary as labor-ers, and should stay home and work. Military training of the negro will cer-tainly intensify the race problem in the south. The South will do the negro's fighting, if he is left in the field." [35]

The Craighead County board's suggestion turned out to be close to the ulti-mate federal policy on African American conscripts, with this qualification: It was not southern whites per se who would do the fighting, but southern poor whites. While blacks were disproportionately drafted, black conscripts did not stand much danger of being sent into combat. World War I was not just a poor man's fight; it was a poor white man's fight.

When the war began, the federal government placed limits on black enlistments in the army's regular black units and African American National Guard units from the northern states, but it drafted blacks in large numbers. Since the army was segregated, black conscripts had to be trained in separate camps from whites or at least in separate facilities within camps. The logical thing would have been to build new camps in the South, whence most conscripts came. But racial tensions in the South and in the nation as a whole ran high in the summer of 1917, with white attacks on black communities in northeastern and midwestern cities. In August black army regulars stationed at Houston, Texas, angered by police harassment, mutinied and attacked the town. Alarmed, southern white political leaders called for the removal of black soldiers from all southern states and adamantly opposed building any new training camps for blacks in their states. With no place to put black conscripts, the federal government delayed their induction until spring 1918. Once inducted, most black conscripts served as supply and labor troops.[36]

As white conscripts entrained for camps, blacks stayed home. This was distressing to black leaders, who hoped blacks' service in the military would earn them citizenship rights. But it was infuriating to southern whites, who found their race for once a disadvantage. The brunt of criticism fell on local draft boards. From Florida, the Jackson County board suggested that in the future the quota should be based on the "population percentage of races in order to prevent the aggravation of racial prejudices." In some places local draft boards stopped conscripting white men until blacks were inducted. But in other places draft boards followed Provost Marshal General Crowder's orders to fill quotas with whites until blacks could be inducted. Training camps for blacks finally opened in spring 1918, and African Americans were then called to service in what Crowder himself acknowledged to be "unduly large percentages" to compensate for the delay.[37]

Conscription, designed ostensibly to allocate the burdens of military service equitably, in practice proved extremely adaptable to the systems of privilege found in southern communities. Those with wealth and political power could obtain exemptions or finagle positions behind the lines. Meanwhile, poor men of both races found that government regulations did not respect their status as husbands or as farmers. United in this degradation, southern workingmen were nonetheless divided by race. While black men faced induction in greater percentages than whites, they were relegated to second-class, mostly noncombatant status once in the army. Southern whites worried about the safety of their boys fumed to see white men mustered into service and placed in combat regiments, while the sons and the servants of the upper class stayed home. Some white southerners opposed the war and the draft for political reasons; many others must have been pushed to rebellion by the implementation of the draft in the region.

Resistance began with political protests sponsored by populist Democrats and socialists. As citizens empowered with First Amendment rights, these grass-roots political leaders attempted to persuade Congress to modify the draft law through traditional methods, including petitions and litigation. Once federal legislation took away white southerners' right to protest politically against the war, thus suddenly transforming the empowered into the powerless, draft resistance continued through methods the anthropologist James C. Scott has labeled "infrapolitical," including evasion, foot dragging, and desertion. Repression transformed resistance, driving the political action of citizens underground and reducing nominally dominant white men to the same methods of protest used by disenfranchised blacks. As an illustration of how repression worked, I offer the case histories of a Texas farmers' union and of an antidraft movement headed by the famous populist leader Tom Watson of Georgia.[38]

In 1917 the Farmers' and Laborers' Protective Association (FLPA) of Texas, a multiracial union for small farmers and tenants, had attracted ten thousand members by its plans to create cooperative stores. Among those members was a government spy. Ensconced as a high officer in the organization, this man reported to the Justice Department's Bureau of Investigation. Probably through him, the department received information about the FLPA's internal debates over conscription. On May 5, 1917, a FLPA state convention in Cisco, Texas, rejected a proposal that the group resist conscription by any means necessary. Confusingly, this radical proposal was called the "majority report," because the group supporting it insisted that their views represented the majority of the organization. However, the "minority report," calling for peaceful resistance within the legal system, was the one adopted by the delegates. Nevertheless, on May 17 the United States attorney stationed at San Angelo reported to the attorney general that grand jury testimony had shown that the "main purpose of organization is to resist conscription and oppose Government power generally." The attorney continued, in telegraphic style: "All members instructed to obtain high power rifle and use when necessary. Members disclosing information threatened with death."[39]

As draft registration got underway on June 5, FLPA members traveled to Dallas for grilling before the federal grand jury, which ultimately indicted fifty-three union members for conspiracy to commit treason. In September, fifty of the alleged conspirators were brought to trial at Abilene. In vain organization officers protested that the Cisco convention had rejected the "majority report" advocating violence. Several of the FLPA officers were convicted and sent to federal prison for terms of up to six years. Despite headlines announcing the destruction of draft resistance in Texas, bureau agents continued to surveil suspected FLPA members well into the autumn of 1918.[40]

The federal government's methods in the FLPA case illustrate the difficulties faced by groups planning peaceful resistance to the draft. In effect, the federal government put the FLPA on trial at Abilene, not for what its members did nor even for their plans to protest the draft by petition, but for the rejected "majority report." Given the bureau informer's rank in the FLPA, the possibility that he acted as an *agent provocateur* cannot be discounted. Using this man's inside information, plus the power of the federal court system, the Department of Justice destroyed the FLPA, foreclosing its plans for political protest.

Although the federal government used conspiracy charges against the FLPA, its most effective weapon against rural dissent was not the lawsuit, but the suppression of the rural radical press. On June 15, 1917, Congress passed the Espionage Act, which with the later Sedition and Trading with the Enemy acts placed severe limitations on freedom of speech and press. In June, post offices began to deny mailing privileges to newspapers containing material critical of the war or war mobilization measures. In July Postmaster General Albert S. Burleson publicly announced that mailing privileges would be denied to publications attributing the war to munitions makers or Wall Street. This was the line taken by socialist newspapers in the Southwest and by Tom Watson's *Jeffersonian,* published in Thomson, Georgia.[41]

Watson's erratic career as newspaper publisher had taken him far from his attempt to build a biracial Populist party in the South in the 1890s. By 1917 Watson's paper was known nationally as a vicious race-baiting, anti-Catholic, anti-Semitic sheet. Watson's diatribes contributed directly to the lynching of Leo Frank in 1915 and to the resurgence of the Ku Klux Klan. But Watson was more than an avatar of "reactionary populism," to use Nancy MacLean's phrase. As his earlier career had indicated, he was capable of great courage in defense of people he considered to be poor, helpless, and oppressed. In January 1917 his political influence in Georgia was greater than it had been for many years. By opposing the war, Watson risked imprisonment and made himself vulnerable to his enemies in Georgia politics, most of whom supported war mobilization.[42]

Contending that the war had been fomented by the wealthy, Watson poured scorn on the idea that the United States was fighting for any sort of ideal:

BOSH!

　Wall Street Capitalists, Chicago Trusts, Standard Oil Magnates, Steel Kings, Coal Kings, Copper Kings, Aair-ship Trusts, Powder Trusts, Food Trusts, Leather

Trusts, Flour Trusts—such human vultures do not precipitate wars for health, pleasure or ideals.

They cause wars and panics for the money they can make out of them.[43]

Watson mustered southern rural whites to political resistance with headlines asking, "Do You Want Your Son Killed in Europe in A Quarrel You Have Nothing to Do With?" In the *Jeffersonian* he provided sample petitions calling for the passage of a bill that would have amended the draft act to confine conscript service to the nation's territorial limits: "After the paper has been signed by all the men who are not afraid the Booger Man will catch'em, mail it to the Representative of your Congressional District." The United States Post Office, the Bureau of Investigation, and local-level mobilization agencies noted with dismay that speakers at protest meetings across the South used arguments from the *Jeffersonian*. Eventually, the bureau filed reports on incidents of draft protest and resistance in Georgia, South Carolina, Tennessee, North Carolina, Alabama, Mississippi, Texas, and Louisiana under Watson's name.[44]

Those reports provide insight into the rationale for southern rural whites' opposition to the draft. Although some rural whites were religious pacifists, most opposed conscription, not warfare. Like Watson, they conceded that the state could levy men for defensive service within the country's territorial limits, but they denied that conscription could be used to raise an army for service overseas. (On this point, Watson cited William Blackstone, who had contended that the first right of an Englishman was to stay at home in peace in his own country.) Anticonscription southerners linked their protests against going to war in France with concerns about growing political repression at home. At Ebenezer, Georgia, a local pastor told a protest meeting that conscription was wrong and added, "I hope our flag will never fly over another country and a European battlefield, but if she does, let her fly free." Some draft protest leaders carried into the movement the same class consciousness raised in prewar opposition to preparedness. The Ebenezer meeting's organizer told the group that poor people were being "hoodwinked" on conscription. But the ultimate rationale for southern white draft resistance is revealed by the crowd's reaction to a circulating antidraft petition. Men rallied their neighbors to sign, saying, "Come on and sign, if you don't want to send your boy to war." This was antiwar resistance at its simplest: a refusal to see precious lives sacrificed for what appeared to be no good reason.[45]

Through the spring and summer of 1917, Tom Watson courted federal prosecution with rhetoric far surpassing, in vitriol and nerve, the statements that resulted in the arrest of the socialist leader Eugene Debs in 1918. Watson raised approximately $100,000 in contributions from his readers to fight the draft in the courts. Serving as counsel for two African American men appealing for release from conscription under *habeas corpus,* he charged that conscription abused states' rights and violated the Thirteenth Amendment's prohibitions of involuntary servitude. Although the litigation failed, Watson announced plans for a "state convention" to be held in Macon, Georgia, "for peaceable protest against the recent usurpations of power by Congress, the President, and the Post Office Department," who, he said, had spat on the Constitution they had sworn to defend. When he received warning that military force would be used against the gathering, Watson called it off, announcing, "The world must be made safe for democracy, even though none is left in these United States." In late August Postmaster General Burleson sent Congress a message labeling the *Jeffersonian* and the socialist paper the *Masses* the two most egregious violators of the Espionage Act. Shortly thereafter, Burleson officially denied Watson's paper its mailing privileges, a development Watson announced with a headline calling the president "Kaiser Wilson." But that paper never reached most of Watson's readers; the post office had not delivered the *Jeffersonian* since mid-July. Cut off from his public, well aware that he was in danger of imprisonment, and in ill health, Watson gave up the fight.[46]

By denying the small radical press mailing privileges, the federal government silenced the voice of political protest from the hinterlands and forestalled any possibility that geographically isolated rural dissent could draw together into a coherent protest movement. From about mid-June through the end of the war, government propaganda dominated the field of public discourse, filling the front pages of prowar southern newspapers. The time frame is significant: draft registration began on June 5, 1917, and the first trainloads of soldiers pulled out of southern depots in August. By the time rural southerners had begun to feel the true impact of conscription, the federal government had made it dangerous, if not impossible, to call for the abolition of the draft. At that point, dissenters had three alternatives: accept the situation and work within it, protest passively through evasion, or fight. By the summer of 1918, southern rural resisters had tried all three.

The easiest, and probably most prevalent, tactic was to acknowledge the legitimacy of the draft system but to demand equal treatment and reform. Thus many rural whites and some blacks wrote letters to federal authorities calling for investigations into abuses perpetrated by local and district draft boards. Charles Hodges, a prominent black farmer from Fayette County, Tennessee, began a letter of complaint by describing the local black community's support for the war: "We have freely taken out Liberty Bonds . . . and donated to the Red Cross and sent our sons at the call of the government to the camps and are wiling to move in any direction that Sec. Baker or Pres. Wilson should say for us to go." Having established his patriotic bona fides, Hodges then detailed the local board's abuse of black registrants.[47]

Also operating within the system were the people of both races who simply begged the authorities for mercy. Unsure as to which of the powers that be were in charge of the draft, many southerners wrote to governors to plead for leniency. A letter from a Tennessee man is typical: "I am up against the greatest trouble of my life, and I appeal to you for help." [48]

The region's poorest, most illiterate, and most politically powerless people could not effectively agitate for better treatment within the system, nor would they have cherished much hope that their pleas would be heard. Therefore poor whites and blacks took up the classic weapons of the weak: evasion, prevarication, and foot dragging. While both races dodged the draft, it was southern black men's primary strategy of resistance.

When the army finally called up black conscripts in spring 1918, many could not be located. According to military regulations during World War I, men who had been drafted and failed to show up for induction were deserters, subject to military discipline. By the spring of 1918, the provost marshal general's office had compiled alarming statistics on the high rate of such desertion among blacks. Provost Marshal General Crowder sent telegrams to the governors of the southern states asking why the black desertion rate was so high. Several governors defended their black constituents, explaining that black men were not lacking in patriotism—indeed, were eager to serve—but were ignorant, illiterate, and migratory, drifting from place to place looking for work. Some southern communities made special efforts to encourage black "deserters" to come in for induction. In other communities, draft boards and local sheriffs neglected to inform blacks of their induction and then arrested them for "desertion" so that they could collect the fifty-dollar reward promised by the provost marshal general. Whether paternalistic or predatory, however, southern authorities from the governor's office down to the county sheriff attributed the high black desertion rate to ignorance and shiftlessness. Both southern and federal authorities denied the possibility that black deserters were acting in a political fashion, choosing not to serve a country that did not respect their rights.[49]

Few records from the period indicate the political sentiments of illiterate, migratory black southern farm workers, and what traces of their thinking do exist are usually filtered through documents prepared by members of the middle class, whether black or white. Most black bourgeois leaders throughout the nation saw the war as a chance for racial advancement; they hoped that blacks' service in the military would bring them first-class citizenship. But we should not assume that when W. E. B. Du Bois issued his famous call for blacks to "close ranks" with whites for the duration, he spoke for the entire race, let alone for members of the black working class in the South. As Theodore Kornweibel Jr. and Steven Reich have shown, some black southerners shared rural whites' beliefs about the class nature of the war, while many resented being asked to support a war for freedom and democracy when both were denied to them. Southern whites understood the contradiction, and it made them afraid. During the war southern whites repeatedly asked the Bureau of Investigation to check into rumors that blacks were planning a race war. They saw signs of revolution in black workers' demands for higher wages, the discontent of house servants, and the growing swell of black migration out of the region. Whites publicly attributed all of this variously to German saboteurs, the National Association for the Advancement of Colored People (NAACP), and black northern newspapers such as the *Chicago Defender,* which provided front-page coverage of lynchings. But the paranoid tone of white southerners' letters to the bureau does not obscure the occasional note of truth, as when southern whites reported that blacks said they had no country. Southern and federal political leaders who refused to see resistance in black draft evasion may have been whistling past the graveyard of the fiction that black southerners accepted Jim Crow. Black southern working-class men's high rates of desertion can be seen as an appropriate strategy of protest for those with no political rights and no expectation of protection from the surrounding white community.[50]

Although southern rural whites, like their black neighbors, used evasion as a method of resistance, they had additional options unavailable to blacks and could often draw on community support. In Dothan, Alabama, where the draft board was particularly corrupt and registrants said that they would rather go to federal prison than to France, Stokely McCardel slashed the board chairman across the face with a knife. When accused of conspiracy to resist the draft law, he said, "D—— the Provost Marshal, and his ruling too," and was carried off to the army. McCardel's departure from Dothan resembled a triumph: Local men came to the train to see him off, gave him gifts of money, and "complimented and congratulated him on beating up a member of the Local Board." Southern draft boards, on the front line of an unpopular policy, bore the brunt of public hostility. An Arkansas farmer wrote his draft board from Camp Beauregard that men with the same family situation as his were "getting loose all the time . . . they . . . are well off to the men own farms and had plenty. I hope to see you all some day and you all are going to suffer for it too . . . you could have turn me loose as well as you did some of them big men around there," signed "your enemy." In Sabine Parish, Louisiana, the board reported that they had "received a letter threatening our Chairman with Death," and the St. Landry, Louisiana, board complained, "we . . . are becoming more or less outcaste and are ostracized by numbers of people."[51]

In north Georgia, the home ground for Tom Watson's draft protests, political draft resistance and desertion converged; local men resisting the draft received help from their communities, sometimes including the very officials charged with administering conscription. In August 1918 the adjutant general of Georgia wrote to the provost marshal general on behalf of the governor, asking that all three members of the local board of Liberty County be removed from office after they refused to subscribe for Liberty Loans. An investigator sent to the county filed reports describing it as a "county of slackers." The local newspaper editor told the agent that "all the county officers here are opposed to the war and have been opposed to the war all along." The chair of the Liberty Loan committee stated, "The people here fought the draft law, they had meetings and raised a fund to employ Thomas E. Watson to resist the draft law." The agent reported, "These men are, in effect, using a deadly peace argument in that county. They are thinking peace and the men sent out from that county . . . will be thinking peace when they leave." While the sheriff and other board members sympathized with draft dodgers in Liberty County, the adjutant general of Georgia reported to Crowder that opposition to the draft in Union County amounted "to almost armed resistance." A deserter in Union County shot a federal marshal, and the federal government charged his entire family with the murder. The adjutant general, charging that the Union County sheriff was in collusion with the deserters, appealed for federal troops to capture a band of men, estimated at between fifty and seventy-five, reportedly hiding out on the mountain. He suggested that rounding them up would require two companies of 250 men each. In August federal authorities mounted the abortive raid into Cherokee County described above, only to have it sabotaged at the Etowah bridge. In fall 1918 a federal agent reported to Crowder that Georgia had "discordant elements, such as political influence, personal-liberty-lovers, and spiritual devotees and malingerers. All of these classes are outlaws, and should be brought to justice." He added, "In North Georgia in the mountains there exists a certain rebellious element who are not easily handled or controlled by law, probably bloodshed would be the result of an enforcement of the law."[52]

Although there is no effective way to quantify dissent in the South, federal statistics on prosecutions initiated July 1917–June 1918 under the Selective Draft Act provide interesting information. Federal authorities' decision to prosecute depended on the politics of the situation and, one suspects, on the energy and enthusiasm of the United States attorneys on the scene. In Georgia men were prosecuted under the draft laws at a rate of .146 per thousand; in Mississippi the rate was .079; and in North Carolina, .073. Georgia's rate is much higher than the rate prevailing in Iowa (.054) or Indiana (.044), although less than that in New York (.256).[53]

By summer 1918, local authorities in the South reported bands of white men hiding out in the region's mountains, forests, and swamps. Among those groups were men who had failed to register for the draft, men who had refused to show up for induction, and those AWOL from army camps, all deserters under Selective Service regulations. In many places local authorities proved unable or unwilling to arrest deserters, and governors called for federal troops. The federal government sent troops to Mississippi and Tennessee as well as Georgia, while state National Guard troops raided resisters in Arkansas. In addition, resistance flared up in rural areas throughout the region, as reflected in small-town newspapers. A sheriff's raid on a family in Carroll County, Tennessee, is typical: When the sheriff came to pick up Dock Whittaker, his family fought. At the end of the fracas, Whittaker was in custody, his sister and father had been arrested for harboring him, his brother (who had fought in his behalf) was dead, and the county sheriff had been seriously wounded.[54]

While the groundswell of draft resistance faded out as the war ended in November, the controversies of the war years continued in postwar politics. Southern politicians whose opposition to the war and to conscription had cost them reelection in 1918 (an election fought under laws restricting free speech) made triumphant comebacks two years later. Among them was Tom Watson, who in 1920 crowned his long and contentious career by winning a Senate seat with a campaign that featured vituperative attacks on the Wilson administration's war mobilization policies.[55]

In his 1918 report on conscription, Provost Marshal General Crowder overstates Americans' compliance with the draft and trivializes the resistance by casting it in the stereotypes of popular magazine fiction of the period. His description includes an anecdote (complete with pseudodialect) in which a black woman turns in her daughter's slacker husband and an account of resistance in North Carolina that features stalwart but ignorant and suspicious mountaineers, "who could not at first comprehend the purpose of the draft," brought to patriotism by a federal agent. Evidence from Crowder's own bureaucratic records indicates the contrary: North Carolina mountaineers, like rural southerners across the region, understood very well the purposes of the draft and defied them. Because they did not express their protest in the language of the Left or even (often) in any discourse at all, it has been obscured. But the desire to be left alone is a principle too, one shared widely by Americans of all political affiliations, as is the belief that the ends of the state do not necessarily supersede the needs of individuals or families. Willing to defend their country, many rural southerners of both races were not willing to die in foreign fields for principles of international law or geopolitical strategy extraneous to their own lives.[56]

The question with which I began remains unanswered: How widespread was public support for Mr. Wilson's war? Like most good historical questions, it may ultimately be unanswerable, given the nature of the documentary record. But sufficient evidence exists to suggest that the public pageant of patriotism staged by Wilson's agents of mobilization did not express the sentiments of a sizable portion of the southern rural population. These rural resisters must be added to the list of other dissenters that already includes many immigrants, German Americans, leftists, and pacifists. As the list grows, the concept of overwhelming public support for the war becomes less and less tenable, leaving us to consider new questions: Did support for the war follow class lines in other regions, as in the South? If so, why? Ultimately, these questions boil down to one simple (if colloquial) query: Whose war was this, anyway?

Notes

Research for this paper was funded by two grants from the National Endowment for the Humanities, a summer stipend, and a year-long Grant for College Teachers; travel grants from the American Philosophical Society and from the Pennsylvania State System of Higher Education Faculty Development Fund; and a sabbatical from Bloomsburg University of Pennsylvania. I wish to thank K. Walter Hickel; Pete Daniel; Crandall Shifflett; Hal Barron; Kriste Lindenmeyer; Jack Kirby; Paul Freedman; Mary Neth; Kay Mansfield; James C. Scott; Tony Allen; Leah Potter; Glenda Gilmore and her graduate students in American studies and history at Yale University; my colleagues at the Yale Agrarian Studies Program, 1999–2000, especially Cindy Hahamovitch and Scott Nelson; Mitch Yockelson at the National Archives in Washington, D.C.; and the staff at: Sterling Memorial Library at Yale; the Shelby County Archives in Memphis, Tennessee; the Tennessee State Library and Archives in Nashville; the Mississippi Department of Archives and History; the Library of Congress Manuscript Division; and the National Archives at College Park, Maryland, and at East Point, Georgia. Readers may contact Keith at keith@bloomu.edu.

1. Howell Jackson, report, June 15–18, 1918, Old German File 17,761, roll 349, Records of the Federal Bureau of Investigation, RG 65 (National Archives, College Park, Md.).

2. Unlike the transcripts of resistance described by James C. Scott, these are not encoded in culture but are written documents, often compiled by agencies of the state. James C. Scott, *Domination and the Arts of Resistance: Hidden Transcripts* (New Haven, 1990).

3. For books indicative of the grip the Great War maintains on the British imagination, see Niall Ferguson, *The Pity of War: Explaining World War I* (London, 1998); John Keegan, *The First World War* (London, 1998); and Pat Barker, *Regeneration Trilogy* (London, 1996). For United States home front history, see David Kennedy, *Over Here: The First World War and American Society* (New York, 1980); Ronald Schaffer, *America in the Great War: The Rise of the War Welfare State* (New York, 1991); and Ellis W. Hawley, *The Great War and the Search for a Modern Order* (New York, 1979). For top-down views of Wilson administration policies, see Arthur S. Link, *Woodrow Wilson and the Progressive Era, 1910–1917* (New York, 1954); Robert H. Ferrell, *Woodrow Wilson and World War I, 1917–1921* (New York, 1985); and Kendrick A. Clements, *The Presidency of Woodrow Wilson* (Lawrence, 1992). On surveillance and civil liberties, see Joan M. Jensen, *The Price of Vigilance* (Chicago, 1968); Theodore Kornweibel Jr., *"Seeing Red": Federal Campaigns against Black Militancy, 1919–1925* (Bloomington, 1998);

H. C. Peterson and Gilbert C. Fite, *Opponents of War, 1917–1918* (Madison, 1957); Roy Talbert Jr., *Negative Intelligence: The Army and the American Left, 1917–1941* (Jackson, 1991); and Athan G. Theoharis and John Stuart Cox, *The Boss: J. Edgar Hoover and the Great American Inquisition* (Philadelphia, 1988).

4. If one book on the World War I draft is all we have, it is nice to have a book this good, and I build on it in this essay. See John Whiteclay Chambers II, *To Raise an Army: The Draft Comes to Modern America* (New York, 1987), 211–13.

5. On the impact of the war on the Left, see Talbert, *Negative Intelligence;* Jensen, *Price of Vigilance;* Melvyn Dubofsky, *We Shall Be All: A History of the Industrial Workers of the World* (Chicago, 1969); Frances H. Early, *A World without War: How U.S. Feminists and Pacifists Resisted World War I* (Syracuse, 1997); David Williams, "The Bureau of Investigation and Its Critics, 1919–1921: The Origins of Federal Political Surveillance," *Journal of American History,* 68 (Dec. 1981), 560–79; and Nick Salvatore, *Eugene V. Debs: Citizen and Socialist* (Urbana, 1982). For the suggestion that repression was rational because it reduced opposition to the war, see Schaffer, *America in the Great War,* 30.

6. In this paper, I have defined rural as nonurban, outside the region's cities. On the martial South, see John Shelton Reed, *One South: An Ethnic Approach to Regional Culture* (Baton Rouge, 1982), 139–53; Bertram Wyatt-Brown, *Southern Honor: Ethics and Behavior in the Old South* (New York, 1982); W. J. Cash, *The Mind of the South* (New York, 1941); Jack Temple Kirby, *Media-Made Dixie: The South in the American Imagination* (Baton Rouge, 1978); and Paul Gaston, *The New South Creed: A Study in Southern Mythmaking* (New York, 1970). Chambers attributes sporadic resistance to sharecroppers, mountaineers, and western Indians, whose actions "posed little threat to the enforcement or legitimacy of Selective Service." See Chambers, *To Raise an Army,* 212. For a blunter account that finds among the participants in the green corn rebellion "much ignorance, religious superstition, and discontent," see Peterson and Fite, *Opponents of War,* 40.

7. On the preparedness movement and its critics, see John Patrick Finnegan, *Against the Specter of a Dragon: The Campaign for American Military Preparedness, 1914–1917* (Westport, 1974); Chambers, *To Raise an Army,* 73–177; and Michael Pearlman, *To Make Democracy Safe for America: Patricians and Preparedness in the Progressive Era* (Urbana, 1984).

8. Finnegan, *Against the Specter of a Dragon;* Chambers, *To Raise an Army,* 103–77; Alex Mathews Arnett, *Claude Kitchin and the Wilson War Policies* (Boston, 1937), 160–84; Seward W. Livermore, *Woodrow Wilson and the War Congress, 1916–1918* (Seattle, 1966), 6.

9. On the "widespread agrarian fear of international complications, militarism, and monopoly," see Dewey Grantham, *Southern Progressivism: The Reconciliation of Progress and Tradition* (Knoxville, 1983), 383–87. I identify correspondents here as rural based on their addresses and as white on the basis of their lack of reference to their own race, as well as their familiarity with politics. Typically, black rural southerners writing white authority figures began their letters by identifying themselves by race and used deferential, careful, and nonpolitical language. Hugh A. White to Claude Kitchin, Dec. 11, 1915, file 72, box 6, Claude Kitchin Papers (Southern Historical

Collection, University of North Carolina, Chapel Hill); W. T. Hefley to Kitchin, Jan. 7, 1916, file 87, box 7, ibid. Not all of Kitchin's mail supported antipreparedness. See, for example, "Resolutions Adopted by the North Carolina Cotton Seed Crushers' Association, at Norfolk, Va.," Dec. 10, 1915, file 72, box 6, ibid.; and A. C. House to Kitchin, Feb. 3, 1916, file 103, box 8, ibid.

10. Despite the president's insistence on the "volunteer" aspect of the continental army, the members of the army's General Staff admitted in congressional hearings that they considered it a step toward universal military training. See Chambers, *To Raise an Army*, 103–24.

11. Arnett, *Claude Kitchin*, 227–36; Chambers, *To Raise an Army*, 153–77.

12. Livermore, *Woodrow Wilson and the War Congress*, 16–24; William F. Holmes, *The White Chief: James Kimble Vardaman* (Baton Rouge, 1970), 306–25. Rep. J. Thomas Heflin of Alabama, a strong supporter of conscription, argued that the draft would protect white womanhood. See *Congressional Record*, 65 Cong., 1 sess., April 26, 1917, pp. 1227–28. For the use of Civil War conscription as an example on both sides of the House debate over the 1917 draft, see ibid., April 25 and 26, pp. 959, 967, 1018, 1051, 1111, 1171–72. V. E. Sigman [signature not clear] to Kitchin, April 7, 1917, file 300, box 20, Kitchin Papers.

13. J. R. Moore to Rep. Edwin Yates Webb, file 249, box 13, Edwin Yates Webb Papers (Southern Historical Collection); *Congressional Record*, 65 Cong., 1 sess., April 25, 1917, p. 1094; Chambers, *To Raise an Army*, 162–64; *Congressional Record*, 65 Cong., 1 sess., April 26, 1917, p. 1234; H. Q. Alexander to senators F. M. Simmons and L. S. Overman and congressmen Webb, Kitchin, and others from North Carolina, file 300, box 20, Kitchin Papers.

14. Chambers, *To Raise an Army*, 157–59, 165–66, 176–77. My statement that southern politicians believed farmers had received a blanket deferment is also based on the John Sharp Williams Papers (Manuscript Division, Library of Congress, Washington, D.C.) and the Webb Papers.

15. John Sharp Williams to C. S. Butterfield, April 25, 1917, box 79, John Sharp Williams Papers (Manuscript Division, Library of Congress, Washington, D.C.); Thad A. Cox to Thomas Rye, Dec. 21, 1917, file 6, box 14, Governor Thomas Rye Papers (Tennessee State Library and Archives, Nashville, Tenn.); F. Fred Johnson to Rye, May 31, 1917, ibid.

16. Eugene Cunningham Branson to George Lanier, Jan. 17, 1918, file 92, box 2, Eugene Cunningham Branson Papers (Southern Historical Collection).

17. W. M. Black to Webb, April 17, 1917, file 251, box 13, Webb Papers; Chas Gibson to Webb, June 18, 1918, file 261, ibid.

18. Chambers, *To Raise an Army*, 180–83. The provost marshal general instructed governors to supply names for district boards, to be composed of one doctor, one lawyer, and one representative each of agriculture, industry, and labor. See Enoch Crowder to all governors, June 18, 1917, file "General Letters May 9, 1917 to [blank]," box 315, Records of the Selective Service System (World War I), RG 163 (National Archives, Washington, D.C.); Local Draft Board Experience Files, ibid. Provost Marshal General Crowder informed Mississippi governor Theodore Bilbo: "Members of boards are

drafted for the service upon which they are engaged." Crowder to Theodore Bilbo, Aug. 16, 1917, file 12, box 1321, Theodore G. Bilbo Papers (Mississippi Department of Archives and History, Jackson).

19. Chambers, *To Raise an Army*, 191; *Second Report of the Provost Marshal General to the Secretary of War, On the Operations of the Selective Service System to December 20, 1918* (Washington, 1919), 108–16; Keegan, *First World War*, 402.

20. Of the 4,883,213 married men registered for the draft between June 5, 1917, and September 11, 1918, only 3,619,466 received dependency deferments. Even after calculating in deferments given for other reasons, 488,537 married men remained eligible for service. *Second Report of the Provost Marshal General*, 108–16, esp. 116. Sen. Henry F. Hollis to Joseph Tumulty, Aug. 25, 1917, file 3735a, series 4, Woodrow Wilson Papers (microfilm, 540 reels, Library of Congress, 1973), reel 353.

21. In 1917 the South's population was at least 75% rural. The percentage rural in 1910 was: Alabama, 82.7; Arkansas, 87.1; Georgia, 79.4; Florida, 70.9; Louisiana, 70.0; Mississippi, 88.5; North Carolina, 85.6; South Carolina, 85.2; Tennessee, 79.8; Texas, 75.9; and Virginia, 76.9. See U.S. Department of Commerce, Bureau of the Census, *Thirteenth Census of the United States: 1910* (11 vols., Washington, 1913), II, 20, 92, 338, 300, 760, 1024, III, 268, 638, 720, 772, 916. In 1913 southern farm laborers could expect to earn about $20 per month. George Brown Tindall, *The Emergence of the New South, 1913–1945* (Baton Rouge, 1964), 33–37, 111, 320; Gavin Wright, *Old South, New South: Revolutions in the Southern Economy since the Civil War* (New York, 1986), 66, 202; *Second Report of the Provost Marshal General*, 192–93.

22. Rep. Frank Clark to Woodrow Wilson, Sept. 10, 1917, file 3735, series 4, Wilson Papers, reel 353; letter from community group, Faxon, Benton County, Tennessee, n.d., filed with correspondence from 1917, file 2, box 15, Rye Papers. In 1920, only 47.5% of the farmers in the South owned their land: 60% of white farmers and 22.4% of black farmers. Although most black farmers were either sharecroppers or renters, most sharecroppers were white. See Wright, *Old South, New South*, 99–123. On hill-country farmers, see Stephen Hahn, *The Roots of Populism: Yeoman Farmers and the Transformation of the Georgia Upcountry, 1850–1890* (New York, 1983); Jeanette Keith, *Country People in the New South: Tennessee's Upper Cumberland* (Chapel Hill, 1995); and Paul Salstrom, *Appalachia's Path of Dependency: Rethinking a Region's Economic History, 1730–1940* (Lexington, Ky., 1994). In 1918 the Selective Service began requiring that conscripts fill out questionnaires and provide financial statements, including information on income, property, and savings. Illiterate or semiliterate southern farmers of both races would have found it impossible to fill out the complicated forms; nor would most have had documentation of their annual income. See file: "Rules and Regulations, PMG," section 268, pp. 126–214, box 317, Selective Service System Records (Washington, D.C.).

23. On the quota system, see Chambers, *To Raise an Army*, 185, 222–26. Tennessee did have one black National Guard unit, Separate Company G, formed in 1899. See Rye to Commanding General [name unclear] 30th Division, Camp Sevier, Greenville, S.C., Nov. 17, 1917, file 3, box 14, Rye Papers.

24. Local Draft Board Experience Files, Selective Service System Records (Washington, D.C.). I pulled the boxes of county-level reports filed for each southern state

and went through all draft board reports that were not from large cities. I may have understated the percentage of communities that encouraged men to avoid the draft. I have counted as "pro-exemption" only communities where boards' answers indicated that many exemptions had been requested with the support of the community.

25. Quotations throughout are given for illustration; the conclusions drawn in the text are based upon the totality of the reports: reports from Hawkins County, Tenn., box 45, Local Draft Board Experience Files, Selective Service System Records (Washington, D.C.); Fentress County, Tenn., ibid.; Washington County, Tenn., ibid.; Gordon County, Ga., box 7, ibid.; Saluda County, S.C., box 43, ibid.; Princess Anne County, Va., box 50, ibid.; Southampton County, Va., ibid.; Gregg County, Tex., box 47, ibid.; Shelby County, Tex., ibid.; Davie County, N.C., box 34, ibid.; Transylvania County, N.C., box 35, ibid.; Wilkes County, N.C., ibid. For quoted passages, see reports from Saluda County, S.C., box 43, ibid.; Princess Anne County, Va., box 50, ibid.; Gregg County, Tex., box 47, ibid.; and Shelby County, Tex., ibid.

26. "Part IV, Classification Rules and Principles, Regulations (1st copy)," box 317, ibid.; *Second Report of the Provost Marshal General,* 108–13; Frederic C. Wardevard to Major Clark, Report of Agent of Department of Justice on the Local Board for Crittenden County, Ark., Dec. 11, 1918, including report of James Maynard, Nov. 15, 1918, on William Richards, file Ark. 17–112, box 86, States File, Selective Service System Records (Washington, D.C.). On the problems in East Tennessee, see file Tenn. 17–28, box 273, ibid., esp. R. L. Deal, report, [1918?]. H. E. Hildebrand to Crowder, Feb. 25, 1918, box 315, ibid.; Local Draft Board report, Milam County, Tex., box 46, ibid. See also a lengthy file documenting the political motivations of the draft board of Turner County, Ga., in file Ga. 17–184, box 110, ibid.

27. These percentages reflect married men deferred for all reasons, including occupation. *Second Report of the Provost Marshal General,* appendix, 401.

28. Monroe County, Tenn., box 45, Local Draft Board Experience Files, Records of the Selective Service System (World War I), RG 163 (National Archives, College Park, Md.); Polk County, Tenn., ibid.; Rhea County, Tenn., ibid.; Hardeman County, Tenn., ibid.; Gibson County, Tenn., ibid.; Walker County, Ala., box 1, ibid.; Dallas County, Ala., ibid.; Perry County, Ala., ibid.; Craighead County, Ala., ibid.; Cherokee County, Ga., box 6, ibid.; Screven County, Ga., box 8, ibid.; Columbia County, Fla., box 6, ibid.; Union County, S.C., box 48, ibid.; Caldwell County, Tex., box 46, ibid.

29. Wilkes County, N.C., box 35, Local Draft Board Experience Files, ibid.; Appomattox County, Va., box 50, ibid.; Franklin County, Tenn., box 45, ibid.; Sequatchie County, Tenn., ibid.; Monroe County, Tenn., ibid.; Polk County, Tenn., ibid.; Rhea County, Tenn., ibid.; Cherokee County, Ala., box 1, ibid.; Crenshaw County, Ala., ibid.; Dallas County, Ala., ibid. On the interplay of race and gender in the plantation belt, see Gerald E. Shenk, "Race, Manhood, and Manpower: Mobilizing Rural Georgia for World War I," *Georgia Historical Quarterly* 81 (Fall 1997), 622–62.

30. For examples, see Geneva County, Ala., box 1, Local Draft Board Experience Files, Selective Service System Records (Washington, D.C.); McIntosh County, Ala., ibid.; Cherokee County, Ala., ibid.; Hawkins County, Tenn., box 45, ibid.; Sequatchie County, Tenn., ibid.; Franklin County, Tenn., ibid.; Suwannee County, Fla., box 6, ibid.;

and Lee County, Tex., box 46, ibid. On charges against the draft board of Clay County, Ark., see O. T. Ward to Crowder, May 30, 1918, file Ark. 17–53, box 86, States File, ibid.; Petition from "farmers and citizens of Clay County, Ark." to Crowder, received Sept. 3, 1918, file Ark. 17–110, box 86, States File, ibid.; L. Hunter to Lloyd England, report, Oct. 18, 1918, ibid.; Local Draft Board Experience Files, box 50, ibid.; and Complaint from Local Board of Frederick County, file Va., 17–106, box 292, States File, ibid.

31. Arthur E. Barbeau and Florette Henri, *The Unknown Soldiers: Black American Troops in World War I* (Philadelphia, 1974), 36.

32. Ibid., 36–49; William L. McCalley to Joel B. Mallett, file Ga. 17–15, box 109, States File, Selective Service System Records (Washington, D.C.); W. S. Price to Sen. Hoke Smith, May 19, 1919, ibid.; Montgomery County, Ala., box 1, Local Draft Board Experience Files, ibid.; Monroe County, Ala., ibid.; Schley County, Ga., box 7, ibid.; Oconee County, Ga., ibid.; Dillon County, S.C., box 43, ibid.

33. Clifton Gray to Adjutant General, Arkansas, report, Sept. 11, 1918, file Ark. 17–81, box 86, States File, ibid.; Milton Wayman Guy to Emmett Scott, July 11, 1918, ibid.

34. File Tex. 17–174, box 280, States File, ibid. R. L. Boatrite, "In Re: Investigation Local Board Dothan, Ala.," July 10, 1918, file Ala. 17–106, box 77, ibid. Similar proprietary attitudes on the part of planters in Georgia are documented in Shenk, "Race, Manhood, and Manpower."

35. Montgomery County, Ala., box 1, Local Draft Board Experience Files, Selective Service System Records (Washington, D.C.); Craighead County, Ark., box 2, ibid.

36. Barbeau and Henri, *Unknown Soldiers,* 21–32, 70–163.

37. Jackson County, Fla., box 6, Local Draft Board Experience Files, Selective Service Records (Washington, D.C.). Other Florida counties reported problems over this issue. See Santa Rosa County, ibid.; Wakulla County, ibid.; Baker County, ibid.; DeSoto County, ibid.; Lake County, ibid.; Manatee County, ibid.; and Suwannee County, ibid. By 1918 conscription policy was reformed in that "white and colored quotas" were assigned to each community. See Chambers, *To Raise an Army,* 224–25. See Crowder to Bilbo, quoted in "Governor (Bilbo) To the District Board for the Northern District of Mississippi," Sept. 10, 1917, file 17, box 1322, Bilbo Papers. Bilbo to Crowder, Sept. 12, 1917, file 18, ibid.; Bilbo to District Boards, Sept. 13, 1917, ibid.

38. Scott, *Domination and the Arts of Resistance,* 198.

39. Robert Wilson, "The Farmers' and Laborers' Protective Association of America, 1915–1916" (M.A. thesis, Baylor University, 1974), iv–vii, 12, 13–75. For evidence that an officer of the Farmers' and Laborers' Protective Association was a government spy, see William Odell to R. L. Barnes, July 3, 1917, reproduced in R. L. Barnes, "In Re: Farmers and Laborers Protective Assoc.," July 7, 1917, Old German File 1889, roll 289, FBI Records. For the United States attorney's statement, see Odell to Attorney General, May 17, 1917, reproduced, ibid.

40. Wilson, "Farmers' and Laborers' Protective Association," 47–75; Barnes, "In Re: Farmers and Laborers Protective Assoc."

41. Schaffer, *America in the Great War,* 13–15.

42. Nancy MacLean, "The Leo Frank Case Reconsidered: Gender and Sexual Politics in the Making of Reactionary Populism," *Journal of American History,* 78 (Dec.

1991), 917–48; C. Vann Woodward, *Tom Watson, Agrarian Rebel* (1938; New York, 1955), 360–410.

43. *Jeffersonian,* July 19, 1917. Although Watson blamed the war on Wall Street, he dropped almost all of his anti-Semitism for the duration of his antidraft crusade.

44. Ibid.; "In Re: Tom Watson," Old German File 17,761, roll 349, FBI Records.

45. "In Re: Tom Watson"; Woodward, *Tom Watson,* 360–410.

46. Woodward, *Tom Watson,* 456–61; *Jeffersonian,* Aug. 2, 1917. Max Eastman, Amos Pinchot, and John Reed, editors of the *Masses,* wrote to President Wilson about the suppression of small papers. The *Jeffersonian* held first place on their list of the disappeared. Max Eastman et al. to Wilson, July 12, 1917, file 4122, series 4, Woodrow Wilson Papers, reel 362.

47. Charles C. Hodges to Scott, July 17, 1918, file Tenn. 17–116, box 273, States File, Selective Service System Records (Washington, D.C.).

48. Ernest W. Morelock to Rye, Sept. 5, 1917, folder 3, box 16, Rye Papers.

49. Governor Brough to Crowder, Nov. 7, 1918, file Ark. 17–109, box 86, States File, Selective Service System Records (Washington, D.C.); Crowder to Rye, telegram, Nov. 4, 1918, file Tenn. 17–149, box 273, ibid. On delinquents, see Adjutant General of Alabama to the Provost Marshal General, report, July 1, 1918, file Ala. 17–33, box 77, ibid.; report from Phillips County, Ark., to the War Department, Aug. 23, 1918, file Ark. 17–62, box 86, ibid. On state and local authorities' predatory behavior toward deserters, see Commanding General 31st Division Camp Wheeler, Ga., to Adjutant General, Army, "Alleged Deserters," report, Nov. 5, 1917, file Ga. 17–14, box 109, ibid.; and W. S. Price to Smith, May 19, 1918, file Ga. 17–15, box 175, ibid. On Mississippi's delinquent rate, see Office of Judge Advocate General to the Provost Marshal General, July 8, 1918, file Miss. 17–108, box 175, ibid.

50. For a depiction of black Americans' service in World War I as patriotic, whole-hearted, and based on the belief that such service would win citizenship rights, see Barbeau and Henri, *Unknown Soldiers.* For revisionist views, see Mark Ellis, "'Closing Ranks' and 'Seeking Honors': W. E. B. Du Bois in World War I," *Journal of American History,* 79 (June 1992), 96–124; Theodore Kornweibel Jr., "Apathy and Dissent: Black America's Negative Responses to World War I," *South Atlantic Quarterly,* 80 (Summer 1981), 322–38; and Steven A. Reich, "Soldiers of Democracy: Black Texans and the Fight for Citizenship, 1917–1921," *Journal of American History,* 32 (March 1996), 1478–1504. On white reactions to black discontent, see Kornweibel, *"Seeing Red";* and Bureau of Investigation report, Old German File 22310, FBI Records. Theodore Kornweibel Jr., ed., *Federal Surveillance of Afro-Americans (1917–1925): World War I, the Red Scare, and the Garvey Movement* (microfilm, 25 reels, University Publications of America, 1985), reel 9.

51. Files Ala. 17–11, 17–65, and 17–108, box 77, States File, Selective Service System Records (Washington, D.C.); Walter Tully to J. L. Green, n.d., file Ark. 17–13, box 86, ibid.; Sabine County, La., Local Draft Board Experience Files, Louisiana, box 17, ibid.; St. Landry County, La., box 18, ibid.

52. Report on Liberty County, Ga., file Ga. 17–103, box 109, States File, ibid.; Report on Union County, Ga., file Ga. 17–179, box 109, ibid. James Ernest Gilreath is listed as

a willful deserter charged with murder in Union County in Final Lists Delinquents and Deserters, Union County, Provost Marshal General Office forms 4003, Georgia, box 17, Records of the Selective Service System (World War I), RG 163 (National Archives, Southeast Division, East Point, Ga.). See also *United States v. Frank Crowley alias Frank Crawley,* Union County, Oct. 1919, case no. 3043, Northern Division of the North District of Georgia, District Court of the United States, ibid.; "Indictment against Rosa Crowley alias Rosa Crawley," March 1919, *United States v. Rosa Crowley alias Rosa Crawley,* file 3393, case no. 3041, ibid.; and *United States v. Frank Crowley alias Frank Crawley,* Nov. 1919, file 3390, case no. 2918, ibid. Joel B. Mallet to Provost Marshal General, report, Oct. 16, 1918, file Ga. 17–167, box 110, States File, Selective Service System Records (Washington, D.C.); W. S. Nash to Crowder, Oct. 8, 1918, Selective Service Report, State of Georgia, ibid.; Tindall, *Emergence of the New South,* 51.

53. Computed from *Report of the Attorney General, 1918* (Washington, 1918), 157–237. (Available at the National Archives, College Park, Md.)

54. Gov. Thomas Rye of Tennessee informed Crowder that he was unable to get local sheriffs to arrest deserters: Rye to Crowder, April 12, 1918, file Tenn. 17–40, box 273, States File, Selective Service System Records (Washington, D.C.). *Carroll County Democrat,* April 12, 1918; *Southern Sentinel* (Tippah County, Miss.), May 2, July 11, 1918; *Alexandria* [Tennessee] *Times,* July 3, 1918; file Tenn. 17–108, box 272, States File, Selective Service System Records (Washington, D.C.). In Arkansas, the draft resisters were Jehovah's Witnesses, according to James F. Willis, "The Cleburne County Draft War," *Arkansas Historical Quarterly,* 26 (Spring 1967), 24–39. See also file Tex. 17–48–4, box 279, States File, Selective Service System Records (Washington, D.C.); file Tex. 17–133, box 280, ibid.

55. Most desertion and sedition cases in the federal court records at the National Archives, Southeast Division, East Point, Georgia, were marked "Nolle Pros." after the armistice. For a discussion that attributes Watson's victory to the popularity he gained as a result of the Frank case, see MacLean, "Leo Frank," 946. But the Frank case was five-year-old news in 1920, while the events of the war years were fresh in the memory of Georgia voters, and Watson campaigned on the war: see *Columbia Sentinel,* Feb. 25, 1920. Woodward, *Tom Watson,* 400–420. Sen. Thomas Hardwick of Georgia, an anti-intervention, anticonscription southern Democrat, was crushingly defeated in 1918 but made a triumphant return by winning the governorship of Georgia in 1920. For the argument that Hardwick's fate shows the formerly isolationist South becoming interventionist as a result of the war, see Anthony Gaughan, "Woodrow Wilson and the Rise of Militant Interventionism in the South," *Journal of Southern History,* 65 (Nov. 1999), 771–808.

56. *Second Report of the Provost Marshal General,* 108–16, 210–12. Residents of North Carolina charged that Crowder's report misrepresented conditions there. The North Carolina legislature passed a resolution in protest, and Crowder apologized; see Crowder to Gov. T. W. Bickett, Feb. 23, 1919, file N.C. 17–153, box 222, States File, Selective Service System Records (Washington, D.C.); Memo from Local Board of Exemptions for Mitchell County to Crowder, Feb. 21, 1919, ibid.; and Resolution 33, H.R. 783, S.R. 660, North Carolina General Assembly, ratified Feb. 26, 1919, ibid.

"Fighting Whiskey and Immorality" at Auburn

The Politics of Southern Football, 1919–1927

Andrew Doyle

On a sunny Saturday afternoon in early November 1927, President Spright Dowell of Alabama Polytechnic Institute, today's Auburn University, walked up the gleaming white marble steps of the Alabama state capitol on his way to a special meeting of his school's board of trustees. The single item on the agenda was a motion to dismiss him from his job. During his seven-year tenure, Dowell had obtained accreditation, raised admission standards, and improved the professional qualifications of the faculty. He had created an administrative bureaucracy and introduced modern accounting, auditing, and purchasing procedures. Prior to his arrival, registration had been a two-week-long nightmare; now it was accomplished in two days. He energetically lobbied the notoriously parsimonious Alabama legislature for increased appropriations, and when sufficient funding was not forthcoming, he orchestrated a fundraising drive that collected over half a million dollars. These funds paid for the construction of nearly two dozen campus buildings and such vital infrastructural needs as a safe and reliable water supply. Yet this solid record was overshadowed by a raging public controversy sparked by the decline of the once-powerful Auburn football program. Dowell had deemphasized football from the beginning of his tenure, and the 1927 team was about to complete the first winless season in school history. To make matters worse, football at rival University of Alabama was thriving. Trustees and football boosters publicly criticized Dowell, and a delegation of students met with Governor Bibb Graves to report that the student body had voted overwhelmingly for his dismissal. The trustees responded by mounting a formal investigation, complete with public hearings. The flurry of charges and countercharges paralyzed the campus and dominated headlines for a month, and the trustees now held Dowell's fate in their hands.[1]

Although he likely knew that he had little chance to keep his job, Dowell remained publicly confident as he entered the showdown in Graves's office. In characteristically blunt fashion, he asserted that his achievements outweighed the puerile clamor of a football-crazed mob. He maintained a contemptuous, self-righteous attitude toward the students and alumni who sought his ouster. He regarded as absurd the notion that a winning football program could be the sine qua non of his tenure in office. He should have known better. Like numerous university presidents before and since, Spright Dowell learned that the vicissitudes of football can make or break a collegiate administration. The trustees' meeting was brief and to the point: Dowell was out, effective at the end of the academic year. He had dismissed his critics as an "irresponsible mass" possessed of a "mob spirit," but in the end, the trustees had sided with the mob.[2]

The Dowell controversy is partially explained as an episode in the long-running struggle between athletics and academics in American higher education. Dowell was resolutely hostile to big-time intercollegiate football, and he was determined that the athletic tail not wag the academic dog at Auburn. He considered the football program "a continuous problem" that threatened to "sidetrack ... the more serious work of the institution." He undertook a quixotic campaign to diminish "the unnatural and exaggerated position which [football] occupies in the eyes of the students and of the public." He suggested that intercollegiate sports were no more important than intramural athletic competition, intercollegiate debate teams, student orchestras, the dramatic club, glee club, or agricultural and engineering societies. Dowell seemed to think that if he lectured the campus community and public zealously enough about the dangers of big-time football, he could convince them that their priorities were misplaced. Colleges, he insisted, existed primarily to "train men of character for the business of life," and football "should not be allowed to sidetrack or eclipse the real purpose for which this institution exists." Yet his call for "sober and sane thinking" regarding football was drowned out by the howls of outrage over the downfall of the Auburn football program.[3]

A career administrator with a master's degree from Columbia University, Spright Dowell was typical in many ways of the southern business progressives of the 1920s who introduced "the gospel of efficiency" to southern governmental and business institutions. The reforms that he instituted at Auburn systematized and rationalized administrative procedures and brought the school into line with national standards in these areas. Yet he disagreed sharply with most progressive southerners over the issue of intercollegiate football. Following the lead of their northeastern counterparts, many southern business leaders, politicians, and academics saw football as a symbol of progress and modernity. The members of the northeastern elite who invented and popularized American football defined it as the perfect sport for a modern, rationalized, industrial capitalist society. Walter Camp, the Yale coach hailed as "The Father of American Football," Caspar Whitney, the sports editor of *Harpers' Weekly*,

Theodore Roosevelt, and many others claimed that football's set plays, hierarchical command structure, and on-field division of labor made it a model of precision, orderliness, and teamwork that replicated the form and function of the modern industrial corporation. Its violence taught the toughness and "virile masculinity" necessary for success in the Darwinian world of corporate capitalism and imperialist competition. In their view, football was the perfect vehicle for inculcating the traits necessary for success in a modern industrial society. The New South progressives who brought football to the South in the 1890s yearned to replicate the northern nexus of factories, cities, and railroads in the region. They embraced social and economic change and welcomed the integration of the South into the American cultural and economic mainstream. Football became identified with the progressive impulse that brought industrialization, urbanization, and a modern bourgeois society with consumerist values to the South.[4]

Progressivism was a big-tent political phenomenon, but the liberal and left variants of progressivism were weak in the South, even in the academic world. Given the general skewing of the southern political spectrum to the right, the power of socially conservative evangelicals, and the southern legacy of traditional conservatism, the term "progressive" can fairly describe those southerners who supported economic modernization and regional integration into the national mainstream. Yet the more conservative progressives were most likely to support football, while liberals and leftists were much more likely to question its value. E. L. Godkin, the editor of the *Nation,* economist Thorstein Veblen, University of Chicago President Robert Maynard Hutchins, the American Association of University Professors, and the Carnegie Foundation were among the steadily increasing number of individuals and groups who rejected the claim that football possessed social, moral, and educational utility. They asserted that it did not build character in young men and argued that it had a profoundly negative impact on academic institutions. By the 1920s, this view was relatively common among left-of-center academics and intellectuals. Few of them, however, resided south of the Mason-Dixon line. Thus, while many nonsouthern college presidents attempting to deemphasize football could count on support from leftists and liberals in their campus communities and among their state's opinion leaders, Spright Dowell could not.

Dowell also stood out among southern college presidents, most of whom strongly supported football. James Kirkland of Vanderbilt, the leading educational reformer in the South from the 1890s through the 1930s, initially believed strongly in the progressive social and educational mission of football. Although he began to deemphasize football at Vanderbilt in the late 1920s and early 1930s, he did so much less radically than Dowell. He also had virtually unassailable authority on his campus and absolute support from his trustees.

S. V. Sanford of Georgia, K. G. Matheson of Georgia Tech, John Tigert of the University of Florida, and John Futrall of the University of Arkansas were all progressive university presidents who actively supported football at their institutions. Closer to home, Dowell's rejection of football stood in stark contrast to his two immediate predecessors at Auburn, Charles C. Thach and William Leroy Broun.[5]

Dowell's primary foil, however, was George Denny, the president of the University of Alabama from 1912 until 1936. Denny regarded football as a public relations vehicle that could increase enrollment, gratify alumni, and create popular support for the university. When he took the helm at Alabama, the student body numbered 390, the annual state appropriation totaled less than $50,000, and a majority of Alabamians viewed the university with feelings that ranged from indifference to overt hostility. The Alabama football program was similarly moribund. When Denny retired in 1936, student enrollment had increased to nearly 5,000, and fourteen major classroom buildings and dormitories had been constructed. He created a graduate program, schools of business and home economics, an extension program that enrolled thousands of students throughout the state, and a summer program for teachers that enrolled over 2,000 students annually. The endowment rose from under $500,000 to over $4,500,000. Denny applied a similar drive to building his football program. Along with Georgia Tech, Alabama became one of the first southern teams to become a national power, winning six conference championships and four national championships between 1924 and 1934. Publicity generated by the football program attracted thousands of out-of-state students after the mid-1920s, many from the Northeast. Their tuition payments were a major reason why Alabama remained solvent during the Depression while Auburn was forced at times to pay faculty and staff in scrip. While his autocratic manner and penchant for spending money earmarked for faculty salaries on campus construction projects made him unpopular among his faculty, Denny faced remarkably little opposition to his support for football. A strong case can be made that Denny made a Faustian bargain by fostering rapid enrollment growth and expansion of the physical plant without a commensurate increase in the size or salary scale of the faculty. Clearly impressed with the university's growth and, perhaps, intoxicated by football, students, alumni, and politicians generally gave Denny high marks for his accomplishments and overlooked his shortcomings.[6]

Although each university president instituted a modern, rationalized administrative system, Denny used it to further the growth of his football program while Dowell used it to cripple his. Dowell's first step toward that goal was to wrest control of the football program from a small clique of coaches and alumni boosters. As was the case at virtually every other big-time football power, an alumni-dominated athletic association exercised preponderant control over the football program while existing as an independent fiefdom outside the control of university authorities. Denny co-opted and worked in partnership with the Alabama Athletic Association; Dowell declared war on Auburn's. Dowell marginalized the alumni's influence by creating an athletic department within the college's administrative structure, putting the coaches on the college payroll, and appointing an athletic director loyal to him rather than to the alumni. The new athletic policy shifted resources away from Auburn's "highly selective and competitive athletics" and instead encouraged widespread student participation in intramural sports. Intramural teams were given access to the lone campus football field, much to the consternation of coaches concerned about damage to the field and competition for practice time. Coaches were forced to teach several physical education courses, leaving them less time to spend with varsity athletes. When the Southern Conference banned freshman eligibility in 1922, only intense lobbying by coaches and athletic boosters induced Dowell to permit the formation of freshman teams at Auburn.[7]

Dowell also denied funding increases to the football program during an era when the cost of fielding a successful team was spiraling upward. He maintained pre-World War I levels of athletic funding, but he lavished funds on the campus YMCA. In a move that enraged athletic boosters, Dowell forced the Auburn athletic association to contribute $25,000 in five annual installments to the 1922 capital campaign. Athletic department funds were used to cover this pledge after the college assumed control of varsity athletic finances. The athletic department did not have sufficient funds in June 1926 to cover this contribution and was forced to borrow against future football gate receipts in order to do so. To add insult to injury, he refused to use any of the funds he raised to build an on-campus stadium. Denny, by contrast, built an on-campus stadium at Alabama.[8]

These fiscal limitations created significant problems, but the Auburn football program, like the school as a whole, persevered despite chronic underfunding. Dowell's truly crippling blows focused on player recruitment, remuneration, and eligibility. Colleges were nominally obliged to meet impossibly rigid standards in these areas. They were prohibited from offering any compensation whatsoever to athletes, including athletic scholarships. Yet the prestige, public-relations value, and gate receipts generated by a winning college football program inevitably tempted administrators and boosters to offer financial inducements to prized recruits. Schools almost uniformly offered athletes bogus academic scholarships, scholarship loans that were never repaid, and, most commonly, well-paying jobs on campus or with businesses controlled by alumni. Many of these jobs required athletes to do little or no work. In addition, boosters, and sometimes even the coaches, disbursed under-the-table payments to athletes from slush funds. Then as now, hypocrisy was an integral feature of intercollegiate athletics. Colleges remained competitive in the increasingly market-driven world of intercollegiate athletics while maintaining a putative loyalty to the amateur ideology that originated in the Victorian English class system. These practices began in the earliest days of college sports in the mid-nineteenth century and had become institutionalized before football had even come to the South in the 1890s. The Carnegie Foundation Report of 1929 garnered headlines when it castigated colleges and universities for their widespread subsidization of intercollegiate athletes. Of the 130 institutions examined by the Carnegie investigators, only 28 did not subsidize their athletes. Of these, only 8 had big-time football programs. After a requisite amount of editorial hand-wringing and fervent protestations of innocence by college officials, everyone returned to business as usual.[9]

Auburn had maintained a relatively good reputation with regards to recruitment and subsidization prior to Dowell's arrival. While no college could comply with these rules and still remain competitive, Auburn had avoided the worst abuses. It had never been known for employing ringers or tramp athletes, and the vast majority of its football players were legitimate students who actually pursued degrees. It had remained relatively unscathed by the football scandals that erupted, died away, and then recurred with monotonous regularity. It did, however, discreetly subsidize its better athletes. Many football players served as waiters in the campus dining hall, a plum position that afforded them both free board and enough income to pay their tuition. Many also received money from a scholarship loan fund, which they often neglected to repay. The active alumni booster network almost assuredly provided cash subsidies to the better players, although records of this are as nonexistent as one might expect.[10]

Auburn's record of coming closer than most schools to meeting standards that few took seriously failed to impress Spright Dowell. There were no shades of gray in his ethical universe. While he admitted in 1922 that "no other institution in the South has had quite so enviable a reputation for so long a period," he remained adamant that major changes must be made. He knew that he could not completely end systematic subsidization of athletes, but he did reduce the number of campus jobs and scholarships available to them. He also insisted that athletes meet all normal academic and disciplinary standards. Football players took full academic course loads during the season, and if afternoon classes conflicted with practice, they skipped practice. A number of football players were expelled for academic deficiencies or for violating the ban on the consumption of alcoholic beverages. No other major southern football power adhered to such a strict policy. Once word of this filtered out, the best athletes began to shy away from Auburn. Dowell compounded this problem by refusing to assist in the recruitment of promising high school athletes, as his predecessor, Charles C. Thach, had done.[11]

Head Coach Mike Donahue chafed at the restrictions placed on the football program. A genial and diminutive native of Ireland whose accent still confounded many southerners despite his having lived in Auburn since 1904, Donahue had overseen Auburn's relatively high ethical and academic standards prior to the implementation of Dowell's more rigid policies. He had graduated from Yale with honors, believed in the concept of "clean sport," and took academics seriously. He had taught both mathematics and Latin at Auburn for a number of years. A beloved and respected figure on campus, he had never had any problems coexisting with faculty and administrators. He also had never been very close to the alumni boosters whom Dowell so thoroughly despised. Yet Donahue had seen enough by the end of the 1922 season, sadly concluding that the football program that he had built was headed for disaster. He left Auburn to accept the head coaching job at Louisiana State University (LSU). Dowell replaced him with John Pitts, a former Auburn football player then working part-time as an assistant coach and part-time as an instructor of mathematics. Pitts continued to receive $1,400 annually for teaching, so the athletic department could get by with paying him only $2,400 for coaching, less than a fourth of the $10,000 that LSU paid Donahue. Also, Dowell possessed greater influence over Pitts, a marginal coaching talent who could never obtain a head coaching position elsewhere, than he would have had over a big-name coach hired from outside the campus.[12]

Predictably, Dowell's actions had a devastating effect on Auburn football fortunes. Donahue's teams had won three conference championships in the seven years prior to Dowell's arrival, and they posted respectable records in 1920, 1921, and 1922. The program floundered, however, under Dowell's recruiting and eligibility restrictions and Pitts's less-than-stellar coaching. In 1924 Auburn finished with a 4–4–1 record, losing four of its five big games against major conference rivals. An alumni faction comprised of leading football boosters waged a noisy public campaign to force Dowell's ouster after the 1924 season. The dissident alumni brought a motion to dismiss Dowell before the board of trustees, but thanks to Governor William W. Brandon's crucial political support the motion failed.[13]

Dowell had dodged a bullet, but this reprieve ultimately bought him only three additional years. He reluctantly appeased his enemies by replacing the hapless Pitts with Dave Morey, a brash young Dartmouth graduate whose talent for self-promotion exceeded his coaching ability. Yet even legendary Notre Dame coach Knute Rockne would have had trouble fielding a competitive team under the conditions established by Dowell. Morey's recruiting efforts were hamstrung by the restrictions on financial inducements, and several of the players that he managed to recruit were kicked out of school for poor grades or for misbehavior. The team remained mired in mediocrity through 1925 and 1926. Disaster struck prior to the opening of the 1927 season, however, when star quarterback Frank Tuxworth was caught sneaking into the women's dormitory after a night of drunken reverie. Dowell was beside himself over this "most unwholesome fraternization between the sexes." Not only was Tuxworth expelled, he was forced to endure a lengthy lecture from Dowell on the necessity of resisting the temptations of the flesh.[14]

Tuxworth's expulsion was Dowell's final and ultimately self-destructive blow to an already reeling football program. Auburn opened the 1927 season with a "warm-up" game against the Hatters of tiny Stetson College, whose nickname could not possibly have been calculated to strike fear into opponents' hearts. The chance of an upset seemed so remote that gamblers did not even give odds on the game. The Auburn team, however, had lost the will to fight, and it suffered one of the most humiliating defeats in its history. One week later, perennial also-ran Clemson defeated Auburn for the first time in over two decades. Clemson students jubilantly rang the campus bell and ignited a bonfire after the news reached their campus, while Auburn students and alumni seethed at this humiliation of their once-proud football program. Morey melodramatically announced his resignation at a pep rally six days after the loss to Clemson. Dowell dismissed this as a "clever stunt" that had inflamed the "mob spirit" of the "irresponsible mass" of students. He was certain that reasonable observers would never take such behavior seriously. In any event, it ignited the crisis that led to his downfall. In an unprecedented challenge to authority, students lit a huge bonfire and plastered the campus with placards bearing the blunt pronouncement "To Hell with Spright Dowell." They also sent emissaries to seek aid from the alumni who had led the fight against Dowell three years earlier. Unlike 1924 the student protesters and dissident alumni found an ally in the governor's office. Bibb Graves had replaced William Brandon as governor in January 1927, and his refusal to support Dowell proved decisive in forcing the latter's resignation.[15]

"Four Great Years of Romping Pleasure"

The decline of the Auburn football program was the proximate cause of Dowell's firing. However, the football controversy was intertwined with the larger social and cultural conflicts that beset the South and the nation during the 1920s. Rapid economic growth over the previous half century had extended industrial capitalism, mass culture, and consumerism into a region that remained conservative and devoted to tradition. An emerging urban society built upon the secular gospel of progress and innovation coexisted uneasily with a rural folk culture informed by agrarian work rhythms and evangelicalism. The influential constituencies of major state universities such as Auburn—students, alumni, business leaders, and the urban upper middle class—possessed a generally progressive worldview. In addition to his antagonism toward big-time intercollegiate football, Dowell's position on other issues alienated a critical mass of university supporters. Most unpopular were his attempts to enforce rigid disciplinary standards on the Auburn campus, the favoritism that he showed to agricultural education vis-à-vis engineering at Auburn, and his political ties to the Alabama Agricultural Extension Service and the Alabama Farm Bureau Federation. Each of these factors earned Dowell the enmity of progressive elements within Alabama and thus played a key role in his ouster.

Although the scope of these changes is often overstated, the 1920s marked a significant social and cultural watershed in America. The spread of a cosmopolitan worldview, the growing predominance of the consumer culture, and the impact of new technology, including the automobile and the new communications media of radio and movies, all worked to undermine Victorian values. Secularization, especially the gradual removal of religion from its central place in the public sphere, reached something of a critical mass during the decade. The changing social role of women and the concomitant liberalization of sexual mores, what contemporaries called the "Revolution in Manners and Morals," were symbolic of the changes associated with modernity. White middle-class youth were at the vanguard of these changes, and in the process they created the first real youth culture in American history. Seeing themselves as a distinct social group with legitimate rights and unfulfilled desires, they became increasingly unwilling to accept uncritically the authority of their elders. Colleges and universities provided a hothouse atmosphere in which the youth culture flourished, nourished by an intensive exposure to new ideas and values in the classroom and in the new media, and intensified by peer-group reinforcement.[16]

Major southern universities were strongly affected by this cultural transformation. They had changed only glacially between the end of the Civil War and the 1890s, stubbornly adhering to the classical curriculum and draconian disciplinary standards. The pace of change quickened between the 1890s and World War I, spurred by educational progressives among the faculty. These cautious reformers were taken aback by the tidal wave of student rebelliousness that suddenly confronted them in 1919 and continued unabated throughout the succeeding decade. Auburn students began chafing at what they regarded as unreasonable disciplinary restraints before the ink on the Armistice was dry. Students openly flouted Prohibition laws, and football weekends in Montgomery, Columbus, Birmingham, and Atlanta became occasions for wild partying. Unsurprisingly, student dances also prompted significant alcohol consumption. Students not only had no compunction about publicly admitting their drinking, they bragged about it. The "Scandals" column of the *Orange and Blue,* the Auburn student newspaper, repeatedly chuckled at the alcohol-fueled misadventures of Auburn students during the 1919–20 school year. An unprecedented spirit of militancy galvanized the Auburn student body in the fall of 1919, just as Dowell was taking office. Students posted placards and scrawled graffiti throughout the town of Auburn, hissed faculty and administrators at assemblies, and openly flouted disciplinary rules. The turmoil attracted unfavorable coverage from the state's daily newspapers. The student newspaper concluded, "We may call it unrest or Bolshevism or any of these terms and not miss it so very far."[17]

Bolshevism it was not. The activism of the Auburn students, like that of college students generally during the 1920s, reflected their desire for greater personal autonomy rather than a radical reordering of society. Yet apolitical as it was, student militancy could be extremely disruptive. In response, administrators at most public universities beat a tactical retreat and liberalized disciplinary codes. Dowell, however, resisted fiercely. An intensely pious Baptist, he fought a relentless battle to improve the "moral tone" of the campus. One of his first actions was to crack down on the *Orange and Blue,* installing an editor who supported his agenda and instituting faculty oversight of the paper. The lively and gossip-filled "Scandals" column disappeared, replaced by editorials voicing support for the president's drive to "improve the social and moral life of the campus." It called for students to quit using vulgar language and insistently touted activities despite their unpopularity among students. It even called for the reinstitution of mandatory daily chapel attendance, a practice that had been extremely unpopular among Auburn students for years and that had been abandoned during the war. Students began calling the newspaper "The Weekly Disappointment." The establishment of a student government, touted as a palliative for student restiveness, instead sparked an abundance of it. Auburn was one of the few major southern universities still without a system by which students had a voice in drafting and enforcing behavior codes. Dowell assured the trustees in 1921 that "we have all but agreed upon a constitution for student government." However, an agreement proved elusive and the pursuit of it divisive. Students overwhelmingly defeated a proposed constitution in a popular vote later that year because they believed that it gave them too little influence over disciplinary decisions. One student complained that without a constitution, Auburn students were relegated to the status of the "ignorant semi-savage Filipino." A constitution was finally adopted three years later, but the long fight generated additional ill-will.[18]

Prohibition and sexual morality were the two most divisive issues in the cultural wars of the 1920s, and, predictably, Dowell and the students clashed over them. Any student caught under the influence of alcohol was immediately expelled from school. Dowell reported that his policies were an effective means of eliminating "ne'er-do-well's and incompetents" from the campus. He appointed Zoë Dobbs, a woman who shared his worldview, to the newly created position of social director and gave her broad authority to regulate campus social life. She and her hand-picked team of local matrons closely monitored the school-sponsored dances, keeping an especially close watch for anyone under the influence of alcohol. In a move that particularly rankled the virtually all-male Auburn student body, young women invited to dances were vetted by Dobbs and her cohorts, and any deemed to be of insufficiently high moral character were denied admission. When dances at fraternity houses proved more difficult to supervise than those in the school gym, Dowell banned them altogether. In an attempt to impose stricter control over fraternity life in general, Dobbs began selecting the fraternity house mothers who lived in the houses. Dobbs observed that the new house mothers provided a "constraining and restraining influence." In addition, Dowell flatly prohibited women from visiting fraternity houses. This rule was enforced so strictly that a young woman was barred from visiting her mother, who was a fraternity house mother. Although Dowell later relented in this particular case, the incident enhanced his reputation for rigid authoritarianism. Dowell also banned movies with strong sexual content from campus. Auburn did not have a privately owned movie theater, so he effectively prevented some of the most popular movies of the day from being seen there.[19]

Auburn students had certainly grumbled about restrictive rules prior to the war, but the level of discontent rose dramatically during the 1920s. Students wanted a significant liberalization of the behavior code, which Dowell was unwilling to grant them. Their anger intensified when they compared their situation to that of their peers at other southern state universities. Exponential advances in communications and transportation, an increasingly pervasive media culture, and the rising generational consciousness that characterized the youth culture increased student awareness of the disparity. In keeping with national trends, authorities at the University of Georgia, Georgia Tech, and the University of Alabama liberalized their behavior codes during the decade.[20]

Once again, Alabama president George Denny provided a striking contrast to Dowell. Denny was relatively tolerant by the standards of the day, and Alabama acquired a reputation as a "party school" during his tenure. The university aggressively recruited female students and permitted unchaperoned dating. Female students were even permitted to ride in automobiles with men.

Dances became ubiquitous, and the presidency of the Cotillion Club was the most desirable office to which a student could aspire. Denny also adopted a see-no-evil approach to Prohibition violations. An Assistant U.S. Attorney in Birmingham complained to Denny in 1923 about fraternities that openly served liquor at social functions. He implicitly accused Denny of condoning this behavior and threatened to slap the university with an injunction unless he cracked down. Likewise, a student's father asserted that Denny either tolerated drinking or was grossly ignorant of activities that were common knowledge. Denny replied that he believed that it was essential to place faith in his students. "The ideal of a college is not that of a reformatory," he declared. An Auburn student who led the 1927 revolt against Dowell wistfully recalled that he and his friends wished fervently that Auburn had a president who was more like Denny.[21]

The polarization of public opinion over Dowell's policy of rigidly enforced morality reflected the bitter conflict between secular modernizers and religious conservatives during the 1920s. Dowell's opponents tended to be less pious and more tolerant of the youthful rebelliousness and more open sexuality of the Jazz Age. His alumni critics viewed him as a "narrow-minded Puritan" who behaved more like a jailer than an enlightened college president. Students complained that a chat with the president felt like an interrogation and that his "stool pigeons" lurked in every corner of the campus. The urban businessmen who led the movement to sack him almost certainly were church members and did not espouse irreligion and hedonism. However, they were sympathetic to the more modern, materialistic, and secular society of the urban, industrialized South, and they had little use for the moral norms that were rooted in the declining world of the southern countryside. Shortly before the 1927 controversy at Auburn broke, editorials in the *Montgomery Advertiser* and *The State* of Columbia, South Carolina, displayed the tolerant attitude that many in the urban middle class took toward college life. In prose that was purple even by the standards of the day, *The State* proclaimed that college boys should "have not a good time, but the best time . . . four great years of romping pleasure in the heyday of their youth." It urged college authorities to "let them romp through life a bit, while the coltish nature is still hot with the mettle of the lush pasture." The *Advertiser* approvingly reprinted the editorial, asserting that college students had a "duty" to have a good time. It declared, "We need not take life any less seriously because it is something to be enjoyed."[22]

"A Question of Morals and Nothing Else"

Religious conservatives vehemently rejected this more permissive value system. "Fundamentalism" is a broad-brush term often used to describe the religious backlash to the changes associated with modernism, but it was only one manifestation of the widespread discontent of conservative evangelicals during the 1920s. It wasn't only Fundamentalists who perceived the new culture of the 1920s as rife with immorality and irreligion and desired the restoration of religion to the more prominent social role it once possessed. The *Alabama Christian Advocate,* the official organ of Alabama Methodism, repeatedly railed against the new youth culture and the attendant evils of drinking, dancing, jazz music, dirty movies, and sexual license. Warren Candler, a Methodist bishop and president of Emory University, likened the modern youth movement to the revolt of Absalom against King David. Dowell was no Fundamentalist, believing as he did in the spirit of scientific inquiry and embracing broadly ecumenical beliefs. He also never issued blanket denunciations of the moral shortcomings of young people, and he defended them against those who did. He was, however, a pious Baptist who taught a weekly Sunday school class, relentlessly promoted the campus YMCA despite student indifference, and waged his vigorous campaign to improve the moral atmosphere at Auburn despite the controversy that it generated.[23]

Many pious Alabamians vigorously applauded his efforts. The executive board of the Alabama Baptist Convention unanimously passed a resolution of support for Dowell during the alumni challenge of 1924. That same year, the *Alabama Christian Advocate* lauded Dowell as "first, last and always a Christian gentleman." Evangelical leaders supported Dowell in 1927 as well. The *Alabama Baptist* offered editorial support for him, and the *Alabama Christian Advocate* stated, "One of his traducers is reported to have said that he was 'too Christian,' as though any man who presides over the youth of the State could be too Christian for any save those who, perchance, place other considerations ahead of moral character." Only days prior to Dowell's ouster, Leland Cooper, a campus YMCA employee, beseeched the governor to look beyond the football controversy to the first principles at issue. After regaling the governor with horror stories about the drunken debauchery at student dances prior to his arrival, Cooper stated that Dowell "has been fighting whiskey and immorality ever since he came here." Dowell was unpopular, she declared, because such principled behavior had become unfashionable. She asserted that those who favored a liberalization of moral standards apparently did not care whether or not their sons and daughters grew up to be "men and women of real upright character." "The present fight," she wrote, "is not against President Dowell, but against the principles for which he stands. The fight is purely a question of morals and nothing else." Dowell framed his final argument to the trustees in similar terms. He declared that the question facing the trustees was whether they would stand for "high standards of conduct and scholarship, for law and order, and for social decency; or whether they shall wink at or ignore poor work, unsportsmanlike conduct, the use of liquor, and social immorality."[24]

Presuming that his reference to unsportsmanlike conduct referred to the excesses of the football program, Dowell's linkage of football and moral issues is significant. His piety may have informed his opposition to big-time football, which was not uncommon among evangelicals of the era. The southern evangelical leadership had vigorously denounced football during the 1890s and made a concerted effort to have it banned. Football, they argued, was too violent, promoted drinking and gambling, and was a shameless emulation of the materialistic and godless culture of the Northeast. Some argued that it glorified the inherently corrupt and sinful human body. William H. Felton, a Methodist minister who served on the University of Georgia Board of Trustees, waged a vigorous if ultimately futile battle against both football and dancing at that school in the 1890s, and conservative Methodist bishops did the same at Vanderbilt. Warren Candler banned football at Emory and successfully lobbied the Georgia legislature in 1897 to make playing football a felony punishable by a year on the chain gang, although it was negated by a gubernatorial veto. President John Franklin Crowell of Trinity College made football a key element of his ambitious plans to reform that school. The conservative Methodist bishops on the board of trustees who had vigorously criticized both his brash liberalism and his football program led a successful movement to fire him in 1894. Wofford, Furman, Emory and Henry, and Wake Forest were among the other denominational institutions that banned intercollegiate football around the turn of the century. The campaign petered out in the early 1900s, and all but Emory resumed their football programs. Most urban middle-class evangelicals liked football and simply ignored the leadership. An occasional echo of the old jeremiads lingered into the 1920s. For example, the *Alabama Christian Advocate* blamed the 1924 campaign against Dowell on the "rather freakish and abnormal" public obsession with football, and an aging Bishop Candler occasionally cut loose with a blast at football. It may have lived on in Spright Dowell's value system, however. He had been a senior at Wake Forest when that school banned football in 1895, and this early experience may have influenced his attitude toward big-time football. His campaign to use a reformed Auburn football program as an "opportunity to inculcate moral standards and ideals" and his parallel campaign to improve the "moral tone" of the campus contained strong overtones of religious piety, and he pursued both with an evangelical fervor.[25]

Football's roots in the progressive movement and its growing prominence in the commercial entertainment industry ground it firmly in the same urban middle-class culture that was least amenable to religious conservatism. Dowell's leading critics were the urban businessmen who dominated the alumni association, and his strongest support came from the evangelicals who tended to live in smaller towns and rural areas. This rural-urban tension can be overstated, as Dowell had a graduate degree from Columbia University and was hardly bereft of support in Alabama cities. However, the social conflicts of the 1920s were strongly informed by this dichotomy, and the third of the issues associated with the Dowell controversy is related to it as well: his alumni critics believed that Dowell spent a disproportionate share of Auburn's limited resources on the School of Agriculture, to the detriment of engineering programs. He was closely allied with Luther N. Duncan, the director of the Alabama Agricultural Extension Service, which was a semiautonomous body with only loose institutional ties to the college. The Extension Service and the Agricultural Experiment Station, although funded primarily by federal monies, received considerable financial support from the college. Dowell defended this outlay of resources while acknowledging that it placed "a burden upon the treasury of the college." The School of Agriculture received significant funding increases throughout his tenure despite a precipitous decline in its enrollment. In 1923–24, 12 percent of Auburn undergraduates were enrolled in the agricultural curriculum, whereas only three years later, that figure had fallen to just over 4 percent. The proportion enrolled in the School of Engineering remained steady at over 40 percent during this same period. Ambitious young Alabamians of the 1920s sought educational training that would facilitate their entry into the urban middle class rather than training that would relegate them to the less prestigious and less remunerative life of the farmer. A majority of Auburn students came from rural areas and small towns, but most saw their education as a means of accessing the opportunities offered in the urban industrial economy.[26]

Henry DeBardeleben, a leading Birmingham industrialist and the leader of Auburn's dissident alumni faction in both 1924 and 1927, declared that "a vast number of the leading industrial men in Alabama" were concerned that Auburn was devoting an insufficient level of resources to engineering. As an example, he cited Dowell's refusal to divert resources from agriculture to fund the creation of a program in textile engineering. He complained that Duncan was using the political influence of the Alabama Farm Bureau and the Extension Service to generate political support for Dowell. DeBardeleben was also a member of the first Auburn football team in 1892 and was probably the single most influential Auburn football booster. Haygood Paterson, a Montgomery businessman who was also a leading alumni booster and former Auburn football player, also complained that agriculture received "more than its share of attention" at Auburn. They found it expedient to publicly disavow that their dispute with Dowell had anything to do with football and focused instead on engineering education and the malign political influence of the Farm Bureau and Extension Service. While they obviously cared more deeply about football than they were willing to admit, they sincerely felt that Dowell was pursuing shortsighted and antiprogressive policies in terms of football, disciplinary policy, and engineering education. Gubernatorial politics likely entered the equation as well. Governor William Brandon had been elected with the support of Duncan and the Farm Bureau, and he had supported Dowell in 1924. His successor, Bibb Graves, had been elected despite Farm Bureau opposition, so political calculation presumably played a role in his decision to support Dowell's ouster.[27]

The conflict between progress and tradition in the 1920s South is the common thread running through the complex web of issues underlying the Auburn football controversy. Dowell's supporters tended to be more pious, to dislike intercollegiate football or at least want to curb the excesses associated with it, and to value the traditional mores of the agrarian South. His opponents were mostly urban businessmen who valued football as both commercial entertainment and as a symbol of modernity and inclusion in the national cultural mainstream. While it is difficult to ascertain how great a proportion of Auburn students objected to Dowell's disciplinary policies, those who did were both numerous and highly disruptive. His critics generally possessed more secular values and were more tolerant of the liberalized morality of the Jazz Age than were Dowell and his supporters. Yet Dowell was a determined reformer during his tenure at Auburn, and his opponents were hardly radicals who rashly rejected the received canon of the southern tradition. Dowell's piety did not prohibit him from introducing modern administrative procedures at Auburn, and the more secular worldview of the students and alumni boosters did not preclude them from Christian belief or church membership. Both Dowell and the men who forced his removal from office embodied the sometimes contradictory elements of progress and tradition that coexisted uneasily within the South during the 1920s.

Notes

1. Dowell either destroyed his personal papers and correspondence or took them with him when he left Auburn, but he did make detailed and (perhaps overly) frank semiannual reports to the board of trustees. Most of the generalizations made in this essay about Dowell's opinions and sentiments have been drawn from material in these reports, which he personally drafted.

2. Report of the President to the Board of Trustees (hereafter referred to as President's Report), 5 November 1927, Dowell Papers, Auburn University Archives; *Montgomery Advertiser*, 5 November 1927, 1, 2, 4.

3. President's Report, 22 February 1923, 7; 13 May 1924, 1–2, 9; 14 February 1924, 1–2.

4. On the links between football and corporate capitalism, see Michael Oriard, *Reading Football: How the Popular Press Created an American Spectacle* (University of North Carolina Press, 1993), esp. ch. 1. For a discussion of the links between football

and southern business progressivism in the 1920s, see Andrew Doyle, "Turning the Tide: College Football and Southern Progressivism," *Southern Cultures* 3 (Fall 1997): 28–51.

5. On Kirkland, see Paul Conkin, *Gone with the Ivy: A Biography of Vanderbilt University* (University of Tennessee Press, 1985), 135–36, 140–41; on the other southern university presidents, see Andrew Doyle, "Causes Won, Not Lost: College Football and Southern Culture," doctoral dissertation, Emory University, 1998, esp. ch. 1.

6. Suzanne Rau Wolfe, *A Pictorial History of the University of Alabama* (University of Alabama Press, 1983), 128–29, and Andrew Doyle, "George Denny, Intercollegiate Football, and the Modernization of the University of Alabama," paper presented at the North American Society for Sport History, French Lick Springs, Indiana, May 2002.

7. President's Report, 22 February 1923, 7; 13 May 1924, 9; Cliff Hare to Thomas Bragg, 1 January 1921, Auburn University Athletic Department Records (hereafter referred to as Auburn Athletic Department Records), File 7, Auburn University Archives; Cliff Hare to W. S. Hurst, 19 October 1922, Auburn Athletic Department Records, File 14.

8. President's Report, 13 May 1924, 8–9; Report of the Director of Student Activities, 13 May 1924, 1 June 1925, Dowell Papers, Auburn University Archives; Auburn Athletic Association Budget, 1921–22, Auburn Athletic Department Records, File 22; *Mobile Register,* 23 October 1927, 1.

9. For a discussion of the chronic problems that American intercollegiate athletics have faced over the issues of player recruitment and eligibility, see, for example, Ronald A. Smith, *Sports and Freedom: The Rise of Big-Time Intercollegiate Athletics* (Oxford University Press, 1988); for a discussion of the Carnegie Report, see John Watterson, *College Football: History, Spectacle, Controversy* (Johns Hopkins University Press, 2000), 158–76.

10. B. L. Shi to Carmichael Simmons, 2 September 1909, Charles Coleman Thach Papers, File 44, Auburn University Archives; "Statement of Business, Smith Dining Hall Association," 1 January 1917, Thach Papers, File 98, Auburn University Archives; Cliff Hare to J. P. Illges, 17 September 1922, Auburn Athletic Department Records, File 10.

11. President's Report, 22 February 1922, 8; Cliff Hare to Wellington Brink, 29 March 1923, File 31, Dowell Papers, Auburn University Archives; transcript of testimony given to the Board of Trustees, 14 October 1927, 21, Dowell Papers, File 15, Auburn University Archives; Cliff Hare to A. C. Crowder, 8 November 1920, Auburn Athletic Department Records, File 5; Hare to J. P. Illges, 26 August 1922; Auburn Athletic Department Records, File 11; A. Clyde Robinson to Bibb Graves, Graves Papers, RC2; G199, File: Schools, Alabama Polytechnic Institute, 1927, Alabama Department of Archives and History; *Montgomery Advertiser,* 22 September 1927, 7.

12. Sam Hendrix, "Irishman Iron Mike Donahue Built on Heisman's Success," *The Auburn Alumnews* 74 (October 1992): 22; undated clipping from *Birmingham News,* Historical Collection, Series I, File: Mike Donahue, Auburn University Archives; Athletic Department Budget, 1923–24, Auburn Athletic Department Records, File 30.

13. Alabama Polytechnic Institute Trustees Minutes, 12 January 1925, 11 February 1925, Auburn University Archives.

14. Transcript of testimony of open meeting of Board of Trustees, 14 October 1927, 12–16, Dowell Papers, File 15, Auburn University Archives; President's Report, 5 November 1927, 22.

15. *Montgomery Advertiser*, 25 September 1927, 6; 8 October 1927, 1; *Atlanta Journal*, 2 October 1927, B-1; President's Report, 5 November 1927, 25.

16. For a discussion of the changing social mores of the 1920s and the impact that they had on college life, see Paula Fass, *The Damned and the Beautiful: American Youth in the 1920s* (Oxford University Press, 1977); Lynn Dumenil, *The Modern Temper: American Culture and Society in the 1920s* (Hill and Wang, 1995), esp. ch. 3.

17. *Orange and Blue*, 31 November 1919, 1; 7 November 1919, 3; 14 November 1919, 2, 3; 6 December 1919, 8; 7 November 1919, 1; 14 November 1919, 2. The works that discuss the transformation of American higher education during the late nineteenth and early twentieth centuries generally focus on nonsouthern schools. Laurence R. Veysey, *The Emergence of the American University* (University of Chicago Press, 1965) is the standard work, but there is no comparable treatment of southern higher education. Institutional histories can offer a view of this process from the perspective of individual schools, although they vary in quality. The best is Conkin, *Gone with the Ivy.*

18. On student rebelliousness, see Fass, *The Damned and the Beautiful*, 123–67, 194–98; *Orange and Blue*, 21 May 1921, 4; 17 December 1921, 2; 20 May 1922, 2; President's Report, 30 May 1921, 9; *Orange and Blue*, 22 October 1921, 1; 28 October 1921, 2; Report of the Director of Student Activities, 13 May 1924, 4, Dowell Papers, Auburn University Archives.

19. President's Report, 22 February 1923, 5–8; Report of the Social Director, 1 June 1925, 18 May 1927, Dowell Papers, Auburn University Archives; *Orange and Blue*, 17 December 1921, 2.

20. Information about the liberalization of behavior codes is from the author's primary research conducted at each of these schools.

21. D. H. Riddle to George Denny, 19 November 1917; Denny to Riddle, 23 November 1917; Jim C. Smith to Denny, 28 March 1923, Denny Papers, William Stanley Hoole Special Collections, University of Alabama. William G. Gilchrist, interviewed by Allen W. Jones, Oral History Collection, Auburn University Archives.

22. Leland Cooper to Bibb Graves, 4 November 1927, Graves Papers, RC2: G199, File: Schools, Alabama Polytechnic Institute, 1927, Alabama Department of Archives and History; Gilchrist interview; *Montgomery Advertiser*, 26 September 1927, 4.

23. On the religious climate during the 1920s, see Dumenil, *The Modern Temper*, ch. 4; the most comprehensive book on American Fundamentalism is George Marsden, *Fundamentalism and American Culture: The Shaping of Twentieth-Century Evangelicalism, 1870–1925* (Oxford University Press, 1980); *Alabama Christian Advocate*, 13 September 1923, 4; 25 September 1924, 2; 30 October 1924, 3; 9 November 1924, 2, 4; 6 January 1927, 2; Dowell defended young people against what he saw as unfair attacks in his President's Report, 21 June 1926, 8; his ecumenical and generally tolerant religious views are in evidence in the portions of virtually all of his reports in which he discusses campus religious atmosphere and the activities of the YMCA.

24. *Montgomery Journal,* 9 December 1924, 2; *Alabama Christian Advocate,* 18 December 1924, 2; 17 November 1927, 2; editorial from *Alabama Christian Advocate,* reprinted in *Alabama Baptist* 92 (December 1927): 3; Leland Cooper to Bibb Graves, 4 November 1927, Graves Papers, RC2: G199, File: Schools, Alabama Polytechnic Institute, 1927, Alabama Department of Archives and History; President's Report, 5 November 1927.

25. See Andrew Doyle, "Foolish and Useless Sport: The Evangelical Crusade Against Intercollegiate Football, 1890–1920," *Journal of Sport History* 24 (Fall 1997): 317–40; *Alabama Christian Advocate,* 9 November 1924, 2; President's Report, 13 May 1924, 9.

26. President's Report, 22 February 1923, 2; 13 May 1924, 1; Report of the Registrar, 9 May 1927, File 13, Dowell Papers, Auburn University Archives.

27. *Montgomery Advertiser,* 18 December 1924, 4; Alabama Polytechnic Institute Trustees Minutes, vol. 7, 143–44; *Montgomery Advertiser,* 11 December 1924, 2.

The Campaign for Racial Purity and the Erosion of Paternalism in Virginia, 1922–1930

"Nominally White, Biologically Mixed, and Legally Negro"

J. Douglas Smith

In September 1922 John Powell, a Richmond native and world-renowned pianist and composer, and Earnest Sevier Cox, a self-proclaimed explorer and ethnographer, organized Post No. 1 of the Anglo-Saxon Clubs of America. By the following June the organization claimed four hundred members in Richmond alone and had added new groups throughout the state, all dedicated to "the preservation and maintenance of Anglo-Saxon ideals and civilization." For the next ten years Powell and his supporters dominated racial discourse in the Old Dominion; successfully challenged the legislature to redefine blacks, whites, and Indians; used the power of a state agency to enforce the law with impunity and without mercy; fundamentally altered the lives of hundreds of mixed-race Virginians; and threatened the essence of the state's devotion to paternalistic race relations.[1]

The racial extremism and histrionics of the leaders of the Anglo-Saxon Clubs have attracted the attention of both legal scholars and southern historians, particularly those interested in the 1924 Racial Integrity Act, the major legislative achievement of the organization, and *Loving v. Virginia,* the 1967 U.S. Supreme Court decision that outlawed three centuries of miscegenation statutes in the United States.[2] Historian Richard B. Sherman, for instance, has focused on the organization's leaders, "a small but determined group of racial zealots," who rejected the contention of most southern whites in the 1920s that the "race question was settled." Sherman, who has written the most detailed account of the legislative efforts of the Anglo-Saxon Clubs, has argued in the pages of the *Journal of Southern History* that the leaders of the organization constituted a "dedicated coterie of extremists who played effectively on the fears and prejudices of many whites." Convinced that increasing numbers of persons with traces of black blood were passing as white, they made a "Last Stand" against racial amalgamation.[3]

While Sherman is certainly correct that the Anglo-Saxon Clubs owed their success to the commitment of their leaders, their views and policies resonated with a much broader swath of the white population. The Anglo-Saxon Clubs did not merely manipulate the racial fears and prejudices of whites but also tapped into the same assumptions that undergirded the entire foundation of white supremacy and championed segregation as a system of racial hierarchy and control. The call for racial integrity appealed especially to elite whites in Virginia who were obsessed with genealogy and their pristine bloodlines. Lady Astor, for instance, reportedly informed her English friends that they lacked the purity of the white inhabitants of the Virginia Piedmont. "We are undiluted," she proclaimed. Author Emily Clark satirized this prevailing view in Richmond when one of her characters remarked, "For here alone, in all America, flourished the Anglo-Saxon race, untainted, pure, and perfect." White elites across Virginia gave their support to the Anglo-Saxon Clubs and allowed Powell's message a hearing: state senators and delegates approved legislation; governors publicly advocated the aims of the organization; some of the most socially prominent women in Richmond joined the ladies auxiliary; and influential newspapers offered editorial support and provided a public platform for the dissemination of the organization's extreme views.[4]

Although Sherman himself does not suggest that the "[race] question was settled" in the 1920s, he does follow the lead of George Brown Tindall and other historians in accepting that most white southerners at the time believed this to be the case. On the one hand, this argument is persuasive: leading whites in the South did not debate the wisdom of segregation. But at the same time, white elites in Virginia struggled on a daily basis to figure out how best to manage white supremacy. In this sense, they knew that the race question was not, nor was likely ever to be, settled. Although later challenges to white supremacy emanated primarily from African Americans in Virginia and throughout the South, the fulminations of the Anglo-Saxon Clubs exposed an ideological fissure in elite ranks between advocates of genteel paternalism and those who favored rigid extremism. Supporters of both courses of action were certain that they knew best how to manage and perpetuate white supremacy.[5]

Virginia's small circle of social and political elites craved order and stability, especially with regard to race relations. Throughout the first half of the twentieth century they spent a great deal of time assuring themselves that "no other state in the Nation has better and more understanding, cordial relations between the races than does Virginia." Like most delusions, this one depended upon a grain of truth, resting primarily on the fact that fewer lynchings occurred in Virginia than in most southern states. Even political scientist V. O. Key Jr. noted that "Virginia's white citizens . . . have demonstrated a relatively acute sense of responsibility toward the Negro—an attitude that may account in part for the fact that its race relations are perhaps the most harmonious in the South." This ethos of paternalism, however, served first and foremost to defend the segregationist status quo and therefore offered African Americans little of substance.[6]

The activities of Virginia's Anglo-Saxon Clubs speak volumes about the mutability of race relations at the height of the classical period of segregation, an era too long portrayed in static terms. The most significant of Virginia's Jim Crow statutes were adopted not in the 1900s and 1910s but in the 1920s and 1930s, a sign to historian Charles E. Wynes that "white Southerners knew that their world was changing." By the 1920s white elites in particular had begun to lose what Dan Carter refers to as their "racial self-confidence." This does not mean that their grip on power had loosened but rather that the management of that power had become increasingly difficult. Ironically, it was the extremists in Virginia who most clearly recognized the implications of this change. John Powell and others reacted with alarm precisely because they understood that paternalistic support for interracial cooperation and black education might ultimately lead to the breakdown, and not the reinforcement, of white supremacy. That all white Virginians did not share their sense of imminent danger terrified John Powell and Earnest Cox.[7]

In addition to exposing a fundamental weakness in the system of managed race relations, the Anglo-Saxon Clubs unintentionally revealed the absurdity of the basic assumption that underlay their mission: it proved impossible to divide the state, or the nation for that matter, into readily identifiable races. The longer they waged their campaign, the more apparent it became that they could not divine the precise amount of nonwhite blood in a given individual. Furthermore, the Anglo-Saxon Clubs met a great deal of resistance from individuals and communities who rejected the clubs' particular construction of racial identity. Communities across the state revealed a variability in race relations that confounded those most committed to a discrete, binary definition of race.

Although attempts to draw a strict color line did not directly affect the majority of black Virginians who never tried nor had any desire to pass as white, John Powell and his supporters engendered a great deal of interracial hostility and ultimately contributed to a crack in the edifice of white supremacy and to an erosion of paternalistic race relations. Many members of Virginia's ruling class had refused to openly support the Anglo-Saxon Clubs precisely because they thought the clubs unnecessarily agitated the race issue. Such elites, however, never questioned the essential rightness and necessity of racial integrity. Before long, they employed the same logic and rhetoric to denounce the demands of black Virginians for equality and justice. But by then, the hollowness and inherent contradictions of managed race relations had been exposed—elite Virginians could not defend the segregationist status quo and simultaneously ensure racial harmony and good will, the very hallmarks of their paternalism.

John Powell, Earnest Cox, and Walter Ashby Plecker, the director of the Bureau of Vital Statistics and the third leading member of the Anglo-Saxon Clubs, drove the organization's agenda, publicized its platform, and formulated legislation. Yet Powell did not act until he felt confident that he had the implicit backing of some of the Old Dominion's wealthiest and most powerful citizens. In January 1921, more than eighteen months before the establishment of Post No. 1, Powell wrote to William T. Reed, a Richmond tobacco magnate and arguably Virginia's most powerful unelected individual. Powell was pleased to report that John Kerr Branch, one of the wealthiest men in the state and a close friend of Reed's, had "expressed wholehearted approval of the purposes of the Anglo-Saxon Clubs and I believe he will really be willing to help our program along. I am sure his changed attitude is the result of your influence."[8]

From the outset Powell and his supporters defined themselves in opposition to the Ku Klux Klan, which had never received the support of the Virginia elite, and asserted their intention to achieve their goals "in the spirit of good sportsmanship and fair play." Powell's claim earned him both explicit and tacit support from many of the same elites who condemned the Klan as a threat to law and order. Leading newspapers, especially the Richmond *Times-Dispatch,* added much needed editorial support. The clubs' early history, however, suggests a much closer connection to the Klan than Virginia's elites ever cared to admit.[9] In fact, just weeks after the establishment of the first post of the Anglo-Saxon Clubs, the *Times-Dispatch* reported that the local chapter of the Klan had seceded from the national organization based in Atlanta. According to J. T. Bethel, an attorney for the Richmond Klansmen, the capital city's lodge had determined that the national Klan was run by "bad characters" whose primary concern was making money. Furthermore, Richmond's membership, including some of the city's "best citizens," found the national organization a "rampant anti-Catholic organization instead of an organization to maintain white supremacy." Consequently, the membership voted to sever its ties with the Klan and joined instead the local chapter of the Anglo-Saxon Clubs in an effort to "retain the best there is in the Klan and to eliminate the worst." While no evidence exists to suggest that Powell himself ever belonged to the Klan, his insistence that he and the Anglo-Saxon Clubs were in no way connected with the Klan was simply not true. Lawrence T. Price, W. C. Maddox, and W. I. Stockton Jr., respectively the chairman, president, and secretary of the Anglo-Saxon Clubs, all appeared in a notarized list of former Richmond

Klansmen who had renounced their membership. By putting a new face on the Klan, Powell was able to legitimize the Anglo-Saxon Clubs in the minds of respectable, elite Virginians.[10]

Although Powell and Cox initially placed their efforts within the broader nativist context of the national debate over federal immigration policy, they soon ceased to mention immigration at all.[11] Instead, they focused their energies toward "achieving a final solution" to the "negro problem." Their ultimate concern, as they suggested in lengthy articles in the *Times-Dispatch,* was to prevent "White America" from devolving into a "Negroid Nation." Writing in July 1923, Powell argued that the passage of Jim Crow laws and the disfranchisement of blacks had "diverted the minds of our people from the most serious and fundamental peril, that is, the danger of racial amalgamation." "It is not enough to segregate the Negro on railway trains and street cars, in schools and theaters," the pianist declared; "it is not enough to restrict his exercise of the franchise, so long as the possibility remains of the absorption of Negro blood into our white population." Powell acknowledged that Virginia's laws already prevented the intermarriage of blacks and whites but warned that such laws did not necessarily "prevent intermixture." He and his colleagues in the Anglo-Saxon Clubs also believed that a 1910 Virginia statute that defined a black person as having at least one-sixteenth black blood no longer protected the integrity of the white race. Pointing to census figures that showed a decrease in the number of mulattoes in Virginia from 222,910 in 1910 to 164,171 in 1920, they argued that an increasing number of people with some black blood must be passing as white. Consequently, a new, "absolute" color line offered the only "possibility, if not the probability, of achieving a final solution."[12]

Powell's analysis of census data, however, points to the absurdity of his campaign to define race in absolute terms. While Powell interpreted the steep drop in mulattoes as proof of increased passing, historian Joel Williamson argues that by the early twentieth century the only significant "mixing" occurred between lighter-skinned blacks and darker-skinned blacks. Even census officials warned in 1920 that "considerable uncertainty necessarily attaches to the classification of Negroes as black and mulatto, since the accuracy of the distinction depends largely upon the judgment and care employed by the enumerators." Mulattoes in Virginia did not become white between 1910 and 1920 but rather became black. In fact, the census bureau did away with *mulatto* as a category for the 1930 enumeration.[13]

Powell and Cox borrowed much of their rhetoric from the science of eugenics and its counterpart, scientific racism. Although they referred most often to northern eugenicists like New York attorney Madison Grant and *Saturday Evening Post* contributor Lothrop Stoddard, the clubs' leading spokesmen need not have looked far from home for intellectual sanction. Virginia, and in particular the University of Virginia in Charlottesville, had become a hotbed of eugenical studies by the mid-1920s. According to historian Gregory Michael Dorr, biology professor Ivey Foreman Lewis and a number of other eugenicists at the university developed a curriculum that "taught that heredity governed all aspects of life, from anatomical form to social organization." By definition, therefore, "eugenics reinforced the social hierarchy that elevated the elite, extolled sedate whites as fit, and considered troublesome whites, poor whites, and all others to be genetic defectives in need of control." Firmly rooted in the ethos of Progressive-era reform, Lewis and his compatriots sanctioned white elite rule in scientific terms and "provided generations of educated, self-consciously modern Virginians with a new method of legitimating the South's traditional social order."[14]

Though never a serious student of eugenics, Powell recognized an opportunity to whitewash his extreme prejudice with a veneer of respectable intellectualism by clothing his ideology in theories of biology and ethnography. Powell latched on to Mendel's theories of heredity to argue that when two races interbred "the more primitive, the less highly specialized, variety always dominates." A widespread belief in the inferiority of blacks allowed the Anglo-Saxons to argue that "every race that has crossed with the Negro has failed to maintain its civilization and culture." Powell warned, therefore, that "one drop of Negro blood makes the Negro." Powell acknowledged that blacks had been forced to come to the United States against their will and consequently remained "innocent of responsibility for the existence of the Negro problem." Perhaps mindful that he needed at least the passive acquiescence of Virginia's paternalistic elites, he added that "these considerations should compel us, in any sentiment of the matter, to treat him not only with meticulous fairness but also with large generosity. Noblesse oblige would permit no less."[15]

Powell and Cox thus underscored the degree to which the Anglo-Saxon movement reflected an admission among whites that they, at the very height of the classical period of segregation, had become powerless to guarantee racial boundaries in absolute terms. "Those of us who live in the South," Cox explained, "will detect with comparative accuracy the presence of colored blood in the individual, but not always are we sure, and in a large number of cases where the race purity of the individual is suspected there is lacking adequate means by which the white race may be protected." Consequently, legislation was necessary to "remove the 'suspect' from uncertainty and place him on the right side of the color line." As evidence of the problem, Powell offered that he stood for forty-five minutes at the intersection of Broad and Second Streets in Richmond. "During this time," reasoned Powell, "I counted among the passers-by over 200 Negroes, of whom only five were black. In addition, I counted over thirty individuals of whom I could not with any degree of certainty state whether they were white or colored." Although Powell clearly worried about the biological breakdown of the color line, he was also concerned that interracial cooperation on social welfare committees and in training schools threat-ened "social and caste distinctions." Knowing that many of his friends in Richmond's elite circles participated in such interracial work, Powell noted the noble motives of these whites but warned of the "advance of social equality under existing conditions." In addition, Powell expressed concern that a younger generation of Virginians lacked the wherewithal to protect the color line. To all these problems, legislation offered the only remedy.[16]

The Richmond *Times-Dispatch,* the most widely read morning paper in the state, enthusiastically embraced the positions taken by the two Anglo-Saxon Club leaders. In an editorial published alongside the pieces by Powell and Cox, the daily concluded that all "thinking men and women in Virginia" had to give the articles "serious consideration." Acknowledging that the Anglo-Saxon platform alone would not "solve the negro problem," the paper did suggest that the platform "will at least express an ideal, and throw every possible safeguard around racial purity."[17]

Two weeks after the appearance of the Powell and Cox articles, Walter Plecker provided an early glimpse of the zeal with which his department, the Bureau of Vital Statistics, would attempt to define Virginians as white or black. Plecker instructed local registrars in Amherst and Bedford Counties, both home to persons of contested racial heritage, "to firmly refuse to admit them as white if they have even a trace of negro blood on either side."[18] This determination to redefine blackness according to a "one-drop" rule, however, flew in the face of Virginia law, which then defined as black those persons with one-sixteenth or more black blood. In essence, Plecker granted himself legislative authority to define race in terms favored by the Anglo-Saxon Clubs before the issue had been considered by the General Assembly. This attempt to tighten the law in matters of miscegenation resonated throughout the South. Beginning immediately after emancipation, all of the southern states adopted or reinforced preexisting laws against miscegenation. Custom and belief dictated to all white southerners that "one-drop" defined a black person, but the law in most states said otherwise. Some states ultimately followed Virginia's lead and adopted a "one-drop" test, but other states kept a "one-eighth" or "one-sixteenth" rule on their books. Some states even maintained one definition of blackness for the purpose of intermarriage and a second definition for all other purposes.[19]

No doubt Plecker's concern was only heightened by the reaction that his instructions prompted from at least one unidentified local registrar, possibly from Bedford County, who expressed a concern about the damage to his own business if he did not register people according to their wishes. The official told Plecker that "these people have their own churches, schools, etc., and do not associate with either class, yet they are registered as white on the voting list, and the only thing I could do without being injurious to my business, was to let the birth registers go on as handed in to me by the midwives as white." Several months later this registrar resigned rather than choose between the health of his business and compliance with Plecker's instructions. Plecker's experience with local registrars not only revealed the degree to which some communities in Virginia rejected his rigid definition of race but also further convinced him of the need for a state law that would leave local officials with no discretion in the matter of racial classification.[20]

With the Virginia legislature not due to convene until January 1924, John Powell and his supporters set about building support for their agenda. Although Powell never realized his grand ambition of turning the Anglo-Saxon Clubs into a nationwide organization, his influence was nevertheless broad. From its first post in Richmond in September 1922, the club apparently reached its peak in 1925 with thirty-one posts in Virginia, plus three in the North. In addition, the Women's Racial Integrity Club of Richmond had at least forty members, many of whom were matrons of the capital's most socially prominent families. Although plans to start chapters in North Carolina and Mississippi apparently never came to fruition, Powell succeeded in garnering support for legislation in other states. Invited to address the Georgia legislature in 1925, his pleas contributed to that state's adoption of a racial integrity measure two years later, the same year that Alabama added a similar statute.[21]

While a number of college clubs appeared on early lists, their membership proved less than reliable. The Hampden-Sydney post objected to the constitution as "too complicated." A week after the first statewide convention in October 1923, M. O. Williams, president of the chapter at Virginia Polytechnic Institute in Blacksburg, told Powell that only ten members remained in his post; several months later, just as Powell, Cox, and Plecker prepared to present legislation to the Virginia General Assembly, Williams resigned his presidency and withdrew his membership. The collegian claimed to remain "in accord with the aims" of the organization, but he had decided that "the method followed by the Anglo-Saxon Clubs does not lead to a solution as I see it."[22]

This kind of unreliable support for his mission, coupled with other, more threatening campus activities, further convinced Powell that the younger generation of whites lacked the necessary commitment and upbringing to maintain racial integrity. A front-page story in the January 10, 1924, issue of the Virginia Tech student newspaper, for example, detailed the proceedings of the Student Volunteer Conference, held in Indianapolis over the Christmas holidays and attended by seven thousand students, including fourteen from Tech. Most of the coverage centered on discussions of race, and no doubt the conclusion of at least half of the participants that racial distinctions should not

be drawn terrified Powell. Students proposed to "eliminate the white superiority complex ingrained in the primary schools," to "utilize every opportunity to
become friends with members of other races," to "begin tackling the problem
by converting our own families!" and to "work for the breaking down of racial discrimination in dormitories, class-rooms, societies, athletics, fraternities, churches—in college life generally." The last two suggestions in particular drew Powell's attention. The student newspaper reported favorably on the
convention as a whole and gave full coverage to the discussions on race. To
make matters worse, M. O. Williams, the former president of Virginia Tech's
Anglo-Saxon Club, had attended as a delegate.[23]

Powell had stumbled upon the genesis of the southern student interracial
movement. In early 1924, as a result of discussions at the Indianapolis conference, collegians established interracial groups in a half-dozen southern cities,
including Lynchburg, Virginia. When a handful of students from Lynchburg
College, Randolph-Macon Women's College, and the Lynchburg Theological
Seminary, a black college, gathered at the Lynchburg YWCA, local citizens
and YWCA officials forced them to meet instead in the city's black slums.
Although the students did not openly challenge legalized segregation, they
proved far more committed to genuine interracial cooperation than did their
adult counterparts. In an effort to break down the psychological and physical barriers imposed by segregation, the students promoted social interaction,
held debates, musicals, literary readings, and even dined together—an absolute taboo in southern society.[24]

In February 1924 Powell and other supporters of the Anglo-Saxon Clubs finally had an opportunity to present their case to the Virginia General Assembly. Sponsors in the house and senate introduced legislation based on Powell's
stated aims: rigid, mandatory registration of all Virginians under the auspices
of the Bureau of Vital Statistics; one year's confinement in the penitentiary for
willfully lying about one's color; mandatory presentation of racial certifica-
tion to local registrars before a marriage license could be issued; prohibition
against whites marrying anyone save another white; and the definition of a
white person as one "who has no trace whatsoever of any blood other than
Caucasian"—the first time Virginia law defined white persons. In addition, to
meet the concerns of white elites who descended from Pocahontas and John
Rolfe (blood traced to that union was considered a badge of status in the Old
Dominion and the sole example of acceptable nonwhite ancestry), supporters created a "Pocahontas Exception": persons "who have less than one sixty-
fourth of the blood of an American Indian and have no other non-Caucasic
blood shall be deemed to be white persons."[25]

Powell headlined the list of the bill's supporters who appeared before a legislative committee on February 12. Citing cases from around the state that

showed the danger of racial mixing, Powell quoted leading northern eugenicists Lothrop Stoddard, Madison Grant, and Franklin Giddings, all of whom
predicted the downfall of white civilization without proper legislation. Powell
repeatedly emphasized that racial integrity was more important than rigid racial separation. Yet, he simultaneously conceived of even the most basic mani-
festations of racial cooperation as inevitably posing a threat to white racial
integrity. Thomas Dabney, a black professor at Virginia Union University, underscored the inherent contradiction in Powell's rhetoric by pointing out how
often Powell "lamented the degree to which barriers between the races were
coming down." In his testimony, for example, Powell specifically mentioned
that the proposals of the Student Volunteer Conference would likely lead to
amalgamation. Powell worried, moreover, that white southern students had
attended this convention. While no credible evidence suggested that miscegenation was actually on the increase, student newspapers and interracial groups
proved to Powell that interracial cooperation was on the rise.[26]

Virginia's black press remained relatively quiet as the racial integrity measure wound its way through the legislature. Aimed at those mixed-race persons who were no longer clearly identifiable as black, the proposed statute did
not affect directly the vast majority of black Virginians who had no desire
to pass as white. The Richmond *Planet* opined that "[w]e do not see that it
concerns any Negro in this state. . . . Every well-thinking colored person who
understands existing conditions wants the line of racial demarcation to remain. They want the white man to 'stay on his side' of the line and they will
do the same thing on their side." Upon the measure's passage, the Norfolk
Journal and Guide added its regret that the measure was intended to preserve
only the integrity of the white race.[27] Nevertheless, Powell's testimony elicited
a stirring rebuke from Gordon Blaine Hancock, a professor at Virginia Union
University, a Baptist minister, and a leading voice on Richmond's interracial
committee. Hancock vehemently denied that blacks in Virginia or anywhere
in the South were interested in racial amalgamation. "What the negro wants,
therefore, is . . . a man's chance and simple justice," wrote Hancock in a letter
to the Richmond *News Leader.* "The negro is not demanding amalgamation[,]
. . . and he resents an implication that he does." Hancock argued that fears
of racial mixing had disingenuously been used as a smokescreen to deny to
blacks benefits of citizenship such as education and neighborhood improvements. Proponents of racial integrity dismissed such objections as evidence
that blacks were "determined to pass over into the white race."[28]

While influential support came from sources like the Richmond *Times-
Dispatch,* some state senators considered the section of the bill that mandated
racial registration an insult to whites. Accordingly, the senate amended the
bill to allow for voluntary registration and, in a further nod to elites, raised the

allowable amount of Indian blood to one-sixteenth. In March 1924 the General Assembly passed and Governor E. Lee Trinkle signed the Racial Integrity Act, a measure that Peggy Pascoe has termed "the most draconian miscegenation law in American history." Several weeks later, the secretary of Post No. 1 of the Anglo-Saxon Clubs thanked Governor Trinkle not only for his support of the bill but for "the promptness of the registration of yourself and family."[29]

Although Powell was the Anglo-Saxon Clubs' leading spokesman, Walter Plecker, as director of the Bureau of Vital Statistics, was without a doubt the group's primary enforcer. From 1924 until his retirement twenty-two years later, Plecker waged a campaign of threats and intimidation aimed at classifying all Virginians by race and identifying even the smallest traces of black blood in the state's citizens. In short, the statistician operated on the belief that a person was guilty of being black until he or she could prove otherwise.

Plecker considered it his mission to encourage as many Virginians as possible to register with the state. Between ten and twenty thousand near-white Virginians, he noted, "possess an intermixture of colored blood, in some cases to a slight extent, it is true, but still enough to prevent them from being white." Such people previously had been considered white, which had allowed them to demand "admittance of their children to white schools" and "in not a few cases" to marry whites. Although such people were "scarcely distinguished as colored," they "are not white in reality." Registration, he argued, would enable the Bureau of Vital Statistics to head off such trouble.[30]

Within days of the passage of the Racial Integrity Act, Plecker sent instructions to county and city registrars, health professionals, and all other persons responsible for the administration of the law. He emphasized the necessity of recording accurately the racial composition of both parents, warned authorities not to accept persons as white if any doubt existed, and described the proper usage of such terms as *mulatto, quadroon, octoroon, mixed,* and *issue.* That fall, Plecker asked school teachers and officials to assist his office in preventing children with even a trace of black blood from enrolling in white schools and urged them to report to his office any uncertainties. Relying on birth and marriage records from 1853 to 1896 in his office's possession, Plecker confirmed that some families in the past had been "correctly listed as colored, but have now succeeded in passing as white, and intermarrying with white people who have no knowledge of the facts." Nevertheless, according to Plecker, "under Mendel's law, the children from such marriages are likely, even after many generations, to present clear marks of colored ancestry."[31]

The enforcement of Virginia's Racial Integrity Act produced profound and devastating consequences in the lives of Plecker's targets. On April 30, 1924, for example, Plecker wrote Mrs. Robert Cheatham of Lynchburg with regard to the racial classification of her child born the previous July, well before the law was passed. According to the birth certificate signed by midwife Mary Gildon, Cheatham and her husband were white. Yet the Lynchburg health department, Plecker revealed, listed her husband as black. "This is to give you warning that this is a mulatto child and you cannot pass it off as white," Plecker wrote. "You will have do to something about this matter and see that this child is not allowed to mix with white children. It cannot go to white schools and can never marry a white person in Virginia. It is an awful thing." In addition, Plecker informed the midwife that "it is a penitentiary offense to willfully state that a child is white when it is colored. You have made yourself liable to very serious trouble by doing this thing." Although John Powell held no state position, Plecker updated him with documents like this one, at the top of which he had scribbled, "This is a specimen of our daily troubles and shows how we are handling them."[32]

The degree to which residents of Amherst and Rockbridge Counties would cause trouble for Plecker became readily apparent in the ensuing weeks. Located in the mountainous western part of the state, these counties comprised one of two regions considered home to significant numbers of mixed-race Virginians. Plecker told Earnest Cox that "our Amherst County colony is up in arms and are [sic] on the verge of a race riot, threatening the life of one of our local registrars for giving out information concerning them." Forty-seven such people had attempted to register as white, even though Plecker could prove they were not. In response, the bureau had instructed all local registrars to refund the registration fee rather than accept them as white.[33]

Plecker's instructions to local registrars led to court challenges in the fall of 1924. A. T. Shields, the clerk of court for Rockbridge County, refused to grant a marriage license to Dorothy Johns and James Connor after determining that Johns had at least a trace of black blood. Johns took Shields to court where witnesses on her behalf testified that she had no black blood. But Plecker and Silas Coleman, a resident of Amherst County, effectively used birth records to show that she descended from the Johns family of Amherst County, all of whom had "colored" ancestors. In response, Johns's attorney argued correctly that "colored" had been used in the nineteenth century to describe Indians as well as blacks and provided witnesses who acknowledged his client's Indian ancestry. Judge Henry Holt, however, sided with the clerk of court that Johns had at least some black blood. At the same time, he objected to aspects of the law itself. In particular, he found that persons wrongly accused of having some nonwhite blood would find it nearly impossible to disprove such charges.[34]

Several weeks later Plecker found himself back in the same court in an almost identical case. This time the clerk of court had refused a marriage license to Atha Sorrells and Robert Painter, believing that Sorrells had at least some black blood mixed with her white and possibly Indian ancestry. Despite the earlier victory, Plecker approached this second case with extreme caution. He urged his star witness in the Johns case, Silas Coleman, to testify a second time despite being "afraid that they will burn your barn and do you other injury." Coleman, however, refused Plecker's request.[35] Now lacking any witnesses to support Plecker's testimony, Judge Holt ruled in favor of the plaintiff and ordered that the clerk grant the marriage license. While the judge expressed support in his opinion for the intent of the Racial Integrity Act, he nevertheless determined that the law depended upon a definition of Caucasian "which in the present state of ethnology has no certain meaning." As Holt noted, a literal interpretation of Virginia's statute according to contemporary ethnography would have denied a marriage license to a white woman and a Hungarian nobleman but would have permitted the marriage of the same woman to an Arab or North African. Furthermore, the jurist argued, nobody could prove without a doubt that he or she did not have somewhere, generations back, a drop of black blood. "Half the men who fought at Hastings were my grandfathers," reasoned Holt. "Some of them were probably hanged and some knighted, who can tell?" Holt insisted that the "rule of reason" must be applied to law, and therefore "an appreciable amount of foreign blood" must exist to fall within the bounds of the Racial Integrity Act. In this case, the evidence showed "no strain present in the applicant of any blood other than white, except Indian, and there is not enough of that to come within the statute."[36]

Although he suppressed personal criticism of Holt, Powell did express an urgent concern with the implications of the ruling. Referring to the birth and marriage records kept by the Bureau of Vital Statistics, Powell warned that Holt's decision, if upheld, "will mean the complete nullification of our most precious possession, our race records, [those of] 1853–1896, our greatest protection against the infusion of negro blood. If this decision is to stand, any negroid in the state can go before a court and say, 'My ancestors are recorded as colored, but that does not mean negro, they were Indians.' He may then be declared white and may marry a white woman." Consequently, exclaimed Powell, "Indians are springing up all over the state as if by spontaneous generation."[37] Powell's devotion to the "race records" underscores one of the most troublesome aspects of the entire history of the racial integrity crusade in Virginia. Birth and marriage records had been kept from 1853 until 1896 and then discontinued until 1912. Five years later the old records were transferred to the Bureau of Vital Statistics. But no evidence exists to suggest that the old record keepers had been especially careful or consistent. Many of the records were incomplete. "Colored" may well have meant black to one registrar and Indian to another. Plecker and Powell, however, recognized no such uncertainty.[38]

Anthropologists and genealogists agree that triracial mixing did occur with some frequency in certain parts of Virginia in the seventeenth, eighteenth, and early nineteenth centuries. Whites, Indians, free blacks, and slaves lived as neighbors, most especially along the peninsulas of the Tidewater between the Rappahannock and James Rivers but also in the western mountain counties that were home to Atha Sorrells and Dorothy Johns. People fell in love, married, and had children. But just as interracial mixing between whites and blacks had slowed to a trickle by the Civil War, so too did mixing between Indians, many of whom also had white blood, and blacks. In fact, Indians understood all too well the social implications of blackness. Throughout the late nineteenth century Indians sought to separate themselves from their black neighbors by establishing their own schools and churches. Over time, some Indians even disavowed cousins with recognizable black features. As late as 1928 Chief George Cook of the Pamunkey tribe proclaimed, "I will tie a stone around my neck and jump in the James River rather than be classed as a Negro."[39] Not once prior to the passage of the Racial Integrity Act did Powell or Plecker suggest that their efforts would be aimed at Virginia's Indians. Yet in the aftermath of the Sorrells decision, as individuals followed the successful tactic and claimed that any mixed blood was of Indian origin, Plecker attempted to define Virginia's Indians out of existence. Although triracial mixing had certainly occurred, all persons of Indian descent did not necessarily have a trace of black blood, a distinction lost on Plecker.[40]

The majority of Virginians claiming Indian status lived along the Tidewater in the eastern Virginia counties of Charles City, New Kent, King and Queen, and King William. Plecker devoted himself to interviewing white residents of these counties in an effort to determine the racial classification of the Indians. E. H. Marston and his brother George, both lifelong residents of Charles City County, assured Plecker that no one had claimed Indian heritage until the passage of Virginia's first Jim Crow laws at the turn of the century. At that time, a group of mixed-race persons organized themselves as the Chickahominy Indians; their first action was to buy train passes that allowed them to ride on whites-only cars. A local registrar in Charles City County confirmed the essence of the Marstons' account with the story of Hill Adkins, a man who chose not to join the tribe because he could not afford the membership fees. According to the registrar, Adkins had said, "I am a negro, and stay with the negroes."[41]

Plecker seized upon such anecdotal, and highly distorted, evidence to bolster his belief that all Indians in Virginia had black blood. In anticipation of the 1930 enumeration, Plecker unsuccessfully pleaded with the director of the federal census not to recognize any Virginians as Indians. Plecker acknowledged that he could not change the status of the Pamunkey and Mattaponi who had lived on reservations in King William County since colonial times. Since these groups had not been taxed and therefore normal records had not been kept, Plecker lacked evidence to prove they were black. Yet Plecker used the information acquired from interviews with persons such as the Marston brothers to disqualify the claims of the Chickahominy of Charles City County and the Rappahannock of King and Queen and Essex Counties. By contrast, Plecker disqualified the mulattoes of Amherst and Rockbridge Counties, whom he identified as the largest (and "lowest socially") group of blacks in the state trying to gain Indian status, based on his reading of the census: the 1900 enumeration showed no Indians in Amherst County, only 7 appeared in 1910, yet there were 304 in 1920. Certainly, reasoned Plecker, these people were not truly Indians.[42]

Throughout 1925 Plecker became increasingly strident in his claims that no Virginia Indians were free from black blood. To combat the success of persons claiming Indian ancestry, Plecker concentrated on tightening loopholes in the 1924 statute. The legislative act of 1910 had not defined whites, but it had defined blacks as those with one-sixteenth or more black blood. (Before 1910 blacks had been defined as persons with one-fourth or more black blood.) Hence, according to the law of 1910, a person with at least a drop but less than one-sixteenth black blood was defined as white and prohibited from marrying a black person. The Racial Integrity Act of 1924, however, also prohibited such a person from marrying a white. Plecker became convinced that an amended law, even if it entailed removing the privileges granted under the "Pocahontas Exception," offered the only means of correcting this statutory contradiction and of preventing certain blacks from continuing to pass as whites or Indians.[43]

In late November Edward P. Bradby, chief of the Chickahominy Indians whom Plecker considered black, wrote Governor Trinkle concerning Plecker's intentions to introduce this new, amended legislation. Though the disingenuous governor claimed to know nothing of Plecker's plans, Trinkle assured Bradby that the chief would have an opportunity to present his case to the General Assembly. Remarking that "the Indians have certainly given me no trouble since I have been Governor," Trinkle expressed a desire to avoid such trouble in the future. At the same time, Trinkle admonished Plecker "to be conservative and reasonable and not create any ill feeling if it can be avoided between the Indians and the State government. . . . I am afraid sentiment is molding itself along the line that you are too hard on these people and pushing matters too fast."[44]

The governor's warning illuminated the contours of the relationship between Virginia's political leadership and the Anglo-Saxon ideologues. Trinkle and the vast majority of state legislators found it politically expedient to support the agenda of the Anglo-Saxon Clubs. After all, as politicians they had often employed racial imagery successfully in their own campaigns and feared having their own stated devotion to white supremacy questioned. Many of them, however, considered certain aspects of the Anglo-Saxon ideology excessive. Enough senators had objected to the mandatory registration statute, for example, to defeat it. As Trinkle realized, Plecker's mission to enforce mandatory registration in his own terms threatened to create a backlash. Yet the nature and power of white supremacy ideology insured that the governor only dared rebuke Plecker in private. Furthermore, Trinkle appears to have been guided more by public opinion than by personal conviction. Interestingly enough, the perception among whites that Plecker had gone too far only extended to his treatment of persons claiming Indian ancestry. No whites publicly doubted the essential rightness of the racial integrity measures. As a result, Trinkle and the rest of Virginia's political elites offered minimal resistance at best to expressions of racial extremism. They proved unable and unwilling to turn off the faucet of race hatred from which they so willingly drank.

Despite the governor's warning, Plecker continued to insist that the Chickahominy group had been classified correctly; Trinkle, in turn, promised that he in no way intended to interfere with Plecker's enforcement of the Racial Integrity Act. At the same time, Trinkle regretted the negative press that "makes it look as if we are probably working on them pretty hard and continually exposing their misfortune of having colored blood. I know this is humiliating if it is true and I was in hopes that this could be handled in a quiet way so as not to emphasize and embarrass them any more than possible." Plecker, however, considered Trinkle's request an impossibility. His job, no matter the negative publicity, was to prevent persons with any black blood from passing. "I am, therefore, unable," Plecker wrote, "to see how it is working any injustice upon them or humiliation for our office to take a firm stand against their intermarriage with white people, or to the preliminary steps of recognition as Indians with permission to attend white schools and to ride in white coaches." [45] More than likely, this exchange only confirmed Plecker's belief that Trinkle's attitude constituted part of the problem in the law's enforcement. A month earlier Plecker had complained about a photograph of Trinkle posing with Chief George Cook of the Pamunkey Indians and his daughter, Pocahontas, that had appeared in the Richmond *Times-Dispatch*. Plecker appealed to "prominent men to protest against this thing" so that the newspapers would stop running such pictures. Plecker also implicitly criticized Trinkle to Governor-elect Harry Byrd. [46]

Plecker's criticism of Trinkle drew a strong rebuke from his boss, the state health commissioner. The occasion was not the first time that Plecker overstepped his bounds as a government employee. As director of the Bureau of Vital Statistics, a division of the public health department, Plecker also was appointed a special agent of the Children's Bureau of the U.S. Department of Labor, charged with disseminating modern health information to new parents. In addition to the authorized mailings, however, in 1925 Plecker used federal franking privileges to send out a pamphlet, *Eugenics in Relation to The New Family and the Law on Racial Integrity.* Designed to arouse young, white newlyweds, especially men, to the dangers that confronted them, Plecker decreed, "Let the young men who read this realize that the future purity of our race is in their keeping, and that the joining of themselves to females of a lower race and fathering children who shall be a curse and a menace to our State and civilization is a crime against society." Educators, health workers, and ministers snapped up more than sixty thousand copies of the pamphlet.[47]

Relatively quiet at the time of the 1924 act's passage, the African American press denounced the dissemination of Plecker's pamphlet. "With the sanction and seal of the great State of Virginia upon his utterances," the Norfolk *Journal and Guide* opined, "Dr. Plecker, as a Virginia health officer, paid by the taxpayers of the State, Negroes included, is industriously engaged in sowing the seeds of bitterest racial discord, from one end of the country to another." Few whites, reasoned the paper, could possibly read Plecker's literature and not develop a bad reaction to blacks. Labor Department officials agreed that Plecker had exceeded his authority and terminated his position.[48]

The loss of his federal position did not slow down Plecker for a moment. He joined Powell and several other colleagues in extending their influence to the censorship of motion pictures through the Board of Censors, established by the Virginia General Assembly in 1922 and charged with reviewing each motion picture submitted for public viewing in the state. Board members understood that their mandate demanded the censorship of films that portrayed blacks and whites in a manner inconsistent with accepted racial norms. In fact, the board stated clearly in an early annual report that it had "scrutinized with peculiar care all films which touch upon the relations existing between whites and blacks. Every scene or subtitle calculated to produce friction between the races is eliminated." The censors worked hard to make sure that Virginians saw only stereotypical images of blacks on the screen: the faithful servant, the ignorant child, and the loathsome criminal. After 1924 the censors consistently explained their decisions in light of the Racial Integrity Act. In addition, Powell and Plecker used the censorship of such films to judge the fealty of white public officials to their agenda.[49]

Most Hollywood productions in the 1910s and 1920s failed to present African Americans in terms other than stereotypically subhuman and so rarely raised the eyebrows of the censors. Those films that dared to address racial issues in a meaningful way and to present blacks in fully human terms were the work of black film entrepreneurs. By the mid-1920s Oscar Micheaux stood at the forefront of those producing these so-called race films. In March 1925 Micheaux's latest film, *The House Behind the Cedars,* engendered significant controversy. Unlike the deliberations on Micheaux's previous two films, however, Micheaux this time readily agreed to re-cut the film according to the censors' wishes; the filmmaker was thus not the actual focus of the uproar. Instead, the board's deliberations became a litmus test for the proper allegiance of white civil servants to the Racial Integrity Act. When Arthur James, an assistant commissioner of public welfare, failed to object to the film with sufficient vehemence, Powell and members of the Anglo-Saxon Clubs threatened to ruin his career.[50] *The House Behind the Cedars,* based on the novel by Charles W. Chesnutt, tells the story of a mulatto woman passing as white, her interracial love affair, and racial grievances held by blacks, all topics that invoked the ire of white Virginians. Not surprisingly, the censors found the movie "so objectionable, in fact, as to necessitate its total rejection." For particularly controversial movies, however, the three-member board often chose to screen the film a second time in the presence of other state officials and private citizens, including, in this case, state labor commissioner John H. Hall Jr., Arthur James of the Department of Public Welfare, Walter Plecker, Earnest Sevier Cox, Louise Burleigh (later the wife of John Powell), a Mrs. Beattie, and a Mrs. Staples. Most of these persons had gone on record as strict advocates of Virginia's Racial Integrity Act. The board's report concluded that movies were not "the medium" for handling touchy subjects such as black grievances and intermarriage between the races. In a nod to the influence of the Anglo-Saxon Clubs, the Virginia Board of Censors noted that "the picture, either purposely or through the maladroitness of the producers, at least indirectly contravenes the spirit of the recently enacted anti-miscegenation law which put Virginia in the forefront as a pioneer in legislation aimed to preserve the integrity of the white race."[51]

Several weeks after the Virginia board reviewed Micheaux's film, Powell returned to Richmond after a prolonged absence. Upon his return, Plecker, Cox, and Burleigh reported that Arthur James had made inappropriate comments at the board of censors meeting. Although the official report indicated only that one viewer had left open the possibility that the film receive a license after significant cuts, Burleigh reported that James had expressed opinions "so opposed to the consensus as to indicate that Mr. James' feeling about the proper position of the races differed fundamentally from that of the other people present and from the accepted standard in Virginia." In particular, James reportedly dismissed the need to make certain cuts in the film because "you can at any time, go up to Atlantic City and see the best people in Richmond dancing in cabarets with negresses." James also offended his accusers by admitting that he would like to see the most competent black lawyers, doctors, and ministers move to Richmond. Burleigh's report reminded Powell of James's response to Plecker's controversial eugenics pamphlet. During a January 1925 visit to James's office, Powell had remarked favorably upon the publication; James, however, had "criticized it severely, stating that Dr. Plecker had gone too far and . . . was using his official position to conduct a campaign of propaganda against the negro."[52]

Powell now informed James that "such views and expressions on the part of a State official—especially one connected with the Board of Public Welfare, constituted, in the present delicate and tense situation, a very real menace to the public." While claiming to recognize James's freedom of speech and thought on a personal level, Powell declared, "I shall not hesitate to criticize the actions and expressed views of public servants whenever they may seem to me unsound or dangerous." Consequently, Powell convened a closed meeting of Anglo-Saxon Post No. 1, whose members decided to ask James to explain his opinions. James denied making the statements ascribed to him, but Powell's informants offered to provide signed statements testifying to their accounts. Powell appeared to relish his role as self-appointed judge and told James that he would happily publicize the results once James had resolved his differences with his accusers. "If, however, you desire," Powell continued, "to institute against me a suit for slander, I must tell you without any hesitation that I should welcome the opportunity to clear up before the public a matter so deeply affecting the public welfare." Several weeks later, Powell sent James the signed statements of Cox and Burleigh and apparently made his point.[53]

Nominally at issue in the James controversy was loyalty to the letter of the Racial Integrity Act. Yet at the same time that members of the Anglo-Saxon Clubs were threatening Arthur James for his insufficient devotion to the law, they launched an assault that ultimately led to the passage of the Public Assemblages Act that required racial separation in all public places. The agitation over the proposed measure demonstrates that Powell and his supporters were not, as they claimed, concerned primarily with biological interracial mixing but rather with ensuring that black Virginians remained second-class citizens. The agitation over the statute left white paternalists struggling to negotiate a middle ground between professions of good will toward their black neighbors and fealty to the dictates of white supremacy. Furthermore, the passage of the measure revealed to black Virginians the emptiness of white elite paternalism.

The dispute that led to adoption of the statute began in February 1925 when Grace Copeland, a close childhood friend of John Powell, attended a dance recital at Hampton Institute's Ogden Hall. Whether or not the large auditorium had sold out because, as one trustee later noted, "the dancers were practically naked and therefore everybody went," Mrs. Copeland arrived late to discover that the only remaining seats were next to a group of black patrons. Three weeks later her husband, newspaper editor Walter Scott Copeland—a respected journalist who served four terms as the president of the Virginia Press Association—wrote a blistering piece in the Newport News *Daily Press* in which he accused the school of teaching and practicing "social equality between the white and negro races." [54] Copeland, moreover, remained unconvinced by the assurance of Hampton's white principal, James Gregg, that the editor had misunderstood the facts of the situation. When the Norfolk *Journal and Guide,* a black newspaper, took umbrage at Copeland's charges, a war of words escalated between the two newspapers. Already distressed by the reports from the censorship board, Powell led the recently organized Hampton post of the Anglo-Saxon Clubs into action on the Copelands' behalf. Over the course of the next year, Powell and Copeland together kept alive the issue of social equality at Hampton Institute: Powell in frequent speeches and behind-the-scenes maneuvering, Copeland through his editorial pages. [55]

Their combined efforts prompted the Norfolk *Journal and Guide* to ask why white opponents singled out Hampton, where white teachers taught black and Native American students, for abuse, when public sentiment in Richmond required that black schools, hospitals, sanitariums, and schools for deaf and blind black children be staffed by whites. "Is it because at Hampton," the weekly asked, "Negroes are treated as *human* beings and at the other places they are treated as *inferior* human beings?" [56] This question penetrated to the heart of the racial debate in Virginia in the 1920s and 1930s. Originally conceived as an institute emphasizing vocational training, white elites in Virginia, including Walter Copeland, had easily supported Hampton's mission. But by the 1920s, many students at Hampton resented the restrictions that limited their growth and advancement and ultimately went out on strike to demand greater intellectual rigor in their curriculum. Many of the same whites who sanctioned and supported manual training balked at the implications of a more classical education and rejected any attempts at further reform. [57]

On November 27, 1925, three hundred members of the Hampton Anglo-Saxon Club listened to speeches by Powell and Copeland and passed a resolution calling on their delegate, Alvin Massenburg, to introduce legislation at the upcoming session of the General Assembly to make illegal the "mixing of audiences at public assemblages." Though aimed at curtailing the arrangements at Hampton, supporters intended the legislation to cover the entire state. On January 20, 1926, thirty-one-year-old George Alvin Massenburg, serving his first term in the House of Delegates, introduced a bill "requiring the separation of white and colored persons at public halls, theaters, opera houses, motion picture shows and places of public entertainment and public assemblages." Popularly known as the Massenburg Bill, the Public Assemblages Act became the broadest and most restrictive measure of its kind in the United States; it defined segregation in Virginia until 1963. [58]

Unlike the debate in 1924 when the General Assembly had considered the Racial Integrity Act, significant opposition did mobilize against the

Massenburg Bill. Led by Norfolk *Virginian-Pilot* editor Louis Jaffe, a number of white newsmen deemed the measure unnecessary. While Jaffe pointed out that all whites believed in racial integrity, they did not all support "Prussianized segregation" that would affect a privately owned assembly hall in a privately endowed black college. Jaffe urged persons who objected to the conditions at Hampton simply to stay away. Aside from newspaper editors, the most prominent opposition to the bill came from several groups of clergy. Members of the Richmond Ministerial Union, the foreign mission board of the Southern Baptist Convention, and the Methodist and Baptist ministers' conferences of Richmond did not like that separate seating would have to be provided for Chinese and Japanese students who attended religious colleges in Virginia as part of missionary efforts. The Reverend Dr. J. F. Love, secretary of the foreign mission board of the Southern Baptist Convention, explained that the legislation would "offer offense to all non-white people and would in China, at this time, cause much irritation and give all Virginia missionaries serious trouble." [59]

Aided by a statement of support issued by a group of Richmond's most prominent white citizens, and perhaps spurred by growing public opposition to the Massenburg Bill, Powell, Cox, and Copeland advocated the measure with rhetoric that reached new levels of extremism. Powell asserted that the situation at Hampton was part of a broader conspiracy among blacks to achieve social equality. He blamed the NAACP and the Norfolk *Journal and Guide,* in particular, for "making this breaking down of the color line a matter of principle." According to J. A. Rogers, a northern journalist of mixed racial heritage who covered the legislative committee hearings on the bill, Walter Copeland testified to the sincerity of his affection for his mammy and in the next breath said with reference to Hampton Institute, "The niggers in that institution are being taught that there ought not to be any distinction between themselves and white people. If you wipe out the color line we are gone." [60]

Rogers concluded after the hearing that blacks in the North could not possibly understand the obstacles faced by blacks in the South. He also claimed to have learned more about the psychology of southern whites from three hours of testimony than from years of personal experience. Any similar debate in a northern legislature, he noted, would have revolved around the desirability of segregation itself. "At that hearing in Richmond," Rogers discovered, "segregation was taken as a prime necessity by both attackers and advocates of the bill." Furthermore, proclamations of white supremacy and Anglo-Saxon racial purity from both sides led the journalist to wonder which side he found the most objectionable. He commented that "if anything, my sympathies were with the advocates for they at least were frank." [61]

On March 22, 1926, the Massenburg Bill became law without the signature of Governor Harry F. Byrd. The chief executive later told James Gregg that he opposed the measure and that he would not have supported it had he still been in the state senate. Nevertheless, Byrd was unwilling to veto legislation passed by such a large majority. More than likely, however, Byrd would have taken no position on the issue had he been in the senate, just as he had abstained from the vote on the Racial Integrity Act two years before. A public stand against any racially charged measure might have threatened the political future of the ambitious young politician.[62]

In the aftermath of the Massenburg Bill's passage, Grace Copeland revealed an ideological side to the Anglo-Saxon Clubs that John Powell and others had tried hard to hide. In a letter to Governor Byrd, Copeland concluded that recent events at Hampton proved the fallacy of educating African Americans. Instead, she agreed with her father "that it was impossible to reason with a negro—that the only way to keep him in his place was to keep him under fear." Copeland's views challenge the primacy of eugenics and miscegenation in the agenda of Powell and his supporters. Powell began his crusade claiming that Jim Crow laws were of secondary importance, but his advocacy of the Public Assemblages Act suggests otherwise. Black students at Hampton Institute sought the very things that Gordon Blaine Hancock had claimed when he refuted any interest in amalgamation among blacks. For Powell and the Copelands, however, education offered the possibility of first-class citizenship. That, more than miscegenation, concerned them first and foremost. As legal scholar Paul Lombardo has written, "The true motive behind the Racial In-tegrity Act of 1924 was the maintenance of white supremacy and black economic and social inferiority. . . . It was an accident of history that eugenic theory reached its peak of acceptability in 1924 so as to be available as a respectable veneer with which to cover ancient prejudice. For Powell, Plecker, and their ilk, eugenical ideology was not a *sine qua non* for legislation but merely a coincidental set of arguments that provided intellectual fuel to the racist fires."[63]

The passage of the Public Assemblages Act angered Virginia's black citizens, especially those who had labored to educate and better themselves within the confines of a white-dominated civil and political society. Although a number of the state's leading black newspapers and businessmen articulated their belief that the legislation was unnecessary since blacks and whites led sufficiently separate lives, the statute's passage served as one more reminder that they could not depend upon the "good will" of white elites for genuine advancement. In addition, the adoption of the Massenburg Bill opened the door for the Virginia General Assembly to saddle the state's black citizenry with additional Jim Crow laws over the course of the next two decades.[64]

Although successful in overcoming opposition to the Public Assemblages Act, Powell and Plecker failed to tighten loopholes created by the "Pocahontas Exception." In 1926 and again in 1928 the General Assembly responded to growing sentiment that the campaign against Indians had gone too far. Others opposed the effort to close the loopholes when the Richmond *News Leader* reported that a proposed bill would make sixty-three "First Families" of Virginia "colored." Those targeted for racial reassignment under the legislation apparently included senators, presidents, governors, generals, novelists, and bishops, all of whom proudly included seventeenth-century Indians among their ancestors.[65]

Nevertheless, Plecker continued his assault on Virginia's Indians. By 1929 Richmond *News Leader* editor Douglas Southall Freeman recognized the damage that Plecker threatened. "In his zeal for racial integrity," Freeman argued, Plecker "has become a propagandist, has sought to play upon emotions and prejudices, and to arouse ill-feeling to the end that new and more drastic laws be enacted." Freeman concluded that "the continued harassment of an inoffensive, isolated people, whose only desire is to be left alone, is a blot on the name of the state, and, indeed, savors of cruelty. It has gone too far."[66] Freeman's attack on the excesses of those devoted to racial integrity evolved from his broader conception of managed race relations. A firm opponent of interracial marriage and sexual relations, Freeman supported the initial goals of the racial integrity crusade. At the same time, he embodied the commitment of elite Virginians to a paternalistic ethos and thus preferred to think of race relations in the Old Dominion as tranquil. Emphasizing civility and good will, Freeman worked tirelessly to alleviate racial tension and to maintain social stability. The essence of his paternalism, however, lay not in a recognition of African Americans as first-class citizens but in a desire to foster what he referred to as "separation by consent," an arrangement by which blacks would agree to live separate lives.[67]

Despite the objections of Freeman and other elites, Powell and Plecker continued to champion racial integrity. With intermarriage and public integration forbidden by legislation, the Anglo-Saxon leaders shifted the focus of their attention to the public schools. Since the mid-1920s, Plecker had informed school superintendents whenever he suspected that children with any black blood had enrolled in schools for whites. Most of these children were expelled and left with no choice but to attend far inferior black schools. Furthermore, aggrieved parents could not appeal Plecker's decisions. As had been the case with intermarriage, persons claiming to be Indian rather than black provided Plecker his greatest frustrations in protecting racial purity. By 1930 he renewed his efforts to define these people as black to keep them out of white schools.[68]

Linking racial integrity and segregated schools assumed a level of critical importance as the General Assembly prepared to meet in January 1930. Revelations that a number of mixed-race children attended white schools in

Essex County provided advocates of a stricter racial-definition law the means of persuasion that they had lacked in 1926 and 1928 when they were seen as unnecessarily harassing the state's Indians. The situation in Essex County first developed in 1928 as local school officials took steps to remove from the white schools children considered mixed. One family resisted, hired a lawyer, and filed suit. In the Circuit Court of Essex County, school officials acknowledged that the children in question had less than one-sixteenth black blood. Consequently, Judge Joseph W. Chinn ruled that the children could not be kept out of white schools.[69]

Chinn based his ruling on what racial integrity advocates had long understood as a loophole in the original legislation. The 1924 Racial Integrity Act defined a white person as an individual with "no trace whatsoever of any blood other than Caucasian," making an exception only for certain Indians, and failed to define a black person. Furthermore, the act specifically prohibited the intermarriage of a white person with a nonwhite person, but it made no mention of the schools. Powell later testified that he had assumed that all persons not deemed white would be automatically classified black. But since the 1924 statute did not amend the 1910 act that termed blacks as persons with one-sixteenth or more black blood, an individual with less than one-sixteenth black blood could not be considered black, and therefore he or she could not be prevented from attending white schools.[70]

A reporter for the Richmond *Times-Dispatch* concluded that under Chinn's ruling "any child having less than one-sixteenth Negro blood, not only can attend a white school, but must attend it, and is by law prevented from attending a colored school." The judge's opinion, moreover, opened the door for persons with less than one-sixteenth black blood to attend any of Virginia's colleges or universities. In the wake of Chinn's decision, local officials understood that their only avenue of relief lay with the state legislature passing a stricter law; consequently, sponsors introduced a measure that defined as black "any person in whom there is ascertainable any Negro Blood"—the so-called one-drop rule.[71]

As the General Assembly began deliberations on the revised statute, a correspondent for the Richmond *Times-Dispatch* visited the Essex County schools that had sparked the controversy. The reporter was shocked at the extent to which the mixed-race children could have passed for white: at one of the schools "only one pupil would have impressed the casual observer as revealing traces" of black features, while the "remaining thirteen could have passed for white anywhere." He also observed that white children and black children "played together on terms of equality" with "no consciousness of any racial barrier." The reporter shared the concern of school superintendent W. G. Rennolds and the commonwealth's attorney James M. Lewis that "many residents of the community have become accustomed to the fact that their children go to school with mix breeds, and show no resentment, active or passive."[72] The seeming acceptance of the white parents whose children attended these schools only heightened in Rennolds and Lewis a determination to see the stricter law passed. Both believed that the Racial Integrity Act's ban on intermarriage "cannot be hoped for if children of both races are permitted to go to school together and regard each other as equals over a period of eight or ten years."[73]

Unanimity among whites in support of the stricter racial definition bill, however, was not to be found. In testimony before the General Assembly, proponents like W. Leigh Carneal, a Richmond architect, cited the Essex County situation, acknowledged that ultimate amalgamation appeared likely, and considered the bill crucial to slowing the process. Similarly, Richard Heath Dabney, a professor of history at the University of Virginia and the father of Virginius Dabney, warned that failure to pass the law would make it possible for persons with some black blood to gain admittance to the university. A parade of opponents, led by clergy who felt the measure again unfairly targeted Indians, also appeared before the legislature. The Dover Baptist Association, an organization that represented sixty-seven churches in Richmond and its outlying counties, including a number of Indian congregations, objected to the "recurring attempts to misrepresent and humiliate" the Pamunkey, Mattaponi, and Chickahominy Indians.[74]

Acting at the request of an aide to Walter Plecker, Rennolds protested to R. Hill Fleet, a member of the Dover Baptist Association, that "unless we can get some legislation, we might as well turn our schools over to both races and save the expense of a dual system of schools." Rennolds's complaint infuriated Fleet, who responded that he was only concerned with protecting the Pamunkey, Mattaponi, and Chickahominy who had been "called Indians for the past fifty years." Fleet agreed that steps should be taken to stop those persons who tried to evade the law with unwarranted claims of Indian ancestry, but he denied the right of Rennolds and his cohorts to "throw those people out of education or any advantages that they might be able to enjoy; cut them loose from any kind of society and damn them as negro on account of the sins of their forefathers, just because one drop of negro blood flows in their veins." As if to punctuate his rejection of rigid racial integrity doctrine, Fleet added that "the milk of human kindness certainly ought to flow in their direction along with the cold blooded law."[75]

Nevertheless, the reality of mixed schools in Essex County overwhelmed such objections, and the House of Delegates passed the revised measure with little dissent. The Virginia Senate did amend the statute to allow those persons with at least one-fourth Indian blood and less than one-sixteenth black blood to remain classified as Indians, but only if they lived on a recognized reservation. This amendment protected the Pamunkey and Mattaponi who had lived on reservations since the eighteenth century, but it did not extend to the Chickahominies of Charles City and New Kent Counties, persons said to have claimed Indian ancestry only after the passage of the first Jim Crow laws at the turn of the twentieth century. Virginia's 1930 Racial Integrity Act allowed for the bizarre possibility that two full-blooded siblings, one living on a reservation, the other living outside such boundaries, would be classified as members of different races. The senate passed the amended version without a dissenting vote, and the house soon concurred.[76]

The Richmond *Times-Dispatch* hailed the measure's passage as "A Long Fight Won" and lauded the law's "great objective" to "maintain the color line in the public schools." The paper commended the legislature for rejecting a suggestion that the issue be submitted to a commission for more thorough study. Before such an investigative body could report to the General Assembly, the *Times-Dispatch* surmised, "there would have been mixed public schools all over the State." In conclusion, the paper praised the efforts of John Powell and Earnest Cox, asserting that "those Virginians who feel that the maintenance of pure white public schools is a worthy thing will recognize their debt to the men who did this job for them." The newspaper's emphasis underscored the degree to which the debate over racial integrity had shifted away from miscegenation and toward the schools, precisely where it would remain for the next three decades.[77]

The Richmond *News Leader* and Norfolk *Virginian-Pilot* provided less generous assessments of the bill's adoption. The Norfolk daily concluded that the bill "involves for a limited group of our population a genuinely tragic predicament." The *News Leader* predicted "endless possibilities of controversy" between the Bureau of Vital Statistics and various Indians. "Even with these faults," the Richmond paper concluded, in a tone that reflected the paternalistic ethos of its editor, "liberal Virginians are apt to accept the bill without a further fight, in the hope that it puts an end to the continuous agitation of the race question before the general assembly. Year after year this has gone on, to the distress of inoffensive people and to the impairment of better racial relations."[78]

As usual in racial matters in Virginia, it required the insight of the state's black press to underscore the depth of hypocrisy and delusion inherent in the passage of the new racial integrity measure. "Traced to its logical end it comes up against a pathetic and rather tragic impasse," editorialized the Norfolk *Journal and Guide*, "which will in reality constitute a defeat of its own purpose. For instance, if a person having only a trace of Negro blood is defined by fiat as a Negro in the face of all his nominally Caucasian instincts, associations, heritage, passions and emotions—in short, against his very nature itself—here is created a problem the ramifications of which are pathetic and delicate to contemplate. He is nominally white, biologically mixed[,] and legally Negro."[79]

In 1931 George S. Schuyler published *Black No More,* a brilliant satire in which Junius Crookman, a black medical researcher and doctor, recognized that "if there were no Negroes, there could be no Negro problem. Without a Negro problem, Americans could concentrate their attention on something constructive." Using a new chemical process that he had invented, Crookman offered black men, women, and children an opportunity to become white and therefore to rid themselves of all the barriers that blackness placed in their way. Before long, African Americans all over the United States underwent the treatment, causing immense consternation as "one couldn't tell who was who." In response, membership in the Knights of Nordica, a clear reference to the Ku Klux Klan, soared, although it became impossible to ascertain the color of new members.[80]

While Schuyler spared no one—black, white, rich, or poor—he saved his sharpest barbs for two white southerners connected with the Anglo-Saxon Association of America. Headquartered in Richmond, its members were "too highbrow" to join the Knights of Nordica; no one could have mistaken the object of Schuyler's wit or wrath. Arthur Snobbcraft, the group's president and a descendant of one of the First Families of Virginia (FFV), had devoted his life to "white racial integrity and Anglo-Saxon supremacy." Dr. Samuel Buggerie, a statistician, "professional Anglo-Saxon," and FFV, believed that millions of lower-class whites had black ancestors. After an intense investigation, Buggerie stunned Snobbcraft with the unexpected and devastating truth that black blood extended deep into the family tree of most FFVs, the two of them included. When a member of Buggerie's research team, a recipient of Crookman's treatment, released the report identifying thousands of upper-class whites as black, Snobbcraft and Buggerie were forced to flee Richmond. When their plane was forced down in Mississippi, the pair were caught and identified by a rabid mob who recognized them from the newspapers. Snobbcraft and Buggerie, the fiercest advocates of Anglo-Saxon purity and superiority, were lynched for being black.[81]

John Powell and Walter Plecker avoided such an ending, of course, but Schuyler's keen powers of observation penetrated to the heart of the campaign for racial purity. Despite its absurdity, the determination of the Anglo-Saxons to identify even the slightest trace of black ancestry in white Virginians appealed to elites obsessed with their own bloodlines and convinced of their own superiority. A number of more thoughtful elites, including Douglas Southall Freeman, never felt the imminent danger that so concerned Powell and

Plecker. But Freeman, like all white elites, did support the essential goals as well as the assumptions that undergirded the movement.

The legislative efforts of the Anglo-Saxon Clubs ended in the early 1930s, but Plecker remained at his post in the Bureau of Vital Statistics until 1946, undisturbed by six Virginia governors. Despite his acknowledgment toward the end of his tenure that no test existed "to determine the race of an individual," he spent his career bluffing and posturing that he could do just that. In his final batch of official correspondence to Powell, an unrepentant Plecker admitted that "in some cases, no mixture was found." Although Plecker died soon after his retirement when he stepped off the curb of a Richmond street and was hit by a car, the Racial Integrity Act continued to intrude upon the lives of Virginians until 1967, forty-three years after its passage, when the United States Supreme Court ruled it unconstitutional. Not until the 1980s did Virginia's Indian tribes receive the official state recognition that had eluded them throughout the 1920s and 1930s and that might have blunted Plecker's attacks.[82]

The rhetoric and actions of the Anglo-Saxon Clubs, along with the responses of blacks and paternalistic whites, underscore the degree to which the maintenance of Jim Crow and white supremacy entailed overt power struggles on a daily basis. Cultural and ideological inertia did not ensure the perpetuation of segregation; instead a panoply of issues demanded constant negotiation and involved continual contestation. John Powell and Walter Plecker strove to define and redefine whiteness and blackness because they feared the blurring of racial boundaries. Although no credible evidence exists to support their claims that miscegenation was on the rise, they themselves recognized more clearly than the paternalists that non-biological breeches in the color line posed an even greater threat to white supremacy. They perceived correctly that basic interracial cooperation and African American education ultimately portended significant changes in Virginia's race relations. Meanwhile, white elites such as Douglas Southall Freeman continued to believe they could manage race relations on their own terms. Tragically, however, these elites failed to prevent adoption of some of the most vile and pernicious legislation in American history. Their decision "to accept the bill without a further fight," combined with a rising tide of black activism in the late 1920s and 1930s, provided conclusive evidence of the erosion of white elite paternalism as a viable strategy for managing white supremacy.[83]

Notes

1. Richmond *News Leader*, June 5, 1923, p. 18 (quotation). For more on Powell's career as a pianist and composer, see Ronald David Ward, "The Life and Works of John Powell, 1882–1963" (Ph.D. dissertation, Catholic University of America, 1973); and

David E. Whisnant, *All That Is Native and Fine: The Politics of Culture in an American Region* (Chapel Hill and London, 1983), chap. 3. For their suggestions and comments on this and earlier drafts, I would like to thank Ed Ayers, Paul Gaston, John Kneebone, Matt Lassiter, Andy Lewis, Phil Troutman, Peter Wallenstein, the participants of the 1999 Cambridge-Tulane Atlantic World Studies Conference, and the anonymous readers for the *Journal of Southern History*.

2. *Loving v. Virginia*, 388 U.S. 1 (1967); Walter Wadlington, "The *Loving* Case: Virginia's Anti-Miscegenation Statute in Historical Perspective," *Virginia Law Review*, 52 (November 1966), 1189–223; Paul A. Lombardo, "Miscegenation, Eugenics, and Racism: Historical Footnotes to *Loving v. Virginia*," *U.C. Davis Law Review*, 21 (Winter 1988), 421–52. In part, Lombardo's purpose is to challenge historians of the eugenics movement who have not paid much attention to the connection between eugenics and anti-miscegenation laws. Gregory Michael Dorr, a historian of the eugenics movement in Virginia, successfully answers Lombardo's challenge in "Assuring America's Place in the Sun: Ivey Foreman Lewis and the Teaching of Eugenics at the University of Virginia, 1915–1953," *Journal of Southern History*, 66 (May 2000), 257–96. Historian Peter Wallenstein touches upon Virginia's 1924 Racial Integrity Act in an insightful piece that looks more broadly at the regulation of interracial marriage from the end of the Civil War to the *Loving* decision in "Race, Marriage, and the Law of Freedom: Alabama and Virginia, 1860s–1960s," *Chicago-Kent Law Review*, 70 (1994), 371–437. For a comparison of miscegenation statutes throughout the United States, see Peggy Pascoe, "Miscegenation Law, Court Cases, and Ideologies of 'Race' in Twentieth-Century America," *Journal of American History*, 83 (June 1996), 44–69; Pauli Murray, ed., *States' Laws on Race and Color* (Athens, Ga., 1950; reprint, Athens, Ga., and London, 1997); and Charles S. Mangum Jr., *The Legal Status of the Negro* (Chapel Hill, 1940), chap. 1.

3. Richard B. Sherman, "'The Last Stand': The Fight for Racial Integrity in Virginia in the 1920s," *Journal of Southern History*, 54 (February 1988), 69–92 (quotations on p. 69). Sherman recognizes the influence of the eugenics movement and connects Virginia's racial integrity campaign to the national anti-immigration movement that reached its apogee with the passage of the National Origins Act of 1924.

4. William Joseph Showalter, "Virginia—A Commonwealth That Has Come Back," *National Geographic Magazine*, 55 (April 1929), 439 (first quotation); Emily Clark, *Stuffed Peacock* (New York and London, 1927), 68 (second quotation). Douglas Southall Freeman, the editor of the Richmond *News Leader*, once described eastern Virginians, who dominated the state in political, social, economic, and cultural terms, as "Shintoists" for whom "genealogy makes history personal" and "kinship to the eighth degree is usually recognized." Federal Writers' Project, *Virginia: A Guide to the Old Dominion* (New York, 1940), 4.

5. George Brown Tindall, *The Emergence of the New South, 1913–1945* (Baton Rouge, 1967), 143–83 (quotation on p. 160). Tindall writes that "in the 1920's the new peculiar institution of Negro subordination had reached its apogee as an established reality in law, politics, economics, and folkways—under attack from certain minorities in the North, to be sure, but not effectively menaced and virtually taboo among respectable whites as a subject for serious discussion. The question was settled." (It should be

noted, however, that Tindall does cite the Anglo-Saxon Clubs as the one organization that did not believe the race question was settled [160 n. 73]). Similarly, Joel Williamson describes the pitched battle between southern white conservatives and racial radicals but concludes that such divisions had given way to a consensus on race after 1915. More recently, Grace Elizabeth Hale has described a culture of segregation and violence that whites used to dominate black southerners and to construct an identity of whiteness in this period. Although she portrays the degree to which race relations remained deeply contested throughout the era of segregation, Hale also lends support to Tindall's conclusion when she writes that "by 1930 white southerners felt so secure within the new racial order of segregation that white supremacy, often politely expressed as interest in 'the Negro question,' received much less public attention." Williamson, *The Crucible of Race: Black-White Relations in the American South Since Emancipation* (New York and Oxford, 1984), 1–7, 234–41; Hale, *Making Whiteness: The Culture of Segregation in the South, 1880–1940* (New York, 1998), 144.

6. *The Virginia Public School System: Report of the Virginia Education Commission, 1944* (Richmond, 1944), 32 (first quotation); V. O. Key Jr., *Southern Politics in State and Nation* (New York, 1949; reprint, Knoxville, 1984), 32 n. 11 (second quotation). W. Fitzhugh Brundage explains the less frequent incidents of lynching in Virginia as a consequence of the state's more varied economy. Brundage, *Lynching in the New South: Georgia and Virginia, 1880–1930* (Urbana and Chicago, 1993), 15–16. For more on Virginia's ruling elite see J. Douglas Smith, "Managing White Supremacy: Politics and Culture in Virginia, 1919–1939" (Ph.D. dissertation, University of Virginia, 1998).

7. Charles E. Wynes, "The Evolution of Jim Crow Laws in Twentieth Century Virginia," *Phylon*, 28 (Winter 1967), 416; Dan T. Carter, "From Segregation to Integration," in John B. Boles and Evelyn Thomas Nolen, eds., *Interpreting Southern History: Historiographical Essays in Honor of Sanford W. Higginbotham* (Baton Rouge and London, 1987), 409. In his survey of the field, Carter refers to studies of Virginia and Georgia that suggest that the onset of segregation statutes at the turn of the twentieth century reflected the "racial self-confidence" of white southerners. My argument here, in contrast, is that the laws passed in Virginia in the 1920s reflected the lack of such confidence.

8. John Powell to William T. Reed, January 24, 1921, Section 1, Reed Family Collection (Virginia Historical Society, Richmond). For more on Reed and his influence see Joseph A. Fry, "Senior Advisor to the Democratic 'Organization': William Thomas Reed and Virginia Politics, 1925–1935," *Virginia Magazine of History and Biography*, 85 (October 1977), 445–69.

9. Richmond *News Leader,* June 5, 1923, p. 18. On the Ku Klux Klan's lack of support among Democratic officials in Virginia, see David M. Chalmers, *Hooded Americanism: The History of the Ku Klux Klan* (3d ed.; Durham, 1987), 230–35.

10. Richmond *Times-Dispatch,* October 18, 1922, pp. 1, 6 (first, second, and third quotations on p. 1; fourth quotation on pp. 1 and 6); Richmond *News Leader,* June 5, 1923, p. 18. In a letter to Dr. Stuart McGuire, Powell insisted, "I am not a leader, nor even a member of the Ku Klux Klan. The Anglo-Saxon Clubs are in no way connected with the Klan. In fact the men who originated the Clubs were so strongly opposed to

the Klan that they took it into the Courts and stopped its activities in the state for more than a year." Powell to McGuire, January 1, 1925, Folder 2, Box 56, John Powell Collection, #7284a (Special Collections, Alderman Library, University of Virginia; hereinafter UVA). See also Nancy MacLean, *Behind the Mask of Chivalry: The Making of the Second Ku Klux Klan* (New York and Oxford, 1994); and Wyn Craig Wade, *The Fiery Cross: The Ku Klux Klan in America* (New York, 1987).

11. Richmond *News Leader,* June 5, 1923, p. 18. It is not entirely clear why Powell and Cox ceased to discuss immigration well in advance of the passage of the National Origins Act in 1924. Virginia's population hovered between 98 and 99 percent native-born throughout the 1920s. It is entirely possible that Virginians simply did not respond to fears over immigration in the same way that they did to concerns over racial mixing. Powell and Cox may have sensed this and tailored their arguments accordingly. See U.S. Bureau of the Census, *Fourteenth Census of the United States, Taken in the Year 1920.* Vol. II: *Population* (Washington, D.C., 1922), table 7, p. 33; and U.S. Bureau of the Census, *Fifteenth Census of the United States, Taken in the Year 1930.* Vol. III, Pt. 2: *Population, Montana–Wyoming* (Washington, D.C., 1932), table 2, p. 1141.

12. John Powell, "Is White America To Become a Negroid Nation?" Richmond *Times-Dispatch,* Sunday Magazine, July 22, 1923, p. 2 (quotations); Earnest Sevier Cox, "Is White America To Become a Negroid Nation?" Richmond *Times-Dispatch,* Sunday Magazine, July 22, 1923, p. 2; Sherman, "'Last Stand,'" 70–71.

13. Joel Williamson, *New People: Miscegenation and Mulattoes in the United States* (New York and London, 1980), 112–15, 126–29; *Fourteenth Census,* Vol. II: *Population,* 16–18 (quotation on p. 16). For more on the variability of census enumerations and racial designations, see Victoria E. Bynum, "'White Negroes' in Segregated Mississippi: Miscegenation, Racial Identity, and the Law," *Journal of Southern History,* 64 (May 1998), 247–76, esp. 255 and 261.

14. Dorr, "America's Place in the Sun," 258 (first quotation), 262 (second quotation), 259 (third quotation). The eugenicists' conviction culminated in the 1924 passage of an involuntary sterilization measure. For nearly fifty years the Commonwealth of Virginia sterilized thousands of persons, white and black, deemed feebleminded, insane, or prone to criminal behavior. Those at the top of Virginia's social order, including Douglas Southall Freeman, commented on the "beneficent effects" of the bill. Furthermore, many of Lewis's students, especially those who went on to careers in medicine and politics, were directly responsible for the enforcement of the sterilization statute; in this respect alone, Lewis's teachings had a profound and long-lasting effect on public policy in the Old Dominion. See also Daniel J. Kevles, *In The Name of Eugenics: Genetics and the Uses of Human Heredity* (Cambridge, Mass., and London, 1995), 110–12; Richmond *Times-Dispatch,* November 26, 2000, p. A1; and Minutes of the *News Leader* Current Events Class, March 10, 1924, Box 177, Douglas Southall Freeman Collection (Manuscript Division, Library of Congress, Washington, D.C.) (Freeman quotation). Lewis's beliefs quite naturally led him to embrace the aims of the Anglo-Saxon Clubs, though he was not a leader of the organization. He never appeared before the legislature on its behalf and did not promote its cause in the state's top newspapers, but he did admire the positions taken by Powell, Plecker, and Cox. As

late as 1929 Lewis urged Walter Plecker "to stand firm in the face of ill considered and ill tempered criticism" and referred to Plecker's efforts as "the most important public service being rendered in Virginia." Dorr, "America's Place in the Sun," 265 n. 23; Lewis to Plecker, October 18, 1929, Box 13, Freeman Collection (quotations). Plecker, in turn, supported the sterilization movement. Plecker, "Racial Improvement," *Virginia Medical Monthly*, 52 (November 1925), 486–89.

15. Powell, "Is White America To Become a Negroid Nation?" 2 (quotations); Sherman, " 'Last Stand,' " 71–74.

16. Cox, "Is White America To Become a Negroid Nation?" 2 (first and second quotations); Powell, "Is White America To Become a Negroid Nation?" 2 (subsequent quotations).

17. Richmond *Times-Dispatch,* July 22, 1923, p. 4.

18. Sherman, " 'Last Stand,' " 75–76 (Plecker quotation on p. 75). See also form letters designed by Plecker for use by the commissioner of revenue, dated July 26, 1923, and by the local registrar, dated June 22, 1922, Folder 1, Box 56, Powell Collection.

19. At the end of the nineteenth century, twenty-six states, mostly in the South and West, prohibited interracial marriage; ultimately at least thirty-eight states adopted such laws, although sixteen southern states retained such statutes by the time of the *Loving* decision in 1967. Peter W. Bardaglio, *Reconstructing the Household: Families, Sex, and the Law in the Nineteenth-Century South* (Chapel Hill and London, 1995), 176–89; Pascoe, "Miscegenation Law, Court Cases, and Ideologies of 'Race,' " 49; Paul Finkelman, "Crimes of Love, Misdemeanors of Passion: The Regulation of Race and Sex in the Colonial South," in Catherine Clinton and Michele Gillespie, eds., *The Devil's Lane: Sex and Race in the Early South* (New York, 1997), 135; Williamson, *New People,* 97–98; Mangum, *Legal Status of the Negro,* 1–17. More than likely, members of the Anglo-Saxon Clubs would have cited the situation that Victoria Bynum has described in " 'White Negroes' in Segregated Mississippi" as proof of the necessity of a "one-drop" rule. Bynum discusses the acquittal of Davis Knight, a "white Negro" who acknowledged having black blood but who could not be convicted under Mississippi's miscegenation law because it defined blackness according to a "one-eighth" rule (265–74).

20. Letter from a local registrar to Plecker, July 28, 1923 (quotations), Plecker to Senator M. B. Booker, February 15, 1924, both in Folder 1, Box 56, Powell Collection.

21. John Powell to Stone Deavours, April 20, 1925, W. C. Neill to James C. Davis, May 19, 1925, Davis to Powell, May 25, 1925, Powell to Davis, May 30, 1925, all in Folder 2, Box 56, Powell Collection; Davis to Powell, August 22, 1927, and "Addresses of W. R. I. Club of Richmond, Virginia, 1926," both in Folder 3, Box 56, Powell Collection; *Richmond, Virginia, City Directory 1926* (Richmond, 1926); *Social Register: Richmond, Charleston, Savannah, Augusta, Atlanta, 1919* (New York, 1918); Henry Brantly Handy, ed., *The Social Recorder of Virginia* (Richmond, 1928); Mangum, *Legal Status of the Negro,* 6–8. The establishment of Anglo-Saxon chapters in the North (at the University of Pennsylvania, at Columbia University, and on Staten Island) reflected the presence of leading eugenicists in those locales. There is no evidence that those posts were ever active. Former Richmond journalist Parke Rouse includes Mrs. E. Randolph (Maude)

Williams among Richmond's most important "dowagers." Williams and a number of her relatives and friends appear on the list of members of the Women's Racial Integrity Club. See Parke Rouse Jr., *We Happy WASPs: Virginia in the Days of Jim Crow and Harry Byrd* (Richmond, 1996), 204.

22. M. H. Bettinger to John Powell, October 13, 1923 (first quotation), M. O. Williams to Powell, November 1, 1923, Williams to Lawrence T. Price, January 31, 1924 (second and third quotations), all in Folder 1, Box 56, Powell Collection.

23. *The Virginia Tech,* January 10, 1924, p. 1 (quotation), Reid Brockenbrough to John Powell, February 2, 1924, both in Folder 1, Box 56, Powell Collection. The article in question was highlighted, either marked for Powell's attention or by Powell himself. In addition, check marks were placed next to some of the specific suggestions.

24. John Stark Bellamy, "If Christ Came to Dixie: The Southern Prophetic Vision of Howard Anderson Kester, 1904–1941" (M.A. thesis, University of Virginia, 1977), 37–40; Tindall, *Emergence of the New South,* 183 n. 160. For more on Howard Kester, the leader of the Lynchburg student interracial group, see John Egerton, *Speak Now Against the Day: The Generation Before the Civil Rights Movement* (New York, 1994), 124–26; and Anthony P. Dunbar, *Against The Grain: Southern Radicals and Prophets, 1929–1959* (Charlottesville, 1981), 18–39.

25. Sherman, "'Last Stand,'" 77 (quotations); June Purcell Guild, *Black Laws of Virginia* (Richmond, 1936; reprint, New York, 1969), 35. The issue of registration only applied to persons born before June 14, 1912. Those born after that date were already registered according to the provisions of the 1912 law that had established the Bureau of Vital Statistics. Sherman, "'Last Stand,'" 78.

26. Richmond *Times-Dispatch,* February 13, 1924, p. 1; "Citation of Cases: Showing Racial Amalgamation and Decadence of Racial Sense," Folder 7, Box 56, Powell Collection; Lothrop Stoddard, "To All Whom This Statement May Concern," February 1, 1924, Franklin Giddings to Powell, February 5, 1924, Madison Grant to Powell, February 1, 1924, all in Folder 1, Box 56, Powell Collection; Sherman, "'Last Stand,'" 71–72, 77–78; Thomas L. Dabney, "Views and Reviews," Norfolk *Journal and Guide,* February 23, 1924, pp. 7, 9 (quotation on p. 9).

27. Richmond *Planet,* February 23, 1924, p. 4, quoted in Brian William Thomson, "Racism and Racial Classification: A Case Study of the Virginia Racial Integrity Legislation" (Ph.D. dissertation, University of California, Riverside, 1978), 128; Norfolk *Journal and Guide,* March 15, 1924, p. 12, cited in Thomson, 132.

28. Gordon B. Hancock to the editor, Richmond *News Leader,* February 23, 1924, p. 19; Plecker to Stone Deavours, April 15, 1925, Folder 2, Box 56, Powell Collection. Douglas Southall Freeman actually sent a copy of Hancock's letter to Powell to see if he thought that the newspaper should print it. Powell's response is unrecorded. Freeman's action is remarkable and suggests the depth of Powell's influence at the time. Freeman to Powell, February 14, 1924, Folder 1, Box 56, Powell Collection. For more on Hancock see Raymond Gavins, *The Perils and Prospects of Southern Black Leadership: Gordon Blaine Hancock, 1884–1970* (Durham, 1977).

29. Sherman, "'Last Stand,'" 78; Pascoe, "Miscegenation Law, Court Cases, and Ideologies of 'Race,'" 59; E. H. Anderson to E. Lee Trinkle, April 17, 1924, "Bureau of

Vital Statistics" Folder, Box 43, Executive Papers, E. Lee Trinkle, 1922–1926 (Library of Virginia, Richmond; hereinafter LVA), hereinafter cited as Trinkle Executive Papers. Thirteen of forty senators and nineteen of one hundred delegates actually abstained from voting, though their reasons are not entirely clear. Commonwealth of Virginia, *Journal of the Senate, 1924* (Richmond, 1924), February 27, 1924, pp. 476–77; Commonwealth of Virginia, *Journal of the House of Delegates, 1924* (Richmond, 1924), March 8, 1924, pp. 774–75.

30. Richmond *Times-Dispatch,* March 19, 1924, p. 2.

31. "Instructions to Local Registrars and Other Agents in Administration of Law," *Virginia Health Bulletin,* 16 (March 1924), copy in Folder 7, Box 56, Powell Collection; W. A. Plecker, "Birth Registration and Racial Integrity Law," *Virginia Journal of Education,* 18 (September 1924), 13 (quotations). In his "Instructions," Plecker defined *mulatto* as an offspring of white and colored, *quadroon* as offspring of mulatto and white, and *octoroon* as offspring of quadroon and white. He used *mixed* and *issue* to refer to any person containing a mixture of white and black in which white predominated. "That is the class," he warned, "that should be reported with the greatest care, as many of these are on the borderline, and constitute the real danger of race intermixture." It is ironic that Plecker insisted that persons with even a trace of black blood would continue to "present clear marks of colored ancestry," while John Powell had cited as evidence for the need of a Racial Integrity Act his own difficulty in being able to tell who was black or white.

32. Plecker to Mrs. Robert Cheatham, April 30, 1924, Plecker to Mary Gildon, n.d., both in Folder 1, Box 56, Powell Collection. Plecker copied these letters on a single sheet and sent it to Powell. Plecker wrote the note (third quotation) at the top of the copy. In a similar update Plecker told Powell, "I struck quite an interesting family in Norfolk County yesterday with ten children, seven of whom are registered with us, three as white, three as colored and one doubtful. Think of the benefit of preventing those ten mixed children from going white." Plecker to Powell, July 30, 1924, Folder 1, Box 56, Powell Collection.

33. Plecker to Earnest S. Cox, August 9, 1924, Plecker to Powell, July 30, 1924, both in Folder 1, Box 56, Powell Collection.

34. Plecker to W. E. Sandidge, October 4, 1924, Folder 1, Box 56, Powell Collection; J. David Smith, *The Eugenic Assault on America: Scenes in Red, White, and Black* (Fairfax, Va., 1993), 71; Sherman, " 'Last Stand,' " 80. Just as census takers did not apply uniform standards in determining who was black and who was mulatto (see note 13), evidence also exists that "colored" may have specifically referred to blacks or, at other times, designated any nonwhite person. See Mangum, *Legal Status of the Negro,* 4–5. In addition, no consistent definition of "Indian" existed in the nineteenth century; racial designations depended upon the whims of enumerators. Furthermore, many of the records in Virginia counties with large Indian populations had been burned or were lost at various points during the century. Thus, any attempt to document the racial classification of persons with Indian ancestry was fraught with difficulty. See Helen C. Rountree, *Pocahontas's People: The Powhatan Indians of Virginia Through Four Centuries* (Norman, Okla., 1990), 188–90.

35. Plecker to Silas Coleman (quotation), Plecker to E. Lee Trinkle, Plecker to A. Willis Robertson, and Plecker to A. T. Shields, all dated November 7, 1924, "Bureau of Vital Statistics" Folder, Box 43, Trinkle Executive Papers.

36. Richmond *News Leader,* November 18, 1924, pp. 1, 4 (first five quotations on p. 4; final quotation on p. 1); Smith, *Eugenic Assault on America,* 71–73; Sherman, "'Last Stand,'" 80–81. In distinguishing between Hungarians and Arabs and North Africans, Holt understood that contemporary ethnography divided humans into five races: Caucasian, Ethiopian, Mongolian, American, and Malay. Hungarians, along with Finns and Turks, were considered Mongolian in origin, while Arabs and North Africans, as well as numerous other, darker-skinned, non-European peoples, were deemed Caucasians. *Senate Reports,* 61 Cong., 3 Sess., No. 662: *Reports of the Immigration Commission: Dictionary of Races or Peoples* (42 vols.; Washington, D.C., 1911), V, 30–33; Matthew Frye Jacobson, *Whiteness of a Different Color: European Immigrants and the Alchemy of Race* (Cambridge, Mass., and London, 1998), 78–80.

37. Powell quoted in Smith, *Eugenic Assault on America,* 74.

38. Powell to Henry Holt, April 6, 1925, Folder 2, Box 56, Powell Collection; Plecker to Powell, June 29, 1946, Folder 6, Box 56, Powell Collection; John Kneebone, "In Jim Crow's Lifetime: Race in Virginia before the Civil Rights Movement" (paper presented at the Virginia Historical Society, April 19, 1996); Smith, *Eugenic Assault on America,* 69–70. I am grateful to John Kneebone, who personally inspected these records, for sharing his conclusions.

39. Rountree, *Pocahontas's People,* 188–218; Virginia Easley DeMarce, "'Verry Slitly Mixt': Tri-Racial Isolate Families of the Upper South—A Genealogical Study," *National Genealogical Society Quarterly,* 80 (March 1992), 5–13; Richmond *Planet,* February 11, 1928, p. 4 (quotation). Even prior to the Civil War, many mixed-race Virginians understood the social and political benefits of claiming Indian rather than black ancestry. See Peter Wallenstein, "Indian Foremothers: Race, Sex, Slavery, and Freedom in Early Virginia," in Clinton and Gillespie, eds., *Devil's Lane,* 57–73. The desire among some ethnic groups to hide or deny black ancestry, born no doubt of the realities of racial discrimination and oppression, continues into the twenty-first century. Contentious debates continue to swirl over the racial ancestry of the Melungeons, a group of mixed-race persons in western Virginia and eastern Tennessee and Kentucky. Like all mixed-race persons in Virginia in the 1920s, Plecker considered the Melungeons to have African ancestors. The Melungeons themselves denied this at the time, and many of them continue to do so today. See the essays by David Henige and Darlene Wilson in "Brent Kennedy's *Melungeons,*" *Appalachian Journal,* 25 (Spring 1998), 270–98; Virginia Easley DeMarce, "Looking at Legends—Lumbee and Melungeon: Applied Genealogy and the Origins of the Tri-Racial Isolate Settlements," *National Genealogical Society Quarterly,* 81 (March 1993), 24–45; and Carol Morello, "Beneath Myth, Melungeons Find Roots of Oppression," Washington *Post,* May 30, 2000, p. A1.

40. Plecker to Samuel L. Adams, December 11, 1924, Folder 1, Box 56, Powell Collection; DeMarce, "'Verry Slitly Mixt,'" 9. DeMarce says in her study that "not all bearers of the family names mentioned here are of tri-racial ancestry; many of the names were common among white settlers in the Upper South." Plecker, on the other

hand, assumed precisely that all persons with the same surname in a given community shared a common racial heritage. As seen in the Johns case, he relied on lists of such names to prove his allegations.

41. "Stenographic Report of an Interview Regarding the So-Called 'Indians' of Charles City County between Mr. E. H. Marston of Charles City County and Dr. W. A. Plecker . . . February 1925," p. 1, "A Statement of the Origin of the So-Called 'Indians' of Charles City County, as Given by Mr. George H. Marston, brother of Mr. E. H. Marston . . . (in February 1925)," and "Mr. D. F. Rudisill, local registrar at Roxbury, gives us Hill Adkins' Reason for not Joining the 'Tribe', February 1925," all in Folder 2, Box 56, Powell Collection. Anthropologist Helen Rountree acknowledges that the advent of Jim Crow laws did, in fact, spur the Chickahominies to organize formally and to assert their "Indianness." But Rountree also documents that they had been encouraged to seek formal recognition in the early 1890s by a white anthropologist and the chief of the Pamunkey Indians, one of two tribes living on state-recognized reservations. Thus Plecker's interpretation appears based on a kernel of truth but clearly relied upon a distorted interpretation of events. Rountree, *Pocahontas's People,* 212–15.

42. Plecker to W. M. Steuart (U.S. census director), January 14, 1925, "Bureau of Vital Statistics" Folder, Box 43, Trinkle Executive Papers; Plecker to Steuart, November 20, 1928 (quotation) and August 30, 1929, "Health—Bureau of Vital Statistics" Folder, Box 24, Executive Papers, Harry F. Byrd, 1926–1930, LVA, hereinafter cited as Byrd Executive Papers.

43. Plecker to Georgia Fraser, March 16, 1925, Plecker to E. Lee Trinkle, October 5, 1925, both in "Bureau of Vital Statistics" Folder, Box 43, Trinkle Executive Papers; Richmond *News Leader,* July 2, 1925, pp. 1, 16, and July 22, 1925, p. 4; Norfolk *Journal and Guide,* July 11, 1925, p. 1; Sherman, "'Last Stand,'" 78–79.

44. E. Lee Trinkle to E. P. Bradby, December 1, 1925 (first quotation), Trinkle to Plecker, December 1, 1925 (second quotation), both in "Bureau of Vital Statistics" Folder, Box 43, Trinkle Executive Papers. Trinkle's claim that he knew nothing of Plecker's intentions seems dubious at best. When Plecker first broached the subject in October, Trinkle advised him to consult with the director of legislative services about preparing new bills for the 1926 General Assembly. Trinkle to Plecker, October 5, 1925, Ibid.

45. Plecker to Trinkle, December 2, 1925, Trinkle to Plecker, December 4, 1925 (first quotation), Plecker to Trinkle, December 5, 1925 (second quotation), "Bureau of Vital Statistics" Folder, Box 43, Trinkle Executive Papers; Richmond *Times-Dispatch,* January 29, 1929, p. 3.

46. Plecker to Hiram Smith, November 19, 1925 (quotation), "Bureau of Vital Statistics" Folder, Box 43, Trinkle Executive Papers; Richmond *Times-Dispatch,* November 12, 1925, p. 9; Plecker to Harry F. Byrd, December 2, 1925, Box 90, Harry F. Byrd Collection, #9700, UVA.

47. Richmond *News Leader,* April 2, 1925, p. 26; State Board of Health, Bureau of Vital Statistics, *Eugenics in Relation to The New Family and the Law on Racial Integrity: Including a Paper Read Before the American Public Health Association* (2d ed.; Richmond, 1925), copy in "Bureau of Vital Statistics" Folder, Box 43, Trinkle Executive

Papers. The language of Plecker's warning, explicitly urging young white men not to join "of themselves to females of a lower race," challenges the conclusions of historian Lisa Lindquist Dorr in "Arm in Arm: Gender, Eugenics, and Virginia's Racial Integrity Acts of the 1920s," *Journal of Women's History,* 11 (Spring 1999), 143–66. She argues that the "key" to Virginia's 1924 Racial Integrity Act was "prescribing the behavior and attitudes of Virginia's white women" (143–44). She adds that Powell and Plecker acted in response to a fear "that social interactions between whites and blacks, specifically between white women and black men, had increased sharply in Virginia during the early 1920s" (143). More specifically, she argues that Powell and Plecker worried that men of unknown racial ancestry "targeted the most innocent victims—presumably naive, young, modern women newly free from traditional familial supervision" (156). Many white Virginians, however, blamed white men, not black men, for whatever miscegenation did occur. Douglas Southall Freeman, for example, argued that it was the "bad habits" of "good-for-nothing" white men who pursued black women that caused the trouble (Minutes, Richmond *News Leader* Current Events Class, November 24, 1924, Box 177, Freeman Collection). Furthermore, the Johns and Sorrells cases involved white men marrying women that Plecker considered black. These women were not modern, freed from the constraints of family, but were relatively isolated persons who lived in rural communities with extended families. Powell and Plecker certainly objected to any form of interracial mixing, and Plecker's remarks included a warning to white women as well, but neither Plecker's admonition nor his experience in enforcing the Racial Integrity Act support Dorr's thesis that white women were the main targets.

48. Norfolk *Journal and Guide,* February 14, 1925, p. 7, p. 12 (quotation), April 4, 1925, p. 1; Richmond *News Leader,* April 2, 1925, p. 8, p. 26; Richmond *Times-Dispatch,* March 31, 1925, p. 1.

49. *Virginia State Board of Censors: 1923 Censorship Law and Rules and Regulations* (Richmond, 1923), 3, copy in "Motion Picture Censorship" Folder, Box 44, Byrd Executive Papers; *Report of the Virginia State Board of Censors, July 1, 1924, to June 30, 1925* (Richmond, 1925), 2 (quotation), copy in Division of Motion Picture Censorship, Record Group 53, State Government Records Collection, #26515, LVA; hereinafter cited as RG 53. In April 1927 the act that reorganized the state government renamed the board the Division of Motion Picture Censorship. This discussion borrows from J. Douglas Smith, "Patrolling the Boundaries of Race: Motion Picture Censorship and Jim Crow in Virginia, 1922–1932," *Historical Journal of Film, Radio and Television,* 21 (August 2001), 273–91.

50. Thomas Cripps, *Slow Fade To Black: The Negro in American Film, 1900–1942* (New York and Oxford, 1993), 170–202; see Smith, "Patrolling the Boundaries of Race," 273–91, esp. 279–85, for the censors' consideration of Micheaux's films *Birthright, Son of Satan,* and *The House Behind the Cedars.*

51. "Films Rejected In Toto Since August 1922," p. 4, Memo on *The House Behind The Cedars* (quotations), both in RG 53; Henry T. Sampson, *Blacks in Black and White: A Source Book on Black Films* (Metuchen, N.J., and London, 1995), 322; Powell to Arthur James, July 8, 1925, Folder 2, Box 56, Powell Collection.

52. Statement of Louise Burleigh, "1926 Jan–June" Folder, Box 3, Powell Collection (first and second quotations); Powell to Arthur James, June 6, 1925, Folder 2, Box 56, Powell Collection (third quotation); Smith, *Eugenic Assault on America,* 51–54.

53. Powell to Arthur James, June 6, 1925 (quotations), Powell to James, July 8, 1925, both in Folder 2, Box 56, Powell Collection; Statements of Earnest S. Cox and Louise Burleigh, "1926 Jan–June" Folder, Box 3, Powell Collection; Smith, *Eugenic Assault on America,* 52–54. Although Powell's antics underscored the lengths to which the Anglo-Saxons went to ensure conformity, the threats failed to derail James's career. James was promoted to commissioner of the Virginia Department of Public Welfare several years after the incident, and he served with distinction in a number of state and federal posts for decades to come. See Richmond *Times-Dispatch,* February 14, 1985.

54. James E. Gregg to William Howard Taft, September 3, 1925, William H. Taft Papers (Manuscript Division, Library of Congress, Washington, D.C.), microfilm, reel 276; Minutes of the Richmond *News Leader* Current Events Class, February 8, 1926, Box 176, Freeman Collection; Raymond Wolters, *The New Negro on Campus: Black College Rebellions of the 1920s* (Princeton, 1975), 237–47 (first quotation on p. 239); Newport News *Daily Press,* March 15, 1925, p. 4 (second quotation). For more on these events see Smith, "Managing White Supremacy," chap. 3; Richard B. Sherman, "The 'Teachings at Hampton Institute': Social Equality, Racial Integrity, and the Virginia Public Assemblage Act of 1926," *Virginia Magazine of History and Biography,* 95 (July 1987), 275–300; and Howard V. Young Jr., "William Howard Taft and Hampton Institute," in Keith L. Schall, ed., *Stony the Road: Chapters in the History of Hampton Institute* (Charlottesville, 1977), 147–54.

55. James E. Gregg to E. Lee Trinkle, July 11, 1925, "Hampton Institute" Folder, Box 21, Trinkle Executive Papers; Gregg to William Howard Taft, September 3, 1925, Taft Papers, reel 276; Sherman, "'Teachings at Hampton Institute,'" 282; Norfolk *Journal and Guide,* March 28, 1925, p. 3, p. 12, April 4, 1925, p. 12, May 9, 1925, p. 12; Henley Guy to Powell, April 9, 1925, Folder 2, Box 56, Powell Collection; Elizabeth Copeland Norfleet, interview with author, Charlottesville, Virginia, December 28, 1996. In 1949, more than twenty years after Copeland's death, the Virginia Press Association named its most prestigious honor the W. S. Copeland Award for Journalistic Integrity and Community Service. In July 2000 Copeland's name was stricken from the award in response to an article that reported Copeland's leadership in the events detailed here. Richmond *Times-Dispatch,* July 23, 2000, p. A1, July 27, 2000, p. A1.

56. Norfolk *Journal and Guide,* July 25, 1925, p. 12 (emphasis in original).

57. On Hampton Institute's origins see Robert Engs, *Freedom's First Generation: Black Hampton, Virginia, 1861–1890* (Philadelphia, 1979). On the 1927 student strike at Hampton, see Wolters, *New Negro on Campus,* 230–75; and Young, "William Howard Taft and Hampton Institute," 155–57.

58. Sherman, "'Teachings at Hampton Institute,'" 288; Norfolk *Journal and Guide,* December 5, 1925, p. 1 (first quotation); Commonwealth of Virginia, *Acts of Assembly, 1926* (Richmond, 1926), 945–46 (second quotation on p. 945); Mangum, *Legal Status of the Negro,* 57. The Massenburg Bill was struck down in 1963 by the Virginia Supreme

Court of Appeals. *Felix J. Brown, et al., v. City of Richmond, et al.,* 204 Va. 471 [132 S.E. 2d 495] (1963); Sherman, "'Last Stand,'" 92.

59. Norfolk *Virginian-Pilot,* February 15, 1926, p. 4 (first quotation); Richmond *News Leader,* February 8, 1926, p. 8, February 9, 1926, p. 1, February 20, 1926, p. 4 (second quotation); Norfolk *Journal and Guide,* February 20, 1926, pp. 1, 7. The Richmond Chamber of Commerce also opposed the measure. Richmond *News Leader,* February 2, 1926, p. 2; Richmond *Planet,* February 7, 1926, p. 1.

60. Richmond *News Leader,* March 3, 1926, p. 26; J. A. Rogers, "'Color' Psychology Amazingly Revealed In State Legislature," Norfolk *Journal and Guide,* February 27, 1926, pp. 1, 9 (first quotation on p. 9; second quotation on p. 1); Sherman, "'Teachings at Hampton Institute,'" 290–91; Wolters, *New Negro on Campus,* 240. It should be noted that Rogers's account is the only one that this author has found in which Copeland reportedly used the word "nigger."

61. Rogers, "'Color' Psychology Amazingly Revealed In State Legislature," 1. Rogers particularly objected to the stand taken by Reverend Love, who expressed such concern over the law's impact on Chinese and Japanese students in Virginia that "one would have thought they were the citizens and the Negro the alien" (1). Love's concern prompted Rogers to note the injustice inherent in "making a law against a group of citizens which the state is afraid to apply to aliens" (9). Nevertheless, mused Rogers in a moment of prophecy, "later, we might be called upon to be loyal in a struggle with Japan" (9).

62. Sherman, "'Teachings at Hampton Institute,'" 295; *Journal of the Senate, 1924,* February 27, 1924, pp. 476–77. The senate records show that Byrd joined twelve others in not voting on final passage of the Racial Integrity Act. In addition, Byrd never went on record opposing the act.

63. Grace Copeland to Harry F. Byrd, October 17, 1927, Byrd to Copeland, November 9, 1927, "Hampton Institute" Folder, Box 24, Byrd Executive Papers; Lombardo, "Miscegenation, Eugenics, and Racism," 425.

64. The legislature extended Jim Crow to buses in 1930; to waiting rooms in bus stations in 1936; to waiting rooms in airports in 1944. Wynes, "Evolution of Jim Crow Laws in Twentieth Century Virginia," 421.

65. Richmond *News Leader,* February 9, 1926, p. 1, February 8, 1926, p. 1; Richmond *Times-Dispatch,* February 14, 1928, p. 1; Sherman, "'Last Stand,'" 85–89.

66. Richmond *News Leader,* September 21, 1929, p. 8 (quotations). Plecker responded with a three-page letter in which he vehemently denounced Freeman's attack and expressed "the hope that you may yet see the light, and be guided by it." Plecker to Freeman, October 22, 1929, "Health—Bureau of Vital Statistics" Folder, Box 24, Byrd Executive Papers.

67. "Separation by Consent," Richmond *News Leader,* May 20, 1930, p. 8; Smith, "Managing White Supremacy," chap. 6.

68. Abraham Branham to Harry F. Byrd, July 3, 1926, "Vital Statistics, Bureau of" Folder, Box 68, Byrd Executive Papers; Plecker to Kate Robinson, December 11, 1926, Box 1, William Gregory Rennolds Collection, #26832, LVA.

69. Richmond *Times-Dispatch,* January 17, 1930, p. 1, January 26, 1930, p. 1; Decision of Joseph W. Chinn, September 22, 1928, Chancery Order Book, Vol. 8, p. 220, and papers pertaining to "In Re Petition of Robinson et al. to County School Board: Petition and Appeal to Circuit Court of Essex County, June Term, 1928," Circuit Court of Essex County. I am grateful to the Honorable Joseph E. Spruill Jr., Judge of Virginia's Fifteenth Judicial Circuit, for locating these records.

70. Commonwealth of Virginia, *Acts of Assembly, 1924,* p. 535 (quotation); handwritten speech of John Powell in favor of House Bill No. 2, introduced 1928, Folder 3, Box 56, Powell Collection.

71. Richmond *Times-Dispatch,* January 26, 1930, pp. 1–2 (first quotation on p. 2), January 17, 1930, p. 1 (second quotation).

72. Richmond *Times-Dispatch,* January 26, 1930, pp. 1–2 (quotations on p. 2).

73. Richmond *Times-Dispatch,* January 27, 1930, pp. 1–2 (quotation on p. 2); L. R. Reynolds to William Gregory Rennolds, April 19, 1928, Box 1, Rennolds Collection.

74. Norfolk *Journal and Guide,* February 8, 1930, pp. 1, 7; Dover Baptist Association, "A Statement In Regard To Senate Bill, No. 49," Folder 4, Box 2, Rennolds Collection (quotation). Richard Heath Dabney, in fact, had for decades warned that granting rights and privileges to blacks would lead to an increase in racial tension. In 1901 he authored a lengthy article in the Richmond *Times* that praised the loyalty of blacks as slaves and warned against "political, social, and industrial equality." See the folder on the article in Box 2, Virginius Dabney Collection, #7690p, UVA.

75. W. G. Rennolds to R. Hill Fleet, January 27, 1930 (first quotation), Fleet to Rennolds, January 31, 1930 (subsequent quotations), both in Folder 4, Box 2, Rennolds Collection; Estelle Marks to Rennolds, January 24, 1930, Folder 7, Box 2, Rennolds Collection; Thomson, "Racism and Racial Classification," 217 n. 25, 243–44.

76. Norfolk *Journal and Guide,* February 15, 1930, p. 3; Richmond *News Leader,* February 11, 1930, p. 1; Richmond *Times-Dispatch,* February 14, 1930, pp. 1, 6; Sherman, "'Last Stand,'" 90.

77. Richmond *Times-Dispatch,* February 12, 1930, p. 8.

78. Editorial from Norfolk *Virginian-Pilot,* quoted in Norfolk *Journal and Guide,* February 22, 1930, p. 8; Richmond *News Leader,* February 14, 1930, p. 8.

79. Norfolk *Journal and Guide,* February 15, 1930, sec. 2, p. 2.

80. George S. Schuyler, *Black No More* (New York, 1931; New York, 1999), 35 (first quotation), 81 (second quotation).

81. Ibid., 119 (first quotation), 120 (second quotation), 122 (third quotation).

82. Plecker to Elsie Graham, August 9, 1940, Folder 4, Box 56, Powell Collection (first quotation); Plecker to Powell, June 29, 1946, Folder 6, Box 56, Powell Collection (second quotation); Smith, *Eugenic Assault on America,* 69–70; Richmond *Times-Dispatch,* August 3, 1947, sec. 2, p. 1; *Loving v. Virginia,* 388 U. S. 1 (1967); Richmond *Times-Dispatch,* March 6, 2000, pp. A1, A6. During his brief retirement, Plecker worked on a book that he intended to prove his assertions about Virginia's Indians. Although no copy of the full manuscript appears to exist, Plecker did prepare a ten-page pamphlet to advertise his work. He died the following month, so it is possible he never finished the book. See Plecker, *Virginia's Vanished Race* (Richmond, 1947),

copy in the holdings of the Virginia Historical Society. Eleven years before *Loving,* the U.S. Supreme Court passed on the opportunity to review the Racial Integrity Act when it let stand the decision of the Virginia Supreme Court in *Naim v. Naim,* 197 Va. 80 (1955). Gregory Michael Dorr, "Principled Expediency: Eugenics, *Naim v. Naim,* and the Supreme Court," *American Journal of Legal History,* 42 (April 1998), 119–59; Wadlington, "The *Loving* Case," 1189–223. After 1930 John Powell turned his attentions to the promotion of Anglo-American folk music, the strand of American music that he had always considered most pure and authentic. See John Powell, "Lectures on Music," *Rice Institute Pamphlets,* 10 (July 1923), 107–63; and Whisnant, *All That Is Native and Fine,* chap. 3.

83. Richmond *News Leader,* February 14, 1930, p. 8.

Spirited Youth or Fiends Incarnate

*The Samarcand Arson Case and Female
Adolescence in the American South*

Susan Cahn

On 12 March 1931, two residential cottages at Samarcand Manor, the North Carolina state training school for delinquent girls, went up in flames. Four days later sixteen Samarcand inmates between the ages of thirteen and nineteen were charged with arson, a capital crime in North Carolina. The accused would stand trial for their lives. Suffering through one of the worst periods of the Depression, North Carolina citizens were diverted and enthralled by the fire, the trial, and surrounding events, which over a period of three months included a state investigation into Samarcand's management, two jail uprisings staged by some of the teenage defendants awaiting trial, and the intervention of one of the state's most famous women, journalist and socialite Nell Battle Lewis, who in her first courtroom appearance stepped in as defense attorney. After much sensation, two suspects were released for lack of evidence, two received suspended sentences, and the remaining twelve were convicted and sentenced to eighteen months to five years in state prison on a plea bargain that reduced the charge to a noncapital offense.[1]

The incident at Samarcand Manor interested me initially for its lurid detail and its spectacular nature (a kind of intellectual ambulance chasing, perhaps). But as I researched the events and public reactions to them, I discovered that these apparently atypical girls may not have been so unusual. Not only were there similar rebellions at other state reformatories, but more to the point, a public debate developed around precisely this question of exceptionalism: were these adolescent firebugs to be understood as uncommonly dangerous and corrupted youth, "fiends incarnate" in the words of one correspondent, or were they typical adolescents replete with the normal passions of late girlhood who had merely been led astray by the unfortunate circumstances of their impoverished and unstable lives?[2]

The Samarcand investigations and trial served as a focal point for a public controversy over the proper understanding of juvenile delinquency in girls. The question of delinquency, in turn, formed part of an even more general effort to come to terms with the sexuality and self-assertiveness attributed to "normal" girls under "modern" definitions of adolescence. Psychologist G. Stanley Hall's landmark 1904 study, *Adolescence,* redefined this period of life—previously characterized by the economic condition of "semi-independence"—as a "psychological" life stage made particularly difficult by the conditions of modern industrial society.[3] Hall and other theorists characterized the teen years as a distinct and prolonged stage of life marked by emotional instability, some measure of antisocial conduct, and identities in crisis. The new psychology viewed sexuality as key to adolescent angst; adolescence was a time in which the body's sexual maturation and increased libido were not yet matched by mature judgment and emotional or physical restraint.[4]

New understandings of adolescence developed contemporaneously with emerging concepts of "modern womanhood" that also underscored sexuality as central to female personality and new ideals of femininity.[5] In the early decades of the twentieth century, the sexuality of teenage girls and young women became a frequent topic of popular attention, ranging from moral outrage over the supposed "white slave trade" to bemused notice that it was now "six o'clock in America."[6] By the 1920s, images of sexually victimized "white slaves" or the more positively portrayed eroticism of the charming "Gibson Girl" and her adventurous sister, the "New Woman," faded before the highly sexualized persona of the middle-class "flapper." Although still a figure of some controversy, the flapper signaled the final break with Victorian reticence and the acceptance of at least some level of independence, assertiveness, and sexual desire among middleclass adolescent girls and young women.[7]

This change elicited more criticism when it appeared among working-class adolescents. Although the figure of the "working girl" could symbolize exuberant and intrepid female modernity, a generation of self-assertive working-class daughters raised fundamental questions about sexual expression, sexual regulation, and the social order. Their audacious dress, their lively presence on city streets, and their brazen sexuality as patrons of dance halls and other popular amusements excited strong reactions from a group of largely middle-class Progressive reformers who worried not only that freer sexual expression placed the "modern" girl in danger of prostitution, abandonment, or abuse, but that her assertive sexuality endangered the society as a whole, lowering moral standards and creating a potentially large number of unwed mothers and so-called "illegitimate" children. Spurred to action by such fears, Progressive reformers returned again and again to the independent, endangered young working-class woman who figured first as the "woman adrift" and later as the teenage "sex delinquent."[8]

Although efforts to define and regulate female adolescent sexuality occurred across the nation during the Progressive and interwar periods, the Samarcand incident brought these issues to a head in the South. By the late 1920s the social dangers raised by assertive, sexually active, young working girls held particular resonance in a region still coming to terms with economic and cultural modernity.[9] White southerners had long exalted and defended the purity of "southern womanhood" as the linchpin of social order. But what did it mean to become a southern woman in modern times when expressions of female sexual agency challenged the pristine virtue of the idealized "Southern Lady"? What were the appropriate behaviors and identities for female adolescents in a fast-changing region that was nevertheless still rooted in traditions of patriarchy and white supremacy? In a society that justified its racial caste system on the grounds that segregation protected the sexual and racial purity of white womanhood, recognition that sexual desire was common to all teenage girls might hasten the collapse of racialized distinctions between white virtue and black vice, not to mention the racial order that such ideas buttressed.

The incident also brought class-based considerations of citizenship to the forefront. The region's commitment to a segregated and unequal racial order depended on cross-class white alliances—a sense of a cohesive white "us" assumed in often-used phrases like "the citizens of our state." The way in which poor whites would be figured into the equation of "us" and "them" was always a live issue in southern politics. But poor, white female delinquents—whose sexualized bodies were often associated with disease, vice, profligacy, and low-grade intelligence—broached the question in its starkest terms.

The 1931 Samarcand arson trial offers an unusually visible example of the process by which public officials and the public at large grappled with changing female adolescent behaviors in the context of regional, racial, and class concerns. Although ostensibly about arson, the trial and surrounding public controversy returned repeatedly to the issue of sexuality—the sexual "delinquency" in these girls' pasts and the sexual energy thought to infuse and explain their riotous behavior. The disruptive actions of troubled and defiant working-class girls forced a moment of reckoning in which the public and the courts had to draw a line between punishable adolescent deviance and understandable adolescent misbehavior; in the process they articulated the modern parameters for female adolescent sexuality.

The fervor and ambivalence that characterized public discussion of the Samarcand incident suggest that these issues were pressing but not easily resolved. State officials and middle-class citizens wavered between a faith in the state's redemptive power to restore the essential goodness of white teenage girls damaged by poverty and personal misfortune and a strong apprehension that female sex delinquents bred both social chaos and degenerate offspring, thereby diluting the quality of the white body politic. In the end, while many sympathetic citizens attempted to incorporate modern definitions of adolescent sexuality into a charitable embrace of white delinquent girls, the state of North Carolina opted for a far harsher approach that treated female delinquents as sexually immoral, physically degenerate criminals subject to severely punitive measures.

The "Girl Problem" in the South

The problem of sexually endangered or active young women was not a new one. Since at least the 1880s, reformers around the nation had dedicated themselves to finding answers to what soon became known as the "girl problem." This phrase conveniently merged three separate problems: the problems of economic and sexual exploitation that girls or young women often encountered in urban industrial settings; the generational tensions occasioned by young women's bold styles and actions, especially their sexual and reproductive behavior; and the conceptual problem of defining the passage from girlhood to womanhood in legal practice and social theory. Efforts to solve the "girl problem" sometimes focused proactively on providing decent jobs, housing, and education to young women in the city. But equal or greater energy went into more punitive legal and penal reforms designed to protect adolescent women from the perceived hazards of modern city life and dangerous youthful inclinations.

Late-nineteenth-century age-of-consent campaigns used statutory rape laws to raise the age at which a girl could legally consent to sexual intercourse. This legal reform attempted to contain adolescent sexuality within a protective framework of childhood innocence. However, subsequent efforts to found girls' reformatories for delinquent females moved beyond an interpretation of innocence. Early-twentieth-century reformers increasingly viewed female offenders as deliberate actors who participated willingly in dangerous or "immoral" activities that, if not criminal by adult standards, were serious enough to warrant incarceration and rehabilitative training.[10]

The earliest reformatories usually grew out of private efforts, but as with many other Progressive Era reforms, activists gradually secured state support. By 1924, there were fifty-seven publicly funded institutions for delinquent girls, with only two states failing to provide at least one reformatory. These "training schools," and a number of private institutions established for the same purpose, served a population of girls and young women who might be as old as twenty-one but typically fell between the ages of thirteen and eighteen.[11]

Southern institutions followed the national pattern but developed some regional distinctions as well. Consistent with the generally later and weaker development of southern Progressivism, juvenile reformatories in the South were often founded later and granted far fewer funds by penurious legislatures.

Southern reform schools were divided as others were by gender, but also by race. States typically established reformatories for white boys, black boys, and white girls, with training schools for black girls left to the private efforts of African American club women.[12] Efforts by African American leaders in North Carolina to obtain state funding for a "Training School for Negro Girls" met continued opposition from whites who, according to the *Charlotte Observer,* believed "that such a large proportion of the negro girls might fall within the scope of such a correctional institution that the state would simply be overrun with inmates."[13] By implication, sexual misbehavior among black girls was so common it did not constitute delinquent behavior, while among white girls it was an exceptional and correctable condition.

A final wrinkle in the picture of southern reformatories was the practice of sending delinquent girls who tested low in intelligence to state schools for feebleminded children. Not unheard of in the North, by the 1930s the practice occurred more extensively in the South where institutions for the feebleminded served as a kind of wastebasket for problem cases of a mental, physical, or moral nature.[14]

Although apparent before World War I, southern concern about female "sex delinquents" crystallized during the war. North Carolina, for example, established Samarcand Manor in 1917 and opened its doors one year later supported by federal funds earmarked for the reduction of venereal disease in wartime.[15] These concerns did not recede in the war's aftermath but rather garnered greater attention due to the crisis in southern agriculture. As farms failed and rural incomes dropped in the 1920s, individuals and families, lured by anticipated employment and the attractions of commercial entertainment and urban sociability, fled rural areas for the cities.

Migrants experienced both satisfactions and disappointments, but middle-class urbanites and reformers focused only on the many problems that accompanied the transition. Chronic unemployment, crime, substandard housing, high venereal and other disease rates, and especially the sight of naive and "loose" young women roaming city streets in search of adventure sparked efforts among social workers and women's organizations to solve a problem dubbed the "crisis of the rural girl in the city for work." Fearing that the restless rural girl's "idle search for excitement" in the years between school leaving and marriage might lead to "calamities which will permanently handicap her," reformers proposed a program of supervised recreation and vocational education to safeguard the adolescent in her transition from rural girlhood to urban marriage and motherhood.[16]

In actuality, such programs rarely materialized and most teenage girls remained outside the scope of gentle efforts at vocational or recreational guidance. The most troublesome cases, however, came to the attention of local police and welfare officials and could result in incarceration at state institutions such as Samarcand. The North Carolina reformatory annually housed between 160 and 260 girls in the late 1920s and early 1930s, averaging 215 for the decade 1926 to 1935.[17] Most were charged with vagrancy or immoral conduct as a result of encounters with the police, county welfare workers, community members who lodged complaints, or family members who opted to place disobedient daughters in the hands of the law. Inmates typically spent between one and three years at Samarcand and while there received treatment for venereal disease if necessary, minimal academic training, and many hours of "vocational training"—obtained while performing the domestic and agricultural tasks necessary to run the institution. If compliance can be deduced from submission to routine, frequent escape attempts suggest that many inmates actively disliked and resisted their treatment. Samarcand girls responded much like other incarcerated delinquents of the period who, according to historian Mary Odem, perceived their reformatory term not as an educational opportunity but as an unfairly harsh and undeserved punishment.[18]

The desire to escape scheduled punishments and the intolerable conditions of the institution prompted Samarcand inmates to set fire to two dormitories, one of them a "disciplinary cottage" where staff meted out punishments. Although most denied setting the fire, upon their arrest and removal from Samarcand to a local county jail the defendants all but indicted themselves when seven of them set fire to mattresses in their jail cells. Several weeks later, still awaiting trial and having been removed to another county jail, five of the inmates once again rioted, reportedly keeping up "a continual stream of verbal vulgarity, curses, and imprecations" as they "set fire to their cell bunks, smashed every window pane they could reach, . . . and finally attacked members of the local fire department who came to their rescue, with pocket knives."[19] Although the fires were quickly doused, many wondered whether the flames that burned inside such rebellious female spirits could be so easily contained.

"Fiends Incarnate" or "Sisters under the Skin": Conflicting Discourses of Female Adolescence

The months of publicity surrounding the Samarcand arson case sparked a statewide discussion on how to perceive such unruly adolescents. North Carolinians pondered whether these were innocent girls, behaving like any other teenagers but for the particularly harsh circumstances in which they found themselves. Or were they—as one newspaper headline wondered— "fiends incarnate," modern day "vixens" who had merely gotten an early start on the road to adult vice and dissolution?[20] Although phrased as an issue of age-appropriate behavior, much more was at stake in this controversy. The question of whether the Samarcand inmates were misguided yet salvageable teenagers or fiendishly carnal women was freighted with political and social implications.

The South of the 1920s and 1930s was lurching unsteadily and painfully toward a modern economy as coal, furniture, textiles, steel, and retail industries drew rural sharecroppers, tenants, and small landholders toward the cities and into the wage economy. Champions of the New South held up modern industries and fast-growing cities as examples of regional prosperity, but they also worried about the instability of the new order. Massive displacement of rural whites and blacks raised social, economic, and political uncertainties soon heightened by the Depression. Moreover, despite the strength of legally implemented racial segregation and black disfranchisement, modern southern race relations always depended on extralegal terrorism to maintain a hierarchy that was never accepted by the region's African American citizens. Hopes for stability rested on continued economic development and the creation of a dependable, well-adjusted, and cohesive white population that supported the existing political and social order.[21]

To many, the unruliness, illicit sexuality, and high rates of out-of-wedlock pregnancy and venereal disease common to female delinquents became emblematic of the instability of the New South. The defiant wills and the sexually precocious, frequently diseased bodies of sex delinquents raised a disturbing specter of social disorder and racial degeneracy within the state's white population. Yet others responded more hopefully, seeing in delinquent girls a raw spirit that if harnessed represented the vigor and spark of modernity. These contrasting views were entertained but ultimately not resolved by the media, concerned citizens, state officials, and trained social workers as they responded to the disturbing behaviors of Samarcand inmates.

The initial response to the fire took place in the press, where articles, editorials, and letters featured competing interpretations of the accused girls' conduct and character. The majority opinion commented that these were foolish, restless girls whose boundless energy and "school spirit" had merely taken a destructive turn due to unfortunate childhoods and the harsh conditions at Samarcand Manor. "These girls are just like girls everywhere," stated one editorialist from Elizabeth City, while a Raleigh reporter concluded that the group of girls who took part in the latest jailhouse ruckus might just as easily "walk into a high school class room [sic] and not be different from the average."[22] These authors implied that whether in high school or reform school, the typical adolescent girl was high-spirited, sexually interested, and drawn toward a reckless search for fun and freedom. While the enthusiasms of adolescence might get any girl into a modicum of trouble, in the case of the Samarcand inmates, poverty and misfortune had led to more serious harm.

In contrast, a minority opinion viewed these girls as a precocious version of sexually immoral, "low-class" women who menaced society. Advocates of this view perceived "a certain corrosion which strikes much deeper than the 'mistake' or 'false step' with which they are credited."[23] Anger and an absence of control were the most noted features of this debased condition. After quoting one girl's explanation that "I just feel mean," an account of the second jailhouse mutiny described faces distorted with rage, eyes gleaming, and hair and clothes disheveled such that "they seemed to be angered to the point of temporary insanity."[24] What in "normal" girls might be an urge for excitement had become in these girls a wanton search for thrills expressed in irrational and uncontrollable fury.

Proponents of both views emphasized two integrally connected themes, the inmates' sexuality and their modernity. In a trial that on the surface had nothing to do with sex, the papers often noted that the girls had been raised in "immoral" environments and had been incarcerated for sexual offenses. Their lawyer, Nell Battle Lewis, compiled a casebook in which she noted the sexual history of each defendant and their age at first intercourse.[25] Beyond these direct references, sexuality often appeared as a subtext in press descriptions of the defendants' rebellious modernity. The girls were described as wearing "attractive silk and cotton prints," rolling their stockings down under their knees, begging visitors for magazines, cigarettes, and, of course, matches. Their incessant thrill-seeking seemed to come from an irrepressible sexual energy linked to modern pleasures. Their juvenile records were sprinkled with references to cafés, automobiles, and "running around" in towns and cities. And they reportedly explained that their final jailhouse fire had been set simply as a means to win release from their cells to a recreation room where they might be allowed to listen to the Victrola and dance.[26]

The thrill-seeking, sexualized adolescent represented a dangerous current in female modernity, a view accentuated by the contrasting presence of a more palatable New Woman, the refined yet dynamic figure of defense counsel Nell Battle Lewis. Although she ended her life as a reactionary defender of southern conservatism, in the 1920s and early 1930s Lewis stood out among southern women as a leading exemplar of New Womanhood. Born to a prominent North Carolina family and educated at St. Mary's College in Raleigh, she lived briefly in the North and then returned to the South to become a columnist for the *Raleigh News and Observer.* She used her column as a podium to advance heretical challenges to the southern pieties of race, religion, gender, and respectability. She rebelled most zealously against the idealized "Southern Lady" and in one 1925 column suggested prophetically that women's rights in the South would have been hastened by "a smashed window or two and a little arson."[27]

Seeming to heed her suggestion, the rebellious Samarcand inmates held an immediate appeal to Lewis. In the late 1920s she had taken an extended break from journalism during which she studied law and passed the bar.[28] When the court-appointed public defender neglected to mount a serious defense she agreed to step in as defense attorney. Throughout the trial the press presented a glowing picture of Lewis as a dynamic and fashionable modern woman who walked intrepidly where male lawyers feared to tread. Her presence in the case offered a version of modernity that was bold and stylish but ultimately asexual, professional, and respectful of the law. As such, Lewis posed a sharp and reassuring contrast to the lawlessness and sexuality of the young women she defended.

Trying to divert attention from her charges' disorderly behavior and hoping to shift blame for the fire from her clients to their keepers, Lewis played up public accusations of institutional neglect and cruelty. The mounting criticism forced the state Department of Public Welfare to launch an investigation into charges that Samarcand staff administered brutal corporal punishments, failed to segregate venereally diseased inmates from non-infected girls (a concern that stemmed from the belief that VD was spread through casual contact or airborne germs), isolated girls for weeks or months at a time in vermin-infested solitary confinement chambers, and generally failed in the goal of rehabilitation. After conducting extensive interviews, investigators issued a lengthy report exonerating the administration of all charges, despite sworn testimony from several recently departed employees about routine brutality. The report did, however, make several criticisms and suggestions, the most urgent a call for the immediate abolition of corporal punishment.[29]

The voyeuristic, almost pornographic discussion of corporal punishment at Samarcand provides additional evidence of the uncertainty with which both state officials and the public viewed delinquent girls. While roundly condemning its use or abuse, most commentators nevertheless reveled in its detail. Reporters and investigators regularly inquired about the number and nature of the beatings, then offered the public graphic descriptions of mature and already sexualized female bodies forced to the ground, stripped, whipped repeatedly with sticks or straps, and left in a bruised and battered condition. The horror these descriptions evoked seemed to contain within it an element of erotic fascination about young, sexually active female bodies being literally and metaphorically exposed for view and "stroked" in a public spectacle of humiliating punishment.[30] Again, such images reflect a public ambivalence about—or a fascinated discomfort with—adolescent bodies. Were they to be protected or punished; who had the right to control and derive pleasure from them; and were these the bodies of children—thus subject to corporal punishment—or adults, for whom such punishments had been outlawed?

The confusion that characterized popular responses and official inquiries was present as well in professional accounts of adolescent psychology and juvenile correction. An example of this phenomenon appears in the writing of Margaret C. Brietz, a city probation officer in Winston-Salem, North Carolina, who supervised former Samarcand inmates and used their case records as the basis for her 1927 master's thesis in sociology.[31] Drawing heavily on contemporary psychological, sexological, and eugenic literatures, Brietz's elaborately-drawn portraits of eighteen Samarcand girls reveal some of the tensions that characterized scientific and social reform thinking on female delinquency in this period.

Brietz, like other contemporary experts, was especially uncertain about the relationship of delinquency to normal adolescence. Three possible interpretations run through her manuscript, starting with the most sympathetic and building toward much harsher conclusions. Delinquent behaviors could be revealing of typical teenage energy, budding sexuality, and a taste for modern pleasures. Thus, early in her 250-page thesis Brietz describes girls suffering from the "normal instability of adolescent years" typified by a youthful "craving for thrills and romance" and a sense of "great upheaval." The fact that adolescent girls experienced "the desires and impulses of adulthood but only a child's self-control" could lead to an occasional "adolescent flare-up" and trouble with the law. In this sympathetic view, adolescence in and of itself could be a cause of delinquency.[32]

As she proceeds through more, difficult cases, however, Brietz appears to lose sympathy with a portrayal of delinquents as normal but misguided adolescents. Instead she approaches delinquency as adolescence gone wrong among a group of "subnormal" teens whose behavior indicates pathology; she becomes more and more critical of her clients' "sickening backgrounds," "abnormal tendencies," deceitfulness, sexual obsessions, and "defective mental capacity."[33] Brietz's revulsion leads her further from modern views of normal adolescent compulsions and closer to a view of hereditary depravity among "defective" adolescents who would soon add to the ranks of a degenerate white population.

This increasing concern with heredity culminates in Brietz's third analysis of sex delinquency as less a marker of adolescence, whether normal or psychopathic, than evidence of adult pathology among "degenerate" white women whose reputed lack of sexual inhibitions and morality had already begun to surface.[34] Although a staple of four decades of American eugenics thought, views of hereditary degeneracy were losing scientific credibility by the late 1920s.[35] Yet in Brietz's work they assumed a modern scientific cast through her eager embrace of intelligence testing as the latest technique of scientific measurement and surgical sterilization as a eugenic corrective to the problem.

Female Delinquents and the Dilemma of White Citizenship

In her conclusion, Brietz unconsciously paints the dilemma faced by reformers, policy makers, and ordinary citizens of the state. She attests that the impulses motivating delinquency "are found to be those operating in the lives of the best of us." Reminding her readers that "we are all 'sisters under the skin,'" Brietz instructs educated citizens neither to punish nor to ostracize the delinquent in any way that would "deny that she is our own." [36] Yet the high number of girls testing low in intelligence—"morons" in her parlance—leads Brietz to question her own guiding premise; by the end of the study she doubts the entire enterprise of rehabilitating "subnormal" girls for a future of domesticity and motherhood. Considering the children borne by such women she exclaims, "What a price!" and concludes that "any program of 'Social Work' which encourages or permits feebleminded individuals to 'become moral' by marriage and parenthood is of doubtful value" to the state.[37]

Brietz wrote as a middle-class professional and reformer coming to terms with young working-class females whose independence, vulnerability, and spunk attracted her sympathy while their sexual improprieties and grievous poverty discomfited and sometimes repulsed her. Was the female sex delinquent one of "our own" or did she belong, as Brietz feared, to a group of genetically inferior people whose costly immorality must not be tolerated. Implicit in this narrative are questions of citizenship that resurfaced in popular press debates about the Samarcand arson case. Who did the state recognize as citizens? Were "immoral" and rebellious working-class white girls dangerous non-citizens who corrupted the body politic, or were they "our girls" who through proper training could be salvaged as productive members of a white citizenry?

The contest between political inclusion and exclusion of white female delinquents was not specific to the South of the 1930s. This issue, however, may have held special resonance in the South, where long before the 1930s white teenage girls had come to play a controversial and symbolic role in regional events. Historians of southern women have explored "unruly" or "disorderly" female sexuality back to the antebellum period, a time when the extramarital or interracial involvements of poor white women were perceived as especially threatening to a social order dependent on white women's sexual purity for the orderly transmission of property and racial identity.[38] These concerns intensified and shifted focus with the advent of industrial development in the turn-of-the-century New South. At issue now was the sexuality of the young white girls who rapidly populated the paid labor force of mill towns and modern cities. Both Nancy MacLean and Jacquelyn Hall have analyzed the 1915 lynching of Leo Frank, a northern-bred Jewish factory supervisor in Atlanta who allegedly raped and murdered his fourteen-year-old employee Mary Phagan. Each argues that this episode reveals deep tensions in southern society over who would control the labor and sexuality of daughters during the transition from family-based agriculture to individual waged labor. Although framed as an issue of female vulnerability and victimization, reactions to the Phagan murder also exhibit an apprehensiveness about the possibility of daughters taking sexual initiatives of their own in direct defiance of traditional lines of gender and generational authority.[39]

By the 1920s, the revitalized Ku Klux Klan drew adherents by capitalizing on these very same fears. Railing against youthful propensities for drink, dance, and sexual experimentation, the Klan exercised a violent brand of moral vigilantism designed to restore paternal authority and traditional sexual mores.[40] Progressive women reformers of the South, although they often represented the tendencies of modernity and elitism the Klan abhorred, also embraced the vulnerability of poor white women to advance a set of reforms that included prohibition, female reformatories, and other state-sanctioned "protective" measures. In an address to the United Daughters of the Confederacy, noted Georgia politician Rebecca Latimer Felton offered this justification for expanded public education, especially for poor white girls: "Why do I particularly mention poor white girls? Because these girls are the coming mothers of the great majority of the Anglo-Saxon race in the South. The future of the race for the next fifty years is in their hands."[41]

By the 1930s, that future seemed to have arrived and it did not look promising. In an era of rapid but painful regional transformation, state governments fretted over how to allocate shrinking resources to ameliorate severe economic problems and hold together a racially tendentious society that now also threatened to split across class seams. In this context it would seem unlikely that teenage girls would garner much attention, especially since new understandings of modern adolescents as sexually interested and active reduced the persuasive power of sentimental defenses of purity. Yet unusual circumstances could still throw teenage daughters into the center of public controversy. For example, Jacquelyn Hall has written about teenage rayon workers in Elizabethton, Tennessee, who held center stage during a 1929 strike that presaged the wave of textile strikes that would soon roll across the southern Piedmont. After a military occupation led to numerous arrests, subsequent courtroom dramas featured disputed standards of appropriate sexual behavior among young female strikers on trial for "disorderly conduct."[42] Two years later, in an incident both similar to and contemporaneous with the outbreak at Samarcand, charges of mistreatment and corruption at the Alabama Girls' Training School led to an equally sensational public controversy.[43] A more devastating example is the Scottsboro Case in which nine African American teenagers in Alabama were charged and quickly convicted of the rape of two white women aged seventeen and twenty-one. Occurring less than two weeks after the Samarcand fire in March 1931, the incident once again placed poor white women—mill girls who perfectly fit reformers' description of the "rural girl in the city for work"—at the center of a trial that generated worldwide controversy. In this case the question of whether disreputable working-class white girls had sexual virtue worthy of protection was answered in favor of cross-class white solidarity against an imagined and unproven threat of predatory black sexuality.[44]

Opinion was less unified in the Samarcand arson case. Although the white electorate generally agreed that the accused posed a danger to the state, they differed on the matter of how "salvageable" such white delinquents were. Competing viewpoints may reflect class divisions in North Carolina—it is possible that members of working-class or lower middle-class communities who understood juvenile problems as part of growing up with limited resources may have been more sympathetic toward sexual delinquency.[45] However, since the historical record consists largely of middle-class commentary, interpretations of white female delinquency appear to have divided less along class lines and more at other points of cleavage—between fundamentalist Christian ideas of sin and more liberal religious views; between allegiances to "traditional" versus "modern" mores; and possibly between more permissive rural attitudes toward sexuality and more propriety-conscious views held by town and urban residents.

Yet if the lines of disagreement remain blurry, the debate that swirled around the Samarcand trial leaves no doubt that white North Carolinians saw the problem of sex delinquency as relevant to building a strong and moral white citizenry. The association between morality and whiteness appears most starkly in case records of girls who were turned in by neighbors or picked up by local authorities for associating voluntarily with African American men. Crossing racial lines was equivalent to crossing the boundary between lawfulness and delinquency, or good and evil. For the most part, though, the racial implications of the citizenship debate remained muted, cloaked as a discussion about the motives, character, and ultimate social worth of the poor white girl, the future mother of the (white) citizens of North Carolina.

Through the press, the public wondered whether the alleged arsonists should be considered valuable citizens—"our own"—or members (and reproducers) of a class of poor whites not worthy of citizenship. One sympathizer went so far as to claim the Samarcand defendants as not only fellow citizens but also spirited modern-day patriots. The author, signing himself or herself "Citizen," asserted that the girls' repeated appeals for liberty demonstrated that they shared "the blood of our patriots."[46] Other less sanguine observers confessed to being baffled by the rebellious personalities of the defendants. A journalist reporting on the second jailhouse riot noted with puzzlement that the "five imprisoned little souls" who had just engaged in riotous revolt now "seemed as gentle and demure as if they had never once dreamed of a mutiny." [47] Confusion could easily turn to suspicion, as it did when a more critical editorialist warned readers, "A chit may look as mild and sweet as you please—and yet be thinking in terms of the torch!" [48] Disturbingly, girls could at one moment seem normal and the next moment fiendish, one moment disarmingly childish and the next alarmingly adult.

The fear that one did not know quite with whom one was dealing in the case of delinquent females carried over as well into the thinking of experts. In what I call a rhetoric of "the masquerading mental defective," child experts of this era became alarmed at the possibility of being tricked by mentally deficient teens who cleverly assumed the guise of intellectual normalcy. Probation officer Brietz, for example, made numerous references to Samarcand inmates whose history of sexual immorality and low IQ scores classified them as "high moron types" but whose charms, verbal agility, and cleverness could create a deceptive facade of intelligence. Describing one such "subnormal" girl with unusual language and music abilities, Brietz labeled her a "defective delinquent with special abilities" whose attractive personality and skills as a "verbalist" were deceptive. She concluded however that this girl's IQ of 67 made her "definitely feebleminded" and therefore a good candidate for sterilization. [49]

Brietz was not alone in her fear that the difference between a sexually dangerous and an apparently normal woman might be undetectable. In a feature essay on the North Carolina training school for feebleminded youth, the Greensboro Daily News warned readers against the girl who gave no outer sign of "inner lack" yet suffered from an "almost irresistible tendency to crime and immorality." The author described a female inmate who "of all the morons there, has an expression most benign" yet has a "record of immorality that is nothing less than appalling." As proof the reporter noted that the inmate had been discovered living with a Negro man and feeling "apparently entirely satisfied with herself and her estate." The article concluded that girls like this "who do not exhibit to the untrained eye the signs of their condition honeycomb the foundations of a state...[and] represent a menace which, if allowed to continue unchecked, cannot be overestimated." [50] Young sexually active women, whose premarital and interracial sexual relations served ipso facto as proof of "mental defect," threatened the foundations of a white supremacist state maintained, in part, through proscriptive controls on youthful white female sexuality.

Sexuality and Self: Samarcand Girls and Modern Sexual Subjectivity

The missing voice in the public discourse about female adolescence is that of the Samarcand inmates themselves. Although rarely given the opportunity to articulate publicly their own points of view, in their many actions and few words we can speculate about the experiences and self-understandings of white working-class southern girls caught in the institutional matrix of the state.

Scholars of popular culture have established that women of the early twentieth century used commercial entertainment, contemporary fashions, and popular narratives from film and dime novels to forge modern subjectivities marked by an expressive, affirmative female sexuality. This "new morality" of sexual modernism was initially pioneered by urban working-class youth, especially girls who boldly insisted on the legitimacy of their sexual desires. These claims were not only condemned by parents and reformers but also pathologized by professional psychiatrists who for a period in the 1910s and 1920s identified the assertive and charming allure of sexually active, white working-class teenagers as symptoms of female "hypersexuality" in need of treatment.[51]

In her study of ideologies of love and romance in the interwar period, Pamela Haag traces the gradual integration of female sexual desire into modern middle-class mores. Challenging the notion that post-Victorian "sexual liberalism" restored sexual subjectivity to women in their newly granted status as modern desiring subjects, Haag argues that modern sexology continued to deny sexual subjectivity to women by locating female passion in an unconscious domain of sexuality, the subconscious. Where men were presumed to be rational, self-possessed sexual actors, women remained dispossessed of a rational sexual self because they were driven by irrational passions unknowable at the conscious level. Adolescence, noted for its stormy irrationality, particularly incriminated young women.[52]

Eventually the desiring female adolescent assimilated into modern sexual norms through class-based narratives of "true love." Middle-class girls embraced a discourse of romantic love articulated as the "real thing"—a love so strong it could not be repressed. Expressed through middle-class narratives of romantic love, adolescent desire was presumed to transport young women toward adulthood along a passionate stream of sexual love channeled safely into marriage and a contained sexual modernity. Working-class adolescent sexuality fell outside of this nexus, perceived as vulgar, unconscious, and often alienated by economic considerations.[53] As such, the working-class adolescent girl—portrayed in various guises as the hypersexual, the juvenile delinquent, the problem girl, or in the South the mentally deficient girl—remained "a law unto herself" and subject to strict, often punitive regulation.[54]

The possibilities presented by modern commercial culture and the persistence of class and racial prejudices within modern sexual ideologies create a framework for examining the feelings and fate of girls imprisoned at Samarcand. Like their more urban, industrialized counterparts in the North, southern adolescent girls facing difficult economic and family conditions often saw in cars, cafés, dancing, and fashionable clothes the promise of self-expression and a better life. Yet it was the pursuit of such pleasures that typically led to incarceration. Most Samarcand inmates were arrested as they sought out the very realms of popular culture that others found so useful in the making of the modern sexual self.

Significantly, they did not enter this world from a position of economic or emotional strength. Institutional records show that the typical inmate came from an impoverished family broken apart by death, violence, or illness.[55] Among the Samarcand defendants, for example, ten of the sixteen girls came from families separated by death, desertion, or divorce. In two of the remaining families, the mother was severely ill, and in a third the daughter lived away from parents due to intolerable home conditions. In only four cases were the girls' families described as having adequate economic resources.[56] Without emotional or financial support from relatives, these young women often entered illicitly the world of popular thrills, becoming involved in crime or simply in sexual relationships that others deemed immoral and impermissible. While joyous participation certainly comprised one aspect of their experience, case records show that frequently accompanying this were severe venereal infections, abusive and decidedly unromantic relations with men, constant mobility, and persistent poverty.

Under these circumstances it may have been particularly difficult for working-class inmates of Samarcand to develop or maintain an identity that combined modernity, sexuality, and social legitimacy. Incarcerated teenagers mirrored other adolescents by utilizing modern pleasures like travel, fashion, and tales of romance to create themselves as "modern," fashioning hopeful narratives in which sexual attractiveness and an adventurous spirit might win them release from the demoralizing drudgery of home and work life.[57] Yet they lacked resources that might have turned creative fantasy into a secure reality. Especially notable is the absence of supportive mediating conditions such as education, intact and economically viable families, birth control, good jobs, and stable peer or residential communities. Troubled teenagers encountered instead a set of prejudices about poor, sexually active young women that denied their viability as knowing sexual subjects. Their tentative efforts to combine modernity, sexuality, and notions of "goodness" were met with charges of sexual deviance and mental defect. They then confronted a set of laws, public institutions, and state officials empowered to use this far more damning narrative to incarcerate them on the basis of their "delinquency."

The few adolescent voices that emerge from the records of Samarcand demonstrate that young inmates resisted such negative interpretations, attempting instead to piece together a positive if inchoate assertion of self that fused modern sensibilities with values absorbed from religion, family, reformatory staff, and peer culture. Self-assertion might simply consist of reckless acts of defiance, such as burning down a dormitory in hopes of being sent home, that in their bravado demonstrate a crude, if self-defeating, expression of will. Other inmates articulated a concept of self based on compliance and an end to transgressive behavior. Most often, though, we see a mixture of obedience and defiance through which inmates struggled to integrate an ignominious past with a bleak present and a hopefully more auspicious future.

Relying on a concept of self based on becoming a "good girl" or "lady," many delinquent girls embraced the tale of sin and repentance laid out by reformatory supervisors. In one awkward but seemingly heartfelt pledge to reform, an inmate wrote to her family: "I have done dirty but that is no reason I can not make a lady out off myself every lady hase had failures and [I] have had mine but it will come out all right some sweet day." [58] This teenager believed that neither her past nor her lack of education and means would prevent her from claiming status as a "lady" if her behavior met the standards set forth by Samarcand Manor. Other girls, however, revealed more conflicted emotions announced in their wildly inconsistent behavior. One former Samarcand inmate who later found herself in the North Carolina Farm Colony (a reformatory for women sixteen and older that admitted many former Samarcand inmates) was described by Samarcand staff as a "strange combination of apparent submission and great defiance." One month before parole she informed her parents that she was turning her life "to good from Bad." Explaining that she prayed nightly to the Lord for mercy, she wrote proudly that "I am being a good girl now." Yet within weeks of her parole this adolescent, who claimed "I am getting so I really love to be good," had been convicted of larceny and sent to state prison. Her frustrated and perplexed caseworker wrote her off as an apparent "dual personality." [59]

Some heartfelt pledges of reform were most likely ruses designed to earn approval, privileges, or early release from Samarcand staff. But others demonstrate genuinely mixed emotions, pulled between a desire to embrace a "higher worthwhile life" and a fierce anger at adults who seemed all too eager to judge and punish. A typical case is a paroled inmate who had been baptized twice while in Samarcand, but upon her release and re-arrest claimed in anger that "she did not give a doggone what we did with her."[60] Reformatory staff reacted with dismay when they encountered such "flippant" responses, like that of a similar inmate who resisted all authority and simply "could not seem to feel that she had 'done much wrong.'"[61] These adolescents stubbornly clung to a sense of their past behavior as legitimate, if not commendable. Although Samarcand rules required that inmates bury their pasts, forbidding them even to mention their preinstitutional life, some delinquent girls demonstrated a remarkable determination to create a sense of self that did not sever the past from hopes for a better future. "Why should I be afraid of anything I've ever done?" asked one unrepentant inmate. "Although my background for the past three years hasn't been so very desirable, what does that count. It's very different now."[62]

Heartened by staff assurances that repentance and reform would produce an end to hardship and incarceration, inmates looked forward to a more socially accepted life yet they refused to view their past as reprehensible or their lives as rent in two by a dissolute "before" and a resolute and godly "after." A woman who had spent much of her adolescence in Samarcand, given up a child for adoption, undergone a forced sterilization, and been repeatedly arrested for drunk and disorderly conduct until placed in the adult women's reformatory acknowledged that at age twenty-one her life had "been spent in drunkness and immorality." With apparent sincerity, she wrote her superintendent that "I have fully made up my mind to do the right thing," resolving to live a life that would please God, her reformatory keepers, her mother, and, in doing so, herself as well. Yet she was unable to disregard an ever-present "blueness," writing in anguish that "I haven't been happy since I've been here or either before I came." She seemed fully aware that while future happiness might depend on harmonious family and community relations, her past difficulties were rooted in those same relationships, at one point complaining bitterly that family members "haven't as much as took time to write hello's since I been here." The rhetoric of reform, however, left no room for informed skepticism or the recognition of contradictions, and she embraced the narrative of repentance offered by female reformatory staff as the only one that promised immediate release and a respectable future. Claiming that "I've never done a wrong but what I wasn't sorry afterward," she admitted her own wrongs and sought redemption. However, read another way this inmate's simple declaration also acknowledges her lingering sorrow and stubbornly bridges past with present, suggesting a complex understanding of herself as a person capable of wrong and right, sorrow and hope, commitment to self and others.[63]

At their most powerful these determined insights found expression as an aggrieved demand for justice and liberty. Samarcand defendant Pearl Stiles composed a letter to the governor of North Carolina that appears to have been intercepted and never delivered. In an appeal for life, Stiles pleaded for herself and eight others being held in the Lumberton jail, explaining to Governor Gardner that "the way we were treated was terrible. We were locked, beat, and fed on bread and water most of the time. Please give me liberty or death. . . . We girls in Roberson County jail is just as innocent of this crime they hold against us as a little child. . . . Please give me liberty or death . . . Mr. Gardner, this is Pearl Stiles writing and I am always trying to be good."

Stiles closed her letter with another declaration of innocence followed by a wish from all the girls to send their love and then this ending: "Will close with good heart. From Miss Pearl Stiles to Mr. Gardner. Lumberton, North Carolina. Answer at once." [64] Employing a rhetoric of revolutionary patriotism, Pearl Stiles not only professed her own and her cellmates' innocence but also laid claim to a loving and "good" heart and to a set of rights to bodily integrity and justice under the law.

In the words of Pearl Stiles, along with those of other inmates claiming either to be wrongly condemned or righteously reformed, we can detect efforts to combine a traditional religious discourse with a language of human rights, the self-possessed body, and a romantic, loving heart—precisely the elements that scholars have identified as providing the basis for modern political and sexual subjectivity among the middle classes. However, Stiles and others in her situation seemed to know that such claims were precarious. She couched her innocence as that of "a little child," since innocence for a sexually delinquent teenager was presumably much harder to come by. Her sense of rights too is as tentative as it is bold, mixed as it is with a claim to victim status and more supplicating declarations of love.

In the end, it was not through language that Samarcand inmates launched their most effective appeals. Far more effective than rhetorical claims to rights or sexual subjectivity were protests issued through rebellious actions. Throughout the published and unpublished institutional records, it is clear that the quickest route out of Samarcand was not reform but defiance. The most difficult inmates were often judged as beyond rehabilitation and promptly sent back to their home communities.[65] Yet this form of protest, not supported by acknowledged rights or by approved social identities, remained a dangerous one. The many expressions of public kindness and concern for Samarcand inmates did not prevent punitive incarceration, violent correction, and routine mistreatment at the hands of state officials. Underneath a rhetoric of sympathy and redemption, the state's actions spoke to an abiding distrust and even revulsion for the adolescent minds and bodies over which it assumed responsibility.

Conclusion

The Samarcand defendants found themselves prisoners in a legal system that mirrored the broader society's uncertainty over whether to classify female delinquents as children or adults. In the end the alleged arsonists experienced the harshest side of both the juvenile and adult justice system. They were incarcerated in the first place for non-criminal status offenses like "running around," "incorrigibility," being "in danger of prostitution" or "beyond parental control," and in one case as an incest victim whose father's conviction as the perpetrator left her without a legal guardian.[66] They were held under indeterminate sentences unique to juveniles and while incarcerated were subject to severe corporal punishment that had been outlawed for adult prisoners. Yet, rebelling against the vagaries of the juvenile justice system landed them in court on adult arson charges that carried the possibility of execution.

With her clients' lives on the line, defense attorney Nell Battle Lewis struck upon a strategy that she hoped would avoid the penalties of adult criminality and steer clear of the culture's uneasiness about adolescence. She argued in court that the defendants must be understood as children on the basis of their low IQs. Through the claim of "feeblemindedness" she sought to paint a picture of environmental deprivation that had left these girls in a state of mental, and thus moral, underdevelopment for which they could not be held responsible. To Lewis, feeblemindedness—in which immorality was seen as both symptom and proof of mental defect—offered up the only potentially convincing defense. But too much about the defendants' behavior indicated either adult passions or adolescent compulsions. The defense strategy failed and the teenagers received adult sentences. They were immediately transferred to the predominantly male state prison where they would occupy cells directly above death row because it was the only fireproof wing of the prison.[67]

The judicial process, like the popular debate over the case, reveals a constant tug between sympathetic inclusion and punitive correction. The ambivalent response to female adolescent sexuality, especially that of white working-class girls, is not specific to the South of the 1930s. We can read the case as an unusually sharp articulation of the persistent tensions that have surrounded adolescent girls whose confident embrace of sexuality is as appealing as it is disturbing to adult society. Yet we can also examine the Samarcand incident for the way experiences of female adolescent sexuality were inscribed in, and articulated through, the class and racial fault lines of modern southern society. Here sociologist and probation officer Margaret Brietz's claim that Samarcand inmates were "sisters under the skin" is quite revealing. It simultaneously portrays poor white girls as of another race—presumed to have a different skin—and members of a white sisterhood whose physical and moral health held the key to the future of the state. How could white citizens of the New South maintain solidarity and social cohesion when confronted by working-class urban problems and sexual behaviors that so reviled middle-class modernists? And how would southerners deal with sexual modernity in girls who violated every tenet of both bourgeois respectability and a still powerful racial code of white female purity? Were these girls to be embraced as southern daughters or rejected as racial degenerates?

State authorities and reformers advanced a view that only through a maternalist state institution, a reformatory staffed and headed by women but kept on course by paternal oversight and funds, could North Carolina hope to prevent its wayward girls—the future mothers of the state—from corrupting the moral or "racial" stock of current and future populations. The rhetoric of enlightened guidance and reclamation provided a veneer for much harsher policies that could literally cut like a knife. During the same years they publicly debated the fate of rebellious daughters at Samarcand, state legislators quietly put in place sterilization laws and procedures used to control the fertility of poor white women in their teens and early twenties. Between 1929 and 1947, 79 percent of North Carolina's 1,901 "eugenic sterilizations" were performed on women. Of the nearly 1,500 females sterilized in this period, 780 were between the ages of ten and nineteen, with white girls significantly overrepresented in this group. Samarcand was one of the main cooperating institutions among various state schools, submitting at least three hundred inmates for sterilization.[68]

Meanwhile, white citizens of North Carolina remained torn. Some viewed Samarcand positively as a "training school" that could produce charm and refinement among poor, uneducated but rehabilitated females. Skeptics, however, refused the suggestion that Samarcand was a working-class "boarding school," nor did they accept the incendiary acts of inmates as merely misguided demonstrations of "school spirit." They persisted in seeing the institution as a breeding ground for revolt and disease among the dangerous classes, a view that in turn sanctioned physical abuse and sterilization as state policies appropriate to the larger goal of shoring up a dependable white citizenry. This contradictory discourse formed the context in which troubled working-class white girls articulated tentative claims to sexual subjectivity and personal dignity as they navigated their own difficult passage from southern girlhood into modern womanhood.

Notes

I would like to thank Nan Enstad, Liz Kennedy, Mary Odem, Nancy Staudt, and Tamara Thornton for incisive comments on earlier drafts of this essay, as well as

Jacquelyn Hall and Joanne Meyerowitz for their helpful readings of the most recent version.

1. Faced with possible execution, the young women pleaded guilty even though only two girls claimed they had anything to do with setting the fires. They were advised that even with the guilty plea, charges would be dropped if their innocence was established. Documentation on the arson trial and on the institutional history of Samarcand comes from several sources: Nell Battle Lewis Papers, North Carolina State Archives (hereafter NCSA); records of the State Board of Public Welfare, Institutions, and Correction (hereafter SBPWIC), some of which are located at the NCSA and others at the Old Record Center (hereafter ORC-NCSA) of the NCSA; "Prisons in North Carolina," clipping file in the North Carolina Collection, University of North Carolina Library (hereafter NCC-UNC), Chapel Hill; and the published "Biennial Reports of the State Home and Industrial School for Girls" (available at NCC-UNC). An undergraduate honors essay by Susan Pearson, "Samarcand, Nell Battle Lewis, and the 1931 Arson Trial" (7 April 1989, NCC-UNC), provides a useful overview of the trial.

2. Elizabeth City *Daily Advance*, 22 April 1931.

3. G. Stanley Hall, *Adolescence: Its Psychology and Its Relations to Physiology, Anthropology, Sociology, Sex, Crime, Religion, and Education* (1904; rev. ed., New York: D. Appleton and Co., 1915).

4. On the new definition of adolescence, see Ruth Alexander, *The "Girl Problem": Female Sexual Delinquency in New York, 1900–1930* (Ithaca, N.Y.: Cornell University Press, 1995), 2.

5. For a general discussion of these changes, see Sara Evans, *Born for Liberty: A History of Women in America* (New York: Free Press, 1989), chaps. 7–8; Nancy Cott, *The Grounding of Modern Feminism* (New Haven, Conn.: Yale University Press, 1987), chap. 5; and Estelle B. Freedman and John D'Emilio, *Intimate Matters: A History of Sexuality in America* (New York: Harper and Row, 1988), chaps. 8–10.

6. On "white slavery," see Ruth Rosen, *The Lost Sisterhood: Prostitution in America, 1900–1918* (Baltimore, Md.: The Johns Hopkins University Press, 1982), 112–36. "Six O'Clock in America," Current Opinion 55 (August 1913): 113–14.

7. Evans, *Born for Liberty*, 175–96.

8. See Joanne J. Meyerowitz, *Women Adrift: Independent Wage Earners in Chicago, 1880–1930* (Chicago: University of Chicago Press, 1988); Mary E. Odem, *Delinquent Daughters: Protecting and Policing Adolescent Female Sexuality in the United States, 1885–1920* (Chapel Hill: University of North Carolina Press, 1995); Regina Kunzel, *Fallen Women, Problem Girls: Unmarried Mothers and the Professionalization of Social Work, 1890–1945* (New Haven, Conn.: Yale University Press, 1993), 36–64; Constance A. Nathanson, *Dangerous Passage: The Social Control of Sexuality in Women's Adolescence* (Philadelphia: Temple University Press, 1991). For general treatments of adolescence and juvenile delinquency, see Joseph E Kett, *Rites of Passage: Adolescence in America, 1790 to the Present* (New York: Basic Books, 1977); and John R. Sutton, *Stubborn Children: Controlling Delinquency in the United States, 1640–1981* (Berkeley: University of California Press, 1988).

9. By "modernizing" I refer to a regional transformation involving large-scale immigration from rural to urban areas, the growth of a manufacturing sector, the extension of a cash-based consumer economy, and a regional self-consciousness of "becoming modern."

10. Odem, *Delinquent Daughters*, 8–37.

11. Twenty-nine of these had been established after 1910, many with federal funds made available during World War I in an effort to eliminate the threat to soldiers' morale and health presented by prostitution and venereal disease. Margaret Reeves, *Training Schools for Delinquent Girls* (New York: Russell Sage, 1929), 18–20, 42–46. See also Odem, *Delinquent Daughters*, 116. On nineteenth-century reformatories, see Barbara Brenzel, *Daughters of the State: A Social Portrait of the First Reform School for Girls in North America, 1865–1905* (Cambridge, Mass.: MIT Press, 1983). On reformatories for adult women, see Nicole Hahn Rafter, *Partial Justice: Women, Prisons, and Social Control,* 2d ed. (New Brunswick, N.J.: Transactions Publishers, 1990).

12. Of the fifty-seven schools examined by Reeves in 1924, nine were for African American girls; of these only four received primary funding by the state; the other five depended on private charity. A later study by the Osborne Association found that the only exception to segregationist policies in southern reformatories was Kentucky, although within the institution itself inmates continued to be segregated by both race and sex. North Carolina funded two institutions for white male delinquents, one for black male delinquents, Samarcand Manor for white female juvenile offenders eighteen and under, and an Industrial Farm Colony for Women, which was a reformatory for adult white women that in practice served an "adult" population the majority of whom were still between seventeen and twenty-one. The legislature of North Carolina also covered a small portion of the costs incurred by the state's Training School for Negro Girls, which was largely kept afloat by funds raised privately by African American community groups. On southern institutions for delinquent juveniles, see Reeves, *Training Schools,* 42–43; and Osborne Association, *Handbook of American Institutions for Delinquent Juveniles,* vol. 2, "Kentucky-Tennessee" (New York: Osborne Association, Inc., 1940); and Osborne Association, *Handbook of American Institutions for Delinquent Juveniles,* vol. 4, "Virginia-North Carolina" (New York: Osborne Association, Inc., 1943).

13. *Charlotte Observer,* 19 February 1939, records of the SBPWIC, North Carolina Training School for Negro Girls, Box 163, ORC-NCSA, folder, n.d., "North Carolina Industrial Training School for Negro Girls, 1919–1934."

14. Steven Noll, *Feeble-Minded in Our Midst: Institutions for the Mentally Retarded in the South, 1900–1940* (Chapel Hill: University of North Carolina Press, 1995).

15. See Pearson, "Samarcand," 5.

16. O. Latham Hatcher, *Rural Girls in the City for Work: A Study Made for the Southern Woman's Educational Alliance* (Richmond, Va.: Garrett and Massie, Inc., 1930). See also, Nora Miller, *The Rural Girl in the Rural Family* (Chapel Hill: University of North Carolina Press, 1935), quote on 106–7.

17. *Biennial Reports of the North Carolina Charitable, Penal, and Correctional Institutions* (Raleigh, N.C.: Capital Printing Co., 1926–1936).

18. Odem, *Delinquent Daughters,* 148.

19. "Samarcand Girls Riot in Moore County Jail," *Moore County News,* 30 April 1931. Other reports on the incident indicate that this one is much exaggerated. Nevertheless, it is the description that the residents of Moore County received.

20. Elizabeth City Daily Advance, 22 April 1931.

21. On the New South, see Dewey W. Grantham, *The South in Modern America: A Region at Odds* (New York: HarperCollins, 1994); Edward Ayers, *The Promise of the New South: Life after Reconstruction* (New York: Oxford University Press, 1992); Jacqueline Jones, *The Dispossessed: America's Underclass from the Civil War to the Present* (New York: Basic Books, 1992); Jack Kirby, *Rural Worlds Lost: The American South, 1920–1960* (Baton Rouge: Louisiana State University Press, 1987); and Jacquelyn Dowd Hall et. al., *Like a Family: The Making of a Southern Cotton Mill World* (Chapel Hill: University of North Carolina Press, 1987).

22. Mrs. Herbert Peele, *Elizabeth City Daily Advance,* 22 April 1931; "Rebellious Girls Set Their Bunks Afire to Get Thrill," *Raleigh News and Observer,* 2 May 1931.

23. Arson clippings in folder, "Samarcand Manor, 1918–1924," SBPWIC-Samarcand, Box 164, ORC-NCSA.

24. "Rebellious Girls," *Raleigh News and Observer,* 2 May 1931; and "Samarcand Girls," *Moore County News,* 30 April 1931.

25. According to Lewis's records, nine of the sixteen defendants (including an incest victim) reported having had intercourse between the ages of twelve and fifteen. Several others denied having had intercourse but were strongly suspected by reformatory officials of acts of prostitution and/or having sexual intercourse.

26. One report quoted a rioter as explaining that after being released from their burning cells and sprayed with water hoses to calm their "rampage," "we went upstairs then and danced about two hours" while jailers cleaned up the rubble. "Rebellious Girls," Raleigh News and Observer, 2 May 1931.

27. Biographical information on Lewis is drawn from her own papers at NCSA and from Darden Asbury Pyron, "Nell Battle Lewis (1893–1956) and 'The New Southern Womanhood,'" in *Perspectives on the American South: An Annual Review of Society, Politics, and Culture,* vol. 3, ed. James C. Cobb and Charles R. Wilson (New York: Bordon and Breach Science Publishers, 1985), 63–85. Lewis's 10 May 1925 *Raleigh News and Observer* column is quoted in Pyron, "Nell Battle Lewis," 70.

28. Pyron, "Nell Battle Lewis," 73–74.

29. Folder "Samarcand Manor, 1925–31," SBPWIC-Samarcand, Box 164, ORC-NCSA.

30. Jacquelyn Dowd Hall has described southern lynchings and the South's fascination with rape as a form of "folk pornography." Hall, "'The Mind that Burns in Each Body': Women, Rape, and Racial Violence," in *Powers of Desire: The Politics of Sexuality,* ed. Ann Snitow, Christine Stansell, and Sharon Thompson (New York: Monthly Review Press, 1983), 335.

31. Margaret C. Brietz, "Case Studies of Delinquent Girls in North Carolina" (master's thesis, University of North Carolina, Chapel Hill, 1927).

32. Ibid., 65, 51.

33. Ibid., 122, 134, 177.

34. Ibid., 171–204.

35. On eugenic thought, see Mark H. Haller, *Eugenics: Hereditarian Attitudes in American Thought* (New Brunswick, N.J.: Rutgers University Press, 1984); and Philip R. Reilly, *The Surgical Solution: A History of Involuntary Sterilization in the United States* (Baltimore, Md.: The Johns Hopkins University Press, 1991).

36. Brietz, "Case Studies," 226.

37. Ibid., 186.

38. Victoria Bynum, *Unruly Women: The Politics of Social and Sexual Control in the Old South* (Chapel Hill: University of North Carolina Press, 1992). On similar dynamics during Reconstruction, see Laura Edwards, "Sexual Violence, Gender, Reconstruction, and the Extension of Patriarchy in Granville County, North Carolina," *North Carolina Historical Review* 68 (July 1991): 237–60.

39. Nancy MacLean, "The Leo Frank Case Reconsidered: Gender and Sexual Politics in the Making of Reactionary Populism," *Journal of American History* 78 (December 1991): 917–48; Jacquelyn Dowd Hall, "Private Eyes, Public Women: Images of Class and Sex in the Urban South, Atlanta, Georgia, 1913–1915," in *Work Engendered: Toward a New History of American Labor,* ed. Ava Baron (Ithaca: Cornell University Press, 1991), 243–72.

40. Nancy MacLean, *Behind the Mask of Chivalry: The Making of the Second Ku Klux Klan* (New York: Oxford University Press, 1994), 98–124, and N. MacLean, "White Women and Klan Violence in the 1920s: Agency, Complicity, and the Politics of Women's History," *Gender and History* 3 (Autumn 1991): 285–303.

41. Rebecca Latimer Felton, "Education of Veterans' Daughters," 1893 speech, quoted in LeeAnn Whites, "Rebecca Latimer Felton and the Problem of 'Protection' in the New South," in *Visible Women: New Essays on American Activism,* ed. Nancy Hewitt and Suzanne Lebsock (Urbana: University of Illinois Press, 1993), 51.

42. Jacquelyn Dowd Hall, "Disorderly Women: Gender and Labor Militancy in the Appalachian South," *Journal of American History* 73 (September 1986): 35482.

43. See newspaper coverage in clippings file, "Reformatories—Ala.—Girls," Southern History Department, Birmingham Public Library.

44. For an analysis of the racialized sexual politics of the case, see James Goodman, *Stories of Scottsboro* (New York: Vintage, 1994).

45. The only access to working-class opinions I found was in the institutional records of parental responses to daughters sentenced to Samarcand. They suggest that although many poor urban and rural parents sought criminal sanctions against their troublesome daughters, they were often dismayed at the harshness of the legal system's response.

46. Fayetteville Observer, 4 May 1931.

47. "Samarcand Girls," *Moore County News,* 30 April 1931.

48. Arson clippings in folder "Samarcand Manor, 1918–1924," SBPWIC-Samarcand, Box 164, ORC-NCSA.

49. Brietz, "Case Studies," 156–60. Similarly, she classified another former inmate with an IQ of 77 as a high-grade moron complicated "by charm of personality and conversational ability." Brietz, 169.

50. "Idiots, Imbeciles, and Morons at Caswell," *Greensboro Daily News,* 10 December 1922.

51. See Kathy Peiss, *Cheap Amusements: Working Women and Leisure in Turn-of-the-Century New York* (Philadelphia: Temple University Press, 1986); Elizabeth Ewen, *Immigrant Women in the Land of Dollars: Life and Culture on the Lower East Side* (New York: Monthly Review Press, 1985); Susan Glenn, *Daughters of the Shtetl: Life and Labor in the Immigrant Generation* (Ithaca, N.Y.: Cornell University Press, 1990); Nan Enstad, "Dressed for Adventure: Working Women and Silent Movie Serials in the 1910s," *Feminist Studies* 21 (Spring 1995): 67–90; Hall, "Disorderly Women," 354–82; Paula Fass, *The Damned and the Beautiful: American Youth in the 1920s* (New York: Oxford University Press, 1977); Beth Bailey, *From Front Porch to Back Seat: Courtship in Twentieth-Century America* (Baltimore, Md.: The Johns Hopkins University Press, 1988); and Elizabeth Lunbeck, "'A New Generation of Women': Progressive Psychiatrists and the Hypersexual Female," *Feminist Studies* 13 (Fall 1987): 513–43.

52. Pamela Haag, "In Search of the 'Real Thing': Ideologies of Love, Modern Romance, and Women's Sexual Subjectivity in the United States, 1920–1940," *Journal of the History of Sexuality* 2, no. 4 (1992): 547–77. On "sexual liberalism," see Freedman and D'Emilio, *Intimate Matters,* chaps. 11–12.

53. Haag, "In Search of the 'Real Thing,'" 547–77.

54. Winifred Richmond, *The Adolescent Girl: A Book for Parents and Teachers* (New York [1929]), 117, quoted in Haag, "In Search of the 'Real Thing,'" 557.

55. Samarcand Biennial Reports, 1920s–1940s, NCC-UNC.

56. Casebook, Lewis Papers, NCSA.

57. Lisa Duggan defines identity as "a narrative of a subject's location within social structure," or as situating "stories" that "traverse the space between the social world and subjective experience . . . connecting self and world." L. Duggan, "The Trials of Alice Mitchell: Sensationalism, Sexology, and the Lesbian Subject in Turn-of-the-Century America," Signs 18 (Summer 1993): 793.

58. N.d., SBPWIC-Samarcand, Box 164, ORC-NCSA.

59. I found limited case record information on Samarcand residents in the records of former inmates later incarcerated at the State Industrial Farm Colony for Women. To protect privacy I do not use names from these case records. Quotes are from Case 463, Farm Colony Records, "North Carolina Board of Correction and Training—State Industrial Farm Colony for Women, Case Histories," ORC-NCSA.

60. Case 410, Farm Colony Records, ORC-NCSA.

61. Case 17, Farm Colony Records, ORC-NCSA.

62. Case 600, Farm Colony Records, ORC-NCSA.

63. Case 670, Farm Colony Records, ORC-NCSA.

64. Letter contained in folder "Samarcand Manor, 1931," SBPWIC-Samarcand, Box 164, ORC-NCSA.

65. The 1931 investigation into Samarcand included the finding that "girls giving a great deal of trouble in [the] institution are discharged. Girls have learned that incorrigibility is the quickest method of getting away and some conduct themselves accordingly." Folder "Samarcand Manor, 1931," SBPWIC-Samarcand, Box 164, ORC-NCSA.

66. Casebook, Lewis Papers, NCSA. The incest victim, incarcerated without any

charge of criminal wrongdoing, was one of those convicted of arson and committed to state prison.

67. "Prisons in North Carolina" clippings file, NCC-UNC.

68. Between 1929 and 1947, 1,494 of North Carolina's 1,901 "eugenic sterilizations" were performed on females, with 1,260 of the total performed on "feebleminded" individuals, a classification that included an overwhelmingly female population. Despite a fantasy narrative presented by the state of overburdened married mothers begging for sterilizations to save their health, over a period of two decades 77 percent of all sterilizations were performed on single individuals, and 76 percent of all sterilized women had either no children or only one or two. In the program's initial decades, white women were consistently overrepresented and African American women underrepresented in sterilizations, most likely because black women remained outside the reach of state institutions and county welfare agencies. This changed by the 1950s, at which time African American women became the primary target of sterilization efforts. See Eugenics Board of North Carolina, "Biennial Reports," NCC-UNC; Moya Woodside, *Sterilization in North Carolina: A Sociological and Psychological Study* (Chapel Hill, N.C.: University of North Carolina Press, 1950); and Johanna Schoen, "The State and Women's Sexuality: The Birth Control and Sterilization Program in North Carolina, 1929-75" (master's thesis, University of North Carolina, Chapel Hill, 1989). See also Edward J. Larson, *Sex, Race, and Science: Eugenics in the Deep South* (Baltimore, Md.: The Johns Hopkins University Press, 1995).

Winning the Peace

Georgia Veterans and the Struggle to Define the Political Legacy of World War II

Jennifer E. Brooks

In traveling around the nation and throughout the European and Pacific theaters during World War II, soldiers from the South encountered cultures, economies, and political ideas beyond the realm of southern tradition. After the war, armed with new exemptions from poll taxes, Georgia soldiers injected a strong dose of uncertainty into state politics.[1] Local dynasties pondered the electoral potential that the veterans represented: Would they vote to defend southern tradition and, by extension, the right of incumbents to rule? Or had wartime service altered their attitude to the southern status quo?

In Georgia black and white veterans confirmed both the worst fears and best hopes of political pundits across the region. They launched numerous powerful and multifaceted assaults on the provincial and undemocratic nature of southern politics, expressing an energetic sense of civic duty and entitlement derived by and large from service in the war. Above all, Georgia's veterans wanted their well-deserved share of political and economic opportunities unleashed by the war. When they returned home from the service, however, they confronted a conservative, complacent, and often reactionary leadership determined to hold onto the power and privileges that had long perpetuated Bourbon rule. For veterans weary of war and anxious to take advantage of new opportunities, postwar Georgia posed a disturbing conundrum: achieving the quality of life they believed they had earned required waging another war—this time at home—against the political, economic, and racial traditions that upheld the one-party South. An account of their efforts to achieve these goals illustrates the difficulty in determining whether World War II was an agent of political change or political continuity in Georgia and the South.

The activities that black and white veterans pursued were fraught with contradiction. For example, those who assaulted the citadels of southern racial tradition confronted other veterans policing the ramparts of white supremacy. These contradictions, however, make veteran activism a useful barometer by which to measure the war's political impact. Through their efforts to implement often conflicting understandings of the war's meaning, southern veterans did much to define the political legacy of the war as disruptive and contradictory for Georgia and the South. They destabilized conservative Democratic hegemony, made racial reform and economic development the key issues of the postwar era, and determined that the politics of growth would prevail over the politics of progressive racial reform. It was a complicated political legacy, one that testified to the war's role in generating considerable political and social turmoil.

African American veterans who returned to Georgia were determined to exercise their rights of citizenship.[2] They organized to protect their veterans' benefits, protested police brutality, and used voter registration drives to increase black political influence. Through it all, Georgia's black veterans asserted a strong moral claim to citizenship, respect, and justice, which they felt should reward their service in the war. Their efforts helped to elevate postwar registration and voting to unprecedented levels, boosted postwar movements for progressive reform—and eventually touched off a reactionary backlash. In the wake of the white primary's demise in Georgia in 1946, this surge in black political activism made race a key issue in postwar politics throughout the state.[3]

Service in the war both increased black soldiers' frustration with racial injustices and boosted their expectations for the future. W. W. Law, a black veteran from Savannah, Georgia, found military service to be a series of disheartening encounters with the barriers and humiliations of Jim Crow. When drafted, Law recalled, "I asked for frontline duty as an infantry soldier. But they assigned me to the quartermaster, as was typical." After he was inducted, he ran into trouble almost immediately. Assigned to Keesler Airfield's aviation battalion in Biloxi, Mississippi, Law clashed with his company commander, a white man from Mississippi. "We were being assigned chores on the base of picking up matchstems and cigarette butts," Law recalled, "and I objected and was called before my commander, and we had a discussion on leadership." Being a headstrong young man, as Law recalled, he informed the commander that "a proper leader would be a person who could inspire his people into formation, and this was not inspirational work." After this discussion, "he found a way to transfer me out because I did not go along with the proceedings."[4]

Historians of black soldiers during the war have demonstrated that experiences such as Law's were far from unusual. Despite such encounters, many black service men remained convinced that the war ultimately would improve black life in the South. "There was a tendency among Negro soldiers," army researchers found, "to expect or hope for an increase in rights and privileges, improved treatment, and better economic status after the war," with southern blacks tending to be more optimistic than those from the North. In fact,

43 percent of those soldiers surveyed expected to have "more rights and privileges" after the war, and 42 percent believed "in the long run Negro soldiers [would] be better off . . . after they got out of the Army than they were before they went into the Army."[5] Confident in the value of their own contribution to victory, many apparently headed home expecting, or at least hoping, to find a changed environment. "A lot of guys . . . didn't expect to find the same situation that we left," explained Tuskegee war veteran Otis Pinkard, in part because many blacks believed that southern whites had a moral imperative to acknowledge and reward blacks' wartime participation by recognizing their civic, political, and economic rights.[6]

Thus, many black veterans returned to Georgia certain that their contribution to victory would give them greater opportunities than they had enjoyed before the war.[7] They soon discovered that few white southerners agreed. Horace Bohannon, a field agent for the Southern Regional Council's Veteran Services Project, noted that white citizens in Ft. Valley, Georgia, for example, nervously anticipated trouble from the "returning Negro veteran . . . dissatisfied with conditions" and expected white southerners to " 'pick on' the returning veteran to try and steer him 'back into his place.' "[8] Both predictions were accurate.

As soon as the war ended, whites in Georgia and throughout the South began a campaign of discrimination against black veterans that impeded both their utilization of wartime skills and their access to the job-training, unemployment, and educational benefits guaranteed by the GI Bill. A group consisting primarily of black teachers, principals, and school administrators attending a summer seminar in 1946 at Atlanta University reported that employment discrimination was widespread. A Bibb County, Georgia, teacher and minister declared, "I believe that the single greatest problem confronting the returning Negro veteran is . . . obtaining employment." An Atlanta area student agreed: "The veterans in my community are having difficulty getting suitable job placement in newly acquired skills. In most cases," he stated, "these men were in a low income bracket prior to the war, but while in service they learned how to do better jobs." Now, he noted, veterans "are unwilling to accept the old job as before." "For myself I was not able to find a job because I was not able to do the kind of work they wanted done," lamented a veteran from Hogansville, Georgia. "I can operate any kind of office equipment but I was refused a job in this line of work." He concluded that "the Negro veterans are merely being pushed around."[9] The American Council of Race Relations found in 1946 that of 246 approved on-the-job federal training programs in Georgia, black veterans participated in only 6.[10] High hopes for a better job, more economic security, and a "chance to make it" came crashing down in the cruel light of the Jim Crow day, and a Warm Springs, Georgia, principal noted that "for the most part, the returning soldiers seem not to be able to readjust themselves."[11]

In the immediate postwar years, however, intransigent southern whites confronted a determined, ambitious, and experienced foe who staunchly resisted the forces of white reaction and southern tradition. Georgia's black veterans organized the Georgia Veterans League (GVL), which was a statewide association headquartered in Atlanta with four chapters throughout the state.[12] According to Horace Bohannon, who was a member, the GVL had two to three hundred members statewide with sixty or so of those in the Fulton County (Atlanta) chapter.[13]

Organized to facilitate black veterans' access to GI Bill benefits, the GVL hoped, according to John B. Turner, the Fulton County commander, "to aid returning veterans in adjusting themselves to community life." Through an office established in Atlanta in early 1946, the GVL's trained black counselors assisted veterans in applying for GI benefits, because, as Bohannon recalled, black veterans often did not "feel quite at home talking to a white representative," and "if you had credential as a representative of a veterans' group . . . you got a much better ear than if you were somebody that [just] got off the train."[14]

More importantly, these veterans quickly learned that "there was no need of applying for a job as radio announcer. . . . You weren't going to get it. . . . You had to stay within these artificial barriers." In order to address this discrimination in wages and hiring, the GVL also pledged to fight for equal pay for equal work and for employment in all professions and occupations. The group also advocated equal park, recreational, public health, and hospital facilities; improved and equal schools for black children; equal justice under the law; and black policemen and firemen. Promising to cooperate with organized labor, black-owned businesses, and organizations working for community improvement, veterans of the GVL aimed to use "every intelligent and honorable means," including the "ballot, publicity, picketing, parades, and boycotts," to combat discrimination, all of which, according to Horace Bohannon, "made a difference in the black community."[15]

Indeed, participation by veterans lent a new moral legitimacy to voter registration campaigns, some of which had begun before or during the war. As Doyle Combs, a World War II veteran and later a leader of the National Association for the Advancement of Colored People (NAACP) in northeast Georgia, eloquently explained, defending the American way of life abroad fostered a deep conviction in the right to political freedom at home. After leaving the army, Combs was determined to vote because "I lost a portion of my body for this country" even though "I didn't have no right to fight whatsoever cause I didn't have no rights in the United States of America, as a black man." Having "lost a portion of my body to protect my own rights," Combs was determined to "die for my rights" and even "kill for my rights" if necessary.[16] The sense of civic entitlement that veterans like Combs articulated underlay the practical realization that the franchise represented the only realistic avenue to increased black political power. "We demand ... full civil and political rights and protection for every person," declared the GVL, and "the League will work for every Negro of age becoming a registered voter." Voter registration was a requirement for membership in the GVL.[17]

Thus, in communities throughout Georgia and the South, black veterans organized, joined, and led voter registration drives that aimed to boost black participation in the first postwar Democratic Party primaries. Their commitment and enthusiasm helped increase black registration and voting to unprecedented levels and disrupted the civic complacency at the heart of Bourbon rule. Two of the most energetic and successful drives occurred in Savannah and Atlanta. Both campaigns drew very large numbers of black citizens to county courthouses to register and to precincts and polls to vote.

An enthusiastic insurgent campaign launched in Savannah by the moderately reformist and business progressive Citizens Progressive League (CPL), a new civic organization consisting primarily of white veterans and citizens, attracted broad interest in the spring of 1946. If enough blacks voted to assist in ousting the mossback political machine headed by Chatham County Attorney John Bouhan, a local Democratic Party boss, blacks surmised, then they might increase their influence with the new city administration and state legislative delegation. With this in mind, a newly organized black World War II–Veterans Association (WW2–VA) launched an enthusiastic voter registration campaign in the early spring, fulfilling its pledge to "take a leading role in politics" in order to improve "the political and economic positions of all of its colored citizens." [18]

Calling on all registered voters and every organization to lend a hand, the WW2–VA conducted a house-to-house canvass and mass meetings to encourage registration and voting. Black citizens responded in overwhelming numbers. Pastors led large numbers of their parishioners to register, and undertakers donated hearses to carry people to the courthouse. On July 5, the last day to register, black citizens—with lunchboxes and children in tow—came in "droves," jamming the courthouse and the surrounding park. They were ready to stand in line all day if necessary to enforce, as one elderly citizen told a reporter, "the will of the Lord that us colored folks vote." [19] Indeed, the voter registration project by the WW2–VA turned out enough black voters to give the margin of victory to the CPL, which swept state legislative and local offices as well as the membership of the county Democratic committee.[20]

In Atlanta, veterans helped to spearhead an equally vigorous registration drive aimed at the 1946 campaigns for governor and the Fifth District congressional seat. The All Citizens Registration Committee (ACRC) registered over twenty thousand black voters in the spring and summer of 1946, and black veterans were crucial to the drive's success.[21] Ex-GI David Watson served as director of ACRC headquarters and executive secretary of the voter drive. In canvassing black neighborhoods, veterans in the GVL drew on the following script to make a powerful moral appeal against blacks' civic apathy and fear. "I spent over two years, a part of which was overseas, in the armed services," veterans told prospective registrants, and "I had hopes that my services would provide *YOU* with freedom from want and fear. Above all else I wanted to maintain *YOUR* freedom of speech. Now that the war has been won," veterans testified, "the most difficult job ahead of us is to win the *PEACE* here at home. . . . If you will become a *REGISTERED VOTER* we may be able to win the *PEACE*." Political participation, veterans argued, was the key to unlocking the restrictive hold of southern racial tradition over black opportunity and freedom. "If we are to be treated fairly in this state, if we want to stop police brutality, get justice in the courts, Negro policemen, equal educational, health, and recreational facilities," GVL leader Clarence Stephens declared, "then we must have a voice in our government. The ballot must be our weapon against the enemies of democracy at home in Georgia."[22]

Initially, the ACRC drive was successful. The campaign registered almost 22,000 new black voters, who became the core of the new black political strength in Atlanta. However, the county-unit system nullified the popular majorities that black voters helped to give Helen Douglas Mankin, the Fifth District congressional candidate, and James V. Carmichael, the gubernatorial candidate. Nonetheless, increased black registration quickly drew official attention. In Atlanta, Mayor William B. Hartsfield and the board of aldermen finally agreed to hire black police officers, while in Savannah the new CPL administration appointed a Negro Advisory Committee, hired nine black police officers, and began school and recreational improvements in black neighborhoods.[23] Black veterans initiated and joined similar registration drives across the state, often boosting voter registration and turnout to historic levels.[24]

As these campaigns illustrate, African American veterans who returned to Georgia and the South believed that their contribution to American victory overseas had real value. Their determination to implement the sense of civic entitlement that resulted had important political repercussions in a region that habitually circumscribed black freedom and opportunity. The organized protests and voter registration drives in which these veterans participated had significant results. In Georgia, these efforts netted between 135,000 and 150,000 registered black voters in 1946 alone. Between 85,000 and 100,000 black citizens actually voted that year, helping provide popular majorities to both Helen Douglas Mankin and James V. Carmichael. Moreover, black voters played a key role in defeating entrenched political machines in Savannah and Augusta in 1946, and in electing a new mayor in Macon in 1947. The following year around

200,000 black citizens registered statewide for the gubernatorial race between Melvin E. Thompson and Herman E. Talmadge. By the time of the *Brown v. Board of Education* decision in 1954, over one million African Americans were registered to vote in the South. By forcefully demanding racial and democratic reform, black veterans helped to disrupt the civic complacency that sustained the Solid South.[25] Their efforts made the issue of racial change especially controversial in postwar elections throughout the state.

Black veterans were not alone in their fight to define the war's political legacy in racially progressive terms. White veterans from the South probably did not expect their military service to generate doubt and uncertainty in their regional loyalties. While many white southerners entered the service certain of the immutability of Jim Crow, some found that the war undermined that conviction.[26] Defending a discriminatory nation against a racially intolerant enemy posed a disturbing irony. War-induced disenchantment with southern racial practices and political traditions turned into outright opposition when veterans were confronted with the persistent vitality of reactionary conservatism at home. They joined black veterans in combating political inequality and injustice and ultimately mounted a spirited attack on the county-unit system, a discriminatory apportionment of state legislative representation and electoral votes that tilted power and policy against the interests of blacks, workers, and urban dwellers. Their efforts provided an interracial component to progressive postwar movements—though they were less successful in battling racial hatred and tyranny at home than they had been overseas.

Despite an official policy of segregation in the armed forces, the exigencies of the war required interaction between black and white GIs. Black servicemen performed their duties ably despite discrimination and mistreatment. In light of this, the notion that they deserved unequal treatment because of their race grew less convincing as the war progressed. "I have spent four and a half years in the army, twenty months overseas," Henry C. Rivers of Griffin, Georgia, remarked, and "I have been around and fought with Negro soldiers and I have nothing to hold against them." A white sergeant from Texas agreed. He had not cared about discrimination before the war, but his wartime experiences convinced him that white southerners should not "abuse the colored people any more" because blacks as well as whites had died serving their country.[27] Few white veterans, however, recalled the liberalizing impact of their wartime service as vividly as did Georgian Harold Fleming.

Fleming had attended Harvard before the war but, as he later recalled, "was still pretty much a victim of [his] own upbringing." Though he looked with "disdain on redneck stuff and on the crasser forms of prejudice [and] discrimination," Fleming was "pretty damn unenlightened" on the racial issues of the day. Upon graduating from Officer Candidate School, he took command of black troops in the Quartermaster Corps on Okinawa. The experience "was critical" in transforming him from a relatively "unenlightened" southern moderate into an outright racial liberal.[28]

Commanding black troops was "a very traumatic kind of experience," Fleming recalled, because "you were a white straw boss in a very discriminatory segregated Army, and you felt discriminated against." As a white officer commanding black troops, "you lived where they lived [and] you were a second class citizen because your privates were black." Fleming took exception to the practice of confiscating black soldiers' ammunition and weapons while they guarded Japanese prisoners of war in remote areas subject to guerrilla attack. White GIs performing the same duty were armed, but "they blatantly . . . made us turn in every round. . . . The big fear of the brass, who were mostly southern . . . was fraternization between the black soldiers and the POWs. They didn't trust them worth a damn." To Fleming, this experience was pivotal. "It was a good way to learn about race relations," he recalled, because "you could really see it plain if you had any sense of fairness and if you weren't just under the total mercy of your prejudices": "It was just the sheer human experience of 'good, God, how can these men stand it, why do they do it?' Here they are being called on to follow the rules, shape up, be a good soldier, work your ass off, be ready to die for your country and then they would crap all over you without apology. 'Not a single one of you black bastards is good enough to be an officer even with your own people. You don't get the Quonset huts. You stay in tents and mud. All the Quonset huts go to a white unit that landed yesterday even though you have been here six months.'" "It was that kind of stuff," Fleming concluded, "and I understood why they were bitter. The amazing thing is that they functioned at all."[29]

Service with black GIs afforded disturbing lessons in racism, and the war's destructiveness also caused soldiers to search for a meaning that justified such tremendous cost in human life and property. In this sense, the war magnified the value of the freedoms and opportunities that most white southerners took for granted. James Mackay, a Georgia veteran and postwar liberal politician, believed that his fifty-two months aboard a Coast Guard cutter during the war "taught [him] what freedom is." As a first lieutenant on a destroyer escort, Mackay saw several shipmates die: "I lost thirty-one shipmates and I had to hose down the brains of my buddies on my own ship." Mackay had been at sea with them long enough to recognize "who they were by looking at their shoes, covered with blankets." Before then, he stated, "I had taken freedom for granted," but when "the executive officer said to me— 'Mackay, is there anything, anything, worth the deaths of these guys. They're not going to live their lives.' And I said 'of course, there's only one thing . . . it is clear that they died to secure the right of all of us to go behind the curtain and cast our ballot without anybody knowing how we voted or having anything to do with how we voted." [30]

Likewise, serving as a Marine Corps chaplain in the Pacific theater during World War II made Joseph Rabun, a Baptist preacher in Telfair County, Georgia, far "more conscious of the precious importance of life and dignity." As a Marine "sky pilot," Rabun came under enemy fire on Guadalcanal, Bougainville, Saipan, and Guam, where he ministered to the dying and wounded. His beliefs about the war, which developed during his Marine Corps service while he was in his late thirties and informed his liberal political views afterward, included the ideas "that the war was fought against the anti-Christ, that the war was fought against forces that would shackle and ground men down instead of set him free; that the war was fought against an ideology which held that because of race one man was better than another." [31]

For Mackay and Rabun and, no doubt, others, the war's devastation seemed a pointless tragedy unless meaning could be found to vindicate the death and destruction it wreaked—and that meaning could not apply only to the fight abroad. If preserving democracy, justice, and freedom justified such a sacrifice overseas, then the same rights had to be defended at home. Many of the organizations through which veterans pursued a progressive agenda explicitly drew this connection. Military service may have educated these veterans in much more than the tactics and strategy of warfare, particularly in exposing the hypocrisy of American racial practices, but it often took the reality of postwar conditions at home to turn disenchantment into active rebellion against the political and racial status quo. [32] Harold Fleming found that the racial violence and political turmoil that plagued postwar Georgia intensified his disillusionment and demoralization, which had begun overseas. "When I came back I was sick of the whole goddamn business," Fleming later recalled, "I was mad at the Army and mad at the system." And then, much to his chagrin, "Talmadge came back in," and then a white mob in Walton County, Georgia, lynched four black citizens in the summer of 1946. These events, which "laid the base for total disgust that built up over the preceding year," made it more than he could bear to think of "settling and having a normal life in that setting when that kind of thing could take place and where you could have a guy saying the things that Talmadge said, reelected governor after all that." However, after a brief return to Harvard, Fleming came back to Georgia in the summer of 1947. That fall, he joined the Southern Regional Council (SRC) at the urging of Ralph McGill, editor of the Atlanta *Constitution*. "I didn't know there was anybody in the South, anybody white," Fleming explained, "who had my egalitarian values or wanted to see society move away from segregation and discrimination." [33]

White veterans like Fleming returned to the South and joined organizations devoted to fighting against discrimination and intolerance and for progressive social change. Many joined the interracial and progressive American Veterans Committee (AVC), which had over twenty chapters in the southern states, including several in Georgia.[34] Through the AVC, white veterans worked alongside black veterans to obtain full GI benefits, to address problems of housing and employment, and especially to challenge discriminatory practices. The Atlanta chapter protested police brutality against black veterans and called for the integration of the city police force. In addition to raffling appliances to raise money and conducting membership drives, the Atlanta area AVC, according to Johnny Glustrom, its president, also worked "for civil rights in close cooperation with other groups." The Atlanta chapter won the national AVC'S new George W. Norris Award for "outstanding work" on behalf of American civil rights in 1950–1951. In particular, the award cited the chapter's efforts to improve housing for black Atlantans, its support of litigation to "eliminate discrimination" in Atlanta schools, and its ongoing and "vigorous" fight against the Ku Klux Klan (KKK).[35]

Not content to rely on pronouncements and petitions, Georgia's progressive white veterans also campaigned for political change. In particular, they worked to elect moderate to liberal candidates who advocated programs and policies in keeping with their own reformist sympathies. In Atlanta they joined black citizens in rallying behind the candidacy of Helen Douglas Mankin in her bid for reelection in 1946 to the House of Representatives from Georgia's Fifth Congressional District.[36] For example, George Stoney, an Army veteran and AVC member, left his job with the federal housing authority in Atlanta to head Mankin's re-election bid. He recruited volunteers from his associates in the AVC who became a core of support for Mankin throughout the myriad difficulties of her campaign. Among those AVC supporters was Calvin Kytle, who backed Mankin because of her impressive record in supporting price controls, President Truman's veto of the anti-labor Case Bill, federal aid to education, veterans' housing, and improved relations between business and labor. "Since March [of 1946]," reasoned Kytle, "Mrs. Mankin represented the one cause for cheer in Georgia's otherwise depressing political situation."[37]

White veterans in the AVC and black veterans in the ACRC helped Mankin win the majority of the popular vote in the Fifth District primary on July 17, 1946. Enthusiasm and commitment, however, could not overcome the power of Georgia's discriminatory county-unit system. Mankin's reactionary opponent, James C. Davis, won enough county-unit votes to nullify her popular majority. This disheartening outcome—achieved, many suspected, through manipulation and fraud—convinced progressive veterans of the futility of trying to accomplish substantive change without first achieving important electoral reform. Veterans believed that freeing Georgia's electorate from the discriminatory restrictions that perpetuated a truncated vote and nullified popular democracy was a crucial first step to fulfilling what they regarded as the war's mandate for democratic reform.[38] Thus, the fight against Germany, Japan, and Italy overseas ultimately generated a battle against the county-unit system at home.

Within a few days of Mankin's defeat, progressive white and black veterans formed Georgia Veterans for Majority Rule (GVMR). The GVMR sponsored two federal lawsuits aimed at overturning the county-unit system as a violation of the Fourteenth Amendment's equal protection clause.[39] The plaintiffs alleged that the unit system of voting deprived the residents of Georgia's more populous counties of the right to have their votes counted on the same effective basis as the votes of residents in less populous counties. As an example, under the county-unit system 106 votes in Georgia's largest county equaled 1 vote in the smallest. Thus, the plaintiffs argued, the county-unit system constituted "a deliberate, express, and unreasonable discrimination in varying degrees against all voters residing in any but the smallest counties."[40]

Progressive veterans organized the GVMR with the assistance of the Southern Conference for Human Welfare in order to raise the money and support necessary to carry their case all the way to the U.S. Supreme Court.[41] White veterans in the AVC were the majority of the staff in the central office in Atlanta, and they led a structure of committees throughout the state to facilitate these efforts. The central committee included James Mackay and Calvin Kytle, while other veterans headed GVMR committees in each congressional district and on several college and university campuses.[42]

Fund-raising letters sent to prospective donors in Georgia explained how these veterans defined their civic obligations and cause in relation to the recent war. "We are a group of Georgia men and women who served in World War II," they stated, "and who are now fighting for a better state. We need your support." Through urban-rural discrimination, GVMR veterans alleged, the county-unit system "had made it possible for corrupt politicians to control votes in our rural areas." Moreover, "as servicemen we saw in other countries the poverty, corruption, and disease that were the product of minority rule," the GVMR proclaimed, and "now as citizen-veterans we mean to do everything we can to wipe out minority rule back here home in Georgia." In fact: "The question of majority rule is the fundamental issue facing the world today. . . . It is the basic principle upon which this nation is founded. It is one man's guarantee against oppression. In defense of majority rule the world has just passed through the greatest conflict in the history of man. . . . We feel strongly that as long as this system persists Georgia is in danger of the same sort of dictatorship we went to war to defeat."[43]

The veterans' impassioned pleas helped to raise funds; nevertheless, they lost the case. The U.S. Supreme Court refused to overturn a lower federal decision sustaining the constitutionality of the county-unit system. Indeed, the climate of fear and suspicion that permeated postwar Georgia made organizing for any progressive cause a difficult and even risky gamble.[44] Like many southern reformers, progressive white veterans proceeded cautiously, straddling the fence when it came to the racial implications of their political attacks. Veterans in the GVMR, for example, sidestepped the race issue by never mentioning it directly as they pursued legal action against the county-unit system. Others vacillated between racial progressivism on the one hand and political expediency on the other. War veteran R. W. Hayes testified before a Georgia state legislative committee against a bill to restore the white primary in 1947. Condemning the bill as "thoroughly undemocratic," he pleaded with the committee to not "sink back to the period of 1865" and to "free Georgia from its Reconstruction complex." After all, he noted, "if the Negro was good enough to carry a gun in the war, and pay taxes, he should vote." He also warned that the White Primary Bill posed "the imminent danger of forcing the colored citizens into a colored bloc due to present antagonism."[45]

Even white veterans who dared to challenge the racial status quo expressed a progressivism that had its racial limits. Given the reactionary climate in postwar Georgia, it was the rare white southerner who had the moral conviction and courage to risk community censure, opprobrium, and personal safety for the cause of black political freedom. Nonetheless, despite their caution and sometimes equivocation, progressive white veterans did challenge the political traditions, racial discrimination, and civic complacency that they believed betrayed the war's democratic purpose. In this sense, the war did serve as agent of social change, not only by heightening the racial consciousness and activism of black soldiers, but also by convincing some white veterans of the moral righteousness of racial reform. Within two years of the war's end, southern veterans of both races had helped an unprecedented number of black citizens become registered voters, mounted a broad and diverse challenge to Jim Crow, and organized to attack the state's most blatantly discriminatory political custom.

In addition to Georgia veterans who were eager to create a more progressive and democratic future for the region, there were reaction- ary white veterans who understood the racial implications of the war's impact in very different terms. These veterans belonged to the Ku Klux Klan and the neo-fascist Columbians, Inc., and supported Governor Eugene Talmadge and the white primary. They expressed an understanding of the war that demonstrated its capacity to produce division and reaction as much as unity and reform. Their support of reactionaries and conservatives determined to defend southern political tradition at all costs limited what progressive veterans were able to achieve and helped turn the state's first postwar elections into a popular referendum on what the racial legacy of the war would be.

Veterans who returned to Georgia in the first year after the war found plenty of reason to be disappointed. At first, economic observers, industrial developers, and the media anticipated the end of the war with nervous optimism, predicting in 1945 that the state would weather the trials of reconversion easily. Rosy predictions, however, gave way to worried ruminations on the layoffs that followed V-J Day.[46] By September 6 employment officials of the State War Manpower Commission announced that there were 36,016 displaced war workers in Georgia, most of whom were seeking jobs comparable in pay, skill, and training to what they had done during the war. It seemed to be a fruitless effort. By January 1946 Savannah reported a "sharp rise since V-J Day" in unemployment, with around three thousand jobless receiving unemployment benefits.[47]

Difficulty in readjusting to civilian life was not unique to southern white veterans. Ex-servicemen and women throughout the United States experienced problems, at least initially, in reintegrating into postwar society.[48] However, conditions that existed in other regions had special racial implications in the Deep South. White veterans encountered economic difficulties just as campaigns for progressive reform were adding to reconversion's destabilization of the local and regional economic, political, and social environment. In this context, some white veterans in Georgia construed the problems of reintegration in specifically racial terms.

Certainly, many areas of the region and state had undergone significant change since the war began. War industries and military cantonments attracted black and white southerners to regional towns and cities, and the wartime boom produced overcrowding and economic competition, which some white veterans deeply resented. Black residents crowding into the outskirts of previously all-white working-class neighborhoods, black-white competition for scarce jobs during the period of reconversion, a wave of black voter registration drives, the occasional individual rebellion against Jim Crow, and ongoing campaigns by the NAACP, the Southern Conference for Human Welfare, and the Congress of Industrial Organizations (CIO) indicated that the battlements of white supremacy were under attack. In the chaotic and competitive environment of postwar reconversion, some white veterans fell back on a long tradition of racial scapegoating to expunge their fears of social change and their frustrations and resentment of postwar conditions.[49]

While infiltrating the Ku Klux Klan in Georgia in 1946 Stetson Kennedy found that the KKK used "horror stories of social equality" to attract veterans, who made up 10 percent or more of its membership. [50] At a September meeting of Atlanta Klavern #1, a young veteran "declared that he was working in the Chevrolet plant in Atlanta and that he was proud that 76 fellow workers were members of the Klan." In fact, "he stated that he and his fellows planned to keep organizing until they had the majority of workmen in Chevrolet in the Klan."[51] Indeed, veterans were often active members in the Georgia Klan's Klavalier Klub, reportedly the "storm trooper arm" or "whipping squad" that carried out so-called direct-line activity.[52] Informants in Georgia's Klavalier Klubs reported that veterans made up about half of those who requested to join the Klan's inner circle. Immediately after the war, these Klubs reportedly intimidated, beat, and murdered more than one black cab driver, reported on alleged interracial transgressions, kidnapped and flogged at least one black citizen, and organized against moderate and liberal candidates for state and local offices.[53]

For those veterans who found the Klan to be too passé or tame, the Columbians, Inc., of Atlanta offered an attractive alternative.[54] Sporting khaki shirts, black ties, and armbands with an SS-like thunderbolt emblem, members of the Columbians vented racial and religious resentments in a pseudo-martial atmosphere. Several sources commented on the active participation of at least a few ex-soldiers in this organization. For example, "Ned," an informant, reported to "AF" that at one meeting, Bill Couch, reportedly an Army officer on terminal leave, "appeared in full uniform wearing the columbians lightning bolt silver emblem on his shirt pocket," and speaker P. M. Adams "praised the 'group of veterans who have sacrificed to get this thing started.'" In addition, John Zimmerlee sported his "G.I. shirt and trousers" as Hoke GeWinner "charged . . . that the reason veterans cannot find housing is that unscrupulous real estate dealers are selling white property to Negroes, thus forcing all whites in the neighborhood to move." In fact, lamented the Atlanta chapter of the American Veterans Committee, "there are veterans in the Columbians. Men who fought as we did: men who fired guns and learned fear, as we did. Did these men, all through the long battles, think they were on the wrong side?"[55]

While the Klan worked to thwart black economic advancement and to enforce a traditional code of racial behavior, the Columbians specialized in policing the lines of residential segregation. During the fall of 1946, veteran members of the Columbians waged a brief campaign of intimidation and violence against African Americans living on the fringes of transitional white neighborhoods in Atlanta. On October 28 three Columbians blackjacked Clifford Hines in an unprovoked attack, ostensibly to protect a white family from "Negroes" moving in. A few days later, Columbian "regulators" prevented Frank Jones, a black man, from occupying his newly purchased house in the Ashby Street section. A Columbian sign demarcated Jones' house for the "White Community only," and various reports put James Akins and R. I. Whitman, veterans of the war, on a picket line in front of the house, carrying signs that read "Zoned for Whites." Authorities arrested three Columbians, including Akins and Whitman, for disorderly conduct and inciting to riot.[56]

The activities of veterans in the Klan and the Columbians reflected their fear of racial reform, of black competition, and of a breakdown in the traditional code of racial behavior. Herman Talmadge, son of Eugene Talmadge (Georgia's reigning demagogue) and a veteran of the Pacific theater, declared that the real issue in 1946 was to "determine whether or not we will fight to preserve our southern traditions and heritages as we fought on our ships at sea and as we fought on foreign soil."[57] Such determination to defend white supremacy had important political ramifications, and the racial legacy of World War II became a source of controversy at the center of many of the state's first postwar elections.

Indeed, in February 1946 Helen Douglas Mankin won the popular vote in a special election for representative from the Fifth Congressional District of Georgia, and the pivotal role of Atlanta blacks rang like a fire bell in the night to racial conservatives alarmed at the potential power of an organized and active black electorate. This fear grew as the All Citizens Registration Committee successfully boosted black registration and voting. Meanwhile, Eugene Talmadge kicked off his fourth bid for the gubernatorial seat. Campaigning largely on a white supremacy platform, Talmadge promised to reinstate the white primary, preserve the county-unit system, and generally keep black southerners "in their place." Talmadge's message attracted veterans already uncomfortable with the direction in which Georgia appeared to be headed.

They avowed allegiance to the reactionary Talmadge and hostility to the liberal Mankin in explicit terms. "I am glad I live in Georgia and not in Fulton County," proclaimed Guy Alford, a combat veteran from Emanuel County: "Helen Douglas Mankin is the biggest political freak or fraud in Georgia [and] certainly has never added or reflected any credit on the Democratic party in Fulton County."[58] Jimmy Gaston of Atlanta announced that he had "awakened while in Guam, Iwo Jima, and Okinawa." As "a veteran of many South Pacific invasions," Gaston declared, he knew "what it means to lose buddies and friends." Thus, "I and all of my friends are for Mr. Talmadge."[59] Similarly, while in the U.S. Navy at Norfolk, Virginia, J. D. Dickens "watched the recent gubernatorial race with considerable interest," regarding Eugene Talmadge as "the only man in the race that could qualify in a real Southern Democratic primary." After five and a half years in the Navy, Dickens added, he looked forward to a Georgia where "Old Gene will be around for the next four years."[60] William Tyson of Nashville, Georgia, took issue with the Atlanta *Journal's* claim that veterans of the recent war would disapprove of Talmadge. "These boys died so we could be free to go to the polls and vote for the man we think most worthy of holding office," Tyson angrily proclaimed. After losing "many friends while serving in the Army, and [with] two brothers wounded in ETO," he planned, along with his brothers, to "go to the polls and vote for Eugene Talmadge." Moreover, he promised, "we will also talk to our many good friends and pull every vote for Mr. Talmadge possible." After all, "we feel it is our duty because we believe Mr. Talmadge is the only man in the race worthy of being governor of Georgia."[61]

Candidates in Georgia's 1946 elections campaigned on platforms that addressed a variety of issues, from road improvements and industrial development to teacher pay raises and veteran services.[62] Conservative and reactionary veterans who publicly articulated a position during these campaigns more often than not neglected to mention these issues. Rather, the key question to them was whether the state and region's political traditions would withstand the racial implications of the war. Christopher De Mendoza, a war veteran, wrote to congressional candidate Prince Preston in order "to open an outlet in my chest to let out what is in it." Noting that Preston's opponent, incumbent Hugh Peterson, had done little for veterans over the years, Mendoza pointed out that Peterson had, to his credit, fought consistently against the "F.E.P.C. and social equality." And that, Mendoza informed Preston, "is exactly what I want you to do." After all, he continued, Georgia "was the best state in the union [until] the influence coming down here from the North" turned it into a haven for "Negroes lovers." Indeed, he added, "It seems to me that the white people are tired and disgusted of been [sic] white and now they want to turn into Negroes." Thus, he continued, "today we are not living in a democratic country but under a dictatorship like Germany, Russia, Italy, and Japan." In fact, "we are slaves under the dictatorship of a bunch of fools in the Congress and 'Negroes lovers' in the Supreme Court."[63]

In Coffee County, a group of veterans ran campaign ads in the local newspaper with a picture of Eugene Talmadge beside a large headline that read "Georgia Can Restore the Democratic White Primary and Retain the County-Unit System." Declaring that, if Talmadge was elected, recent court rulings would not defeat the white primary in Georgia, the veterans advocated writing the county-unit system into the state constitution. In case these arguments were not compelling enough, they spelled out the consequences of a Talmadge defeat: "Here is what will happen if our Democratic white primary is not restored and preserved," one ad read. "The Negroes will vote in a block" and dictate to white citizens who should be elected. "Proof of this was shown in the recent election in the Fifth Congressional District where the vote of one Negro ward carried the election. . . . The same thing can happen all over Georgia," they warned, "if Negroes are allowed to vote in the Democratic White Primary and if the county Unit System is abolished." Remember, veterans ominously added, "if Georgia, now feeling progressive tremblors that could shake the entire South, elects Talmadge Governor again, not even a Supreme Court ruling will prevent a return to 'White Supremacy' as only Talmadge can support it." To "Preserve our Southern Traditions and Heritage," citizens should "Vote for Talmadge and a White Primary!"[64] Thus, predicted Don Prince of Atlanta: "Eugene Talmadge will be elected governor of Georgia because the veterans who hail from this state will vote almost in a bloc for the man who has kept faith with them. . . . A person must be very naive to believe that the white primary is not the main and vital issue in this present campaign."[65]

Openly adopting the rhetoric, ideology, and extralegal tactics of the recently defeated enemy discredited the extreme reactionism of the Georgia Klan and the Columbians. City, state, and county authorities essentially broke up both organizations through infiltration and prosecution.[66] The more mainstream variant of southern conservatism, however, fared much better. White veterans helped elect Eugene Talmadge as governor in 1946, supported Herman Talmadge's claim to that office in 1947 and 1948 (following Eugene Talmadge's death in 1946), and voted in the state legislature to enact the white primary bill thereafter.[67]

In fact, the momentum for democratic and racial change seemed to have waned nationally and regionally by 1947, as the developing Cold War with its virulently anticommunist tinge undercut the legitimacy of progressive social reform.[68] In the South, both black and white veterans made the political equality of blacks an important issue in the battle to redirect the region's future. Their conservative counterparts circumscribed what they could achieve and contributed to the reactionary climate that hindered all political challengers in the South, progressive or moderate. Even white veterans who pursued very moderate agendas found it prudent to reaffirm their commitment to racial stability.

Indeed, many returning white veterans found neither racial discrimination nor social change nearly as disturbing as the slow economic growth and venal officials that hampered many southern communities. Military service had a direct influence on their political attitudes because it had exposed them to a more modernized world. The paved highways, efficient sanitation systems, advanced educational facilities, and public health services encountered in the course of their wartime journeys often revealed glaring deficiencies at home.[69] In many southern communities during the war, shortages and hidebound officials had perpetuated and exacerbated shoddy infrastructure and meager services; and postwar complacency promised to continue that pattern, even as the demand for services and diversified development increased. For many southern white veterans, the war exerted a dual influence—exposing them to a level of development unattained at home *and* convincing them that corruption, inefficiency, electoral fraud, and machine politics impeded their postwar opportunity for prosperity.

Moreover, much like their progressive counterparts—black and white—these veterans brought home a sense of civic entitlement that chafed under the thumb of local and state political incumbency. Their energetic efforts to oust entrenched Bourbon leaders, to campaign for development and growth, and to eradicate bureaucratic inefficiency and governmental corruption, however, developed more from a burning desire for economic modernization than from a progressive mandate derived from the war.

This ambition had important political repercussions. Armed with a new and critical perspective on home, Georgia's white veterans returned to mount insurgent revolts against old-guard leadership and political machines sustained by electoral fraud, corrupt patronage, and civic apathy, none of which conformed to the principles of honest and democratic government that many believed they had fought to defend.[70] In 1946 alone, white veterans mounted a strong challenge to Eugene Talmadge's reactionary bid for governor, toppled the Cracker regime in Augusta, and overturned the political machine led by John Bouhan in Savannah.[71] The political shock waves that these insurgencies generated reverberated throughout Georgia's cities, towns, and rural communities, drawing an unprecedented number of citizens into state and local politics. The diversity and demands of a new, more engaged constituency—a political by-product of the war—compounded the political turmoil of the postwar era and heightened pressure on the state's traditional leadership either to change or to relinquish power to a new generation.[72]

For many of Georgia's white soldiers and sailors, World War II was a disconcerting experience—and not simply because of the hard lessons of combat. "You were exposed to the world," recalled Griffin Bell, a former U.S. attorney general and veteran of World War II, and furthermore, "you had different ideas than the parochial world you had lived in before you went into the military." J. H. Bottoms, a boatswain's mate in the Navy, agreed: "I was born and reared in Georgia and never realized what a place it really was until I got out of it."[73]

Discovering what kind of place Georgia "really was" came, in part, from encountering a level of development and modernization not found at home. Entering the military at a time when Georgia was still struggling to overcome the burden of the Great Depression, veterans were frequently amazed at the development, prosperity, and sophistication of other states and nations. Private James Moffett marveled at the cultural sophistication in Tokyo after attending a concert by the Nippon Philharmonic Orchestra, and he wondered why Atlanta came up short in comparison: "It's generally believed in various sections of the country . . . that the South is backward in every respect," he noted. After all, "less than a year after V-J day," the Japanese "have mustered an orchestra capable of giving a concert comparable to many heard in the United States." Yet, Atlanta, "can't compare insofar as culture . . . is concerned, with a city that has been the objective of bombing and foreign occupation." John J. Flynt, a veteran and candidate for the state legislature, remarked during his 1946 political campaign that "in comparison with some of the places [I have] seen . . . there [is] much to be done back home . . . in health, education, housing, and roads."[74]

What seemed to impress Georgia's white veterans even more than what they saw, however, was what they heard. Homesick for the cotton fields, provincial towns, and scruffy cities of the Empire State of the South, Georgia's servicemen and women encountered far less sympathy than recrimination and ridicule from nonsoutherners (and even foreigners), who rarely let pass an opportunity to belittle their state. Discovering that their own home defined "bad government" and "backwardness" in the minds of other Americans was a humbling experience that few veterans forgot.

The tenure of Eugene Talmadge as governor in the 1930s and early 1940s was indelibly linked in the minds of many of the state's servicemen and women with the embarrassment of hailing from a state so poorly regarded by the rest of the nation and world.[75] Georgia's GIs entered the armed forces with Talmadge's reputation already well established. However, his reckless attack on the University of Georgia's Board of Regents in 1941 became a new source of embarrassment, and Georgia's soldiers cringed at the remarks and ridicule it earned. "At least forty of my company are Northerners" who watched Talmadge's feud with the board of regents unfold "with great interest," wrote one soldier to a friend in Atlanta: "What could I say about my home state after such a farce was enacted?" "Small wonder," he lamented, "that Northerners have such views about the South." Filipinos in Manila put Georgia Sergeant Norman Tant on the spot by questioning him about the racial implications of Talmadge's behavior. "I was ashamed and I could give no adequate explanation," he later recalled, and to Tant, as well as many other GIs, Talmadge's actions "stank 10,800 miles from Georgia."[76]

Not surprisingly, many of Georgia's white veterans found Talmadge's reactionary bid for governor in 1946 an unpleasant reminder of the many unflattering remarks they had just endured. "I had an opportunity to see Georgia from the outside," complained Thomas Y. Lovett of Athens: "I had the humiliation of being constantly reminded that my state was one of the most backward in the nation, and we Georgians were often called the electors of dictators and demagogues for governors." J. C. Huddleston had the same opinion. "You would be surprised at the things that have been said by people from other states about the kind of rule the state of Georgia [has had]." In fact, "what they know and say about Talmadge would fill several volumes. . . . [M]ost of them classify him alongside of Hitler."[77] "Hitler, Mussolini, and Tojo [are] gone," noted veteran E. G. Wilkes of Atlanta, and soon, he predicted,

"Eugene Talmadge is joining them. Never has a man done more to retard the progress and growth of a state." In fact, Wilkes noted, "men from all sections of the nation during my six-year cruise in the Navy couldn't understand why the people of Georgia would elect a man like Talmadge." As far away as Japan, embarrassed GIs were "sick and tired," explained Captain Frank Morrison, "of being ragged and ribbed about [the] loud-mouthed, demagogic and dishonest government we have in Georgia."[78]

Nonsoutherners not only took shots at Georgia's colorful political heritage, but they also pointed out the economic and social problems that plagued the state presently. Recalling that no one had "greater regard for Georgia" when he entered the service, Lewis Adams Jr. of Carrollton was soon "shocked and awakened" by "the many unfavorable but true things" his shipmates knew about his home state. Adams grew too embarrassed to claim his place of birth because he tired of hearing "how low Georgia stood in comparison with other states in education, how high it stood in illiteracy, physical unfitness, syphilis, murder, etc."[79] A Georgia soldier stationed in Orlando, Florida, remarked to a reporter that a soldier away from home liked nothing better "than being able to brag to his buddies about conditions at home." Still, "he likes to do it honestly," and nothing, he ruefully admitted, was "so irritating as having to 'take it' when somebody launches an attack on his state which he knows is justified."[80]

For many of Georgia's GIs, a welcome reprieve from such insults came with Talmadge's defeat and Ellis Arnall's election as a moderately progressive governor in 1942. The image of poverty, backwardness, and reactionary, corrupt politics that dogged them in the early years of the war began to fade as the new governor demonstrated a more modern, businesslike, and democratic approach to state government. Georgia became the embodiment of urbane and progressive government rather than its antithesis, and the state's servicemen and women appreciated the difference.[81]

Bill Boring, a reporter for the Atlanta *Constitution* who had served in North Africa during the war, first heard of Arnall while he was in Egypt, where the accolades for the new governor surprised and pleased him. Accustomed to hearing, "From Georgia, huh? It's a great state but how does a man like that Talmadge get elected Governor?" Boring "got a big lift in Cairo" when someone spoke well of Arnall, "particularly since all my life I had been accustomed to listening to indignities heaped upon my governor." Similarly, a "Cracker in service" noted that Arnall "really made a name for Georgia, and brought her forward from the lowest depths of corrupt government to a democracy admired by 47 states."[82] Lt. P. D. Cunningham agreed. While stationed in Walla-Walla, Washington, he welcomed Arnall's election as a chance for the "boys away from home [to] stop apologizing for Ol' Gene's antics."[83]

The setbacks and hardships that many veterans encountered when they returned home transformed war-induced revelations into active opposition to the Bourbon status quo. Proud and ambitious soldiers who had basked in the praise showered on Arnall's administration came home to find the reactionary, undemocratic, archaic, and venal habits that had prompted negative comment outside the South still alive and well even after four years of war.

Georgia's white veterans consistently articulated a conviction that they *had* fought for principles, values, and rights irreconcilable with the continued rule of undemocratic and corrupt government at home. Survival may have been the driving force for most soldiers during the war, but defending democracy and "good government" against dictatorship and "bad government" became the meaning that many white veterans drew from their participation after they returned. This "recovered" sense of mission defined the war as a fight against government removed from popular influence and unrestrained by concerns of political honesty, racial harmony, and community betterment. The lessons of the recent war, veterans explained, demanded vigilance against the same thing at home. Sergeant Harry Baxter of Ashburn, Georgia, noted that veterans who "have made sacrifices in the name of democracy to overthrow dictators and tyrants in Europe and Asia" will not "return to power in their home state men who have shown beyond a doubt that they have all the characteristics and instincts of would be dictators." This mandate for vigilance against home-grown dictators was enmeshed with a conviction that service in the war earned one a right to economic prosperity.[84]

Veterans have returned to home and families "to try to fulfill the way of life which they dreamed of and planned for during the war years," stated James W. Green of Atlanta, and they "want to be assured of a way of life which will warrant their having fought the most costly war in history." Thus, reminded Green, "let us not forget the purpose behind these four years of sacrifice and death." C. W. Carver of College Park in Atlanta spent three and one-half years in the Pacific theater "fighting for a better place to live," while H. P. Dasher and his "buddies" passed the war "in their foxholes, dodging bullets, [and] dreaming of home and what they could come back to."[85]

However, wartime dreams of postwar abundance and prosperity faded amid job shortages and housing scarcities as the country lurched through reconversion. The war had fueled Georgia's economic growth but not sufficiently to guarantee a better standard of living right away to all returning veterans.[86] The complaints made to Georgia's newspapers revealed smoldering frustration with postwar conditions, particularly regarding employment and housing. "We expected to find things a little tough," remarked "Ex-Sarge" in Atlanta, "but little did we dream how things could have gotten in such a rotten state of affairs." Noting that her husband served in the Army for five years, including almost two years overseas, Mrs. W. R. Lewis expressed her "thorough disgust" at the treatment meted out to returning veterans. Laid off only two months after his discharge, her husband searched fruitlessly for comparable work. "At 36 he's told he's too old to work," Mrs. Lewis complained, though, she pointedly noted, "He wasn't too old for the Army." And, she claimed, even firms participating in the GI Bill's on-the-job training program preferred veterans with relevant experience. "Human memory is short-lived," Mrs. Lewis bitterly concluded. World War II veterans were "being given the 'run-around' just as veterans were after the last war."[87] Other veterans blamed job shortages on labor disputes that brought important sectors of the economy to a standstill shortly after V-J day. "GIs returning to 'civilization' are having difficulty in finding 'on-the-job' training in this strike-ridden land," proclaimed a "$20 GI" to the Atlanta *Journal*. Seeking to find jobs for themselves and other returning servicemen, Valdosta veterans petitioned the federal government to hire them to operate plants closed by strikes "if the strikers refuse to resume work."[88]

For many of Georgia's white veterans, housing shortages, inflated prices, and menial jobs called into question the whole purpose behind the war. They wondered why the oft-heralded economic impact of war mobilization had fallen so short of their dreams of abundance and prosperity. The ridicule that Georgia's soldiers had endured during the war illuminated the state's political and economic shortcomings, but postwar conditions demonstrated in very personal terms the cost of maintaining a long tradition of civic apathy and political corruption. War mobilization put local institutions and leadership to the test by straining not only resources and services but also popular faith in the fitness of incumbents to rule. Traditional excuses for spending as little as possible to maintain streets, schools, and sewage systems, to regulate the proliferation of vice and crime, to build public housing, and to develop plans to recruit industry fell flat in the wake of the development and spending that came with the war.

Thus, a newly critical perspective born in the war gained credence under the pressure of homefront conditions. Veterans believed that complacency caused communities to languish while opportunities to capitalize on wartime growth passed by. Meanwhile, local administrations, machines, and factions throughout Georgia routinely stuffed ballot boxes and defrauded voters of the democracy and clean government that many believed they had fought to defend. Veterans grew disgusted with parochial and conservative leaders who seemed ill-suited to govern; as a result, in 1946 white veterans across the state invaded the public arena in order to claim their rights to "good government," honest elections, and economic opportunity.

In Georgia, veterans flocked to support the "good government" campaign of James V. ("Jimmy") Carmichael against gubernatorial candidates Eugene

Talmadge and Eurith D. Rivers, two former governors whose past administrations evoked memories of bayonet rule, national ridicule, and indictments for scandal and fraud. White veterans organized Carmichael-for-Governor Clubs in counties and towns throughout the state (as well as in Tokyo, Japan), appeared with Carmichael regularly on the stump, and made numerous speeches on his behalf at rallies and over the radio.[89]

Veterans liked Jimmy Carmichael because his platform advocating fiscal conservatism, industrial development, agricultural diversification, improved education, and a positive national image reflected their own vision of what constituted "good government." Veterans in the Student-League-For-Good-Government proclaimed that Talmadge's former administration amounted to "Six years of . . . Virtual Dictatorship" and "Four Years of Rivers Was Greed, Graft, and Shame," and that it was "small wonder that daily more and more thinking Georgians are turning to efficient, clean-cut Jimmy Carmichael." In fact, World War II veteran C. W. Carver noted that "The State of Georgia will always be in a rut and looked down upon by the other 47 states as long as we allow reckless politicians to have the run of the state. I spent three and one-half years in the Pacific fighting for a better place to live," he added, and "in order to have that place we must have good government." Thus, "here's one vote for Carmichael."[90]

John Sammons Bell, a veteran of the Pacific war, campaigned actively for Carmichael, and Bell's powerful, well-crafted appeal linked participation in the war with opposition to Talmadge. He had entered the Army in 1941, received the Purple Heart and the Bronze Star for his participation in the Pacific theater, and joined the Carmichael campaign when he returned home. "In the South Pacific, four of us were sitting on the Russell Islands," announced Bell in a WSB Radio broadcast shortly before the election. "The fighting in Guadalcanal was over [and] we were making preparations" for the next invasion. With his three friends, Bell declared, he discussed returning home, and "each and every one of those four soldiers said when we get back home, we are going to do our best to make America a better America." Only Bell survived the war, however, and upon his return, he proclaimed, "I feel it a bounden duty to carry on their fight for good government." Veterans supported James Carmichael and opposed Eugene Talmadge, Bell trumpeted, because "we are determined to continue in peace to fight for the things we fought for in war." Thus, "we shall keep the faith of our battle dead" by voting for Carmichael.[91]

Veterans' programs for modernization and political change revealed their faith in "good government" and economic development as panaceas for the state's persistent problems. To black and progressive white veterans *progress* meant reforming the region's worst racial habits. To pro-modernization veterans it meant modernizing the economy, making the administration of government efficient and fiscally responsible, cleaning up ramshackle towns and overcrowded cities, and repairing and expanding old infrastructures. All of this, as if by magic, would attract new industries, boost agriculture, elevate the incomes of all southerners, and thereby resolve the region's racial, social, and economic ills.

Veterans in the B-29ers-for-Carmichael Club spelled out a platform that Carmichael and his veteran supporters articulated throughout the state.[92] Carmichael pledged to keep Georgia out of debt, never to increase taxes unless the increase was for education and was approved by the voters, to improve veterans' services as well as general health and pension programs, and to accomplish all of this "within the Georgia income." Home rule promised local control over local matters, and improved rural roads and agricultural markets helped farmers. Governed by the maxim that "the very foundation of good government is economy," Carmichael promised to run the state "like you run your business" because good government was crucial to "create an atmosphere that will attract industry."[93]

Veterans in other cities and towns throughout Georgia followed suit, pledging to bring prosperity, national respect, and honest politics to their communities.[94] The state's strongest urban machines, in Augusta and Savannah in particular, faced strong challenges from veterans who were disgusted with electoral fraud, economic stagnation, corruption, arbitrary tax assessments, and rule by decree. White veterans led anti-machine coalitions of civic reformers and businessmen against the incumbents sustained by the Cracker Party in Augusta and the Bouhan machine in Savannah. Similar efforts took place in Gainesville, McRae, Americus, and many other Georgia communities in the state's first postwar elections of 1946.[95]

Veterans' calls for modernization proved to be popular, attracting unprecedented numbers to the polls and pushing registration and voting to record levels in Americus, Columbus, Brunswick, Gainesville, Augusta, Savannah, and statewide. More citizens than ever before, black or white, turned out to state their concerns for the future and to express a new political voice that grew, in large part, from the war's impact. "Now that I'm home again and settled," explained Columbus veteran Walter Player as he registered to vote, "I think it's important to participate in elections, exercising a vote in our democratic form of government."[96] In communities in which citizens directly experienced machine rule and economic stagnation—and because local elections were not affected by the county-unit system—the postwar campaign for modernization often unseated the forces of southern political and economic tradition, at least temporarily. The Citizens Progressive League defeated the Bouhan machine in Savannah, and the Independents broke the hegemony of the Cracker Party in Augusta.[97] Statewide, however, the county-unit system combined with the threat of black voting defeated James V. Carmichael.[98]

The fight for modernization and good government in Georgia sounded remarkably progressive and farsighted. Ultimately, however, it expressed a conservative vision that failed to fulfill the imperative for democratic reform induced by the war. Many white veterans believed that entrenched and corrupt machines were dictatorial—but not because they denied civic and economic rights to black southerners and workers but because their corruption, intimidation, and reaction infringed on the rights and ambitions of *white* southerners. Ballot-box stuffing and political intimidation violated every citizen's constitutional right to an equal voice in public affairs, but, even more insidiously— according to many white veterans—such practices perpetuated a corrupt and backward image that discouraged industrial recruitment. For the majority of white veterans, the key postwar issue was modernization, particularly the creation of more democratic and honest administrations that created jobs to raise the standard of living to a level that most veterans felt they deserved. The majority of politically active white veterans in Georgia articulated a vision of progress that reflected an unwavering popular faith in the restorative powers of economic development and governmental efficiency.

The racially tense atmosphere of 1946, however, precluded the separation of issues of race from those of modernization. Veterans challenging the political status quo confronted a race-baiting response designed to command the support of white citizens by arousing their racial fears. From Talmadge in the gubernatorial race to Roy V. Harris and the Crackers in Augusta to opponents of the CPL in Savannah, race became the rhetorical ploy that old-guard defenders enlisted to offset the moral advantage veterans enjoyed in challenging their control.[99]

Deflecting these attacks required, at best, mastering a delicate balancing act, since most white veteran campaigns directly benefited from the recent expansion of the black electorate. Thus, these veterans made a fateful choice by adopting a Janus-faced approach to change that rejected anything that impeded modernization while affirming whatever promised to sustain racial stability.

James V. Carmichael's struggle to respond to Talmadge's race-baiting attack suggests how difficult this balancing act could be. Talmadge tried to paint Carmichael as the newest vanguard of a liberal Yankee plot to integrate the South, as indicated by his pledge to obey federal law by allowing blacks to vote in Georgia's Democratic primary.[100] The Carmichael campaign tried to negate this attack by combining an assault on the resurgent Ku Klux Klan and Talmadge's racial extremism with a strong defense of Georgia's county-unit system. [101] More explicitly, pro-Carmichael veterans regularly took to the stump to proclaim their candidate's southern loyalties and the immutability of Jim Crow. Lon Sullivan, a veteran of both world wars, dismissed the importance of the race issue by reminding Georgians that "No negroes go to white schools in Georgia, and they never will. We have no Negro sheriffs, policemen, or congressmen," he added, "and we never will." Veteran George Doss Jr., an avid Carmichael supporter and chairman of the Student League for Good Government, agreed. Talmadge had been predicting for twenty years that blacks would "take over" Georgia, Doss argued, yet that had not happened. Rather than offer a positive program, Talmadge "screams 'Nigger, Nigger, Nigger'" to cloak the real issue: good government versus his own past gubernatorial record. In fact, Doss explained, "we all know that letting the Negro vote in our primary will not bring the results that he claims." "You know Georgians well enough to know that whites and Negroes are never going to mix in schools, restaurants, picture shows or other public places and institutions," Doss assured white voters, and "in every county in Georgia there are far more whites than Negroes registered." Thus, "there is no county where the Negro can possibly gain control." As for Carmichael, proclaimed the B-29ers-for-Carmichael Club, "he adheres to Southern racial traditions."[102] Though Carmichael later regretted his defense of the county-unit system, the veterans who supported him apparently did not question the irony in defining good government as a vehicle for modernization rather than as a guarantor of real political democracy, even as the county-unit system defeated their own candidate.[103]

Other campaigns proclaimed the southern loyalties of white veterans even more explicitly. In Augusta, Independents successfully campaigned against the long incumbent Cracker Party by promising to end local bossism and establish a modern and efficient administration and by declaring their commitment to white supremacy. "We independent candidates bow to no one in their love for and loyalty to the traditions of the South," trumpeted the Independents, and "You know that we are against FEPC. You know we are southerners through and through."[104]

The war fostered among most politically active white veterans a desire for economic development, prosperity, modernization, and clean, efficient government. These were goals important enough to moderate the racial attitudes of some veterans, as in the case of Savannah's Citizens Progressive League, and to compel others to neglect the needs and demands of black southerners in favor of maintaining white support, as in the case of veterans who supported Carmichael and opposed the Crackers in Augusta.[105]

More important than *who* won these battles, however, was what remained once the political dust of the postwar forties had settled. Despite the dynamic growth sparked by the war, despite the moderation of racial attitudes that sometimes came with serving alongside black soldiers, despite a keen desire to improve Georgia's image in order to attract industry, and despite a fairly broad sense of civic entitlement and obligation, the persistent strength of southern racial tradition still limited political change. Indeed, the struggle between change and tradition that defined southern veteran activism continued to animate southern political discourse and events in the following decades. The progressive racial reform that black and white veterans pursued bore fruit in the civil rights movement of the 1950s and 1960s. Reactionary veterans continued to lead the region in the massive resistance to integration that followed the *Brown* decision in 1954. Both the progressive impulse to southern reform and the extreme reaction against it, however, lost out to the ascendance of the Chamber of Commerce policies that white veterans helped to legitimize. Indeed, the conservative growth ethos popularized by veterans in their campaigns for political and economic change became the guiding philosophy behind the policies and expansionism of the Sun Belt era. The industry and development that transformed the southern landscape in the decades following World War II helped to produce a region that expanded faster and grew more rapidly than the rest of the country but also remained, in many ways, poor and racially divided.

The embodiment of Georgia's contradictory political legacy was Herman Talmadge. A Pacific War veteran instrumental in his father's 1946 reelection campaign for governor, Talmadge carried on in his father's footsteps with his assumption of the governorship in 1947 (extra-legally) and 1948. He crafted a strong statewide political machine sustained by a program that offered unprecedented expenditures for education, public services, and industrial recruitment and a stalwart defense of Jim Crow. Talmadge pushed through a 3 percent sales tax to fund the Minimum Foundation program, which effectively created the first real public education system in the state. Moreover, over the course of his administrations, he introduced a tax-reform program conducive to attracting industry and built ten thousand miles of new roads. Talmadge also tried to reestablish the white primary as his first act as governor in 1947 and continued to rant against blacks, integration, the NAACP, the federal courts, and communism, earning a reputation as one of the region's foremost defenders of white supremacy. Subsequent Georgia governors Marvin Griffin and Ernest Vandiver followed suit. All were veterans of World War II.[106]

Veteran activism defined the political legacy of World War II as an engine of significant economic and political change that traveled, by and large, along a quintessentially southern track. It produced a program for change more moderate than the reactionary provincialism of prior days but offered little social and economic uplift to needy black and white southerners. The veterans who won the fight against fascism overseas ensured that the South's approach to change remained enmeshed in the contradictions and ironies of its past.

Notes

1. A new state constitution, drafted and ratified under the direction of Governor Ellis Arnall's wartime administration, abolished the poll tax for all of Georgia's citizens. On this and other electoral law changes that occurred under Arnall's administration during the war see Numan V. Bartley, *The Creation of Modern Georgia* (2d ed.; Athens and London, 1990), 194–95.

2. For general discussions of the impact of the war on African Americans and the struggle for black civil rights see Mary Penick Motley, ed., *The Invisible Soldier: The Experience of the Black Soldier, World War II* (Detroit, 1975); Phillip McGuire, *Taps for a Jim Crow Army: Letters from Black Soldiers in World War Two* (Santa Barbara, Calif., and Oxford, Eng., 1983); Richard M. Dalfiume, *Desegregation of the U.S. Armed Forces: Fighting on Two Fronts, 1939–1953* (Columbia, Mo., 1969); Harvard Sitkoff, *The Struggle for Black Equality, 1954–1980* (New York, 1981); and Neil A. Wynn, *The Afro-American and the Second World War* (New York, 1975).

3. The Supreme Court decision abolishing the southern white primary rendered in *Smith v. Allwright* in 1944 was applied to Georgia through the *Primus King* case decided in early 1946. On the *King* case see Bartley, *Creation of Modern Georgia*, 201.

4. Law finally came to believe that his not receiving an overseas assignment was "a blessing in disguise," since many of the men with whom he had trained did not return. See W. W. Law interview, November 15 and 16, 1990, Transcript Series E, Georgia Government Documentation Project, Special Collections and Archives (William Russell Pullen Library, Georgia State University, Atlanta [this collection hereinafter cited as GGDP]).

5. Samuel A. Stouffer *et al.*, *Studies in Social Psychology in World War II*. Vol. I: *The American Soldier: Adjustment During Army Life* (Princeton, N. J., 1949), 513–14 (first quotation) and 515 (second and third quotations); and Joyce Thomas, "The 'Double V' Was for Victory: Black Soldiers, the Black Protest, and World War II" (Ph.D. dissertation, Ohio State University, 1993), 171.

6. Robert J. Norrell, *Reaping the Whirlwind: The Civil Rights Movement in Tuskegee* (New York, 1985), 60–61.

7. Horace Bohannon found that most black ex-servicemen in Georgia had definite, if modest, postwar goals. What they most wanted, he recalled, was "a decent job. They wanted to work. They wanted to make it." After all, Bohannon noted, "they had lived, they'd seen other circumstances, they'd seen other peoples. And by now they knew that all every man wants is a job, and security for his family and so forth." See Horace Bohannon interview, June 16, 1989, manuscript #2854, audio tapes (Hargrett Library, University of Georgia, Athens [hereinafter cited as Bohannan interview]).

8. Horace Bohannon to George Mitchell, Ft. Valley, Ga., January 11, 1945, document series VII: 3, Southern Regional Council Archives (Special Collections, Robert W. Woodruff Library, Atlanta University Center), microfilm, reel 188, frame 257.

9. "Statements by Teachers, Principals, and Administrators," Atlanta University Seminar, Summer 1946, document series VII: 35, Southern Regional Council Archives, microfilm, reel 189, frames 1289–94.

10. Figures, as well as a detailed examination of the experience of black veterans

in the South and their access to the GI Bill, may be found in David Onkst, "'First a Negro . . . incidentally a Veteran': Black World War Two Veterans and the G.I. Bill of Rights in the Deep South, 1944–1948," pp. 18 and 29–30 (manuscript in possession of author).

11. "Statements by Teachers, Principals, and Administrators."

12. Southern black veterans often established their own organizations rather than joining segregated chapters of the American Legion or the Veterans of Foreign Wars. Information on such veteran organizations in Alabama, Mississippi, and Tennessee may be found in Birmingham *World*, March 8, 1946; Atlanta *Daily World*, October 1, 1946, p. 6; Jackson *Advocate*, September 7, 1946; and Memphis *World*, August 23, 1946.

13. Bohannon interview.

14. "14 Points of Action of GVL, Inc.," December 1945, document series VII: 4, Southern Regional Council Archives, microfilm, reel 190, frame 931 (first quotation); and Bohannon interview (second quotation). Veteran services organizations such as the American Legion (which required segregated chapters), as well as government offices, usually had white counselors who often did not prioritize serving black veterans. According to Bohannon, black veterans often felt more comfortable with, and received better service from, black counselors when trying to navigate through the inevitable bureaucratic red tape involved in applying for federal or state benefits.

15. Bohannon interview (first and third quotations); and "14 Points of Action of GVL, Inc." (second quotation). See also Paul Douglas Bolster, "Civil Rights Movements in Twentieth-Century Georgia" (Ph.D. dissertation, University of Georgia, 1972), 106.

16. Doyle Combs interview, October 13, 1989, audio tape, Transcript Series E, GGDP.

17. "14 Points of Action, GVL, Inc."

18. Savannah *Herald*, April 24, 1946, p. 6 (first quotation) and June 5, 1946, p. 7 (second quotation). Supporting the CPLgave black citizens of Savannah an opportunity to gain political influence by helping overthrow an entrenched political machine that had provided few services for blacks since its inception in the 1930s. See editorial in the Savannah *Tribune*, December 12, 1946, pp. 4 and 8.

19. Savannah *Morning News*, May 1, 1946, p. 12; and Savannah *Evening Press*, July 5, 1946, p. 18 (quotations). For more details on the Savannah voter registration campaign see Savannah *Herald*, May 1, 1946, pp. 2 and 9; R. W. Gadsen interview, July 10, 1947, for "Who Runs Georgia?" unpublished manuscript, Transcript Series B, GGDP; Bolster, "Civil Rights Movements in Twentieth-Century Georgia," 119; and Alexander Heard interview, July 17, 1991, accession #A-344, transcript, Southern Oral History Program (Southern Historical Collection, Louis Round Wilson Library, University of North Carolina, Chapel Hill).

20. Savannah *Morning News*, May 13, 1946, p. 10, July 2, 1946, p. 16, and July 18, 1946, p. 14; Savannah *Herald*, July 25, 1946, p. 8; and Bolster, "Civil Rights Movements in Twentieth-Century Georgia," 123.

21. The All Citizens Registration Committee was a new umbrella organization that encompassed several black civil rights groups in Atlanta and Fulton County.

On the ACRC voter registration campaign see David Andrew Harmon, "Beneath the Image: The Civil Rights Movement and Race Relations in Atlanta" (Ph.D. dissertation, Emory University, Atlanta, 1993), 33–56; Bolster, "Civil Rights Movements in Twentieth-Century Georgia," 116 ff; Jacob Henderson interview, July 24, 1992, videotape; and Jacob Henderson interview, June 8, 1989, transcript, Transcript Series E, both in the GGDP. Campaign material from the ACRC drive also may be found in the Clarence Bacote Collection (currently being processed), and in the Atlanta Urban League papers, box 7, document series 2, manuscript #597, Grace Towns Hamilton Papers (both in Special Collections Department, Robert Woodruff Library, Atlanta History Center). Also see Birmingham *World,* March 19, April 30, and May 7, 1946.

22. Veterans' Division memo, folder 1, box 7, document series 2, manuscript #597, Hamilton Papers (first quotation); Atlanta *Daily World,* March 31, 1946, pp. 1, 2 (second quotation), March 28, 1946, p. 7; and Birmingham *World,* March 19, 1946.

23. Harmon, "Beneath the Image," 47 and 72; and Bolster, "Civil Rights Movements in Twentieth-Century Georgia," 117 and 122.

24. On similar activities throughout Georgia, see Birmingham *World,* January 15, 1946, p. 5 and April 19, 1946, p. 4; Atlanta *Journal,* May 23, 1946, p. 1 and June 14, 1946, p. 1; Atlanta *Daily World,* March 28, 1946, p. 2; Augusta *Chronicle,* February 10, 1946, p. 1; Brunswick *News,* November 1, 1945, p. 8 and March 21, 1946, p. 8; and Columbus *Enquirer,* June 2, 1946, p. 10-C and September 27, 1946, p. 7-A.

25. Donald L. Grant, *The Way It Was in the South: The Black Experience in Georgia* (New York, 1993), 363–65 and 368–70. In Mississippi, for example, black veterans' efforts to oust Senator Theodore G. Bilbo failed to rid the state of its most notorious reactionary. Nonetheless, veterans' courage in testifying against "the Man" in a later congressional investigation of electoral chicanery encouraged others to take action. By 1950 some 20,000 black Mississippians were registered to vote, far short of their overall percentage in the population but a significant start, nonetheless, in a state known for its rabid racism. See Kenneth H. Williams, "Mississippi and Civil Rights, 1945–1954" (Ph.D. dissertation, Mississippi State University, 1985), 89–99 and 108; and Steven F. Lawson, *Black Ballots: Voting Rights in the South, 1944–1969* (New York, 1976), 128.

26. Hodding Carter, editor of the Greenville, Mississippi, *Delta Democrat Times,* who was a World War II veteran, believed that his observation of the British attitude toward Egyptian colonials and natives while serving as Middle East editor for *Yank* magazine awakened him to the destructiveness of discrimination, prodding him toward a moderate racial liberalism in his editorials after the war. Congressman Frank E. Smith of Mississippi learned through his experiences with integration at Fort Sill, Oklahoma, that "compelling authority" could cause widespread acceptance of racial change, and he ultimately became somewhat of a racial moderate in Congress, at least by Mississippi standards. See Ann Waldron, *Hodding Carter: The Reconstruction of a Racist* (Chapel Hill, 1993), 128–29; Frank E. Smith, *Congressman from Mississippi* (New York, 1964), 59, 66–67, and 71–72; and James C. Cobb, *The Most Southern Place on Earth: The Mississippi Delta and the Roots of Regional Identity* (New York and Oxford, 1992), 210–11.

27. Atlanta *Constitution,* July 17, 1946, clipping (first quotation), Scrapbook #7 entitled "1946 Gubernatorial Campaign," James V. Carmichael Papers (Special Collections

Department, Robert W. Woodruff Library, Emory University); and Morton Sosna, "More Important than the Civil War? The Impact of World War II on the South," in James C. Cobb and Charles R. Wilson, eds., *Perspectives on the American South: An Annual Review of Society, Politics, and Culture.* Vol. IV (New York, 1987), 154–55 (second quotation).

28. Harold Fleming interview, January 24, 1990, accession #A-363, transcript, Southern Oral History Program (hereinafter cited as Fleming interview).

29. Ibid. (all quotations); and Washington (D.C.) *Washington Post,* September 6, 1992.

30. After the war, Mackay became an avid defender of the democratic political rights of all Georgians and developed a reputation as a maverick southern liberal in the state and national legislatures. See James Mackay interviews, March 18, 1986, and March 31, 1987, transcript, Transcript Series B, GGDP (hereinafter cited as Mackay interview).

31. Atlanta *Constitution,* February 16, 1947, 10-A, and February 9, 1947, 4-A. See also Joseph Rabun interview for "Who Runs Georgia?" unpublished manuscript, Transcript Series B, GGDP.

32. White veterans with burgeoning, but as yet untapped, progressive inclinations returned to a state beset both by the forces of change and a reactionary resistance to reform. The growing presence of the (CIO), the reformist efforts of the Southern Regional Council (SRC) and the Southern Conference for Human Welfare (SCHW), and the political activism of black veterans, the NAACP, and other organizations generated a resurgent Ku Klux Klan, reactionary campaigns for public office, and a wave of racial violence and antiunionism. See Numan V. Bartley, *The New South, 1945–1980* ([Baton Rouge], 1995), for the conservative trends of the postwar years in the South.

33. Fleming interview; and Washington *Post,* September 6, 1992. The race baiting that occurred following the war, as Georgia conservatives worked to reinstate a white primary, moved Joseph Rabun to mount a protest that ultimately cost him his pulpit. Rabun convinced the Georgia Baptist Convention to condemn Eugene Talmadge's white supremacy campaign in the fall of 1946, and he testified in early 1947 before a state legislative committee against a bill to reinstate the white primary. Rabun had lived "by those beliefs" ever since his conversion, he told an Atlanta reporter, but now "he had faced 100 days of battle-fire for them; he had known four years of war." Thus, he declared, "It was little enough that as a private citizen I should exercise my right as such in a democracy, to speak in behalf of them." Quoted in Atlanta *Constitution,* February 16, 1947, p. 10-A. Rabun's comments inspired much controversy among his congregants, particularly since the church was the home of the Talmadge family. After resisting calls to resign, Rabun eventually stepped down from that pulpit later in 1947. See Joseph Rabun interview, p. 2, for "Who Runs Georgia?" unpublished manuscript, Transcript Series B, GGDP; and Atlanta *Constitution,* February 9, 1947, p. 4-A. Also see John Egerton, *Speak Now Against the Day: The Generation Before the Civil Rights Movement in the South* (New York, 1994), 423–24.

34. The AVC condemned racial segregation and discrimination and worked to advance progressive causes and candidates. See Atlanta *Daily World,* November 14, 1946, p. 3; Birmingham *World,* May 10, 1946, p. 7; Egerton, *Speak Now Against the Day,* 340,

382, 468; and AVC pamphlet, Robert Thompson Biographical File (Special Collections, Woodruff Library, Atlanta University Center).

35. *The Bellringer*, XI (October 20, 1947), 1, box 13 (first quotation), Glenn Rainey Collection (Special Collections Department, Robert W. Woodruff Library, Emory University); AVC pamphlet, Robert Thompson Biographical File (second quotation). For more on the American Veterans Committee in Georgia, see Atlanta *Constitution*, July 10, 1946, p. 4 and July 23, 1946, p. 3; "Southern Activity," American Veterans Committee bulletin, March 1948, folder entitled "American Veterans Committee, 1944–55," box 5, Gilbert Harrison Papers (Library of Congress, Washington); Marcus Gunter to George Mitchell, December 15, 1946, document series VII: 6, Southern Regional Council Archives, microfilm, reel 188, frames 456–523; Robert Thompson interviews, June 5, 1989, audiotape and transcript, Transcript Series E and G, GGDP; and Annie McPheeters interview, June 8, 1992, transcript, Transcript Series J, GGDP.

36. Lorraine Nelson Spritzer, *The Belle of Ashby Street: Helen Douglas Mankin and Georgia Politics* (Athens, 1982), 98.

37. Atlanta *Constitution*, July 9, 1946, p. E-1 (first and second quotations); George Stoney became acquainted with the community of Atlanta liberals as a researcher for Gunnar Myrdal's *An American Dilemma: The Negro Problem and Modern Democracy* (New York and London, 1944). "Josephine Wilkins and Maggie Fisher [of the Southern Conference for Human Welfare's Georgia Committee]," he recalled, "suggested that I work for Helen Douglas Mankin." See George Stoney interview, June 13, 1991, transcript #A-346, Southern Oral History Program. Many of Mankin's positions paralleled those taken by the national AVC. See, for example, Atlanta *Daily World*, October 8, 1946, p. 3.

38. Convinced that "sinister forces might be back of all this," (meaning the county-unit system's nullification of Mankins and Carmichael's popular majorities), a coterie of Atlanta liberals affiliated with the Southern Conference for Human Welfare, the Southern Regional Council, and the Urban League obtained a Rosenwald Fund grant to ferret out the "hidden influences" that ostensibly ran the state. Progressive white veterans Calvin Kytle and James Mackay carried out the research to discover "Who Runs Georgia?" After interviewing numerous politicians, editors, writers, and community leaders, Mackay and Kytle concluded that a cabal of large economic interests, particularly the Georgia Power Company and the railroads, essentially controlled politics throughout the state. Mackay and Kytle compiled their interviews and conclusions into a manuscript that remained unpublished until recently by the University of Georgia Press. According to Kytle, however, at the time it became "the most famous unpublished report of Georgia politics because the Talmadge people stole it" and enlisted it in the next campaign. See Calvin and Elizabeth Kytle interview, January 1, 1991, interview #A-365, transcript, Southern Oral History Program; and Mackay interview.

39. Plaintiffs for the two lawsuits were Mrs. Robert Turman of the League of Women Voters, Cullen Gosnell, chairman of the political science department at Emory University, and Earl P. Cooke, a law student at Georgia Tech and veteran of World

War II. These suits were styled on *Thurman and Gosnell* v. *J. Lon Duckworth* and *Cooke* v. *Fortson*. See Atlanta *Journal,* August 2, 1946, p. 1.

40. Ibid.

41. "A group of veterans is out today to raise $40,000 in a month's time to wage a political battle against minority rule," announced one Savannah newspaper as veterans in the GVMR set up a central office in Atlanta from which to coordinate their fund-raising efforts. See Savannah *Morning News,* September 22, 1946, p. 27.

42. GVMR members included Alexander Heard, a navy veteran from Savannah who headed the committee in the First Congressional District; George Doss Jr. of the Student League for Good Government at the University of Georgia; James M. Crawford, veteran of seventeen months service as an enlisted man in the infantry and in the Army's Tenth Armored Division; Elizabeth Penn Hammond, veteran of forty months as an enlisted woman and officer in the WAVES; and Richard T. Brooke, veteran of seventeen months as an enlisted man in the Navy. See "Personal Histories," Georgia Veterans for Majority Rule, August 1946, document series VII: 43, Southern Regional Council Archives, microfilm, reel 190, frames 730 and 733.

43. Georgia Veterans for Majority Rule, October 1946, frame 413, reel 63, document series V-1, entitled the Lucy Randolph Mason Papers in *Operation Dixie: The CIO Organizing Committee Papers, 1946–1953* (Special Collections, Perkins Library, Duke University) (first and second quotations [this collection hereinafter cited as Mason Papers]); Georgia Veterans for Majority Rule [undated], document series Pt. 4, NAACP Papers, microfilm (John C. Hodges Library, University of Tennessee, Knoxville) reel 7, frames 729–31 (third and fourth quotations).

44. Lucy Randolph Mason remarked on the "pall of fear" hanging over Georgia after Eugene Talmadge's reelection as governor, making organizing for any progressive causes difficult. See Lucy Randolph Mason to Barry Bingham, September 8, 1946, frame 343, and Lucy Randolph Mason to Eleanor Roosevelt, September 8, 1946, frame 344, both in document series V-1, Mason Papers, reel 63; and V.O. Key Jr., *Southern Politics in State and Nation* (New York, 1949), 121. For more on this veteran organization, including the obstacles it faced, see Jennifer E. Brooks, "From Hitler and Tojo to Talmadge and Jim Crow: World War Two Veterans and the Remaking of Southern Political Tradition" (Ph.D. dissertation, University of Tennessee, Knoxville, 1997), Chap. 5; Mackay interview; Savannah *Morning News,* August 11, 1946, p. 21; Atlanta *Constitution,* August 11, 1946, p. B-2; "Personal Histories," Georgia Veterans for Majority Rule, reel 190, frames 731–33; Georgia Veterans for Majority Rule, October 1946, document series V-1, Mason Papers, reel 63, frame 413; and Georgia Veterans for Majority Rule [undated], document series Pt. 4, NAACP Papers, reel 7, frames 729–31.

45. Atlanta *Constitution,* February, 1947, pp. 1 and 4. On testimony at the committee hearing see Egerton, *Speak Now Against the Day,* 389.

46. "While it is important to not be too optimistic," stated a reporter for the Atlanta *Constitution* in June 1945, "many practical Atlantans feel sure this area will meet the shock of transition from war to peace with less pain that many other areas." Specifically, "there will be some sort of job . . . available to everyone wanting to work." On

predictions of full employment see Atlanta *Constitution,* April 22, 1945, p. E-1, June 24, 1945, p. 1 (quotation), August 19, 1945, p. 2-B, August 21, 1945, p. 1, August 22, 1945, p. 1, August 24, 1945, p. 1, August 26, 1945, p. 9-A, and August 27, 1945, p. 1; and Savannah *Evening Press,* April 27, 1946, p. 14.

47. On unemployment at the end of the war see Savannah *Morning News,* January 24, 1946, p. 14 (quotation), and April 5, 1946, p. 14; Atlanta *Constitution,* September 6, 1945, p. 8; and Atlanta *Journal,* January 13, 1946, p. 9-D. According to the Georgia Department of Labor in February 1946, employment in the state dropped "from a peak" of "502,500 in the third quarter to 1943" to 435,000 soon after V-J day. "The drop was attributed to cutbacks in shipyards and war plants," reported the Atlanta *Journal,* as well as in "textile plants engaged in war production." See Atlanta *Journal,* February 5, 1946, p. 6. The *Coffee County Progress* reported that in Douglas, the county seat, "the volume of unemployed exservicemen . . . is still unusually high." See Douglas (Ga.) *Coffee County Progress,* May 16, 1946.

48. In the Midwest, returning veterans hoping to become independent farm operators found that high prices made affording good land difficult, even with the help of GI Bill credit benefits. See New York *Times,* April 28, 1946, p. IV-8.

49. For a discussion of the chaotic social and economic aftermath of the war for the South and the United States generally see Bartley, *Creation of Modern Georgia,* 179, 197–98, and 199–203; George Brown Tindall, *The Emergence of the New South, 1913–1945* (Baton Rouge, 1976), 687–73; Bartley, *New South,* 1–73; and Richard Polenberg, *War and Society: The United States, 1941–1945* (Philadelphia, New York, and Toronto, 1972), 99–153.

50. Lucy Randolph Mason to John Roy Carlson, April 15, 1946, document series V-1, Mason Papers, reel 63, frame 269.

51. Report on Atlanta Klavern #1, September 23, 1946, folder 3, box 1, Stetson Kennedy Papers (Special Collections and Archives, William Russell Pullen Library, Georgia State University, Atlanta), microfilm, reel 1.

52. The following sources describe the Klan's "strong-arm" inner circle: Klavalier Klub Meeting, May 1, 1946, folder 3, box 1; "Information Relative to the Klavalier Klub," folder 4, box 1; and Report on the Atlanta Ku Klux Klan, May 6, 1946, folder 3, box 1, all in Kennedy Papers, reel 1.

53. Klan report, Atlanta, May 6, 1946, folder 3, box 1; report on Klavalier Klub meeting, May 1, 1946, folder 3, box 1; Klavalier Klub Activities, 1948, folder 4, box 1; Report on meeting of Atlanta Klavern #1, April 29, 1946, folder 3, box 1; "Info Relative to Klavalier Klub," 1948, folder 4, box 1; Meeting of Klavalier Klub, May 15, 1946, folder 3, box 1; Report by John Brown, Atlanta Klavern #1 meeting, April 8, 1946, folder 3, box 1; Report by John Brown, Atlanta Klavern #297 meeting, April 18, 1946, folder 3, box 1, all in Kennedy Papers, reel 1. Also see Atlanta *Journal,* September 16, 1946, p. 5.

54. Brief discussions of the Columbians may be found in the following sources: Brooks, "From Hitler and Tojo to Talmadge and Jim Crow," Chaps. 1 and 4; J. Wayne Dudley, "'Hate Organizations' of the 1940s: The Columbians, Inc.," *Phylon,* XLII (September 3, 1981), 262–74; Spritzer, *Belle of Ashby Street,* 117. Also see Atlanta *Daily*

World, November 1, 1946, p. 1 and November 5, 1946, pp. 1 and 6; Atlanta *Journal,* October 30, 1946, p. 1, October 31, 1946, pp. 1 and 8, November 1, 1946, p. 9, November 3, 1946, p. 3, December 10, 1946, p. 1, and December 11, 1946, p. 4. Informants infiltrating this organization reported regularly on its activities to Ralph McGill, editor of the Atlanta *Constitution.* See, for example, Grey to AF, October 1, 1946, and Ned to AF, November 8, 1946, folder 1, box 51, Series V: Subject Files, Ralph McGill Papers (Special Collections Department, Robert W. Woodruff Library, Emory University). Stetson Kennedy played a key role in this infiltration, and his papers include a variety of firsthand information on the Columbians. See folder entitled "Columbians," Kennedy Papers, reel 1.

55. AF to Ned, September 3, 1946, folder 1, box 51, Series V: Subject Files, McGill Papers (first quotations); *The Bellringer,* I (September 7, 1946), 2, SRC Archives, reel 190 (last quotation).

56. See Dudley, "'Hate Organizations' of the 1940s," 269; Atlanta *Daily World,* November 5, 1946, pp. 1 and 6; "Atlanta Version of Mein Kampf," folder 6, box 1, reel 1; Ned to AF, November 2, 1946, folder entitled "Columbians," reel 1, both in Kennedy Papers. Although a few veterans joined the Columbians, it is possible to assign too much significance to their association with the group. The Columbians had trouble sustaining its membership, not only because of competitive, obviously twisted egos among the leadership but also because few southerners, veteran or civilian, could stomach an organization that closely parroted the antics and philosophy of the Nazis. Nonetheless, the presence of some veterans illustrates the extent to which they would go to defend southern racial tradition.

57. Herman Talmadge, speech delivered for Eugene Talmadge, May 4, 1946, transcript and audiotape, accession #Draft APR.1992.3, GGDP.

58. Guy Alford to Prince Preston, July 31, 1946, folder entitled "Emmanuel," box 33, Preston Papers (Richard B. Russell Library, University of Georgia).

59. Atlanta *Journal,* May 9, 1946, p. 14.

60. Ibid., August 20, 1946, p. 8.

61. Ibid., June 7, 1946, p. 18.

62. See, for example, Atlanta *Constitution,* July 19, 1946, p. 4, July 21, 1946, pp. 1 and 13, and July 24, 1946, p. 8; Atlanta *Journal,* July 14, 1946, p. 10-A; Savannah *Evening Press,* May 27, 1946, p. 2; Augusta *Chronicle,* March 31, 1946, pp. 1 and 2; La Fayette (Ga.) *Walker County Messenger,* August 22, 1946, p. 1.

63. While "in the First World War we used to sing 'The Yanks Are Coming,'" Mendoza added, "now we are going to sing 'The negroes are coming.'" Christopher De Mendoza to Prince Preston, July 12, 1946, folder entitled "Liberty," box 33, Preston Papers.

64. Douglas (Ga.) *Coffee County Progress,* June 20, 1946 (first quotation), and July 4, 1946 (remaining quotations).

65. Atlanta *Journal,* July 1, 1946, p. 10.

66. See ibid., December 10, 1946, p. 1, December 11, 1946, p. 4, and January 5, 1947, p. B-1.

67. State Representative Garland T. Byrd, a combat veteran elected in 1946 from Taylor County, proclaimed that a "Herman Talmadge Victory Is a Victory for Veterans!" in the *Statesman,* a pro-Talmadge political rag published in Hapeville, Georgia, and associated with Roy V. Harris, the Augusta Cracker politico. See Atlanta *Statesman,* January 2, 1947. Over three hundred World War II veterans in Floyd County reportedly drafted a petition sympathetic to Herman Talmadge and critical of press coverage of the two-governors controversy. "We the undersigned, being veterans of World War II, who fought for fairness and justice in the world," they declared, "have a firm determination to bring about fairness and justice in Georgia." Thus, "We . . . are absolutely and completely for Herman Talmadge and pledge to him (a fellow veteran) our full support in his legal and moral right to the Governorship of the State of Georgia." See Atlanta *Statesman,* January 13, 1947. For the controversy, see Bartley, *Creation of Modern Georgia,* 204. State Representative Culver Kidd, a war veteran from Baldwin County elected in 1946, recalled supporting Herman Talmadge during the gubernatorial controversy, which earned him an appointment as chairman of the Institutions and Property Committee. John J. Flynt, yet another veteran elected to the state legislature in 1946, recalled taking a "bad beating" in the press and from his hometown constituency in Spalding County for supporting Talmadge and his white primary bill. See Culver Kidd interview, October 3, 1988, transcript, Transcript Series B, and John J. Flynt interview, July 13, 1947, for "Who Runs Georgia?" unpublished manuscript, Transcript Series B, both in GGDP.

68. See Bartley, *New South,* 38–73, for an incisive discussion of "The Rise and Fall of Postwar Liberalism."

69. Having "been around the country and in a few other cities," for example, "Just Another GI" found that when looking at New Orleans, "I have not got too much to brag about." "If New Orleans is the 'Pride of the South'," he added, "there should be more beautiful places to visit and . . . they should be kept clean. . . . Several soldier friends of mine visited New Orleans before they were in the army and some don't ever want to go back." New Orleans *Times Picayune,* January 26, 1946.

70. The same phenomenon marked postwar politics in virtually every southern state. Submitting to a "dictatorial" ring that thrived on ballot-stuffing, nepotism, and profiteering at the public expense seemed unconscionable to veterans in Yell County, Arkansas, for example, who promised in 1946 to wage the "damnedest campaign you ever saw" against local bossism. "We were told we were fighting for democracy," these ex-soldiers explained, but "democracy [does not] exist in Yell County, so we're still fighting for it." Atlanta *Constitution,* August 11, 1946, p. 10-A. The Battle of Athens stands as the most widely known postwar veterans' revolt. In Athens, Tennessee, disgust with the practices of a corrupt county ring compelled veterans not only to run their own candidates for office but also to wage a heated gunbattle to prevent the election from being stolen. A sensationalized image of gun-wielding, crusading hillbilly veterans shooting it out with brutish, corrupt courthouse thugs blazed across national headlines in the summer of 1946. "If democracy is good enough for Germany and the Japs," declared one Athens combat veteran, "it's good enough for McMinn County!" See Stephen C. Byrum, *The Battle of Athens* (Chattanooga, Tenn., 1987), 3–4 (quotation

from "combat veteran"), 7–8, and 119; *Newsweek,* August 12, 1946, pp. 30–32, September 9, 1946, p. 38, and January 27, 1947, pp. 25–26; Jennings Perry, "Rebellion in Tennessee," *Nation,* August 10, 1946, p. 147; *Commonweal,* August 16, 1946, pp. 419–20; Theodore H. White, "The Battle of Athens, Tennessee," *Harper's Monthly,* CXCIV (January 1947), 54–61; and Lones Seiber, "The Battle of Athens," *American Heritage,* XXXVI (February/ March 1985), 72–79.

71. The Cracker Party of Augusta was a long-incumbent Democratic Party organization in Richmond County headed by Roy V. Harris, reactionary former speaker of the Georgia House. For more on the Cracker Party and the veteran-led Independent revolt against it in 1946 see James C. Cobb, "Colonel Effingham Crushes the Crackers: Political Reform in Postwar Augusta," *South Atlantic Quarterly,* LXXVIII (Autumn 1979), 507–19.

72. Voter turnout for the 1946 gubernatorial election was more than twice the turnout in the 1942 election in which Ellis Arnall had defeated Eugene Talmadge. See William Anderson, *The Wild Man from Sugar Creek: The Political Career of Eugene Talmadge* (Baton Rouge, 1975), 210–11; Joseph L. Bernd, *Grass Roots Politics in Georgia: The County Unit System and the Importance of the Individual Voting Community in Bifactional Elections, 1942–1954* (Atlanta, Ga., 1960), 66–71; and Harold Paulk Henderson, *The Politics of Change in Georgia: A Political Biography of Ellis Arnall* (Athens and London, 1991), 50, 145, and 166–68.

73. Griffin Bell interview, September 19, 1990, transcript, Transcript Series B, GGDP (first quotation); and Atlanta *Journal,* April 29, 1946, p. 10 (second quotation). Many observers at the time noticed, and were pleased by, the broadened perspective of the state's returning white soldiers. "Georgians . . . returning from lands all over the earth are bringing in new visions and ideas," reported the Gainesville *Eagle,* and having "seen and experienced many new things . . . they can do much to broaden the horizons of Georgia today." The Augusta *Chronicle* agreed, remarking that "most, if not all, of these young men are quite different in their outlook and actions from the timid, apathetic, secure in the rut, average run of the mine [*sic*] citizen." See Gainesville *Eagle,* May 9, 1946; and Augusta *Chronicle,* March 9, 1946, p. 4.

74. Atlanta *Constitution,* August 7, 1946, p. E-1 (Moffett quotation) and July 21, 1946, p. 14-A (Flynt quotation). Veterans in other southern states remarked on and acted from similar experiences. Arkansas veteran Orval E. Faubus, who rose to political prominence in Governor Sidney S. McMath's administration and later became one of the South's leading architects of massive resistance, was influenced by the modern world he had observed in Germany during and after the war. Having used the enemy's good roads, Faubus recalled thinking that "Germany was a poor country and I wondered what they would think if they knew that when I, a representative, of a wealthy country, went back I would have to get a mule to get home." See Diane D. Blair, *Arkansas Politics and Government: Do the People Rule?* (Lincoln, Neb. and London, 1988), 17. In Polk County, Tennessee, heartened by the success of their comrades in nearby Athens, veterans formed a Good Government League in 1946 to oust the Crump-allied Burch Biggs machine, declaring to Congressman Estes Kefauver that "Machine Rule has brought decay and stagnation to Progress in Polk County, and

citizens have at last rebelled." See R. E. Barclay to U.S. Representative Estes Kefauver, October 14, 1946, telegram, folder entitled "Qualifying Petitions, 1944–6," box entitled "1946 Political Files," Estes Kefauver Collection (Special Collections, Hoskins Library, University of Tennessee–Knoxville).

75. Few would dispute, in fact, that during his terms as agricultural commissioner and as governor in the thirties and the early forties Talmadge had provided plenty of ammunition to fuel Yankee ridicule. Not every politician was in a position to make political capital out of an investigation into his misuse of funds, but Talmadge was. As Georgia's commissioner of agriculture, one of Talmadge's most infamous feats was his use of state money to purchase from local farmers eighty-two carloads of Georgia hogs, which were shipped to Chicago for sale, all without any legal appropriation of funds for that purpose. Ardently opposed to the New Deal, Talmadge responded to the hog farmers' dilemma during the Great Depression with an illegal appropriation of state funds to buy and market Georgia hogs. In the ensuing controversy, prompted, in part, by the state's loss of approximately $13,000 on the deal, Talmadge publicly declared that "If I stole, it was for farmers," which delighted his wool-hat followers but embarrassed uptown Georgians. As governor, Talmadge's antics reached new heights of absurdity, reactionism, and downright meanness. Talmadge pastured a cow on the statehouse lawn, kept the state government in a state of martial law for months in order to consolidate his control of state agencies, and declared those who served in the Civilian Conservation Corps to be "bums and loafers." In 1934 he remarked that "the next President . . . should be able to walk a two-by-four," a comment that splashed across national headlines. That same year, Talmadge called out the state national guard in a brutal suppression of Georgia workers in the Great Textile Strike of 1934, during which thousands were incarcerated in barbed-wire prison camps, and one worker was beaten to death in front of his family. The following year, Talmadge provoked an impasse with the Georgia General Assembly by vetoing old-age pensions, seven constitutional amendments, and hundreds of local measures. Later in 1935, the legislature adjourned without appropriating money to operate the state government in 1936. In the ensuing imbroglio, Talmadge defied state law and political convention by having the state adjutant general physically remove the state treasurer from office and then try to open the state vault with blowtorches. Such antics, and there were plenty of others, gained not only widespread local coverage but also directed national attention to Georgia's "banana republic" politics. Talmadge publicly bragged about having read *Mein Kampf* seven times just as war broke out in Europe, and more and more observers drew a connection between his style of rule and the dictatorships overseas. In the wake of the 1936 conflict with the legislature, newspapers in Georgia remarked that Talmadge "is getting to be worse than Hitler or Mussolini," and that he was a "paper-mache dictator" who administered "lynch law" in Georgia. Nor did Talmadge try to deflect his critics, declaring around 1942 that "I'm what you call a minor dictator. But did you ever see anybody that was much good who didn't have a little dictator in him?" Quotations in Anderson, *Wild Man from Sugar Creek*, 57–58, 59, 60, 73, 194.

76. "Arnold" to James Setze Jr., July 15, 1941, folder 1, box 1 entitled "Letters to James Setze Jr., 1940–August 1941" (first quotations), World War II Miscellany Papers (Special

Collections Department, Robert W. Woodruff Library, Emory University) (hereinafter Setze Letters); Atlanta *Constitution,* May 15, 1946, clipping, Scrapbook #6, Carmichael Papers (Tant quotation). "Frank" wrote to James Setze about reading of "the Georgia students and Governor Talmadge in Life and Time. That sure is a mess." "Larry" wrote to Setze from Missouri: "It sure is a disgrace that Talmadge's meddling caused such a loss of prestige to the University of Georgia." See "Frank" to James Setze Jr., undated, folder 2, box 1, and "Larry" to James Setze Jr., January 11, 1942, folder 3, box 1, both in Setze Letters.

77. Atlanta *Journal,* July 26, 1946, p. 18 (first quotation), and May 28, 1946, p. 10 (second quotation).

78. Atlanta *Constitution,* July 16, 1946, p. E-1 (first quotation); and clipping, circa 1946, Scrapbook #6, 1946 Gubernatorial Campaign, Carmichael Papers (second quotation).

79. Atlanta *Journal,* May 22, 1946, clipping, Scrapbook #6, Carmichael Papers.

80. "Georgia soldier," Orlando, Florida, August 15, 1944, clipping, folder entitled "Servicemen's reactions to Georgia," box 16, Lamar Q. Ball Collection (Georgia Department of Archives and History, Atlanta).

81. Governor Arnall's accomplishments included a new state constitution, a consti-tutional board of regents, a state board of education, a law providing absentee ballots to out-of-state and overseas soldiers, lowering voter eligibility to eighteen years of age, abolishing the poll tax for all citizens, significantly increased expenditures for educa-tion, a teacher-retirement plan, and liquidating the long-standing state debt without raising taxes. See Bartley, *Creation of Modern Georgia,* 194.

82. Atlanta *Constitution,* July 3, 1946, p. 1 (first quotation); and Atlanta *Journal,* May 10, 1946, p. 18 (second quotation).

83. Cunningham to James Setze Jr., September 29, 1942, folder 6, box 1, Setze Letters.

84. Sgt. Harry Baxter, July 2, 1946, WSB Radio broadcast, transcript, accession # Draft APR.1993.18, GGDP.

85. Atlanta *Journal,* October 28, 1946, p. 10 (first quotation), May 15, 1946, p. 12 (sec-ond quotation); and Atlanta *Constitution* August 23, 1946, p. E-1 (third quotation).

86. War mobilization fostered significant economic growth in Georgia and the South, boosting the region's overall industrial capacity by almost 40 percent. Along with new aircraft, munitions, rubber, and chemical industries came the expansion of traditional ones like textiles, lumber, and mining. This growth, combined with in-creasing agricultural prices, generated more income, which encouraged the develop-ment of a nascent consumer market in the South. In Georgia, wartime development boosted per capita incomes from 57 percent of the national average in 1940 to 73 per-cent in 1960. The arrival of over 1,600 new manufacturing establishments between 1930 and 1947 and the emergence of a burgeoning consumer market spurred diversification and expansion of jobs in both the white- and blue-collar sectors of the economy. The prosperity induced by World War II seemed an abrupt change after years of unrelent-ing depression, a change that promised to eradicate the South's image as a "benighted" region burdened by its past and saddled with an unwelcome, though deserved, reputa-

tion as the nation's "number one economic problem." While pump-priming federal spending did much to boost southern economic growth, it failed to "neutralize the South's economic heritage." Much of this development was uneven, favoring the Gulf Southwest within the South and larger cities within Georgia. In addition, with much of this development centered on war production, reconversion shut down plants that were important sources of wartime employment. Huntsville, Alabama; Columbia, Tennessee; and Brunswick, Savannah, and Marietta, Georgia, for example, all suffered immediately after the war from the closure of war industries, which contributed to local racial tensions and political instability. See Tindall, *Emergence of the New South,* 694 and 700–701; and Bartley, *Creation of Modern Georgia,* 186–87 and 181–83.

87. Atlanta *Journal,* February 19, 1946, p. 10 (first quotation) and July 23, 1946, p. 10 (second quotation).

88. Ibid., March 13, 1946, p. 10 (first quotation); and Atlanta *Constitution,* February 10, 1946, p. A-15 (second quotation).

89. For examples of veterans' support of Carmichael's gubernatorial campaign see clippings from Atlanta *Constitution,* April 28, 1946, and from Atlanta *Journal,* April 30, 1946, Scrapbook #6, Carmichael Papers; Atlanta *Journal,* May 5, 1946, p. 16-A, May 12, 1946, p. 18-A, May 14, 1946, p. 6, and June 13, 1946, p. 6; and Waycross *Journal Herald,* May 16, 1946, p. 1.

90. Student-League-for-Good-Government, advertisement, folder 5 entitled "Georgia Politics," Kennedy Papers, reel 2 (first quotation); and Atlanta *Journal,* May 22, 1946, clipping, Scrapbook #6, Carmichael Papers (second quotation).

91. John Sammons Bell, Fulton County-for-Carmichael-Club, WSB Radio broadcast, July 11, 1946, accession # Draft APR.1993.22.uc-m84-20/56b & 55b, GGDP.

92. The B-29ers-For-Carmichael Club also included former employees of the Bell Bomber plant in Marietta, Georgia, managed by Carmichael. See B-29ers-for-Carmichael Club, WSB Radio broadcast, July 5, 1946, transcript, accession # Draft APR.1993.20.uc-M84-20/49b & 46a, GGDP.

93. B-29ers-For-Carmichael Club; James V. Carmichael, WSB Radio broadcast, June 15, 1946, transcript, accession # Draft APR.1993.9.c-M84-20/29a & 29b, GGDP. See also Atlanta *Journal,* May 26, 1946, p. 6-A.

94. Smaller communities in Georgia that experienced veteran insurgencies, or in which veterans were particularly active, included Telfair County, Douglasville, La Fayette, Rabun County, Emanuel County, Milledgeville, Athens, Clarkesville, Valdosta, Waycross, Albany, Talbotten, Cartersville, and La Grange.

95. Similar campaigns occurred across the South. Ex-serviceman Sidney Mc-Math rode a wave of veteran support to become governor of Arkansas in 1948. In 1946 veterans helped exserviceman DeLesseps S. Morrison oust the Long Machine in New Orleans and seize the mayoralty, while ex-soldiers in Alabama facilitated the formation of a long-lasting political machine by electing populist-progressive and veteran James E. Folsom to the governorship. See Jim Lester, *A Man for Arkansas: Sid McMath and the Southern Reform Tradition* (Little Rock, Ark., 1976); Edward F. Haas, *DeLesseps S. Morrison and the Image of Reform: New Orleans Politics, 1946–1961* (Baton Rouge, 1974).

96. Columbus *Enquirer,* May 26, 1946, p. 10-D and June 2, 1946, p. 10-C (first and second quotations).

97. See note 71 above for information on the Independents, a veteran-led insurgency against the Cracker Party in Augusta.

98. James Carmichael received a solid plurality of votes, around 700,000, but the majority of county-unit votes went to Talmadge. See Bartley, *Creation of Modern Georgia,* 203–4.

99. In announcing his campaign for governor in 1946, Talmadge minced few words in appealing to his constituency's southern and racial nationalism. Declaring that the white primary issue was the most important question facing the region and the state of Georgia, Talmadge then announced that "alien and communistic influences from the East are agitating social equality in our state." In fact, he alleged, "they desire negroes to participate in our white primary in order to destroy the traditions and heritages of our Southland." Thus, "if elected Governor," Talmadge promised, "I shall see that the traditions which were fought for by our grandparents are maintained and preserved . . . unfettered and unhampered by radical Communistic and alien influences." Talmadge capitalized also on national controversies and implied that the outcome of the gubernatorial race would affect issues that actually could be settled only by Congress. In a speech at Summerville, for example, Talmadge attacked "socialized medicine" and the "FEPC," pretending to explain how these questions threatened white supremacy in Georgia. "If they get across the FEPC and the socialized medicine, too," Talmadge alleged, "if you apply for a doctor, they might send you to a Negro doctor right here in this county." See Montgomery *Advertiser,* April 7, 1946, p. 25; and Eugene Talmadge, undated, WSB Radio broadcast, transcript, accession # Draft APR.1993.79.uc-M84-20/113a, 106, GGDP. Probably the only Georgia politician who could approach Talmadge in racial hyperbole and demagoguery for political effect was Roy V. Harris of the Cracker Party in Augusta. As an incumbent state legislator whose reelection was opposed by the Independents, Harris led the Crackers in attacking their opponents as carpetbaggers intent on eliminating the white primary in Georgia. Dubbing the white primary as the vehicle used by "the old Confederate veterans to wrest control of this state from the hands of the carpet-baggers, scalawags, and negroes," a political ad for the Cracker legislative candidates proclaimed the importance of maintaining a racially exclusive primary. The "colored people" who "vote as a bloc" and "take orders from Washington and New York" aim to defeat southern congressmen, pass a permanent FEPC bill, and end segregation in all public facilities as well as promote intermarriage "of the races." The result, the Crackers warned, would be "the end of Augusta's development and growth" because "we will either have race riots or the white people will leave the community." Having declared white supremacy to be the overarching issue, the Crackers then tried to put the Independents on the spot by challenging them to take a position on the white primary. "This is the most important election in Georgia since we got rid of the scalawags, carpetbaggers, and Negro government," trumpeted Harris, yet "I have been asking this question [about the white primary] for two weeks but I have received no answer." See Augusta *Chronicle,* April 13, 1946, p. 8 and April 12, 1946, pp. 1 and 9.

100. Rather than attacking Carmichael directly, Talmadge often focused his most vitriolic efforts on his old rival Ellis Arnall, who had endorsed his opponent. His race-baiting attacks on Arnall for refusing to defend the white primary, for example, labeled Arnall as the leader of a Yankee-liberal-union-black plot to overturn Georgia's racial traditions, a conspiracy that Carmichael's election as governor would only further. "Ellis 'Benedict' Arnall opened the breach in the dike that has protected Southern manhood, Southern womanhood, and Southern childhood for three quarters of a century," Talmadge accused, and Arnall had gone "further than any white man in America to promote [racial equality] in Georgia." Quoted in Henderson, *Politics of Change*, 166. On Talmadge's racial antics during the gubernatorial campaign of 1946 see Anderson, *Wild Man from Sugar Creek*, 229–31; and Bartley, *Creation of Modern Georgia*, 201–3.

101. Throughout the campaign, Carmichael sought to make the Klan the only racial issue, linking both Talmadge, endorsed by the Georgia Klan, and Rivers, a former member, to the reconstituted KKK. At Vienna, Georgia, Carmichael flayed his opponents for granting the Klan significant influence during their gubernatorial administrations. "Georgia cannot have prosperity if the governor uses tax money to endow the imperial wizard of Ku Klux Klan," he declared. In fact, Carmichael even tried enlisting a folksy ruralism to offset Talmadge's distinctive vernacular advantage. "Sometimes, I've thought of Georgia . . . as a field attacked by crows," Carmichael proclaimed in one speech before a rural audience: "There are crows that wear costumes of red suspenders [i.e., Talmadge], and there are crows that wear black bow ties as their insignia [i.e., Rivers] . . . . when these two flocks of crows get together after dark . . . they cannot be told apart because they all wear white nightshirts . . . . And instead of going Caw, Caw, Caw as they do in the daytime, they go: Klux, Klux, Klux." See Jackson (Miss.) *Advocate*, May 25, 1946, p. 1; Birmingham *World*, May 24, 1946, p. 1; and James Carmichael speech, WSB Radio broadcast, June 1, 1946, transcript, accession # Draft APR.1993.4, GGDP. Carmichael often emphasized the need to obey the law and respect the courts as a way to deflect his opponents' attack on the white primary issue. "The welfare of any community . . . depends upon the maintenance of law and order, or respect for the courts, of reasonableness in dealing with one another," Carmichael stated, and Talmadge's and Harris's antics aimed "to disturb the good relations that exist in Georgia between the races" inviting a "disregard for law and . . . an invitation to lawless chaos." Thus, he continued, "my platform means that the county unit system will be preserved as a part of our law and that control of Georgia politics will remain with the people of our state and will not pass to Roy Harris and his stooges." Preserving the county-unit system and all other laws regulating primary elections, Carmichael promised, "means that the statutes against fraud, against ballot box stuffing, against fake registration lists, against the voting of dead folks on election day, will not be repealed in the interests of any political gain." See James V. Carmichael, June 15, 1946, WSB Radio broadcast, transcript, accession # Draft APR 1993.9.c-M84-20/29a & 29b, GGDP.

102. Lon Sullivan speech, WSB Radio broadcast, July 13, 1947, accession # Draft APR.1993.14.uc-M84-20/32b and 59a (first quotations); George Doss Jr., WSB Radio

broadcast, July 6, 1946, audiotape, accession # Draft APR.1993.10.uc, GGDP (second quotations). The B-29ers also hurried to affirm Carmichael's southern "legitimacy" by proclaiming "here's Jimmy's stand" on race relations: "He adheres to southern racial traditions. [He] was born in, reared in, lives in, and expects to die in Cobb County, Georgia." B-29ers-For-Carmichael Club, WSB Radio broadcast, July 5, 1946, transcript, accession # Draft APR.1993.20.uc-M84-20/49b & 46a, GGDP (third quotation).

103. In an interview shortly after the election, Carmichael confided that his capitulation on the county-unit system—he personally regarded the system as evil and undemocratic—rendered him unsuitable to be governor. See James V. Carmichael interview, July 23, 1947, for "Who Runs Georgia," unpublished manuscript, Transcript Series B, GGDPGGDP.

104. Augusta *Chronicle,* April 13, 1946, pp. 1–2, and April 14, 1946, p. 7.

105. In Savannah, where black veterans helped an upstart reformist coalition of white veterans defeat the corrupt John Bouhan machine, the Citizens Progressive League fulfilled African American demands to improve city services to black neighborhoods, appoint a Negro Advisory Committee, and hire black police officers. Racial conservatism in the CPL, however moderate compared to other administrations in the South, nonetheless soon caused a rupture in the relationship between CPL Mayor John Kennedy and the new Negro Advisory Committee. Black war veteran W. W. Law, a supporter of the CPL and member of the committee, resigned when Mayor Kennedy refused to allow integrated lines for viewing the traveling Freedom Train exhibit. See W. W. Law interview; Savannah *Evening Press,* May 27, 1946, p. 2; Savannah *Tribune,* November 28, 1946, pp. 1 and 8, February 6, 1947, pp. 1 and 7, and May 8, 1947, pp. 1 and 7; Savannah *Morning News,* October 27, 1946, p. 4; and Savannah *Herald,* February 6, 1947, pp. 1 and 8.

106. See Henderson, *Georgia Governors;* and Bartley, *Creation of Modern Georgia.*

"Nothing Else Matters But Sex"

Cold War Narratives of Deviance and the Search for Lesbian Teachers in Florida, 1959–1963

Stacy Braukman

> Lesbianism, which has been promulgated and perpetuated by many female
> teachers, has now infiltrated, or is now being practiced by school girls aged
> 12–18. The situation is of such nature that many parents have become very
> much aroused. . . . It has been reported that the young ladies carry knives
> and other weapons to force others to submit to their desires. . . . Certainly
> this is not only fertile ground in which to breed communism, but it's also
> against the very grain of marriage, normal life, and manhood.
> unsigned letter, Records of the Florida Legislative Investigation Committee

Harrowing images of bullying, knife-wielding teenage girls, paranoid
reports of lesbian infiltration, dire warnings about the social and political consequences of female sexual deviance: this 1963 letter from a group of
Palm Beach, Florida, ministers, businesspeople, and parents to state Senator
Charley E. Johns captures perfectly, if melodramatically, the fears that had
both driven and sustained Johns's brainchild, the Florida Legislative Investigation Committee (FLIC)—popularly known as the Johns Committee—for
the previous five years. During the cold war, as the South and the rest of the
country grappled with enemies real and invented, Florida's investigating committee served as an important example of the lengths to which political demonization could go, as well as a reminder that the ghosts of McCarthyism
continued to haunt America well into the 1960s.

The Johns Committee spent nine years, between 1956 and 1965, combating
subversives within the state, which came to include civil rights activists, homosexuals, and leftist intellectuals. It had been created as part of the great tide
of massive resistance that swept over the South in the wake of the two Brown
decisions mandating an end to educational segregation by race in 1954 and
1955. The committee's original aim was to cast public doubt on the loyalty of
members of the National Association for the Advancement of Colored People.
By the early to mid-1960s, it had also begun keeping close tabs on lesbian and
gay teachers as well as growing student activism, "indecent literature," and left-
wing teaching in the state's universities. Its primary target, however, remained

homosexuals. Seizing the psychiatric model of homosexuality as pathological, the cultural model of homosexuality as predatory and youth directed, and the political model of homosexuality as subversive, the FLIC was in many ways a logical embodiment and extension of postwar anxieties about the undermining of traditional political, sexual, and racial values and, in turn, the health and vigor of the state and the nation.

What follows is an examination of one segment of those hunted by the Johns Committee in the late 1950s and early 1960s: lesbians. For the purposes of this article, lesbians are singled out and analyzed in a way that would have run counter to the committee's understanding of the "problem" of homosexuality. That is, the FLIC itself drew little distinction between female and male homosexuals—it saw both as not only individuals suffering from a personality disorder but also as innately hypersexual and predatory. Donna Penn has written that the postwar tendency among psychiatric and social science experts to emphasize lesbians' sexual degeneracy and criminality was most often expressed by linking the figure of the lesbian to that of the prostitute. In this way, Penn claims, social commentators made previously "unnoticed" lesbians "visible to the unsuspecting public" by discursively associating them with prostitutes and constructing both as the "essence of female sexual deviance and danger."[1] There are two problems with this interpretation. First, drawing connections between homosexuality and prostitution was not unique to lesbians during this period; in fact, one could make the case for a greater, more deep-seated cultural fear of adult males luring younger boys into the underworld of hustling and prostitution.[2] Second, within the context of the cold war view of homosexuality as a disease or condition that could be spread through recruitment and association, and pervasive anxieties about American youth, it is perhaps more useful to note the ways in which the lesbian became discursively connected not to the prostitute but to the male homosexual. In the construction of the "homosexual menace," in order to justify the expulsion of both women and men from the military and the civil service, differences between lesbians and gay men had to be downplayed and lesbians subsumed within the category of "homosexual."

The FLIC's search for lesbian teachers in Florida exemplifies this postwar conflation of female and male homosexuality in the construction of a new political enemy. Between 1959 and 1963, the committee questioned dozens of lesbians, pressured countless others into relinquishing their teaching positions, and had many students quietly removed from state universities. Although they made up only about 20 percent of the total number of suspected homosexuals questioned by the committee's investigators, lesbians were not excluded from the cold war model of same-sex desire as morally suspect, psychologically damaged—and damaging—and inherently subversive.[3]

As far as the FLIC was concerned, lesbians fit somewhere in the new cold war discourse of sexual and political perversion, but just where they fit was not clear to Johns and his colleagues. Their uncertainty resulted to some degree from the numerous and often conflicting meanings of "lesbian" in the years following World War II. Popular images of the working-class, butch "bar dyke," the mannish lesbian athlete, and the masculine prison lesbian coexisted with those of the college-educated, highly cultured, and intellectual spinster and the "fem," whose ability to pass as heterosexual rendered her an invisible, insidious threat.[4] The ambivalence toward lesbians that marked the FLIC's public school investigations can also be attributed to the prevailing wisdom that men's sexual deviance posed a far greater threat to children, to public safety, and even to national security than did women's. Rather than formulating a distinctive approach to questioning suspected lesbians, investigators focused on the same aspect of homosexual life that they did with male suspects: the performance of specific sexual acts, experiences with children or teenagers, and a willingness to direct or redirect one's sexual desire toward the opposite sex. Within this schema, lesbians became sexual predators—albeit ones less threatening than gay men—and a menace to the health and safety of youth and carriers of subversion into Florida classrooms.

During the course of its public school campaign, the committee encountered a wide range of women and yet clearly attempted to fit them into a narrow definition of same-sex pathology that equated aggressive, youth-directed sexuality with that of gay men. Some of the female witnesses admitted to having lesbian encounters, others grudgingly confessed their full-fledged lesbian identity, and many who were named by others went to great lengths to deny the accusations—even as they handed over their teachers' certificates at the end of a grueling interrogation. Black and white women, middle class and working class, teachers and nurses, prisoners and reform school girls, and women in the armed services all found themselves confronted by charges of deviance and came face-to-face with an investigating committee bent on expurgating what it viewed as a scourge from the state's public schools.

By the time the FLIC was organized in the fall of 1956, the federal government and the armed forces had already purged hundreds of employees and soldiers for engaging in homosexual acts. A growing awareness of the presence of gay subcultures in the midst of a much-hyped period of suburban normalcy, a need for a scapegoat in the cold war against the Soviet Union, and a popular view of same-sex desire as a form of mental illness all contributed to the creation of the figure of the homosexual as a security risk, a subversive, and a predator.[5] The FLIC modified this view to fit the special needs of a growing state in a strife-torn region. In early 1959 it broke new ground among state legislative investigating committees by searching for homosexuals in Florida's public educational system, beginning with a purge of fourteen faculty and staff members from the University of Florida.[6]

There is no firm evidence pointing to the precise reason that Johns chose homosexuals—and homosexual teachers in particular—as a substitute target. As early as September 1954, when he served as acting governor following the death of Governor Dan McCarty, a series of highly publicized raids on gay bars in Miami inspired Johns to launch a "campaign against perversion" there.[7] Later, in the spring of 1957, the committee tapped into investigative reports from the Hillsborough County Sheriff's Department, which had uncovered the presence of several gay men on the staff of a Tampa tuberculosis hospital. During that inquest, the dean of boys at a local high school was named as a homosexual; this led the sheriff's office to a two-month foray into the public school system in the Tampa Bay area that summer. Because the Johns Committee was preoccupied with countering the legal maneuverings of the NAACP, however, it took no action on the findings. Not until the fall of 1958—by which time the FLIC had been hamstrung by an injunction prohibiting any further action against the civil rights organization—would the issue of lesbian and gay teachers take center stage. Johns, the committee chair that year, dispatched investigators to the University of Florida. Some historians have suggested that the pro–civil rights stand taken by a handful of professors there first attracted the committee's attention.[8] Others speculate that Johns's son, who attended the university, repeated to his father the campus gossip swirling around several "effeminate" members of the faculty. One scholar has argued that "rumors and innuendo offered the FLIC a long-awaited opportunity to create a conspiracy that linked homosexuality, subversion, and integration" in order to justify its continued existence to the state legislature.[9]

But the committee did not have to imagine or invent a conspiracy. Instead, it drew upon a variety of cultural narratives that had long constructed communists and civil rights activists as sexual deviants and homosexuals as political deviants.[10] The committee's wide-ranging campaigns in the name of anticommunism only served to strengthen the discursive links among these familiar enemies. The University of Florida investigation convinced Charley Johns that the new target his committee had found merited further probing, that the University of Florida represented only the tip of the iceberg of the strange and frightening problem that somehow had infiltrated his state and was getting uncomfortably close to his own home. (Johns hailed from Bradford County, which abuts the northeastern edge of Alachua County, home to the university.)

Although the FLIC did not invent the belief that homosexuals—who bore a striking and sinister resemblance to communists and "race agitators"—subverted American institutions, it did help to construct the idea of homosexual teachers as a pressing cold war issue. In doing so, the committee also solidified new definitions of "subversive" that bound together integrationists and sexual deviants. In a report on the University of Florida investigation, the FLIC acknowledged that homosexuality in schools was "not new." The new danger, it claimed, lay in the spread of homosexuality, which seemed to be happening at a disturbingly high rate.[11]

Homosexuality-as-social-ill did not debut on the American landscape in the 1950s, but the fear of its spread came to the fore during this period, closely tied to the sense that other forms of subversion, especially communism and racial protest, were also proliferating. Observers have credited the research of Alfred Kinsey with opening up a cultural space for discussing sexuality. Thanks in large part to the avuncular biologist from Indiana University, the pages of *Time, Newsweek, Good Housekeeping,* and *Reader's Digest,* along with newsrooms, colleges, and kitchens, resounded with talk of sex. Much of it dwelt upon the surprising frequency of same-sex desire and behavior uncovered by Kinsey. For the hundreds of thousands of Americans who flocked to bookstores and turned Kinsey's two reports into best-sellers in 1948 and 1953, it came as a shock that fully 10 percent of adult males and 3 percent of females considered themselves exclusively homosexual and that more than one-third of the men and one-fifth of the women in the reports had engaged in homosexual acts. Surely, Americans thought, it had not always been so, but now it seemed plausible that just about anyone could be harboring secret queer desires.[12]

The perception of a rising tide of homosexuality was bolstered by the expanding media coverage of Kinsey's research, the military and federal government purges of gays and lesbians in the late 1940s and early 1950s, and local police raids on gay bars across the nation. With all this talk, this "endless stream of negative headlines and news articles," the homosexual menace seemed to loom ever-larger by the 1950s.[13] Florida's investigating committee, like many other antisubversive groups that flourished during the cold war, believed that sexual perversion was seeping into and undermining the institutions held as cornerstones of American democracy: the family, the government, and the schools.

Donna Penn has argued that the postwar anxiety about lesbians in particular "had less to do with women choosing other women as sexual objects than with the degree to which lesbians, particularly butch women who in their very appearance defied strict adherence to prescribed gender roles, challenged what it was to be a woman in American society."[14] The example of the FLIC, however, with its focus on sexual object choice—and on the physical, erotic acts performed between people of the same sex, whether female or male—cautions against such a generalization. Occasional references to masculine characteristics or mannerisms are scattered throughout the interviews with lesbians, but it is clear that these were not linked, in the committee's view, to the sexual behavior of the women under investigation. In fact, investigators considered gender inversion a signifier of homosexuality much more frequently in their dealings with men, but even then it remained secondary to the issue of sexual practices.

During their search for homosexual teachers, committee investigators, led by R. J. Strickland, a former Tallahassee vice squad detective, were most interested in collecting details about the sexual histories of lesbians and gay men. In questioning suspects, the intent was to determine the degree to which each individual under investigation was a "practicing" homosexual based on the acts she or he had performed. Members of the FLIC hoped to be able to assess what sort of threat the teacher posed to students as well as the likelihood that she or he could return to or assume a "normal" heterosexual life. As a 1959 committee report put it, "With respect to medical prognosis for cure (stopping homosexual conduct), homosexuals fall into several classes, depending upon such factors as age of the individual, the degree and extent of his homosexual conduct, the period of time over which he has engaged in same, and his individual desire to correct his sexual deviation."[15] This model rested on the belief that an individual progressed over time—by increased association with other homosexuals and participation in the full spectrum of sex acts—toward "real" homosexuality, at which point any hope for a cure vanished. The figure of the authentic homosexual was thus essentialized and assigned supposedly immutable characteristics, most important a desire to recruit others by enticing them into homosexual acts. For legislators serving on the committee, the key to determining a person's location within this continuum was sex. Investigators scrutinized virtually every conceivable aspect of their targets' sex lives, compelling them to describe specific acts and the role played in each (most often articulated by questioners as "passive" or "aggressive") to measure their potential for corrupting Florida's children.

In tracing the process by which this state institution both interpreted and constructed homosexual identity, the question of motives remains central. To be sure, as other historians have shown, there was an element of political posturing at work among anticommunists.[16] In Florida after World War II, the small group of rural, conservative, white Democrats who held disproportionate power in the state legislature watched warily as new residents poured into the state from outside the South, swelling the population in urban areas and bringing in ever-larger numbers of moderate Democrats and Republicans. As this happened, a movement arose in support of reapportioning the state legislature. At the same time, lawmakers faced the challenge of funding Florida's university and public school systems to keep pace with the postwar population explosion. Between 1940 and 1950, Florida's total population increased by 46 percent. In 1950, the urban population stood at 1.8 million and the rural population at approximately 1 million. Ten years later, the number of urban dwellers had doubled to 3.7 million, while those in rural areas constituted 1.3 million.[17] Much of this upsurge came from massive immigration from the South, the Midwest, and the Northeast. While the Panhandle and the northeastern part of Florida retained a largely white, Protestant populace and saw virtually no population growth, the southern and central urban areas attracted residents from a wide range of ethnic and religious groups, including Cubans, Spaniards, Italians, Greeks, and Jews. Although for most of the twentieth century Florida had boasted a higher rate of urbanization than any other state in the South, the differences between city and countryside became increasingly pronounced after World War II. Diversified economies and peoples often translated into different values and priorities.

Most important, in such urban centers as Miami, Tampa–St. Petersburg, and Orlando, recent arrivals to the state tended to be less invested in maintaining white supremacy than were conservative, native-born Floridians who lived in farming communities and small towns.[18] Confronted by change and by a direct challenge to their political power, legislators representing rural counties created and supported the Johns Committee in order to demonstrate their concern for the safety and welfare of the citizens of Florida—and in particular, the youth of Florida. The committee in effect advertised the "problem" of increasing homosexuality and then promised to solve it—all in the public eye. Although the one-on-one questioning occurred behind the closed doors of motel rooms, principals' offices, and police interrogation rooms all across Florida, the results—arrests, resignations, firings—made news and were strategically detailed by the committee in press releases and biennial reports to the legislature.

The disproportionate attention to male homosexuals mirrored the widespread belief that men—even gay men—were naturally more predatory and aggressive, and therefore more dangerous, than women. As Estelle Freedman has argued, the popular stereotype of the gay man as child molester first took hold in the 1930s, when astronomical unemployment among male breadwinners disrupted family life and led many men to abandon their traditional roles of husband and father. The figure of the unattached male became a symbol of economic and social breakdown. Moreover, psychiatric research into sexual deviance and sensationalized newspaper accounts of sex crimes (often those committed against children) together stirred the public's fears both of the "inadequately masculine" (the homosexual) and the "hypermasculine" (the "sexual psychopath").[19] Each was believed to prey upon children as a way of satiating his unnatural desires. Further, the common practice of anonymous sex between men in public places such as parks and restrooms made them at once a more visible presence within local communities and a more vulnerable target of the police and the criminal justice system.

Still, given the popular conflation of male homosexuality and pedophilia that persisted well into the postwar years and beyond, it is significant that lesbian teachers were also viewed by the Johns Committee as a menace to young people. There was some precedent for these fears in the lesbian pulp novels that proliferated in the 1950s and in the psychiatric and social scientific literature of the day. Here lesbians were represented as masculine, voracious, maladjusted hunters of heterosexual women and girls.[20] In his 1957 work, *Is Homosexuality a Menace?* one freelance investigator and armchair psychologist proclaimed: "The female who is held captive by a lesbian soon becomes a mental and physical wreck, who suffers from the pangs of hell and remorse, but like a drug addict she is unable to ward off the repeated advances made towards her by the octopus-like creature who continually saps her strength."[21] It was not a stretch for committee members to imagine such monsters running amok in Florida's schools and universities.

The FLIC's 1959 report to the legislature spelled out its mission and beliefs, as well as listing the "facts" gathered from the University of Florida investigation. The report set the tone and direction for the four-year search for homosexuals that followed. The "salient facts" developed during the inquiry included that the extent of homosexual activity in the state's school system was "absolutely appalling"; that homosexual activity became "more prevalent as you progress upward on the educational scale"; that lesbians and gay men were "almost entirely the product of environment and practice" and "made by training, not born"; and, most significantly, that homosexuals recruited others to their way of life—and that "a surprisingly large percentage of young people are subject to be influenced into homosexual practices if thrown into contact with homosexuals who desire to recruit them."[22] Committee members drew upon a cultural narrative of pathology that explained the causes of and solutions to the "problem" of homosexuality and simply fit their findings into it. Moreover, by citing the authority of medical and psychiatric experts to bolster its case against homosexual teachers, the committee sought to affirm its own legitimacy and adopt a dispassionate, objective, "scientific" approach to the problem.

The chief investigator first encountered lesbians in 1959, when, armed with the names of several women jailed for "crimes against nature," he paid a visit to the State Prison for Women in Lowell, a small, north-central Florida town. He hoped to extract information about any lesbian teachers they might know. Of the twelve women whose testimony appears in the committee's papers, most had only a middle-school education. Some worked in bars, some in factories, others hustled for a living. Many were regulars in the bar scene in Tampa and St. Petersburg.[23] One twenty-year-old from Texas told Strickland that she had "never heard of a woman being homosexual until I came to Florida and there were a lot of them on Skid Row and I guess that's what got me interested in it."[24] In spite of the class differences that may have separated them from teachers, their networks overlapped enough so that these women were able to offer Strickland the names of several lesbians who were currently teaching in Florida's public schools and even one female dean at Hillsborough High School in Tampa.

During these initial prison interviews Strickland limited himself to identifying teachers and eliciting information about the harm they caused young people. For example, at one point in his questioning of a reluctant witness, he assured her that he was not interested in the details of her personal life but wanted only to gather facts in order to "help some small child that has become involved in this thing." His view of the central problem—that of adults corrupting "small children"—echoed a familiar refrain from the sex-crime panics of the 1930s and the homosexual panics of the 1950s; now, however, lesbians were given attributes previously reserved for male sexual deviants. Another woman, thirty-nine years old and serving time on drug charges, recounted what she saw as an unhealthy attachment between her seventeen-year-old daughter and two physical education teachers who lived together. According to the mother, the girl "seemed to want to do things for them more than for me, and that sort of annoyed me a little." She "was over there quite a lot, more than I thought was proper." At the end of the interview the woman confessed that she "never really, you know, just discussed it in a serious way with her to try and get her to—." Frustrated, she stopped herself in midsentence and said simply, "I know that I really feel that these teachers did have an influence on her. I really do."[25]

Such testimony reaffirmed the committee's beliefs about homosexuals in general and specifically the similarities between lesbians and gay men in their capacity to contaminate young people. It also led Strickland, two years later, to the Florida Industrial School for Girls in Ocala.[26] A prisoner at Lowell had testified that, as a student at the girls' reform school, she had had sex with an instructor there. She had also informed Strickland that sex among students was common and that teachers and administrators did little, if anything, to prevent it.

A 1956 compilation of articles from the Acorn (the school's newsletter), titled *Our Way of Life at the Florida Industrial School for Girls,* was put together by the staff as a showcase of students' writing and drawing talents. It also outlined the rules and regulations governing the lives of young women sent there by the state's juvenile courts but suggested that they had a positive experience. Students followed a rigid schedule of work and classes. They awoke each morning at 6:30. Work crews were outside by 7, while those attending classes enjoyed a more leisurely breakfast period between 7:30 and 8:20. School began promptly at 9 and lasted until 4:15, with an hour for the noonday meal. A former resident described the outdoor work detail, in which girls would "dig ditches, haul logs and bum them, clear fields, mow lawns." This backbreaking labor was reserved for students who failed to receive passing grades—based on academic performance but with special attention as well to standards of behavior, among them obedience, attitude, neatness, courtesy, honesty, and initiative. Indoor work assignments included kitchen detail, cleaning school buildings, sewing, and laundry. As the school newsletter explained, girls "are not sent [here] for punishment but rehabilitation and training." A student's "length of stay is solely dependent upon her behavior." [27]

The Acorn's cheerful descriptions of hard physical labor and its sunny outlook on the rigorous grading system, dress code, and methods of discipline fail to account for the stories of rampant lesbianism told by Yvonne Marie Ross, age fifteen, to R. J. Strickland on July 15, 1961, at her Gainesville home. Upon her release from the institution (after several unsuccessful escape attempts) in 1960, she relayed these tales to her father, who in turn contacted Charley Johns and alerted him to the problems of aggressive lesbian students, rumored lesbian instructors, and administrators looking the other way. He enclosed a copy of his daughter's seven-page narration of the goings-on, including a long list of girls' first names, courtship rituals, types and degrees of sexual behavior, and lists of code words and numbers used by students to avoid detection by watchful housemothers and teachers.[28] Coupled with testimony taken at Lowell back in 1959, this was more than enough to convince Johns to send his chief investigator to Gainesville.

According to Yvonne, she arrived at the reform school on October 15, 1959, and spent the first two weeks in isolation. This "orientation period as we prefer to call it," noted the Acorn, was designed to get each newcomer "accustomed to 'our way of living.'" After two weeks, the girl would be assigned to a work crew and to a "cottage." [29] Yvonne ended up at the Office Building, which housed not only the administrative offices and staff quarters but also two large dormitory rooms on the second floor, each containing thirteen beds. A red-tile hallway lined by pink walls connected the rooms. She spent six weeks there with girls ranging in age from eleven to seventeen. Here she claimed to have witnessed a wide variety of lesbian behavior. During her interview, Yvonne read aloud to Strickland from her handwritten account: "They start out with sweetying. This is courtship. They have making-out parties, where a group of partners are together. They kiss and fondle each other. The more making-out parties they have, the more they want each other. They finally get to the stage where nothing else matters but sex." Her tone became increasingly dramatic as she relayed her perceptions of what her schoolmates did with each other and why: "When the girls get worse off, they go through an act that we call eating. They put lips to vagina and they tongue each other; they kiss and fondle each other in any way and anywhere that will give them a better feeling. This becomes more serious until it's done every chance possible." [30] This characterization of lesbians as insatiable and obsessed with sex, as well as the use of the phrase "worse off" to denote degrees of affliction, mirrored the ideas that the committee had been absorbing and using in its campaign against homosexual teachers. This witness offered a firsthand account of the process by which "normal" girls became introduced to homosexual activity, and their progression through various stages of sexual experience to the final, inevitable fate of becoming a "real" lesbian.

The young witness declared at the outset of her interview that she had "heard rumors" of lesbianism at the school before she was sent there. Yvonne confirmed to the investigator the truth of such talk: "They just show off, I mean they are skilled at doing it, they know how to do things like that, they just lead it on, do it slow until you finally agree with them." [31] The depiction of the gradual process of transforming girls into lesbians—imperceptibly, yet with deliberation and purpose, in a way that seemed to make resistance impossible—sat squarely in line with the committee's understanding of how homosexuals, regardless of their sex, were "made." Moreover, this interpretation explained away her own complicity in any same-sex erotic behavior. It also rang true in the context of the cold war anxiety over indoctrination—the fear of an arrogant ("they just show off"), devious "other" seducing the innocent with cold calculation.

In addition to explaining "our way of living" in prose, the Acorn also featured comic strips drawn by students. These are crude, superficially upbeat renderings of daily life at the institution. One, "A Typical Saturday," shows two girls happily cleaning their room, helping their housemother, and hanging their clothes out to dry. Next, we see the pair sharing a shower during "Shower Time." After lunch and reading period, the girls prepare for "Movie Time." One demands of the other: "Be my partner for the show." They walk to and from the show holding hands, as do two other girls. The seemingly most innocuous frame has one girl exclaiming after supper: "Those hot dogs were good!" But in the light of Yvonne's testimony, her words take on a comical double meaning: "In order to gain a sexual feeling," she told Strickland, her schoolmates used "such items as bottles, hot dogs, or pickles, etc. or anything possible." [32] Taken as a whole, the comic strips reflect the culturally acceptable bonds between young women. They are unselfconscious representations of affection and closeness among adolescent girls, which were beginning to fall under suspicion at midcentury. But they also hint at what the committee and the wider culture saw as the potentially sinister turns these bonds could take at a same-sex institution with inadequate supervision. They reveal the spaces that were made available for forging romantic and sexual relationships between girls. The Johns Committee viewed these spaces as highly dangerous, as contributing to and even encouraging the spread of lesbianism among teenage girls in Florida.

Yvonne's testimony likely confirmed Strickland's suspicions about the aggressively corrupting influence of lesbians, but her stories revolved around sex among students. She said little of the transgressions of instructors there. One person identified at the women's prison in Lowell, however, was Vonceil Benson, a teacher living in Jacksonville Beach who had received a master's degree from Florida State University in 1958 and who had taught at the Florida Industrial School for Girls. Strickland interviewed her on January 11, 1961, at the Duval County Courthouse in the company of the personnel director of the county superintendent's office. When the investigator read the testimony of a former student who claimed to have had sex with Benson, she coolly denied the accusation: "Mr. Strickland, if I may say so, this testimony of girls who made their way through life by lying, is hardly disturbing to me. It may be disturbing to you but I certainly do not take this seriously from these girls." She went on, "Now any adults you have, I would take that more seriously but I certainly don't think that anyone can make any such statements about me in truth." In fact, Benson went on to deny any sexual relationships with women. When asked if she had ever gone to Jimmy White's or the Knotty Pine (two gay bars in Tampa) she admitted to visiting the latter, but merely "as a joke—just looking at the people that congregated there."[33] Clearly she knew enough about these bars to understand why it would be a "joke," or a spectacle, to go there and watch the crowds.

On the same day of Benson's interview, Strickland also questioned her roommate, a physical education teacher at Fletcher High School in Jacksonville. This woman also proclaimed ignorance about homosexuality in general, stated that she had never been approached by a homosexual, and finally denied knowledge of any gay or lesbian teachers in the state. She did, however, offer up the names of several women she knew who played on a softball team in Jacksonville but added that she did not think they had ever been in any "trouble."[34] There is no way to prove that Benson and her roommate were lesbians (or lovers), or to determine whether Benson ever crossed the student-teacher line at the reform school. The clues in both women's statements, however—references to women's softball, familiarity with gay bars, teaching physical education—in addition to having been identified as lesbians by other women, confirmed more benign stereotypes of female homosexuality. Strickland, for one, took for granted that he would find lesbians who played softball and who populated physical education departments around the state. That he chose not to pursue more of them again testifies to a comparative disinterest or at least ambivalence toward lesbians, in favor of targeting men.

The transcripts of the interrogations conducted by Strickland, which comprise thousands of pages of his interactions with suspected, accused, and admitted homosexuals, offer more than fragmentary evidence about gay communities; they provide as well a glimpse into the workings of the right-wing imagination. They also reveal a wide range of responses to investigators' prying: from outright refusal to answer (which was rare, because witnesses were commonly told that if they did not cooperate they would be subjected to a public hearing), to delicate sidestepping and careful hedging (a more common occurrence), to remorseful confession (also fairly common). We can only speculate about the mix of emotions that washed over each woman in the interrogation room (often set up in any location that was convenient: a motel room, a police station, a county superintendent's office) as she faced investigators, along with administrators, her principal, and police officers. A tape recorder sat on the table beside her. The scene must have had the awful air of official legitimacy, although in fact Strickland lacked the legislative and constitutional authority to compel witnesses to testify. Virtually none of the committee's victims realized this, or even if they did, the threat of public disclosure proved in the majority of cases to be a powerful deterrent against resistance.

The record contains few clues as to how investigators first devised their blueprint for interrogating suspected homosexuals, but over the course of five years they followed it closely.[35] The interview began with the basic facts of the witness's life—full name, age, educational background, and employment history. But the inquisitor wasted little time in getting to the point, asking some variation of "Have you ever been involved in any type of homosexual activity?" (a new twist on the familiar "Are you now or have you ever been a member of the Communist Party?"). This was commonly followed by a question about being "approached" by a homosexual. Because the committee operated on the premise that female and male homosexuals were predatory by nature, this was a critical step in determining whether the witness had been the aggressor or the victim. The woman was then asked how long she had been involved in homosexual activity. Often Strickland asked leading questions, as when he queried one suspect: "Do you feel like you've acquired this through association and environment, the places that you were staying around, and the people with whom you were associating?"[36]

Then came the coaxing and prodding to elicit intimate details about sexual activity and exhaustive naming of specific acts performed with other women. On October 10, 1962, for example, Strickland questioned a thirty-year-old physical education teacher from Brentwood Junior High in Pensacola named Lala Swicegood. A former roommate of the band director at the school (who had just resigned from her position earlier that day after being interrogated),

Swicegood had taught there for three years. At first she claimed ignorance of any matters relating to homosexuality. When the chief investigator informed her: "This Committee holds in file statements from other people who state that they have had such practices with you," she denied the accusations outright. As happened often, Strickland turned off the tape recorder and spoke with the witness off the record. When the interview resumed, Swicegood's story changed dramatically. After she admitted to some "petting" with her ex-roommate, the investigator prompted her:

Q. It was the injection of the finger into the vagina?
A. Correct.
Q. And the caressing of the breast and kissing?
A. Correct.
Q. And were you the aggressive partner or was she the aggressive partner?
A. Worked both ways.
Q. It was mutually?
A. Yes.

Not satisfied with these answers, and in his own mind likely searching for every possible shred of "evidence" upon which to build a case against Swicegood, Strickland followed up:

Q. Did you reach a climax, a sexual climax through these arts?
A. I have never reached a climax.
Q. Through this type of act. Did _____ reach a climax?
A. Yes.
Q. Did you, how did you know she did?
A. Her reactions.
Q. Did she tell you she did?
A. Yes.
Q. You could see the fluid?
A. Yes.[37]

Why dwell on the particulars of lesbian sex? Why did investigators need to know whether two women reached orgasm during sex? What larger truth was revealed to Strickland by finding out that Lala Swicegood saw her partner's "fluid"? In addition to the committee's claim of determining objective facts about individual women and men, and measuring the likelihood of "saving" them from homosexuality, other explanations are possible. We can smile knowingly about the stereotype of the straight male's penchant for girl-on-girl sex fantasies (and certainly this may have played a part in it) or wonder whether questioners received voyeuristic thrills in the interrogation room, but neither theory fully accounts for the similar detail with which gay men were asked to recite their sexual activities. It is also possible that this obsessive, prurient line of questioning served as a form of ritual humiliation, by forcing women and men to sit surrounded by an assortment of authorities—representatives of the state, the law, the public school system—and confess their participation in acts that were reviled by the wider culture, by religious tradition, and by the medical profession.

Strickland did not limit this approach to adults. In October 1961, he traveled to the tiny Panhandle town of Wewahitchka to look into complaints about a group of girls at the local high school who had formed something called the Bongo Club. Rumor had it around school that they were lesbians. Of the many girls he interviewed, his discussion with a thirteen-year-old named Opal stands out. She told him that she had kissed girls in the past but felt reluctant to divulge anything more. Finally, persuaded by Strickland's cajoling, Opal described an unpleasant sleepover incident with one of her friends:

Q. Were you sleeping in pajamas?
A. Gowns.
Q. Did she try to put her hand under your gown?
A. Yes, sir.
Q. Did she ever succeed in getting her hand under your clothes?
A. Yes, sir.
Q. And that's when you stopped her?
A. Yes, sir.
Q. Did she say anything about using her mouth on any part of your body?
A. No, sir.
Q. She didn't mention that?
A. No, sir.
Q. Did she try to put your breasts in her mouth?
A. No, sir.
Q. Just felt of those with her hands?
A. Yes, sir.
Q. Did this arouse any emotion in you at all?
A. No, sir.
Q. In other words, you had no feeling about it, is that true?
A. Well, I felt like slapping her.[38]

Intrusive as his tactics may seem, Strickland no doubt saw them as necessary to get to the root of the problem. Homosexuality, he and the committee believed, needed to be understood in all stages, and even more important, it had to be stopped early on. Groups such as the Bongo Club only reinforced this notion. As he explained to another uncooperative Wewahitchka teen, "People just don't want to be affiliated or connected with someone who is involved in this type of thing. Your friends just shed off of you, away from you. They dodge you. They don't want to be seen publicly. So if we can save any of these people from this type of future life, don't you think you're doing them a deed instead of doing them harm?" [39]

As Strickland, his assistant investigators, and law enforcement officers across the state scoured public schools and universities for female and male homosexuals, they contributed to the hardening of a cold war model of sexual deviance that located it as a tool for political subversion, a sign of mental illness, and a grave threat to young people and to the future of the state. The construction of a singular "homosexual menace" necessitated that lesbians be explained as sharing certain characteristics with their male counterparts, namely an aggressive sexuality and a compulsive need to seduce and recruit youth. The impulses that guided the strange career of the Johns Committee had less to do with political expediency than with the prevailing national and regional obsession with subversion, indoctrination, and conspiracy. To a certain extent we must take the committee at its word: its leaders seemed honestly to believe that homosexual teachers threatened the normal, healthy development of Florida's youth, just as did communists and Negroes in integrated schools. We can pause along the way, scratch our heads in bemusement, and question the unconstitutional and morally objectionable lengths to which the FLIC went during its near-decade-long reign, or the degree to which committee members had their own personal or psychosexual stake in the proceedings. But at the same time, we must accept, with caution, the Johns Committee's own understanding of its crusade to protect Florida's children and closely examine the processes by which it was carried out.

The FLIC used medical and popular ideas about homosexuals and communists to argue that lesbians and gays did untold damage in the classroom, where vulnerable, naive adolescents were easy prey to recruitment into homosexuality by deviant teachers. In so doing, the committee built upon the postwar emphasis on the nuclear family, normative heterosexuality, and traditional gender roles as a critical line of defense against communism at home. Elaine Tyler May and other scholars have underscored the importance of this domestic ideology within cold war culture. But they have, for the most part, ignored how anxieties about integration, communism, and homosexuality played out on the battleground of public schools and universities.[40] The FLIC is one of the most dramatic examples of a state-funded organization's attempts to combat these "enemies" on the schoolhouse steps: keeping white schools white; monitoring teachers' political beliefs and curricula; and rooting out lesbians and gay men from the classroom.

In Florida, the ideas about homosexuality formulated in medical and social science literature and in the popular media were filtered by institutions of the state and put into action, used against real women and men, with real consequences. The Johns Committee grouped lesbians and gay men together into the category of "homosexual"; constructed them as a menace to youth; and proceeded to interrogate, spy, and prod in order to confirm widely held beliefs about homosexuality. During the cold war, the figures of the lesbian and the male homosexual took on added meanings that transformed earlier fears of gender inversion or child molestation; they now became infused with even more insidious associations of security risks, infiltrators, recruiters. Schools and universities, already sites of a reinvigorated battle for racial justice, also came to be seen as places where homosexuals and communists could operate covertly to undermine the morals of young people. The FLIC chose schools as the grounds upon which to unleash an aggressive attack against these subversives, who could be rooted out only after shining the light of medical and scientific "truth" on their sexual habits and histories, only after exposing them as sex-crazed seducers of the young. It is in this imposition of an alternative "reality" on to the lesbian and gay subculture—one that distorted and altered it— that we can locate the fears, values, and ideologies that informed and shaped the politics and culture of the postwar years.

This cold war construction of the "homosexual menace," further complicated by race and politics, came to conflate a wide range of individuals into a single category that was founded on the model of sexual predation and the need to recruit new, preferably young members (as an unnatural means of "reproducing" themselves). Thus, when Johns Committee investigators and legislators sought out—and found—lesbian teachers, they employed the same list of questions about sexual experiences and used the same rationale for removing them from public schools, as they did with gay male suspects. But just as importantly, the committee often overlooked or downplayed the presence of white and Black lesbians in the midst of what they perceived as a greater danger—civil rights activists and homosexual men.

This ambivalence about lesbians enabled investigators to claim that they were as potentially harmful as their male counterparts yet to treat them as something of an afterthought. This was likely the result of an underlying recognition that, in fact, female and male homosexuals were different. Gay men's access to and uses of public space were markedly different from lesbians, as were their social networks, dating rituals, sexual practices and attitudes, and a whole host of other cultural markers. The FLIC and the larger culture feared and exaggerated the threat of gay male promiscuity and public sexuality and thus subjected gay men to more frequent arrest and prosecution (and in the case of the Johns Committee, removal from schools and universities).[41] Yet, in the name of state and national security, they also attempted to place lesbians—in the military, civil service, and public schools—within the new cold war construction of the homosexual, fittingly, through guilt by association.

Notes

1. Donna Penn, "The Sexualized Woman: The Lesbian, the Prostitute, and the Containment of Female Sexuality in Postwar America," in *Not June Cleaver: Women and Gender in Postwar America, 1945–1960*, ed. Joanne Meyerowitz (Philadelphia: Temple University Press, 1994), 365, 369.

2. One infamous scandal over young men and prostitution, which received national attention in the mid-1960s, is dissected in John Gerassi, *The Boys of Boise: Furor, Vice, and Folly in an American City* (New York: Macmillan Co., 1966). For its part, the Johns Committee worked with the Dade County Police Department and Sheriff's Office to uncover a male prostitution and pornography ring in 1961. Investigators questioned more than a dozen teenage boys who had worked the streets of Miami and treated them as victims of predatory adult male homosexuals.

3. Of the approximately 320 suspected homosexuals whose interviews appear in the committee's files, roughly 255 are men and 65 are women.

4. Madeline Davis and Elizabeth Lapovsky Kennedy, "Oral History and the Study of Sexuality in the Lesbian Community: Buffalo, New York, 1940–1960," *Feminist Studies* 12 (spring 1986): 7–26; Estelle B. Freedman, "The Prison Lesbian: Race, Class, and the Construction of the Aggressive Female Homosexual, 1915–1965," *Feminist Studies* 22 (summer 1996): 397–423; Margaret Gibson, "The Masculine Degenerate: American Doctors' Portrayals of the Lesbian Intellect, 1880–1949," *Journal of Women's History* 9 (winter 1998): 78–103; Susan K. Cahn, "From the 'Muscle Moll' to the 'Butch' Ballplayer: Mannishness, Lesbianism, and Homophobia in U.S. Women's Sport," *Feminist Studies* 19 (summer 1993): 343–68; and Jennifer Terry, *An American Obsession: Science, Medicine, and Homosexuality in Modern Society* (Chicago: University of Chicago Press, 1999).

5. John D'Emilio, "The Homosexual Menace," in his *Making Trouble: Essays on Gay History, Politics, and the University* (New York: Routledge, 1992); Allan Berube, *Coming Out under Fire: The History of Gay Men and Women in World War II* (New York: Penguin Books, 1990); Geoffrey S. Smith, "National Security and Personal Isolation: Sex, Gender, and Disease in the Cold-War United States," *International History Review* 14 (June 1992): 307–37.

6. For a discussion of state anticommunist investigating committees, see M.J. Heale, *McCarthy's Americans: Red Scare Politics in State and Nation, 1935–1965* (Athens: University of Georgia Press, 1998); see also Ingrid Winther Scobie, "Jack B. Tenney and the 'Parasitic Menace': Anti-Communist Legislation in California, 1940–1949," *Pacific Historical Review* 43 (May 1974): 188–211; and Philip Jenkins, *The Cold War at Home: The Red Scare in Pennsylvania, 1945–1960* (Chapel Hill: University of North Carolina Press, 1999).

7. Johns to Mayor Abe Aronovitz, 7 Sept. 1954, quoted in James T. Sears, *Lonely Hunters: An Oral History of Lesbian and Gay Southern Life, 1948–1968* (Boulder: Westview Press, 1997), 22–23.

8. D'Emilio, "Homosexual Menace," 63.

9. James A. Schnur, "Closet Crusaders: The Johns Committee and Homophobia, 1956–1965," in *Carryin' On in the Lesbian and Gay South,* ed. John Howard (New York: New York University Press, 1997), 134.

10. Two works that explore the origins and effects of beliefs about the relationship among communism, civil rights activism, and sexual promiscuity are Robin D. G. Kelley, *Hammer and Hoe: Alabama Communists during the Great Depression* (Chapel Hill: University of North Carolina Press, 1990); and Kenneth O'Reilly, *"Racial Matters": The FBI's Secret File on Black America, 1960–1972* (New York: Free Press, 1989). The most concise accounts of the political demonization of lesbians and gay men after World War II are D'Emilio, "Homosexual Menace"; and Smith. See also John Howard, *Men Like That: A Southern Queer History* (Chicago: University of Chicago Press, 1999).

11. Charley E. Johns, "Homosexuality in Public Education" (Report of the FLIC, 1959), LeRoy Collins Administrative Correspondence, box 101, folder 16, Florida State Archives, Tallahassee. The belief that homosexuality was spreading appears in numerous committee reports and depositions.

12. James H. Jones, *Alfred C. Kinsey* (New York: Norton, 1997). See also Terry, chap. 9.

13. Edward Alwood, *Straight News: Gays, Lesbians, and the News Media* (New York: Columbia University Press, 1996), 23–26.

14. Donna Penn, "The Meanings of Lesbianism in Post-War America," *Gender and History* 3 (summer 1991): 201.

15. Johns, "Homosexuality in Public Education," 7.

16. See, for example, Richard M. Fried, *Nightmare in Red: The McCarthy Era in Perspective* (New York: Oxford University Press, 1990); and Earl Latham, *The Communist Controversy in Washington: From the New Deal to McCarthy* (Cambridge: Harvard University Press, 1966).

17. U.S. Bureau of the Census, Census of Population: 1950, vol. 2, Characteristics of the Population, pt. 10, Florida (Washington, D.C.: GPO, 1952), table 10; Census of Population: 1960, vol. 1, Characteristics of the Population, pt. 11, Florida (Washington, D.C.: GPO, 1963), table 13.

18. David R. Colburn and Richard K. Scher, *Florida's Gubernatorial Politics in the Twentieth Century* (Tallahassee: University Presses of Florida, 1980), 16–17.

19. Estelle B. Freedman, "'Uncontrolled Desires': The Response to the Sexual Psychopath, 1920–1960," in *Passion and Power: Sexuality in History,* ed. Kathy Peiss and Christina Simmons (Philadelphia: Temple University Press, 1989), 203.

20. Lillian Faderman, *Odd Girls and Twilight Lovers: A History of Lesbian Life in Twentieth-Century America* (New York: Penguin, 1991), 145–47; D'Emilio, "Homosexual Menace," 57–73.

21. Arthur Guy Mathews, *Is Homosexuality a Menace?* (New York: Robert M. McBride Co., 1957), 20.

22. Johns, "Homosexuality in Public Education," 3–4.

23. The transcripts of the prison interviews contain no clues as to the racial and

ethnic identity of the women questioned by Strickland, with the exception of one witness who stated that her father was Spanish.

24. Testimony, 19 Aug. 1959, Records of the Florida Legislative Investigative Committee (hereafter cited as FLIC Papers), Florida State Archives, box 7, folder 22, p. 137.

25. Testimony, 18 Aug. 1959, FLIC Papers, box 7, folder 22, pp. 54,127–28.

26. It is telling that, despite convincing evidence of teacher-student lesbian activity, Strickland waited for two years to follow up on the case. Lesbians were not high on the list of committee targets, and between 1959 and 1961 male homosexuals and Black activists in the civil rights movement took precedence.

27. *Our Way of Life at the Florida Industrial School for Girls* (Ocala, 1956), 4, Papers of the Florida Children's Commission, box 3, folder 6, Florida State Archives.

28. A copy of Ross's notes on the Florida Industrial School for Girls can be found in the FLIC Papers, box 9, folder 5.

29. *Our Way of Life,* 1.

30. Testimony, 15 July 1961, FLIC Papers, box 9, folder 5, pp. 18–19.

31. Testimony, 15 July 1961, p. 5.

32. *Our Way of Life,* 17; testimony, 15 July 1961, p. 18.

33. Vonceil Benson testimony, 11 Jan. 1961, FLIC Papers, box 8, folder 76, p. 4, 8.

34. Ibid, 9.

35. The committee employed junior investigators who occasionally questioned witnesses, both with and without R. J. Strickland. Mark Hawes, chief counsel to the committee, also was called upon to perform interrogations.

36. Testimony, 18 Aug. 1959, p. 54.

37. Lala Swicegood testimony, 10 Oct. 1962, FLIC Papers, box 10, folders 145, 146, pt. 1, p. 7; pt. 2, p. 3; ibid., box 10, folder 146, pt. 2, pp. 8–9.

38. Testimony, n.d., FLIC Papers, box 11, folder 130, p. 5.

39. Testimony, n.d., FLIC Papers, box 11, folder 123, p. 9.

40. Elaine Tyler May, *Homeward Bound: American Families in the Cold War Era* (New York: Basic Books, 1988); Ellen W. Schrecker, *No Ivory Tower: McCarthyism and the Universities* (New York: Oxford University Press, 1986).

41. John D'Emilio, Sexual Politics, Sexual Communities: The Making of a Homosexual Minority in the United States, 1940–1970 (Chicago: University of Chicago Press, 1983), chaps. 5 and 6.

"It Was Like All of Us Had Been Raped"

Sexual Violence, Community Mobilization, and the African American Freedom Struggle

Danielle L. McGuire

On Saturday, May 2, 1959, four white men in Tallahassee, Florida, made a pact, one of their friends testified in court later, to "go out and get a nigger girl" and have an "all night party." That evening, they armed themselves with shotguns and switchblades and crept up behind a car parked alongside a quiet road near Jake Gaither Park. At about 1:00 a.m. on May 3, Patrick Scarborough pressed a sixteen-gauge shotgun against the driver's nose and ordered Richard Brown and his companions out of the car. Dressed in formal gowns and tuxedoes, the four African Americans—all students at Florida A&M University who had spent the evening dancing at the Green and Orange Ball—reluctantly stepped out of the car. Scarborough forced the two black men to kneel, while his friend David Beagles held the two black women at knifepoint. When Betty Jean Owens began to cry, Beagles slapped her and told her to "shut up" or she "would never get back home." Waving his gun, Scarborough ordered Richard Brown and his friend Thomas Butterfield back in the car and told them to leave. As Brown and Butterfield began to move toward the car and then slowly drove away, Edna Richardson broke free and ran to the nearby park, leaving Betty Jean Owens alone with their attackers. Beagles pressed the switchblade to Owens's throat and growled, "We'll let you go if you do what we want," then forced her to her knees, slapped her as she sobbed, and pushed her into the backseat of their blue Chevrolet; the four men drove her to the edge of town, where they raped her seven times.[1]

Analyses of rape play little or no role in most histories of the civil rights movement, even as stories of violence against black and white men—from Emmett Till to Andrew Goodman, Michael Schwerner, and James Chaney—provide gripping examples of racist brutality.[2] Despite a growing body of literature that focuses on the roles of black and white women and the operation of gender in the movement, sexualized violence—both as a tool of oppression and as a political spur for the movement—has yet to find its place in the story of the African American freedom struggle.[3] Rape, like lynching and murder, served as a tool of psychological and physical intimidation that expressed white male domination and buttressed white supremacy. During the Jim Crow era, women's bodies served as signposts of the social order, and white men used rape and rumors of rape not only to justify violence against black men but to remind black women that their bodies were not their own.

African American women frequently retaliated by testifying about their brutal experiences. I argue that, from Harriet Jacobs to Ida B. Wells to the women of the present, the refusal of black women to remain silent about sexualized violence was part of a long-standing tradition. Black women described and denounced their sexual misuse, deploying their voices as weapons in the wars against white supremacy. Indeed, their public protests often galvanized local, national, and even international outrage and sparked campaigns for racial justice and human dignity. When Betty Jean Owens spoke out against her assailants, and when the local black community mobilized in defense of her womanhood in 1959, they joined in this tradition of testimony and protest.

The arrest, trial, and conviction of Owens's white rapists by an all-white jury marked a dramatic change in the relations between this tradition of testimony and a tradition of silence that Darlene Clark Hine has termed the "culture of dissemblance."[4] The verdict not only broke with southern tradition but fractured the philosophical and political foundations of white supremacy by challenging the relationship between sexual domination and racial inequality. For perhaps the first time since Reconstruction, southern black communities could imagine state power being deployed in defense of their respectability as men and women. As a result, the 1959 Tallahassee rape case was a watershed event that remains as revealing now as it was important then.

The sexual exploitation of black women had its roots in slavery. Slave owners, overseers, and drivers took advantage of their positions of power and authority to rape slave women, sometimes in the presence of their husbands or families. White slave owners' stolen access to black women's bodies strengthened their political, social, and economic power, partly because colonial laws made the offspring of slave women the property of their masters.[5] After the fall of slavery, when African Americans asserted their freedom during the interracial experiment in democracy that briefly characterized Reconstruction, former slaveholders and their sympathizers used violence and terror to reassert control over the social, political, and economic agency of freedpeople. At the heart of this violence, according to Gerda Lerner, rape became a "weapon of terror" to dominate the bodies and minds of African American men and women.[6]

"Freedom," as Tera Hunter notes, "was meaningless without ownership and control over one's own body." During Reconstruction and Jim Crow, sexualized violence served as a "ritualistic reenactment of the daily pattern of social dominance," and interracial rape became the battleground upon which black men and women fought for ownership of their own bodies. Many African American women who were raped or assaulted by white men fought back by speaking out. Frances Thompson told a congressional committee investigating the 1866 Memphis race riot that seven armed white men broke into her house on a Tuesday afternoon, "drew their pistols and said they would shoot us and fire the house if we did not let them have their way with us." Four of the men raped Frances, while the other three choked and raped sixteen-year-old Lucy Smith and left her close to death. In 1871, Harriet Simril testified in front of a congressional committee investigating Ku Klux Klan terror during Reconstruction that she was beaten and "ravished" by eight men in South Carolina who broke into her house to force her husband to "join the democratic ticket." Essic Harris, appearing before the same committee, reported that "the rape of black women was so frequent" in the postbellum South that it had become "an old saying by now." Ferdie Walker, who grew up during the height of segregation in the 1930s and 1940s in Fort Worth, Texas, remembered being "scared to death" by a white police officer who often exposed himself to her while she waited at the bus stop when she was only eleven years old. The sexual abuse of black women, she recalled, was an everyday occurrence. "That was really bad and it was bad for *all black girls*," she recalled.[7]

John H. McCray, editor of the *South Carolina Lighthouse and Informer,* reported that it was "a commonplace experience for many of our women in southern towns . . . to be propositioned openly by white men." He said, "You can pick up accounts of these at a dime a dozen in almost any community." African American women that I interviewed in Birmingham, Alabama, in March 2003 echoed Ferdie Walker's and McCray's comments. Nearly all of them testified about being sexually abused or intimidated by white men— particularly bus drivers, police officers, and employers.[8]

The acclaimed freedom fighter Fannie Lou Hamer knew that rape and sexual violence was a common occurrence in the segregated South. *For Freedom's Sake,* Chana Kai Lee's biography of Hamer, is one of the few histories of the modern-day civil rights movement that openly deals with and documents the legacy of sexual assault. Hamer's grandmother, Liza Bramlett, spoke often of the "horrors of slavery," including stories about "how the white folks would do her." Bramlett's daughter remembered that "this man would keep her as long as he want to and then he would trade her off for a little heifer calf. Then the other man would get her and keep her as long as he want—she was steady having babies—and trade her off for a little sow pig." Twenty of the twenty-three children Bramlett gave birth to were products of rape.[9]

Hamer grew up with the clear understanding that a "black woman's body was never hers alone." If she was at all unclear about this lesson, the forced hysterectomy she received in 1961 and the brutal beating she received in the Winona, Mississippi, jail in 1963 left little room for confusion. After being arrested with other Student Nonviolent Coordinating Committee (SNCC) activists for desegregating a restaurant, Hamer received a savage and sexually abusive beating by the Winona police. "You bitch," one officer yelled, "we going to make you wish you was dead." He ordered two black inmates to beat Hamer with "a long wide blackjack," while other patrolmen battered "her head and other parts of her body." As they assaulted her, Hamer felt them repeatedly "pull my dress over my head and try to feel under my clothes." She attempted to pull her dress down during the brutal attack in order to "preserve some respectability through the horror and disgrace." Hamer told this story on national television at the Democratic National Convention in 1964 and continued to tell it "until the day she died," offering her testimony of the sexual and racial injustice of segregation.[10]

By speaking out, whether it was in the church, the courtroom, or a congressional hearing, black women used their own public voices to reject the stereotypes used by white supremacists to justify economic and sexual exploitation, and they reaffirmed their own humanity. Additionally, African American women's refusal to remain silent offered African American men an opportunity to assert themselves as *men* by rallying around the protection of black womanhood. Many other men, however, remained silent since speaking out was often dangerous, if not deadly. Most important, women's testimonies were a political act that exposed the bitter ironies of segregation and white supremacy, helped to reverse the shame and humiliation rape inflicts, and served as catalysts in mobilizing mass movements.[11]

Only after local and national groups were organized, black women's testimony began to spark public campaigns for equal justice and protection of black womanhood. In this respect, World War II served as a watershed for African Americans—especially in the South. Black women's testimony and the willingness of black leaders to protect black womanhood must be viewed as part of these resistance movements. For example, in Montgomery, Alabama, the organizational infrastructure that made the Montgomery bus boycott possible in 1955 stemmed in part from decades of black women's activism and a history of gendered political appeals to protect black women from sexual assault. The majority of leaders active in the Montgomery Improvement Association in 1955 cut their political teeth demanding justice for black women who were raped in the 1940s and early 1950s.[12]

In 1944, the kidnapping and gang rape of Mrs. Recy Taylor by six white men in Abbeville, Alabama, sparked what the *Chicago Defender* called "the strongest campaign for equal justice to Negroes to be seen in a decade." Taylor, a twenty-four-year-old African American woman, was walking home from the Rock Hill Holiness Church near Abbeville on September 3 when a carload of six white men pulled alongside her, pointed a gun at her head, and ordered her to get into the car. They drove her to a vacant patch of land where Herbert Lovett pointed his rifle at Taylor and demanded she get out of the car and "get them rags off or I will kill you and leave you down here in the woods." Lovett held her at gunpoint while each of the white men took turns "ravishing" her. After the men raped her, Lovett blindfolded her, pushed her into the car, and dropped her off in the middle of town. That night, Recy Taylor told her father, her husband, and Deputy Sheriff Lewey Corbitt the details of her harrowing assault.[13]

Within a few weeks, the Committee for Equal Justice for Mrs. Recy Taylor formed and was led on a local level by Rosa Parks, E. D. Nixon, Rufus A. Lewis, and E. G. Jackson (editor of the *Alabama Tribune*), all of whom later became pivotal figures in the Montgomery bus boycott. By utilizing the political infrastructure designed to defend the Scottsboro boys a decade earlier and employing the rhetoric of democracy sparked by World War II, Parks, Nixon, and their allies secured the support of national labor unions, African American organizations, women's groups, and thousands of individuals who demanded that Gov. Chauncey Sparks order an immediate investigation and trial. "The raping of Mrs. Recy Taylor was a fascist-like, brutal violation of her personal rights as a woman and as a citizen of democracy," Eugene Gordon, a reporter for the *New York Daily Worker,* wrote in a pamphlet about the case; "Mrs. Taylor was not the first Negro woman to be outraged," he argued, "but it is our intention to make her the last. White-supremacy imitators of Hitler's storm troopers [will] shrink under the glare of the nation's spotlight." Gordon closed by universalizing the rape: "The attack on Mrs. Taylor was an attack on all women. Mrs. Taylor is a Negro . . . but no woman is safe or free until all women are free."[14] Few African Americans were surprised when the Henry County Grand Jury twice failed to indict the white men—despite the governor's belief that they were, in fact, guilty. Still, Recy Taylor's testimony launched a national and international campaign for equal justice that must not be ignored.[15]

Five years later, African Americans in Montgomery, Alabama, rallied to the defense of a twenty-five-year-old black woman named Gertrude Perkins. On March 27, 1949, Perkins was walking home when she was arrested for public drunkenness and attacked by two white police officers in uniform. After forcing her into their squad car, they drove her to the edge of town and raped her repeatedly at gunpoint. Afterwards, they threw her out of their car and sped away. Somehow, she found the strength to stagger into town, where she went directly to Rev. Solomon Seay Sr.'s house. Awaking him, she told him the details of her brutal assault through sobs and tears. "We didn't go to bed that morning," remembered Seay; "I kept her at my house, carefully wrote down what she said, and later had it notarized." Seay sent Perkins's horror story to the syndicated columnist Drew Pearson, who let the whole country know what happened in his daily radio address before Montgomery's white leaders knew what hit them.[16]

The leaders of the local Interdenominational Ministerial Alliance, the Negro Improvement League, and the National Association for the Advancement of Colored People (NAACP), led by E. D. Nixon and the Reverend Mr. Seay, joined together to form the Citizens Committee for Gertrude Perkins. Mary Fair Burks and her newly formed Women's Political Council may have been involved since one of their early goals was to "aid victims of rape." Although the community mobilized on behalf of Perkins, a grand jury failed to indict the assailants a few weeks later, despite running the full process of "the Anglo-Saxon system of justice." Still, Joe Azbell, editor of the *Montgomery Advertiser*, thought Gertrude Perkins, who bravely spoke out against the men who raped her, "had as much to do with the bus boycott and its creation as anyone on earth." The Perkins protest did not occur in isolation. In February 1951, Rufus A. Lewis, whose influence was crucial to the 1955 campaign, led a boycott of a grocery store owned by Sam E. Green, a white man, who was accused of raping his black teenage babysitter while driving her home. Lewis, a World War II veteran and football coach at Alabama State University, organized other veterans and members of the Citizens' Coordinating Committee in the successful campaign to close the store and bring Green to trial.[17]

The 1955 Montgomery bus boycott itself can be viewed as the most obvious example of the African American community coming to the rescue of a black woman, Rosa Parks, though not because of rape. When Parks sat down in a bus's "no-man's land" and was arrested for refusing to give up her seat to a white man, Montgomery blacks found the *perfect* woman to rally around. "Humble enough to be claimed by the common folk," Taylor Branch notes, Rosa Parks was "dignified enough in manner, speech, and dress to command the respect of the leading classes." Rosa Parks fit the middle-class ideals of "chastity, Godliness, family responsibility, and proper womanly conduct and demeanor" and was the kind of woman around which all the African Americans in Montgomery could rally. It is clear that her symbolic role as icon of virtuous black womanhood was decisive in Montgomery. Rev. Martin Luther King Jr.'s first speech at Holt Street Baptist Church stressed this point. "And since it had to happen," the young preacher told the crowd, "I'm happy it happened to a person like Mrs. Parks. Nobody can doubt the height of her character; nobody can doubt the depth of her Christian commitment."[18]

By selecting Rosa Parks as the symbol of segregation instead of other, less exemplary black women who had been arrested on buses earlier in 1955, black leaders in Montgomery embraced the "politics of respectability" and adhered to what Darlene Clark Hine calls the "culture of dissemblance" as a matter of political necessity amidst the burning white backlash that the 1954 Supreme Court decision in *Brown v. Board of Education* sparked.[19] The White Citizens' Councils, a kind of uptown Ku Klux Klan, led the movement for massive resistance to school integration by relying heavily on sexual scare tactics and white fears of racial amalgamation. As a result, any gender or racial impropriety on the part of African Americans could be viewed as threatening the social order. For the supporters of segregation, "integration always meant miscegenation." Headlines in the *Citizens' Council* warned that "mixed marriage," "sex orgies," and accounts of black men raping white girls were "typical of stories filtering back from areas where racial integration is proceeding 'with all deliberate speed.'"[20]

In this environment, respectability and dissemblance required that silence surround black sexuality, a "cult of secrecy" that helped counter negative stereotypes and kept the inner lives of African Americans hidden from white people. This self-imposed reticence, Hine argues, "implied that those [African American women] who spoke out provided grist for detractors' mills and, even more ominously, tore the protective cloaks from their inner selves."[21] Silence as strategy did not emerge in the mid-twentieth century; it had been a staple of black clubwomen's politics since Reconstruction, when whites continued to use racist violence and sexual abuse to shore up white supremacy.

The culture of dissemblance does not mean there was an unbroken wall of silence. There are moments in history when the pain of violation or the opportunity for justice forced women to come forward to speak out against their abusers. Yet this code of secrecy, a political imperative during the Montgomery bus boycott, helped create a void in the historical record. As a result, violence toward black women has not been as "vividly and importantly retained in our collective memory," Elsa Barkley Brown claims, as the lynching of and violence against black men.[22]

In many ways, this culture of dissemblance silenced more than the survivors of rape; it also trained historians of the black freedom struggle to ignore the subject of black women's dissemblance. Over the past two decades, historians have sharpened their focus on the gendered meanings of respectability, but they have lost sight of the role rape and the threat of sexual violence played in the daily lives of African American women as well as within the larger black freedom struggle.[23] Yet throughout the Jim Crow South, African American women such as Recy Taylor in 1944, Gertrude Perkins in 1949, and Betty Jean Owens in 1959 refused to shield their pain in secrecy, thereby challenging the pervasiveness of the politics of respectability. Following in the footsteps of their Reconstruction-era counterparts, they testified about their assaults, leaving behind critical evidence that historians must find the courage to analyze.

To be sure, black women's refusal to remain silent about sexual violence during and after slavery suggests that the culture of dissemblance functioned in tension and in tandem with a tradition of testimony. Even after respectability became the key to black women's symbolic place in the civil rights movement in the early 1950s, however, a number of African American women continued to speak out publicly about being raped, and African American community members rallied to their defense. Unfortunately, too many of these stories remain buried in the archives, yellowing newspapers, or the memories of the survivors, contributing to the historical amnesia about black women's experiences. And Montgomery, Alabama, was not the only place in which attacks on black womanhood fueled protests against white supremacy. Betty Jean Owens's experience in Florida is evidence that a significant story has been missed across the South.

When the four armed white men in Tallahassee forced Thomas Butterfield and Richard Brown to get into their car and drive away, leaving Betty Jean Owens and Edna Richardson at the mercy of their assailants, the two black men did not abandon them but drove around the corner and waited. As the blue Chevrolet disappeared down the street, Brown and Butterfield hurried back to the scene. Edna Richardson, the black woman who was able to get away, saw her friends from her hiding spot, called out to them, and then ran to the car. Hoping to save Owens, the Florida A&M students rushed to the local police station to report the crime.[24]

Similar situations in other southern towns had typically left African Americans without police aid. The officer on duty that night in Tallahassee was Joe Cooke Jr., a nineteen-year-old intern from the all-white Florida State University. Much to the surprise of the three black students, he agreed to look for Owens and her assailants. After a lengthy search, one of the students finally spotted the blue Chevrolet and shouted, "That's it!" It was just after 4:00 a.m. Deputy Cooke turned on his flashers and drove alongside the car. Attempting to escape, the kidnappers led Cooke "twisting and turning through the dark streets of Tallahassee at speeds up to 100 miles per hour." One of the white men suggested "dumping the nigger," but William Collinsworth replied, "we can't now, he's on our tail." Finally, Collinsworth pulled the car to the curb, grabbed his shotgun, and got out of the car. Deputy Cooke drew his pistol and ordered all four to line up against the car or, he threatened, "I will shoot to kill."[25]

As they waited for assistance from Cooke's supervisor, they heard muffled screams coming from the car. Richard Brown and Deputy Cooke peered through the rear window and saw Betty Jean Owens, bound and gagged, lying on the backseat floorboards. Brown tried to help her out of the car, but, as her feet touched the ground, she collapsed. Cooke drove Betty Jean Owens and her friends to the local colored hospital at Florida A&M while Deputy Sheriff W. W. Slappey arrested the four white men and drove them to the jailhouse. [26]

Laughing and joking on the way to the police station, the four white men apparently did not take their arrest seriously, nor did they think they had done anything wrong. Collinsworth, for example, worried less about the charges against him than about the safety of his car. Deputy Sheriff Slappey revealed his disgust when he handed the men over to Sheriff Raymond Hamlin Jr. "They all admitted it," Slappey said; "they didn't say why they did it and that's all I'm going to say about this dirty business." William Collinsworth, David Beagles, Ollie Stoutamire, and Patrick Scarborough confessed in writing to abducting Betty Jean Owens at gunpoint and having "sexual relations" with her. When Sheriff Hamlin asked the men to look over their statements and make any necessary corrections, David Beagles, smiling, bent over the table and made one minor adjustment before he and his friends were hustled off to jail.[27]

If the four white men did not take their arrests seriously, students at Florida A&M University flew into a rage. Many of them were veterans of the Tallahassee bus boycott in 1957, a Montgomery-inspired campaign that highlighted the trend in students' preference for direct action rather than the more respectable and slower litigation favored by the NAACP throughout the 1940s and 1950s. When the students heard news of the attack on Owens and the subsequent arrest of four white men, a small group planned an armed march to city hall to let city officials know that they were willing to protect black womanhood the same way whites "protected" white womanhood—with violence or at least a show of force. Mainstream student leaders persuaded them that an armed march was "the wrong thing to do" and patched together a "Unity" demonstration on Sunday, May 3, only twelve hours after Betty Jean Owens was admitted to the hospital and the four white men were taken to jail.[28]

Fifteen hundred students filled Lee Auditorium, where Clifford Taylor, president of the Student Government Association, said he "would not sit idly by and see our sisters, wives, and mothers desecrated." Using language white men in power could understand, student leaders professed their "belief in the dignity, respect, and protection of womanhood" and announced that they would petition the governor and other authorities for a "speedy and impartial trial." [29]

Early the next day, a thousand students gathered in the university's grassy quadrangle with signs, hymns, and prayers aimed at the national news media, which sent out stories of the attack across the country. The students planned to show Tallahassee and the rest of the nation that white men could no longer attack black women without consequence. Student protesters held signs calling for "Justice"; other posters declared, "It could have been YOUR sister, wife, or mother." Some students linked the attack in Tallahassee to larger issues related to the black freedom struggle: two students held up a poster depicting scenes from Little Rock, Arkansas, which read, "My God How Much More of This Can We Take." [30]

It was the deeply personal violation that rape inflicts, however, that gave the students their focus. Patricia Stephens Due remembered feeling helpless and unsafe. She recalled, "We all felt violated, male and female. It was like all of us had been raped." The student leader Buford Gibson, speaking to a crowd, universalized the attack when he said, "You must remember it wasn't just one Negro girl that was raped—it was all of Negro womanhood in the South." [31] By using Betty Jean Owens as a black Everywoman, Gibson challenged male students to rise up in protest and then placed the protection of black womanhood in their hands. Gibson's exhortation inspired students at Florida A&M to maintain their nonviolent demonstration, unlike white men who historically used the protection of white womanhood to inspire mob violence against black men.

At about the same time, white men in Poplarville, Mississippi, used the protection of womanhood as justification for the lynching of Mack Charles Parker, a black man who was charged with the kidnapping and rape of a twenty-four-year-old white woman who could barely identify him in a police lineup. On April 25, 1959, two days before his trial, a group of eight to ten white men obtained keys to Parker's unguarded jail cell, savagely beat him, and then dragged him down three flights of stairs and out of the building while he screamed "I'm innocent." Federal Bureau of Investigation (FBI) agents located Parker's bloated body floating in the Pearl River on May 4, 1959, just two days after four white men gang-raped Betty Jean Owens. [32] The Parker lynching cast a shadow over Tallahassee, brutally reminding the black community that white women's bodies were off limits, while the bodies of black women were fair game.

Accelerating media coverage, student-led protests, and a threat to boycott classes at Florida A&M forced Judge W. May Walker to call members of the grand jury into special session in Tallahassee on May 6, 1959. Over two hundred black spectators, mostly students, squeezed into the segregated balcony at the Leon County Courthouse to catch a glimpse of Betty Jean Owens and her attackers before they retreated into the secret hearing. Still undergoing hospital treatment for injuries inflicted during the attack and for "severe depression," Owens was accompanied to the courthouse by a nurse, the hospital administrator, and her mother. [33]

Gasps and moans emanated from the balcony when, after two hours behind closed doors, William Collinsworth, David Beagles, Patrick Scarborough, and Ollie Stoutamire emerged, calmly faced the judge, and pleaded innocent to the charge of rape, making a jury trial mandatory. African Americans in the balcony roared with disapproval. Dr. M. C. Williams, a local black leader, shouted, "four colored men would be dead if the situation had been reversed. It looks like an open and shut case." Defense attorneys for Collinsworth and Scarborough argued for a delay, insisting that public excitement threatened a fair trial, but Judge Walker ignored their objections. For the first time in Florida history, a judge sent the white defendants charged with raping an African American woman back to jail to await their trial. Echoing the sentiments of the people around him, a young boy traced "we want justice" in the dust on the railing of the segregated balcony.[34]

Justice was the last thing the black community expected. In the thirty-four years since Florida began sending convicted rapists to the electric chair instead of the gallows, the state had electrocuted thirty-seven African Americans charged with raping white women. Before this, Florida led the country in per capita lynchings, even surpassing such notoriously violent states as Mississippi, Georgia, and Louisiana. From 1900 to 1930, white Floridians lynched 281 people, 256 of whom were African American. Throughout its history, Florida never executed or lynched a white man for raping a black woman. In this respect, Florida followed the entire region. Florida's violent history included the "little Scottsboro" case involving Samuel Shepard, Walter Irvin, and Charles Greenlee, black men accused of raping a white woman in Groveland, Florida, in 1949. After the U.S. Supreme Court overturned their guilty verdicts in 1951, Sheriff Willis McCall picked up Shepard and Irvin from Raiford State Prison to transfer them back to the county. On the way there, McCall pulled to the side of the road and asked the two handcuffed men to change the tire and then shot them both in the chest. He radioed his boss and muttered, "I got rid of them; killed the sons of bitches." Walter Irvin survived the shooting, but Samuel Shepard died that day.[35]

In Tallahassee, memories of the "little Scottsboro" case hung over many members of the African American community in 1954 when the state electrocuted Abraham Beard, a seventeen-year-old black youth accused of raping a white woman. Apart from the races of the accuser and the accused, the Beard case featured a cast of characters almost identical to that of the Tallahassee case five years later: an all-white jury had tried and convicted Beard in the same courtroom where Betty Jean Owens faced her attackers. Judge W. May Walker presided, and for Betty Jean Owens, that foundation began to crumble.[36]

News that four white men would actually face prosecution for raping a black woman plunged both whites and blacks into largely unfamiliar territory. It not only highlighted the bitter ironies of segregation and "social equality" but allowed African Americans to publicize them. According to the *Pittsburgh Courier,* the arraignment made the "arguments for white supremacy, racial discrimination, and segregation fall by the wayside" and the arguments against school desegregation seem "childishly futile." "Time and again," another newspaper editor argued, "Southern spokesmen have protested that they oppose integration in the schools only because it foreshadows a total 'mingling of the races.' The implication is that Negroes are hell-bent for intimacy, while whites shrink back in horror." "Perhaps," the writer argued, "as Lillian Smith and other maverick Southerners have suggested, it is not quite that simple." [37]

While prominent members of the white community expressed their shock and horror at the rape, they continued to stumble into old narratives about race and sex. The indictment helped incite age-old fears of miscegenation and stereotypes of the so-called black beast rapist. William H. Chafe argues that "merely evoking the image of 'miscegenation' could often suffice to ring the alarm bells that would mobilize a solid phalanx of white resistance to change." For example, white women around Tallahassee began to speak openly about their "fear of retaliation," while young white couples avoided parking "in the country moonlight lest some Negroes should be out hunting in a retaliatory mood." Reflecting this fear as well as the larger concern with social equality, Florida legislators, like other lawmakers throughout the South, passed a series of racist bills designed to segregate children in schools by sex in order to circumvent the *Brown v. Board of Education* decision and "reduce the chances of interracial marriage." [38] The extent to which the myth of the black beast rapist was a projection of white fears was never clearer than when the gang rape of a black woman conjured up terror of *black-on-white* rape. The fact that the black community rallied around Betty Jean Owens and her womanhood threatened white male power—making the myth of the black savage a timely political tool.

Black leaders from all over the country eagerly used the rape case for their own political purposes as well. Most focused on the lynching of black men in similar cases, placing the crime against Betty Jean Owens into a larger dialogue about the power struggle between black and white men. As A. D. Williams, a black businessman in Tallahassee, put it, "the white men are on the spot." Rev. Dennis H. Jamison felt that the indictment of four white men indicated a "better chance at Justice than any involving the races in the South," but, he added, "still no white men have ever been executed." Elijah Muhammad, leader of the Nation of Islam, expressed this viewpoint forcefully. Using almost the exact same language as white supremacists, he accused the "four devil rapists" of destroying the "virginity of our daughters." "Appeals for justice," he fumed, "will avail us nothing. We know there is no justice under the American flag." [39] Nearly all the editorials in major black newspapers echoed his sentiments.

Ella Baker, director of the Southern Christian Leadership Conference (SCLC), felt that the evidence in the Tallahassee case was so strong that "not even an all white Florida jury could fail to convict." Reminding whites of their tendency to mete out unequal justice toward black men, she warned, "with memories of Negroes who have been lynched and executed on far less evidence, Negro leaders from all over the South will certainly examine every development in this case. . . . What will Florida's answer be?" The *New York Amsterdam News* called for equal justice, noting that the "law which calls for the death sentence does not say that Negro rapists should be punished by death and white rapists should be allowed to live." The *Pittsburgh Courier* bet on acquittal, despite the fact that the case "is as open and shut as a case can be." [40]

Martin Luther King Jr., at the annual SCLC meeting in Tallahassee a few days after the indictment, praised the student protesters for giving "hope to all of us who struggle for human dignity and equal justice." But he tempered his optimism with political savvy, calling on the federal government to force the country to practice what it preached in its Cold War rivalry with the Soviet Union. "Violence in the South can not be deplored or ignored," King declared, directing his criticism at President Dwight D. Eisenhower; "without effective action, the situation will worsen." [41] King exploited a political context in which America's racial problems were increasingly an international issue. The British Broadcasting Corporation (BBC) broadcast segments of the Florida A&M University student speeches condemning the rape and racial injustice, while newspapers throughout Europe closely watched the case unfold. "It is ironical that these un-American outrages occur as our representatives confer in Geneva to expand democratic principles . . . it might well be necessary and expedient," King threatened, "to appeal to the conscience of the world through the Commission on Human Rights of the United Nations." This international angle was a strategy shared by mainstream integrationists, leftist radicals, and black nationalists alike. Audley "Queen Mother" Moore, leader of the Universal Association of Ethiopian Women, Inc., petitioned the United Nations Human Rights Commission in person to end the "planned lynch terror and willful destruction of our people." She tied issues of race, gender, sex, and citizenship together by demanding Justice Department assistance for Betty Jean Owens's rape case, an FBI investigation of the Mack Charles Parker lynching, and basic voting rights. [42]

Robert F. Williams, militant leader of the Monroe, North Carolina, chapter of the NAACP, suggested African Americans stand their ground and defend themselves. The Parker lynching, the Tallahassee rape case, and two Monroe, North Carolina, cases in which white men stood accused of attacking black women forced Williams to defend racial pride and black womanhood. On May 6, 1959, B. F. Shaw, a white railroad engineer, had been exonerated on charges of beating and kicking a black maid at the Hotel Monroe, even though he did not show up for court. That same day, white jurors giggled while Mrs. Mary Ruth Reed, a pregnant black woman, testified that Lewis Medlin, a white mechanic, beat and sexually assaulted her in front of her five children. Medlin's attorney argued that he was just having a little fun, that he was married to a "lovely white woman . . . the pure flower of life," whom he would not dare leave for "that." The jury deliberated for less than ten minutes before returning the not guilty verdict. It was the defilement of black womanhood and the humiliation of black manhood that inspired Williams to hurl his infamous vow to "meet violence with violence." His exhortation set off a national controversy, culminating at the 1959 NAACP convention where Executive Secretary Roy Wilkins suspended Williams for his remarks. Williams defended his position by citing the tragedy in Tallahassee. Had the "young black men who escorted the coed who was raped in Tallahassee" been able to defend her, Williams argued, they would have been justified "even though it meant that they themselves or the white rapists were killed." [43]

Roy Wilkins shared Williams's gender and race politics but not his methods for achieving them. In a letter to Florida governor LeRoy Collins, Wilkins invoked the lynchings of Mack Charles Parker and Emmett Till, noting that the victims' skin color alone kept them from receiving a fair trial and that their deaths threatened political embarrassment at home and abroad. "Full punishment has been certain and swift in cases involving a white victim and a Negro accused," he said, "but the penalty has neither been certain nor heavy in cases involving a Negro victim and a white accused. . . . For these reasons," Wilkins warned, "all eyes will be upon the state of Florida." [44]

On June 11, 1959, at least four hundred people witnessed Betty Jean Owens face her attackers and testify on her own behalf. Owens approached the witness box with her head bowed. She wore a white embroidered blouse and a black-and-salmon checked skirt with gold earrings. The African American press had cast her in the role of respectable womanhood by characterizing her as a God-fearing, middle-class college co-ed "raised in a hard-working Christian household" with parents devoted to the "simple verities of life that make up the backbone of our democracy." Unlike white women, who were often able to play the role of "fair maiden" before a lynch mob worked its will on their alleged attackers, Betty Jean Owens had to tell her story knowing that the four white men who raped her might go unpunished. Worse, Owens had to describe the attack in front of hundreds of white people in a segregated institution that inherently denied her humanity. [45] Though it may seem unnecessary, even lurid, to bear witness to the details of her testimony today, it is crucial that we hear the same testimony that the jurors heard. Owens's willingness to identify those who attacked her and to testify against them in public broke the institutional silence surrounding the centuries-long history of white men's sexual violation of black women, made a white southern judge and jury recognize her womanhood and dignity, and countered efforts to shame or stereotype her as sexually unchaste. As a result, her testimony alone is a momentous event.

Owens remained strong as state prosecutor William Hopkins asked her to detail the attack from the moment she and her friends left the Florida A&M dance. This she did powerfully and emotionally. "We were only parked near Jake Gaither Park for fifteen minutes," she said, when "four white men pulled up in a 1959 blue Chevrolet." She identified Patrick Scarborough as the man who pressed the shotgun into her date's nose and yelled, "Get out and get out now." When Owens began to cry, David Beagles pressed a "wicked looking foot long knife" to her throat and forced her down to the ground. He then pulled her up, slapped her, and said, "You haven't anything to worry about." Owens testified that Beagles pushed her into the car and then "pushed my head down in his lap and yelled at me to be quiet or I would never get home." "I knew I couldn't get away," she stated; "I thought they would kill me if I didn't do what they wanted me to do." [46]

She continued with the horrid details. As the car pulled off the highway and into the woods, "the one with the knife pulled me out of the car and laid me on the ground." Owens was still wearing the gold and white evening gown as they tugged at the dress and "pulled my panties off." She pleaded with them to let her go and not hurt her when Beagles slapped her again. She then told how each one raped her while she was "begging them to let me go . . . I was so scared, but there was nothing I could do with four men, a knife, and a gun . . . I couldn't do anything but what they said." Owens testified that the men eagerly watched one another have intercourse with her the first time around but lost interest during the second round. "Two of them were working on taking the car's license plate off," she said, "while the oldest one" offered her some whiskey. "I never had a chance to get away," she said quietly; "I was on the ground for two or three hours before the one with the knife pushed me back into the car." After the men had collectively raped her seven times, Ollie Stoutamire and Beagles blindfolded her with a baby diaper and pushed her onto the floorboards of the car, and they all drove away. When she heard the police sirens and felt the car stop, she pulled the blindfold down and began yelling for help. After police ordered the men out of the car, Owens recalled, "I was so scared and weak and nervous that I just fell on the ground and that is the last thing I remember." [47]

Betty Jean Owens then described the physical injuries she sustained from the attack. "One arm and one leg," she said, "were practically useless" to her for several days while she was at the hospital. A nurse had to accompany her to the grand jury hearing a few days after the attack, and she needed medication for severe depression. She also had a large bruise on her breast where the bodice stay from her dress dug into her skin as the four men pressed their bodies into hers. Asking her to identify some of the exhibits, Hopkins flipped open the switchblade used the night of the attack, startling some of the jurors. Immediately the four defense attorneys jumped up and vehemently called for a mistrial, arguing that "by flashing the knife Mr. Hopkins tried to inflame the jury and this prejudiced their clients' constitutional rights to a fair trial." Judge Walker denied their motion, signaling Hopkins to continue. When asked whether she consented, Owens clearly told Hopkins and the jury, "No sir, I did not."[48]

Defense attorneys grilled Owens for more than an hour, trying to prove that she consented because she never struggled to get away and that she actually enjoyed the sexual encounter. "Didn't you derive any pleasure from that? Didn't you?" the attorney Howard Williams yelled repeatedly. He kept pressing her, "Why didn't you yell or scream out?" "I was afraid they would kill me," Owens said quietly. She showed signs of anger when Williams repeatedly asked if she was a virgin in an attempt to characterize her as a stereotypical black jezebel. Owens retained her composure, refused to answer questions about her chastity, and resisted efforts to shame her. The defense made a last-ditch effort to discredit Owens by arguing that, if the young men had actually raped her and threatened her life, she would have sustained more severe injuries.[49]

Proceeding with the state's case, William Hopkins called the doctors, both black and white, who examined Owens after the attack. They told the jury that they found her in a terrible condition and that she "definitely had sexual relations" that caused the injuries that required a five-day hospital stay. Richard Brown, Thomas Butterfield, and Edna Richardson took the stand next. They all corroborated Owens's testimony, adding that after the attack Owens was "crying, hysterical, and jerking all over." Brown testified that Scarborough pointed the shotgun into his car window and ordered him and Butterfield to kneel in front of its headlights. Defense attorney John Rudd asked Brown on cross-examination, was it a "single or double barrel shotgun they pointed into your car?" Brown replied, "I only saw one barrel, sir." Laughter rolled down from the balcony, upsetting Rudd. "I can not work with this duress and disorder at my back, a boy's life is at stake here!" Judge Walker called for order and reprimanded the spectators.[50] When the prosecution finally rested its case at 8:30 P.M. on June 11, defense attorneys moved for a directed verdict of acquittal, claiming the state failed to prove anything except sexual intercourse. Judge Walker vigorously denied the motion and insisted the defense return the next day to present their defense.

Amid a sea of people in the tiny courtroom, David Beagles, an eighteen-year-old high school student, sat rigidly on the stand, pushing a ring back and forth on his finger as he answered questions from his attorney. His mother buried her head in her arms as she listened to her son tell the jury his side of the story. Beagles testified that he had a knife and William Collinsworth had a shotgun. The four of them were out "looking around for Negroes who had been parking near Collinsworth's neighborhood and bothering them." When they came upon the Florida A&M students, Beagles admitted holding the switchblade but then said he put it away when he saw they were dressed in formal wear. He admitted that they ordered Brown and Butterfield to drive away but insisted that he "*asked* the girls to get into the car." He denied the rape, arguing that Owens consented and even asked them to take her "back to school to change her dress." Under cross-examination, Beagles admitted that he "pushed her, just once . . . not hard," into the car, that he said, "If you do what we want you to, we'll let you go," and that he blindfolded her with a diaper after the attack. Defense attorney Howard Williams then asked Judge Walker to remove the jury as Beagles detailed the confession he made the night of the crime. Williams argued that when police officers arrested the young men, they "were still groggy from a night of drinking," making their confessions inadmissible. Under Hopkins's cross-examination, however, Beagles admitted that he was not pressured to say anything, that his confession was voluntary, and that he actually looked over the written statement and made an adjustment.[51]

Patrick Scarborough, who admitted that he was married to a woman in Texas, testified that he had intercourse with Owens twice but emphatically denied using force. When Hopkins questioned him, Scarborough admitted that Owens pleaded, "please don't hurt me," but he insisted that she offered "no resistance." He denied kissing her at first and then said he kissed her on the neck while he had sex with her.[52]

Defense attorneys focused on discrediting Owens instead of defending their clients because the prosecution repeatedly drew self-incriminating information from them. State prosecutor Hopkins argued that "they simply have no defense." Defense attorneys tried to use each man's ignorance to prove his innocence, highlighting their low IQ's and poor educations. When that failed, they detailed the dysfunctional histories of each defendant, as though to diminish the viciousness of the crime by offering a rationale for the men's depravity. Character witnesses for William Collinsworth, for example, described his sordid home life and drinking problem. Nearly every member of Collinsworth's family took the stand, spilling sorrowful stories about their poverty and dysfunction. His sister, Maudine Reeves, broke down on the stand and had to be rushed to the hospital. His wife, Pearlie, told the jury through sobs and tears that he was "not himself when he was drunk," but when he was sober "you couldn't ask for a better husband." On the stand, she failed to mention what her letter to the judge had made explicit: that her husband regularly beat her. When that did not seem to work, defense attorneys switched gears and attempted to portray their clients as reputable young men who were incapable of rape. Friends and family members all testified that these young men "were good boys," and that in particular Ollie Stoutamire, a cousin of Tallahassee police chief Frank Stoutamire, had "nothing but pure and moral intentions." [53]

Finally, the defense appealed to the jury's prejudices. Collinsworth blamed his actions on the "Indian blood" pulsing through his veins; the Pensacola psychiatrist Dr. W. M. C. Wilhoit backed him up when he argued, "It is a known fact that individuals of the Indian race react violently and primitively when psychotic or intoxicated." When Collinsworth added alcohol to his "Indian blood," Wilhoit argued, "he was unable to discern the nature and quality of the crime in question." The attorney for Ollie Stoutamire, city judge John Rudd, blamed "outside agitators." The defendants are "being publicized and ridiculed to satisfy sadists and people in other places," Rudd yelled during closing arguments. "Look at that little skinny, long legged sixteen-year-old boy. Does he look like a mad rapist who should die . . . should we kill or incarcerate that little boy because he happened to be in the wrong place at the wrong time?" [54]

In their summations to the jury, defense attorneys S. Gunter Toney and Harry Michaels followed Rudd's lead. Michaels insisted that "the crime here is insignificant . . . the pressure, clamor, and furor are completely out of proportion." Pointing to Scarborough, Michaels told the jury, "his motives, intentions, and designs that night were wholesome, innocent and decent." The fact that Owens could "have easily walked ten feet into the woods where nobody could find her," Michaels said, proved she consented. Waving her gold and white gown in front of the jury, he pointed out that it was "not soiled or torn," which he said proved no brutality was involved. Finally, he called for an acquittal, arguing that the jury could not possibly convict on the basis of "only one witness—the victim, and confessions that admitted only one fact—sexual intercourse." Sitting in the segregated balcony, Charles U. Smith, a sociologist at Florida A&M University, said he gasped when he heard Howard Williams yell, "Are you going to believe this nigger wench over these four boys?" [55]

In his summation, prosecuting attorney William Hopkins jumped up, grabbed the shotgun and Betty Jean Owens's prom dress, and appealed to the jury for a conviction. "Suppose two colored boys and their moron friends attacked Mrs. Beagles' daughter . . . had taken her at gunpoint from a car and forced her into a secluded place and regardless of whether they secured her consent or not, had intercourse with her seven times, leaving her in such a condition that she collapsed and had to be hospitalized?" Betty Jean Owens, he said, "didn't have a chance in the world with four big boys, a loaded gun and a knife. She was within an inch of losing her life. . . . She was gang-raped SEVEN times." "When you get to the question of mercy," he told the jury, "consider that they wouldn't even let that little girl whimper."[56]

Restless spectators, squeezed into every corner of the segregated courthouse, piled back into their seats when jurors emerged after three hours of deliberation with a decision. An additional three hundred African Americans held a silent vigil outside. A. H. King, the jury foreman and a local plantation owner, slowly read aloud the jury's decision for all four defendants: "guilty with a recommendation for mercy." The recommendation for mercy saved the four men from the electric chair and, according to the *Baltimore Afro-American*, "made it inescapably clear that the death penalty for rape is only for colored men accused by white women." A. H. King defended the mercy ruling by arguing that "there was no brutality involved" and insisted, implausibly enough, that the decision would have been the same "if the defendants had been four Negroes."[57] Judge Walker deferred sentencing for fifteen days, cleared the courtroom, and sent the four white men to Raiford prison.

African Americans who attended the trial quietly made their way home after the bittersweet verdict. Betty Jean Owens's mother told reporters that she was "just happy that the jury upheld my daughter's womanhood." Rev. A. J. Reddick, former head of the Florida NAACP, snapped, "If it had been Negroes, they would have gotten the death penalty." "Florida," he said, "has maintained an excellent record of not veering from its pattern of never executing a white man for the rape of a Negro," but he acknowledged that the conviction was "a step forward." Betty Jean Owens showed a similar ambivalence in an interview by the *New York Amsterdam News*. "It is something," she said; "I'm grateful that twelve white men believed the truth, but I still wonder what they would have done if one of our boys raped a white girl."[58]

Florida A&M students, who had criticized Butterfield and Brown for failing to protect black womanhood a week earlier, were visibly upset after the trial. In fact, letters to the editors of many African American newspapers condemned the two men and all black men for failing to protect "their" women. Mrs. C. A. C. in New York City felt that all Negro men were "mice" and not worthy of respect because "they stand by and let the white men do anything they want to our women." She then warned all black men that they "would never have freedom until [they] learn to stand up and fight." In a letter to the *Baltimore Afro-American,* a black man accepted her challenge: "unless we decide to protect our own women," he argued, "none of them will be safe." Some African American women felt they should protect themselves. A white woman sent her black maid home one day after she came to work with a knife, "in case any white man came after her," reported the *Tallahassee Democrat*. Still, many felt that "someone should have burned."[59]

Despite their anger at the unequal justice meted out, some African Americans in the community considered the guilty verdict a victory. The Reverend C. K. Steele Jr., head of the Tallahassee chapter of the SCLC, said it showed progress, reminding others that four white men "wouldn't have even been arrested twenty years ago." The Reverend Leon A. Lowery, state president of the Florida NAACP, saw a strategy in the mercy recommendation. He thought that it could help "Negroes more in the long run" by setting a precedent for equal justice in future rape cases.[60] After Judge Walker handed down life sentences to the four white men, some African Americans in Tallahassee applauded what they felt was a significant step in the right direction; many others, however, exhibited outrage. Roy Wilkins openly praised the verdict as a move toward equal justice but acknowledged in a private letter the "glaring contrast that was furnished by the Tallahassee verdict." In light of the recent lynching of Mack Charles Parker, no one really had to wonder what would have happened had the attackers been black. Editors of the *Louisiana Weekly* called the trial a "figment and a farce" and insisted that anyone who praised the verdict "confesses that he sees nothing wrong with exacting one punishment for white offenders and another, more severe for others."[61]

Any conviction was too much for some whites who felt that sending four white men to jail for raping a black woman upset the entire foundation of white supremacy. Many believed the guilty verdict was the result of a Communist-inspired NAACP conspiracy, which would ultimately lead to miscegenation. Letters to Judge Walker featured a host of common fears and racist stereotypes of black men and women. Fred G. Millette reminded the judge that a conviction "would play into the hands of the Warren Court, the NAACP, and all other radical enemies of the South . . . even though the nigger wench probably had been with a dozen men before." Mrs. Laura Cox wrote to Judge Walker that she feared this case would strengthen desegregation efforts, posing a direct threat to white children who might attend integrated schools. "If the South is integrated," she argued, "white children will be in danger because the Negroes carry knives, razors, ice picks, and guns practically all the time." Petitioning Judge Walker for leniency, Mrs. Bill Aren reminded him to remember that "Negro women like to be raped by the white men" and that "something like this will help the Supreme Court force this low bred race ahead, making whites live and eat with him and allow his children to associate with the little apes, grow up and marry them."[62]

It is ironic that a rape case involving a black woman and four white men would conjure up images of the black brute chasing white women with the intent to mongrelize the white race. The Tallahassee case attests to the persistence of such images decades after Reconstruction, when the mythological "incubus" took flight, justifying mob violence and a reign of terror throughout the South. Anxieties about the black beast rapist and fears of miscegenation conveniently surfaced when white men feared losing their monopoly on power. As Frederick Douglass noted nearly a century earlier, the myth of the black man as a rapist was an "invention with a well defined motive." [63] The rape of Betty Jean Owens reminds us that the maintenance of white supremacy relied on *both* the racial and sexual domination of black men *and* women.

While the verdict was likely the confluence of localized issues—a politically mobilized middle-class African American community, the lower-class status of the defendants (who were politically expendable), Florida's status as a "moderate" southern state dependent on northern tourism, and media pressure—it had far-reaching consequences. [64] The Tallahassee case focused national attention on the sexual exploitation of black women at the hands of white men, leading to convictions elsewhere that summer. In Montgomery, Alabama, Grady F. Smith, a retired air force colonel, was sentenced to fourteen months of hard labor for raping a seventeen-year-old African American girl. In Raleigh, North Carolina, Ralph Lee Betts, a thirty-six-year-old white man, was sentenced to life imprisonment for kidnapping and molesting an eleven-year-old African American girl. And in Burton, South Carolina, an all-white jury sent a white marine named Fred Davis to the electric chair—a first in the history of the South—for raping a forty-seven-year-old African American woman. In each case, white supremacy faltered in the face of the courageous black women who testified on their own behalf. [65]

Betty Jean Owens's grandmother recognized the historic and political significance of the verdicts. "I've lived to see the day," she said, "where white men would really be brought to trial for what they did." John McCray, editor of the *South Carolina Lighthouse and Informer,* wondered if the convictions in Tallahassee and elsewhere pointed to "defensive steps" taken by the South to "belatedly try to disprove that it discriminates against colored people." Still, he realized the importance of guilty verdicts. "This forced intimacy," he argued "goes back to the days of slavery when our women were the chattel property of white men." For McCray, the life sentences indicated a new day: "Are we now witnessing the arrival of our women? Are they at long last gaining the emancipation they've needed?" [66]

John McCray's connection between the conviction of white men for raping black women and black women's emancipation raises important questions that historians are just beginning to ponder. How did the daily struggle to gain self-respect and dignity, rooted in ideas of what it meant to be men and women, play out in the black freedom struggle? It is not just a coincidence that black college students, struggling for their own identity and independence, sparked the sit-in movement soon after Betty Jean Owens was brutally raped. In Tallahassee, Patricia Stephens Due, who felt that the rape symbolized an attack on the dignity and humanity of all African Americans, organized the city's first Congress of Racial Equality (CORE) chapter just six weeks after Owens's trial. Florida A&M CORE members launched an uneventful sit-in campaign that fall, but, like other black students throughout the South, successfully desegregated local lunch counters, theaters, and department stores in the spring of 1960. The students later led the "jail, no bail" tactic popularized by SCLC and SNCC.[67] While the rape alone may not have been the galvanizing force that turned students into soldiers for freedom, the sexual and racial dynamics inherent in this case speak to larger themes in the African American freedom struggle.

The politics of respectability—Betty Jean Owens's middle-class background, her college education, and her chastity—may have enabled African Americans on the local and national level to break through the "culture of dissemblance" and speak out against her rape. But it was the convergence of the politics of respectability, Owens's testimony, and African Americans' growing political influence on the national and international stage in the late 1950s that made the legal victory possible. Still, the long tradition of black women's testimony, stretching back to slavery and Reconstruction, makes it clear that some elements of the Tallahassee case were not aberrations. The testimonies and trials of Betty Jean Owens, Gertrude Perkins, and Recy Taylor, to name just a few, bear witness to these issues, forcing historians to reconsider the individual threads that make up the fabric of African American politics. Black women not only dissembled where it was necessary but testified where it was possible. Not only silence but often protest surrounded the sexualized violence against African American women. If we are fully to understand the role of gender and sexuality in larger struggles for freedom and equality, we must explore these battles over manhood and womanhood, frequently set in the context of sexualized violence, that remain at the volatile core of the modern civil rights movement.

Notes
This article would not have been possible without the gracious historians, teachers, family, and friends who always seemed willing to go out of their way to provide encouragement, support, and intellectual engagement. For this I am eternally grateful. Thank you especially to Steven Lawson, Nancy Hewitt, Tim Tyson, and Steve Kantrowitz and the Harmony Bar Writers Collective, all of whom spilled gallons of ink on this essay. They are members of a beloved community that is made up of some of the best folks around. A hearty thanks goes out to Davarian Baldwin, Martha Bouyer, Herman Bennett, David S. Cecelski, Bill Chafe, Paul Clemens, Dorothy Sue Cobble, John Dittmer, Lisa Elliott, Ann Fabian, Glenda Gilmore, Christina Greene, Darlene Clark Hine, Charles Hughes, William Jones, Temma Kaplan, Le Club, Jan Lewis, Tim and Dee McGuire, Richard and Grace McGuire, Katherine Mellen, Jennifer Morgan, Perri Morgan, Adam Rosh, Karl and Marcia Rosh, Regan Shelton, Phyllis St. Michael, Stephen Tuck, William L. Van Deburg, Craig Werner, and Deborah Gray White. I am

also grateful to Joanne Meyerowitz, Kathleen Brown, Victoria Walcott, and the anonymous referees of this essay for their insightful comments and criticisms.

1. *New York Amsterdam News,* June 20, 1959, p. 37. Jimmy Carl Cooper, a white youth, testified that David Beagles told him he planned to go out and get "some nigger 'stuff'" and noted that "stuff was not the word used": Trezzvant W. Anderson, "Rapists Missed Out on First Selection," *Pittsburgh Courier,* June 20, 1959, p. 3. A cleaned-up version reported that Beagles had plans to get a "Negro girl": "Four Convicted in Rape Case," *Tallahassee Democrat,* June 14, 1959, p. 7. "I Was Scared," *Pittsburgh Courier,* June 20, 1959, p. 1. "Four Begin Defense in Trial on Rape," *New York Times,* June 13, 1959, p. a13. See also criminal case file #3445, *State of Florida v. Patrick Gene Scarborough, David Ervin Beagles, Ollie Odell Stoutamire, and William Ted Collinsworth,* 1959 (Leon County Courthouse, Tallahassee, Fla.) (copy in Danielle L. McGuire's possession). Thanks to the Leon County Courthouse for sending me the file. Because the original trial transcript is no longer available, I have had to rely on newspaper reports, particularly those in African American newspapers: the *Baltimore Afro-American,* the *Louisiana Weekly,* the *New York Amsterdam News,* the *Pittsburgh Courier,* and the *South Carolina Lighthouse and Informer.* The fact that the transcript is missing is verified in the case file notes of *Patrick G. Scarborough v. State of Florida,* 390 So. 2d 830 (Fla. Dist. Ct. App., 1980). See also Robert W. Saunders, "Report on Tallahassee Incident," May 9, 1959, box A91, series III, National Association for the Advancement of Colored People Papers (Manuscript Division, Library of Congress, Washington, D.C.). Thanks to Timothy B. Tyson for finding this information for me.

2. The murders of Emmett Till in 1955 and Andrew Goodman, Michael Schwerner, and James Chaney in 1963 are considered pivotal moments in the civil rights movement. Their stories are given prominent attention in the PBS *Eyes on the Prize* series and Hollywood films such as the 1988 thriller *Mississippi Burning.* For monographs on these murders, see, for example, Nicolaus Mills, *Like a Holy Crusade: Mississippi 1964—The Turning Point of the Civil Rights Movement in America* (Chicago, 1992); and Stephen J. Whitfield, *A Death in the Delta: The Story of Emmett Till* (Baltimore, 1991).

3. Historians have only recently begun to explore how gender and sexuality affected the civil rights movement. Early efforts to include gender often took the form of "a women's history tacked onto men's history of civil rights": Steven F. Lawson, "Civil Rights and Black Liberation," in *A Companion to American Women's History,* ed. Nancy A. Hewitt (Oxford, Eng., 2002), 411. On the ways women changed the civil rights movement and how it changed their lives as well, see, for example, Vicki L. Crawford, Jacqueline Anne Rouse, and Barbara Woods, eds., *Women in the Civil Rights Movement: Trailblazers and Torchbearers, 1941–1965* (New York, 1990); and Belinda Robnett, *How Long? How Long? African-American Women in the Struggle for Civil Rights* (New York, 1997). Recent works place black and white women and their long-standing traditions of community organizing and resistance in the forefront of the movement; see, for example, Charles M. Payne, *I've Got the Light of Freedom: The Organizing Tradition and the Mississippi Freedom Struggle* (Berkeley, 1995); and Barbara Ransby, *Ella Baker and the Black Freedom Movement: A Radical Democratic Vision* (Chapel Hill, 2003).

4. On the "culture of dissemblance," see Darlene Clark Hine, "Rape and the Inner

Lives of Black Women in the Middle West: Preliminary Thoughts on a Culture of Dissemblance," *Signs*, 14 (Summer 1989), 912–20.

5. On the way gender and sexuality structured racial slavery, see, for example, Kathleen Brown, *Good Wives, Nasty Wenches, and Anxious Patriarchs* (Chapel Hill, 1996), 128–36; Kirsten Fischer, *Suspect Relations: Sex, Race, and Resistance in Colonial North Carolina* (Ithaca, 2002); and Deborah Gray White, *Arn't I a Woman? Female Slaves in the Plantation South* (New York, 1985).

6. Gerda Lerner, ed., *Black Women in White America: A Documentary History* (New York, 1972), 172. See also, for example, Jacquelyn Dowd Hall, "'The Mind That Burns in Each Body': Women, Rape, and Racial Violence," in *Powers of Desire: The Politics of Sexuality*, ed. Ann Snitow, Christine Stansell, and Sharon Thompson (New York, 1983), 328–49; and Leslie A. Schwalm, *A Hard Fight for We: Women's Transition from Slavery to Freedom in South Carolina* (Urbana, 1997), 37, 44–45, 119–21.

7. Tera W. Hunter, *To "Joy My Freedom: Southern Black Women's Lives and Labors after the Civil War* (Cambridge, Mass., 1997), 34. Winthrop Jordan, *White over Black: American Attitudes toward the Negro, 1550–1812* (Chapel Hill, 1968), 141. Frances Thompson quoted in Lerner, ed., *Black Women in White America*, 174–75; Harriet Simril quoted ibid., 183–85; see also Hannah Rosen, "'Not That Sort of Woman': Race, Gender, and Sexual Violence during the Memphis Riot of 1866," in *Sex, Love, Race: Crossing Boundaries in North American History*, ed. Martha Hodes (New York, 1999), 267–93. Essic Harris quoted in Elsa Barkley Brown, "Negotiating and Transforming the Public Sphere: African American Political Life in the Transition from Slavery to Freedom," *Public Culture*, 7 (1994), 112 n. 18; Ferdie Walker quoted in William Chafe, Raymond Gavins, and Robert Korstad, eds., *Remembering Jim Crow: African Americans Tell about Life in the Segregated South* (New York, 2001), 9–10.

8. John H. McCray, "South's Courts Show New Day of Justice," *Baltimore Afro-American*, July 11, 1959. Theralene Beachem interview by McGuire, March 19, 2003, audiotape (in McGuire's possession); Gloria Dennard interview by McGuire, March 19, 2003, audiotape, ibid.; Linda S. Hunt interview by McGuire, March 19, 2003, audiotape, ibid.; Mrs. Lucille M. Johnson interview by McGuire, March 16, 2003, audiotape, ibid.

9. Chana Kai Lee, *For Freedom's Sake: The Life of Fannie Lou Hamer* (Urbana, 1999), 9. On the "perilous intersection of race, gender, and sexualized brutality," see Timothy B. Tyson, *Radio Free Dixie: Robert F. Williams and the Roots of Black Power* (Chapel Hill, 1999), 2, 94. Though over a half century old, two of the best articulations of the sexual subtext of segregation that exist are John Dollard, *Caste and Class in a Southern Town* (Madison, 1937); and Lillian Smith, *Killers of the Dream* (New York, 1949).

10. Lee, *For Freedom's Sake*, 9–10, 78–81. Although Lee argues that Hamer was "inclined to dissemble when it came to sex, race, and violence" (ibid., 78–81), Lee's own evidence suggests that Hamer testified publicly to the sexualized aspects of her beating in Winona, Mississippi, and her forced sterilization as often as she kept them hidden; see ibid., 54, 59, 79, 80–81, 89, 198–42, 196 n. 2. See also Kay Mills, *This Little Light of Mine: The Life of Fannie Lou Hamer* (New York, 1993).

11. See Deborah Gray White, *Too Heavy a Load: Black Women in Defense of Them-*

selves, 1894–1994 (New York, 1999), 60–66. John Lewis Adams, "'Arkansas Needs Leadership': Daisy Bates, Black Arkansas, and the National Association for the Advancement of Colored People" (M.A. thesis, University of Wisconsin, Madison, 2003). Thanks to John Adams for sharing his research with me. On "reversing the shame," see Temma Kaplan, "Reversing the Shame and Gendering the Memory," *Signs*, 28 (Autumn 2002), 179–99. Jo Ann Robinson, *The Montgomery Bus Boycott and the Women Who Started It: The Memoir of Jo Ann Gibson Robinson*, ed. David J. Garrow (Knoxville, 1987), 37.

12. On the impact of World War II, see, for example, Timothy B. Tyson, "Wars for Democracy: African American Militancy and Interracial Violence in North Carolina during World War II," in *Democracy Betrayed: The Wilmington Race Riot of 1898 and Its Legacy*, ed. David Cecelski and Timothy B. Tyson (Chapel Hill, 1998), 254–75; and Harvard Sitkoff, "Racial Militancy and Interracial Violence in the Second World War," *Journal of American History*, 58 (Dec. 1971), 661–81. My preliminary dissertation research indicates that African Americans throughout the South used World War II as a wedge to publicize southern injustice, especially sexual violence by white men. Between 1942 and 1950, African American women accused white men of rape, testified about their assaults, and sparked community mobilization efforts in a number of southern towns, often securing convictions, mostly on minor charges with small fines assessed.

13. Fred Atwater, "$600 to Rape Wife? Alabama Whites Make Offer to Recy Taylor Mate," *Chicago Defender*, n.d., clipping, Recy Taylor case, folder 2, Administrative Files, Gov. Chauncey Sparks Papers, 1943–1947 (Alabama Department of Archives and History, Montgomery); N. W. Kimbrough and J. V. Kitchens, "Report to Governor Chauncey Sparks," Dec. 14, 1944, ibid.; John O. Harris, N. W. Kimbrough, and J. V. Kitchens to Gov. Chauncey Sparks, "Supplemental Report, December 27, 1944," ibid. See also "Grand Jury Refuses to Indict Attackers," *Pittsburgh Courier*, Feb. 24, 1945, folder 3, ibid.; "This Evening," *Birmingham News*, Feb. 21, 1945, ibid.; and "Second Grand Jury Finds No Bill in Negro's Charges," *Dothan Eagle*, Feb. 15, 1945, ibid.

14. On Scottsboro's political infrastructure, see Dan T. Carter, *Scottsboro: A Tragedy of the American South* (New York, 1971); and James Goodman, *Stories of Scottsboro* (New York, 1994). Over thirty national labor unions and many more locals supported Recy Taylor. See "Press release," Feb. 3, 1945, folder 4, box 430, Earl Conrad Collection (Cayuga Community College Library, Auburn, N.Y.). Other organizations that played an active role in Recy Taylor's defense include the Southern Conference for Human Welfare, the National Council of Negro Women, the Southern Negro Youth Congress, the National Negro Congress, the International Labor Defense, and the Birmingham and Montgomery branches of the NAACP: "Partial Sponsor List," Dec. 28, 1944, ibid.; Earl Conrad, Eugene Gordon, and Henrietta Buckmaster, "Equal Justice under Law," pamphlet draft, ibid.

15. See Kimbrough and Kitchens, "Report to Governor Chauncey Sparks"; Harris, Kimbrough, and Kitchens to Sparks, "Supplemental Report." See also "Grand Jury Refuses to Indict Attackers," *Pittsburgh Courier*, Feb. 24, 1945; "Dixie Sex Crimes against Negro Women Widespread," *Chicago Defender*, n.d., Scrapbook Collection, Conrad Collection; "Alabama Rapists Came from Church to Join White Gang in Sex Crime,"

Chicago Defender, March 24, 1945, ibid.; and "Alabama Has No Race Problem, Claims Official," *Chicago Defender*, n.d., ibid.

16. See *Montgomery Advertiser*, April 5, 1949, p. 8A; ibid., April 6, 1949, p. 1B; ibid., April 7, 1949, p. 2; S. S. Seay, *I Was There by the Grace of God* (Montgomery, 1990), 130–31. "Drew Pearson Changes Mind; Criticizes City," *Montgomery Advertiser*, May 3, 1949, p. 1A; ibid., May 21, 1949, p. 1A; "Anglo-Saxon System of Justice," ibid., May 22, 1949, p. 2B.

17. "Rape Cry against Dixie Cops Fall on Deaf Ears," *Baltimore Afro-American*, April 9, 1949, p. 1; Stewart Burns, ed., *Daybreak of Freedom: The Montgomery Bus Boycott* (Chapel Hill, 1997), 7; Joe Azbell quoted in "Cradle of the Confederacy," transcript, *Will the Circle Be Unbroken*, Southern Regional Council Web site (March 1997; not currently available; printout in McGuire's possession). Rufus A. Lewis story in Townsend Davis, *Weary Feet, Rested Souls: A Guided History of the Civil Rights Movement* (New York, 1998), 34.

18. Taylor Branch, *Parting the Waters: America in the King Years, 1954–1963* (New York, 1988), 130. Marissa Chappell, Jenny Hutchinson, and Brian Ward, "'Dress modestly, neatly . . . as if you were going to church': Respectability, Class, and Gender in the Montgomery Bus Boycott and the Early Civil Rights Movement," in *Gender in the Civil Rights Movement*, ed. Peter J. Ling and Sharon Monteith (New York, 1999), 87. Branch, *Parting the Waters*, 130.

19. Black leaders in Montgomery decided against using the arrests of Claudette Colvin, an unwed pregnant teenager, and Mary Louise Smith, the daughter of a local drunk, as test cases for desegregating the buses; see Branch, *Parting the Waters*, 123–28; Lynn Olson, *Freedom's Daughters: The Unsung Heroes of the Civil Rights Movement from 1830–1970* (New York, 2001), 94–95; and Chappell, Hutchinson, and Ward, "'Dress modestly, neatly . . . as if you were going to church,'" 84.

20. Neil R. McMillen, *The Citizens' Council: Organized Resistance to the Second Reconstruction, 1954–1964* (Urbana, 1994), 184, 186; see also Numan V. Bartley, *The Rise of Massive Resistance: Race and Politics in the South during the 1950s* (Baton Rouge, 1969), 83–84; and Tom P. Brady, *Black Monday: Segregation or Amalgamation, America Has Its Choice* (Winona, Miss., 1955). The White Citizens' Councils counted approximately 250,000 members throughout the South.

21. Hine, "Rape and the Inner Lives of Black Women in the Middle West," 915.

22. Brown, "Negotiating and Transforming the Public Sphere," 146.

23. Historians of the modern day civil rights movement are beginning to build upon work that chronicled the ways respectability, dignity, and manhood and womanhood shaped the strategies and goals of the middle- and working-class black activists during Reconstruction and the Progressive Era; see, for example, Glenda Gilmore, *Gender and Jim Crow: Women and the Politics of White Supremacy in North Carolina, 1896–1920* (Chapel Hill, 1999); and Evelyn Brooks Higginbotham, *Righteous Discontent: The Women's Movement in the Black Baptist Church, 1880–1920* (Cambridge, Mass., 1993).

24. "Deputy Tells of Confessions," *Tallahassee Democrat*, June 12, 1959.

25. Saunders, "Report on Tallahassee Incident."

26. "Deputy Tells of Confessions," *Tallahassee Democrat,* June 12, 1959. Original reports stated that Owens was "bound and gagged," but she later testified that she was only blindfolded; after she pulled the blindfold down, she appeared to have been gagged.

27. "Four Whites Seized in Rape of Negro," *New York Times,* May 3, 1959, p. A45.

28. On the Tallahassee bus boycott, see Glenda Alice Rabby, *The Pain and the Promise: The Struggle for Civil Rights in Tallahassee, Florida* (Athens, Ga., 1999), 9–46. Robert M. White, "The Tallahassee Sit-ins and CORE: A Nonviolent Revolutionary Sub-movement" (Ph.D. diss., Florida State University, 1964), 65.

29. White, "Tallahassee Sit-ins and CORE," 65.

30. "Rapists Face Trial," *Famuan,* 27 (May 1959), 1, 3; "Negroes Ask Justice for Co-ed Rapists," *Atlanta Constitution,* May 4, 1959, p. 2; "Four Whites Seized in Rape of Negro," *New York Times,* May 3, 1959, p. A45; ibid., May 5, 1959, p. A23; "Mass Rape of Co-ed Outrages Students," *Louisiana Weekly,* May 9, 1959, p. 1; *L'Osservatore Romano,* June 12, 1959; *Herald Tribune–London,* June 13, 1959; "Jury to Take Up Rape of Negro Co-ed," *Atlanta Constitution,* May 5, 1959, p. 5.

31. Patricia Stephens Due telephone interview by McGuire, March 4, 1999 (notes in McGuire's possession). See also Tananarive Due and Patricia Stephens Due, *Freedom in the Family: A Mother-Daughter Memoir of the Fight for Civil Rights* (New York, 2003), 40–41. White, "Tallahassee Sit-ins and CORE," 65.

32. See Howard Smead, *Blood Justice: The Lynching of Mack Charles Parker* (New York, 1988); Tyson, *Radio Free Dixie,* 143; "Lynch Victim Mack Parker's Body Is Found," *Tallahassee Democrat,* May 5, 1959.

33. "4 Indicted in Rape of Negro Co-ed," *New York Herald Tribune,* May 7, 1959, p. 5; Moses Newson, "Leaves Hospital to Give Testimony," *Pittsburgh Courier,* May 16, 1959, pp. 1–2.

34. M. C. Williams quoted in "Packed Court Hears Not Guilty," *Pittsburgh Courier,* May 16, 1959, pp. 1–2; "Judge Instructs Jury Here," *Tallahassee Democrat,* May 6, 1959, p. 1; "Sobbing Co-ed Bares Ordeal," *Baltimore Afro-American,* May 16, 1959, p. 1; "Indictment for Rape," criminal case file #3445, *Florida v. Scarborough, Beagles, Stoutamire, and Collinsworth;* "Four Plead Not Guilty to Rape," *Tallahassee Democrat,* n.d., clipping, folder 4, box 912, W. May Walker Papers (Special Collections, Robert Manning Strozier Library, Florida State University, Tallahassee).

35. Claude Sitton, "Negroes See Gain in Conviction of Four for Rape of Co-ed," *New York Times,* June 15, 1959, p. A1. Statistics are from David R. Colburn and Richard K. Scher, *Florida's Gubernatorial Politics in the Twentieth Century* (Gainesville, 1995), 13. Willis McCall quoted in Steven F. Lawson, David R. Colburn, and Darryl Paulson, "Groveland: Florida's Little Scottsboro," in *The African American Heritage of Florida,* ed. David R. Colburn and Jane L. Landers (Gainesville, 1995), 298–325, esp. 312.

36. See Moses J. Newson, "The Wind Blew, the Sky Was Overcast," *Baltimore Afro-American,* June 20, 1959; Moses J. Newson, "Abraham's Shadow Hangs Low over Tallahassee," ibid.; and Moses J. Newson, "His Mother Can Never Forget Him," ibid.

37. "Another Dixiecrat Headache," *Pittsburgh Courier,* June 20, 1959; "The Other Story," n.d., clipping, folder 1, box 912, Walker Papers.

38. William H. Chafe, "Epilogue from Greensboro, North Carolina," in *Democracy Betrayed,* ed. Cecelski and Tyson, 281–82. "Senate to Get Racial Measures," *Tallahassee Democrat,* June 14, 1959, p. 1; "Pent Up Critique on the Rape Case," ibid., May 14, 1959.

39. *Pittsburgh Courier,* May 30, 1959, p. 3; "Mr. Muhammad Speaks," *Pittsburgh Courier,* May 16, 1959.

40. Ella Baker quoted in *Pittsburgh Courier,* May 30, 1959, p. 3; see also Ransby, *Ella Baker and the Black Freedom Movement,* 210; "Enforce the Law," *New York Amsterdam News,* May 9, 1959; "What Will Florida Do?," *Pittsburgh Courier,* May 16, 1959.

41. "King Asks Ike to Go to Mississippi," *Baltimore Afro-American,* May 23, 1959; see also Martin Luther King Jr. to Clifford C. Taylor, May 5, 1959, in *The Papers of Martin Luther King,* ed. Clayborne Carson et al. (vol. 6, Berkeley, forthcoming). Thanks to Kieran Taylor for sending me this information.

42. "Report from Europe," *Baltimore Afro-American,* May 23, 1959; "King Asks Ike to Go to Mississippi," ibid. For the impact of the Cold War on civil rights, see, for example, Mary L. Dudziak, *Cold War Civil Rights: Race and the Image of American Democracy* (Princeton, 2000); and Thomas Borstelmann, *The Cold War and the Color Line: American Race Relations in the Global Arena* (Cambridge, Mass., 2001). "Appeal to U.N. to Stop Race Violence," *Louisiana Weekly,* May 9, 1959, p. 1.

43. Tyson, *Radio Free Dixie,* 145–51, esp. 148, 149; ibid., 163–65.

44. Roy Wilkins to LeRoy Collins, May 6, 1959, box A91, series III, NAACP Papers.

45. *Tallahassee Democrat,* May 4, 1959. On the "fair maiden," see Hall, " 'The Mind That Burns in Each Body,' " 335.

46. "I Was Scared," *Pittsburgh Courier,* June 20, 1959; see also "Did Not Consent," *Tallahassee Democrat,* June 11, 1959; "Rape Co-eds Own Story," *New York Amsterdam News,* June 20, 1959, p. 1; *Atlanta Constitution,* June 12, 1959; "Negro Girl Tells Jury of Rape by Four," *New York Times,* June 12, 1959, p. A16. Coverage of Owens's testimony was nearly identical in newspapers cited.

47. "Did Not Consent," *Tallahassee Democrat,* June 11, 1959; ibid.; ibid.; "I Was Scared," *Pittsburgh Courier,* June 20, 1959, p. 1; "Did Not Consent," *Tallahassee Democrat,* June 11, 1959; ibid.; see also *Charlotte Observer,* June 12, 1959, p. 1A.

48. "Did Not Consent," *Tallahassee Democrat,* June 11, 1959; "I Was Scared," *Pittsburgh Courier,* June 20, 1959; "State's exhibits" (knife) in criminal case file #3445, *Florida v. Scarborough, Beagles, Stoutamire, and Collinsworth,* 1959.

49. "Rape Co-eds Own Story," *New York Amsterdam News,* June 20, 1959, p. 1; "I Was Scared," *Pittsburgh Courier,* June 20, 1959, p. 1; see also "Four Begin Defense in Trial on Rape," *New York Times,* June 13, 1959, p. A13.

50. Doctors quoted in "Rape Co-eds Own Story," *New York Amsterdam News,* June 20, 1959, p. 1; also in "Four Begin Defense in Trial on Rape," *New York Times,* June 13, 1959, p. A13; friends quoted in "Did Not Consent," *Tallahassee Democrat,* June 11, 1959; John Rudd and Richard Brown quoted in "Deputy Tells of Confessions," ibid., June 12, 1959.

51. Anderson, "Rapists Missed Out on First Selection," *Pittsburgh Courier,* June 20, 1959, p. 3; "Four Begin Defense in Trial on Rape," *New York Times,* June 13, 1959,

p. A13; Howard Williams quoted in "Rape Defendants Claim Consent," *Tallahassee Democrat*, June 13, 1959.

52. "Negro Co-ed Gave Consent, Rape Defendants Tell Jury," *Atlanta Constitution*, June 13, 1959.

53. William Hopkins quoted in "Four Convicted in Rape Case; Escape Chair; 2 hr 45 min Verdict Calmly Received in Court," *Tallahassee Democrat*, June 14, 1959, p. 1; Pearlie Collinsworth and friends quoted in "Rape Defendants Claim Consent," ibid., June 13, 1959; Maudine Reeve's history of Ted Collinsworth, "State's exhibit #15," criminal case file #3445, *Florida v. Scarborough, Beagles, Stoutamire, and Collinsworth*, 1959; letter from Mrs. W. T. Collinsworth, "State's exhibit #16," ibid.

54. W. M. C. Wilhoit's testimony in "Motion for Leave to File Notice of Defense of Insanity," May 28, 1959, criminal case file #3445, *Florida v. Scarborough, Beagles, Stoutamire, and Collinsworth*, 1959. "Four Begin Defense in Trial on Rape," *New York Times*, June 13, 1959, p. A13; John Rudd quoted in "Four Guilty of Raping Negro; Florida Jury Votes Mercy," ibid., June 14, 1959, p. 1; Arthur Everett, "Four Convicted in Florida Rape Case," *Washington Post*, June 14, 1959; "Insanity Plea Prepared as Rape Case Defense," *Tallahassee Democrat*, May 28, 1959; "Mental Exam Set for Collinsworth," ibid., May 29, 1959; "Four Begin Defense in Trial on Rape," *New York Times*, June 13, 1959, p. A13.

55. "Four Guilty of Raping Negro; Florida Jury Votes Mercy," *New York Times*, June 14, 1959, p. A1. Charles U. Smith interview by Jackson Lee Ice, 1978, in Jackson Lee Ice Interviews, Florida Governors Manuscript Collection (Special Collections, Strozier Library); verified in Charles U. Smith telephone interview by McGuire, March 9, 1999 (notes in McGuire's possession).

56. "Precedent Seen in Rape Trial," *Tampa Tribune*, June 15, 1959; *Tallahassee Democrat*, June 14, 1959, p. 1.

57. "Verdict," June 14, 1959, criminal case file #3445, *Florida v. Scarborough, Beagles, Stoutamire, and Collinsworth*, 1959. "Guilty as Charged," *Baltimore Afro-American*, June 20, 1959; A. H. King quoted in "No Brutality Proof, Says Florida Jury," *Atlanta Constitution*, June 15, 1959, p. 1.

58. Sitton, "Negroes See Gain in Conviction of Four for Rape of Co-ed," *New York Times*, June 15, 1959, p. A1; "I'm Leaving Dixie," *New York Amsterdam News*, June 20, 1959.

59. Apparently students at Florida A&M ostracized Thomas Butterfield and Richard Brown for failing to protect Betty Jean Owens and Edna Richardson; students thought they ought to have shown some "physical resistance" rather than run away from the "point of a knife and gun": "I'm Leaving Dixie," *New York Amsterdam News*, June 20, 1959. "Hits Negro Men," ibid., June 6, 1959, p. 8. "Williams Was Right," *Baltimore Afro-American*, June 27, 1959; "Four Convicted in Rape Case," *Tallahassee Democrat*, June 14, 1959, p. 7; "I'm Leaving Dixie," *New York Amsterdam News*, June 20, 1959.

60. Sitton, "Negroes See Gain in Conviction of Four for Rape of Co-ed," *New York Times*, June 15, 1959, p. A1. "Negroes Say They Will Use Tallahassee Case as Precedent in Rape Trials," *Tampa Tribune*, June 15, 1959. Later that summer, Leon A. Lowery and others helped launch a successful campaign to highlight the unequal justice meted out

for black men accused of raping white women. See also Trezzvant W. Anderson, "Four Florida Rapists Near Chair," *Pittsburgh Courier,* July 4, 1959.

61. Roy Wilkins to Fredrick Cunningham, June 23, 1959, box A91, series III, NAACP Papers; "This Is Not Equal Justice," *Louisiana Weekly,* July 4, 1959.

62. Fred G. Millette to Judge W. May Walker, June 15, 1959, box 912, folder 1, Walker Papers; Mrs. Laura Cox to Judge Walker, June 15, 1959, ibid.; Mrs. Bill Aren to Judge Walker, June 15, 1959, ibid.

63. On the "incubus," see Glenda Gilmore, "Murder, Memory, and the Flight of the Incubus," in *Democracy Betrayed,* ed. Cecelski and Tyson, 73–93. Frederick Douglass quoted in Martha Hodes, *White Women, Black Men: Illicit Sex in the Nineteenth-Century South* (New Haven, 1997), 206.

64. For information on Florida's "moderate" racial politics, see Tom Wagy, *Governor LeRoy Collins of Florida: Spokesman of the New South* (University, Ala., 1985); and Steven F. Lawson, "From Sit-in to Race Riot: Businessmen, Blacks, and the Pursuit of Moderation in Tampa, 1960–1967," in *Southern Businessmen and Desegregation,* ed. Elizabeth Jacoway and David R. Colburn (Baton Rouge, 1982), 257–81.

65. Cases cited in Kimberly R. Woodard, "The Summer of African-American Discontent," unpublished paper, Duke University, 1992 (in McGuire's possession). See also "Death to Be Demanded in Rape Case," *Baltimore Afro-American,* July 4, 1959; John H. McCray, "Marine Doomed to Electric Chair in S.C. Rape Case," ibid., July 11, 1959, p. 1; Clarence Mitchell, "Separate but Equal Justice," ibid.; "Girlfriend Turns in Rape Suspect," ibid., Aug. 1, 1959; Trezzvant Anderson, "Negroes Weep as Georgia White Is Acquitted," *Pittsburgh Courier,* Sept. 2, 1959.

66. "The Tallahassee Case: A Turning Point in South," *New York Amsterdam News,* July 18, 1959; John H. McCray, "South's Courts Show New Day of Justice," *Baltimore Afro-American,* June 11, 1959.

67. Richard Haley, "Report on Events in Tallahassee, October 1959–June 1960," folder 7, box 10, series 5, Congress of Racial Equality Papers (Wisconsin Historical Society, Madison).

"An Oasis of Order"

The Citadel, the 1960s, and the Vietnam Antiwar Movement

Alex Macaulay

In the spring of 1970, a few hours before dawn, a car passed through Lesesne Gate and entered The Citadel, the Military College of South Carolina. The driver was a former cadet who had resigned earlier in the school year for undisclosed reasons. Beside him sat a stack of papers with The *Vigil* emblazoned across the top of each sheet. For several months, the former cadet and two of his friends from the senior class had collaborated to produce the underground newspaper that exposed the alleged injustices, inequities, and censorship that plagued The Citadel's campus. When the cadets awoke for the 6:30 breakfast formation, they would take copies of the unauthorized publication and read its take on the administration's one-sided views of events occurring outside The Citadel's gates and the regular student newspaper's reluctance to defend students interests. They would see complaints about the poor quality of mess hall food and the double standard separating cadet officers and privates. Although the *Vigil*, like many aspects of student activism at The Citadel, lacked the scope and longevity of similar ventures at other colleges, the intrigue, rebelliousness, and mystery surrounding the paper fascinated many cadets, and they welcomed each edition. These same qualities appalled the more militarily inclined members of the corps, who saw the publication as seditious, tendentious, and inappropriate for the structured, orderly environment of a military college. School officials agreed and pledged to uncover and expel the *Vigil*'s irresponsible publishers.[1]

It is not all that shocking that student unrest and underground newspapers came late to The Citadel. Many people see the college as a socially isolated institution, more attuned to the 1860s than the 1960s. In *Confederates in the Attic,* journalist Tony Horwitz calls the school "arguably the most mummified institution in America." A former faculty member claims that "perhaps more than any other institution of higher education The Citadel best reflects the cultural values of the Old South." Historian Timothy Tyson describes the college as "perhaps the most hidebound institution in tradition-steeped South Carolina."[2]

Although some depict The Citadel as an institution "locked in pre–Civil War concrete," such assessments constitute a simplistic view of both the school and the South that downplays white southerners' participation in the changes that swept the region in the decades following World War II. Except for mention of the Civil Rights movement, southern colleges and universities are often left out of general discussions about 1960s campus unrest, with Merle Haggard's "Fightin' Side of Me" and "Okie from Muskogee" framing perceptions of the region during this era. Numerous authors have demonstrated the important impact young black southerners had on the antiwar and student movements, but many young white southerners were also swept up in the political ferment of the period—and not just as opponents of "peaceniks" and "integrationists."[3]

As a military college, The Citadel placed students—the dynamic core of the national antiwar movement—in a disciplined, structured, and hierarchical environment that personified what many of their dissenting peers opposed. The layout of the campus itself seemed designed to keep student protests at bay. To deliver the *Vigil*, for example, the driver of the vehicle had to pass a guardhouse and then turn right onto the Avenue of Remembrance, so named in honor of American soldiers who had died while serving their country. Then, as now, first-year cadets had to walk in the gutters along the Avenue, a tradition that not only reminded freshmen of their lowly position among the cadet corps, but also reminded all cadets of the sacrifices made by U.S. servicemen and women.

After rolling by the library and Summerall Chapel, the car, with its load of subversive newspapers, then had to stop at the intersection of Jenkins Avenue and the Avenue of Remembrance. On the right stood Mark Clark Hall, the relatively new student activities building named after the famed World War II general and staunch "Cold Warrior" who also served as The Citadel's eleventh and probably most influential president. Across the street from Mark Clark Hall stood Jenkins Hall. This building contained the Commandant's Office and the offices of the over two dozen active-duty military personnel who taught courses for the Reserve Officers' Training Corps (ROTC) and oversaw the operations of the eighteen cadet companies. It was only after reaching the end of Jenkins Avenue that the driver could turn left and begin unloading his cargo in front of the four barracks that housed the corps of cadets.

The ideological barriers to dissent at The Citadel proved just as intimidating as the structural ones. For much of the school's history, being a "Citadel Man" meant following orders, conforming to societal standards, and exhibiting an uncompromising patriotism. While some cadets clung to these tenets, others worried that a decade shaped by youthful protest might pass without their participating in some way. The extent to which many cadets overcame these considerable institutional and regional constraints to formulate alternative assessments of the qualities good Citadel men ought to possess offers valuable insight into the momentum and nature of the antiwar movement, and at the same time, it complicates common perceptions of the South during this era.

The 1960s marked a transitional period in The Citadel's history in many ways. General Mark W. Clark had served as the school's president since 1954, and he was an outspoken critic of integration. The school would not admit its first African American cadet until 1966, a year after Clark retired. The ideological justifications of the public college's men-only admissions policy took shape under the general, and The Citadel's corps of cadets remained all-male long after he left. Coining the term that would become the school's mantra, Clark explained that The Citadel's system was "inextricably tied to our 'whole man' concept of education," a concept, "which we emphasize above all else," whereby cadets were trained "mentally, physically, morally, and militarily." Clark and others argued that as a result of this training, "America's elite manhood comprises our Corps of Cadets," and with their sense of self-worth tied directly to their image as "whole men," cadets boasted that "here, as in few other American colleges, the aim is to train leaders: leaders of thought and action, leaders of opinion, leaders of men." [4]

Preparing future "leaders of men" for the "eventual showdown with communism" was Clark's top priority, and he made certain that through "constant and respectful display of the Stars and Stripes on campus, through patriotic music, through the chaplain's sermons, through [his] talks to the Corps . . . and through military instruction," the "atmosphere on The Citadel campus is calculated to renew constantly a feeling of patriotism among cadets." As part of this process, the general instituted a "Greater Issues" lecture series whereby cadets listened to a string of influential Cold Warriors "condemn communism, praise Clark for his patriotic leadership, and commend [the corps's] preparation to defend civilization." [5]

Immersed in the teachings and terminology of the Cold War, cadets found protest rallies and student antiwar demonstrations difficult to fathom. In November 1960 well over half the corps watched a Federal Bureau of Investigation film on the "Communist inspired riots" outside a meeting of the House Un-American Activities Committee in San Francisco. Outraged over student opposition to ROTC on other campuses, a Citadel undergraduate listed the military's declining popularity as "one of the most alarming signs of the decay of the spirit and character of the youth of America today." Clark and other school officials fostered these sentiments, casting the corps as a bulwark against the "deterioration of American youth" and reminding cadets that a military education instilled students with the "moral fiber" needed to keep America strong.[6]

Throughout the early 1960s, editorials in the student newspaper, the *Brigadier,* implored U.S. officials to take a stronger stand against Soviet aggression, blasting the American government's "poor leadership" and "timid foreign policy." After the Bay of Pigs fiasco in 1961, one cadet criticized John F. Kennedy's "half hearted" efforts in Cuba but praised the president for sending more military advisors to South Vietnam. Under the headline "Practice Can Make Perfect," he argued that increased military intervention, not only in Vietnam, but also in Laos, Cambodia, and Berlin, might prevent the United States from "losing the Free World yard by yard, village by village, country by country."[7]

Following the 1962 Cuban Missile Crisis, reporters for the *Brigadier* welcomed Kennedy's strong stand as long overdue, and one writer encouraged the student body to prepare for war. Invigorated by the events that distressed students at universities like Columbia or Berkeley, many cadets began to distance themselves even further from their civilian peers. They cast The Citadel as a bastion of patriotism and morality, condemning their rebellious colleagues as "weak willed and more than willing to go along for a joy ride." Enthusiastic alumni praised the cadets' rejection of the "filth of the big coed colleges [and] the immature element of questioning and doubting and non-conforming." In late 1963 an article in the *Brigadier* published the results of a national survey of college students conducted by the conservative *National Review* that asked the question: "If the United States should find itself in such a position that all other alternatives were closed save world war with the Soviet Union, would you favor a) war, or b) surrender?" Taking some liberties with the question's wording, the reporter announced that at one school 46 percent chose "unconditional surrender," while on another campus 49 percent "preferred slavery to liberty, if a struggle was involved." Faced with these statistics, the author deplored the sad state of his generation and declared the United States must continue fighting these internal as well as external enemies.[8]

By mid-decade the cadets' disdain for dissent and protest collided with the increased militancy and exposure of the antiwar movement. Angered at Lyndon Johnson's escalation of the air and ground war in Vietnam, teachers and students on over one hundred campuses across the country held teach-ins. In 1965 public rallies in Washington, D.C., Berkeley, and New York drew crowds totaling in the tens of thousands, but Citadel students wanted no part of the demonstrations. That same year the organizers of the International Days of Protest, a national antiwar rally scheduled for October, sent The Citadel a letter asking how students there planned to participate in the event. The *Brigadier* staff responded to this "not-too-flattering request" with a massive rebuttal titled "Vietnam Survey: Why the Protests are Wrong." Describing Southeast Asia as "a current scene of communist aggression and the free world's struggle to stop it," the reporters equated U.S. withdrawal with appeasement, repeating Johnson's claim that "our honor and word are at stake in Vietnam."[9]

Numerous other factors drove the wedge between the corps and the antiwar demonstrators deeper. The rising antimilitarism of the 1960s contributed to a sharp drop in applicants, and Mark Clark's successor, General Hugh P. Harris, warned the college's governing Board of Visitors that "the roof is coming down faster than many realize." Many South Carolinians had begun to question the necessity of a half-filled, state-supported military college, and Harris looked for ways to enhance the college's reputation and enrollment. During his presidency, The Citadel integrated, launched a graduate program, began accepting transfer students, admitted veteran students, and allowed women to attend evening classes. These initiatives troubled many alumni, who responded in stereotypically southern fashion, warning that "too much change" would cost the school its distinct place in society. Others scolded Harris for catering to the demands of "outside forces," setting the school on the road to "decadence" and transforming The Citadel from a "man's college" into a "boy's school." Charlestonian Alice Beckett argued that the enrollment of noncadets devalued a Citadel education because the corps could start "cheating and rubbing elbows with Communists like at the University." These concerns fueled rumors that the school planned to abandon its military traditions, admit females into the cadet corps, and discard the plebe system.[10]

While he never planned to abolish the school's plebe system, Harris and others worried that hazing at The Citadel had gotten out of hand. In *The Lords of Discipline,* Pat Conroy, a 1967 Citadel graduate, recounts the horrors of his freshman year in gruesome detail. In his latest work, *My Losing Season,* Conroy describes the plebe system he endured as "mind-numbing, savage, unrelenting, and base." Many people associated with The Citadel dismiss the novelist's accounts as literary hyperbole, and Conroy himself accepts the skepticism of older graduates, who see no similarities between their freshman year and the one he describes. He explains, however, that by the early 1960s "the system had evolved into the extreme form of mob violence my classmates and I experienced."[11]

Although exactly when and why this evolution took place isn't clear, it is possible that social and political imperatives combined with explicit and implicit directives from Citadel officials encouraged, or at least condoned, cadet aggressiveness. Conroy remembers General Clark boasting "that the school would have the toughest plebe system in the world." "I personally attest that he succeeded admirably," Conroy added. The 1963 Citadel *Catalogue* lauded the college's method of producing "young men with alert minds and sound bodies, who have been taught high ideals, honor, integrity, loyalty, and patriotism." This assessment carried the rather ominous message that "these personal qualities must be deeply ingrained in order that neither time nor trouble will erase them from his personality." [12]

With Vietnam looming over most Citadel graduates, some cadets might have viewed plebe year as a means of preparing young men for the gruesome realities of a strange and discouraging war. Others seemed to believe that pushing freshmen to their physical and emotional limits insured that Citadel cadets would "continue to stand proudly apart from the permissiveness and decadence that surround us." Not coincidentally, by mid-decade, as more and more Americans challenged traditional mores by wearing their hair longer and shaggier, Citadel freshmen began sporting "baldy" or "knob" haircuts. While previous classes had received a "buzz" cut during their first week on campus, this new "tradition" required freshmen to have their scalps shaved practically bare. Due to the fourth classmen's shorn appearance, upper-classmen began referring to plebes as "knobs," and alumni from earlier eras remember their shock upon seeing the new haircuts for the first time. [13]

By 1968 General Harris was aware of "impressive evidence" that hazing at The Citadel had spiraled out of control. While labeling these problems "severe," Harris waffled as to whom to blame for the system's deficiencies. Speaking before a class of incoming freshmen, the general announced, "The only harm to The Citadel that I know is being done is by about 5 percent who came here, cannot cope, and then go home and start rationalizing their weaknesses to mama." At least privately, however, Harris realized much of the trouble stemmed from abusive practices that had become accepted aspects of plebe year. In May he informed the Board of Visitors that the college "must consider refinement or elimination of features which normal, intelligent, open-minded parents cannot accept." [14]

While struggling to corral rowdy upperclassmen, Harris and the Board of Visitors looked for ways to bolster the college's standing. The antiwar movement tarnished The Citadel's luster, but the war itself offered school officials ample opportunity to polish the institution's image as local, state, and national publications praised the battlefield heroics of Citadel alumni in Vietnam. The college held frequent ceremonies honoring graduates killed or wounded in the war, and these commemorations are vividly remembered by cadets from that era. "The most haunting thing for me at The Citadel was when a Citadel cadet died in Vietnam," one former student recalled. "That night, when it was announced, they did echo taps. I'll never forget that as long as I live." [15]

Between 1963 and 1976, sixty-seven Citadel alumni died in Vietnam; forty-three between 1966 and 1969. During this time, the dedications of campus memorials, the unveiling of portraits, and the playing of echo taps strengthened the ties between the corps and U.S. military personnel. Hearing frequent reports of their friends dying overseas, most cadets despised antidraft demonstrations. Referring to protestors who burned their draft notices, one cadet screamed, "This is not our generation! These 'people' do not represent us." He called them traitors and regretted that "the American fighting man is dying so that these bearded, draft-dodging, dope-addicted, Communist-inspired, pseudo-intellectual, coward[s] have the liberty and sanctuary" to disparage America.[16]

Although the corps's empathy for American soldiers heightened their disgust for antiwar demonstrators, it also opened the door for a wider critique of the war. In the *Shako,* a literary magazine containing poems, short stories, and essays written by cadets, a student poet lamented that "10,000 men may die before the sunrise / and leave a million children wondering." This discontent eventually spilled over into cadets' assessments of their college as the corps began to criticize Citadel administrators and challenge school policies. Unlike his predecessor, Harris sought to loosen the administrative reins on the cadets, and his hands-off approach allowed for more dissent among the student body. Cadets began complaining publicly about old furniture in the barracks and stringent uniform regulations. Others questioned the administration's tendency to stress military duties over academic ones. To protest what they saw as nitpicky regulations, one group of cadets painted an image of Mickey Mouse on the water tower overlooking the campus. This admittedly limited rebelliousness fostered a certain degree of ideological tolerance within the corps. A few students defended citizens' right to protest and warned that outlawing dissent because it might damage the United States' position in Vietnam "is one of the most dangerous courses that we could take."[17]

However, with some state policymakers still calling The Citadel "a luxury our state cannot afford," legislative threats to cut the school's funding quelled the corps's burgeoning unrest. Taking their cue from members of the Board of Visitors who continued blaming the school's woes on "outside forces," the besieged cadets saw the antiwar movement as an assault on themselves and their institution.

When an antiwar organization mailed the *Brigadier* a letter arguing that the U.S. government had deliberately misinformed the public about Vietnam, the paper called the charges insulting to those serving overseas, and wondered, "if honor is the most cherished principle of the cadet's life," what motivated those who opposed the war. In the *Shako,* a poet heard "democracy dying" over "the protests of cowards," while an essayist ridiculed those who protested while "soldiers died for their right to shirk." In November 1967, under the caption "No Hippies," an exasperated cadet cried that "the recent round of antiwar, anti-draft, anti-military, in fact, just about anti-everything demonstrations puts into a glaring light not only the growing disenchantment with the Vietnam War, but also sheds a most unfavorable light on the younger generation." He denounced the protestors as "neither intellectual nor American" and urged the government to crack down on these members of society.[18]

The rage of "No Hippies" startled many members of the corps. One student pleaded for some form of compromise between "the fanatical stance of the true hippie" and the close-minded "nationalist who sets Victorian imperialistic sanctions above all else." Cadet Allen Beiner conceded the right to dissent but argued that legal protest fell short of destroying draft cards and burning the flag. Foreshadowing a shift in cadet opinion, Beiner affirmed his support for the war but questioned the government's commitment to winning it.[19]

The Tet Offensive in January 1968 seemed to validate Beiner's concerns, and that year marked a turning point in the corps's attitude towards both the war and its protestors. Many cadets accused politicians of hamstringing the military, and the 1968 yearbook honored alumni killed overseas while denouncing both "the protests of dissenters and promises of politicians." In May, Tom Brown, an assistant editor for the *Brigadier,* contributed a column on "The Right of Dissenting Opinions." Quoting Voltaire and drawing analogies to Socrates and Jesus, he defended the right to debate "antiquated university regulations, oppressive governments, students' rights and civil rights." In that same issue, the newspaper's editor established a framework for dissent at The Citadel, acknowledging the benefits of constructive criticism but urging that cadets "not go too far. And never let those College Joes' knock [The Citadel]." [20]

With this in mind, several members of the corps adopted aspects of the student movement that were compatible with their situation at a military college. Reminiscent of the Berkeley slogan "I am a student. Do not spindle, tear, or mutilate," an editorial in the *Brigadier* reminded school officials of students' individuality as well as their importance to the institution. Some argued for a reduced focus on the military and an increase in liberal arts courses. Tom Brown rendered a light-hearted, humorous evaluation of the Yippies without mocking or dismissing their views.[21]

Even moderate dissent worried school officials, however, especially since they spent much of 1968 cultivating the institution's image as an island of patriotic stability amidst a sea of chaos. Throughout that tumultuous year, Harris received numerous letters praising him for maintaining campus order. One correspondent claimed that the "college stands out like a bright beacon" in troubled times. In Florida a Rotary Club member bragged that "one of those fine cadets can take care of five hippies." Parents congratulated Harris for pursuing true educational goals that counteracted the "hippie, Drop-out, Campus Riot, city riot-torn America we have today." When colleagues at other schools sought advice on how to avoid campus unrest, Harris replied smugly that "a disciplined environment" kept The Citadel unmarred by protest.[22]

Maintaining this "disciplined environment" proved more troublesome than Harris seemed willing to admit. When the administration refused to allow Brown to publish a cartoon of the Biblical figure Samson being taunted by calls of "Fag" and "Long-Hair Freak," censorship of the *Brigadier* became an issue. Each edition had to meet the approval of Harris's assistant, Colonel Dennis Nicholson, who admitted removing passages he deemed "extremely detrimental" to the institution. In contrast, senior cadet Arthur von Keller complained to Harris that "no criticism of any sort is allowed in any *student* publication." Eventually, the administration allowed the newspaper to run the cartoon, but not before Brown resigned his post as assistant editor due to Nicholson's excessive censorship.[23]

General Harris's self-proclaimed "oasis of order" proved to be a mirage during the 1969–1970 school year. Wishing to "radically change the ultra-conservative *Brigadier* of the past," the paper's new editor-in-chief, Jim Lock-ridge, encouraged students and faculty to submit articles reevaluating school policies. He broadened the paper's coverage of outside events, hoping to strike a balance within a school "military in its structure" but "primarily academic in its nature." Inspired by the "rising social revolution" that had already begun to ebb, he urged the corps to think critically of the government, society, and especially The Citadel.[24]

Many cadets heeded Lockridge's call. Several complained bitterly about the school's haircut policy. Others lobbied for new uniform requirements, longer furloughs, and televisions in the barracks. The cadets' lingering siege mentality tempered their protests, however, as they sought to improve their college without damaging its reputation. They regarded changes in the uniform policy, requests for appliances in the barracks, and decreased administrative intervention as positive goals but treated "gripes" about mandatory chapel attendance, drill, and Friday afternoon parades as threats to The Citadel's uniqueness. "None of us wants our school to become another Clemson," the cadets acknowledged, urging one another to keep this in mind the next time anyone muttered, "I hate this place."[25]

In an effort to stem cadet unruliness, Harris mixed tough talk with minor concessions. He reduced the number of Saturday morning inspections, shortened drill periods, relaxed uniform requirements, increased the number of furloughs, and agreed to recruit a more diverse group of "Greater Issues" speakers. At the same time, Harris emphasized the cadets' obligation to preserve the school's image, warning them of the threats posed by liberal legislators and societal antimilitarism.[26]

Harris's response failed to satisfy all cadets, and early in his senior year, Tom Brown and two friends began publishing the *Vigil*. Claiming to bring "to the surface the suppressed bitterness of a liberal minority," it blasted the administration's control of the *Brigadier* and wailed about the poor quality of mess hall food. Not all students appreciated this critique of their institution, and they answered the *Vigil* with a conservative underground paper called *Common Sense*. Although most cadets dismissed the latter publication as a rightwing "propaganda rag," one that was possibly sponsored by school officials, the use of an underground newspaper to defend the establishment against another underground newspaper underscores the corps's divided reaction to the tumult of the 1960s. In the end, despite its popularity, the *Vigil* disappeared after only three installments when school officials threatened to uncover and expel the "small minority activist group in the cadet corps."[27]

By this time, many cadets had softened their positions on the war and the protestors. A handful accepted that the conflict in Southeast Asia was not the result of a "plot for world-wide communist expansion." Some even considered the war futile. The *Brigadier* printed several cartoons ridiculing the U.S. government's heavy handedness in stifling dissent. In November 1969, the Charleston *Evening Post* asked students from The Citadel, the College of Charleston, and nearby Baptist College for their opinions on an upcoming antiwar rally in Washington, D.C. All three condemned the protestors' actions, but only The Citadel spokesman conceded the activists' right to dissent. Another cadet opposed the goals of the fall "moratoriums," antiwar events that one observer has described as a "cascade of local demonstrations, vigils, church services [and] local petition drives," but respected this effort at legal, responsible protest. Reportedly, one Citadel student even participated in this nationwide event by wearing a black armband on the designated day.[28]

In the midst of this growing unrest at The Citadel, the May 1970 shootings at Kent State shocked the nation. Students at forty-four colleges engaged in some sort of demonstration. Several schools shut down for days, some for semesters. In an attempt to commiserate with those at other schools, Jim Lockridge printed an unauthorized copy of the *Brigadier* entirely devoted to Kent State. The front page featured a giant fist slamming down on the body of a bleeding student.[29]

The paper recorded a wide spectrum of reactions among the corps. In contrast to calls for sober reflection and openminded tolerance, cadet Doug Nelson berated the students, comparing their protests to Nazi book burnings and declaring, "To hell with tradition and down with sedition." Several cadets cheered the deaths of "four long hairs," while others reminded their classmates that cadets and "long hairs" shared common bonds as students. Most cadets sympathized with the National Guardsmen, but events closer to home muted the cadets' indictment of the protestors. Students at the University of South Carolina (USC) clashed with police and the National Guard on May 11, and some state legislators demanded harsh punishments for the demonstrators.

One politician wanted to "annihilate" the offenders. Students at The Citadel undoubtedly had friends at USC and proposals to "annihilate" them bothered many. For the most part, cadets wanted a break from the turmoil and called for a stable medium between violent protest and forceful repression.[30]

While cadet activism declined after May 1970, the corps did not return to its staunchly conservative ways. Antiauthoritarian attitudes crippled corps unity and confounded school officials. With increasing regularity, cadets grew their hair longer, refused to salute officers, and resisted most aspects of the military. When alumni commented on the students' low morale, lack of discipline, and ragged appearance, the administration issued more punishments, accelerating the corps's slide. Drug use became a problem, and in November three cadets were arrested and expelled for selling amphetamines. Rather than condemn this illegal activity, students argued that because school rules banned coffee makers in the barracks, students used speed to study for exams or prepare for inspections. In the same issue that reported the bust, the *Brigadier* staff ran an article describing a "Marijuana High."[31]

As the national antiwar movement gave way to a "popular antiwar mood," The Citadel followed suit. By 1971 even General Harris hoped for an "honorable end to this undeclared, half-executed, and now unwanted war." For the first time, cadets acknowledged the existence of a credibility gap, and they issued sustained critiques of the U.S. government and its role in Vietnam. One embittered young man pointed out that, despite the protests, politicians ignored the rallies, schools repaired damaged buildings, and friends of his died in a far-off land. Faced with these results, the cadet concluded that American society was "going to hell."[32]

The fact that students attending a military college with deep roots in a region often noted for its patriotism found aspects of the antiwar movement compatible with their ideals of citizenship and duty attests to the ideological malleability and broad appeal of the protestors' message. Intrigued by the energy of the protestors, certain members of the corps opened themselves up to new ideas and tried to promote cadet activism. Youthful rebelliousness and exuberance appealed to these cadets, but so did the military ideals of duty, honor, and country. As the corps vacillated between defending students' right to dissent and defending their school against outside dissenters, many cadets eventually came to realize that questioning the war, challenging school officials, and criticizing school policies did not necessarily constitute a treasonous attack on America or American soldiers. Ultimately, many Citadel students decided to end their presumed isolation and start marching in step with their collegiate peers.

An emphasis on and a redefinition of manliness and manly behavior linked many Citadel cadets to their leftist contemporaries. In keeping with the early

Cold War's emphasis on conformity and conservatism, good Citadel men, and by extension good Americans, of the 1940s and 1950s were expected to conform, acquiesce, obey. During the 1960s, however, as the Cold War consensus crumbled, men rebelled, agitated, and questioned authority. Many cadets followed suit, and in doing so, they regarded themselves as no less manly than earlier alumni. The chauvinism of the cadets as well as their rebelliousness corresponded with many of the New Left's views on proper gender roles. Many in both groups seemed convinced that waging war and protesting war were practices best left to men.[33]

The extent and volatility of student activism at The Citadel and other southern schools may have paled in comparison to that of their peers in other parts of the country, but it was not inconsequential. Such behavior corresponds with historian Rod Andrew's identification of a distinct "southern military tradition" that "combined elements of militarism" with "a heritage of individualism, personal autonomy, and rebellion *against* authority." This tradition encouraged Citadel students to embrace antiauthoritarian and nonconformist attitudes but reject calls for revolution. Ideologically opposed to the most extreme and visible elements of the antiwar movement, many Citadel students nonetheless challenged authority and worked to reform their campus more so than their country.[34]

In their efforts to de-romanticize popular perceptions of the 1960s, many scholars make it a point to note that during this era "*most* students moved through the standard labyrinth of courses, examinations and graduate requirements." In *Campus Wars* historian Kenneth Heineman reminds readers that "it is vital to study institutions where the majority of students and faculty were either prowar or apathetic—a more perfect mirror of American society in the 1960s." Although these points are well taken, they tend to present student activism as an either/or proposition, when in actuality it was more personal and complex. The resulting somewhat Manichean view of the era diminishes the activities of less "radical" students by failing to take into account local, seemingly less dramatic variations of what might qualify as "radicalism."[35]

In his history of Vanderbilt University, historian Paul Conkin acknowledges the importance of location and community in shaping and evaluating campus unrest, arguing that viewed within a regional context the actions of many southern students in the late 1960s "seemed almost revolutionary." Clarence Mohr makes the same observation in his study of Tulane University, noting that the behavior of young southerners was "measured . . . by a different and less permissive social yardstick." While cadets, like most students of the era, refrained from seizing buildings, calling for revolution, or rioting in the streets, they did break from tradition by protesting college regulations, questioning authority, and adopting countercultural modes of dress and behavior.

In doing so, they confronted an institutional and regional culture that leaned heavily toward a defense of the status quo. The relative conservatism of The Citadel's "radicals" exposes the artificiality of pitting "revolutionaries" against "the silent majority," suggesting that the era's social and political battle lines were neither as polarized nor as rigid as many believe. Taking this into account when evaluating student activism at The Citadel and other southern campuses might serve the dual purpose of continuing to demystify the 1960s, while at the same time acknowledging the prominence rather than the absence of youthful rebelliousness.[36]

Notes

1. Abe Peck, *Uncovering the Sixties: The Life and Times of the Underground Press* (Pantheon Books, 1985), xv.

2. Tony Horwitz, *Confederates in the Attic: Dispatches from the Unfinished Civil War* (Vintage Books, 1998), 66; Charles Reagan Wilson and William Ferris, eds., *The Encyclopedia of Southern Culture* (University of North Carolina Press, 1989), 277; Timothy B. Tyson, "Dynamite and the 'Silent South': A Story from the Second Reconstruction in South Carolina," in *Jumpin' Jim Crow: Southern Politics from Civil War to Civil Rights,* ed. Jane Dailey, Glenda Elizabeth Gilmore, and Bryant Simon (Princeton University Press, 2000), 279–80.

3. The "pre–Civil War concrete" line came from Vice Admiral James Stockdale following his tumultuous one-year stretch as The Citadel's president, *Newsweek,* 1 September 1980, 83. Melton McLaurin, "Country Music and the Vietnam War," *Perspectives on the American South: An Annual Review of Society, Politics, and Culture,* vol. 3, ed. James C. Cobb and Charles R. Wilson (Gordon and Breach Science Publishers, 1985), 145, 146, 148–49, 153, 155–56, 158; James C. Cobb, "From Muskogee to Luckenbach: Country Music and the Southernization of America," *Redefining Southern Culture: Mind and Identity in the Modern South* (University of Georgia Press, 1999), 82.

4. *Brigadier,* The Citadel Archives and Museum, Charleston, South Carolina, 3 December 1955, 18 May 1957, 6 December 1958, 14 February 1959, 15 April 1961; Charleston *News and Courier,* 12 March 1968; W. Gary Nichols, "The General as President: Charles P. Summerall and Mark W. Clark as Presidents of The Citadel," *South Carolina Historical Magazine* 95 (October 1994): 315, 326–27, 332–33; Alex Macaulay, "Black, White, and Gray: The Desegregation of The Citadel, 1963–1973," *Warm Ashes: Issues in Southern History at the Dawn of the Twenty-First Century,* ed. Winfred B. Moore, David H. White, and Kyle S. Sinisi (University of South Carolina Press, 2003), 320–36; Nancy Mace with Mary Jane Ross, *In the Company of Men: A Woman at The Citadel* (Simon & Schuster, 2001).

5. Nichols, "General as President," 324, 327; Board of Visitors, "Minutes," The Citadel Archives and Museum, Charleston, South Carolina, folder 22, document 471; Board of Visitors, "Minutes," folder 23, document 648; *The Brigadier,* 20 November 1954, 17 December 1954, 15 January 1955, 23 April 1955, 21 May 1955, 8 January 1958, 15 October 1960.

6. *Brigadier,* 13 February 1960, 27 February 1960, 15 October 1960, 12 November 1960, 15 April 1961, 15 December 1961, 17 February 1962.

7. *Brigadier,* 16 January 1960, 4 November 1961, 18 November 1961, 19 May 1962, 16 April 1963.

8. Todd Gitlin, *The Sixties: Years of Hope, Days of Rage* (Bantam Books, 1987), 89–90, 117; William O' Neill, *Coming Apart: An Informal History of the 1960s* (Quadrangle, 1971), 65; *Brigadier,* 19 May 1962, 3 November 1962, 9 November 1963, 18 April 1964, 16 May 1964, 31 October 1964.

9. Kirkpatrick Sale, *SDS* (Random House, 1973), 186; Nancy Zaroulis and Gerald Sullivan, *Who Spoke Up? American Protest Against the War in Vietnam, 1963–1975* (Doubleday, 1984), 38–42, 56, 63–64; Allen Matusow, *The Unraveling of America: A History of Liberalism in the 1960s* (Harper & Row Publishers, 1994), 320, 318; Charles DeBenedetti and Charles Catfield, *An American Ordeal: The Antiwar Movement of the Vietnam Era* (Syracuse University Press, 1990), 110–11, 123, 162; *Brigadier,* 6 November 1965, 4 December 1965.

10. *Brigadier,* 28 November 1964, 18 March 1967, 13 May 1967; Charleston *Evening Post,* 12 March 1968; Board of Visitors, "Minutes," 22 March 1968, documents 736–41; Board of Visitors, "Minutes," 25 November 1969, documents 213, 219, 220; "A Self Study: The Citadel, 1972," 17, I-9, I-10, III-83, III-20, III-21, III-23, III-24, documents in possession of author; Charleston *News and Courier,* 12 March 1968, 12 November 1968; Board of Visitors, "Minutes," 17 March 1967, documents 541–44; Alice Beckett to Harris, 29 September 1965, General Hugh P. Harris Papers, box 41, folder 5, The Citadel Archives and Museum, Charleston, South Carolina; 1972 Citadel *Catalogue,* The Citadel Archives and Museum, Charleston, South Carolina, 210; Board of Visitors, "Minutes," 21 March 1969, document 122; Board of Visitors, "Minutes," 20 March 1970, document 319.

11. Board of Visitors, "Minutes," 1 October 1965, documents 177–80; Board of Visitors, "Minutes," 31 May 1968, document 8, 12; Harris to Reuben H. Tucker, 19 November 1965, box 50, folder 2, Harris Papers; Memo to Tucker from Harris, 27 September 1965, box 50, file T, Harris Papers; Memo to Tucker from Harris, 11 November 1965, box 50, file T, Harris Papers; Memo to Tucker from Harris 27 September 1967, box 50, folder 2, Harris Papers; Board of Visitors, "Minutes," 6 January 1967, documents 464, 468–76; "Commandant's address to cadre," 31 August 1966, box 50, folder 2, Harris Papers; Pat Conroy, *The Lords of Discipline* (Bantam Books, 1982), 127–206; Pat Conroy, *My Losing Season* (Doubleday, 2002), 98, 100; Interview with Bill Marett, 22 December 2001.

12. Conroy, *Losing Season,* 100; 1963; Citadel *Catalogue,* 40–41.

13. Harris to Dr. Horace Greeley, 2 May 1969, box 44, folder 7, Harris Papers; Memo from Association of Military Colleges and Schools of the United States, box 48, folder 2, Harris Papers; L. H. Jennings to Harris, box 46, folder 3, Harris Papers; Catherine Manegold, *In Glory's Shadow: Shannon Faulkner, The Citadel, and a Changing America* (Alfred A. Knopf, 1999), 121; *Brigadier,* 15 October 1960; Interview with Frank Mood, 18 May 2002.

14. "Report to the President and Board of Visitors The Citadel By the Special Advisory Committee on the Fourth Class System," The Citadel Archives and Museum, Charleston, South Carolina, 9; Board of Visitors, "Minutes," 31 May 1968, document 8;

Board of Visitors, "Minutes," 27 January 1968, document 728; Manegold, *Glory's Shadow*, 83.

15. *Brigadier,* 3 November 1962, 10 April 1965, 15 May 1965; Charleston *Evening Post,* 23 September 1967; Board of Visitors, "Minutes," 26 May 1966, document 308; *Time* 80.17 (26 October 1962): 40; Interview with Michael Barrett, 14 January 1998; Interview with Henry Kennedy, 24 October 1997; Interview with James Lockridge, 26 January 1998; Interview with Philip Hoffmann, 29 October 1997; Interview with William Riggs, 7 December 1997; Interview with Douglas Rich, 21 January 1998; Interview with James Cassidy, 23 January 1998.

16. "The Citadel War Record—Vietnam Casualties," The Citadel Archives and Museum, Charleston, South Carolina; Kenneth Heineman, *Campus Wars: The Peace Movement at American State Universities in the Vietnam Era* (New York University Press, 1993), 140; DeBenedetti and Catfield, *An American Ordeal,* 195; Zaroulis and Sullivan, *Who Spoke Up?,* 47, 54, 58, 112–14; *Brigadier,* 2 May 1964, 6 November 1965, 4 December 1965, 26 February 1966, 29 April 1967 (quotation), 2 March 1968.

17. Harris to Reuben H. Tucker, 19 November 1965, box 50, folder 2, Harris Papers; *Brigadier,* 26 February 1966, 12 April 1966, 8 October 1966, 13 January 1967, 25 February 1967; *Shako,* Fall 1966, The Citadel Archives and Museum, Charleston, South Carolina.

18. Board of Visitors, "Minutes," 6 January 1967, documents 468–76; Board of Visitors, "Minutes," 17 March 1967, documents 541–44; Robert Daniel to Alumni, 22 August 1968, box 44, folder 1, Harris Papers; *Brigadier,* 22 October 1966, 3 December 1966, 18 March 1967, 8 April 1967, 29 April 1967, 23 September 1967, 4 November 1967; *Shako,* 30 May 1967.

19. *Brigadier,* 18 November 1967.

20. *Brigadier,* 13 January 1968, 2 March 1968, 6 April 1968, 11 May 1968; 1968 *Sphinx,* The Citadel Archives and Museum, Charleston, South Carolina, 330.

21. *Brigadier,* 19 October 1968, 9 November 1968, 19 April 1969, 10 May 1969; *Shako,* Spring 1969.

22. Heineman, *Campus Wars,* 186; Zaroulis and Sullivan, *Who Spoke Up? ,* 149, 153, 156, 200; Matusow, *Unraveling of America,* 390, 391; *Brigadier,* 13 January 1968, 2 March 1968, 6 April 1968; Walter Albrecht to Harris, 7 June 1968, box 41, folder 1, Harris Papers; Memo from Colonel McAlister to Harris, 24 April 1968, box 50, folder 7, Harris Papers; Martha Sweeney to Harris, 12 September 1968, box 43, folder 1, Harris Papers; Harris to Dr. V.R. Easterling, 6 August 1968, box 44, folder 3, Harris Papers.

23. *Brigadier,* 13 January 1968, 8 March 1969; D.D. Nicholson to R.L. Bergmann, 9 November 1968, box 41, folder 9, Harris Papers; Arthur von Keller to Harris, no date, box 46, folder 4, Harris Papers (emphasis in original); Interview with Thomas Brown, 5 February 1999.

24. Harris to Arthur von Keller, 2 June 1969, box 46, folder 3, Harris Papers; Board of Visitors, "Minutes," 20 March 1970, document 319; Board of Visitors, "Minutes," 21 March 1969, document 122; Board of Visitors, "Minutes," 25 November 1969, document 205; *Brigadier,* 13 September 1969, 11 October 1969, 14 February 1970, 7 March 1970, 17 April 1970, 24 April 1970, 11 December 1970; Memo to James Duckett from James Whitmire, 15 August 1969, box 41, folder 14, Harris Papers; Lockridge interview.

25. *Brigadier,* 14 February 1970, 7 March 1970, 11 December 1970.

26. "Faculty Coffee Klatch," 8 April 1968, box 49, folder 4, Harris Papers; Harris to George Lott, 28 April 1969, box 47, folder 1, Harris Papers; Harris to Horace Greeley Jr., 2 May 1969, box 44, folder 7, Harris Papers; "Talking Papers for Discussion Topics on Monday Morning Program," box 48, folder 3, Harris Papers; "Speak to All Students," 12 September 1969, box 36, Harris Papers.

27. *Brigadier,* 7 March 1970; Board of Visitors, "Minutes," 20 March 1970, document 311; Brown interview.

28. Charleston *Evening Post,* 8 November 1969; Anne Cote to Harris, no date, box 47, folder 1, Harris Papers; *Brigadier,* 21 March 1970, 11 April 1970, 24 April 1970, 8 May 1970, 15 May 1970; Gitlin, *The Sixties,* 379; Brown interview; Interview with Laurence Moreland, 22 October 1997.

29. Heineman, *Campus Wars,* 256; DeBenedetti and Catfield, *An American Ordeal,* 279–80; *Brigadier,* 15 May 1970; Lockridge interview.

30. *Brigadier,* 8 May 1970, 15 May 1970; Charleston *News and Courier,* 12 May 1970, 13 May 1970, 14 May 1970.

31. *Brigadier,* 23 October 1970, 13 November 1970, 25 February 1972; Board of Visitors, "Minutes," 11 September 1971, document 2; Board of Visitors, "Minutes," 25 February 1971, document 681; "Self-Study," II-7, III-7, VII-27; Board of Visitors, "Minutes," 20 December 1970, document 608; Board of Visitors, "Minutes," 18 March 1971, document 684; Board of Visitors, "Minutes," 11 September 1970, document 1; Board of Visitors, "Minutes," 17 March 1972, document 88; Board of Visitors, "Minutes," 12 February 1971, document 657; Board of Visitors, "Minutes," 31 January 1972, document 60; Board of Visitors, "Minutes," 11 February 1972, document 74; Board of Visitors, "Minutes," 17 March 1972, document 80; Board of Visitor, "Minutes," 9 December 1972, document 400; Board of Visitors, "Minutes," 10 February 1973, document 746.

32. DeBenedetti and Catfield, *An American Ordeal,* 300, 317; Harris to Frank Pace, 29 April 1971, box 49, folder 1, Harris Papers; *Brigadier,* 1 October 1971, 29 October 1971, 13 October 1972, 17 March 1972, 24 March 1972, 28 April 1972; *Shako,* Winter 1971.

33. Doug McAdam, *Freedom Summer* (Oxford University Press, 1988), 107–11.

34. Rod Andrew, *Long Gray Lines: The Southern Military School Tradition, 1839–1915* (University of North Carolina Press, 2001), 2, 3, 4 (emphasis in original), 7.

35. James J. Farrell, *The Spirit of the Sixties: The Making of Postwar Radicalism* (Routledge, 1997), 169 (emphasis in original); Heineman, *Campus Wars,* 5, 80–81, 150–51.

36. Paul Conkin, *Gone with the Ivy: A Biography of Vanderbilt University* (University of Tennessee Press, 1985), 613, 625–30; Clarence Mohr and Joseph E. Gordon, *Tulane: The Emergence of a Modern University, 1945–1980* (Louisiana State University Press, 2001), 192, 269–70, 305.

The Fickle Finger of Phosphate

Central Florida Air Pollution and the Failure of
Environmental Policy, 1957–1970

Scott H. Dewey

After the election of November 1994, when the Republican party dramatically gained control of the United States House of Representatives for the first time in decades, the new House leadership promised to join the Republican-dominated Senate in changing the relationship between the federal government and the states. Decrying "federal mandates" that states were obliged to fulfill at great expense, Republicans demanded an end to federal domination and a restoration of the primacy of state governments in many aspects of public policy. Such an agenda figured importantly in the widely touted "Contract with America" advocated and implemented by Newt Gingrich, the new Speaker of the House. The so-called contract between congressional Republicans and the American people undertook to shrink the size and reach of the federal government in the domestic policy area by means of tax cuts, a constitutional requirement for a balanced budget, a moratorium on further federal rules, provisions to require that all federal regulations be subject to risk assessment and cost-benefit analysis, and limits on congressional mandates over lower levels of government.[1] The Republicans who were clustered around Gingrich followed the example of the charismatic, deeply conservative former president, Ronald Reagan, who had also made federal mandates one of the prime targets of his so-called new federalism throughout the 1980s. In the 1980s and the 1990s, Republican conservatives blasted what they characterized as the waste and inefficiency of federal programs, suggesting that the federal government could do almost nothing right and that states and localities could do everything better. Pro-business, antiregulatory lawmakers from conservative southern states such as Georgia and Texas figured prominently in the crusade to return power to the states. While most citizens were never as fervent in these attitudes as the archconservative true believers, such ideas resonated widely in a nation grown weary of federal bureaucracy and gridlock, and even many Democratic politicians joined the move toward granting autonomy to state and local governments on various issues.

Among the many items targeted for devolution to the states were federal environmental mandates, which many conservatives, industrialists, and developers had hated since the sweeping federal environmental legislation of the 1960s and 1970s. In their eagerness to liberate local development interests from costly burdens and obligations imposed by federal environmental statutes, many lawmakers insisted that state and local governments could protect the environment better and more cheaply than unwieldly federal bureaus. However, federal environmental laws and programs proved to be more popular with the American public than Republican leaders had supposed, and they were not able to dismantle and replace the existing federal system of environmental protection to the extent they had wished. Nevertheless, with environmental policy as with other issues, the Reagan-era cry, "Get the government off the backs of the people," still echoes throughout the nation, while in many quarters, state and local governments are still presumed to be more capable than the federal government.[2]

However, the competence of state and local governments is expounded within a context of limited historical awareness. For critics of federal environmental policy, it is enough to complain of the failings of the federal government without ever offering proof of the capacity of lower levels of government to perform the same functions. Yet, with few exceptions, states and localities have a very poor record on environmental protection throughout the early post–World War II years, when Americans became more concerned about the natural environment but the federal government hesitated to intervene in what was traditionally a state and local prerogative. Indeed, the more recent federal policies, with all their shortcomings, compare very favorably with the long record of false starts and inactivity compiled by state and local governments on environmental issues such as pollution control—even in the face of persistent public complaints. Moreover, contrary to the assumptions of many localist conservatives, the federal government, far from actively intruding in state and local environmental affairs, entered the field of pollution-control enforcement very reluctantly. After meager results from many years of deliberately maintaining a limited role and seeking to coax states and cities to fulfill their regulatory and public health responsibilities, the federal government finally began to pass and enforce national environmental standards.[3]

The present study focuses on one illuminating example of how public environmental policy worked when the states had primacy in such matters and the federal government had a very limited advisory role. The case in question arose in central Florida, where a huge phosphate mining and processing industry developed in order to process the local mineral riches into chemical fertilizer. The industry's emissions produced air pollution severe and damaging enough to make the local atmosphere one of the most noxious and notorious in the United

States.[4] The phosphate industry, long resistant to costly pollution-control measures, heavily influenced the politics and economy of central Florida and the entire state. Florida officials were therefore reluctant to push the industry too hard—particularly since Florida and other southern states used lax regulatory standards and low taxes to lure businesses from other areas.[5]

Meanwhile, federal officials, although aware of air pollution in central Florida, were constrained by Eisenhower-era concepts of states' rights, which made them unable or unwilling to act. Of course, postwar federalism also handicapped the development and implementation of policies other than environmental protection, particularly in the South. Although the whole nation shared the postwar reaction against the expansion of federal power under President Franklin D. Roosevelt's New Deal, southern politicians and government officials were especially sensitive about states' rights because of the lingering practice of racial segregation enforced by southern state governments, which viewed the federal government as the primary threat to that practice. Regardless of white southerners' fears, the civil rights movement is the classic example of the failure of federalism during the 1950s and the early 1960s—with a series of presidential administrations reluctant to face the political fallout from actively using the power of government to secure basic rights for African Americans in the South. Southern hypersensitivity over states' rights also may have helped to make southern leaders even more suspicious than their counterparts in other regions toward federal intervention in issues besides racial segregation.[6]

As with civil rights policy, expansion of federal authority to regulate the nation's air quality came slowly, gradually, and reluctantly, only after persistent nonfeasance by lower governments. The federal air pollution–control program had begun officially in 1955 with a modest three-year program of research and technical assistance to help states confront the problem. This limited effort was expanded significantly under the first Clean Air Act, passed in 1963, which gave federal officials a carefully constrained enforcement role. However, the federal government could intervene in interstate or intrastate situations only after a formal request from the governor of an involved state, and such requests were seldom forthcoming. Even in cases of interstate air pollution, where the federal government had greater power and at least one aggrieved governor was more likely to request aid, federal officials held hearings but—before the tough new Clean Air Act amendments of 1970 established federal primacy—were unable to effect significant improvements. With intrastate pollution, the federal government was even less effective because most of the willfully apolitical health scientists and engineers in the federal control program steadfastly supported the status quo of ineffectuality, inertia, and ever more research. Such tendencies are exposed in the case of central Florida.[7]

The history of the Florida phosphate industry is typical of the state's resource-extraction industries and of the perennial, unusually pronounced boom-and-bust cycle of Florida's frantic, unregulated economic development. Like much of the former Confederate South, Florida, still largely a frontier area into the postbellum period, had almost no industry throughout the nineteenth century, and when industries did emerge, they were usually geared either to agriculture or to extracting raw materials. After the Civil War, railroads were built all across the Sunshine State to haul first cotton, then oranges, grapefruits, cattle, and timber, as well as the many Yankee tourists already beginning to seek the sun and refuge from cold northern winters. After the appearance of phosphate-mining ventures during the last decade of the nineteenth century, other typical southern resource-extraction industries followed during the twentieth century, including lumbering and wood-pulp paper production, a foul-smelling, heavily polluting business that came to dominate large areas of Florida's panhandle and northern peninsular counties during the post–World War II years.[8]

Most of Florida's major industries—including tourism, which broke the pattern of typical southern resource extraction and later dominated the state's economy—went through wild swings of boom and bust during the period between the end of the Civil War and the beginning of World War II. A boom in railroad construction and real estate touched off by the northern discovery of Florida's benign climate during the 1870s and 1880s went spectacularly bust in the mid-1920s—though it had facilitated the state's sudden population increase of nearly 1,000 percent between 1860 and 1930. The same pattern applied to Florida's citrus-growing industry, which expanded throughout the state, even to its northern counties until recurrent freezes coupled with sagging prices drove citrus permanently southward, to the central part of the state, where it remained.[9]

The story was much the same for Florida's phosphate industry. The first great phosphate boom began in 1889 with the discovery of major hard rock deposits in north central Florida near Ocala and Dunellon. The resulting "Phosphate Fever" was much like an oil boom, as capitalists flooded in to exploit nature's gift. Eighteen mining operations at work in 1891 grew to 215 the following year and more than 400 by mid-decade. By 1894 Florida had already become the largest producer of phosphates in the Union, but with the onset of recession during the 1890s, the industry faced bankruptcy and consolidation. As with oil, copper, and other mineral extractive enterprises, a few corporate giants came to dominate the Florida phosphate industry, and only 19 phosphate companies remained in business at the end of 1914. During the same period, phosphate mining grew more capital- and energy-intensive, gradually excluding small operators as the industry moved away from the hard-rock phosphate deposits of northern Florida and began using large quarrying draglines and flotation plants to harvest the softer, more scattered "land pebble" deposits of central Florida, mostly in Polk and Hillsborough Counties east of Tampa.[10]

World War II brought boom times back to the Florida phosphate industry by disrupting production elsewhere in the world and hugely increasing total demand. In 1941 United States phosphate production reached a record high, and Florida accounted for 82 percent of the total. Production and profits continued to skyrocket during the postwar years. By 1960 the industry employed more than seven thousand workers in Polk and Hillsborough Counties and supplied 22 percent of the tax income of Polk County. Production doubled between 1950 and 1963 to meet the worldwide need for fertilizer, and by 1965 Florida's annual production of nearly sixty-five million long tons of phosphates represented 86 percent of the United States total and almost 30 percent of the world's total. Increasingly during the 1960s the extraction of phosphates was performed by some of the largest, most powerful corporations in the nation. Giant oil companies—among the few concerns with the massive capital and technological resources necessary to enter large-scale phosphate production— were attracted by the industry's potential for growth as a rapidly expanding global population created demand for chemical fertilizer. These companies gradually bought up phosphate manufacturers and nearly tripled production capacity between 1963 and 1967.[11]

The emergence of a major extractive industry monopolized by a handful of large, powerful corporations greatly altered the culture of the mostly rural area devoted to raising cattle and citrus fruit. For many residents of Polk and Hillsborough Counties, the most crucial change began, almost unnoticed, in the late 1940s and early 1950s, when phosphate-mining companies branched out into the chemical processing of fertilizer. Dust and spoil, but little else, had been the by-products of the extraction, separation, and crushing of mineral phosphates; the processed phosphate had been shipped elsewhere without further chemical refining. However, after 1948, when the Armour Agricultural Chemical Company opened its first local plants to produce chemical fertilizer and sulfuric acid (used in the production of superphosphate and phosphoric acid), the phosphate industry's emissions into the air and water grew progressively more obvious to residents of the two counties.[12]

Phosphorus, nitrogen, and potassium are necessary for soil fertility and are critical in the cellular metabolism of most life forms. The same three elements are the main ingredients of commercial fertilizer, offered in varying proportions to suit different soils. Atoms of phosphorus, a common element in the earth's crust, are usually found chemically bonded to other elements to form salts. The presence of salts containing chemically bonded phosphorus made possible the development of the Florida phosphate industry, and by-products of processing the substance severely polluted the air, land, and water in the state's mining districts.[13]

The phosphates in raw rock phosphate are rendered largely unusable by the presence of fluorine, which bonds tightly to the tricalcium phosphates, making them insoluble in water and hence unavailable to plants and, indirectly, to animals. Plants growing in soils deprived of available phosphorus have difficulty developing and reproducing, while animals grazing on phosphorus-starved lands frequently show stunted growth and malformed bones. Because of the tendency of fluorine to lock in phosphate ions, these symptoms of phosphorus deprivation ironically can appear on lands containing abundant but unavailable phosphates.[14]

During the nineteenth century, however, agricultural scientists discovered that treatment with either heat or sulfuric acid (a process known as "beneficiation") unlocks phosphates and produces usable forms of the material. Since the acid method of beneficiation was cheaper, it soon came to dominate the manufacture of superphosphate, a monocalcium phosphate compound with more available phosphorus. The introduction of large facilities in central Florida to produce sulfuric acid and react it with raw mineral phosphates exposed the surrounding environment to a host of new chemical by-products, such as sulfuric acid and sulfur oxides. Industrial pollution-control techniques, and the recognition of the need for them, were minimal at best in the late 1940s, and chemical by-products were simply emitted into the air and water. A further level of beneficiation brought further pollution, for, in order to make triple superphosphate—which derived more soluble, usable monocalcium phosphate—the raw phosphates were treated with phosphoric acid, itself derived by reacting rock phosphate with sulfuric acid. Florida's phosphate industry kept adding new, complicated chemical processes with additional sources of pollution such as the production of elemental phosphorus and the reacting of phosphates with ammonia to produce diammonium phosphate, a fertilizer base containing nitrogen as well as phosphorus. Each stage of processing involved increased complexity and potential pollution from the chemical plants.[15]

Various sulfur- and nitrogen-oxide by-products of the chemical processing of phosphates were potentially harmful when released into the environment. Most significant for local residents was the fluorine tightly bonded to the phosphate rock and accounting for around 4 percent of the total weight of phosphate mined. During treatment with sulfuric or phosphoric acid, fluorine compounds—along with various relatively harmless silicates and other impurities in the soil matrix—were separated from the phosphates. The resulting mixture of liberated impurities led to new combinations, such as fluorosilicic acid, released during the processing, drying, and curing of phosphates. These fluorides—compounds containing fluorine—from the phosphate processing plants were emitted as dusts or gases that blew freely through the surrounding countryside, with the chemically active fluorine atoms in them ready to react anew with whatever they contacted.[16]

Airborne fluorides are not only a potentially serious human health hazard if present in high enough concentrations but are also harmful to many of the traditional mainstays of the local economy, including cattle, citrus fruit, vegetables, and gladioli. Gladioli are unusually sensitive to fluorine and may not form flowers properly or at all if exposed. Various other ornamental plants, fruit trees, and leafy vegetables are also sensitive to fluorine as well as sulfur dioxide, as truck farmers and commercial flower growers near major cities in Florida and around the nation learned to their dismay, as industrial and urban air pollution around them worsened and spread.[17]

Hardest hit in central Florida's Polk and Hillsborough Counties were the major livestock and citrus industries, although at first, few farmers knew what afflicted their animals and crops.[18] In 1949 Florida was one of the largest cattle-producing states in the nation, and Polk County had more cattle than any other county in Florida. Florida was also the nation's biggest supplier of oranges, limes, lemons, and grapefruit, and Polk was in the center of the state's citrus belt, producing a quarter of the state's citrus crop and 16 percent of the whole nation's citrus during the 1950s. However, by that time, Polk County was also the center of the nation's phosphate industry, the lion's share of which was within a twenty-five-mile radius of Bartow and included Lakeland and Mulberry in western Polk County, as well as slivers of Hillsborough County to the west and Manatee County to the southwest. Central Floridians were soon to learn that the agricultural mainstays and the refining industries were largely incompatible.[19]

After 1948 local farmers and ranchers saw citrus yields fall markedly and cattle sicken. Citrus leaves began to yellow around the edges and fall off prematurely, and generally stunted growth patterns were observed on both fruit and fruit trees. At the same time local cattle ranchers began to note in their animals stiff leg joints, strange knobs on ribs and leg bones, inexplicable starvation, and prematurely rotted teeth. Although it took a few years before scientists established the connection between these occurrences and the phosphate industry's fluoride emissions, by the early 1950s state citrus experts and veterinary researchers at universities in Florida and Georgia had found the link.[20]

As understanding gradually dawned on them, local citizens mobilized to confront and abate the threat. A citizens' committee of citrus growers, ranchers, and other unhappy residents formed in Polk County during the early 1950s and took the lead in documenting evidence of fluorine damage, presenting such data to state and local authorities by 1954 at the latest. In 1955, as a result of this agitation, the state legislature created an interim joint committee to investigate the many public complaints of industrial air pollution in central Florida. The committee held numerous public hearings in Polk and Hillsborough Counties between 1955 and 1957, then issued a report to the state legislature recommending that it establish a state air pollution–control commission with authority to enact all needed control regulations. During the same period, the Florida State Board of Health began a limited program of sampling for atmospheric sulfur oxides and fluorides in central Florida. In 1955 the board of health was given statutory authority to adopt all rules and regulations necessary "to control pollution of the air . . . in any place whatsoever," but a later federal report remarked curtly, "No substantial action resulted from adopting this law." [21]

Following the interim joint committee's report and the board of health's inaction, the state legislature passed the Florida Air Pollution Control Law on June 18, 1957. This act created the Florida Air Pollution Control Commission (APCC), a panel of nine members representing government, industry, and the general public, to hear and take action on complaints about air pollution in the state. The commission was given authority to establish air pollution–control districts covering parts or the whole of one or more counties following a public hearing to determine the necessity of such a district. The public hearing was to be held if county commissioners requested it, or if 15 percent or more of the freeholders in an area petitioned for it, or on the commission's own initiative. The APCC was also given the power to promulgate rules and regulations regarding aerial contamination, which were to be enforced by the board of health. Chronic polluters were to be warned and given a chance to correct their problems voluntarily; however, if such "conference, conciliation, and persuasion" was not effective within a given time, the commission was authorized to give to an incorrigible polluter an ultimatum backed with the threat of an injunction against all further violations. This air pollution–control law was similar to early anti-pollution legislative efforts in other states and cities, including the potentially troublesome provision for divided authority between the APCC and the state board of health. The original law was amended in 1959 to change the composition of the commission to ten members, including three state government officials serving ex-officio, two representatives of industry, two "discreet citizens" representing the general public, a sanitary engineer, and one representative each from the cattle and citrus industries.[22]

After Governor Leroy Collins appointed the first nine commission members to their four-year terms in September 1957, residents of Polk County quickly petitioned for a hearing on the necessity of establishing an air pollution–control district in the phosphate belt. In October 1957 the directors of Florida Citrus Mutual, an association of central Florida citrus growers, adopted, in conjunction with other local citizens' organizations, an angry resolution addressed to the APCC, which claimed serious economic harm to local citrus growers and cattle ranchers as well as injury to human health and demanded immediate action. Consequently, air pollution in the phosphate belt was one of the main items on the agenda of the first meeting of the APCC on December 12, 1957. By March 1958 the commission had created Florida's first air pollution–control district, which covered Polk County. In July 1959 a similar district was created for Hillsborough County, and on June 10, 1960, the two districts were merged to form the Polk-Hillsborough County Air Pollution Control District, which for several years was the only one in the state.[23]

Meanwhile, the Florida APCC began setting standards for air pollution in its districts. In March 1959 they adopted regulations for acceptable levels of fluoride in pasture grass in Polk County, and the same standard—forty parts per million (ppm)—was applied to Hillsborough County in October 1959. In July 1960 new regulations were established for fluorides in gladioli in the two-county area, and that December a new rule requiring APCC review of engineering plans for new industrial construction or alteration was passed. During the same period, the board of health officials responsible for running the Polk-Hillsborough County Air Pollution Control District began to survey levels of ambient fluorides and sulfur oxides in the air and fluorine concentrations in local vegetation. They also collected from local industries information on emissions and started negotiations with company officials toward abating pollution.[24]

Florida officials hoped that these policy initiatives would allow local problems to be addressed and solved at the state and local level, without interference from federal authorities. However, during the late 1950s and early 1960s, like their counterparts in other areas of the nation, Florida officials were reluctant to confront a powerful, polluting industry that increasingly dominated the economy of central Florida, and the cries of local citizens for protection from pollution brought soothing responses but little action. At the same time, the federal air pollution–control program remained mired in 1950s federalism, able to offer polite suggestions but unable to produce results.[25]

The federal government's participation in Florida's air pollution–control efforts began tentatively in 1957, just a few years after the state government began paying attention to the problem, which had developed since World War II. That April, Dr. Harry Heimann, director of the Operational Research Section of the Air Pollution Medical Program of the United States Public Health Service (USPHS), went to Jacksonville, Florida, to discuss public health and other issues related to air pollution with Dr. John MacDonald of the Florida State Board of Health's Division of Industrial Hygiene, then the leading state agency in air pollution control. The main topic of discussion was the state's most obvious air polluter, the phosphate industry of Polk County. In a subsequent report to his superiors in the federal bureaucracy regarding the seven triple superphosphate plants then operating around Bartow and Mulberry, Heimann reported "undocumented and documented . . . effects of fluoride on grazing animals, damage to conifers, and irritation of eyes and throat among the people" and suggested the Bartow-Mulberry area as a "'single-industry' type of community of the kind we were interested in studying at some future time." [26]

From May 28 to June 7, 1957, in the wake of Heimann's visit, staff members of the federal Occupational Health Program, a division of the USPHS, joined Florida authorities in making a preliminary in-plant survey of work-related health problems in the phosphate industry. This study collected information about the processes involved in manufacturing agricultural phosphates and compiled statistics on the workforce and on the ages and operating characteristics of individual plants. The state and federal researchers were also able to identify air pollution as the likeliest source of any job-related health problems that might emerge. In testing the levels of workers' exposure in different parts of the phosphate-processing operation, researchers found that "some work areas had extremely high concentrations of dusts and fluorides, both gaseous and particulate," and, though such exposures were generally "brief and intermittent," the scientists recommended that "management study these operations and assure adequate protection of the worker" against noxious dust and gases. While the visiting scientists found no clear evidence of either acute symptoms of fluoride poisoning or of illness from subacute, chronic exposure, they did admit that the lack of information—such as workers' health records or previous medical studies of fluoride exposure—made it impossible to form conclusions about health risk. [27]

One month later, in July 1957—as part of the federal research project in co-operation with Florida—C. Stafford Brandt, a plant pathologist and official in the USPHS's Air Pollution Engineering Program, made a trip to Lakeland, Florida, in Polk County, to observe reported fluoride damage to local citrus groves. Researchers at Florida State University's Citrus Experiment Station at Lake Alfred had by then discovered that fluorides caused a unique pattern of chlorosis (blotchy, uneven distribution of chlorophyll, indicating sickly leaves) in local citrus trees that could be reproduced experimentally by spraying or dusting trees with fluoride compounds. However, the diagnosis of fluoride-chlorosis was ambiguous because soil nutrient deficiencies could also cause chlorosis; for instance, manganese deficiency produced a pattern similar to that caused by excessive fluoride exposure. Brandt reported that the whole picture was further complicated by the area's highly leached, sandy soils, which provided few nutrients. Citrus growers had to add nutrients by using fertilizers and sprays. It was difficult to sustain the correct balance of minerals and, consequently, "deficiency and toxicity symptoms [were] common in many groves." Brandt failed to note that, notwithstanding such considerations, citrus culture had been extensive and profitable in the area for decades. While citrus growers alleged that fluoride-chlorosis reduced the yield and productivity of their groves, Brandt noted that no precise evidence or estimate of the extent of damage had yet been advanced. The only anti-pollution steps were by state citrus experts, who were merely monitoring the problem. He somewhat high-handedly concluded, "In view of the strictly local and minor importance of this symptom in relation to the entire citrus industry of the State, this attitude by the State Station is understandable and justifiable." In this statement and many others, Brandt displayed a tendency common to professional scientists—treating the observations of laymen with disdain.[28]

Brandt was also suspicious of claims that pollution had damaged local livestock. Despite his lack of veterinary training, Brandt explained the experimental and diagnostic difficulties in determining whether the emissions from phosphate plants were harming cattle. He emphasized various other factors and variables that might have contributed to the apparent rash of fluorosis in cattle—high natural fluoride levels from phosphatic local soils or malnutrition and substandard care of animals in Polk County, which Brandt characterized as "the fringe of the cattle-producing area," where he found cattle-raising operations "somewhat marginal." He concluded, "Undoubtedly, fluorosis does occur" but maintained that it would be difficult to distinguish the effects of air pollution from those of natural fluoride levels. Brandt's lack of expertise in animal health did not prevent him from casting doubt on the validity of local ranchers' claims of unprecedented damage.[29]

Despite his disdain for the allegations of Polk County residents, Brandt found that industrial pollution was visible and serious, and he criticized local phosphate refiners for their nonchalant approach. He observed, "The industry cannot hide from the casual observer that there is a dust problem and that in certain areas, vegetation has been injured and even destroyed as a result of the dust or fumes. Cooperation among the individual companies in the approach to these problems would appear to be nonexistent." Brandt remarked that only two companies were doing any research whatsoever on the effect of their emissions on vegetation and that "no exchange of information between [these] two companies" was taking place. Some of the phosphate refiners were also "operating producing [citrus] groves," but, as Brandt resignedly noted, "The public relations possibilities of these company-operated groves has not been exploited except to a limited extent." As with many federal scientists of the day, Brandt wrote reports that suggest, by their general tone, that he identified more closely with corporations and the scientists employed by them than with citizens who lacked scientific training.[30]

In February 1958 Brandt returned to central Florida to survey local conditions and was accompanied by a higher federal air pollution-control official, Dr. Arthur C. Stern of the USPHS's Robert H. Taft Sanitary Engineering Laboratory in Cincinnati. The two men joined members of the Florida Air Pollution Control Commission, industrial representatives, and other interested citizens on a day-long field trip around Polk County to inspect damage to animals and citrus groves and the control measures implemented by the phosphate industry. On the morning of February 28 the air pollution experts reviewed emissions control efforts at three major phosphate-processing facilities. Later, they were shown damage to citrus groves and livestock. Although Stern was an engineer whose primary expertise was in air pollution control, not plant or animal physiology, he did not share Brandt's doubts about the damage of fluoride emissions to regional agriculture. He noted that in numerous citrus groves across the county, in addition to severe frost damage and signs of nutritional deficiency, "the distinctively chlorotic leaf pattern which is allegedly due to fluorides was evident." Pointing to earlier experiments that produced the same patterns using fluoride sprays and the confinement of this pattern to the phosphate refining area, Stern contradicted Brandt's earlier skepticism about the diagnosis, concluding, "This evidence is quite sound and is probably sufficient." The federal visitors also saw evidence of fluorosis in cattle, although Stern also noted that complicating factors such as poor animal nutrition made it difficult to attribute all symptoms to fluorosis. After attending a meeting of the Florida APCC, receiving accumulated data on local fluoride emissions, and discussing the potential role of the federal government in assisting the state's air pollution–control efforts, Brandt and Stern left for Washington, D.C.[31]

The scientifically and politically complicated Florida air pollution problem had developed during a period when the federal government had only begun to make tentative steps into the field of pollution control; its power remained limited and its role uncertain. During their February 1958 inspection, Stern and Brandt demonstrated some of the approaches of federal officials toward state and local air pollution. First, within the limits of assumptions regarding federalism, they responded to the public outcry in pollution-afflicted areas. Stern presented the possibility that citizens could effectively demand governmental action against fluoride pollution, informing the Florida APCC that widespread and recurrent public complaints clearly indicated the need for an air pollution–control district and further explaining how the federal government could offer limited research and technical assistance. Brandt, on the other hand, seemed to discourage citizens from complaining about fluoride emissions and denied the effects of pollution. For instance, he alleged that the cattle he had seen during his tour were poorly managed and hence were borderline malnourished relative to better-fed and better-tended animals in other states—an observation subsequently challenged by a University of Florida veterinarian. He also noted that natural fluoride in the water might account for some of the observed problems and concluded that the subject required more intensive study. He appears to have discounted citizens' claims that there had been no similar conditions in local plants and animals before the superphosphate plants were established, a technocratic attitude typical of a period when there was great faith in the objectivity of science and scientists—and very little in the observations of laypeople.[32]

Besides revealing an emerging dichotomy between an activist federal approach and a quietist one, Stern and Brandt's performance in Polk County also displayed two approaches to the quandary presented by research versus action—the conflict between experts demanding almost impossibly strict standards of scientific proof before taking action versus advocates of less rigorous standards of scientific proof followed by immediate action. Brandt dwelt upon variables that cast doubt upon the existence of an air pollution problem, ignored the obvious environmental damage because its cause could not be proved beyond a doubt, and, lacking rigorous proof of causation, hesitated to take corrective action. Even though he was aware of complicating factors, Arthur Stern, like most subsequent observers, admitted the existence of significant environmental damage and advocated action to control pollution. This debate over gathering sufficient scientific evidence before taking action— within both the federal air pollution–control establishment and wider scientific and engineering circles—tended to split observers into two camps: those who shared the health concerns of the public and were inclined to act against polluters and those who believed the claims of industry that there were no demonstrable ill effects from emissions and were persuaded to intervene on behalf of the public only by undeniable scientific evidence. Most federal scientists during this period had the same training as industrial scientists, often came to government from the private sector, and tended toward the quietistic approach. For many years, such attitudes remained an impediment to a meaningful federal role in air pollution control. Despite the scientists' desire to be politically neutral, their tacit defense of the status quo and of inactivity inevitably had economic and political ramifications for industry and the public.[33]

After the creation of Florida's first Air Pollution Control District in Polk County in March 1958, state control officials sought help from the federal government to stretch their inadequate budget; they requested aid for research programs and the loan of costly, advanced air pollution sampling and monitoring equipment. Specifically, Florida officials hoped that the USPHS would provide experts to make initial veterinary and epidemiological studies in order to define the nature of the environmental damage, including dental surveys to ascertain whether fluoride pollution was affecting the teeth of local children. However, Dr. Wilton M. Fisher, director of the federal Air Pollution Medical Program (APMP), took a narrow view of the federal role and rejected most of these requests, noting that Florida's anti-pollution concerns were directed less toward public health than toward plant and animal health. He regretted that, though the USPHS "could gain considerably by working with [Florida officials] in this new, almost unexplored, area of total community study," recent federal budget reductions made such cooperation impossible. While the federal government periodically agreed to lend to the Polk County Air Pollution Control District sophisticated and sometimes untried new monitoring equipment, which was frequently unreliable, it was unwilling to lend scientists and technicians for any significant period and offered only "technical assistance or consultation on a short-term basis." Regarding the state's request for help in conducting a full veterinary survey of the effects of fluoride emissions on livestock, Fisher politely suggested that the Florida authorities ask the United States Department of Agriculture (USDA) for a federal veterinarian to assist with their studies of the effects of pollution on animal health.[34]

The USDA, however, was not very interested, either, so instead of a full veterinary survey, Polk County received a visit from Dr. Norman L. Garlick, a veterinary livestock inspector with the USDA's Agricultural Research Service—Animal Disease Eradication Division, who made a brief inspection tour with state and local officials. Garlick, whose veterinary expertise contrasted with earlier federal visitors, found that particular local animals "demonstrated the extreme maximum of dental fluorosis" as well as obvious exostoses on the leg and rib bones, and he noted that calves raised under such conditions would have shortened productive life spans. Besides affirming that local livestock were being poisoned by airborne fluorides from nearby phosphate plants, Garlick, better able to judge than Brandt, observed that cattle ranching in Polk County was a significant and prosperous business: 110,000 head of beef cattle grazed on 900,000 acres of range land, plus a further 7,000 dairy cows and "an important beef cattle purebreeding industry." In short, the USDA expert had no doubt about the existence of serious air pollution, and he emphasized the potential for significant economic damage to the county. He urged further studies to assess effects and to determine safe exposure levels, but there is no evidence that other federal officials followed his suggestion.[35]

Federal officials were frequently reminded of the Florida situation by the letters and complaints that flowed in from angry citizens who were convinced that local air pollution threatened their health and prosperity. They despaired of prompting their reluctant state officials into action. Federal air pollution–control authorities also received worried pleas for help and reassurance from local officials facing a firestorm of public protest over the phosphate industry's emissions. In late January 1959 John H. Dewell, acting attorney for Polk County, sent a request for information to Harry G. Hanson, director of the USPH's Taft Laboratory, emphasizing local citizens' concerns about the effects of fluorides on human health. Dewell alleged that at a recent meeting of the Florida Air Pollution Control Commission, a representative from the state board of health had stated "as an established fact that there was no hazard to human health associated with the air pollution condition now existing in Polk County, Florida," and that "as a result of this fact the U.S. Public Health Service could not participate in any program directed to the elimination of the said air pollution condition." Dewell requested thorough scientific confirmation and evidence of such findings from the federal authorities to reassure "the numerous complaining citizens from whom we receive almost daily inquiries," since, as he continued, "[a] responsible group of vitally interested citizens of this County have in the past few years accumulated data which indicated that under U. S. Public Health Service standards human health was endangered," leading both citizens and county commissioners to have become "greatly alarmed." [36]

Dewell's polite letter of concern touched off considerable discussion within the medical and engineering branches of the federal air pollution–control program. In the initial draft of his response, Hanson protested that the state official at the recent meeting had probably misinterpreted what he had heard, since the USPHS had "worked closely with the Florida State Board of Health in air pollution matters for the last several years." Professing his agency's interest in further efforts to control the region's industrial fluoride emissions, Hanson noted the earlier visits for investigation and consultation by USPHS staff and other federal officials, and he pointed to the agency's ongoing efforts to help Polk County secure federal grant funds and to recruit a chemist skilled in the analysis of fluorides in vegetation to train chemists for the Polk County pollution abatement program. In his draft, Hanson did admit, "No definitive studies have been made in the area to determine whether a hazard to human health exists." However, he argued that Florida air pollution–control authorities had adopted a sound approach by using their limited resources to control problems for which definite information existed, such as damage to cattle and vegetation. Livestock and plants were more sensitive to fluoride emissions than humans were, so if conditions were improved to such a point that plants and animals were no longer afflicted, then risk to human health would be alleviated. Hanson did not add that, given the basic complexities of air pollution science and epidemiological research, compounded by the limited budgets of both the Florida and federal air pollution–control programs, any thorough research program would be a prolonged undertaking that still might not produce conclusive answers. The scientists of the USPHS viewed problems in terms of extended research programs and sought to downplay the emotional and political aspects of issues such as air pollution, including the public's understandable desire for definite answers regarding health risks.[37]

Perhaps because Hanson's draft response was not sufficiently reassuring, Dr. Richard A. Prindle, acting chief of the Air Pollution Medical Program, answered Dewell. Prindle offered a prepared statement of his staff's estimation of the possibility that airborne fluoride threatened human health, which the USPHS medical experts found very unlikely. Nevertheless, Prindle added, the staff's opinion would not preclude federal participation "in any program directed towards further study and appraisal of fluoride air pollution problems and their control," and he promised the USPHS would continue to work on their problems "to the extent that our funds and personnel will allow."[38]

Other governmental entities also wanted the USPHS to tell them not to worry. The Florida State Board of Health had received a similar request for reassurance on the health issue from Polk County officials, and the board turned to the federal government for a response. Of greater concern to Florida officials, some residents of central Florida had threatened to sue the phosphate companies over fluoride emissions. In order to defuse this tense and politically problematic situation, state officials wanted "a statement from the Public Health Service saying that there is no evidence of human health effects as a consequence of fluoride community air pollution in the Polk County area." In an internal memorandum to his superiors on January 29, 1959, Richard Prindle observed that the earlier survey by the USPHS Occupational Health Program of in-plant fluoride exposure among phosphate workers had become "the subject of a bargaining problem between industry and the union," and the local phosphate industry had hired Dr. Louis C. McCabe, formerly with the federal Bureau of Mines, former director of the Los Angeles County Air Pollution Control District, and one of the country's best-known experts on air pollution, to conduct research and offer expert testimony supporting the industry regarding employees' complaints about workplace pollution. The threatened lawsuits, the uneasy labor relations, and increasing evidence of significant damage to citrus and livestock created concern among various constituencies in the central Florida phosphate belt. The state board of health hoped that the federal government could soothe fears, which state and local officials evidently had been unable to do. Florida officials suggested that the USPHS point out that the occupational health survey had found no evidence of fluorosis and that unless an upcoming state investigation of the teeth of local school children produced evidence of mottling and stains characteristic of fluorosis, then citizens had no grounds for worry. The various branches of the USPHS concerned with air pollution and occupational and dental health immediately began to prepare the reassuring statement requested by Florida officials.[39]

The subsequent USPHS statement on the human health hazard from air-borne fluorides in Polk County began by conceding that air pollution had damaged vegetation and livestock and then observed that many plants accumulated fluoride in much greater quantities than would be found in the ambient air and animals that grazed on such plants would have an elevated exposure to fluorides. Studies of livestock fluorosis in other areas of the United States had found symptoms when concentrations of fluoride in the air ranged from 0.01 to 0.4 micrograms per cubic meter of air, which was about one-ten thousandth of the threshold human occupational exposure limit of 2.5 milligrams of fluoride per cubic meter of air that the American Conference of Governmental Industrial Hygienists had declared a safe average concentration for workers to face "eight hours a day, five days a week, without adverse health effects." USPHS officials thus concluded that "effects may become manifest in foraging cattle long before there are evident changes in humans from inhalation." Since the mission of the federal officials was to discount the possibility of serious damage to human health, they did not go on to observe that no one had yet properly studied or set standards for exposure to lower concentrations of aerial fluoride twenty-four hours a day or for the exposure of children, the elderly, and other sensitive individuals, standards that would differ from the workplace exposure of healthy adult males.[40]

Discussing the various ways that humans could be exposed to fluorides, the report noted that the earlier USPHS occupational health survey of phosphate-processing plants in Polk County had found extremely high concentrations of fluorides in some work areas. However, despite workers' complaints about health effects, the report's authors found that "no factual evidence has been provided to us that would indicate that health effects from air-borne fluorides have occurred in this area." Since outdoor concentrations were of course generally much lower than in the phosphate plants, the authors stated that "it is our opinion that at the present time the available data do not indicate the existence of a hazard to human health as a result of air-borne fluorides in the community." Urging further research, the report concluded that "the reduction of the fluoride levels in the community to the point where no further damage occurs to cattle would be a highly commendable aim" and "would assure levels with a great margin of safety for humans, as well as contributing to the solution of obvious economic problems." With this generally soothing disclaimer, the USPHS passed the issue back to Florida officials, who found the report to be just what they had wanted. Federal authorities thus helped state officials and a polluting industry to contain public dissatisfaction for a time, reflecting their understanding of the mission of the federal antipollution program—providing uncritical support for state authorities and maintaining cautious distance from angry citizens.[41]

About this same time, a federal air pollution–control expert visited central Florida as part of a program of limited consultation and technical assistance to state pollution-control agencies. This visit and its aftermath—the "Rossano affair"—caused unexpected tension between federal and state officials and further revealed some of the fundamental weaknesses of the early federal air pollution–control program.[42]

From March 30 to April 3, 1959, August T. Rossano Jr., chief of the Office of State and Community Services in the federal Air Pollution Engineering Program, made a tour of inspection around Polk County with Harry Seifert, director of the Polk County Air Pollution Control District. On the way from the Tampa airport, they inspected orange groves and took samples that, upon analysis, showed very high fluorine concentrations in both fruit and foliage. Over the next two days, besides reviewing the Polk County District's offices and laboratory, Rossano toured two local phosphate plants. On April 2, after discussions with Seifert about "program plans, procedures, and problems," Rossano inspected deformed bones that revealed fluorosis in local cattle, which had been collected by Seifert and Dr. Garlick of the USDA. He then saw parts of Polk County that were exposed to extensive plumes of emissions from the phosphate mills "dense enough to seriously affect visibility on the highway." Rossano also met with a local livestock veterinarian who had mapped the geographical distribution of the many diagnosed cases of fluorosis in cattle, which Rossano found "well interspersed among the phosphate plants." The morning of April 3 Rossano flew to Washington, before returning to his usual post in Cincinnati.[43]

Unfortunately for Rossano, he also had made statements to local journalists at press conferences arranged by Seifert. Rossano told reporters from the Lakeland *Ledger* and Tampa *Tribune* that because a full 75 percent of the phosphate produced in the nation was mined in the area around the Florida county, he "assumed," based on similar situations, that there could be danger from pollution. Noting the substantial tourist, retirement, agricultural, and industrial "enterprises" in the area, Rossano declared that a way would have to be found for them to coexist harmoniously. He emphasized that none of the enterprises should be banned in favor of others but that the one causing problems for others would have to be cleaned up. Going beyond the careful balancing of economic equities, Rossano, in contrast to his superiors in the USPHS who had recently helped Florida officials to gloss over the matter, warned about the possible danger to human health. Rossano truthfully reminded local citizens, "[W]e don't know what effects the fluorides will have on children in their formative years." Observing the definite presence of fluorosis in cattle, he declared, "We can't wait until fluorosis begins to damage humans before we act." [44]

Rossano also offered direct criticism of state programs and recommended a more activist approach. "There seems to be a good deal of confusion between the State Board of Health and the State Air Pollution Control Commission," he stated, and while allowing that "money alone" would not solve the local problem, he called for more funding and for clarification of regulatory laws and of the duties and functions of pollution contol agencies. The federal expert also implicitly criticized the gradual pace of action in Polk County. Stressing the significance of air pollution to the economy and health of Florida and the rest of the nation, he described the current local control effort as "only lip service." He found the sixty-five thousand dollars originally allocated by the state legislature for two years of expenses for air pollution control "very little" relative to the size and importance of local pollution. He further opined that Polk County should contribute to its own air pollution–control district rather than leaving that responsibility entirely in the hands of the state. As he pointed out, "Why should outsiders not bothered with the problem finance it all?" As a veteran of the greatest battle against air pollution up to that time, Rossano noted that Los Angeles County had spent four million dollars the previous year to fight air pollution. He approvingly noted recent examples of joint federal-local cooperation on funding and conducting air pollution surveys. Thus, Rossano argued, Floridians could do a better job in attacking air pollution, and the federal government could help them to do so. [45]

Considering the extensive evidence of underfunding, understaffing, and loose organization in Florida's air pollution–control program, including Harry Seifert's valiant efforts to conduct a meaningful countywide monitoring and control effort with only two assistants and inadequate equipment, Rossano's criticisms seem fairly gentle. However, various Florida officials resented Rossano's public statement. On April 3 they read the *Tribune* interview, and the same day, Dr. Elwood R. Hendrickson, professor of sanitary engineering at the University of Florida at Gainesville and chairman of the APCC, called Arthur Stern of the USPHS's Taft Laboratory in a fury over the criticism of the state program, declaring that he and Dr. Wilson T. Sowder, Florida's state health officer, were personally affronted by Rossano's statement. According to Hendrickson, Rossano had charged that they were "doing it all wrong" and that they provided "insufficient support to Seifert." Hendrickson and Sowder both believed that the visiting federal official had "cut [the] ground out from under [the] State" and its air pollution–control efforts.[46]

Rossano discounted Hendrickson's complaints. In explaining his actions and statements in Polk County to Stern, Rossano claimed that the writer of the article had quoted him selectively to emphasize the shortcomings of the existing Florida control program and to give the piece a slightly more incendiary tone in order to cater to a reading public "quite 'fed up' with existing vacillation."

Rossano indicated that he empathized with the public in its frustration over state inactivity on controlling air pollution and had little sympathy for Hendrickson and other Florida officials, observing, "The need for clarification of duties, better communication, and leadership and more support can be backed up by facts." He also suggested that Hendrickson's anger over the facts revealed in the article might have stemmed from a guilty conscience.[47]

Regardless of Rossano's views, the whole matter snowballed. The following day, Dr. Louis McCabe, who was then employed by the Polk County phosphate industry to conduct air pollution studies in order to protect the industry from legal liability, called Harry Heimann, assistant chief of the federal Air Pollution Medical Program, complaining of the "good deal of excitement in [the] mid-Florida area" arising from Rossano's press conference and various statements "critical of the local Commission and the industry involved." In a memo to Richard Prindle, chief of the Air Pollution Medical Program, Heimann noted that McCabe wished to discuss the matter with Prindle and Vernon G. MacKenzie, of the federal Air Pollution Engineering Branch, because McCabe "had received a letter from the legal persons representing the local industries" that "was condemnatory of Rossano and the Public Health Service." Like the Florida state health officials, the phosphate industry lashed out angrily and defensively when noxious conditions that it had produced and was failing to correct were publicly exposed by a representative of the federal government. Heimann suggested to McCabe that Rossano should also be invited to the meeting with Prindle and MacKenzie so that he "could himself deny having made the statements," since, as Heimann noted, "I did *not* believe that the remarks attributed to Rossano by the newspapers were in fact made by Rossano." McCabe was to arrange a meeting with the other three men.[48]

That same day, April 6, Dr. Clarence M. Sharp of the state health department's Bureau of Preventable Diseases wrote a letter to Harry Seifert sharply criticizing him for what had transpired. Noting that he had received the clipping from the Tampa *Tribune* along with an angry call from Dr. Hendrickson and David B. Lee, another sanitary engineer connected with the state health department, Sharp blasted Rossano for his indiscretion in revealing the actual state of affairs, claiming that he had never seen "a more flagrant violation of Federal-States Relationship [*sic*] than the statement made by Dr. Rossano," who had inflamed the "explosive situation" in Polk County. Sharp also blamed Seifert for the unwanted exposure, charging him with having coached Rossano on what to say. Reflecting on the damage in near-apocalyptic terms, Sharp concluded, "I am requesting and directing that no more consultants be brought into Polk County without first clearing it with Dr. Sowder, Dr. Hardy, Mr. Lee or with this office. If we get out of this new embarrassing situation with a program at all I will be extremely surprised."[49]

Sharp's angry letter to Seifert shows the difficulty of conducting a meaning-ful federal air pollution–control program at a time when federal powers in such areas remained very limited and states jealously guarded their rights against federal incursions—except when they could get money from Uncle Sam with no strings attached. Federal officials could dangle modest incentives to stimu-late cooperation and significant control efforts on the part of the states, but they were powerless to tell state officials how to conduct their programs, and, evidently, even gentle criticism of disorganization and inactivity caused state officials and industrialists to throw tantrums. This sort of relationship seemed to suit the USPHS well enough. According to their professional and institu-tional ethos, they were scientists, not politicians; they generally wished to keep their work strictly scientific and "above politics"; they assumed, incorrectly, that thorough scientific understanding would lead automatically and directly to effective control efforts; and for a long time it seemed not to bother them that their elaborate scientific investigations produced very little concrete action and progress. They were ill equipped to respond when politics and emotionalism intruded into their white-coated world of technical expertise and were able only to fall back on their standard policy of not offending state officials.[50]

Within the USPHS, the matter continued to ripple outward. Interestingly, the hapless Rossano received backhanded support from various knowledge-able federal air pollution experts. In a memo to Rossano's chief in the Bu-reau of State Services, Vernon G. MacKenzie noted Rossano's criticism of "the organization, administration, and financial support" of Florida's air pollu-tion–control program, adding, "From program knowledge of the situation in Florida, some of these criticisms would appear to be justified; however, voicing them through a newspaper interview rather than privately to the State would appear undesirable." MacKenzie concluded that in the future, any federal con-sultants reviewing Florida's control efforts should "report directly to the State" and avoid the newspapers. In a similar vein, Howard W. Chapman from the USPHS's regional office in Atlanta wrote a confidential letter to Assistant U.S. Surgeon General Mark D. Hollis, mentioning the "rather severe" repercussions from the Rossano affair. He further observed, "From my personal knowledge of the air pollution program in Florida, I believe that Rossano's observations are essentially correct, however, it probably would have been better if some things had been left unsaid. . . . In Rossano's defense, indeed, he walked into a very complex and confusing situation." As the experts agreed, Rossano's prob-lem was not with truth but with spin control.[51]

Despite MacKenzie and Chapman's defense of Rossano, the matter did not die quietly. That same day, April 7, Dr. Wilson Sowder wrote an indignant letter to U.S. Surgeon General Leroy E. Burney, complaining that "statements attributed to Doctor Rossano upset a good many people and will not be helpful to our Air Pollution Control Program here in Florida." Sowder also criticized Rossano for suggesting that the county contribute toward a state program directed exclusively toward solving its particular problem, though this was the practice at the time in most other states; in many places, air pollution–control programs remained chiefly a local responsibility that sometimes received partial state funding. In concluding his angry missive, Sowder fumed, "I need not go into detail as to the impropriety of these statements"—regardless of their accuracy. He charged Rossano with having done lasting harm to the Florida program and alleged, "He did not act in accordance with the long standing policy and practice of the Public Health Service by assisting us in a courteous, tactful and diplomatic manner."[52]

Besides attempting unsuccessfully to placate Sowder, Dr. W. H. Aufranc, regional medical director of the Atlanta USPHS office, also issued a report to Surgeon General Burney on the Rossano affair. The regional director sharply criticized Rossano for exceeding his authority, proclaiming, "The fact that most of the statements credited to Mr. Rossano by the press, are probably true, does not in any way excuse him for having unwisely made them to the press in an atmosphere of criticism of many Local and State officials." Noting a long acquaintance with Rossano and respect for his technical knowledge, Aufranc puzzled over how such an experienced USPHS officer could have allowed himself "to be placed in a position of making public statements critical of the persons he was supposed to be assisting." In a virtual epitaph for the federal role in Polk County, Aufranc concluded, "In view of the present tenseness of the situation in Florida, it would seem unwise to either offer or solicit opportunities to offer any type of help on this problem in Florida for the time being." Given the USPHS's firmly non-interventionist self-conception, apparently no one in the agency saw anything inappropriate in the federal government retreating before the wrath of demonstrably ineffectual state officials.[53]

In early May 1959 Surgeon General Burney responded to Sowder's letter, regretting the whole incident and assuring that "all of our personnel concerned will make special efforts to see that this does not happen again." The Rossano affair had reached the highest level within the USPHS, which did not bode well for the career of the outspoken officer. Rossano ultimately was transferred out of the State and Community Services division of the federal program and into USPHS automotive emissions research in California, probably a demotion. Rather than dealing directly with the inadequacies of the Polk County air pollution–control program or the hobbling limitations of the existing system of polite but ineffectual federalism in air pollution control, the USPHS and the Florida agencies in effect killed the messenger who brought bad tidings.[54]

In the wake of the Rossano affair, Florida officials reorganized the state's air pollution–control program. In late June 1959 David B. Lee, director of the Florida State Board of Health's Bureau of Sanitary Engineering and secretary of the Florida APCC, visited the office of Ralph C. Graber, assistant chief of the USPHS Air Pollution Engineering Program, and informed him that at the APCC's next meeting in July, Lee expected Sowder to propose that air pollution–control activity be shifted from the Health Department's Division of Industrial Hygiene to Lee's own Bureau of Sanitary Engineering. Since Harry Seifert, director of Polk County's Air Pollution Control District, came from the Division of Industrial Hygiene and was partly blamed by fellow state health officials for the Rossano affair, this administrative reshuffling almost certainly was designed in part to force Seifert out. After this, Lee planned to request a USPHS review of the technical and administrative aspects of the Polk County program in order to recommend changes in policy and operation, including an increase in staff, which still consisted only of Seifert, one "sanitarian," two chemists, and one secretary. Lee also announced his plans to establish a statewide air sampling network.[55]

Everything happened as Lee planned, and the USPHS agreed to send Ralph Graber and Jean J. Schueneman, Rossano's replacement, to review and report on the Polk County program in early September 1959. Their subsequent report stated, politely and privately, much of what Rossano had said publicly about a control program in disarray. They called for legislative changes to include "damage to property, and the reasonable enjoyment of property and life [in other words, the legal concept of nuisance], in the definition of air pollution in the Florida Air Pollution Control Law" and noted that the existing standard based only on demonstrated major damage to human, plant, or animal health was inadequate. Echoing Rossano, Graber and Schueneman went on to write, "It was apparent that considerable uncertainty has existed regarding the roles and responsibilities, and the lines of communication, among the several entities concerned with air pollution activities in the Florida State Board of Health." They recommended, in obvious indirect reference to past disorganization, that such relationships should be workable, clear, and set forth in writing, and that "once they are agreed to, it would be most desirable that they be adhered to by the entities concerned." The report also concluded that public education and information activities should be significantly improved, regularized, and expanded. In further agreement with Rossano's earlier findings, the two USPHS officials noted that staffing of the Polk County program was so inadequate that professional employees were engaged in "washing of glassware" and other "sub-professional activity"; as such, "staff should be so augmented to release these personnel for the technical and public relations aspects of the activity."[56]

In a victory for Lee over Seifert, the Graber-Schueneman report stated, "The Director of the Winter Haven [Polk County] office should be responsible solely to the Director of the Bureau of Sanitary Engineering, who should set the policies and program within which the field office must operate." In an apparent indirect reference to Seifert, who had tried hard to be responsive to angry local citizens, the report continued, "In this way, the Winter Haven group would not be directly subject to wishes of official and citizen groups, and individuals, for modification of program and policy." Although there probably was a need for more centralized leadership and organization, the state air pollution–control program was to be insulated still further from the concerns of local citizens, who were subject to property damage at the very least. Graber and Schueneman also offered other criticism on experimental technique, data handling, and meteorological monitoring. Lee took advantage of this report and reorganization to squeeze out Seifert, who was soon replaced by Kay K. Huffstutler, who was always careful to keep good relations with the phosphate companies, if not always with concerned citizens.[57]

In the wake of Rossano's abortive effort at public truth telling to stimulate action, the federal air pollution–control program's role in Florida in fact reverted to near impotence and remained so until the end of the 1960s. As with many other states that were not solving their air pollution problems during this period, Florida received modest federal research grants to study characteristics of pollution developing in cities such as Miami, Jacksonville, and Tampa as well as in rural areas where the paper or phosphate industries operated.[58] When desperate citizens contacted federal officials in a vain effort to circumvent largely inactive state pollution-control authorities, federal staffers could only remind them that the existing federal air pollution-control law allowed a "program of research, technical assistance, and training in the field of air pollution" but specified that "the control of air pollution shall be primarily the responsibility of the states and communities."[59]

Even the weak federal laws of the 1960s were too strong for some Florida officials, who remained protective of their right to determine—or prevent—air pollution-control efforts within the Sunshine State. In a letter to a federal official in December 1963, David B. Lee observed, "I can truly say that there are no Federal-State relations in this program." He claimed that he had tried to contact Vernon G. MacKenzie and Arthur C. Stern in the new federal Division of Air Pollution (DAP) to discuss the situation, but, he sniffed, "they emulated . . . the new Federal government which will by-pass state agencies." Lee and Sowder had been horrified by the original draft of the federal Clean Air Act of 1963, which threatened "very rapid hearings without state people being notified," and they remained unhappy with the law as passed, which "still gives the Secretary [of Health, Education, and Welfare] direct connection

... to the local areas without the advice and counsel of the states." He longed for the "smooth Federal-state program" in the earlier federal law of 1955, which had been even more toothless than the 1963 measure. Lee and his fellow Floridians, however, were wrong to worry that the federal government might intervene in Polk County without their express permission; the limited federal enforcement provisions of the Clean Air Act of 1963 were much too weak and dilatory for that.[60]

The federal program did participate in some other activities in the state of Florida during the 1960s, most of which were typical of their strictly limited role prior to 1970. For instance, in 1960, federal staffers joined Florida control officials and university scientists in putting together a *Report on Florida's Air Resources*, which sought to catalogue the sources, varieties, and characteristics of air pollution throughout the state and offer recommendations for controlling it, the sort of study the USPHS conducted in various other states and regions. While federal officials initially hoped that such a standard study might increase the possibility of improving environmental laws in Florida, there is little indication that this cumulation of facts and statistics, released in early 1961, directly affected air pollution control in the state. The state also invited federal officials to join in largely unproductive preliminary discussions of emissions standards for the phosphate industry. As usual, scientific research alone offered no solution for a complex legal, political, and economic problem.[61]

Meanwhile, Florida authorities continued fruitlessly to study and nibble around the edges of the issue. A good example is their proposal late in 1960 to investigate pesticides containing fluoride as a possible cause of damage to gladioli grown commercially around Tampa. Discussing a letter from Kay K. Huffstutler, USPHS scientist C. Stafford Brandt, not one to jump to unwarranted, inflammatory conclusions, saw the proposed study as merely a diversionary tactic, observing impatiently, "I know of no one who has examined the area who does not accept the premise that the gladiolas [*sic*] of the Tampa region are affected by fluorides and that the fluorides are air-borne and not the result of management practices. I fail to see the point in continuing to dodge the issue." Even the cautious Brandt felt that Florida officials were protecting local phosphate interests, whose emissions were by then causing serious economic damage in Hillsborough County (Tampa) as well as in Polk County.[62]

One rare exception to the rule of federal avoidance of activism in central Florida occurred in relation to the first lawsuit brought by Florida state authorities against a phosphate plant. On June 5, 1963, Vincent Patton of the state board of health telephoned the DAP to request federal assistance in providing "either direct testimony or deposition" regarding "the effects of SO2, sulfuric acid mist and fluoride on people, animals, and vegetation" for legal action that the board was taking against the Armour and Company fertilizer plant at

Fort Meade, Florida—the first and only time during the 1950s and 1960s that Florida authorities went beyond "conference, conciliation, and persuasion" in confronting chronic polluters. This particular facility had ignored a permit requirement, and Florida authorities sued the company in a symbolic gesture to assuage public demands for punishment of all the other phosphate plants that regularly exceeded emissions standards. Vernon MacKenzie, director of the DAP and one of the more activist federal control officials, requested permission to make Harry Heimann and Stafford Brandt available for this purpose, arguing, "We believe that this request is in the best interest of the Public Health Service. It is both in an area of our activity and in an area in which we wish to give support to the Florida State Board of Health."[63]

Predictably, not all members of the federal air pollution program shared MacKenzie's eagerness to enter the Florida proceedings. Early in July, when he first found out about this new responsibility, Brandt fumed to MacKenzie about his not having been "consulted prior to any commitment made for my services" nor having been "immediately informed of the full nature of the commitment and the nature of the action involved." Again displaying the self-conception of USPHS officers and their agency as one of scientific research and apolitical technical assistance and advice, Brandt was offended at the prospect of the federal program taking a side in a political or legal dispute. MacKenzie responded that it was unusual for the USPHS to join such an action but affirmed that USPHS rules and regulations allowed its employees to give testimony when state or local agencies were party to cases and the USPHS saw an opportunity to advance program objectives. Encouraging Florida authorities to take legal action for the first time—generally a rough indicator of the seriousness of a control program—represented such a situation. To the disappointment of central Florida pollution fighters, this particular case was settled out of court and did not signal new assertiveness on the part of Florida control officials.[64]

After the sustained public outcry in central Florida led Polk and Hillsborough Counties to be included on the schedule for the 1964 field hearings of the Senate Subcommittee on Air and Water Pollution chaired by Senator Edmund S. Muskie, in mid-to-late December 1963, the DAP produced briefing booklets for the senators' use on major local and regional air pollution in the United States, including one on central Florida. The agency also collected the names of Florida citizens and officials who had participated in the thirtieth and thirty-first meetings of the Florida APCC in May and August 1963 because they might wish to testify before the visiting subcommittee. Beyond that, however, the hearings were left to Senator Muskie and the legislative branch of the federal government, which was slightly more activist regarding federal intervention on air pollution than the executive branch throughout the 1960s. At the hearings, held in Tampa in late February 1964, Florida officials explained the workings of their air pollution–control program, painting a generally rosy picture and warning against excessive federal intervention, while a phosphate industry representative claimed there was no proof of air pollution damage but welcomed further research on the topic. By contrast, various local residents testified that they had suffered severe damage from phosphate industry emissions, and they complained of inactivity from state officials and threats of relocation from industry officials. The residents begged for direct federal intervention, but the visiting senators and other federal officials could only remind them that the federal government had authority to do no more than offer modest research support and technical assistance without a formal request from a state's government.[65]

The federal air pollution–control bureaucrats continued to monitor policy developments in Florida through the rest of the 1960s. They received copies of hearings transcripts from the Florida APCC regarding ongoing pollution in the phosphate belt as well as newer problems in cities such as Jacksonville and Miami, and they continued to receive angry or plaintive letters from citizens in the region. Federal air pollution–control officials were bemused to read Elwood Hendrickson's statement that federal authorities he had spoken to felt that Florida's program was "on the right track" when apparently no one had expressed that opinion; they were similarly amazed to learn of Florida officials testifying that the sulfur oxides emission problem in central Florida was minimal, when in fact ambient concentrations were "extremely high," and all available evidence pointed to a high level of local sulfur oxide emissions. They followed the ongoing and highly emotional political and legal battle occurring in the Sunshine State, and they sought to offer unsolicited advice to a delegation of the Florida state legislature regarding how to improve their inadequate state air pollution–control law. At one point, federal officials even considered offering to help conduct a Florida study on the effects of sulfur oxides on human health and offering to meet with the Florida APCC to discuss implementation after the publication of new federal air quality criteria on sulfur oxides. The federal officials observed hopefully, "This situation would serve as the basis of an interesting intrastate abatement action, if an appropriate request for such action were to reach the Secretary [of Health, Education, and Welfare]"; of course, by then they should have known not to expect a request of that sort from Florida authorities.[66]

The federal air pollution–control program had almost no role in Florida at all throughout the rest of the 1960s. Despite the pressing and highly visible need for meaningful control of air pollution in the phosphate belt, Florida officials dragged their heels and avoided cooperation with agencies that might expose the inadequacies of their control efforts. The issue was finally resolved by private citizens who sidestepped governmental officials and took the matter into their own hands. Finally, in the mid-to-late 1960s, despairing of help from state government, residents of central Florida started having success in private lawsuits against phosphate companies, forcing phosphate operations to compensate them for damaging their property. In such suits, courts accepted evidence of fluoride poisoning in cattle more readily than evidence of citrus damage. Cattle ranchers were larger operators than citrus growers and had higher-priced legal counsel. Even state air pollution–control officials began urging phosphate companies to purchase the land of their angry neighbors in order to quell local protest. With larger land areas around them as buffer zones to absorb heavier concentrations of fluorides or sulfur oxides, emissions from phosphate plants were less likely to produce concentrations of contaminants exceeding state limits on the land of their more distant neighbors. During this same period, and probably as a result of new costs for land purchases, the phosphate companies completed the installation of expensive new equipment to control their emissions—though they worked at their own pace. By 1969, after fifteen to twenty years of suffering by local residents, state officials claimed that air pollution in the phosphate belt had been abated to the limits of existing technology.[67]

There were also changes in Florida's environmental policy during the late 1960s and early 1970s. In 1967 the state passed stricter controls on fluoride emissions and replaced the earlier, weak Air Pollution Control Commission with a somewhat stronger agency, the Florida Air and Water Pollution Control Commission. In the early 1970s Florida underwent a striking renaissance of environmental awareness, more so in the cities and tourist areas, less so in the backwoods. At this time, the Sunshine State partly turned away from traditional, pro-development boosterism, discovered new concerns about quality of life and regulation of growth, and passed new laws on land and water conservation and other environmental issues.[68]

As with the more dramatic civil rights movement, change in the pollution-control arena came mostly after the federal government was dragged into the issue against its will. In the late 1960s, facing the swelling chorus of complaints from their citizens, Florida and other states operated in the shadow of impending federal intervention on air pollution control and other environmental problems. The federal Air Quality Act of 1967 represented a final effort to leave air pollution control in the hands of state and local authorities without more direct federal compulsion, and a number of states that had been lagging on the matter made a somewhat greater show of activity during the late 1960s, if only to avoid federal intervention, which state officials and industrialists already clearly foresaw would follow if they did not promptly reduce pollution. These tardy efforts were not enough to keep pace with the surge in general environmental awareness and concern that swept the United States around 1970, nor were they enough to satisfy the many critics of the federal air pollution–control program who during the late 1960s increasingly called for more direct federal involvement to budge states out of their inertia. In this way, the threat of federal intervention drove state policy even before the Clean Air Act amendments of 1970, which ordered the states to address air pollution promptly and finally authorized the federal government to intervene without the states' permission if they failed to reduce pollution. This law also authorized the federal government to set emissions standards that the states would have to meet. Although air pollution persists in the United States, the 1970 federal enactment limited the ability of states to market themselves as "pollution havens" and provided a foundation for considerable progress since that time.[69]

In its foot-dragging on confronting serious industrial air pollution, Florida was more typical than extraordinary among states in the 1950s and 1960s. Its hesitance to challenge the phosphate companies, coupled with federal officials' aversion to action beyond research, condemned residents of the phosphate belt to nearly two decades of serious economic and physical damage. To the extent that this hesitation resulted from zealous adherence to scientific niceties—the demand of state and federal scientists for unreasonably large amounts of data before enforcing anti-pollution statutes—the Florida case calls into question the value of such rigorous scientific investigation as a foundation for policy. To the extent that the hesitation was born of narrow political and economic considerations, there is simply no justification for permitting the physical and economic damage, and the case of the central Florida phosphate belt stands as a warning against leaving matters of environmental protection to lower levels of government, which are more easily swayed by short-term considerations. Following the national outcry over environmental conditions and the resulting federal laws and enforcement actions of the late 1960s and early 1970s, greater environmental protections—patterned on federal enactments—have been written into state and local law, and perhaps states and localities reliably can assume greater responsibility in environmental matters. Nevertheless, any environmental policy marked by the "new federalism" that does not guard against states' backsliding toward inactivity and favoritism to industrial polluters—a situation once characteristic of industry-hungry southern states such as Florida—is a policy fraught with ecological peril.[70]

Notes

1. "Focus Shifts to Senate After 'Contract with America' Speeds through House," *Chemical and Engineering News*, LXXIII (April 24, 1995), 29–31.

2. Congressional Republicans started to backtrack on their more overtly anti-environmental positions around the time of the elections of 1996, when national polls

revealed relatively widespread national public support for federal environmental programs. Regarding the virulent anti-environmentalism of the Reagan administration and its ultimate blunting by popular support for environmental protection see, for example, Samuel P. Hays, *Beauty, Health, and Permanence: Environmental Politics in the United States, 1955–1985* (Cambridge, Eng., and other cities, 1987), 491–526; Kirkpatrick Sale, *The Green Revolution: The American Environmental Movement, 1962–1992* (New York, 1993), 48–53; Victor B. Scheffer, *The Shaping of Environmentalism in America* (Seattle and London, 1991), 178–82; and Philip Shabecoff, *A Fierce Green Fire: The American Environmental Movement* (New York, 1993), 203–30.

3. For helpful background on the process of federal assumption of former state or local responsibilities in the policy arena see James L. Sundquist, *Politics and Policy: The Eisenhower, Kennedy, and Johnson Years* (Washington, 1968); and Martha Derthick, "Crossing Thresholds: Federalism in the 1960s," *Journal of Policy History,* VIII (No. 1, 1996), 64–80. For further information on the legislative history of the federal environmental enactments of the 1950s and 1960s see Sundquist, *Politics and Policy,* 331–71; Randall B. Ripley, "Congress and Clean Air: The Issue of Enforcement, 1963," in Frederic N. Cleaveland et al., *Congress and Urban Problems: A Casebook on the Legislative Process* (Washington, 1969), 224–78; James E. Krier and Edmund Ursin, *Pollution and Policy: A Case Essay on California and Federal Experience with Motor Vehicle Air Pollution, 1940–1975* (Berkeley, Los Angeles, and London, 1977); and Robert Gilkey Dyck, "Evolution of Federal Air Pollution Control Policy, 1948–1967" (Ph.D. dissertation, University of Pittsburgh, 1971).

4. See "Air Pollution," *Life,* LXVI (February 7, 1969), 38–50, especially pp. 46–47.

5. Regarding the efforts of Florida and other southern states to attract industry before and after World War II see James C. Cobb, *Industrialization and Southern Society, 1877–1984* (Lexington, Ky., 1984). As an example of Florida's willingness to trade environmental purity for industrial jobs see David Helvarg, *The War Against the Greens: The 'Wise-Use' Movement, the New Right, and Anti-Environmental Violence* (San Francisco, 1994), 371–79.

6. Regarding the federal government and the civil rights movement, see generally Taylor Branch, *Parting the Waters: America in the King Years, 1954–63* (New York and other cities, 1988).

7. Derthick offers the Clean Air Act amendments of 1970 as an example of "partial preemption" by the federal government, whereby the states were left with the responsibility to implement, maintain, and enforce national air quality standards, but the federal government itself had clear, explicit authority to step in and enforce standards if states failed to do so. See Derthick, "Crossing Thresholds," 76. For discussion of the failure of 1960s pollution-control policy to resolve one of the nation's worst interstate air pollution problems, that of the New York City metropolitan area, see Harvey Lieber, "The Politics of Air and Water Pollution Control in the New York Metropolitan Area" (Ph.D. dissertation, Columbia University, 1968); and Joseph F. Zimmerman, "Political Boundaries and Air Pollution Control" (M.A. thesis, Graduate School of Public Affairs, SUNY–Albany, 1968). The untitled 1955 law, later referred to as the Federal Air Pollution Control Act, was P.L. 84–159. The first Clean Air Act of 1963 (which derived

its name from a British enactment of 1956) was P.L. 88–206. Other significant federal measures seeking to reinforce the existing system of state and local primacy followed in 1965, 1966, and 1967 before the Clean Air Act Amendments of 1970, P.L. 91–604.

8. Raymond F. Dasmann, *No Further Retreat: The Fight to Save Florida* (New York and London, 1971), 52; Charlton W. Tebeau, *A History of Florida* (Coral Gables, Fla., 1971), 271–78 and 409–10; and Charles I. Harding, Samuel B. McKee, and J. J. Schueneman, *A Report on Florida's Air Resources* (Jacksonville, 1961), 28.

9. Tebeau, *History of Florida*, 181, 271–78, 416–18, and 431; Michael V. Gannon, *Florida: A Short History* (Gainesville, Fla., 1993), 60–61 and 77–85; and David Nolan, *Fifty Feet in Paradise: The Booming of Florida* (San Diego, New York, and London, 1984), 118. Regarding another significant agricultural enterprise in Florida see Joe A. Akerman Jr., *Florida Cowman: A History of Florida Cattle Raising* (Kissimmee, Fla., 1976).

10. Arch Frederic Blakey, *The Florida Phosphate Industry: A History of the Development and Use of a Vital Mineral* (Cambridge, Mass., 1973), 24–35, 56–57, and 78–84; and Lewis D. Harris, "The Florida Phosphate Industry and Air Pollution" (M.A. thesis, Florida State University, 1967), 12.

11. Blakey, *Florida Phosphate Industry*, 90–95 and 100–104; Harris, "Florida Phosphate Industry and Air Pollution," 7–11 and 13–14; and Harding, McKee, and Schueneman, *Report on Florida's Air Resources*, 23.

12. Blakey, *Florida Phosphate Industry*, 94–95 and 108–9; and Harding, McKee, and Schueneman, *Report on Florida's Air Resources*, 22. Harding et al. attribute the phosphate mining companies' decision to move into chemical processing to increased freight rates following World War II, which raised the cost of transporting bulky raw materials.

13. Blakey, *Florida Phosphate Industry*, 1–4 and 109; and Harris, "Florida Phosphate Industry and Air Pollution," 2.

14. Blakey, *Florida Phosphate Industry*, 109; and Harris, "Florida Phosphate Industry and Air Pollution," 2.

15. Harris, "Florida Phosphate Industry and Air Pollution," 4 and 27–35; and Harding, McKee, and Schueneman, *Report on Florida's Air Resources*, 22–27.

16. Harris, "Florida Phosphate Industry and Air Pollution," 21 and 30–33; Harding, McKee, and Schueneman, *Report on Florida's Air Resources*, 24–25; and *Florida Health Notes*, "Clean Water—Clean Air" (Special Edition), XLVIII (December 1956), 221, in File: "Florida (Polk County)," Air Pollution Engineering Branch, Correspondence, 1959–1960, Identification Number NN3-090-91-003, Records of the U.S. Public Health Service, Record Group 90 (National Archives, Washington, D.C. [hereinafter cited as APEB Correspondence, 1959–1960, RG 90]).

17. In sufficient doses, fluorine interferes with the operation of living cells by inhibiting various enzymes that conduct the most basic life processes, such as glycolysis and oxidative metabolism—the breaking down and combustion of stored sugars to provide energy for cellular functions—as well as more specialized functions of particular cells. For further information on the effects of fluorides on animal, plant, and human health, see generally National Research Council, Committee on Biologic Effects of

Atmospheric Pollutants, *Fluorides* (Washington, 1971); National Research Council, Committee on Animal Nutrition, Subcommittee on Fluorosis, *Effects of Fluorides in Animals* (Washington, 1974); National Research Council, Subcommittee on Health Effects of Ingested Fluoride, *Health Effects of Ingested Fluoride* (Washington, 1993); and John C. Esposito, *Vanishing Air: The Ralph Nader Study Group Report on Air Pollution* (New York, 1970), 69 and 183–85.

18. In his dissertation on the economics of air pollution in the Florida phosphate belt, Thomas Crocker offers some state and federal agricultural census data on livestock and citrus production in Polk County, Florida. Unfortunately, this information does not show how much damage was occurring to agriculture in the phosphate belt, because as cattle and citrus operations were gradually driven out of southwestern Polk County where the fluoride air pollution was, other (or sometimes even the same) ranchers and citrus growers expanded their operations in parts of the county that were not afflicted with air pollution. Records for the whole county thus do not show the damage in the phosphate belt alone. See Thomas D. Crocker, "Some Economics of Air Pollution Control" (Ph.D. dissertation, University of Missouri, 1967), 55 and 64.

19. Harris, "Florida Phosphate Industry and Air Pollution," 14; Harding, McKee, and Schueneman, *Report on Florida's Air Resources,* 43–44; and Statement of Commissioner Doyle Conner in U.S. Senate, Committee on Public Works, Subcommittee on Air and Water Pollution, 88 Cong., 2 Sess., *Clean Air: Field Hearings Held on Progress and Programs Relating to the Abatement of Air Pollution* (Washington, 1964), 777–79 (hereinafter cited as *Clean Air: Field Hearings*).

20. Harris, "Florida Phosphate Industry and Air Pollution," 38–45; and Statement of Donald S. McLean in *Clean Air: Field Hearings,* 781 and 792

21. Blakey, *Florida Phosphate Industry,* 110; *Florida Health Notes,* 221–22; Statement of Edwin N. Lightfoot in *Clean Air: Field Hearings,* 742; Statement of Robert W. Rutledge in *Clean Air: Field Hearings,* 808; and "Polk-Hillsborough," undated report c. December 20, 1963, File: "Cooperation 2—Florida," Division of Air Pollution Subject Files, 1963–1964, Accession Number 67-A-1655, RG 90 (quotation).

22. Harding, McKee, and Schueneman, *Report on Florida's Air Resources,* 51–52.

23. Ibid.; Blakey, *Florida Phosphate Industry,* 110; Statement of Edwin N. Lightfoot, 742; Statement of Robert W. Rutledge, 808; and letter, Herman F. Steele to Florida Air Pollution Control Commission, October 19, 1957, and attached Resolution of Florida Citrus Mutual, File: "Cooperation 2—Florida," Division of Air Pollution Subject Files, 1963–1964, RG 90.

24. Harding, McKee, and Schueneman, *Report on Florida's Air Resources,* 52.

25. For further discussion of the conflict between angry citizens and state officials over fluoride pollution in central Florida during the 1950s and 1960s see Scott Hamilton Dewey, "'Don't Breathe the Air': Air Pollution and the Evolution of Environmental Policy and Politics in the United States, 1945–1970" (Ph.D. dissertation, Rice University, 1997), 486–561.

26. "Visit to Florida Board of Health, Division of Industrial Hygiene," memo from Harry Heimann, M.D., April 17, 1957, File: "Florida Air 3–1–1," APEB Correspondence, 1959–1960, RG 90 (quotation); and "Division of Special Health Services—Air Pol-

lution Medical Program: Trip Report," memo from Harry Heimann, April 25, 1957, File: "721.3—to Florida," Air Pollution Medical Program, Project Records, 1955–1960, Identification Number NN3-090-91-003, RG 90 (hereinafter cited as APMP Project Records, 1955–1960, RG 90).

27. U.S. Department of Health, Education, and Welfare, Public Health Service, Occupational Health Program and Florida State Board of Health, *Industrial Hygiene Survey of the Phosphate Industry in Polk County, Florida* (Washington, 1958), 1–17 (quotations on p. 17).

28. "Trip Report—Lakeland, Florida—July 24–26, 1957," memo from C. Stafford Brandt to Arthur C. Stern, July 31, 1957, File: "Florida Air 3–1–1," APEB Correspondence, 1959–1960, RG 90.

29. Ibid.

30. Ibid.

31. "Trip Report (A. C. Stern and C. S. Brandt)—Tampa, Florida—February 27–28, 1958," memo from Arthur C. Stern to Harry G. Hanson, March 7, 1958, File: "Florida Air 3–1–1," APEB Correspondence, 1959–1960, RG 90.

32. Ibid. Some veterinary experts disagreed with Brandt's characterization of the local ranching industry. Brandt later explained his comments about the shoddy care that livestock received in central Florida to Dr. George K. Davis, Animal Nutritionist at the University of Florida's Agricultural Experiment Station, in order to "clarify any misunderstanding that may have arisen" from his public statements about the handling of livestock in the area. Davis, among other experts, was certain that fluorosis existed among Polk County livestock. See letter from Brandt to Davis, March 25, 1958, File: "Florida Air 3–1–1," APEB Correspondence, 1959–1960, RG 90. For a classic critique of the technocratic assumptions of many government and corporate scientists during the 1950s and early 1960s see Rachel Carson, *Silent Spring* (Boston, 1962).

33. For an excellent and remarkably balanced brief discussion of the ongoing politics of science in the environmental arena see Hays, *Beauty, Health, and Permanence,* 329–62.

34. Harry E. Seifert to Frank Tetzlaff, March 5, 1958; Tetzlaff to Seifert, March 10, 1958; Seifert to Tetzlaff, March 24, 1958, File "Florida Air 3–1–1," APEB Correspondence, 1959–1960, RG 90; "Air Pollution Study—Florida," memo from Wilton M. Fisher, M.D., April 15, 1958, ibid.; "Telephone Conversation with Dr. A. V. Hardy, Florida State Board of Health, Saturday, April 26, 1958," memo from Wilton M. Fisher, April 28, 1958, ibid.; Wilson T. Sowder, M.D., to Fisher, May 6, 1958, ibid.; Fisher to Sowder, May 21, 1958, ibid.; "Meeting with Dr. A. V. Hardy," memo from Wilton M. Fisher, April 21, 1958, File "721.3—to Florida," APMP Project Records, 1955–1960, RG 90 (quotation); two further Fisher memos, May 5, 1958, ibid.; and "Florida Fluorides," memo from Richard A. Prindle, M.D., May 20, 1958, ibid.

35. Letter and livestock inspection report from Dr. Norman L. Garlick, D.V.M., June 2, 1958, 4–7, File: "Florida Air 3–1–1," APEB Correspondence, 1959–1960, RG 90.

36. John H. Dewell to Harry G. Hensen [*sic*], January 26, 1959, ibid.

37. Draft letter, Harry G. Hanson to John H. Dewell, February 2, 1959, File "721.3— to Florida," APMP Project Records, 1955–1960, RG 90. See also actual letter from

Hanson to Dewell, February 9, 1959, and memo from Richard A. Prindle, February 4, 1959, ibid.

38. Richard A. Prindle to John H. Dewell, February 27, 1959, File "721.3—to Florida," ibid. See also two drafts of this letter nearby in file.

39. Julian C. Durrance to Wilson T. Sowder, January 28, 1959, File "Florida Air 3-1-1," APEB Correspondence, 1959–1960, RG 90; "Statement on health hazards relating to air-borne fluorides in Florida," memo from A. L. Chapman, February 9, 1959, ibid. (first quotation); "Florida State Health Department's Request for Public Health Service Statement on Air Pollution Fluorosis," memo from Richard A. Prindle, January 29, 1959, File: "721.3—to Florida," APMP Project Records, 1955–1960, RG 90 (second quotation); "Health Hazards and Air-borne Fluorides in Florida," memo from Norman F. Gerrie, February 12, 1959, ibid.; and letter from Richard A. Prindle to Wilson T. Sowder, February 16, 1959, ibid.

40. Draft "Statement" [re: health hazards of airborne fluorides], undated, but from early February 1959, File: "721.3—to Florida," APMP Project Records, 1955–1960, RG 90.

41. Ibid.

42. Harry Seifert to Frank Tetzlaff, February 24, 1959, File: "Florida Air 3-1-1," APEB Correspondence, 1959–1960, RG 90; and August T. Rossano Jr. to Harry Seifert, March 6, 1959, ibid.

43. "Trip Report—Tampa, Florida—March 30th–April 3, 1959," memo from August T. Rossano to Arthur C. Stern, April 16, 1959, ibid.

44. "Expert Sees Danger From Phosphate Here," Lakeland *Ledger,* Thursday, April 2, 1959, clipping in File: "Florida Air 3-1-1," APEB Correspondence, 1959–1960, RG 90.

45. Vance Johnston, "Agencies Confused Over Polk Air Pollution Situation" [Tampa *Tribune,* Friday, April 3, 1959], clipping in File: "Florida Air 3-1-1," APEB Correspondence, 1959–1960, RG 90.

46. Handwritten telephone notes from Arthur C. Stern, April 3, 1959, ibid.

47. August T. Rossano to Arthur C. Stern, April 5, 1959, ibid.

48. "Florida Fluorides Situation—Telephone Call from Dr. Louis McCabe," memo from Harry Heimann, M.D., April 6, 1959, ibid.

49. Clarence M. Sharp to Harry E. Seifert, April 6, 1959, ibid.

50. For sharp criticism of the federal air pollution–control program's persistent research focus through the late 1960s see Esposito and Silverman, *Vanishing Air.* For a more recent reflection on the USPHS's persistent, often ineffectual research orientation regarding air pollution control see Lynne Page Snyder, " 'The Death-Dealing Smog Over Donora, Pennsylvania': Industrial Air Pollution, Public Health, and Federal Policy, 1915–1963" (Ph.D. dissertation, University of Pennsylvania, 1994).

51. MacKenzie was at that time assistant chief for research and development in the Division of Sanitary Engineering Services, and later director of the Division of Air Pollution created after 1960 and the most important architect of the federal control program. See "Newspaper Interview With Dr. Rossano," memo from Vernon G. MacKenzie, April 7, 1959, File "Florida Air 3-1-1," APEB Correspondence, 1959–1960, RG 90; and Howard W. Chapman to Mark D. Hollis, April 7, 1959, ibid.

52. Wilson T. Sowder to Leroy E. Burney, M.D., April 7, 1959, ibid.

53. "Dr. Sowder's letter of April 7," memo from W. H. Aufranc to Leroy E. Burney, April 13, 1959, ibid.

54. Leroy E. Burney to Wilson T. Sowder, May 7, 1959, ibid.; "Air pollution technical assistance—Florida," memo from Frank Tetzlaff, April 13, 1959, ibid.; Mark D. Hollis to David B. Lee, April 20, 1959, ibid.; and August T. Rossano to Harry E. Seifert, July 15, 1959, ibid.

55. "Air Pollution Program, Florida State Board of Health," memo from Ralph C. Graber, July 9, 1959, ibid.

56. Wilson T. Sowder to W. H. Aufranc, July 22, 1959, File: "Florida Air 3-1-1 AP 61," Division of Air Pollution Subject Files, January–August 1961: Accession Number 65-A-0286, RG 90; H. B. Cottrell, M.D., to Sowder, August 13, 1959, ibid.; "Report on a Review of Certain Air Pollution Activities of the Florida State Board of Health," undated but from early September 1959, File "Florida Air 3-1-1," APEB Correspondence, 1959–1960, RG 90 (quotations); and "Trip Report—Jacksonville and Winter Haven, Florida, September 2, 3, 4, 1959," memo from Jean J. Schueneman, September 24, 1959, ibid.

57. "Report on a Review of Certain Air Pollution Activities," File: "Florida Air 3-1-1," APEB Correspondence, 1959–1960, RG 90; and letter to Frank Tetzlaff from unidentified correspondant with the Health Department of Hamilton County, Florida, November 2, 1959, ibid. This unidentified correspondent implied that Lee was determined to remove Seifert. Regarding Huffstutler and his relations with the industry and the public see Blakey, *Florida Phosphate Industry*, 113; and Dewey, " 'Don't Breathe the Air,' " 542–45.

58. For statistics on the minimal efforts of most state and local governments to control air pollution during the 1960s see J. Clarence Davies III, *The Politics of Pollution* (New York, 1970), 125–30; and Ripley, "Congress and Clean Air," 226–27.

59. See, for example, Thomas F. Williams to Jane H. May, April 29, 1959, File: "Florida—AP/61," Division of Air Pollution Subject Files, RG 90 (quotations); Richard A. Prindle to Senator George A. Smathers, September 18, 1962, File "Cooperation 2—Florida," Division of Air Pollution Subject Files, 1963–1964, RG 90; Thomas F. Williams to Donald S. McLean, August 8, 1963, ibid.; Vernon G. MacKenzie to Harriett Lightfoot, March 30, 1964, File: "OCC: Florida Air Pollution Commission," National Center for Air Pollution Control, 1967–1968: Accession Number 70-A-4011, RG 90; and Vernon G. MacKenzie to Harriett A. Lightfoot, May 27, 1966, ibid.

60. David B. Lee to Emil C. Jensen, December 26, 1963, File: "Cooperation 2—Florida," Division of Air Pollution Subject Files, 1963–1964, RG 90. Regarding the Clean Air Act of 1963 and its enforcement provisions see Ripley, "Congress and Clean Air."

61. Harding, McKee, and Schueneman, *Report on Florida's Air Resources;* Arthur C. Stern to Albert V. Hardy, May 20, 1960, in File: "Florida Air 3-1-1 AP 61," Division of Air Pollution Subject Files, January–August 1961, RG 90; "Air Pollution—Florida," memo from Roy O. McCaldin, May 25, 1960, ibid.; David G. Stephan to Wilson T. Sowder, June 26, 1960, ibid.; "State-Wide Air Pollution Survey," memo from David B.

Lee to Sowder, July 1, 1960, ibid.; "Draft of Cooperative Project Agreement for Florida State-Wide Survey of Air Pollution," memo from Vernon R. Hanson, July 6, 1960, ibid.; "Cooperative Project Agreement—Florida," memo from Ralph C. Graber, July 11, 1960, with attached, undated "Cooperative Project Agreement," ibid.; Roy O. Mc-Caldin to David B. Lee, August 11, 1960, ibid.; "Trip Report—Jacksonville and Gainesville, Florida, September 6 through 8," memo from Roy O. McCaldin, September 16, 1960, ibid.; "Trip Report, Jacksonville, Florida, October 11–12, 1960," memo from Jean J. Schueneman, October 24, 1960, ibid.; "Trip Report—Jacksonville and Gainesville, Florida, November 28–30," memo from Schueneman, December 7, 1960, ibid.; "Preliminary Summary of Report on Air Pollution in the State of Florida," memo from Schueneman, December 8, 1960, with attached "Preliminary Summary of a Report on Air Pollution in the State of Florida, target date (unmet) December 14, 1960," ibid; Schueneman to Lee, January 11, 1961, ibid.; Schueneman to Charles I. Harding, January 31, 1961, ibid.; Schueneman to Sowder, February 17, 1961, ibid.; Jean J. Schueneman to Elwood R. Hendrickson, May 19, 1961, File "Florida—AP/61," ibid.; "Trip Report—Gainesville, Florida, June 20–22," memo from Paul A. Humphrey, June 27, 1961, ibid.; and "Trip Report—August 14, 1961 Meeting at Winter Haven, Florida, for the Purpose of Standardizing Phosphate Industry Source Sampling Procedures (Fluorides)," memo from K. L. Johnson, September 1, 1961, ibid.

62. "Florida State Board of Health Letter of November 28, 1960 by K. K. Huffstutler," memo from C. Stafford Brandt to Arthur C. Stern, December 7, 1960, File "Florida Air 3–1–1," APEB Correspondence, 1959–1960, RG 90; and Stern to Huffstutler, December 29, 1960, ibid.

63. Blakey, *Florida Phosphate Industry*, 111; "Request of Florida State Board of Health for Testimony," memo from Vernon G. MacKenzie, June 7, 1963, File "Cooperation 2—Florida," Division of Air Pollution Subject Files, 1963–1964, RG 90 (quotation); David B. Lee to MacKenzie, June 18, 1963, ibid.; and "Request of Florida State Board of Health for Expert Testimony," memo from R. J. Anderson, July 24, 1963, ibid.

64. "Polk County Air Pollution Action," memo from C. Stafford Brandt to Vernon G. MacKenzie, July 5, 1963, File "Cooperation 2—Florida," Division of Air Pollution Subject Files, 1963–1964, RG 90; and "Polk County Air Pollution Action," memo from Vernon G. MacKenzie to C. Stafford Brandt, July 18, 1963, ibid. Although pollution-control programs prefer not to go to court, most of the successful ones, like that in Los Angeles County, had to be ready to do so frequently.

65. "Brief Summary of Air Pollution Status in Polk-Hillsborough County, Florida, and Metropolitan Area, New York," memo from Austin N. Heller, December 20, 1963, File "Cooperation 2—Florida," Division of Air Pollution Subject Files, 1963–1964, RG 90. For examples of citizen requests for federal intervention see Statement of Edwin N. Lightfoot, 746–47; Statement of Donald S. McLean, 798–800; and Statement of Paul B. Huff, 807–16, all three in *Clean Air: Field Hearings*. Regarding the Senate subcommittee hearings see Dewey, "'Don't Breathe the Air,'" 513–35.

66. Harriet Lightfoot to the Florida State Board of Health and the Florida Air Pollution Control Commission, February 11, 1966, File: "OCC: Florida Air Pollution Commission," National Center for Air Pollution Control, 1967–1968, RG 90; Vernon G.

MacKenzie to Harriet A. Lightfoot, May 27, 1966, ibid.; "Minutes—Meeting of the Florida Air Pollution Control Commission, Tampa, Florida, April 15, 1966," 2–3 and 7–9, ibid.; "Meeting of Florida Air Pollution Control Commission, April 15, 1966," memo from S. Smith Griswold to Vernon G. MacKenzie, July 1, 1966, ibid. (first and second quotations); "Minutes—Meeting of the Florida Air Pollution Control Commission, Lakeland, Florida, June 3, 1966," ibid.; "Transcript: Proceedings of Hearings—Possible Effect of Fluorides on Citrus—before the Florida Air Pollution Control Commission, Lakeland, Florida, June 2–3, 1966," 2, ibid.; "Transcript: Proceedings of Hearings—Sulfur Oxide Emissions—before the Florida Air Pollution Control Commission, Lakeland, Florida, June 3, 1966," 1–4, ibid.; "Minutes of Florida Air Pollution Control Commission, April 15, 1966," memorandum from Dr. E. Blomquist, Arthur C. Stern, and Ralph C. Graber to Vernon G. MacKenzie, July 6, 1966, ibid. (third quotation); "Minutes of Florida Air Pollution Control Commission—April 15, 1966," memorandum from Gene B. Welsh to Vernon G. MacKenzie, July 19, 1966, ibid.; and "Minutes of Florida Air Pollution Control Commission, April 15, 1966," memorandum from Gene B. Welsh to Vernon G. MacKenzie, October 14, 1966, ibid.

67. Crocker, "Some Economics of Air Pollution Control," 199–204; and Blakey, *Florida Phosphate Industry,* 112–13.

68. Blakey, *Florida Phosphate Industry,* 112; R. Bruce Stephenson, *Visions of Eden: Environmentalism, Urban Planning, and City Building in St. Petersburg, Florida, 1900–1995* (Columbus, Ohio, 1997), 145–48; and *State of Florida* ex rel. *Shevin* v. *Tampa Electric Company,* Florida Appeals, 291 So. 2d. 45 (1974). Again, regarding Florida's unreconstructed industrial boosterism and laxity on pollution in certain backwoods areas through the 1980s see Helvarg, *War Against the Greens,* 371–79.

69. For an overview of changes in the national mood and federal air pollution policy up to 1970 see Dewey, "'Don't Breathe the Air,'" 630–62.

70. Regarding the South's continuing record of relatively low interest in environmental issues among residents and legislators compared to other regions, outside of exceptional examples such as Chattanooga, Tennessee, see Hays, *Beauty, Health, and Permanence,* 47–50; and James P. Lester, "Federalism and Environmental Policy," in Lester, ed., *Environmental Politics and Policy: Theories and Evidence* (Durham, 1995), 43–45 and 366–77. There is no reason why states cannot establish strong environmental protections of their own, and some writers, such as Hays in *Beauty, Health, and Permanence* (453–57 and 518–20), have pointed out that some states took the initiative in environmental policy when the federal government lagged behind during the 1980s. Yet without strong federal controls, factors such as fears of industry relocation, competitive disadvantage, and economic recession might drive states back into a race to relax or not enforce standards.

The Politics of Race and Public Space

Desegregation, Privatization, and the Tax Revolt in Atlanta

Kevin M. Kruse

Throughout the late 1950s, as much of the segregated South convulsed in "massive resistance" to court-ordered desegregation, one city stood alone in its apparent willingness to abide by the law of the land—Atlanta, Georgia. As other cities and states resisted racial change in any form, Atlanta desegregated a wide variety of public spaces, including its municipal golf courses, city bus lines, public parks, and pools. Supported by a coalition of upper-class white businessmen and an active black community, the city's political leaders complied with court-ordered desegregation in hopes of making Atlanta the model for yet another New South. The city was moving forward, they boasted, not just in its bank accounts and business ledgers but in terms of the ways the races were learning to live and even thrive together. Indeed, by the end of the decade, national observers marveled at the differences between Atlanta and other Southern cities. Here, they pointed, was an "oasis" in a dry desert of ignorance, a "mecca" for right-thinking members of both races. While Atlanta had admirers across the country, it was ultimately Mayor William Hartsfield who came up with the lasting description of his city's attitude. "Atlanta," he liked to brag, "is the City Too Busy to Hate."[1]

Many observers, of the time and since, have accepted the city's claims that it largely obeyed the law and, in doing so, helped close the racial divide. In truth, of course, the story is more complicated. First and foremost, the actual distance between the races remained, even as the legal barriers between them were struck down. Although the two terms are commonly conflated, *desegregation* did not, in practice, mean the same thing as *integration*. While readily apparent across the country, this fact was perhaps clearest in the close quarters of metropolitan space. In most cities, the white population eventually acquiesced to court-ordered desegregation, but that did not mean whites were personally willing to share municipal public spaces with blacks. A majority of whites recoiled from social contact between the races, which they disdained as "interracial intimacy." Accordingly, in Atlanta and other cities across America, as public spaces desegregated, whites abandoned them, effectively resegregating these spaces almost immediately. As this article demonstrates, the desegregation of urban public spaces brought about not actual racial integration but instead a new division in which the public world was abandoned to blacks and a new private one was created for whites.

The second complication of Atlanta's apparent success story is related to the first. Court-ordered desegregation, instead of closing the old divide between blacks and whites, actually aggravated a new one between classes of whites. In the eyes of working-class whites, the desegregation of urban public spaces was nothing short of a disaster. The thought of sharing urban space with blacks was anathema to them, as it was to most whites of this time and place. But unlike upper-class whites, Atlanta's working-class whites had long held a close connection to neighborhood parks and pools, municipal golf courses, and modes of public transportation. They used those facilities regularly and had, under the auspices of legalized segregation, come to think of such municipal services as "their" buses, "their" golf courses, "their" parks, and "their" pools. Upper-class whites had no similar attachment because they, unlike the poor, had private alternatives. They belonged to private country clubs, had access to private pools, and drove private cars. Accordingly, they knew the desegregation of the city's public spaces would not affect them in any meaningful way. To the shock of working-class whites, who had long assumed that all white Southerners stood united in support of segregation, the city's white elite not only went along with court-ordered desegregation but then had the gall to brag about it in public-relations speeches.

The new combination of class and racial inequality, which surfaced in the wake of court-ordered desegregation, drastically reconfigured metropolitan politics in Atlanta and countless other cities throughout the region and nation. In the immediate sense, working-class whites rebelled against the city's drives for civic improvements, which they assumed would henceforth benefit only blacks, and retreated instead into the private world pioneered by their upperclass counterparts. But in a broader sense, this potent mix of racial discrimination and class difference spread beyond the city limits and into the suburbs. There, the politics of inequality could be reconstituted in a new setting and on new terms, which, on the surface, seemed unconnected to the racial and class struggles of the city. A growing body of literature has demonstrated how, in the 1960s and especially the 1970s, such suburbs in the rapidly growing South and Southwest—since christened the Sun Belt—gave middle- and upper-class whites the chance to create new enclaves apart from the inner cities.[2] From this suburban Sun Belt, a new conservative movement emerged, one that soon dominated the Republican Party and then national politics, too.[3] At first, observers dismissed that political movement as a temporary backlash, representing what one observer simplified to "the Three R's: rightism, racism, and repression."[4] However, given the later prominence and longevity of the new conservative ascendancy, several recent studies have taken the time to analyze its more intriguing components in depth—such as the "tax revolt" of the late 1970s[5] and the attendant privatization of public services in the 1980s and 1990s, ranging from the establishment of private security forces to the current campaign for tuition vouchers for private education.[6] While such scholarship has generally assumed that such conservative trends emerged from an established suburban Sun Belt in the late 1970s and 1980s, this article argues, to the contrary, that those trends were already apparent before the rise of the suburbs, inside cities such as Atlanta, as early as the 1950s.

In locating the origins of these phenomena in urban, not suburban, politics, this article seeks to understand the origins of the conservative "counterrevolution" in its proper environment. Problematically, many accounts start their stories only after the white suburbs had become an accomplished fact. By solely examining the conservative political outlook in that overwhelmingly white and predominantly upper-middle-class environment, these observers have often failed to appreciate the importance of race and class in the formation of this new conservative ideology. Confined to such a homogenous setting, it is perhaps easy to understand how some have accepted without question the claims of some conservative activists that their movement was (and still is) "color blind" and unassociated with "class warfare."[7] Indeed, in most suburbs, with no other colors in sight and no other classes in contention, such claims may seem plausible. For how could suburban conservatism be shaped by issues that simply were not there? But once the conservative politics of the Sun Belt are correctly situated in the crucible of urban politics, surrounded by different races, multiple classes, and competing social interests, they can be seen in a rather different light.

For it was inside the city that much of the later agenda and ideology of suburban conservatives first took shape. It was *during* the process of white flight, not after it, that two defining elements of modern conservatism originally emerged. First, in the reaction to court-ordered desegregation of municipal spaces and services, white Atlantans decided to flee those public spaces and create private alternatives in their stead. In the beginning, this was a path taken only by upper-class whites who had the financial wherewithal to do so. But as all whites saw that privatization could effectively be used to perpetuate racial separation, they too came to embrace the approach. Second, and on a related note, as whites fled from these public spaces, they fought to take their finances with them. And so, they staged an early, though often overlooked, tax revolt, rebelling against the use of their taxes to support municipal spaces and services that they no longer used. Thus, white flight from cities like Atlanta was not simply physical, as white residents abandoned the central city for lilywhite suburbs. Their withdrawal first unfolded in a less literal sense, as they withdrew their support—political, social, and financial—from a city and a society that they believed had already abandoned them.

Public Desegregation and Private Resegregation

As a rule, Southern cities distributed public space to the races in distinctly separate and decidedly unequal ways. This pattern was perhaps clearest in the physical nature of public space, in that municipal authorities generally granted each race distinct spaces to call its own.[8] In Atlanta, public space was meted out in disproportionate measures. For instance, in the distribution of public park space, the small lands conceded for black use were woefully underfunded and underdeveloped. A 1954 report from the Atlanta Urban League noted that although blacks represented over a third of the city's population, they could use just 3 of 132 park spaces operated by the Atlanta Parks Department. The distribution of recreational facilities, the report pointed out, was just as bad. There were ninety-six tennis courts in the city, for instance, but blacks could play on only eight, none of which was lighted. The city ran eight community centers, but blacks could use just one; likewise, only one of the city's seven gyms admitted blacks.[9]

The most glaring discrepancy in the distribution of these services, however, stood in the municipal golf courses. While blacks had at least some access to other sites, they were barred completely from the city's five golf courses. Nearly a quarter million whites used these courses each year, but if Atlanta's blacks wanted to play a round, they had to haul their equipment beyond the city limits to the privately owned Lincoln Country Club. Realizing that the provision of public spaces was most obviously imbalanced in this area, civil rights activists thus targeted the golf courses first. On July 19, 1951, a foursome arrived at the Bobby Jones Municipal Golf Course—Dr. Hamilton Holmes, an elderly physician; his sons Alfred, a former Southern Amateur champion, and Oliver Wendell, a seminary student; and Charles T. Bell, a family friend and real-estate agent. They were a respectable, middle-class group. However, as the golf pro pointed out, they were also black. Because of that detail, he refused to let them play, citing a city ordinance barring blacks from "public areas designated for whites." Despite the letter of local law, Atlanta's politicians understood the foursome's challenge presented a serious problem. Nervous officials in the Parks Department announced that plans were "in the blueprint stage for a Negro golf course." Years passed, however, with no steps made toward creating a course for blacks. Meanwhile, two new ones were built for whites.[10]

Accordingly, Hamilton Holmes filed a federal suit in June 1953, demanding that all of Atlanta's courses be opened to blacks. A year later, Judge Boyd Sloan of the U.S. District Court ruled that there was "no legal obligation" for the city to offer public courses. But if it did, it had to allow everyone access. Though Sloan found in favor of the black plaintiffs, he left room for some continued separation of the races. "Segregation," the *Atlanta Journal* assured its readers, "can be maintained." Black leaders, however, were not satisfied. Several of the NAACP's leading legal minds, including Thurgood Marshall and Robert Carter, were brought on board to handle the appeal. Emboldened by recent successes against segregated education, they pressed the case to the U.S. Supreme Court, hoping the justices would strike down other semblances of segregation as well. On November 8, 1955, the Court did just that, ruling unanimously that lower courts had been wrong to apply the "separate but equal" doctrine to municipal facilities. Blacks had to be admitted to Atlanta's golf courses on a completely equal basis.[11]

Segregationists were outraged. Blacks did not want equality, they charged; they wanted social intimacy. "They do not want to play on golf courses where only Negroes are playing," spat former Governor Herman Talmadge. "They want to play with White men and women and they are determined to force themselves on the White players." Blacks should have respected whites' desire for separate facilities. "Instead," he said, "they yell for the Supreme Court like spoiled brats." Governor Marvin Griffin, Talmadge's successor, predicted the ruling would be "a definite disservice to their own people." Other segregationists likewise claimed the ruling could only lead to chaos. "It is obvious," noted Attorney General Eugene Cook, that "the pattern set by the Supreme Court will have its inevitable conclusion in a breakdown of harmonious race relations and in an eruption of intimidation, violence and bloodshed."[12]

In what would emerge as a recurring theme of white resistance, these segregationists offered a drastic solution. Unwilling to let municipal spaces be integrated, they instead urged the city to abandon its public lands altogether. Former Governor Talmadge, for instance, pressed Atlanta to sell its municipal parks and playgrounds to private interests who could keep them white. The Supreme Court's ruling, he predicted dourly, would encourage most states to take such measures and thus would "probably mean the end of most public golf courses, playgrounds, and things of that type." Governor Griffin agreed. "I can make the clear declaration that the state will get out of the park business before allowing a breakdown in segregation in the intimacy of the playground," he announced. If he had been in charge of the courses when the ruling came down, the governor would have "plowed them up next morning and planted alfalfa and corn."[13]

But Mayor Hartsfield was in charge, not Governor Griffin, and he took a different approach. "Atlanta has a good reputation before the nation, and we hope to preserve it," the mayor announced. "I have no doubt that Atlanta, as usual, will do the right thing." Publicly, he refused to say what "the right thing" would be. Privately, he carefully prepared for peaceful compliance with the court's orders. Hartsfield first convinced Judge Sloan to delay the delivery of the desegregation order until the Christmas holidays, to give the city time to comply. In the meantime, Hartsfield worked to orchestrate the courses' peaceful desegregation. First, he met with leaders of the black community to secure their cooperation. "The Negro leadership was agreeable to any plan that would desegregate the golf courses without incident," Police Chief Herbert Jenkins recalled, "and agreed to make no move to integrate the courses until the city had an opportunity to work things out." Next, the mayor met with the nearly one hundred employees of the golf courses. There were just two choices, he told them—comply or close. Reminded that closing the courses would cost them their jobs, the employees voted unanimously for compliance. As a final touch, Hartsfield closed off the locker rooms and shower facilities, hoping that might lessen whites' fears of interracial intimacy. To the press, he claimed with a straight face that the lawsuit had nothing to do with it: "We decided that since most people travel to and from the courses today, the showers just weren't needed any more." By the time Judge Sloan finally handed down the decree to desegregate on December 23, 1955, Hartsfield had thus carefully laid the groundwork for calm compliance.[14]

Now faced with the official order, Hartsfield said Atlanta would "accept [it] without question." Still, he tried to downplay the importance of the ruling. "Golf, by its very nature, is a segregated game," he rationalized, "and neither necessary nor compulsory." He listed other Southern cities that had already desegregated courses without trouble and reminded whites that other public facilities, such as playgrounds and swimming pools, would still be segregated. Following Hartsfield's recommendations, the same group that had first sought to play four years earlier announced they would finally tee off at the Bobby Jones course the next day. "It was Christmas Eve," the mayor later explained, "and we counted on everybody being full of the Christmas spirit, not to mention tired from all that shopping and going to parties." Not everyone was in the holiday mood, however. During the night, a number of angry whites sneaked onto several courses and scrawled obscenities in yellow paint across the pavilions and benches. But Hartsfield was prepared. He had work crews out before dawn, painting over every word. When reporters arrived at the Bobby Jones course, there was no trace of the vandals' work. But there was also no trace of the Holmes family. Fearing an outbreak of violence, the mayor convinced them to play another course. "They had promised the television people they would appear," Hartsfield recalled. "I said, 'Those TV boys aren't interested in watching you hit the ball. They want to get pictures of you getting beat up!'" In the end, his careful preparations paid off. When the foursome arrived at the North Fulton course instead, there was no ugliness.[15]

Though the desegregation seemed to go smoothly, whites in neighborhoods near the two courses were outraged. At first, they had assumed it would never happen. When the original desegregation order came down from the Supreme Court, the local *Northside News* sarcastically addressed the likelihood of black golfers coming to "their" courses. "Oh, we'll be able to tell when the invader's really coming, in person," the editors scoffed. "They'll be yelling 'Fo', white boy! Don't you heah me yellin' fo' at you? The saints is marchin' in.'" But when desegregation actually did arrive, these editors saw it as a personal attack. "There are seven public golf courses in Atlanta," they pointed out. "Only two are in the North Side, the other five being much more convenient to the Holmes boys and their friends who live in southwest Atlanta." Blacks had targeted Northside courses not because they were the city's finest, the paper charged, but because they stood in neighborhoods that were still all white. "Under the NAACP strategy," it warned, "the Negro invading forces strike first at the Pearl Harbors and not at the nearby Asiatic islands. The first attack must humble the self-satisfied whites who believe that the Negro problem will never strike close to their homes. That, itself, is an incident Northsiders need to note."[16]

Tellingly, the paper charged that the city's white elites would, in time, rid all the city's public spaces of segregation. "With a smugness that would be laughable were it not so alarming," they wrote bitterly, "the *Atlanta Journal* declares that the admission of Negroes to white golf courses does not mean that Negroes will be permitted to use the swimming pools with white people. That is like saying the infant who learns to crawl will not learn to walk." No, the golf courses were only the beginning. And it was all Hartsfield's fault. "How are people expected to hail a New Year with delight when they just saw . . . the current mayor of Atlanta hand them a black bombing on their golf courses?" the editors worried at the start of 1956. "They know they can expect from such a mayor the sudden announcement some time this year that he and the merchants welcome the integration of whites and blacks in swimming pools, in all restaurants, on all buses—and maybe, in the public schools."[17]

Because of white outrage, the golf courses remained—quite literally—contested terrain for years after their official desegregation. In the summer of 1959, for instance, whites in the city's southwest learned that black golfers were planning to hold a "National Negro Golf Tournament" on the eighteen-hole course at Adams Park. Whites were furious. A "large contingent of aroused residents" marched to the mayor's office, demanding he stop it. "The whites were by no means the rough element that bothers trouble," judged the *Atlanta Journal-Constitution*; "they were people of middle income, living in a nice section." But the mayor dismissed them. As one white resident remembered with disgust, "City officials (which in Atlanta means the mayor) refused to take a stand, pleading impotence." So whites "defended" the course themselves. "With dogged determination," he noted with pride, "the white people publicized plans to clutter the course from daybreak until dusk, for the duration of the tournament, and the Negroes backed down. The National Negro Golf Tournament was called off." [18]

White resentment over the desegregation of golf courses, though potentially explosive, never reached a state of true crisis. Whites could, of course, simply refuse to play desegregated courses. But if they decided to play, they would rarely encounter any black players. Golf was, as the mayor pointed out, a "segregated game" in which there was little or no contact between groups. Without contact, there would be little conflict. In other public services and public spaces, however, the degree of personal contact would become much more pronounced. Indeed, as segregation spread to the close confines of city buses, the shared facilities of municipal parks, and most important, the common waters of public swimming pools, white fears of "interracial intimacy" would reach new heights. And, accordingly, so would the new patterns of segregationist resistance and white withdrawal.

Unlike golf courses, which had excluded blacks altogether, Atlanta's buses and streetcars were shared by both races. Of course, inside that space, blacks were relegated to the rear of the vehicle, in a reminder of their supposed "place"— both physical and social—in southern society. There, at the back of buses, they were subject to a host of insults and attacks, not the least of which came at the whim of frequently racist and often dangerous white drivers. Throughout the 1930s, 1940s, and early 1950s, the black community tried to secure better treatment on city buses but managed to accomplish little. After the desegregation of Atlanta's golf courses, however, the city's black leaders launched a concerted challenge against bus segregation. Once again, they found support from the city's upper-class whites, their partners in the mayor's political coalition. And once again, their actions further accentuated the dividing line between their white allies and the growing ranks of their white enemies. [19]

The movement against bus segregation in Atlanta started six months after the more-famous bus boycott in Montgomery, Alabama. In early June 1956, a group of black activists, led by the Rev. John T. Porter, spread out in the front seats of an Irwin Street bus. At the next stop, several whites boarded, paid their fares, and stopped dead in the aisle, stunned by what they saw. The operator whirled around and shouted at Rev. Porter, "Boy! Get up, move to the back, and let those folks sit down." The minister refused to move. "Boy! I am talking to you!" the driver yelled again. For several minutes, the two sides remained motionless, but ultimately, the protestors backed down and left. A few weeks later, Rev. Porter tested another segregation statute—the rule that blacks had to leave by the back door. When the bus he was riding reached the corner of Walton and Broad, Rev. Porter got up and walked to the front exit. The driver told him to leave by the back, but the minister proceeded out the front. Outraged, the driver suddenly closed the mechanical doors as the preacher was halfway through them, pinning him there. Only through his own efforts was he able to free himself.[20]

These initial challenges gained strength and support when the Supreme Court settled the Montgomery boycott in November 1956, striking down segregation on its city buses and other modes of public transportation. Emboldened by the ruling, the Rev. William Holmes Borders and other ministers launched the "Love, Law, and Liberation Movement" to apply the decision in Atlanta. In keeping with the city's approach to race relations, they met with Mayor Hartsfield to discuss their plans in advance. All they wanted to do, they told him, was to secure grounds for challenging the state's segregation statutes in court. Always mindful of his city's public image, Hartsfield asked if there were any way it could be done without arresting the ministers. "Impossible," they replied. Without arrests, they would lose face in the black community. Confronted with the challenge, Hartsfield yet again orchestrated the actual desegregation. The first step involved a peaceful test. Together, the Love, Law, and Liberation Movement and the Atlanta Transit System carefully arranged the challenge beforehand. "We are going to ride until these buses are desegregated," Rev. Borders announced to a crowd of 1,200 at his Wheat Street Baptist Church. "If they take the bus to the barn, we'll ride it to the barn and then get another. We'll take every bus in Atlanta to the barn if necessary." Despite these bold words, the challenge was meant to be as conservative as possible. Ministers alone would ride the buses, they announced. Public support was not sought and, indeed, directly discouraged. In addition, while they would be breaking the rules of segregation, the ministers promised not to violate taboos of interracial intimacy. "We will not sit by a white person," Rev. Borders cautioned. "Under no circumstances will any of us sit by a white woman."[21]

The next morning, January 9, 1957, twenty ministers boarded a bus, paid their fares, and as the driver later remembered, "took seats in my trolley coach wherever they pleased to sit." The incident did not take him by surprise. "I was aware," he attested, "that there had been talk of an attempt by certain colored persons to board a vehicle of my employer and ride such a vehicle on a 'desegregated' basis." The driver said nothing to the ministers but refused to move. "It's not going anywhere," someone shouted from outside, and all the white passengers filed off the bus, except one. An Atlanta Transit System manager soon arrived, telling the driver to switch the sign to "special" and drive the bus straight to the barn—just as Rev. Borders had predicted. As the driver carried the singing and praying ministers away, one reporter remembered, a "cavalcade of press and television cars" stretched out behind the bus, saving every moment for public scrutiny. Once at the barn, the ministers exited—by the front door—and left the scene without any ugliness. In fact, the only clash occurred when a white passenger tried to take a camera away from a white reporter who had just taken his photo.[22]

After the challenge, the ministers' arrest was just as carefully scripted. At Hartsfield's direction, Police Chief Jenkins went through the formality of obtaining warrants for their arrest, even though no one—not the mayor, the police chief, the county solicitor, not even the judge himself—thought the ministers should be punished. "He said that he did not believe the warrants would be worth the paper they were written on," Jenkins said of the judge, "but if I believed it would help defuse a potentially explosive situation, he would issue them." Jenkins hoped the ministers could quietly come to the police station on their own; Hartsfield even offered to send city limousines. But Rev. Borders insisted on the spectacle of being carried away in the paddy wagon. Obligingly, the police chief asked him for a convenient time and place for the arrest and arranged for two of his most level-headed men, Captain J. L. Moseley, white, and Detective Howard Baugh, black, to lead the detail. The arrest was an even bigger event than the ministers' ride the day before. Huge crowds came out to Wheat Street to watch. "The people knew why we were there, why the police were there," Rev. Borders recalled. "People quit work. They stopped cooking meals. They left beauty shops. They came out of stores. They thronged the streets." So many turned out, however, that the paddy wagon was unable to leave until Rev. Borders climbed out and asked the crowd to part. Moseley and Baugh chatted amiably with the ministers all the way to the station, and a Time-Life representative rode along, chronicling his trip in the South's first integrated paddy wagon. At the station, the ministers were booked, bonded, and released within two hours. Their brief visit included time in a detention cell, but the door was never even closed.[23]

By the end of the day, everyone involved was satisfied. The ministers had secured grounds for a test case against state segregation laws and were satisfied to fight it out in the courts. "We've accomplished our objective," Rev. Borders told his supporters. "The fight will be in the courts and we won't attempt to ride the buses integrated again until it's settled." At the same time, the mayor safeguarded the positive public image of his city. "Atlanta has an excellent record before the nation for its good race relations," Hartsfield crowed. "We in Atlanta have felt that this was a desirable thing, not only for the sake of decency but from the standpoint of business as well." After the bitterness of the Montgomery boycott, the nation marveled at how smoothly, almost effortlessly, Atlanta had again desegregated its public space.[24]

Indeed, unlike other cities in the South, where whites responded to desegregation with violent attacks, Atlanta witnessed little in the way of violence.[25] To be sure, Rev. Borders soon grew accustomed to answering phone calls for "that damn bus preacher" and heard that whites would dynamite his church in retaliation. But nothing happened. Instead of attacking the activists behind bus desegregation, Atlanta's segregationists struck back by boycotting the buses themselves. For years, whites had predicted that desegregation would drive white patrons away and bring the end of public transportation altogether. "In our opinion," the *Metropolitan Herald* noted after the initial challenges, "the eventual sufferers will be those who will be left with no means of public transportation to get to and from their jobs, as transit systems are forced to go out of business." Likewise, once the court case had been won, segregationists again urged whites to abandon the buses. Attorney General Eugene Cook, for instance, praised white passengers for leaving the bus when Rev. Borders and the other ministers first arrived. Similarly, the head of the segregationist States' Rights Council of Georgia encouraged white flight. "White people should refuse absolutely to be integrated on the city busses of Atlanta," he urged. "In no event should white people remain seated when these NAACP agitators become disorderly and unruly in sitting by them." These leaders' revulsion resonated deeply with their fellow whites. "There is nothing more intimate and integrated," one Atlantan wrote disgustedly in 1959, "than a black nigger sitting beside a white girl on the trolley."[26]

Just as they had reacted to desegregated golf courses, whites claimed that desegregated bus lines were "lost" to them and looked for private alternatives. Early in the boycott, for instance, a Northern man had warned Chief Jenkins about what would happen to Atlanta's transit system as whites inevitably fled in fear. "As of today, Detroit, Chicago, [and] Cleveland public transportation systems are mere shells of their former place in public utility," he noted. "They are almost abandoned to the private car—bumper to bumper, one man to a vehicle—definitely to avoid Integration." Whites and blacks simply could not coexist, the man insisted. "Too many toes were stepped on with no apologies, for it is noted that negroes do not apologize for a social error," he sneered. "Too many women were molested; too many men were knifed, too many bus drivers were attacked in trying to maintain order on public vehicles."[27]

Indeed, white patronage on Atlanta's buses did plummet after the January 1957 challenge to desegregation. The Atlanta Transit System compared its usage from the previous year and found significant and steady declines across the board. By that May, passenger fares had dropped off 7 percent; by November, they were down 13 percent. "It was felt," the board recorded, "that this decline was definitely influenced by publicity on desegregation and by the recent court suit filed by the NAACP in respect to segregation on Atlanta buses." The drop-off in white usage, however, was due not to the *actual* desegregation of the buses but instead to the *threatened* desegregation of them. The ministers' lawsuit took two years to work its way through the courts; meanwhile, they urged blacks to abide by segregated seating patterns. Apparently, they did. An Atlanta University sociology student rode the buses in April and May 1957, for instance, and found that the old patterns of segregation persisted. "Of the total number of white passengers riding the buses, the largest number preferred to sit from 'front to center,'" he noted on a rush-hour bus. "Whites did not change their seats for Negroes. Most of the white passengers boarded by the front entrance and departed by the front exit." That might have been expected, but the observer found that blacks abided by the old codes as well. "Negro passengers elected in the majority of the cases viewed to sit from 'center to rear,'" he observed on a residential line. "Most of the Negroes boarded by the front entrance and departed by the center exit." In three weeks, he witnessed only a single conflict between blacks and whites, and a verbal one at that.[28]

Even after the Supreme Court ruled in favor of the ministers and forced the official desegregation of Atlanta's buses in January 1959, blacks rarely challenged the old rules of race and place. "You are free to ride anywhere you choose," Rev. Borders told a rally of 2,500 after the decision. But he cautioned restraint. "We don't want one single incident, and that is what we are working for," he announced. Blacks should be neat, be orderly, and never sit next to white women. In all, Borders and his fellow ministers did little to encourage integration. As Rev. B. J. Johnson announced, "There will be no concentrated mass effort to ride desegregated." Thus, months after the decision, city buses remained effectively segregated. "So far, here in Atlanta, I have not seen a single negro on the street cars sitting by a white person," a white man wrote in March 1959. "I don't think they, in the mass, are anxious to mix with us anywhere."[29]

White riders, however, were even less anxious to "mix" with blacks. Census reports from 1960 demonstrate that as some had predicted, whites had indeed fled the system and taken to private cars in large numbers. In several neighborhoods, working-class whites now used private cars to get to their jobs instead of public transportation, by a 2-to-1 margin. Meanwhile, blacks in neighboring tracts—sections that likely shared bus routes with these white areas—trended in precisely the opposite direction, choosing public transportation over private cars by a 2-to-1 margin. A private survey of bus usage from 1960 echoed the fact that blacks were becoming a predominant presence on the lines as working-class whites fled. Although African Americans represented only a third of the city's population, the report noted, they made up "59 percent of the bus patronage during the rush period." Over the next decade, as bus desegregation picked up speed, so too did white flight from the lines.[30]

The anger of working-class whites over the "loss" of Atlanta's bus lines paled in comparison to their outrage over the desegregation of municipal parks. Although the desegregation of the golf courses had opened new recreational space for black use, the discrepancies in space and funding were still staggering as the 1950s came to a close. A study from 1960 showed that municipal facilities were still offered on a decidedly unequal basis—20 football fields for whites, none for blacks; 22 baseball diamonds for whites, 3 for blacks; 16 recreation centers for whites, 3 for blacks; 119 tennis courts for whites, 8 for blacks; 12 swimming pools for whites, 3 for blacks. The major municipal parks were still predominantly white spaces, with 42 reserved for whites but just 3 for blacks. Accordingly, in 1961, civil rights activists launched a legal campaign to desegregate the city's parks.[31]

As with the golf courses, the city's political leaders tried to evade the issue. City attorneys stalled for time, challenging everything from the class-action nature of the lawsuit to the fact that the plaintiffs were representing themselves. Once the case received serious attention from District Court Judge Boyd Sloan—the same judge who desegregated the city's golf courses in 1955—the city's attorneys suddenly claimed that the issue was moot. The parks were already desegregated, they said. Park officials and police officers denied enforcing the segregation statutes and insisted that it was merely "by custom and practice" that the races in Atlanta tended to "segregate themselves in the use of the public facilities and otherwise." Despite the official claims of innocence, Atlanta's parks and recreational facilities were still very much segregated, if in subtler ways. At the Bitsy Grant Tennis Center, for instance, blacks were turned away in May 1961 on the grounds that they had failed to sign up for courts in advance. When another group appeared there in August, they found the courts full of white players, including Georgia Tech's famed football coach Bobby Dodd. They walked downstairs to register, but in the short time it took to get there, the manager cleared the courts and announced they were now "closed for repairs." The District Court saw through the city's subterfuges, however, and ordered Atlanta's parks, pools, recreation centers, and tennis courts to desegregate—fully and officially—in 1962 and 1963.[32]

Again, large numbers of working-class whites fiercely opposed the desegregation of public parks. More than anything, they were outraged that the city's public pools would be desegregated in June 1963. "That summer people talked about the integration of the swimming pools and little else," Police Chief Jenkins remembered. "Frankly, the police hoped for a rainy summer, for there were more eyeballers and agitators driving around trying to see how many Negroes were using the pools than there were people swimming." On the first desegregated day at Piedmont Park, for instance, between 40 and 60 people swam in the pools, while a crowd of 250 whites stood outside the fences and watched. Hoping to cut down on the number of clashes between white and black teenagers, the city employed high school coaches to manage the pools that summer and kept uniformed police and plainclothes detectives on hand as well. Aside from a few fistfights, the early weeks of pool desegregation went by calmly.[33]

In truth, pool desegregation went smoothly not because whites accepted the decision but because they had decided, once again, to flee these desegregated public spaces. For many whites, integrated pools represented a level of interracial intimacy they simply could not stomach. Indeed, the image of black and white children swimming together was so repugnant to them that some segregationist groups sent photographers to Atlanta's pools to get pictures for future propaganda. Such a reaction from die-hard segregationists was to be expected, but even those who embraced integration in other areas refused to support shared use of pools. For instance, religious groups who welcomed interracial gatherings often drew the line at integrated swimming. "They had quite a few negroes at Lake Junaluska last year and they took part in all the activities," noted one man about a retreat held by the Methodist Church. "However, when four or five of the negroes decided to go in the pool one afternoon, they immediately drained the pool." Many whites—segregationists or not—believed that blacks carried diseases that might be spread in shared waters. "For the protection of all swimmers," one woman proposed, "would it not be possible for the City to require health cards for admission?" Likewise, a segregationist outside the Piedmont Park pool handed out leaflets to everyone entering. "The negro race is a reservoir of venereal infection," they read. "Will you expose yourself and your children to the deadly threat? Keep your children, especially, out of the public pools." Rumors of health hazards became so prevalent that the *Atlanta Journal* had to remind its readers that syphilis and gonorrhea "are not spread by water, food, or air."[34] In all likelihood, however, such warnings only reinforced whites' assumptions that a great number of blacks really did carry such diseases. Not surprisingly, white attendance at the pools plummeted. Even Chief Jenkins, who had prayed for a rainy summer, was alarmed by the "noticeable drop" in attendance. On opening day the year before, for instance, the popular pools at South Bend and Oakland City took in 400 visitors each; on the first day of desegregated use, attendance was down to 155 and 259, respectively.[35]

As whites abandoned the pools, they asked the city to follow suit. And in many ways, it did. The next summer, for instance, hours of operation were scaled back at most pools. The change had been made, Mayor Ivan Allen Jr. noted, "so as to lessen racial tension wherever possible." But the city did more than simply reduce the operating hours of its pools; it also reduced their size and scope. Instead of the old system, in which large pools served broad sections of the city, Atlanta launched a new "neighborhood pool policy," which relied on smaller "walk-to" pools in individual neighborhoods. Since those neighborhoods were still effectively segregated, such a move could easily be seen as a way around the order to desegregate. For some whites, however, these changes in policy were still not enough. They demanded an end to public pools altogether. In Candler Park, for instance, 850 whites signed a petition calling for the closing of their neighborhood pool, which they claimed had been "a menace to the peace and tranquility of the community" since it desegregated. When such pools were closed, segregationists delighted in it. In 1966, for example, a tour-bus driver entertained visitors with a joke about the changes at Grant Park. "There used to be a swimming pool here," he announced to the tourists, "but when the integrationists made us let Nigras in we fixed them by filling it in and now it's a bear pit." His riders laughed appreciatively.[36]

Unwilling to share public space with blacks, white Atlantans once again looked for a private alternative. In the case of the public parks, some whites hoped to transfer municipal lands to private hands. For instance, the head of the Atlanta Council of Civic Clubs called for the privatization of the entire park system, citing "social changes . . . largely due to the racial situation." Community civic clubs, neighborhood churches, and "patriotic and historical organizations" could take ownership of the parks, he suggested, and thereby maintain the racial patterns in them. Ultimately, privatization of large city parks was simply not feasible. Private pools, however, were a more realistic alternative, and many whites rushed to start construction in their own backyards. In fact, the demand for private pools was so sudden and severe that a number of fly-by-night construction crews cropped up in the city to fleece desperate customers. Eventually, Atlanta's legitimate builders had to form a new organization, the Greater Atlanta Swimming Pool Association, just to clean up the industry's reputation.[37]

Working-class whites, of course, could not afford their own pools. For them, the only alternative to swimming at an integrated pool was not swimming at all. Thus, while almost all whites complained about the self-imposed "sacrifices" they were making in their flight from desegregated public spaces, once again, only the working class had no real alternative. They angrily attacked upper-class whites as hypocrites who pushed a social policy on others but escaped its ramifications themselves. "Don't forget to report on how many of the Atlanta Mayor's official family did or did not attend the opening of the city swimming pools for a nice integrated swim," complained one man to the *Atlanta Constitution*. As he and many others realized, neither the mayor nor his allies in the white business elite would be affected by the desegregation of public parks, pools, or golf courses, since they held memberships in exclusive, still-segregated private clubs. (Indeed, the most exclusive of these—the Peachtree Golf Club and Piedmont Driving Club—did not accept black members until well into the 1990s.) "Integration for everyone but the *Rich* high & fancy," is how one angry white put it. "When the black horde (masses) start banging on the doors of your fine homes & segregated districts & segregated clubs & pools you will sing a different tune. Oh yes & how you will. Integration is just fine as long as it doesn't touch (*in your* opinion) God's chosen few and their Ivory Castles."[38]

Thus, as Atlanta desegregated its parks and pools, working-class whites again reacted in a familiar pattern. First and foremost, they believed that these urban spaces, which they considered their own, had been "stolen" from them and given to another race. As before, working-class whites once again understood the process of court-ordered desegregation not as one which brought down barriers to black citizens but, rather, as one which erected new barriers for themselves. Second, in their anger, they blamed not just black Atlantans but the upper-class whites who had aided and abetted the entire process of desegregation. That anger quickly took the form of a full-fledged tax revolt inside Atlanta and, in time, greater white flight from it.

White Flight and the Tax Revolt

White flight from desegregated public spaces was all the more bitter because whites felt that these public spaces were theirs and theirs alone. This resulted partly from the history of urban segregation. For most whites in Atlanta, these spaces belonged to them as a racial birthright. But whites' sense of ownership of these public spaces went much deeper than that. As they saw it, whites paid the vast majority—or in some interpretations, all—of the taxes collected by the city. Whites alone had paid for these public spaces, their reasoning went, so whites alone should be allowed to use them. When the city opened these public spaces to blacks, therefore, whites felt that their birthright had quite literally been stolen from them.

The perception that whites paid far more in taxes than blacks did was quite common in Atlanta during the late 1950s and early 1960s. To be sure, because of discriminatory policies of public and private lending institutions and real estate agencies, comparatively few black Atlantans owned their own homes. In direct terms, therefore, only a small portion of Atlanta's black population paid property taxes. But indirectly, through often exorbitant rental payments on their homes and businesses, blacks did contribute their full share to the city's tax base. White Atlantans remained ignorant of such facts and assumed that they alone shouldered the vast majority of the tax burden. In some cases, this assumption was expressed in a benign, though paternalistic, way. "The white people have paid lots more taxes for schools, highways, and the other necessities of life than the colored people have paid," one Atlantan claimed, "but we have no regret about that because we have tried to be a help to them." Many of his fellow citizens, however, expressed plenty of regret. "Where would the Negroes be if it were not for the taxes of the white people?" one woman wanted to know. "Very few of them pay any taxes." "Do you know the Atlanta's population is one-third niggers?" read a typical segregationist pamphlet. "They are paying five per cent of the taxes and receive a strong margin of seventy-five per cent of the tax for their race." [39]

This supposed disparity between the tax burdens of whites and blacks took on a strongly racist tone, as whites charged that they unfairly bore the financial burden for a welfare system that catered to blacks. "I believe in them having good things but in their own *negro sections* and I believe in them working by the sweat of their brow as 'God' states in the Bible instead of hand-outs from White organizations," one man complained. "Welfare office, etc. give them about $50 of white peoples tax money for every illegitimate 'youngster' they have & do they breed fast?" "A majority of negro women have no morals and breed like swine," another agreed, "and the white people of the city are taxed to keep them and their illegitimate offspring up." Segregationists used this popular sentiment to disparage blacks' calls for desegregation and other civil rights measures. A mock application for membership in the NAACP, for instance, appeared in Atlanta in 1957. "I believe in equality that niggers is better than white folks is," the pledge read, "and that the White folks should pay more taxes and us Niggers should have more and more welfare." In a similar vein, this segregationist poem surfaced in the city:

> Po' white folks must labor, 'tween sun and sun,
> To pay welfare taxes whilst we has de fun,
> We doan pay no taxes, we doan make no goods,
> We just raise little niggers, way back in the woods.
> Dey pay us to vote and rewards us to sin,
> While dem sweet demmycrates keeps de checks cumming in,
> We waits every month for the slips and de figgers,
> An dats all we do—we is damn lucky niggers.

For angry whites, the implication was clear. "SHALL YOU CONTINUE TO PAY FOR THEIR PLEASURE?" one segregationist sheet asked. "While they sit in the shade and spoon in the moon light, multiplying like rats, we continue to bleed ourselves with heavy taxes to carry the socialistic burden of feeding and clothing them. They do not remain as slaves and therefore are certainly not your wards." [40]

When white neighborhoods were "threatened" by the approach of black buyers, resistance groups often tapped into the resentment over taxes to rally angry whites. Many of them, for instance, called themselves "taxpayers' organizations," "taxpayer leagues," or "property owners' associations." Even those that went by other names still stressed the rights of white taxpayers in their propaganda. "We are faced with the problem of encroachment upon our community, by the Negro race," warned one group in 1958. "If our community is lost, then who will be the loser, except you the property owners and taxpayers. You can not as a property owner, taxpayer, man, woman, or child, sit by and let this situation go as it appears. You must have the intestinal fortitude to stand up and fight these battles wherever and whenever you can. "With the desegregation of public facilities, these whites invoked their beleaguered role as taxpayers even more." Common use of recreational and sanitary facilities supported by taxation—of which the Negroes pay about one-thirtieth—together with all forms of public transportation, seems inescapable," one Atlantan lamented in 1958. "But the die-hard segregationist can still claim and retain his prerogative of strap-hanging in the crowded trolley, wisely holding his temper and tongue. Similarly, he can exercise, for himself and his progeny, the option of staying away from contaminated swimming-pools and bathing at home." Because of their refusal to share public spaces with blacks, whites essentially made their old complaint come true. Their taxes were being used to fund services largely enjoyed by blacks. Whites refused to acknowledge that this was a result of their own racism, however, and instead blamed the city for "surrendering" these spaces to blacks.[41]

White anger over the desegregation of public spaces and the tax revolt soon made itself felt in city politics. The Hartsfield administration and its admirers often cited Atlanta's successful desegregation of public spaces as proof of the city's progress. And, increasingly, local segregationists equated the two as well. In the eyes of working-class whites, the "progress" that the mayor and his allies often bragged about had come at their expense—in the losses of their public spaces and taxes. One Atlantan, for instance, told Hartsfield that he and his neighbors were sickened by what the mayor called "progress." They saw it another way: "Many of the progress viewers now live in the county [outside] of the city. You see, their neighborhoods were taken over by the negro race. Their neighborhoods became slums." Another woman shared this assessment. "I will certainly give the mayor credit for giving one of the largest swimming pools in West End to the Negroes," she complained, "and replacing it with a pool about the size of a pocket handkerchief." For such Atlantans, the city's growth meant nothing alongside their own perceived losses. Municipal services offered by the city meant nothing either. In 1953, one of Hartsfield's supporters described a conversation he had with a neighbor, in which he tried to stress the civic improvements Hartsfield had championed. "I asked my next door neighbor how often her Garbage was taken up under the old plan," he reasoned, "and if she had ever seen a street sweeper before." But there was only one thing on her mind: "Her cry is 'nigger, nigger, nigger.'" In the end, the woman became so enraged that she and the mayor's supporter had to be pulled apart.[42]

By the end of the 1950s, therefore, the city's pursuit of progress had become, in the minds of working-class whites, a zero-sum game in which every gain for blacks was a loss for whites. This attitude was perhaps best seen in a poem Chief Herbert Jenkins found in 1959, tacked to a bulletin board at police head-quarters. Tellingly, the piece was titled "The Plan of Improvement," in a mock tribute to a 1952 program for Atlanta's expansion, which Hartsfield had cham-pioned. The poem began with a sarcastic look back at the course of residential racial change and then focused on the desegregation of public spaces:

> I'll try something different for plan number two
> This time the city's golf courses will do.
> They'll mix in the Club House and then on the green
> I might get a write up in Life Magazine.
> And now comes the schools for plan number three
> To mix them in classrooms just fills me with glee;
> For I have a Grandson who someday I pray
> Will thank me for sending this culture his way.
> And for my finale, to do it up right,
> The buses, theatres and night spots so bright;
> Pools and restaurants will be mixed up at last
> And my Plan of Improvement will be going full blast.

As the poem suggests, a hidden undercurrent of working-class white resent-ment grew out of the politics of race and public space. Increasingly distrustful of the city's moderate leadership and increasingly resentful of the course of racial change, these whites soured on the talk of progress, which was central to both.[43]

In the early 1960s, as Atlanta's leadership continued to press for progress with a new plan for civic improvements, these whites drew the line. The new spaces would be desegregated as well, they reasoned, and therefore, they would stay away. So why should they fund them? The growing white backlash on issues of race and public space became clear in the battles over two bond initiatives in 1962 and 1963. The first bond issue called for $80 million for a number of im-provements on schools, streets, sewers, and other public works, as well as show-case proposals for a new civic auditorium and a new cultural center at Piedmont Park. Mayor Ivan Allen Jr. touted the auditorium as a way for the city to attract national conventions and hold large events, but working-class whites saw it as another space exclusively for blacks. A crude cartoon circulated by the

Klan, for instance, depicted a black speaker—labeled "Martin Luther Coon"—addressing an integrated audience. "I's been advised by de mayor dat de white folks is going to raise dere bond taxes and build us a new auditorium for future NAACP meetings," the caption read. "We is making progress." The proposal for a cultural center caused even greater controversy. Located in the heart of the city, Piedmont Park was perhaps the most prized public space in Atlanta, one originally landscaped by the famed Olmsted Brothers. Mayor Allen hoped to add to its value with a new cultural center but soon found that the politics of race and public space were more complicated than he imagined. Prior to the vote, the Woodruff Foundation, a charitable group founded by Coca-Cola magnate Robert Woodruff, donated $4 million to the project, with the provision that the foundation's name be kept out of it. "The redneck elements started screaming that the Piedmont Park plan was really an effort to integrate the park," Mayor Allen later recalled, "and that the $4 million anonymous gift was 'nigger money.'" Meanwhile, real-estate agents warned surrounding neighborhoods that the cultural center would spark a mass migration of blacks to the area, rumors that only increased white anger. "Piedmont Park suddenly blew up in my face," Allen remembered, "and became a raging racial issue."[44]

Not surprisingly, the bond initiative was soundly defeated. As the *Atlanta Journal* noted, nearly 58,000 turned out at the polls, "a record number as far as bond referendums go." Basic improvements in schools and street works lost narrowly, but the auditorium and cultural center died in a "smothering defeat." The latter proposal, for instance, was rejected by a margin of almost 2 to 1, with the vast majority of opposition coming from working-class and even middle-class whites. In their minds, the reason was clear. The tax burden for the projects, one man complained, would rest on "90 percent of the white people," while blacks would get most of the benefits. Others agreed. "I think that this is another step," one man reasoned, "where the taxpayers are tired of paying hard-earned money for things that they will not be able to enjoy because of the prospect of forced integration, which means that the facilities would be used almost entirely by the Negroes." As Atlanta drifted toward ever more desegregation, he added, "the white people who pay all the bills have decided to stick a little closer and vote accordingly." Mayor Allen tried again the next year, introducing a second bond initiative pared down to the "bare essentials." Though most of the controversial aspects from the year before had been excluded, whites still fought the initiative. A routine letter from Allen to the local NAACP, for instance, was doctored to imply that the mayor took orders from civil rights groups. Copies appeared across the city, with a warning at the bottom. "Don't give the 'CAPTIVE MAYOR' of the Minority Bloc a blank check to use against the OTHER voters and tax-payers of Atlanta," the sheet warned.

"VOTE AGAINST BONDS!" Allen responded by pouring $25,000 into a public-relations campaign for the measure and marshaling the votes of upper-class whites and the black community. Only then did the bond pass. Still, there was sizable protest. "The negative vote came from sections of the city and county where white segregationist sentiment traditionally is strongest," the *Atlanta Journal* noted. "And the vote went heaviest against projects where integration or benefits for Negroes might have appeared to be involved—urban renewal, parks, libraries, the auditorium." Indeed, as the vote demonstrated, for many working-class whites, *public works* and *benefits for Negroes* meant the same thing.[45]

Ultimately, the politics of privatization and the tax revolt would find even greater strength and support in the world of suburbia. Within the city limits, whites had bitterly resisted the sharing of both public space and municipal tax revenues with blacks, but outside Atlanta, they found very few blacks with whom they would be forced to share on either count. (The northern suburbs around Atlanta—the predominant choice for white migrants in the 1960s and 1970s—ranged from 95 to 99 percent white in population in 1970.) Given the lack of meaningful integration in such suburbs, the politics of privatization and the tax revolt might have been expected to fade in importance there. In fact, they grew only stronger. The movement for privatization, to be sure, reached new heights in suburbia. As architects Andres Duany and Elizabeth Plater-Zybek noted, "The suburb is the last word in privatization, perhaps even its lethal consummation." Admittedly, in the suburbs around Atlanta, whites returned to some public institutions, such as parks, but in many other aspects of public life, they pushed privatization to unprecedented levels. In public transportation, for example, suburban counties around Atlanta not only refused to join the metropolitan mass-transit system but also resisted the creation of any *local* public transportation whatsoever. Private cars became the only means of transportation; in one booming county, cars soon outnumbered people. Likewise, in the broader functions of local government, these suburbs came to privatize a wide range of duties, from entering data and cleaning buildings to teaching schoolchildren and feeding prisoners.[46]

The tax revolt, meanwhile, found greater strength in suburbia as well. As whites moved from an urban world of multiple races and classes to a suburban world of greater racial and class homogeneity, it became much easier for them to free themselves from what they regarded as an unfair tax system. Rather than having to rely on the older, more-direct appeals to race or class difference, which were of course becoming increasingly unpopular in the public mind, these whites merely needed to adopt a localist argument, one that insisted on keeping tax revenues at home, not redistributing them across the metropolitan

area. As such local phenomena of suburban isolation spread across the country, the seeds for the nationwide tax revolt of the late 1970s were effectivel-
sown. By the time that revolt made its presence known in national politics, th-
important roles of race and class had been largely obscured, enabling the leaders of the suburban tax rebellion to tell themselves, and the country, that their-
was a color-blind conservatism devoid of any class warfare. Although whit-
suburbanites have largely forgotten the origins of their outlook, their politic-
are, in no small measure, a product of the urban struggles over race and class-
an outgrowth of the city they once sought to escape and still seek to avoid.[47] ,

Notes

For their helpful comments and criticism, the author thanks the receptive audience
who heard earlier presentations of this article at the University of Pennsylvania, th-
University of Georgia, Princeton University, and the annual meeting of the America-
Historical Association, as well as the anonymous reviewer for the *Journal of Urba*-
History.

1. See, for instance, *Christian Century,* June 3, 1953; *Newsweek,* March 15, 1954-
Saturday Evening Post, October 31, 1953; *Atlanta Journal-Constitution,* January 18'
1970. On Atlanta's approach to race relations, see Karen Ferguson, *Black Politics in*
New Deal Atlanta (Chapel Hill: University of North Carolina Press, 2002); Ronald H.
Bayor, *Race and the Shaping of Twentieth-century Atlanta* (Chapel Hill: University of
North Carolina Press, 1996); Gary Pomerantz, *Where Peachtree Meets Sweet Auburn*:
A Saga of Race and Family (New York: Scribner, 1996); Frederick Allen, *Atlanta Ris*-
ing: The Invention of an International City, 1946–1996 (Atlanta, GA: Longstreet Pres-
1996); Clifford M. Kuhn, Harlon E. Joye, and E. Bernard West, eds., *Living Atlanta: An*
Oral History of the City, 1914–1948 (Athens: University of Georgia Press, 1990); Davi-
Garrow, ed., *Atlanta, Georgia, 1960–1961: Sit-Ins and Student Activism* (Brooklyn, NY-
Carlson, 1989); Clarence N. Stone, *Regime Politics: Governing Atlanta, 1946–1988* (Lawrence: University of Kansas Press, 1989); Floyd Hunter, *Community Power Succession*-
Atlanta's Policy-makers Revisited (Chapel Hill: University of North Carolina Pres-
1980); Harold H. Martin, *William Berry Hartsfield: Mayor of Atlanta* (Athens: University of Georgia Press, 1978); Ivan Allen Jr., *Mayor: Notes on the Sixties,* with Paul Hemphill (New York: Simon and Schuster, 1971); Floyd Hunter, *Community Power Structur*-
A Study of Decision Makers (Chapel Hill: University of North Carolina Press, 1953). e:

2. The phrase *Sun Belt* first appeared in Kevin Phillips, *The Emerging Republica*-
Majority (New Rochelle, NY: Arlington House, 1969), esp. 437–43. See also Kirkpatric-
Sale, *Power Shift: The Rise of the Southern Rim and Its Challenge to the Eastern Estab*-
lishment (New York: Random House, 1975); David C. Perry and Alfred J. Watkins, *The*-
Rise of the Sunbelt Cities (Beverly Hills, CA: Sage, 1977); David R. Goldfield, *Cotto*-
Fields and Skyscrapers: Southern City and Region, 1607–1980 (Baton Rouge: Louisian-
State University Press, 1982); Carl Abbott, *The New Urban America: Growth and Pol*-
tics in Sunbelt Cities (Chapel Hill: University of North Carolina Press, 1987); Raymond-
Mohl, ed., *Searching for the Sunbelt: Historical Perspectives on a Region* (Knoxville
:

University of Tennessee Press, 1990); Bruce Schulman, *From Cotton Belt to Sunbelt: Federal Policy, Economic Development, and the Transformation of the South* (New York: Oxford University Press, 1991); Jack Bass and Walter DeVries, *The Transformation of Southern Politics: Social Change and Political Consequences Since 1945* (Athens: University of Georgia Press, 1995); Numan V. Bartley, *The New South: 1945–1980* (Baton Rouge: Louisiana State University Press, 1995), 417–54. (Princeton, NJ: Princeton University Press, 2001); Earl Black and Merle Black, *The Rise of Southern Republicans* (Cambridge, MA: Harvard University Press, 2002).

3. See Jonathan Rieder, "The Rise of the 'Silent Majority,'" in Steve Fraser and Gary Gerstle, eds., *The Rise and Fall of the New Deal Order* (Princeton, NJ: Princeton University Press, 1989), 243–68; William C. Berman, *America's Right Turn: From Nixon to Bush* (Baltimore: The Johns Hopkins Press, 1994); Mary C. Brennan, *Turning Right in the Sixties: The Conservative Capture of the GOP* (Chapel Hill: University of North Carolina Press, 1995); Lisa McGirr, *Suburban Warriors: The Origins of the New American Right* (Princeton, NJ: Princeton University Press, 2001); Earl Black and Merle Black, *The Rise of Southern Republicans* (Cambridge, MA: Harvard University Press, 2002).

4. Sale, *Power Shift*, 153–205.

5. See Robert Kuttner, *Revolt of the Haves* (New York: Simon and Schuster, 1980); Alvin Rabushka and Pauline Ryan, *The Tax Revolt* (Stanford, CA: Hoover Institution, 1982); David O. Sears and Jack Citrin, *Tax Revolt: Something for Nothing in California* (Cambridge, MA: Harvard University Press, 1982); Thomas Byrne Edsall, *Chain Reaction: The Impact of Race, Rights, and Taxes on American Politics*, with Mary Edsall (New York: Norton, 1992); Bruce J. Schulman, *The Seventies: The Great Shift in American Culture, Society, and Politics* (New York: Free Press, 2001), 193–217; Robert O. Self, *American Babylon: Race and the Struggle for Postwar Oakland* (Princeton, NJ: Princeton University Press, 2003).

6. See Mike Davis, *City of Quartz: Excavating the Future in Los Angeles* (New York: Verso Books, 1990); Joel Garreau, *Edge City: Life on the New Frontier* (New York: Anchor Books, 1991); Edward J. Blakely and Mary Gail Snyder, *Fortress America: Gated Communities in the United States* (Washington, DC: Brookings Institution, 1999).

7. For an astute critique of "color-blind" conservatism, see Matthew D. Lassiter, *The Silent Majority: Suburban Politics and the Sunbelt South* (Princeton, NJ: Princeton University Press, forthcoming).

8. C. Vann Woodward, *The Strange Career of Jim Crow* (New York: Oxford University Press, 1955); Howard N. Rabinowitz, *Race Relations in the Urban South, 1865–1890* (New York: Oxford University Press, 1978); David R. Goldfield, *Black, White and Southern: Race Relations and Southern Culture, 1940 to the Present* (Baton Rouge: Louisiana State University Press, 1990); Don H. Doyle, *New Men, New Cities, New South: Atlanta, Nashville, Charleston, Mobile, 1860–1910* (Chapel Hill: University of North Carolina Press, 1990).

9. Gail Anne D'Avino, "Atlanta Municipal Parks, 1882–1917: Urban Boosterism, Urban Reform in a New South City" (Ph.D. diss., Emory University, 1988); Dana F. White, "Landscaped Atlanta: The Romantic Tradition in Cemetery, Park, and Suburban Development," *Atlanta Historical Journal* (Summer/Fall 1982): 104; Atlanta

Urban League, "A Report on Parks and Public Recreational Facilities for the Negro Population of Atlanta, Georgia" [1954], Box 5, Grace Towns Hamilton Papers, Atlanta Historical Society, Atlanta (hereafter GTH).

10. Calvin Trillin, *An Education in Georgia: Charlayne Hunter, Hamilton Holmes, and the Integration of the University of Georgia* (Athens: University of Georgia Press, 1991), 15; Louis Williams, "William B. Hartsfield: The Reluctant Accommodationist and the Politics of Race in Atlanta, 1900–1961" (Ph.D. diss., Georgia State University, 1996), 234; *Atlanta Daily World*, July 20, 1951; *Atlanta Constitution*, December 24, 1955; W.W. Law, interview by Cliff Kuhn and Tim Crimmins, November 15, 16, 1990, transcript, Georgia Government Documentation Program, Georgia State University, Atlanta (hereafter GGDP); Atlanta Urban League, "A Report on Parks and Public Recreational Facilities for the Negro Population of Atlanta, Georgia" [1954], Box 5, GTH; *Atlanta Journal*, July 8, 1954.

11. *Atlanta Daily World*, June 27, 1953, and July 9, 1954; *Atlanta Journal*, July 8–9, 1954, and November 8, 1955; *Atlanta Constitution*, May 25, 1954, July 9, 1954, and November 8, 1955; *Atlanta Journal-Constitution*, July 11, 1954; Williams, "Hartsfield: Reluctant Accommodationist," 259–60; *Holmes v. City of Atlanta*, 350 U.S. 879 (1955). Shortly after *Brown*, the Fourth Circuit Court of Appeals had ruled that the city of Baltimore could no longer segregate its public beaches; *Dawson v. Mayor*, 220 F. 2d 386 (1955). The city appealed the ruling, but the Supreme Court unanimously affirmed the decision on November 8, 1955; *Mayor v. Dawson*, 350 U.S. 877 (1955). That same day, the Court applied their affirmation of the Baltimore case as a governing precedent for the Atlanta golf-course case. See Richard Kluger, *Simple Justice: The History of Brown v. Board of Education and Black America's Struggle for Equality* (New York: Vintage, 1975), 750; Bernard Schwartz, *Super Chief: Earl Warren and His Supreme Court: A Judicial Biography* (New York: New York University Press, 1983), 126; Mark V. Tushnet, *Making Civil Rights Law: Thurgood Marshall and the Supreme Court, 1936–1961* (New York: Oxford University Press, 1994), 301.

12. Herman E. Talmadge, *You and Segregation* (Birmingham, AL: Vulcan Press, 1955), 29; *Atlanta Constitution*, November 9, 1955.

13. *Atlanta Journal*, November 8, 1955; Douglass Cater, "Atlanta: Smart Politics and Good Race Relations," *Reporter*, vol. 17, July 11, 1957, 19.

14. *Atlanta Journal*, July 8, 1954, November 9, 1955, December 23, 1955; *Atlanta Constitution*, November 10, 1955; William B. Hartsfield, *Cities and Racial Minorities: Atlanta's Approach* (Washington, DC: National League of Cities, n.d.; reprinted from Marshall-Wythe Symposium, College of William and Mary, 1964), 57; Herbert T. Jenkins, *Keeping the Peace: A Police Chief Looks at His Job* (New York: Harper, 1970), 34, 37; Williams, "Hartsfield: Reluctant Accommodationist," 262.

15. *Atlanta Journal*, December 23–24, 1955; *Atlanta Constitution*, December 23, 1955; Fred Powledge, "Black Man, Go South," *Esquire*, August 1965, 75; Cater, "Atlanta: Smart Politics and Good Race Relations," 19; *Atlanta Journal-Constitution*, December 25, 1955.

16. *Northside News*, November 16 and December 29, 1955.

17. *Northside News*, December 29, 1955, and January 4, 1956.

18. George Brownlee to Editor, *Jacksonville Journal,* October 10, 1959, Box 38, James C. Davis Papers, Emory University, Atlanta (hereafter JCD); *Atlanta Journal-Constitution,* October 11, 1959.

19. Taylor Branch, *Parting the Waters: America in the King Years, 1954–1963* (New York: Simon & Schuster, 1988), 143–68, 173–205; Harvard Sitkoff, *The Struggle for Black Equality, 1954–1992* (New York: Hill and Wang, 1993), 37–56; David Levering Lewis, *King: A Biography* (Urbana: University of Illinois Press, 1978), 46–80.

20. Plaintiff's Petition, Rev. *Samuel W. Williams and Rev. John T. Porter v. Georgia Public Service Commission, et al.,* Civil Action No. 6067, U.S. District Court (hereafter *Williams v.* GPSC); copy in Box 116, Mule-to-Marta Collection, Archives, Atlanta Historical Society, Atlanta (hereafter MM).

21. *Browder v. Gayle,* 352 U.S. 903 (1956); Catherine A. Barnes, *Journey from Jim Crow: The Desegregation of Southern Transit* (New York: Columbia University Press, 1983), 120–26; Typewritten Draft, Atlanta Transit System, Box 35, MM; Robert L. Sommerville to A. T. Walden, Draft of Letter, January 8, 1957, Box 35, MM; Williams, "Hartsfield: Reluctant Accommodationist," 74, 264–65; James W. English, *Handyman of the Lord: The Life and Ministry of the Reverend William Holmes Borders* (New York: Meredith Press, 1967), 90; *Atlanta Daily World,* January 8–9, 1957; *Atlanta Journal,* January 9, 1957.

22. *Atlanta Daily World,* January 10, 1957; Affadavit, Ganis V. Daniel, Driver, Atlanta Transit System, January 14, 1957, Box 35, MM; Plaintiff's Petition, *Williams v. GPSC*; Cater, "Atlanta: Smart Politics and Good Race Relations," 18.

23. H. T. Jenkins to Paul Webb, Solicitor, Atlanta Judicial Circuit, Fulton County Court House, January 10, 1957, Box 18, Herbert T. Jenkins Papers, Atlanta Historical Society, Atlanta (hereafter HTJ); Herbert T. Jenkins, *Forty Years on the Force: 1932–1972* (Atlanta, GA: Center for Research in Social Change, 1973), 108; Pomerantz, *Where Peachtree Meets Sweet Auburn,* 217; Martin, *Hartsfield,* 119; Jenkins, *Keeping the Peace,* 39; *Atlanta Daily World,* January 11, 1957; English, *Handyman of the Lord,* 93; Cater, "Atlanta: Smart Politics and Good Race Relations," 18.

24. *Atlanta Journal,* January 9, 10, 1957; *Atlanta Constitution,* January 11, 1957; Cater, "Atlanta: Smart Politics and Good Race Relations," 18–21.

25. See Barnes, *Journey from Jim Crow.*

26. English, *Handyman of the Lord,* 90, 97; *Metropolitan Herald,* June 20, 1956; *Atlanta Journal,* January 9, 11, 1957; William T. Bodenhamer, Press Release, January 9, 1957, Box 32, JCD; A. L. Ellis to James C. Davis, January 28, 1959, Box 38, JCD.

27. L. B. Parrish, Detroit, to Herbert Jenkins, December 29, 1956, HTJ.

28. Minutes, Atlanta Transit System, Directors Meetings, June 26, 1957, November 27, 1957, December 18, 1957, Box 2, MM; Paul Douglas Bolster, "Civil Rights Movements in Twentieth-century Georgia" (Ph.D. diss., University of Georgia, 1972), 172–73; Herman Randolph Phillips, "Patterns of Racial Segregation on City Buses in Atlanta, Georgia" (master's thesis, Atlanta University, 1957), 36–38.

29. Bolster, "Civil Rights," 172–73; *Atlanta Journal,* January 19, 1959; *Atlanta Constitution,* January 20, 1959; Fenton M. Dancy to James C. Davis, March 21, 1959, Box 38, JCD.

30. U.S. Bureau of the Census, *U.S. Censuses of Population and Housing: 1960,* Final Report PHC(1)-8, Census Tracts, Atlanta,GA (Washington, DC: Government Printing Office, 1961),Tables P-1 and P-3, Census Tracts F-47, F-48, F-49, F-50; Bayor, *Race and Atlanta,* 191.

31. Bayor, *Race and Atlanta,* 151; "A Second Look: The Negro Citizen in Atlanta," Atlanta Committee for Cooperative Action, January 1960, copy in Box 116, MM; *Atlanta Journal,* June 26, July 25, August 21, 28, 1961.

32. *Atlanta Journal,* July 25, 1961, August 21, 24, 1961, August 28, 1962; Eliza K. Paschall, *It Must Have Rained* (Atlanta, GA: Center for Research in Social Change, Emory University, 1975), 54–55.

33. Jenkins, *Forty Years on the Force,* 115; *Atlanta Journal,* June 12, 1963; Eliza Paschall to Mayor Ivan Allen Jr., June 17, 1963, Box 3, Eliza Paschall Papers, Emory University (hereafter EP); Telex Report, June 25, 1963, Box 1, Newsweek, Atlanta Bureau Files, Emory University, Atlanta (hereafter NAB).

34. Eliza Paschall to Mayor Ivan Allen Jr., June 17, 1963, Box 3, EP; Ernest D. Key to Ralph McGill, June 15, 1963, Box 24, Ralph E. McGill Papers, Emory University, Atlanta (hereafter REM); Mrs. William E. Reynolds to Ralph McGill, June 6, 1963, Box 24, REM; Telex Report, June 25, 1963, Box 1, NAB; Thomas McPherson Jr. to Ernest Lent, June 13, 1963, Box 3, EP. During the Great Depression, white Atlanta experienced a similar panic over the supposed connections between blacks and syphilis in the city. See Ferguson, *Black Politics in New Deal Atlanta,* 112–15, 128–30.

35. Jenkins, *Forty Years on the Force,* 115; *Atlanta Journal,* June 13, 1963.

36. *Atlanta Journal,* June 5, 1964; *Atlanta Constitution,* July 19, 1963; Rabbi Jacob Rothschild to Robert Sommerville, President, Atlanta Transit System, September 23, 1966, Box 7, Rabbi Jacob M. Rothschild Papers, Emory University, Atlanta (hereafter JMR).

37. *Atlanta Journal-Constitution,* June 25, 1961; Allen, *Atlanta Rising,* 122.

38. Edward Norton to Ralph McGill, June 12, 1963, Box 24, REM; Pomerantz, *Where Peachtree Meets Sweet Auburn,* 515, 547; James O. Smith to McGill and Eugene Patterson, July 3, 1963, Box 24, REM.

39. A. W. McBerry to President Dwight D. Eisenhower, December 10, 1958, Box 38, JCD; Mrs. W. C. Todd to Ralph McGill, September 30, 1957, Box 24, REM; Flyer, "Act for God and Country—Help Defeat Communism" [1960], Box 56, REM.

40. Anonymous [Atlanta] to Ralph McGill and Eugene Patterson, September 26, 1966, Box 25, REM; E. A. Rogers to Edward D. Staples, June 11, 1956, Box 31, JCD; "N.A.A.C.P. Application" [1957], Box 31, JCD; "The Black Spangled Banner" [c. 1963], Box 25, REM; Flyer, "Act for God and Country."

41. Charles Abrams, *Forbidden Neighbors: A Study of Prejudice in Housing* (New York: Harper, 1955), 181; Flyer, Fourth Ward Zoning Committee, "UNITED WE STAND!" [May 1958], Box 24, Atlanta Urban League Papers, Atlanta University, Georgia (hereafter AUL); Lawrence W. Neff, Pamphlet, "Jesus: Master Segregationist" [April 1958], Box 38, JCD.

42. "An Atlantan" to William Hartsfield, May 1, 1957, Box 13, William B. Hartsfield Papers, Emory University, Atlanta (hereafter WBH); Mrs. J. T. McKibben, Letter to

the Editor, *Atlanta Journal,* March 13, 1957; Joe Prendergast to William Hartsfield, March 31, 1953, Box 11, WBH.

43. Handbill, "The Plan of Improvement" [January 1959], Box 6, WBH.

44. *Atlanta Journal,* August 3, 1962; Handbill, United Klans [n.d., 1962], Box 30, WBH; White, "Landscaped Atlanta," 102–4; Ivan Allen Jr., *Mayor: Notes on the Sixties,* with Paul Hemphill (New York: Simon& Schuster, 1971), 70.

45. Martin, *Hartsfield,* 181; *Atlanta Journal,* August 3, 6, September 28, 1962, March 10, 29, April 4, May 9, 10, 13, 16, 17, 1963; *Atlanta Journal-Constitution,* May 12, 1963; Mimeographed Letter, Mayor Ivan Allen Jr. to Dr. C. Miles Smith [1963], Box 3, Josephine Wilkins Papers, Emory University, Atlanta.

46. *Atlanta Journal-Constitution,* May 3, 1987, June 1, 1995, July 14, 1995; William Schneider, "The Suburban Century Begins," *Atlantic Monthly,* July 1992, 37.

47. For compelling treatments of the connections between race, class, and the tax revolt, see Edsall and Edsall, *Chain Reaction,* and Self, *American Babylon.*

Globalization, Latinization, and the *Nuevo* New South

Raymond A. Mohl

In 1992 Fellipe Patino settled in Russellville, Alabama, along with his wife, Patricia, and their children, Juan and Alma. They were among a small handful of Hispanics living in Russellville at the time. During the previous four years, Fellipe had traveled back and forth from Mexico to Florida for work while his family remained behind in Mexico. Still earlier, he had made numerous annual migrations to work in California agriculture. Patino was drawn to heavily rural, mostly white, northwest Alabama by the opportunity to work in the Gold Kist poultry plant in Russellville, where, he was told by fellow Mexicans, he could almost double the wages he earned as a migrant farmworker in Florida. The Russellville poultry plant had opened in 1990, but Gold Kist managers had had trouble securing a stable labor force locally. Like other chicken processors in Alabama and elsewhere, Gold Kist found in Hispanic workers like Patino the reliable, low-cost labor pool they needed to maintain efficient production. By the end of the 1990s, population of the Russellville area had become more than one-third Hispanic, some thirty-five hundred of about ten thousand people. By that time, the Patino family had bought a home. The children enrolled in local schools and endured ethnic harassment from American schoolmates, but ultimately they became fluent in English and adjusted to life in small-town Alabama. The family missed the Mexican homeland to a degree, but by the end of the 1990s the Mexican community in Russellville was large enough to provide many homeland comforts: native foods such as flat tacos, hot peppers, and goat meat; Mexican movie videos; Spanish-language soap operas on satellite television; weekend soccer leagues; familiar church services on Sundays; Spanish-speaking workers in government agencies; and Hispanic clerks in local retail stores.[1]

The Patinos adapted to life in Russellville's "Little Mexico." But as the new residents came to feel more at home, the town's white population gradually became uneasy about the ethnic change that upset the stability of small-town southern life. Initially, newcomers from south of the South were received cautiously, but in generally positive ways. They worked hard and spent their money locally, boosting rental housing, retail stores, and the used-car market. They provided about one-third of the labor force in the Gold Kist plant and contributed to the economic turnaround of the local economy. By the late 1990s, however, as the Mexican population continued to grow, local reaction turned less positive. Increasingly, Russellville locals complained about the newcomers' preference for the Spanish language and about the rising costs for health care, social services, schooling, and police services. A few raised the disturbing specter of a rejuvenated Ku Klux Klan that might scare off the Hispanics and restore the familiar whiteness of the past. Whatever their intentions, these discontented whites had little appreciable effect in stemming the flow of new immigrants to the area. Despite rising ethnic tensions in Russellville and elsewhere in Alabama, the Patino family seemed permanently settled in their new place.[2]

The scene is much the same in northeast Alabama, where tens of thousands of additional Hispanics have settled. Near Gadsden, in the small town of Attalla, Raul and Guadalupe Cantellano live in a small, ramshackle house with fifteen other family members, including six children, three of them married with children of their own. Raul had worked as a migrant farm laborer in Florida and Alabama in the 1980s and early 1990s, leaving his family behind in Mexico. In 1994 he brought his family to live in Alabama, settling at first into agricultural labor but eventually getting a job at the Cagle poultry plant in nearby Collinsville. After obtaining green cards permitting work in the United States, Cantellano's three adult sons and their wives all found jobs at the Cagle plant, where Hispanics comprised 63 percent of the work force by 1999. Guadalupe Cantellano works at home, caring for younger children, cooking ten pounds of tortillas a day, and raising chickens in the backyard. The Cantellanos have paid off the mortgage on their moderately priced home, own four used cars, and collectively earn a good income at the Cagle plant. Raul speaks no English and remains illiterate in Spanish, and his adult sons never had much education in Mexico. But like other Hispanic newcomers, they expect that educational opportunity in the United States will enable their younger family members to break the cycle of poverty and low-skill, low-pay work that characterizes Hispanic life in the American South.[3]

As these family stories suggest, Dixie is experiencing a dramatic demographic, economic, and cultural transformation. These transformations have resulted from two patterns of powerful change that are connected and that have coincided in the state of Alabama and in the South generally. Major shifts in the global economy have produced new forms of both deindustrialization and economic investment. New free trade policies such as the 1994 North American Free Trade Agreement (NAFTA) have encouraged the migration of capital and labor. A restructuring of regional, national, and global economies has undermined older forms of production in the South, such as in agriculture, steel, textiles, and apparel. At the same time, new economic investment has poured into the region as American and foreign capital seek cheap labor, new markets, and government incentives. The region's new economy features foreign-owned auto plants in Tennessee, Kentucky, Alabama, Mississippi, and South Carolina; high-tech research and manufacturing in Atlanta, Austin, Huntsville, and North Carolina's Research Triangle Park; biomedical research in Birmingham and other major medical centers; and the new food processing plants for poultry, hogs, and seafood that have sprung up all over the rural South. In the past decade, about half of all poultry processing has come to be concentrated in four low-wage, antiunion southern states—Alabama, Arkansas, Georgia, and North Carolina. In addition, rapid population growth in southern states and Sun Belt cities has created an immense service economy and a consequent demand for low-wage labor.[4]

Global economic change has also created new transnational labor migration patterns. Immigration scholars have noted the historic and deeply entrenched symbiotic relationship between Mexican immigrants and the American economy. Mexico's proximity to southwestern labor markets, immigration scholar Kitty Calavita has suggested, made it possible to easily "expand and contract" the migrant labor force over time in relation to demand. Indeed, throughout much of the twentieth century, Mexican labor migrants found willing employers in agriculture, manufacturing, and service work. During the 1920s, Mexican workers replaced European immigrants in midwestern steel and meatpacking plants, and they found railroad construction and maintenance jobs throughout the West. The immigration quota system established in the 1920s effectively shut off European immigration but did not apply to Mexico. When job losses nationwide mounted during the Great Depression, Mexican workers in the United States were "repatriated" in massive numbers. With new farm labor demands during and after World War II, the newly instituted bracero program legalized the temporary recruitment of as many as four million Mexican migrant farm workers annually. The bracero program officially ended in 1964, but Mexican farmworkers continued their migratory ways. As anthropologist Thomas Weaver has written, "the bracero movement institutionalized migrant networks for the flood of undocumented workers that followed its demise."[5]

During the bracero period and until the late 1980s, most Mexican border crossers sought agricultural and manufacturing jobs in California and the southwestern states, with a sizeable number also heading to the Chicago area. Economic crisis in Mexico in the early 1980s brought to power a new government that promoted free market economic policies. This new economic program encouraged global trade and investment in Mexico, especially American trade and investment, but it did little to improve the economic situation of most Mexicans. These changes coincided with new American immigration policy, primarily the 1986 Immigration Reform and Control Act (IRCA), which beefed up border controls and imposed tough new sanctions on employers who willfully hired undocumented immigrants. Because of worsening economic conditions in Mexico and despite the new American immigration law, Mexicans continued to seek work and higher wages in the United States. However, as sociologist Douglas S. Massey and colleagues have noted, the new border controls eventually "diverted the migratory flows away from traditional points of destination," such as California, thus transforming Mexican immigration "from a regional into a national phenomenon." The same forces encouraged undocumented workers to stay longer, or even permanently, to avoid the now more difficult border crossings that had been more easily managed in earlier years.[6]

IRCA influenced labor migration flows in other ways, as well. Under pressure from big agricultural interests and proimmigrant groups, Congress added an amnesty provision to IRCA, legalizing 2.3 million Mexicans who could document at least five years of work and residence in the United States. Those amnestied subsequently had full labor rights and the freedom to move within the country in search of better opportunities. They also gained the right to bring family members from Mexico, potentially as many as 9.2 million additional Mexican migrants. In addition, IRCA policies eventually encouraged amnestied Mexicans and their families to seek citizenship—an outcome speeded by Mexican legislation in the late 1990s permitting dual U.S.-Mexican citizenship. IRCA's amnesty provisions suggested the contradictions in American immigration policy, seeking to curb illegal Mexican migration while simultaneously granting permanent residency to millions. The surge of Hispanic migration to the South coincided with the new immigration provisions introduced by IRCA, as both illegal and amnestied Mexicans found new labor markets in the Southeast. By the end of the 1990s, the dispersal of Hispanic population from traditional areas of settlement had intensified dramatically. Documenting this new migration pattern, an Urban Institute study in 2001 demonstrated that "California's net population loss from internal migration of foreign-born households during the 1990s was 363,000," mostly Mexican-born immigrants. Amnesty provisions of IRCA encouraged internal migration from heavily Hispanic states such as California, while new job opportunities in the South determined new destinations. Labor recruitment played a role in the dispersal of Hispanic population, as well, as poultry companies and construction firms advertised for workers in Spanish-language newspapers in Mexico, California, and the Southwest.[7]

Taken together, the globalization of markets and capital *and* new American immigration policy diversified the migratory flows of Mexican labor. Within a few years of passage of IRCA, for example, hiring of legal and illegal Hispanic workers had become "a cornerstone of changing labor relations" in southern poultry processing plants. Hispanic labor flows to the South intensified in the wake of NAFTA, which failed to produce promised wage increases in Mexico and fostered further immigration. Large American companies recruited workers directly from Mexico, reflected in 2002 in the message conveyed on a huge billboard in Tijuana, Mexico, sponsored by Gold Kist: "Mucho Trabajo en Russellville, Alabama" [There's plenty of work in Russellville, Alabama]. Similar billboards elsewhere in Mexico advertised job opportunities in North Carolina. Consequently, newcomers from below the border, mostly amnestied or illegal Mexicans, have now become ubiquitously visible in isolated small towns and rural places, as well as in sprawling metropolitan regions such as Atlanta, Nashville, Memphis, Louisville, Birmingham, Charlotte, Greensboro, Raleigh-Durham, Greenville, South Carolina, and Arlington, Alexandria, Norfolk, Virginia Beach, and Fairfax County in Virginia. As labor researcher Hector Figueroa noted in 1996, "Latino labor in the United States is a product of the complex forces that have integrated Latin America into the orbit of U.S. capitalism." Nothing has changed since that time to alter Figueroa's conclusions.[8]

New immigration has fueled the South's changing economy, but it has had other consequences, too. Black and white once defined the racial landscape of the American South, but multicultural and multiethnic rather than biracial now describe society in many southern places. As one Alabama editorialist noted in 2000, "Life in the South used to be defined in shades of black and white. But a growing wave of Hispanic immigrants is adding brown to that color scheme." "A world of racial technicolor is exploding in the South," the *Christian Science Monitor* reported in 1999, "as the ethos of black and white that has defined the region for more than a century diminishes." "The future is brown," Richard Rodriguez has argued in a recent book, *Brown: The Last Discovery of America* (2002), which makes the case that Hispanic migrations to the United States over time have tended to blur racial distinctions and break down racial and ethnic barriers across generations, especially through intermarriage and sexual contact. The seemingly permanent Hispanic influx to the South, a *Washington Post* reporter suggested in 2000, has been "changing forever the old idea of what a southerner is." In northeast Atlanta, journalist Anne Hull wrote, the heavy concentration of Hispanic and Asian immigrants along a fifteen-mile stretch of Buford Highway "has come to symbolize the transformation of the white and black South." In Hull's opinion, with its multiple clusters of immigrant apartment complexes, shopping centers, churches, restaurants, and groceries, Atlanta "represents the two-tone world of the past that is now giving way to a new society." The silent wave of Latin migration that has transformed much of America is now working its way through the South.[9]

Hispanic migration to the Deep South was barely noticeable to most in the 1980s, but the migratory flow surged dramatically in the 1990s. Texas and Florida had long had heavy concentrations of Hispanics—Texas because of its proximity and historic connections to Mexico, and Florida because of the massive waves of Cubans, Nicaraguans, and other Latin exiles, immigrants, and internal migrants that began to arrive in the 1960s. In the 1990s, new and different migration streams deposited Latin newcomers all over the southern United States. Texas and Florida continued to attract Hispanics in substantial numbers, but in virtually every other southern state the Hispanic growth rate surpassed the national growth rate in Hispanic population by three, four, five, or six times. And unlike the 1980s, by the mid-1990s southerners in destination towns and cities found it difficult to ignore the sudden intensity of ethnic change. Verifying these patterns, a few social scientists by the mid-1990s had begun writing about the powerful surge of Hispanic migration to the South.[10]

U.S. Census Bureau statistics tell part of the story of this astonishing shift in population patterns. During the 1990s, for example, the Hispanic population surged nationally by a hefty 61.2 percent, rising from 22.4 million in 1990 to 35.3 million in 2000. By 2003, new census counts confirmed that Hispanics surpassed African Americans as the nation's largest minority, "a symbolic benchmark of some significance," asserted writer and policy analyst Robert Suro. Hispanic population gains nationally were impressive, but statistical evidence of recent Latino migration to the South has been even more dramatic. The most startling example is that of North Carolina, where the census recorded a sizzling 394 percent growth rate for Hispanics in the 1990s. The decennial growth rate was similarly very high in other southern states: 337 percent in Arkansas, 300 percent in Georgia, 278 percent in Tennessee, 212 percent in South Carolina, 208 percent in Alabama, and by lesser but still substantial amounts in other southern states (see table 1). Aside from Texas and Florida, the Hispanic population in southern states in 2000 ranged from a low of 39,500 in Mississippi to a high of 435,000 in Georgia. Virginia, with almost 330,000 Hispanics, and North Carolina, with 379,000, also ranked high on the list. Overall, the 2000 census revealed a decennial increase of almost 4.6 million Hispanics in the South, bringing the total Hispanic population of twelve southern states to a little over 11 million. Another census report in September 2003 revealed that between 2000 and 2002, Georgia had the fastest growing Hispanic population, rising an astonishing 17 percent over two years to 516,500. The same report documented that Atlanta had the highest Hispanic growth rate among the nation's twenty largest metropolitan areas. Interim

TABLE 1. Hispanic Population Growth in Twelve Southern States, 1990–2000

State	1990 Hispanic Population	2000 Hispanic Population	Percent Growth 1990–2000	Percent of Total Population
North Carolina	76,745	378,963	393.8	4.7
Arkansas	19,876	86,866	337.0	3.2
Georgia	108,933	435,227	299.5	5.3
Tennessee	32,742	123,838	278.2	2.2
South Carolina	30,500	95,076	211.7	2.4
Alabama	24,629	75,830	207.9	1.7
Kentucky	22,005	59,939	172.4	1.5
Mississippi	15,998	39,569	147.3	1.4
Virginia	160,403	329,540	105.4	4.7
Florida	1,574,148	2,682,715	70.4	16.8
Texas	4,339,874	6,669,666	53.7	32.0
Louisiana	93,067	107,738	15.8	2.4
South	6,498,920	11,084,967	70.6	12.6

Source: U.S. Census, 1990, 2000.
Note: States ranked by percentage Hispanic growth, 1990–2000.

census studies also showed that Hispanic populations continued to rise rapidly in other southern states. Alabama, for example, recorded a 12.7 percent Hispanic increase between 2000 and 2002.[11]

Many recent Hispanic migrants to the South have settled in small towns and rural areas for agricultural and poultry work. But large numbers of newcomers have chosen urban destinations as well. Metro Atlanta, with 269,000 Hispanics in 2000, provides the most startling example of this pattern of urban migration. According to the census, fully 62 percent of all Hispanics in Georgia reside in the twenty-county Atlanta metropolitan area. This new urban pattern is common throughout the South. North Carolina cities along the Interstate-85 corridor had huge increases in Hispanic migration during the 1990s. The newcomers are now heavily represented in the state's metro population, typified by the 77,000 Hispanics in metro Charlotte, 73,000 in Raleigh-Durham–Chapel Hill, and 62,000 in Greensboro-Winston-Salem. Virginia, too, has striking numbers of Hispanics, including 219,000 in the Virginia portion of the Washington, D.C., metro area. Suburban Fairfax County alone has almost half of that number, about 107,000 or more than 11 percent of Fairfax's total population. Similar urban concentrations of Hispanics can be found in most of the South's other metropolitan areas (see table 2).[12]

The 2000 census also provided a better sense of Hispanic diversity in the South. The census broke down the Hispanic population into four major categories: Mexican, Puerto Rican, Cuban, and "Other Hispanic or Latino," a reference to those from other Central American and South American nations. Generally, observers have tended to identify the South's new Hispanic immigrants and migrants as primarily or almost exclusively Mexican. This may actually be the case in selected small towns, but statewide census statistics demonstrate not only diversity of national origin but wide disparities among southern states. For example, with the exception of Texas and Arkansas, where the proportions of Mexicans surpass 70 percent of all Hispanics, in no southern state do Mexicans exceed about two-thirds of all Hispanics, and in some states the Mexican proportion is quite low: 30 percent in Louisiana, 22.4 percent in Virginia, and 13.6 percent in Florida. The statistics for the "Other Hispanic" category also suggest surprising ethnic differentials among southern states. For instance, the proportion of "Other Hispanic" ranges from a low of 22.5 percent in Texas to a high of 62.5 percent in Virginia, with most states in the 25 to 35 percent range. Even in Florida, generally thought of as dominated by Cubans, that group is surpassed numerically by Hispanics from Central and South America. Finally, excepting Florida, the proportions of Cubans and Puerto Ricans in the South tend to be much lower than the other two categories (see table 3). This Hispanic diversity, of course, can also be traced in the population statistics for individual southern cities, counties, and metropolitan areas.[13]

TABLE 2. Hispanic Population Growth, Selected Southern Metropolitan Areas, 1990–2000

Metro Area	1990 Hispanic Population	2000 Hispanic Population	Percent Growth 1990–2000
Atlanta	57,169	268,851	370.3
Birmingham	3,989	16,598	316.1
Charleston	7,512	13,091	74.3
Charlotte	10,671	77,092	622.4
Fayetteville, Ark.	1,526	26,401	1,630.1
Greensboro–Winston-Salem	7,096	62,210	776.7
Greenville-Spartanburg, S.C.	5,120	26,167	411.1
Jackson, Miss.	1,944	4,240	118.1
Lexington, Ky.	3,117	11,880	281.1
Little Rock	4,164	12,337	196.3
Louisville	5,765	16,479	185.8
Memphis	7,986	27,520	244.6
Nashville	7,665	40,139	423.7
New Orleans	53,226	58,545	10.0
Norfolk–Newport News–Va. Beach	32,329	48,963	51.5
Raleigh–Durham–Chapel Hill	9,019	72,580	704.7
Virginia Part of Wash., D.C. Metro	102,489	218,778	113.5

Source: U.S. Census, 1990, 2000.

TABLE 3. Diversity of Hispanic Population, Twelve Southern States, 2000

State	Mexican	Puerto Rican	Cuban	Other	Total
Alabama					
Hispanic Pop.	44,522	6,322	2,354	22,632	75,830
% Hisp. Pop.	58.8	8.3	3.1	29.8	
Arkansas					
Hispanic Pop.	61,204	2,473	950	22,239	86,866
% Hisp. Pop.	70.5	2.8	1.1	25.6	
Florida					
Hispanic Pop.	363,925	482,027	833,120	1,003,643	2,682,715
% Hisp. Pop.	13.6	18.0	31.1	37.4	
Georgia					
Hispanic Pop.	275,288	35,532	12,536	111,871	435,227
% Hisp. Pop.	63.3	8.2	2.9	25.7	
Kentucky					
Hispanic Pop.	31,385	6,469	3,516	18,569	59,939
% Hisp. Pop.	52.4	10.8	5.9	31.0	
Louisiana					
Hispanic Pop.	32,267	7,670	8,448	59,353	107,738
% Hisp. Pop.	30.0	7.1	7.8	55.1	
Mississippi					
Hispanic Pop.	21,616	2,881	1,508	13,564	39,569
% Hisp. Pop.	54.6	7.3	3.8	34.3	
North Carolina					
Hispanic Pop.	246,545	31,117	7,389	93,912	378,963
% Hisp. Pop.	65.1	8.2	1.9	24.8	
South Carolina					
Hispanic Pop.	52,871	12,211	2,875	27,119	95,076
% Hisp. Pop.	55.6	12.8	3.0	28.5	
Tennessee					
Hispanic Pop.	77,372	10,303	3,695	32,468	123,838
% Hisp. Pop.	62.5	8.3	3.0	26.2	
Texas					
Hispanic Pop.	5,071,963	69,504	25,705	1,502,494	6,669,666
% Hisp. Pop.	76.0	1.0	0.4	22.5	
Virginia					
Hispanic Pop.	73,979	41,131	8,332	206,098	329,540
% Hisp. Pop.	22.4	12.5	2.5	62.5	

Source: U.S. Census, 2000.

Census statistics reveal only part of the Hispanic migration story, however. Actual Hispanic population counts are much higher, perhaps as much as twice as high in many southern cities, counties, and states, according to local sources. For example, the 2000 census counted 39,500 Hispanics in Mississippi, but state economic planner Pete Walley conceded that the actual number "could be well over 100,000." Similarly, Memphis had 23,400 Hispanics according to the census, but local leaders contend that "the real population is probably closer to 100,000 in the metro area." The census reported 13,000 Hispanics in Charleston, South Carolina, but knowledgeable observers offer 50,000 as a more likely Hispanic population total for the city. Some 435,000 Hispanics resided in Georgia, according to the 2000 census, but at least one Georgia demographer suggests the actual number is closer to 800,000, or about 10 percent of the state's population. The Census Bureau, in fact, has routinely undercounted minorities, including new immigrants, many of whom are undocumented and thus avoid any contact with government agencies. As South Carolina journalist James Shannon of the *Greenville News* noted in 2002, "documentation issues make many members of this demographic group less inclined to sit still for official head counters." Indeed, the Census Bureau admitted early in 2001 that its national population count for 2000 could be off by as much as 2.7 to 3.9 million people, most of whom were Hispanics, African Americans, and Native Americans. Nevertheless, census statistics provide important evidence for tracking rapid demographic and ethnic change in the South.[14]

Case studies of several southern states and cities provide a more revealing snapshot of the recent Hispanic migration and its impact. Centrally located in the Deep South, Alabama became an important destination for Hispanic immigrants and migrants in the 1990s. The Census Bureau count for 2000 placed the number of Hispanics in the state at about 76,000. Those who work with the Hispanic communities—public health professionals, social workers, church people, school and police officials—place the actual Hispanic population of Alabama, mostly Mexicans, at considerably more than 100,000 at the turn of the twenty-first century. Hispanics are spread throughout the state, in both rural and urban areas. Metropolitan Birmingham has the largest concentration of newcomers, some 16,600 according to the 2000 census—an increase of more than 300 percent from 1990. Other major cities such as Montgomery, Mobile, and Huntsville have anywhere between 4,000 and 7,000 Hispanics each. Local estimates suggest that doubling the census numbers for Alabama's largest cities would be more accurate. In north Alabama, where the poultry and garment industries are concentrated, small cities and towns such as Gadsden, Anniston, Cullman, Decatur, Russellville, Albertville, Collinsville, Oneonta, and a few others have substantial numbers of Hispanics as well. "Little Mexicos" are sprouting up in north Alabama neighborhoods, trailer parks, and apartment complexes.[15]

Jobs and economic opportunity have provided the magnetic pull attracting Hispanics to Alabama, and to the rest of the South as well. As immigration scholar George J. Borjas has written, "the same economic incentives that drive global trade flows motivate workers to move across international borders." The booming American economy of the 1990s, with the lowest unemployment rates in decades, created a demand for cheap, reliable, nonunion labor. An ongoing economic crisis in Mexico through the 1980s and 1990s helped drive legal as well as undocumented newcomers to the United States. Many labor migrants came directly from rural and small-town Mexico, but many others, such as Fellipe Patino and Raul Cantellano, had already worked in Texas, Florida, California, or elsewhere before arriving in Alabama.[16]

This new immigrant labor force has become an essential ingredient in Alabama's rural and urban economies. In small north Alabama towns, Hispanics are heavily employed on chicken farms and in poultry processing plants; in hosiery, garment, textile, carpet, furniture, and plastics manufacturing; and in agriculture, where they pick and pack tomatoes, peaches, strawberries, potatoes, cucumbers, and watermelons. Notably, former migrant agricultural workers are settling down permanently in north Alabama towns, many moving into factory jobs and chicken plants. Hispanics are fewer in number but still very much in evidence in south Alabama, where they provide migrant agricultural labor, replant timberland, process seafood, and work dairy farms, truck farms, and sawmills. In metropolitan areas such as Birmingham, they work in restaurants, landscaping, roofing, building construction, and car washes. They clean rooms and make beds in Birmingham area hotels. A major portion of the janitorial work in Birmingham's downtown and edge-city office buildings is done by Hispanic service workers, under contract with large building-maintenance firms. The hotels, cleaning companies, construction and landscaping firms, and poultry processors all found in Hispanics a cheap, reliable, and nonunionized labor force at a time when national labor markets were very tight. The Hispanic immigrants, in turn, found numerous ethnic niches in the American economy.[17]

As with other immigrants in past eras, the initial Hispanic newcomers were primarily young, single men who shared cramped housing, worked in teams or crews, and sent earnings to families back home. News of job opportunities in Alabama spread quickly to their villages and towns in Mexico and elsewhere. Through a familiar process of chain migration, homeland relatives, neighbors, and friends joined compadres in specific Alabama towns and work places. In a style reminiscent of employment practices of the industrial era, Alabama plants and firms relied on their Hispanic workforce as a recruitment mechanism. Mexicans, especially, returned home often, eventually bringing wives, children, and even aging parents to the United States. They began putting down more permanent roots, sending children to American schools, and buying homes and property.[18]

The pattern of migration, work, and settlement is much the same elsewhere. For example, Gainesville, Georgia, claimed at one time to be the "Poultry Capital of the World." Gainesville lost its top poultry ranking in recent years, even as production increased and Hispanic migration surged. Low wages and difficult working conditions drove black and white American workers from the industry. But in the 1980s and 1990s, rising demand for processed chickens, or broilers, both nationally and globally, led to recruitment of primarily Mexican workers, who often shifted from migrant agricultural labor to poultry work. Kinship and community networks facilitated the recruitment of additional Hispanic workers for replacement jobs and for new poultry plants. Moreover, substantial numbers of Hispanic women found employment in the chicken industry. In 2000, over twenty-seven thousand Hispanics in Gainesville and Hall County made up 20 percent of the population, and they dominated the workforce in the county's chicken plants. They began arriving in Gainesville for poultry work in the 1980s, primarily from California. The numbers rose dramatically in the 1990s, with most coming directly from Mexico and a smaller number from other Central American countries. For the chicken processing companies, Hispanics represented an ideal low-pay, low-turnover, nonunion labor force, but the workers found benefits as well. They were able to bring families to the United States, send children to local schools, and look forward to upward mobility. By the end of 2002, for instance, Hispanic children accounted for 47 percent of the total enrollment in the Gainesville city schools. The new Hispanic immigrants have built dynamic ethnic communities, become a stable presence in the Gainesville area, and shown little inclination to return permanently to Mexico or other Latin homelands.[19]

In the far northwest corner of Georgia, signs proclaim Dalton to be the "Carpet Capital of the World." In the early 1990s, local carpet factories experienced strong demand, but production was hampered by high worker turnover and persistent labor shortages. Many of the area's 120 carpet factories turned to Hispanic workers, some of whom were already working in north Georgia poultry plants or in agriculture. Through chain migration, others came from California, Texas, and Mexico—mostly amnestied Mexicans and family members, but others were undocumented. By the official count of the census takers, Dalton and Whitfield County had 18,500 Hispanics in 2000, or 22 percent of county population, but unofficial estimates from the INS and university researchers proclaim as many as 40,000 to 45,000 Hispanics in the Dalton area. As in Gainesville, these newcomers have put down roots, built stable communities, and helped to revive dying and abandoned business sections of Dalton and other rural towns. At the same time, they have had a costly impact on local schools and services. Carpet manufacturers rave about the newcomers' work ethic, but some local residents have expressed concerns about costs, consequences, and unwanted change.[20]

Dalton and Gainesville are far from isolated examples of the diverse, new Hispanic migration to the South. Poultry workers in Morganton, North Carolina, include some four hundred Maya from two mountain towns in

Guatemala. Arriving through chain migration, many by way of another Maya community in Florida, they have reconstituted their old communities and sustained traditional cultural values.[21] At the Smithfield Packing Company plant in Tar Heel, North Carolina, the largest hog butchering plant in the world, some three thousand Hispanic workers hack meat from hog carcasses on moving conveyor belts. Mostly Mexican and mostly illegal, according to *New York Times* investigative reporter Charlie LeDuff, the Hispanic meat cutters are replacing black workers who regularly quit in large numbers; the Smithfield plant has a 100 percent annual turnover rate.[22] In small fishing villages along the North Carolina coast, hundreds of Mexican women with special h-2b visas have replaced African American women in the seasonal crab processing industry.[23] Throughout the Southeast, farm labor has been transformed in the past decade or so, as Hispanic workers now make up a huge percentage of the farm labor force. In Georgia, Hispanics comprise over 80 percent of the state's ninety thousand migrant and seasonal farm workers. In North Carolina, 90 percent of farm laborers are Hispanic. In rural Forest Hill, Louisiana, Mexicans fill all the laboring jobs at the state's largest plant nursery. In Morgan City, Louisiana, hundreds of Mexican skilled craftsmen work as welders, fitters, and carpenters in local shipyards. In Lexington, Kentucky, they work on horse farms and tobacco farms. In North Carolina and Virginia, tobacco growers now hire primarily Latinos for tobacco farm work. Some fifteen thousand Hispanic migrants, working on temporary visas, replant timberland for reforestation companies in Arkansas, Georgia, Alabama, and elsewhere in the South.[24] In Charleston, Memphis, Birmingham, Charlotte, Atlanta, and other cities, Hispanics fill jobs in construction, landscaping, factories, hotels, restaurants, and custodial work, and in the vast urban/suburban service sector. In suburban Fairfax County, one of the wealthiest counties in the nation, Hispanics from many different nations work as maids, janitors, landscapers, and truck drivers; they also work as computer engineers, doctors, businessmen, and government bureaucrats.[25]

Hispanics in the rural and urban South have become an important component in the region's low-wage, low-skill economy, especially in manufacturing, construction, agriculture, and food processing. They work mostly for minimal pay, often under difficult and dangerous working conditions, especially in poultry and meat processing plants. "Meatpacking," Eric Schlosser noted in his exposé *Fast Food Nation* (2001), "is now the most dangerous job in the United States." Job training and instruction in work-safety rules and regulations, especially in the Spanish language, are minimal in the slaughterhouses. "Taylorization" in poultry plants, the imposition of a time-work discipline, has speeded up the shop-floor production process and pushed workers to the limits of endurance. Repetitive work with sharp knives on the disassembly lines in these plants often results in serious lacerations, back and shoulder problems, and disabling carpal-tunnel injuries. At one poultry plant in North Carolina, company personnel reported as early as 1989 that it was "normal procedure" for 60 percent of the workers "to visit the company nurse every morning to get painkillers and have their hands wrapped." Farmworkers are exposed to harmful chemicals and pesticides. Few such workers have access to health insurance, primarily because few employers provide such coverage. Fatality rates among Hispanic construction workers rose substantially in the late 1990s. Threats of deportation by crew chiefs and plant managers keep illegal workers in line, despite work hazards. Hispanic workers, the U.S. Occupational Safety and Health Administration (OSHA) reported in 2001, faced "a 20 percent greater risk of being killed on the job than black and white workers combined." [26]

Given these circumstances, labor union organizers have targeted new Hispanic immigrants in an effort to revive union activism in the traditionally antiunion South. With the number of Latino workers rising, they "represent the future" for labor unions at a time when the unionized work force nationally has experienced a deep decline, Atlanta journalist Sheila M. Poole reported in 1998. Union proponents contend that effective organizing among Hispanics will result in higher wages and safer working conditions, the outcome in a nationally profiled organizing drive among Latino janitors by the Service Employees International Union (SEIU) in Los Angeles. [27]

Union organizers in the Hispanic South have not had much success. At the Smithfield plant in Tar Heel, organizers from the United Food and Commercial Workers Union (UFCW) recruited Hispanic workers during a collective bargaining election in 1997. Fearing that unionization would bring unwanted attention to their illegal immigration status, most Hispanics voted against the idea, and the union went down in defeat by a two-to-one vote. But at the Case Farms poultry plant in Morganton, North Carolina, where Maya immigrants from Guatemala comprised 90 percent of the labor force, workers staged several wildcat strikes and work stoppages in 1995 to protest low wages and abusive treatment. Organizers from the Laborers International Union of North America (LIUNA) seized the opportunity, and workers eventually voted for the union as its collective bargaining agent. The Morganton organizing campaign had a negative ending, however, as Case Farms engaged in obstructive antiunion tactics and in 2001 ended union negotiations altogether. However, in some areas of the South, poultry and catfish workers are represented by UFCW. In other efforts, both the Farm Labor Organizing Committee (FLOC) and the National Poultry Workers Organizing Committee are currently engaged in organizing North Carolina's Latino workers. In Greensboro, the Union of Needletrades, Industrial, and Textile Employees (UNITE) has been training Hispanic organizers and incorporating Latino culture into union programs. Reflecting this new union activism, in 2003 the Immigrant Workers Freedom Rides generated considerable support for immigrant rights in southern states such as Georgia and North Carolina.[28]

As these organizational efforts suggest, building a Latino union base in the South has been a difficult process, with few success stories. Some labor leaders, such as Kevin Blair of the FLOC, believe that "employers pit African American and Latino farmworkers and meatpackers against each other to increase productivity and to keep them from organizing labor unions." Yet the new immigrant workforce in the region remains ripe for organization, which may be speeded by a major policy shift by the national AFL-CIO. Long opposed to immigration and critical of immigrant job competition, in February 2000 national labor leaders reversed course, supported a more lenient immigration policy, and vowed to "make immigrants more enthusiastic about joining unions." Labor economist Vernon M. Briggs Jr. has challenged that policy shift, contending that "as long as mass immigration is allowed to flood low wage labor markets," little pressure can be asserted to improve wages and working conditions for American workers.[29]

The surge of Hispanic workers in the South has placed wage issues in the spotlight. Black spokespersons and some scholars have argued that Hispanics have displaced black workers and kept wages low for all workers. As early as 1979, *Ebony* magazine complained that undocumented Mexican immigrants in southern agricultural states such as Florida and North Carolina posed "a big threat to black workers." In many southern places, Hispanics now fill the jobs that used to be held by blacks. Employers' seeming preference for Hispanic workers, often praised as being more compliant and having a strong work ethic, has rankled black communities across the South. Similarly, in many part of the urban South, Hispanics have been settling in traditionally black neighborhoods where rents seem more reasonable. Not surprisingly, black resentment about job competition and unwelcome neighbors has surfaced in the urban and rural South.[30]

These issues have emerged in striking ways in Tar Heel, North Carolina. Charlie LeDuff's report on the Smithfield packing plant there portrayed a tension-filled shop-floor situation. Blacks resented Hispanic job competition and blamed the newcomers for declining wage rates. Smithfield's Hispanic workers—who now make up 60 percent of the plant's workforce—had resentments and suspicions of their own. Verbal and physical confrontations between the two groups became commonplace by the end of the 1990s. As LeDuff wrote in 2000, "While Smithfield's profits nearly doubled in the past year, wages have remained flat. So a lot of Americans here have quit and a lot of Mexicans have been hired to take their places. But more than management, the workers see one another as the problem, and they see the competition in skin-tones. . . . The enmity spills out into the towns." LeDuff captured Tar Heel's uneasy racial standoff in a comment from one of his black informants from the plant: "There's a day coming soon where the Mexicans are going to catch hell from the blacks, the way the blacks caught it from the whites." The sudden surge of Hispanic workers and their dominance in many workplaces has nurtured black concerns about job competition and low wages.[31]

Many immigration scholars, however, reject the wage-competition argument. They contend that the new Latino immigrants are filling jobs that no one else wants. Job turnover in the fields and in food processing plants has been extremely high, they contend, as much as 100 percent a year in some industries. Hispanics, they say, are filling "replacement" jobs abandoned by black workers who have rejected low pay and excessively demanding work. Some labor researchers have described a pattern of ethnic succession in southern labor markets in which Hispanics "are replacing African American or white workers who leave the worst jobs in those industries [textiles, furniture manufacturing, custodial, and meat processing], rather than displacing them from the more desirable jobs in the industry." A North Carolina sociologist echoed that view in 2000: "It looks like the whites are moving out, the blacks are moving up, and the Latinos are filling in at the bottom." [32]

In many metro areas, Hispanics have filled new jobs created by expanding urban and regional economies during the 1990s. For example, a Russell Sage Foundation study in 1996 concluded that new immigrants "are fitting into occupational slots created by economic and demographic growth." Similarly, a University of Memphis study, conducted in 2000, reported that given the growing labor market in the South, "Latino workers have tended not to displace local workers, but rather to fuel economic growth in most regional economies." [33] But not all experts agree on this subject. Indeed, the economic consequences of immigration have been a hotly debated subject among economists and policy experts for more than a decade, with some emphasizing the positive benefits of immigration and others the economic costs as measured in job losses and wage cuts among American citizens.[34]

Whatever the reality, blacks and Hispanics have been at odds over jobs, neighborhoods, and cultural differences for almost a decade. In some places, emerging hostility has led to open conflict and black-on-Hispanic violence. In other places, civic leaders, union organizers, and advocacy groups have sought to mediate emerging ethnic and racial conflicts. In North Carolina, groups such as Black Workers for Justice and the Latino Workers Association created an African-American/Latino Alliance to find common ground among blacks and Hispanics. In Durham, the Piedmont Peace Project, the North Carolina Black-Latino Reconciliation Project, and the Operation TRUCE Campaign engaged in similar work. In April 2002 in Raleigh, the Martin Luther King Jr. Resource Center sponsored a "town hall meeting" discussing issues dividing blacks, whites, and Hispanics. In Birmingham, the Civil Rights Institute, the Community Foundation of Greater Birmingham, and Operation New Birmingham have each reached out to Hispanic newcomers and sought to ease tensions over jobs and housing. Nevertheless, as a consequence of recent Hispanic migration, new patterns of racial and ethnic conflict linger unresolved throughout the South.[35]

Interracial conflict in southern factories and farms has intensified concern about the impact of illegal immigration to the region. Many of the newcomers are legal or amnestied immigrants; others are "guest workers" who work in the United States on H-2A or H-2B visas, special federal programs that permit entry of seasonal agricultural or seafood workers when U.S. Department of Labor officials certify that no Americans can be found to do those jobs. However, a large but unknown number of Hispanic workers in the South are illegal immigrants. Teodoro Maus, Mexico's consul general in Atlanta, admitted to a reporter in 2000 that probably more than half of Georgia's almost half-million Latinos were illegal. In small north Alabama towns, illegals make up half or more of all Hispanic newcomers. IRCA, passed in 1986, required employers to ask new employees for documentation proving their eligibility to work in the United States. Virtually all large employers comply with this requirement, but they have no obligation to verify the documentation provided by new employees. The business of providing false documentation—social security cards or green cards, for instance—thrives in new immigrant communities. In Memphis, for example, undocumented workers can buy fake social security cards for as little as $100 that will pass muster at company hiring offices. In Chapel Hill, North Carolina, the cost of fake social security and resident alien cards ranges from $50 to $150. Once they successfully navigate the border crossing from Mexico, illegals easily travel to southern states on a Hispanic network of bus and van routes traversing the interstate highways. From a tiny bus station on Buford Highway, for instance, regular bus and van service connects Atlanta with more than four dozen Mexican destinations. In Memphis, four bus companies provide regular transportation service to numerous Mexican cities. Their destinations already determined through home-village networks, the newly arrived quickly find work in the ethnic niches already carved out in local economies.[36]

Enforcement efforts to combat illegal Latin immigration have been weak to nonexistent. In Georgia, INS district officials agreed that carpet and poultry processing firms heavily employed undocumented workers, but they also admitted, as the *Atlanta Journal-Constitution* reported in 2000, that those industries "haven't faced major raids in years." Reporter Matt Kempner interviewed one Mexican worker who said he had "been moving back and forth between countries for more than eight years, traveling to South Carolina, Florida, North Carolina, and Georgia. He's never run into overly curious immigration agents or bosses too picky to accept his false documents." After one highly publicized raid in 1992 on two large farms in North Carolina, the INS did little through the rest of the 1990s to enforce immigration law in the state. In Alabama, INS raids on workplaces have been few and far between, but occasional raids on poultry plants typically round up hundreds of illegal workers for deportation. In June and September 1995, for instance, the INS raided Hudson Foods and Gold Kist poultry plants in northeast Alabama, arresting and deporting more than 250 illegal workers. In July 1997, an INS raid at the Tyson Foods plant in Ashland, Alabama, netted 106 illegal Hispanic workers—72 Mexicans, 33 Guatemalans, and 1 Honduran. Another 50 or so workers ran off and eluded capture. Those arrested numbered about 15 percent of the Tyson plant's workforce, suggesting the sizeable dimensions of illegal immigration in the poultry industry. Tyson Foods claimed that it followed the letter of the law by demanding documentation and denied any efforts to recruit illegal workers. Nevertheless, in December 2001 the U.S. Justice Department charged Tyson Foods and six of its managers with running a smuggling ring that recruited illegal Hispanic workers for fifteen Tyson plants in ten, mostly southern, states. In March 2003, a federal judge dismissed some charges, and a jury eventually acquitted Tyson Foods and its managers of the remaining charges. Immigrant smuggling became an issue in Alabama, too. In 1999 when INS agents raided an apparel plant in Henegar, Alabama, they uncovered not only illegal workers but also a company-run smuggling ring that over a decade had recruited hundreds of Mexicans from the central Mexican town of Queretaro for work in company plants in Georgia and Alabama.[37]

Although government prosecutors lost the Tyson case, the indictment of the big chicken processor in 2001 and a subsequent INS investigation in 2003 of hiring practices at Wal-Mart, the nation's largest employer, seemed to represent a new determination on the part of the INS to enforce immigration law after years of benign neglect. Indeed, throughout the urban and rural South, an underground labor market built on illegal immigrant workers has thrived without much regulation or control. As one Border Patrol agent in Mobile noted in 2000, "I couldn't tell you a corner of the state of Alabama that doesn't have some illegal immigration population." Yet until recently Alabama had only one permanent INS agent, stationed in Birmingham, and six Border Patrol agents, all assigned to Mobile. North Carolina, one of the top destinations for Hispanic migrants in the 1990s, had only eighteen immigration agents in 2000. National efforts to beef up the Border Patrol and crack down on illegal immigration have failed miserably, but perhaps this was a purposeful national strategy during the 1990s when labor markets were tight. The fact is, as a writer for *Foreign Affairs* put it, "Immigration policy today is driven by businesses that need more workers—skilled and unskilled, legal and illegal. Somehow, the process has gotten out of control." The sense that illegal Hispanic migration in the South is "out of control" has brought demands for INS action and intensified anti-immigrant feelings in some places. These perceptions have hardened in the wake of the September 2001 terrorist attacks on the United States.[38]

Not surprisingly, given their often tenuous immigration status, low incomes, language difficulties, and cultural differences, Hispanics in the South have experienced adjustment problems. However, churches, schools, libraries, and public agencies have responded in positive ways to the new immigrants. The Catholic Church and numerous Protestant denominations have embraced the newcomers, offering Spanish-language religious services, English classes, employment assistance, and varied social services. Migrant Head Start programs in many southern communities provide educational and nutritional benefits to the children of migrant farmworkers. Public schools in small towns and large cities are struggling to provide ESL classes to a growing number of Latino children. Public health agencies are confronting serious problems in serving a new population without proper immunizations and mostly without health insurance. Medical providers, police, and emergency management personnel are getting training in Spanish.[39] The League of United Latin American Citizens (LULAC) now has state directors in several southern states. Various public and private nonprofit groups have also organized to serve and advocate for new Latino southerners: the Hispanic Interest Coalition of Alabama in Birmingham, El Centro Legal Latino in Birmingham, the North Alabama Hispanic Association in Huntsville, the Alabama Democratic Hispanic Caucus, the National Interfaith Committee for Worker Justice, the Georgia Poultry Alliance, the Hispanic Center for Social Assistance in Memphis, the Latino Memphis Conexion, the Latin American Resource Center in Raleigh, El Pueblo Inc. in North Carolina, the Mexican American Legal Defense and Educational Fund and the Latin American Association in Atlanta, the Mississippi Immigrants Rights Alliance, and dozens of similar groups throughout the South. When the National Council of La Raza held its national meeting in Miami in July 2002, Latino leaders from southern states met to plan a Southeast regional network linking diverse local Hispanic organizations.[40]

While many agencies and groups have responded positively to the South's Hispanic newcomers, a more hostile response has also become evident in some places. For instance, Spanish language use has become controversial. Every southern state except Texas and Louisiana enacted official English legislation in the 1980s and 1990s. In Alabama, after a north Alabama legislator complained that "the Spanish are creeping in," the state legislature in 1989 initiated a statewide referendum on an official English amendment to the state's constitution. Supported by the Alabama English Committee, an affiliate of the national organization U.S. English, the amendment was approved by 88.5 percent of Alabama voters in 1990. Throughout the 1990s, language debates flared in Alabama over such issues as Spanish-language driver's tests and homestead tax exemptions for non-English speakers. When a Birmingham area auto dealership ran Spanish-language ads on television in 2000, local talk radio personalities discovered Birmingham's "immigration problem." They attacked the car dealership for pandering to foreigners and incited a controversy over the rising number of immigrants in the city. Hispanic activist Hernan Prado shot back a response in the Spanish-language newspaper, *El Reportero,* blasting the race-hate mentality that would "drag this state back to the shameful days when Alabama was best known for its Ku Klux Klan rallies and church bombings in Birmingham." A *Washington Post* reporter noted at the time that "many in the Birmingham area are uncomfortable with the notion that their city could take on the characteristics of a Miami." [41]

More overt expressions of anti-immigrant sentiment surfaced, as well. In May 1997 in Oneonta, Alabama, a small town north of Birmingham, a local white supremacist group affiliated with the America First Committee announced plans for a demonstration march to protest the "Mexican invasion" of the area. At the time, Oneonta had several hundred Hispanic families, but the number rose during summers as migrant workers arrived to pick strawberries, tomatoes, and other crops. William Riccio, state organizer and spokesman for the white supremacist group, lived in Birmingham, not Oneonta, and he had an unsavory background. A former Grand Dragon of the Alabama Ku Klux Klan, he had been associated with various KKK, "militant patriot," and skinhead hate groups since the 1970s. The demonstration was needed, Riccio asserted, because the Hispanics were "causing the crime rate to go up and creating a drain on the economy." Many were illegal immigrants, he said; they were "holding jobs that should go to white residents," and their presence affected "the stability of Blount County." Riccio's request for a parade permit anticipated that three hundred to five hundred people, including Klansmen and skinheads, would march in Oneonta's anti-immigrant demonstration. As townspeople began to perceive the planned demonstration as a Klan event, many of them defended local Hispanics as hardworking and law-abiding neighbors. The America First parade was postponed and then cancelled altogether, and subsequent plans for an anti-immigrant rally at the court-house in downtown Oneonta were also cancelled. But the controversy revealed underlying resentment in some quarters about the way Alabama was changing. [42]

Anti-immigrant hostility also flared up in nearby Cullman, Alabama. Almost 99 percent white, Cullman County had fewer than one thousand

Hispanics in 1999, according to U.S. Census estimates. That was too many for some people. In January 1998, after an immigration protest meeting, three men were arrested for burning the Mexican flag, as well as flags of the United Nations and the Communist party. Many of those attending the rally were KKK leaders and right-wing militia members, some from Georgia and a few from as far away as California and Canada. James Floyd, the local leader of the "Stand Up for Cullman" protest, vociferously argued for a permanent halt to Hispanic immigration, which, he believed, would ultimately challenge Cullman's white majority population. "I like my own people more than others," Floyd later asserted, "and I'm not ready for a world without borders." Apparently, he was not alone; at least one hundred people who sympathized with that view attended the Cullman protest. So much for globalization in that part of Alabama.[43]

In Siler City, North Carolina, a small town of about five thousand west of Raleigh, similar anti-immigrant sentiment flared in 2000. Hispanic migration in the late 1990s took the local community by surprise, so much so, one writer noted, that "longtime residents can scarcely grasp what has happened." Mexicans, Guatemalans, and Nicaraguans made up 80 percent of the workforce in Siler City's two poultry plants; Hispanic children comprised over 40 percent of the town's elementary school students. The town's almost abandoned downtown retail district began to sprout Hispanic shops and restaurants. Siler City's lone radio station aired complaints about the newcomers on morning talk shows but turned the airwaves over to Spanish-language music and programming in the evening. One woman seemed to sum up the general attitude in a complaint to a reporter: "They just came in and took over." Chatham County commissioners demanded that the INS crack down on Hispanic illegals, without result. In February 2000, a local white supremacist invited David Duke to Siler City to address an anti-immigration rally. The notorious ex-Klansman from Louisiana, who had just organized his own anti-immigrant group, the National Organization for European American Rights, jumped at the opportunity to promote white supremacy. A few hundred people showed up to hear Duke denounce the Hispanic newcomers: "To get a few chickens plucked, is it worth losing your heritage?" Duke asked. Two years later, in July 2002, a white-supremacist group called National Alliance, based in West Virginia, conducted an anti-immigrant rally in Gainesville, Georgia. "Hispanics in Gainesville have completely taken over," rally organizer Chester Doles complained, and he went on to say "we will take our borders back." Another white, anti-immigrant group, Georgians for Immigration Reduction, has lobbied state lawmakers to curb illegal immigration. One member of the organization expressed his concerns to an Atlanta reporter during a demonstration: "We're not out here waving the rebel flag. Our only concern about the

[Georgia] flag is that it might be a Mexican flag one day." Although not wide-spread, anti-immigrant activities such as those in North Carolina, Georgia, and Alabama have exposed deep-seated concern in some places about the way Hispanic newcomers have been changing traditional patterns of small-town southern life.[44]

The new American nativism has not deterred Hispanics from seeking a new and better life in the American South. Like other immigrants to the United States in earlier times, they have found strength in their communal activities and cultural heritage. They have quickly created a vibrant cultural life based on homeland foodways, kinship activities, and musical traditions—a cultural life centered not just in the home but in hundreds of restaurants, grocery stores, music and dance clubs, and in traditional holiday festivals. Mexican national holidays and important religious events become occasions to celebrate ethnic culture. Customary religious practice, such as universal veneration of the Mexican national patron saint, the Virgin of Guadalupe, has sustained cultural persistence. Latin groceries and many restaurants supply not only familiar food but Spanish-language newspapers, Latin movie videos, music tapes and CDs, religious icons, home-style clothing (from white baptism dresses to cowboy boots and hats), and check-cashing and money-wiring services. They also serve as community gathering places, and they provide employment to some as cooks, waiters, and food service workers. Latin soccer teams and leagues all over the South provide leisure time activities for young men and Sunday outings for entire families, smoothing the transition to life in America. Some thirty-two soccer teams, for instance, make up the Latin American Soccer League of Birmingham, each team complete with sponsors and colorful uniforms. In 2002 in North Carolina, organizers from twenty-six Hispanic soccer leagues sponsored a statewide Hispanic soccer championship play-off, the North Carolina Copa Tecate Fiesta del Futbol. Hispanic bands and dance clubs offer familiar forms of weekend entertainment. Spanish-language newspapers and radio stations have sprouted all over the South, keeping the newcomers informed and sustaining language, culture, and tradition.[45]

The South's growing Hispanic population has important political implications. For European immigrants of the industrial era, participation in the American political process served as an integrating and Americanizing force—a pattern that may eventually emerge among Hispanics in the South. With about 50,000 registered Hispanic voters in 2002, Georgia stands on the cutting edge of Latin politicization in the region. Political analysts project 250,000 Hispanic voters in the state in the next decade, so Republican and Democratic party leaders are gearing up for the future. And, as Walter Woods of the *Atlanta Business Chronicle* suggested in 2002, "the future is in the numbers." Indeed, Woods wrote, "Georgia politics in 2015 may look a lot like present day Texas, New York and California, where the Hispanic vote decides elections." The 2002 election provided a preview of that future, as three Hispanic candidates—two Democrats and one Republican—were elected to the Georgia legislature from metro Atlanta districts. Equally important, both parties scrambled for votes among Georgia's Hispanics, who are considered liberal on social issues but conservative on economic matters. Some African Americans resented efforts to lure Hispanic voters into the Democratic corner, fearing loss of position and power to new ethnic rivals, but other Atlanta black leaders have been more welcoming, suggesting the potential for coalition politics. The new ethnic politics is unlikely to disappear from the southern political scene anytime soon. Indeed, the recent success of Hispanic candidates in Georgia signals the arrival of a new political force in the South—one that will only strengthen over time as the citizenship process inevitably produces more Hispanic voters. More immediately, Georgia's new Hispanic legislators have the opportunity to bring issues of importance to their constituents to the political arena—controversial issues such as redistricting, affirmative action, minority contracting, jury service, driver's licenses for illegal immigrants, and tuition and scholarships for undocumented students. Georgia has taken the lead among southern states in bringing new Latino residents into the political arena, but in Alabama and other states political parties are also recruiting potential Hispanic voters.[46]

Globalization has brought a transnational, low-wage Hispanic labor force to the land of Dixie—a pattern of human migration that has produced substantial cultural and demographic change in a region where change has always been slow and received with skepticism, if not hostility. As the twenty-first century begins, this process of southern ethnic and cultural change has been intensifying. Farms and factories and employers of all kinds now seek out Latino workers for their work ethic and their willingness to work for low pay. After a decade or more of intense Hispanic immigration to the South, people now generally seem more aware of the ways the region is changing, but the speed and strength of these changes in some places, especially in small towns, has caught many white and black southerners by surprise. Local print media and television have begun to pay closer attention to the impact of Hispanic migration, as have businessmen and politicians. Several southern states have created offices of Hispanic or Latino affairs. Southern university scholars have begun analyzing the policy implications of the new Hispanic immigration.[47] As the Latino newcomers become more numerous, more settled, and more established, they will undoubtedly become more organized, more politically mobilized, and perhaps more amenable to union organization. Many black southerners believe that Hispanics have taken jobs and depressed wages, but there are also signs of interracial activism and alliance among the two groups.

Ethnic and linguistic change has also spawned new forms of nativism and stoked concerns about the social and economic costs of immigration. This is the nuevo New South. Ready or not, Dixie appears to be on the cusp of a long-term process of Latinization, mirroring what has already happened in other parts of the United States.

Notes

A slightly different version of this article appeared under the same title in the *Journal of American Ethnic History* 22 (Summer 2003): 31–66. A few paragraphs in this essay have been adapted from my earlier article "Latinization in the Heart of Dixie: Hispanics in Late-Twentieth-Century Alabama," *Alabama Review* 55 (October 2002): 243–74.

1. Rose Livingston, "Russellville Blends Hispanic Flavor," *Birmingham News,* October 5, 1997; Livingston, "Hispanic Families Seek Better Life Here," *Birmingham News,* October 5, 1997.

2. Livingston, "A New Home," *Birmingham News,* October 5, 1997; Livingston, "Meeting Needs of New Residents," *Birmingham News,* September 21, 1997; Patty Fernandez-Rocha, "Hispanic Resident Sets High Goals," *Florence (Ala.) Shoals Times-Daily,* August 28, 2000.

3. Livingston, "Settlers Build a Lifestyle," *Birmingham News,* September 18, 2000; Manuel Torres, "The Latinization of the South," *Mobile Register,* June 28, 1999.

4. James C. Cobb, "The Sunbelt South: Industrialization in Regional, National, and International Perspectives," in *Searching for the Sunbelt: Historical Perspectives on a Region,* ed. Raymond A. Mohl (Knoxville: University of Tennessee Press, 1990), 25–46; David R. Goldfield and Thomas E. Terrill, "Uncle Sam's Other Province: The Transformation of the Southern Economy," in *The South for New Southerners,* ed. Paul D. Escott and David R. Goldfield (Chapel Hill: University of North Carolina Press, 1991), 135–56; Karsten Hulsemann, "Greenfields in the Heart of Dixie: How the American Auto Industry Discovered the South," in *The Second Wave: Southern Industrialization from the 1940s to the 1970s,* ed. Philip Scranton (Athens: University of Georgia Press, 2001), 219–54; Douglas S. Massey, "March of Folly: U.S. Immigration Policy after NAFTA," *American Prospect,* no. 37 (March–April 1998): 22–33; Robert D. Manning and Anna Cristina Butera, "Global Restructuring and U.S.-Mexican Economic Integration: Rhetoric and Reality of Mexican Immigration Five Years After NAFTA," *American Studies* 41 (Summer/Fall 2000): 183–209; Altha J. Cravey, "The Changing South: Latino Labor and Poultry Production in Rural North Carolina," *Southeastern Geographer* 37 (November 1997): 295–300; "The Globalization Game," *Southern Exposure* 26 (Summer/Fall 1998): 21–58; James Green, "Gone South," *American Prospect* 11 (November 20, 2000): 51–53.

5. Kitty Calavita, "Mexican Immigration to the USA: The Contradictions of Border Control," in *The Cambridge Survey of World Immigration,* ed. Robin Cohen (Cambridge: Cambridge University Press, 1995), 236–44, 236; Thomas Weaver, "Time, Space, and Articulation in the Economic Development of the U.S.-Mexico Border Re-

gion from 1940 to 2000," *Human Organization* 60 (Summer 2001): 105–20, 111; Paul Ehrlich, Loy Bilderback, and Anne E. Ehrlich, *The Golden Door: International Migration, Mexico, and the United States* (New York: Ballantine Books, 1979); Philip Martin, "There Is Nothing More Permanent than Temporary Foreign Workers," Center for Immigration Studies, *Backgrounder* (April 2001): 1–3.

6. Douglas S. Massey, Inge Durand, and Nolan J. Malone, *Beyond Smoke and Mirrors: Mexican Immigration in an Era of Economic Integration* (New York: Russell Sage Foundation, 2002), 24–51, 105–41, 127; Alejandro Portes, "Labor Functions of Illegal Aliens," *Society* 14 (September/October 1977): 31–37; Terrence Haverluk, "The Changing Geography of U.S. Hispanics, 1850–1990," *Journal of Geography* 96 (May/June 1997): 134–45; Jorge Durand, Douglas S. Massey, and Emilio A. Parrado, "The New Era of Mexican Migration to the United States," *Journal of American History* 86 (September 1999): 518–36; Jean-Claude Buhrer, "The U.S. Honey-Pot Lures Mexico's Dispossessed," *Manchester Guardian Weekly,* December 27, 1987; Wade Graham, "Masters of the Game: How the U.S. Protects the Traffic in Cheap Mexican Labor," *Harper's,* July 1996, 35–50; David M. Heer, *Undocumented Mexicans in the United States* (Cambridge: Cambridge University Press, 1990); Thomas J. Espenshade, "Unauthorized Immigration to the United States," *Annual Review of Sociology* 21 (1995): 195–216; Jorge Durand, Douglas S. Massey, and Fernando Charvet, "The Changing Geography of Mexican Immigration to the United States, 1910–96," *Social Science Quarterly* 81 (March 2000): 1–15; Gilbert G. Gonzalez and Raul Fernandez, "Empire and the Origins of Twentieth-Century Migration from Mexico to the United States," *Pacific Historical Review* 71 (February 2002): 19–57; Rob Chambers, "Wages Are Driving Force Behind Latest Emigration," *Atlanta Journal-Constitution,* April 19, 1998; Robert Robb, "Tightened U.S. Border Policy Keeps Mexicans Trapped Here," *Arizona Republic,* December 3, 2002.

7. Massey, Durand, and Malone, *Beyond Smoke and Mirrors,* 49–50, 136–38; Calavita, "Mexican Immigration to the USA," 238–41; Jeffrey S. Passel and Wendy Zimmerman, *Are Immigrants Leaving California? Settlement Patterns of Immigrants in the Late 1990s* (Washington, D.C.: Urban Institute, 2001), 13; "Hispanics Drawn to Triangle More Than Other Large Communities," Associated Press, July 31, 2002.

8. David Griffith and David Runsten, "The Impact of the 1986 Immigration Reform and Control Act on the U.S. Poultry Industry: A Comparative Analysis," *Policy Studies Review* 11 (Summer 1992): 118–30, 124; Neil Taylor (immigration attorney in Russellville), telephone interview with the author, January 13, 2003; Kirk Ross, "Economic System Rests on Fragile House of Cards," *Chapel Hill News,* March 31, 2002; Hector Figueroa, "The Growing Force of Latino Labor," *NACLA Report on the Americas* 30 (November/December 1996): 18–22, 22; David Griffith, "Consequences of Immigration Reform for Low-Wage Workers in the Southeastern U.S.: The Case of the Poultry Industry," *Urban Anthropology* 19 (Spring–Summer 1990): 155–84; Carlos A. Heredia, "Downward Mobility: Mexican Workers after NAFTA," *NACLA Report on the Americas* 30 (November/December 1996): 34–38; Massey, "March of Folly"; Manning and Butera, "Global Restructuring and U.S.-Mexican Economic Integration"; Jeff Faux, "How NAFTA Failed Mexico," *American Prospect* 14 (July/August 2003): 35–37;

James H. Johnson Jr., Karen D. Johnson-Webb, and Walter C. Farrell Jr., "Newly Emergent Hispanic Communities in the United States: A Spatial Analysis of Settlement Patterns, In-migration Fields, and Social Receptivity," in *Immigration and Opportunity: Race, Ethnicity, and Employment in the United States,* ed. Frank D. Bean and Stephanie Bell-Rose (New York: Russell Sage Foundation, 1999), 263–310.

9. "Folks Very Much Like Us," *Huntsville Times,* February 25, 2000; Suzi Parker, "Hispanics Reshape Culture of the South," *Christian Science Monitor,* June 1, 1999; Richard Rodriguez, *Brown: The Last Discovery of America* (New York: Viking, 2002), 35; Sue Anne Pressley, "Hispanic Immigration Boom Rattles South," *Washington Post,* March 6, 2000; Anne Hull, "Old South Goes with the Wind," *Washington Post,* December 8, 2002; Hull, "Highway: A Haven for Immigrants," *Washington Post,* December 9, 2002; Elizabeth Kurylo, "Immigrants Shaping Face of Atlanta," *Atlanta Journal-Constitution,* February 23, 1997. See also Barbara Ellen Smith, "The Postmodern South: Racial Transformations and the Global Economy," in *Cultural Diversity in the U. S. South: Anthropological Contributions to a Region in Transition,* ed. Carole E. Hill and Patricia D. Beaver (Athens: University of Georgia Press, 1998), 164–78; Eric Bates, "Beyond Black and White," *Southern Exposure* 22 (Fall 1994): 10–15; Steven A. Holmes, "Figuring Out Hispanic Influence," *New York Times,* August 16, 1998.

10. Frank D. Bean and Marta Tienda, *The Hispanic Population of the United States* (New York: Russell Sage Foundation, 1987), 152–63; Mike Davis, *Magical Urbanism: Latinos Reinvent the U.S. Big City* (London: Verso, 2000), 1–9. On Hispanics in Texas, see Emilio Zamora, *The World of the Mexican Worker in Texas* (College Station: Texas A&M University Press, 1993) and David Montejano, *Anglos and Mexicans in the Making of Texas, 1836–1986* (Austin: University of Texas Press, 1987). On Hispanics in Florida, see Raymond A. Mohl, "The Latinization of Florida," in *Florida's Heritage of Diversity: Essays in Honor of Samuel Proctor,* ed. Mark I. Greenberg, William Warren Rogers, and Canter Brown Jr. (Tallahassee: Sentry Press, 1997), 151–68, 230–34; Larry Rohter, "A Puerto Rican Boom for Florida," *New York Times,* January 31, 1994.

11. U.S. Census, 1990, 2000. Census data on Hispanics for 1990 and 2000 is available on the Internet at http://factfinder.census.gov. See also Lynette Clemetson, "Hispanics Now Largest Minority, Census Shows," *New York Times,* January 22, 2003; Andres Viglucci and Tim Henderson, "Hispanics Become Largest Minority in U.S.," *Birmingham News,* June 19, 2003; Mark Bixler, "Georgia Tops Nation in Hispanic Growth," *Atlanta Journal-Constitution,* September 18, 2003; Erin Sullivan, "Hispanic Population Boom," *Birmingham Post-Herald,* June 19, 2003; Jay Reeves, "Black, Hispanic Numbers Growing," *Birmingham News,* September 19, 2003.

12. U.S. Census, 2000; Deirdre A. Gaquin and Katherine A. DeBrandt, eds., *County and City Extra: Special Decennial Census Edition* (Lanham, Md.: Bernan, 2002); MDC, Inc., *The State of the South, 1998* (Chapel Hill: MDC, Inc., 1998), 10–12; Audrey Singer et al., *The World in a Zip Code: Greater Washington, D.C. as a New Region of Immigration* (Washington, D.C.: Brookings Institution, 2001); Micki Neal and Stephanie A. Bohon, "The Dixie Diaspora: Attitudes Toward Immigrants in Georgia," *Sociological Spectrum* 23, no. 2 (2003): 181–212; Rafael A. Olmeda, "Latinization of the United States

Spreads into Some Unexpected Regions," *Fort Lauderdale Sun-Sentinel*, July 31, 2002; Haya El Nasser, "Immigrants Emigrating from Calif. and N.Y.," *USA Today*, August 22, 2003.

13. U.S. Census, 2000; Evelyn Nieves, "Hispanics Polled See Themselves as Diverse," *Washington Post*, December 18, 2002.

14. Deborah Bulkeley, "Spanish-Speaking Households on the Rise in Mississippi," Associated Press, September 30, 2002; Michael Paulk, "The Latino Connection," *Memphis Business Journal*, September 23, 2002; Jim Parker, "Hispanic Workers," *Charleston Post and Courier*, October 21, 2002; James Shannon, "The Changing Face of Upstate: The Hispanics," *Greenville News*, September 24, 2002; Brian Basinger, "Latino Candidates Eye Offices, History," *Athens Banner-Herald*, July 7, 2002; Bates, "Beyond Black and White," 12–13; Leah Van Wey, "Newcomers in Numbers," *Southern Exposure* 27 (Summer 1999): 21; Carlos Conde, "Down for the Count?" *Hispanic* 12 (October 1999): 60–66; Bailey Thompson, "Can the South Cope with Yet Another Cultural Challenge?" *Huntsville Times*, February 6, 2000; Mike Salinero, "Distrust of Officials Makes Counting Hispanics Hard," *Huntsville Times*, March 21, 2000; Jay Reeves, "Census: Undercount in AL," *Huntsville El Reportero*, April 1, 2001; Haya El Nasser, "Political Fight Brews Over Census Correction," *USA Today*, February 15, 2001; "Undercount Examined," *USA Today*, March 28, 2001; Cindy Rodriguez, "Revised Census Estimate Points to Total of 285M," *Boston Globe*, February 15, 2001; and, more generally, Barry Edmondston, "The Case for Modernizing the U.S. Census," *Society* 39 (November/December 2001): 42–53.

15. Marie Jones, "Habla Espanol? Hispanic Culture Integrating Itself into Birmingham," *Birmingham Weekly*, March 5, 1998, 10–11; Jamie Kizzire, "Hispanics' Clout Rising in Alabama," *Birmingham Post-Herald*, June 27, 2000; Manuel Torres, "Hispanic Presence Grows in Mobile," *Mobile Register*, June 28, 1999; Rebecca Charry, "Cultures Clash and Adjust," *Birmingham Post-Herald*, March 18, 1997; "Official: State Lacks Agents for Immigration," *Decatur Daily News*, March 16, 2000; Rose Livingston, "Seeking a Better Life," *Birmingham News*, April 30, 1996; Jeb Phillips, "Habla Espanol?" *Birmingham Post-Herald*, March 15, 2001; Benjamin Niolet and Rose Livingston, "Hispanic Figure Still Low," *Birmingham News*, March 15, 2001; Livingston, "Franklin Official: Hispanic Count Off by Thousands," *Birmingham News*, March 16, 2001; "Changing Alabama," *Birmingham Post-Herald*, March 17, 2001.

16. George J. Borjas, *Heaven's Door: Immigration Policy and the American Economy* (Princeton: Princeton University Press, 1999), 86; Alejandro Castro (teacher and community organizer), interview with the author and Eric Knudsen, Birmingham, March 19, 1997.

17. Manuel Torres, "The Latinization of the South," *Mobile Register*, June 28, 1999; Carol Robinson, "Hispanic Community Grows," *Birmingham News*, March 21, 1999; Rose Livingston, "The Migrant Stream," *Birmingham News*, July 12, 1999; Connie Baggett, "Changing Work Force," *Mobile Register*, August 8, 2000; Steve Mayo, "Migrant Work Force Declining," *Montgomery Advertiser*, November 19, 2000; Bill Caton, Niki Sepsas, and Chianti Cleggett, "Searching for Magic: Hispanics in the City,"

Birmingham Magazine, May 2001, 100–107; Dale Short, "Mexico in the Heart of Dixie," UAB Magazine, Summer 2001, 2–9; Roy L. Williams, "Employers Say Immigrants Ease Critical Worker Shortage in Area," Birmingham News, September 9, 2001; Glenny Brock, "Service Stronghold," Birmingham Weekly, July 10, 2003, 6–7. On the "settling out" pattern where Hispanic farm workers move into permanent jobs and create stable communities, see Daniel Rothenberg, With These Hands: The Hidden World of Migrant Farmworkers Today (New York: Harcourt Brace, 1998), 181–204.

18. Marcos McPeek Villatoro, "Mexican in Alabama," Southern Exposure 22 (Fall 1994): 26–27; Villatoro, "Birth of a Mestizo Nation," Southern Exposure 27 (Summer 1999): 18–20. For a fascinating study of chain migration patterns in the Atlanta area, see Mark Bixler, "The Latino Network," Atlanta Journal-Constitution, April 15, 2001.

19. Greig Guthey, "Mexican Places in Southern Spaces: Globalization, Work, and Daily Life in and around the North Georgia Poultry Industry," in Latino Workers in the Contemporary South, ed. Arthur D. Murphy, Colleen Blanchard, and Jennifer A. Hill (Athens: University of Georgia Press, 2001), 57–67; Hayes Ferguson, "The Nuevo South: Changing Faces," New Orleans Times-Picayune, December 29, 1997; Gainesville Times, November 3, 2002.

20. Ruben Hernandez-Leon and Victor Zuniga, "'Making Carpet by the Mile': The Emergence of a Mexican Immigrant Community in an Industrial Region of the U.S. Historic South," Social Science Quarterly 81 (March 2000): 49–66; James D. Engstsrom, "Industry and Immigration in Dalton, Georgia," in Latino Workers in the Contemporary South, 44–56; Victor Zuniga and Ruben Hernandez-Leon, "A New Destination for an Old Migration: Origins, Trajectories, and Labor Market Incorporation of Latinos in Dalton, Georgia," in Latino Workers, 126–35; Jim Dyer, "The Dreams of Rigo Nunez," Atlanta Journal-Constitution, January 24, 1999.

21. Leon Fink and Alvis Dunn, "The Maya of Morganton: Exploring Worker Identity within the Global Marketplace," in The Maya Diaspora: Guatemalan Roots, New American Lives, ed. James Loucky and Marilyn M. Moors (Philadelphia: Temple University Press, 2000), 175–95; Leon Fink, The Maya of Morganton: Work and Community in the Nuevo New South (Chapel Hill: University of North Carolina Press, 2003); Allan F. Burns, Maya in Exile: Guatemalans in Florida (Philadelphia: Temple University Press, 1993).

22. Charlie LeDuff, "At a Slaughterhouse, Some Things Never Die," New York Times, June 16, 2000.

23. Lane Windham and Eric Bates, "H-2B," Southern Exposure 20 (Spring 1992): 57–61; David Griffith, The Estuary's Gift: An Atlantic Coast Cultural Biography (University Park: Pennsylvania State University Press, 1999), 71–98; David Griffith, Jones's Minimal: Low-Wage Labor in the United States (Albany: State University of New York Press, 1993), 51–81, 115–47; Griffith, "New Immigrants in an Old Industry: Blue Crab Processing in Pamlico County, North Carolina," in Any Way You Cut It: Meat Processing and Small-Town America, ed. Donald D. Stull, Michael J. Broadway and David Griffith (Lawrence: University Press of Kansas, 1995), 153–86; Anne Hull, "Una Vida Mejor," St. Petersburg Times, May 9, 10, 11, 1999; Emily F. Selby, Deborah P.

Dixon, and Holly M. Hapke, "A Woman's Place in the Crab Processing Industry of Eastern Carolina," *Gender, Place and Culture* 8 (2001): 229–58; Andrew Olsen, "Clawing Their Way Out," *Washington Times,* September 9, 2002.

24. Debra Sabia, "Challenges of Solidarity and Lessons for Community Empowerment: The Struggle of Migrant Farm Workers in Rural South Georgia," *SECOLAS Annals: Journal of the Southeastern Council on Latin American Studies* 30 (March 1999): 95–109; John D. Studstill and Laura Nieto-Studstill, "Hospitality and Hostility: Latin Immigrants in Southern Georgia," in *Latino Workers,* 68–81; Thomas A. Arcury et al., "Pesticide Use and Safety Training in Mexico: The Experience of Farmworkers Employed in North Carolina," *Human Organization* 60, no. 1 (2001): 56–65; Ned Glascock, "Foreign Labor on Home Soil," *Raleigh News and Observer,* August 29, 1999; Hayes Ferguson, "The Nuevo South: Chasing American Dream to a Small La. Town," *New Orleans Times-Picayune,* December 28, 1997; Katherine M. Donato, Carl L. Bankston, and Dawn T. Robinson, "Immigration and the Organization of the Offshore Oil Industry: Southern Louisiana in the Late 1990s," in *Latino Workers,* 105–13; Valarie Honeycutt and Andy Mead, "From the Border to the Bluegrass: Why Hispanics Come and What They Leave Behind," *Lexington Herald-Leader,* December 20, 22, 1998; Chris Poynter, "More Hispanics Find a Job—and a Home," *Louisville Courier-Journal,* July 20, 1999; Steven Greenhouse, "Migrants Plant Pine Trees but Often Pocket Peanuts," *New York Times,* February 14, 2001; Rick Mines, "Ethnic Shift in Eastern Crop Agriculture: Replacement or Displacement?" (unpublished paper, Changing Face Conference, Newark, Delaware, September 1997), http://migration.ucdavis.edu/rmn/.

25. Keith F. West, "Hispanic Population Boom Portends Change," *Charleston Regional Business Journal,* April 9, 2001; Michael Kelley, "Latino Memphis," *Memphis Commercial Appeal,* September 21, 1997; Rebecca J. Dameron and Arthur D. Murphy, "An International City Too Busy to Hate? Social and Cultural Change in Atlanta, 1970–95," *Urban Anthropology* 26 (Spring 1997): 43–69; Jane Kitchen, "The Hispanic Boom," *Hispanic* (January–February 2002): www.hispaniconline.com/magazine; Peter Whoriskey and Sarah Cohen, "Immigrants Arrive from Far and Wide," *Washington Post,* November 23, 2001; "Boom in Immigrants Transforming County," *Washington Post,* June 6, 2002.

26. Joe Fahy, "No Pain, No Gain," *Southern Exposure* 17 (Summer 1989): 35–38; Eric Schlosser, *Fast Food Nation: The Dark Side of the All-American Meal* (Boston: Houghton Mifflin, 2001), 169–90, 172; Steve Stiffler, "Inside a Poultry Plant: An Ethnographic Portrait," *Labor History* 43 (August 2002): 305–13; Barbara Goldoftas, "Inside the Slaughterhouse," *Southern Exposure* 17 (Summer 1989): 25–29, 27; Javier Lopez, "Diary of a Poultry Worker," *Southern Exposure* 31 (Spring 2003): 48–53; E. Richard Brown and Hongjian Yu, "Latinos' Access to Employment-based Health Insurance," in *Latinos: Remaking America,* ed. Marcelo M. Suarez and Mariela M. Paez (Berkeley: University of California Press, 2002), 236–53; Dave Williams, "Uninsured Hispanics Are a Growing Concern Among Health Leaders," *Savannah Morning News,* October 2, 2002; Thomas A. Arcury and Sara A. Quandt, "Chronic Agricultural Chemical Exposure Among Migrant and Seasonal Farmworkers," *Society and Natural Resources* 11 (1998): 829–43; Sara A. Quand et al., "Migrant Farmworkers and Green Tobacco Sickness:

New Issues for an Understudied Disease," *American Journal of Industrial Medicine* 37 (March 2000): 307–15; Thomas A. Arcury et al., "Farmworker Reports of Pesticide Safety and Sanitation in the Work Environment," *American Journal of Industrial Medicine* 39 (May 2001): 487–98; Rebecca C. Elmore and Thomas A. Arcury, "Pesticide Exposure Beliefs Among Latino Farmworkers in North Carolina's Christmas Tree Industry," *American Journal of Industrial Medicine* 40 (August 2001): 153–60; Joyce Hedges, "Hispanic Workers Face Disparate Risk, Are Overrepresented in Hazardous Jobs," *Occupational Safety and Health Reporter* 31 (January 11, 2001); Jim Hopkins, "Deaths of Hispanic Workers Soar 53%," *USA Today*, March 25, 2002.

27. Sheila M. Poole, "Unions Seek Latinos to Bolster Numbers," *Atlanta Journal-Constitution*, April 19, 1998; Harold Meyerson, "Street vs. Suite: Why L.A.'s Janitors Will Win Their Strike," *L.A. Weekly*, April 7, 2000; Meyerson, "A Clean Sweep," *American Prospect* 11 (June 19, 2000): 24–29; Roger Waldinger et al., "Helots No More: A Case Study of the Justice for Janitors Campaign in Los Angeles," in *Organizing to Win: New Research on Union Strategies*, ed. Kate Bronfenbrenner et al. (Ithaca: Cornell University Press, 1998), 102–19. See also Ruth Milkman, ed., *Organizing Immigrants: The Challenge for Unions in Contemporary California* (Ithaca: Cornell University Press, 2000).

28. LeDuff, "At a Slaughterhouse, Some Things Never Die,"; Craig Whitlock, "Immigrant Poultry Workers' Struggle for Respect Draws National Attention," *Raleigh News and Observer*, November 30, 1996; Fink and Dunn, "The Maya of Morganton"; Fink, *The Maya of Morganton;* Griffith, "New Immigrants in an Old Industry," 159; Erica Hodgin, "Heat's on Farm Labor System," *Raleigh News and Observer*, August 10, 1999; "On the Line: Latinos on Labor's Cutting Edge," *NAFTA Report on the Americas* 30 (November/December 1996): 18; Yolanda Rodriguez, "Immigrants Ride for Rights," *Atlanta Journal-Constitution*, September 30, 2003; Lindsey Listrom, "Activists Rally for Immigrant Rights," *Durham Daily Tar Heel*, October 1, 2003.

29. Janita Poe, "Latino Leaders to Target Problems in South," *Atlanta Journal-Constitution*, July 24, 2002; Ian Urbina, "Southern Bellwether: Unions Won't Survive Unless They Organize Down in Dixie," *In These Times* 26 (March 4, 2002): 16–18; Vernon M. Briggs Jr., "American Unionism and U.S. Immigration Policy," Center for Immigration Studies, http://www.cis.org/articles/2001/back1001.htm. More generally, see Hector L. Delgado, *New Immigrants, Old Unions: Organizing Undocumented Workers in Los Angeles* (Philadelphia: Temple University Press, 1993); Vernon M. Briggs Jr., *Immigration Policy and the American Labor Force* (Baltimore: Johns Hopkins University Press, 1984); Briggs, *Mass Immigration and the National Interest*, 2nd ed. (Armonk, N.Y.: M. E. Sharpe, 1996); Briggs, *Immigration and American Unionism* (Ithaca: Cornell University Press, 2001); Ruth Milkman, "Immigrant Organizing and the New Labor Movement in Los Angeles," *Critical Sociology* 26 (2001): 59–81.

30. Jacquelyne J. Jackson, "Illegal Aliens: Big Threat to Black Workers," *Ebony*, April 1979, 33–40. See also Frank D. Bean and Stephanie Bell-Rose, "Immigration and its Relation to Race and Ethnicity in the United States," in *Immigration and Opportunity*, 1–28.

31. LeDuff, "At a Slaughterhouse, Some Things Never Die."

32. Andres Viglucci, "Hispanic Wave Forever Alters Small Town in North

Carolina," *Miami Herald,* January 2, 2000; Mark Bixler, "Unwilling Neighbors," *Atlanta Journal-Constitution,* November 21, 2000; Ben Stocking, "Side By Side: Worlds Apart," *Raleigh News and Observer,* May 4, 1997; Charlie LeDuff, "Some Things Never Die," *Raleigh News and Observer,* July 2, 2000; Ned Glascock, "Latinos Now Filling Bottom-Rung Jobs," *Raleigh News and Observer,* October 29, 2000; Cynthia Tucker, "Latino Growth a Wake-up Call for Black Folks," *Atlanta Journal Constitution,* March 18, 2001; Dahleen Glanton, "Hispanic Influx in Deep South Causes Tensions—with Blacks," *Chicago Tribune,* March 19, 2001; Julianne Malveaux, "Blacks Hold Mixed Views on Immigrants," *USA Today,* August 31, 2001; Ron Nissimov, "Some Blacks Irritated by Immigrant Influx," *Houston Chronicle,* August 25, 2002.

33. Reynolds Farley, *The New American Reality: Who We Are, How We Got Here, Where We Are Going* (New York: Russell Sage Foundation, 1996), 200; Marcela Mendoza, David H. Ciscel, and Barbara Ellen Smith, "Latino Immigrants in Memphis, Tennessee: Their Local Economic Impact" (Working Paper 15, Center for Research on Women, University of Memphis, 2001), 4.

34. For key sources in the debate among the experts, see "Social Science and Public Policy: Immigration and its Consequences," *Transaction: Social Science and Modern Society* 22 (May/June 1985): 67–76; Peter H. Schuck, "The Great Immigration Debate," *American Prospect,* no. 3 (Fall 1990): 100–118; Julian L. Simon and Rita James Simon, "Do We Really Need All These Immigrants?" in *Second Thoughts: Myths and Morals of U.S. Economic History,* ed. Donald N. McCloskey (New York: Oxford University Press, 1993), 19–25; Julian L. Simon, *The Economic Consequences of Immigration* (Oxford: Blackwell, 1989); George J. Borjas, *Friends or Strangers: The Impact of Immigrants on the U.S. Economy* (New York: Basic Books, 1990); Richard A. Wright, Mark Ellis, and Michael Reibel, "The Linkage between Immigration and Internal Migration in Large Metropolitan Areas in the United States," *Economic Geography* 73 (April 1997): 234–54; Daniel S. Hamermesh and Frank D. Bean, eds., *Help or Hindrance? The Economic Implications of Immigration for African Americans* (New York: Russell Sage Foundation, 1998); Bean and Bell-Rose, eds., *Immigration and Opportunity;* George J. Borjas, *Heaven's Door: Immigration Policy and the American Economy* (Princeton: Princeton University Press, 1999); Nelson Lim, "On the Back of Blacks: Immigration and the Fortunes of African Americans," in *Strangers at the Gates: New Immigrants in Urban America,* ed. Roger Waldinger (Berkeley: University of California Press, 2001), 186–227; Roger Waldinger and Michael L. Lichter, *How the Other Half Works: Immigration and the Social Organization of Labor* (Berkeley: University of California Press, 2003).

35. Thomas A. Tweed, "Our Lady of Guadalupe Visits the Confederate Memorial," *Southern Cultures* 8 (Summer 2002): 79–80; Stocking, "Side By Side"; Scott Jenkins, "Blacks, Hispanics Hoping to Break Cultural Barriers," *Salisbury (N.C.) Post,* May 2, 2001; Scott Jenkins, "Hispanics, Blacks Gather to Bridge Culture Gaps," *Salisbury (N.C.) Post,* May 6, 2001; Glascock, "Latinos Now Filling Bottom-Ring Jobs"; "Race Relations Topic of Town Meeting," Raleigh *News and Observer,* April 25, 2002; "Hispanic Forum Overwhelming Success," [Birmingham Civil Rights Institute] *Vision* 3 (January–March 2002): 1; Community Foundation of Greater Birmingham, *Birmingham,*

A City of Roots and Wings: A Special Report on Race Relations and Diversity Survey (Birmingham: Community Foundation of Greater Birmingham, 2003).

36. Philip Martin, "Do Mexican Agricultural Policies Stimulate Emigration?" in *At the Crossroads: Mexico and U.S. Immigration Policy,* ed. Frank D. Bean et al. (Lanham, Md.: Rowman and Littlefield, 1997), 102–3; Matt Kempner, "The Big Wink: Labor Needs Bend Immigration Rules," *Atlanta Journal-Constitution,* January 23, 2000; Roberto Suro, "Boom in Fake Identity Cards for Aliens," *New York Times,* February 19, 1992; Steve Thompson, "The Paper Chase," *Chapel Hill News,* March 31, 2002; "Fake Social Security Cards Sold to Illegal Immigrants," *Athens Banner-Herald,* November 26, 2002; Mendoza, Ciscel, and Smith, "Latino Immigrants in Memphis, Tennessee," 7.

37. Kempner, "The Big Wink"; Ned Glascock and Craig Whitlock, "Law vs. Reality," *Raleigh News and Observer,* November 30, 1998; Nick Patterson, "Illegals Find It Hard to Fit into Society," *Birmingham Post-Herald,* March 17, 1997; Patterson, "Industry Says It Does Not Seek Out Illegals," *Birmingham Post-Herald,* March 3, 1997; Rose Livingston, "Illegal Aliens Arrested," *Birmingham News,* July 7, 1997; Jodi Wilgoren, "U.S. Indictment Charges Smuggling of Workers," *Fort Lauderdale Sun Sentinel,* December 23, 1997; Robert L. Jackson, "Tyson Foods Is Indicted in Immigrant Smuggling," *Los Angeles Times,* December 20, 2001; Bill Poovey, "Tyson, Managers Plead Innocent," *Birmingham News,* January 25, 2002; "Tyson Indicted," *Rural Migration News* 8, January 2002, http://migration.ucdavis.edu/rmn/; Sherri Day, "Jury Clears Tyson Foods in Use of Illegal Immigrants," *New York Times,* March 27, 2003.

38. Greg Schneider, "Grand Jury, Wal-Mart Probe Hiring of Workers," *Washington Post,* October 25, 2003; Abigail Goldman, "Wal-Mart to Review All Workers After Immigration Raids," *Los Angeles Times,* October 25, 2003; Rose Livingston, "INS Agent Shortage Called 'Dangerous' for Alabama," *Birmingham News,* March 16, 2000; Manuel Torres, "The Latinization of the South," *Mobile Register,* June 28, 1999; LeDuff, "At a Slaughterhouse, Some Things Never Die"; James Goldsborough, "Out-of-Control Immigration," *Foreign Affairs* 79 (September/October 2000): 89–101, 89.

39. On churches, see Trish Wilson, "More Latinos Leaving Catholicism for Baptist Faith," *Raleigh News and Observer,* April 23, 1995; Yonat Shimron, "Catholic Welcome of Latinos Uneven," *Raleigh News and Observer,* October 25, 1996; Jessie Burchette, "Methodists Trying to Welcome Hispanics," *Salisbury (N.C.) Post,* July 29, 1999; Greg Garrison, "Jehovah's Witnesses Draw Hispanics," *Birmingham News,* December 5, 1999; "Church Adapts to Hispanic Immigrants," *Huntsville El Reportero,* July 16, 2000; Tom Smith, "Russellville Church Brings Multitudes of Cultures Together," *Florence (Ala.) Shoals Times-Daily,* June 28, 2000; John Gerome, "A More Ethnic City," *Birmingham News,* September 29, 2000; Leslie Scanlon, "Churches Respond to Needs, Fervor," *Louisville Courier-Journal,* January 16, 2000; Frank Roberts, "Some Build Bridges to Growing Ranks of Hispanics," *Norfolk Virginian-Pilot,* June 22, 2002; Linda Parham, "Church Offers Lifeline to Area Hispanics," *Birmingham News,* October 8, 2002; David Cho, "Energetic Worship Excites Hispanic Catholic Church," *Birmingham News,* November 29, 2002; Leigh Anne Monitor, "Faith Breaks Language Barrier," *Birmingham Post-Herald,* March 22, 2003; Patricia Campion, "One Under God? Religious Entrepre-

neurship and Pioneer Latino Immigrants in Southern Louisiana," *Sociological Spectrum* 23, no. 2 (2003): 279–301.

40. Raymond A. Mohl, notes from meeting of Central Alabama Alliance for Latino Health, Birmingham, April 12, 2001; "Hispanic Association Formed in Huntsville," *Huntsville El Reportero,* November 1999; Tom Smith, "Coalition Works to Eliminate Barriers," *Florence Shoals Times-Daily,* July 24, 2000; Charda Temple, "Hispanic Caucus Seeks Stronger Voice in State," *Birmingham News,* February 9, 2003; Kempner, "The Big Wink"; Kelley, "Latino Memphis"; Ned Glascock, "Estimate Alarms Hispanic Advocates," *Raleigh News and Observer,* December 21, 1997; Ruth Sheehan and Ned Glascock, "Spanish Lessons," *Raleigh News and Observer,* February 22, 1998; Rich Badie, "Latino Civil Rights Group to Open Office in Atlanta," *Atlanta Journal-Constitution,* November 29, 2001; Mark Bixler, "Face of the Future," *Atlanta Journal-Constitution,* April 24, 2002; Yolanda Rodriguez, "New Leader to Expand Latin American Association," *Atlanta Journal-Constitution,* July 24, 2002; Bulkeley, "Spanish-Speaking Households on the Rise in Mississippi"; Janita Poe, "Latino Leaders to Target Problems in the South," *Miami Herald,* July 24, 2002.

41. Raymond Tatalovich, *Nativism Reborn? The Official English Language Movement and the American States* (Lexington: University Press of Kentucky, 1995), 182–85, 194–224; Tatalovich, "Official English as Nativist Backlash," in *Immigrants Out: The New Nativism and the Anti-Immigrant Impulse in the United States,* ed. Juan F. Perea (New York: New York University Press, 1997), 78–102; Robert D. King, "Should English Be the Law?" *Atlantic Monthly,* April 1997, 55–64; Gary Strauss, "Can't Anyone Here Speak English?" *USA Today,* March 2, 1997; Carol Schmid, "Immigration and Asian and Hispanic Minorities in the New South: An Exploration of History, Attitudes, and Demographic Trends," *Sociological Spectrum* 23, no. 2 (2003): 129–57; *Birmingham News,* April 27, 1989, June 6, 1990; Mary Orndorff, "High-Court to Review English-only License Test," *Birmingham News,* September 27, 2000; Kevin Sack, "Don't Speak English? No Tax Break, Alabama Official Declares," *New York Times,* June 4, 1999; Rose Toussaint-Almanza, "American Citizen, No English? You Will Not Receive Service from Government Agencies," *Huntsville El Reportero,* November 1, 1999; Elaine Witt, "Ad Controversy Befouls Our Southern Hospitality," *Birmingham Post-Herald,* January 25, 2000; Jamie Kizzire, "Hispanics' Clout Rising in Alabama," *Birmingham Post-Herald,* June 27, 2000; Hernan Prado, "Racial Slurs from Alabama Radio Station," *Huntsville El Reportero,* May 1, 2000; Dave Bryan, "Hispanics Make Headway in Old South," *Washington Post,* October 10, 2000. See also Geoffrey Nunberg, "Lingo Jingo: English-Only and the New Nativism," *American Prospect* no. 33, July-August 1997, 40–47; William Branigin, "As Hispanic Numbers Rise, Some Say No to Spanish," *Birmingham News,* February 7, 1999.

42. Suzy Lowry, "White Supremacists Plan Oneonta March," *Oneonta Blount Countian,* May 21, 1997; Suzy Lowry, "White Supremacists Withdraw Second Application for Parade Permit," *Oneonta Blount Countian,* June 4, 1997; "Ku Klux Klan Gives Mixed Signals," *Oneonta Blount Countian,* June 18, 1997; Gita M. Smith, "Klan Targets Hispanics Welcome in Alabama," *Atlanta Journal-Constitution,* June 17, 1997.

43. Beth Lakey, "Three Arrested at Protest," *Cullman Times,* January 18, 1998; Rose

Livingston, "Hispanics Fear Trouble After Cullman Rally," *Birmingham News,* January 29, 1998; Manuel Torres, "The Latinization of the South," *Mobile Register,* June 28, 1999; "Advocacy: Essential for Hispanic Ministries," United Methodist Church, General Board of Global Ministries, *Hispanic Ministries Newsletter* 6 (December 1998/January 1999); Kelly Hamilton, "Mexico Comes to Cullman, Alabama," graduate seminar paper, Department of History, University of Alabama at Birmingham, 2002.

44. Ben Stocking, "A Surging Latino Population Calls Siler City 'Home,'" *Raleigh News and Observer,* January 14, 1996; Ned Glascock and Ruth Sheehan, "Backlash Greets Newcomers," *Raleigh News and Observer,* February 23, 1998; Sue Anne Pressley, "Hispanic Immigration Boom Rattles South," *Washington Post,* March 6, 2000; Andres Viglucci, "Hispanic Wave Forever Alters Small Town in North Carolina," *Miami Herald,* January 2, 2000; Tom Steadman, "Immigration: A Small Town Struggles to Cope with Change," *Greensboro News and Record,* April 16, 2000; Sergio Bustos, "Small Towns Shaped by Influx of Hispanics," *USA Today,* May 23, 2000; Barry Yeoman, "Hispanic Diaspora," *Mother Jones,* July/August 2000, 35–41, 76; "White Supremacists to March in Hall County," *Athens Banner-Herald,* July 11, 2002; "Faces Change, But Immigration's Positive Impact Remains," *Athens Banner-Herald,* July 20, 2002; Rick Badie, "Group Says Debate Isn't About Race," *Atlanta Journal-Constitution,* February 19, 2003; Atha J. Cravey, "The Changing South: Latino Labor and Poultry Production in Rural North Carolina," *Southeastern Geographer* 37 (November 1997): 295–300.

45. Tweed, "Our Lady of Guadalupe Visits the Confederate Memorial," 72–93; Joan Flocks and Paul Monaghan, "Viva Mexico!: Mexican Independence Day Festivals in Central Florida," in *Southern Heritage on Display: Public Ritual and Ethnic Diversity within Southern Regionalism,* ed. Celeste Ray (Tuscaloosa: University of Alabama Press, 2003), 167–93; Sarah Lundy, "Festival Hispano Celebrates Cultures," *Charleston Post and Courier,* September 8, 2002; Marie Jones, "Habla Espanol? Hispanic Culture Integrating Itself into Birmingham," *Birmingham Weekly,* March 5, 1998; Carol Robinson, "Hispanic Community Grows," *Birmingham News,* March 21, 1999; Mark Bixler, "The Latino Network: Old Ties Renewed in Metro Area," *Atlanta Journal-Constitution,* April 15, 2001; Kevin Sack, "Far from Mexico, Making a Place Like Home," *New York Times,* July 30, 2001; Glenny Brock, "Taking Stock: Family Groceries Reflect Birmingham's Growing Diversity, *Birmingham Weekly,* October 18, 2001; Regina Wright, "Mexican Holiday, Decatur Style," *Decatur Daily News,* May 5, 2000; Gigi Anders, "Nuestro Mundo," *Raleigh News and Observer,* September 20, 1998; "Ethnic Diversity in Birmingham Nightlife," *Huntsville El Reportero,* October 1, 2000; Matt Tidmore, "A League of Their Own," *Birmingham News,* October 4, 2000; "Liga Latino Americana de Futbol," *Gadsden Latino,* May 16, 2001; Jim Young, "Hispanic Soccer Title to be Decided Sunday," *Greensboro News and Record,* September 20, 2002; Dawn Wotapka, "A Latino Superstore Takes Shape," *Raleigh News and Observer,* May 26, 2000; Patricia Dedrick, "Going Gourmet with Goats," *Birmingham News,* July 18, 2003; Eric Velasco, "Bueno!" *Birmingham News,* October 17, 2003.

46. Walter Woods, "A Wave of Political Change," *Atlanta Business Chronicle,* March 22, 2002; Yolanda Rodriguez, "Atlanta's Edge: Latino Diversity," *Atlanta Journal-Constitution,* June 26, 2002; Betty Liu, "Latinos Flex Their Muscles in Georgia

Poll," *Financial Times (London),* August 20, 2002; Mark Bixler, "Latino Candidates: Victories Signal Growing Clout," *Atlanta Journal-Constitution,* November 7, 2002; Yolanda Rodriguez and Sheila M. Poole, "Electoral Jolt Leaves Groups Guessing," *Atlanta Journal-Constitution,* November 20, 2002; Janita Poe, "Budding Coalition," *Atlanta Journal-Constitution,* September 24, 2003; Kim Baca, "Few Hispanics Voting in S.C., Records Show," *Columbia The State,* June 11, 2001; Tom Gordon, "Democrats Reach Out for Hispanic Vote," *Birmingham News,* October 6, 2002. For national implications of Latino voting, see Don Campbell, "The Coming Fight Over Latino Power," *USA Today,* April 23, 2001; Harold Meyerson, "The Rising Latino Tide," *American Prospect* 13 (November 18, 2002): 22–25.

47. Cruz C. Torres, *Emerging Latino Communities: A New Challenge for the Rural South* (Hattiesburg: Southern Rural Development Center, Mississippi State University, 2000); Linda Garrett, *Looking for a Better Life: Latinos in Georgia, Myths and Realities of the Immigrant Journey* (Athens: Institute on Human Development and Disability, University of Georgia, 2000); Jorge H. Antiles and Stephanie A. Bohon, *The Needs of Georgia's New Latinos: A Policy Agenda for the Decade Ahead* (Athens: Carl Vinson Institute of Government, University of Georgia, 2002).

CREDITS

Stacy Braukman is the assistant editor of *Notable American Women: A Biographical Dictionary*.

Jennifer E. Brooks is associate professor of history at Auburn University. She is author of *Defining the Peace: Race, World War Two Veterans, and the Remaking of Southern Political Tradition*.

Susan Cahn is associate professor of history at the State University of New York, Buffalo. She is a coeditor of *Women and Sports in the United States: A Documentary Reader* and the author of *Coming on Strong: Gender and Sexuality in Twentieth-Century Women's Sport*.

Scott H. Dewey teaches history at California State University, Los Angeles. He is the author of *"Don't Breathe the Air": Air Pollution and U.S. Environmental Politics, 1945–1970*.

Andrew Doyle is associate professor of history at Winthrop University. He is the author of *Causes Won, Not Lost: College Football and Southern Culture, 1888–1917* (forthcoming).

Sarah Gualtieri holds a joint appointment in the departments of history and American studies and ethnicity at the University of Southern California. She is currently working on a book that examines the history of Arab racial formation in the United States.

Lu Ann Jones, associate professor of history at the University of South Florida, is the author of *Mama Learned Us to Work: Farm Women in the New South* and a coauthor of *Like a Family: The Making of a Southern Cotton Mill World*.

Jeanette Keith is professor of history at Bloomsburg University of Pennsylvania. She is the author of *Rich Man's War, Poor Man's Fight: Race, Class and Power in the Rural South during the First World War* and *The South: A Concise History*.

Kevin M. Kruse is associate professor of history at Princeton University. He is the author of *White Flight: Atlanta and the Making of Modern Conservatism* and a coeditor of *The New Suburban History*.

Alex Macaulay is assistant professor of history at Western Carolina University. His book on The Citadel in the 1960s is forthcoming from the University of Georgia Press.

Danielle L. McGuire received her Ph.D. from Rutgers University. "It Was Like All of Us Had Been Raped," which received the 2004 Louis Pelzer Memorial Award, is drawn from her dissertation and is currently being revised for publication as a book.

Raymond A. Mohl is a professor of history at the University of Alabama at Birmingham. He is author of *South of the South: Jewish Activists and the Civil Rights Movement in Miami, 1945–1960; Urban Policy in Twentieth-Century America;* and *The Making of Urban America.*

Scott Reynolds Nelson is Legum Associate Professor of History at the College of William and Mary. He is the author of *Iron Confederacies: Southern Railways, Klan Violence, and Reconstruction* and *Steel Drivin' Man: John Henry, the Untold Story of an American Legend.*

Leslie Schwalm is associate professor of history and women's studies at the University of Iowa. She is the author of *A Hard Fight for We: Women's Transition from Slavery to Freedom in South Carolina.*

J. Douglas Smith is visiting assistant professor of history at Occidental College in Los Angeles, California. He is author of *Managing White Supremacy: Race, Politics, and Citizenship in Jim Crow Virginia.*

1. Moved to "fraternities, campus."

Syrians and, 104. *See also*
desegregation; segregation
interracial sexual behavior, 4, 180,
184–85, 189, 218, 221; rape, 300, 302–5,
307–19
itinerant merchants, 67–82; and African
American consumers, 80–82;
"Rawleigh man," 76–80; Watkins
Medical Company, 76–80

Jews: European, 101; in Florida, 284; as
itinerant peddlers, 67, 68, 70, 82, 108;
Latvian, 101; and whiteness, 92, 99,
101, 108. *See also* anti-Semitism
Johns Committee. *See* Florida Legislative
Investigation Committee (FLIC)
Johnson, Guy, 39, 42, 43, 45, 58

Kennedy, John F., 330
King, Martin Luther, 310, 400
Kinsey, Alfred, 282
Ku Klux Klan: compared to White
Citizens' Councils, 400; connection to
Anglo Saxon Clubs, 170–71; and
Hispanic immigrants, 409, 427–28; in
the 1920s, 219; in post–World War II
Georgia, 246–48, 251, 259; during
Reconstruction, 300; and Syrian
immigrants, 104; and Tom Watson, 133

labor contract system, 19, 20, 21–22,
25, 55
labor unions: and civil rights movement,
302; and Hispanic immigrants, 421–22
Leadbelly, 45
lesbians. *See* homosexuality
Loving v. Virginia, 167

marriage: draft exemption for, 125, 128;
interracial 4, 106, 171–94
Mason, Claiborne R., 51–52, 53, 54, 55, 56
massive resistance, 261, 278, 304, 381
mentally challenged, treatment of. *See*
feebleminded, treatment of

midwives, 24, 174, 178
missionaries, 14, 187
Montgomery bus boycott, 301–4, 389
Muhammad, Elijah, 309
music, 38–42, 50–53, 56–60; evils of jazz,
160; Hispanic, 428–29; patriotic, 330;
and salesmen, 75, 78
Muslims: Ottoman, 96, 100; Nation of
Islam, 309; whiteness of, 100, 103,
106–9

NAACP: accused of conspiring for social
equality, 187; in Atlanta, 385–91, 397,
400; defends Gertrude Perkins, 303,
306; Florida branch, 316, 317; and
Johns Committee, 4, 278, 281; Monroe,
North Carolina, chapter, 310–11;
during World War I, 137; after World
War II, 261, 275
National Guard, 120, 123, 131, 139, 272, 337
Native Americans: claim to heritage as
criminal defense, 315; and question of
whiteness in Virginia, 167, 179–83,
190–92
North American Free Trade Agreement
(NAFTA), 409, 412

overseers: resistance to, 14, 15, 16–17, 19,
22–24; sexual exploitation by, 299
Owens, Betty Jean, 298–99, 304–19

pacifism, 120, 140
phosphate industry, 347–50;
environmental damage by, 350–51,
353–354, 360
plantations. *See* rice plantations
Plecker, Walter, 170, 173–74, 177–84,
188–94
Pocahontas Exception, 175, 181–82
poultry, 23, 28; bartering with, 67, 74, 75,
80; and parasites, 77, 79; processing
plants, 408, 409, 411, 412, 418–19, 421,
425, 428
Powell, John, 167, 169–77, 179, 184–94